SpringerWienNewYork

Marianna Sigala
Luisa Mich
Jamie Murphy (eds.)

Information and Communication Technologies in Tourism 2007

Proceedings of the International Conference in Ljubljana, Slovenia, 2007

SpringerWienNewYork

Dr. Marianna Sigala
School of Business
University of the Aegean, Chios, Greece

Dr. Luisa Mich
Dipartimento di Informatica e Studi Aziendali
Universitá degli Studi di Trento, Trento, Italy

Dr. Jamie Murphy
School of Business
University of Western Australia, Crawley, Western Australia, Australia

Printed in Austria
SpringerWienNewYork is a part of Springer Science + Business Media
springeronline.com

Typesetting: Camera ready by authors
Printing: Novographic Druck G.m.b.H., 1230 Wien, Austria
Printed on acid-free and chlorine-free bleached paper
SPIN 11971641

With 147 Figures

ISBN 978-3-211-69564-7 SpringerWienNewYork

Preface

Welcome to the 14th ENTER Conference!

In 1993, academics from universities in Austria, Germany and Switzerland collaborated with the Tyrolean Tourist Board to arrange a conference focusing on tourism and technology. They named the fledgling conference ENTER, "a name derived simply from the 'enter' key on all PC keyboards" (G. Inkpen). Over the years, ENTER has steadily matured into perhaps the premier global conference of information and communication technologies (ICT) in travel and tourism.

ICT advances and organisational innovation continue unabated, affecting every tourism organisation and stakeholder. Similarly the conference title, as well as the conference itself, take on new perspectives. In their efforts to follow trends and foster new thinking, ENTER organisers and chairs improve and update the conference through new sessions and themes. Andy Frew, the ENTER 2007 Conference Chair and esteemed IFITT family member, recently observed that as "we ENTER the new millennium for tourism predicated on global connectedness – immortal electrons, quo vadis?" For example, the soft and humanitarian aspects of ICT merit consideration and examination. As Luisa Mich, a Research Track co-chair, notes, ENTER also reflects the hospitality and tourism aspect of welcoming guests and making them feel comfortable.

In this vein, the conference theme, *Connecting Destinations: New Technologies, New Thinking, New Solutions*, reflects efforts to gather state-of-the art academic research and industry applications to address the challenges of ICT advances fostering a global networked and connected village. Through its rich programme, the conference enables fruitful and multidisciplinary exchanges of knowledge and experience on the concept of connectedness, including hard technology perspectives, industry solutions, as well as the new thinking and e-business models that they enable. Apart from the three familiar landmarks – PhD workshop, Research Track, and Industry & Innovation Track – this year's conference features a three-day eDestinations Summit focusing on destination management with leading academic and industry figures.

The high-tech conference venue in the city centre of Ljubljana, Slovenia, is an ideal gathering place for practitioners and researchers to fertilise new ideas related to connectedness. In the middle of Europe, Ljubljana is easily accessible for international participants and gives them the opportunity to experience and network in a part of the world where connectedness is a recent concept. Ljubljana, a rich cultural capital that combines tradition and modern technologies, is a useful hub and access point to connect with new emerging and dynamic destinations. Referring to the ENTER 2007 Research Track, its key objective is to disseminate research findings on new research theories, methodologies and applications. ENTER's conference proceedings typically represent the global corpus of state-of-the-art ICT travel and tourism research. This year's Research Track raised the quality bar even higher. Of the record number of papers received and subjected to a double-blind review system by at least three reviewers, the conference proceedings include 50 full research papers. The diverse studies – e.g., theoretical, empirical, experimental, case studies and policy – address myriad topics, themes, disciplines and approaches, so that any conference participant or reader of these proceedings will find several studies meeting their interests and expectations.

Submissions that provided useful findings, practical implications or new ideas, but in some way fell short of full-paper level, are included in both the presentation programme and in the CD conference proceedings as works in progress. This promising research deserves inclusion in ENTER's sessions and constructive feedback from leading academics and professionals for advancing the research. As in previous years, the Research Track features two sections: full research papers and works in progress. Both academics and professionals chair the presentations in order to enhance knowledge transfer and cross-fertilisation. Recognising that the quality of ENTER's research programme depends heavily on reviewers' time and expertise, the Research Track decided to identify and award outstanding reviewers. Their constructive feedback and comments help authors enhance their work. We believe that recognising top reviewers with an Outstanding Reviewer Certificate furthers strengthening conference paper quality and motivates more reviewers and better reviews.

Finally, the Research Track programme would not have materialised without the efforts of all authors that submitted or presented their studies. Thus, we thank all authors for their contributions to the conference, as well as all the reviewers for their continuing commitment and support. The IFITT organising committee also deserves recognition, as well as Nicola Zeni, a PhD candidate at the University of Trento, who despite his stressful and demanding doctoral programme, dedicated countless time and effort installing and maintaining the online paper review system. Last but not least, the chairs of the Research Track give their heartfelt thanks to Andy Frew for his continuous support and expert guidance, as well as making this long and demanding journey enjoyable and fun. Dear friends, dear colleagues, dear all, thank you so much for making the ENTER 2007 Research Track a reality!

ENTER is a large international family that is always keen to embrace new members – welcome! So we hope you enjoy the rich and varied research programme, but most of all catch up with old friends, meet new faces and have fun!

Marianna Sigala
Luisa Mich
Jamie Murphy

Ljubljana, 2007

Contents

1 Recommender/Support Systems

2 Consumer Behaviour

3 Mobile Tools and Applications

4 Virtual Communities

5 eBusiness Models

6 Website Design and Functionality

7 Destination Systems and Networks

8 User Perspectives

9 eMarketing

10 Measurement and Metrics

11 Strategy

12 Online Services

13 eLearning

Index of Authors

Research Review Committee

Fourteenth International Conference on Information and Communication Technologies in Travel and Tourism, Ljubljana, Slovenia, January 24–26, 2007

RESA - An Automated Speech Based Hotel Room Booking Call Centre Agent

Klemens Waldhör[a]
Claudia Freidl[a]
Fritz Fessler[b]
Gert Starha[c]

[a] Tourismus Research Center Krems GesmbH
{klemens.waldhoer, claudia.freidl}@kremsresearch.at
[b] Voice Business GesmbH
fritz.fessler@voicebusiness.net
[c] List TourConsult GmbH
g.starha@list.at

Abstract

In this project an automated call centre agent (RESA) for hotel booking via telephone was developed. RESA supports standard bookings of hotel rooms using a software solution based on human language technology (HLT), especially speech technology. This article concerns itself with the implementation of RESA, describes some evaluation results and discusses the advantages of using such a technology for the guest and the hotel.

Keywords: speech technology, booking engine, call centre, call centre agent.

1 Introduction

This article describes the development of an automated call centre and its telephone agent for guests – called RESA. New technologies and hotel concepts require the improvement of booking offers, but people who are not familiar with the usage of new technologies are in general excluded from progress in this area. In addition, most of the new booking engines require guests to have access to the Internet. Furthermore guests are often in situations where they have no Internet access, e.g. while travelling by car or by train. Access making use of mobile phone technology like GPRS (General Packet Radio Service; GPRS is a mobile data service available to users of GSM mobile phones.) or UMTS (Universal Mobile Telecommunications System; UMTS is the mobile telephone system standard of the third-generation of mobile phone technologies.) is still very time consuming, expensive and also unnecessarily complicated for users who are not accustomed to the Internet.

Using human speech as a medium of communication is still the outstanding and the most natural technology for most people. People are accustomed to this type of communication through their whole life and it is one of the first communication methods they learn. And still most people prefer telephone calls when booking hotel rooms. Thus it is natural to apply HLT to the hotel booking area.

An automated speech based booking engine and its agent RESA can be used by everyone who can handle a telephone. This article deals with the development of such a prototype and its evaluation.

Applying speech technology in this area of tourism is not really new item. VerbMobil (Wahlster, 1993) for example tried to support communication between different native language speakers, e.g. when talking about meeting dates. Another example is Pavel, a beer guide for Pilsen (www.speech-experts.com). Golfscore, nominated for the Voice Award 2006, is a system that calculates the handicap of a golfer via voice call based on course rating, slope, and personal rating by entering the relevant scores (www.voice-award.de). Automated time table information systems like the one of Deutsche Bahn (DB-Dialog), Verkehrsverbund Nordrhein Westfalen (NRW) or Salzburger Verkehrsverbund (SVV) are frequently used to provide and get travel information over the phone. Up to date travel information for the roads in Switzerland can be accessed with the short phone number 163 operated by Viasuisse (www.viasuisse.ch).

2 RESA

The project idea has its roots in the extension of a successful low-budget hotel concept realised in Austria. This concept differs from usual guest accommodations in that: modern rooms with Internet access and essential equipment, 24 hour check-in possibility and check out is not necessary. The main difference from other hotels is the (nearly complete) absence of hotel staff. Check-in, food, and beverages are provided by vending machines. The reception is occupied only at peak times in the morning and in the evening. In the remaining time, guests can book rooms via the internet, a call centre or directly at the hotel via a machine called 'Hotelomat'.

The goal of RESA is to enhance the existing 'human based' call centre with a software solution based on HLT for automatic voice recognition and an automatic dialogue system. At the beginning, the system should handle calls if all call centre agents are busy. At the next stage, the system should be able to handle more complicated calls, focusing on complaints as well as being able to cope with many foreign languages.

3 System Architecture

In theory (Balentine & Morgan, 1999; Furui, 2001; IEEE, 2002; Jelinek, 1999; Jurafsky & Martin, 2000; O'Shaughnessy, 2000; Rabiner & Juang, 1993), there are two approaches to dialogue design in HLT applications:

System-controlled dialogue: the user is led through the menu step by step User-controlled dialogue: free dialogue, the system only interrupts if information is missing or if input is not understood.

Needless to say that the second approach is more natural, but many technical problems jeopardize an efficient use of this method. In fact, many people are not familiar with the handling of speech computers and their limitations, which leads to uncertainty, inhibition and even frustration.

Therefore one of the most important concerns was to create a comfortable dialogue situation for callers. For this reason, disruptive factors like monotony should be excluded. For the first prototype a system-controlled dialogue was used.

Another focal point was the ability of the system to communicate with the user (Huang, 2001). There are two different ways of achieving this:

Ex ante recorded statements from a speaker which were regarded as adequate
Automated text-to-speech system (TTS) – any text can be produced by a synthetic computer voice

The speech recognition module translates the guest call into internal representation (W3C, 2006). For the first prototype, a controlled-speech dialogue based on call centre recordings was implemented. It was necessary to integrate as many options as possible to simulate a natural conversation. The aim was that guests should not recognize whether they were talking to a natural person or to the automated system.

However, even an excellent system needs a fallback system. Therefore, it is necessary to give the caller the option to get in touch with 'human' support. In this case, the caller will be forwarded to a call centre agent. In addition guests should always have the option to choose a human agent. Another challenge was the development of the interface between RESA and the web booking engine. The linguistic core architecture of the system (shown in figure 1) should enable voice-operated communication and usage of the web booking engine at the same time.

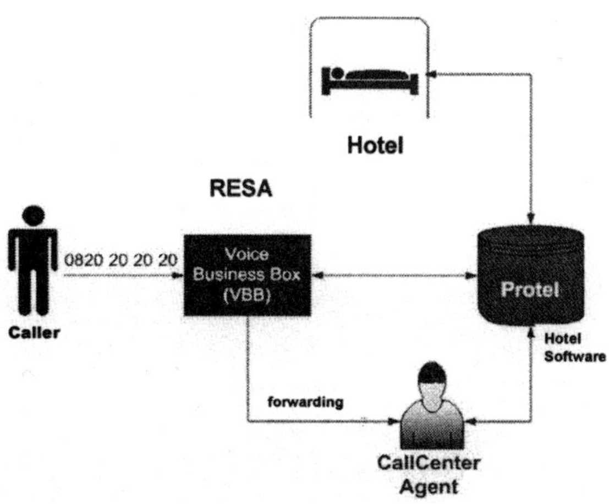

Fig. 1. General System Architecture

The core of this system is the Voice Business Box (VBB). Costumers can reach the VBB with every phone, no matter if it is a conventional landline telephone, a mobile phone or a terminal which enables Voice-over IP (VoIP). The functionality of the VBB is shown in figure 2.

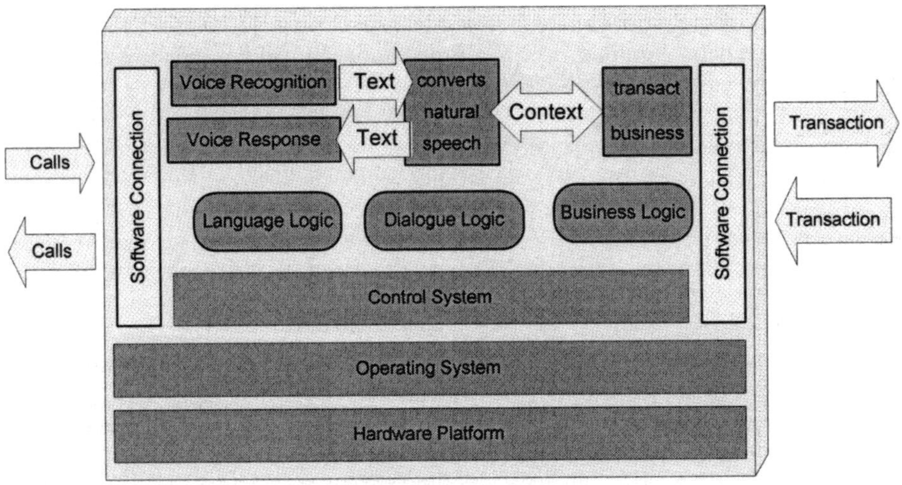

Fig. 2. Voice Business Box Architecture

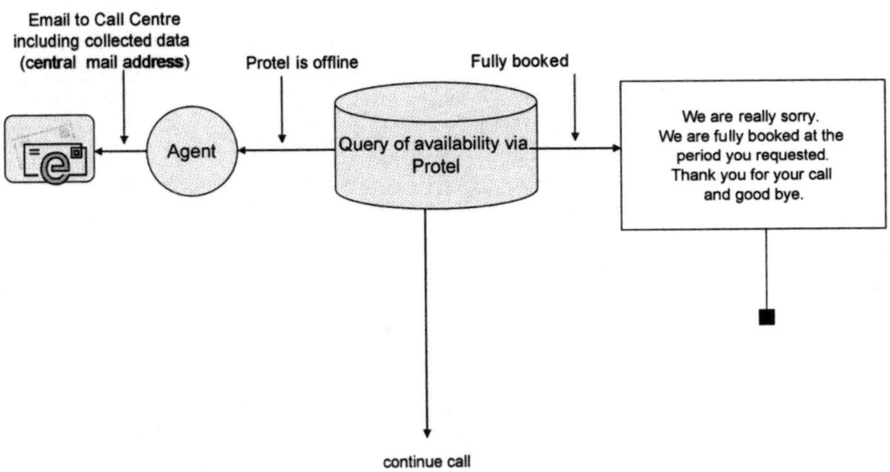

Fig. 3. Connecting RESA and booking engine

A connection to the booking software is necessary to check the availability of free rooms. Figure 3 demonstrates how the booking engine is integrated in this process.

In the following a transcript of a recorded dialogue in German is shown. Figure 4 describes the system process of the marked text sequence in more detail.

Text generated by RESA is shown in standard letters, answers from the caller in *italic* (Figure 5).

Some notable remarks

RESA is speaker-independent, thus meaning that there is no training required for RESA to understand a speaker. This is an absolute necessity .because the callers con not to be expected to be familiar with the usage of such a system.
RESA can handle different time and date formats and can determine which format the user enters based on the present situation (like today, 12th of March, in two weeks, etc., relative and absolute dates).
At any point the user can switch to a human agent – provided that one is free.
RESA can send a SMS with the booking details to the user so that he has something written in his hands.

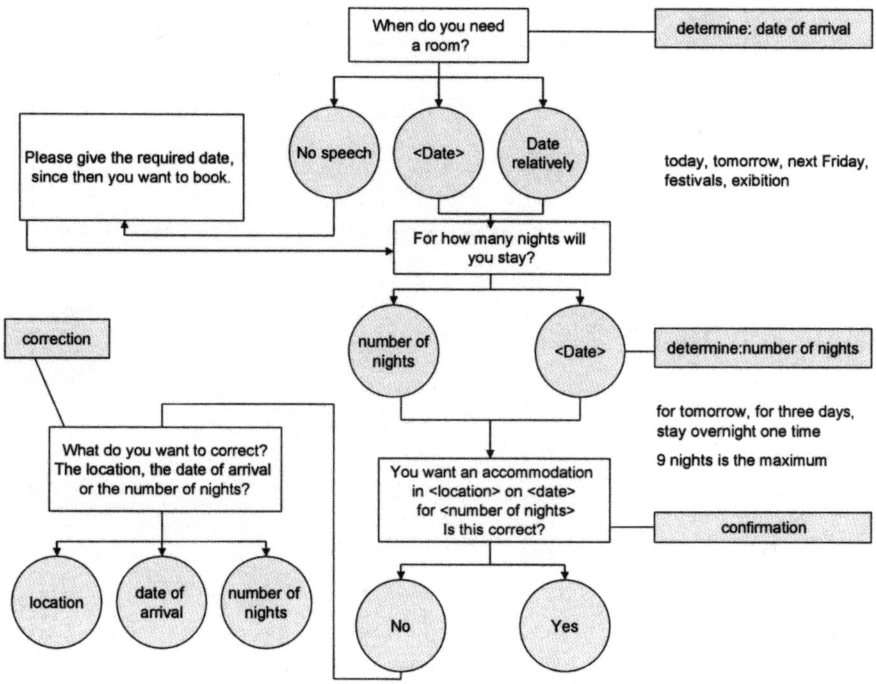

Fig. 4. Dialogue Flow Extract

Welcome to Orange Wings. You are connected with Resa our automated booking system. You can book a room with me by credit card or speak to the next free staff member. Just say Resa or staff member.

- *Resa*

You can interrupt me any time and with the word help I will explain the system to you.

For which location do you need a room?

- *Krems*

When to you need a room?

The day after tomorrow onwards

How many nights will you stay?

-For one night

You want a room in Krems from the August, 10 for one night. Is this correct?

- *Yes*

Which category would you prefer? Available are standard rooms for € 46, apartments for € 76 or rooms for the disabled for € 46.

- *Standard*

Would you like a smoker or a non-smoker room?

- *Non-smoker*

You want a non-smoker standard room. Is this correct?

- *Yes*

The price for your stay in Krems from the August, 10 for one night amounts to 46€. Would you like to make a reservation with credit card now?

- *Yes*

Fig. 5. Transcript of a booking dialogue from German to English

4 Evaluation

The goal of the evaluation was to identify any weaknesses in the dialogue structure before putting RESA into operation. The functionality of the first prototype was tested in a field experiment, for which a student sample was selected. Altogether the test persons held 66 phone calls. The subjects had to carry out different, precisely defined tasks. The tasks given corresponded to real booking situations. For example:

You need a room for two nights in Krems for next weekend. Book a standard, non-smoking room.

The test call was recorded by RESA. In addition, the test persons were videotaped. After the call the test persons were interviewed and their experiences with the system were reflected in terms of a structural evaluation. The following criteria were considered:

- volume
- pitch of the voice
- pronunciation
- pace
- comprehension
- comprehensibility of dialogue
- phrasing of dialogue
- length of dialogue
- confirmation (repetitions)

All in all the system worked well. The real weak point was the length of the dialogue, which was basically caused by repetitions. But those were necessary to verify the received information.

Another important finding was that in some cases the recognition of numbers was difficult and people had to repeat those data. Since numbers form an integral part of the payment process by credit card eliminating this weakness resulted in an essential improvement of the final prototype.

In addition, the participants had the option to give individual feedback which in general was positive. Once again the length of the dialogue and the high number of repetitions was criticized. Figures 6 and 7 show some results of the evaluation. More than 40% noted that the system worked well, nearly 15% said very well. Only six percents gave negative feedback. Obviously, the results of this evaluation contributed to the further development of the prototype.

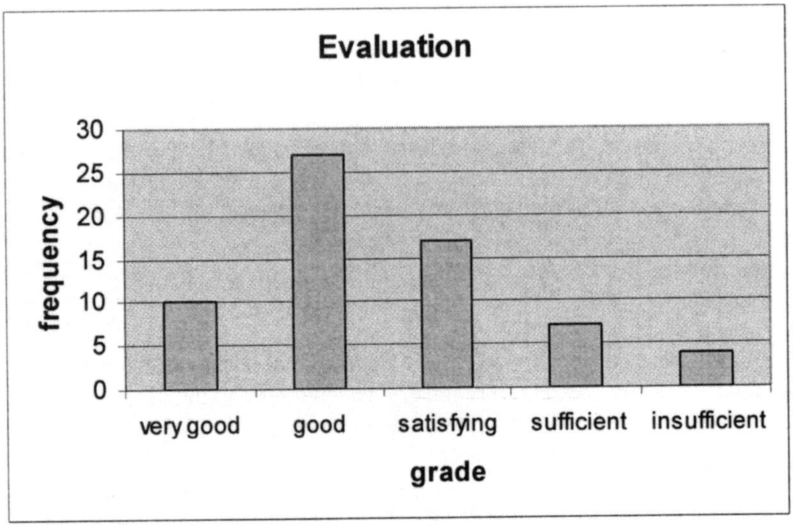

Fig. 6. Evaluation with grades

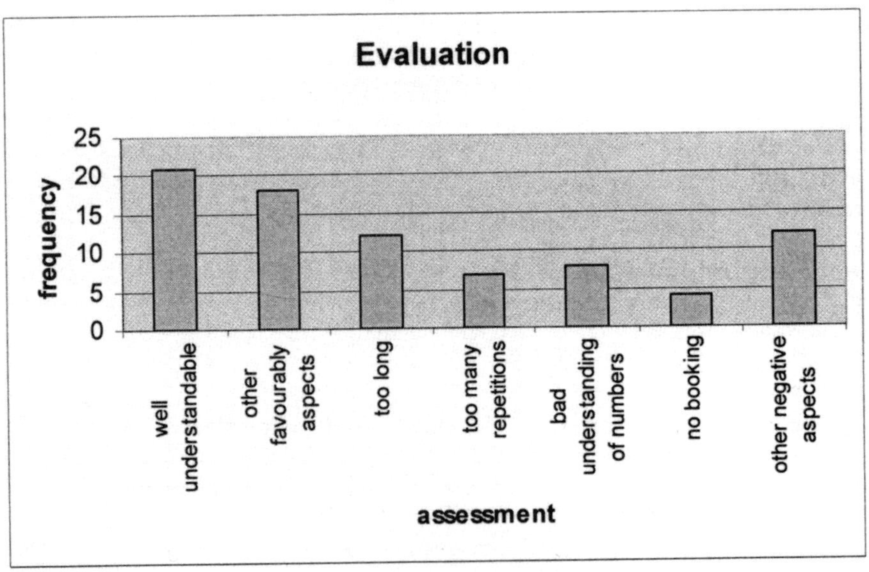

Fig. 7. Qualitative Evaluation

5 Advantages

What are the advantages for a hotel chain to implement such a solution?

The first main advantage of the system is to save money. This is possible because of the following two reasons:

Due to the increasing amount of calls the number of call centre agents needs to be extended. Human resources are still a main cost factor here. In addition bookings are done at different peak times thus the resource demand depends on day time and the day of the week. Using an automated system helps the hotel chain to get those costs under control as a reasonable amount of the calls can be handled by RESA.

It always takes some time until call centre agents have acquired the necessary information to handle guest requests. Thus in peak situations the call centre cannot just switch from one agent to the next but in order to give good support the agents need training. And training costs money.

Other advantages are not directly associated with costs but will bring indirect profit.

Since RESA is always available incoming calls do not have to wait for a free agent. The guest can immediately start the booking dialogue. This clearly enhances the customer relationship aspect for the hotel.
RESA does not get tired or bored by the same guest calls. It is always in the same mood, very patient and is not affected by possible irritations by customers.
In most situations bookings nearly have the same structure and layout. For most calls they can be handled automatically. Those calls can be easily carried out by RESA. The human call centre agents can concentrate on more difficult booking cases like cancellations, bookings for groups, handicapped people etc.

6 Enhancements

As already mentioned, RESA will be further enhanced in the future. The dialogue system will also provide the ability to manage complaints. For example, it should give support for arrival or the handling of devices like the multimedia station in hotel rooms. Multilingualism is another important point because language skills of call centre agents are often very limited. But higher qualified staff generates higher costs. Implementing an efficient software solution would be more cost effective in the long run. The goal is to answer as many calls as possible with the automated system, so the call centre agents have time for more complicated needs and problems of the guests (2nd level support).

A further ambitious goal is to explore the option of a free dialogue situation, thus the caller can specify his booking in a single sentence or a series of sentences like "I want to book a room in Krems for three days starting with next Monday. And it should be a non-smoker room. How much is it?" This type of dialogue support will clearly enhance the user acceptance. With the nominal end of the project in about two years time RESA should at least handle some simple dialogue situations of this kind.

The concept of RESA is also suitable for other hotels and hotel chains, but not limited to the hotel business. It can also be useful for other tourism areas, like hotlines of tourism destinations or even airlines, where they are already used in some cases (Euromap, 2002). In these cases many dialogue situations are similar to the current RESA implementation and only a few fragments would have to be exchanged. Thus with an automated speech system it is possible to handle more calls and avoid annoying waiting time for the customers.

References

Balentine, B. & Morgan D. P. (1999). *How to build a speech recognition application.* Enterprise Integration Group.

Euromap (2002). Travelling the last kilometre to the customer: Opportunities and obstacles for human language technology solutions in the tourism sector; (http://www.hltcentral.org/usr_docs/members_only/task_forces/Tourism/Final_Report_tourism.pdf).

Furui, S. (2001). *Digital Speech Processing, Synthesis, and Recognition* (2. Auflage). Marcel Decker.

Huang, X. et al. (2001). *Spoken Language Processing, Theory, Algorithms, System Development.* Prentice Hall.

IEEE (2002) Transactions on Speech and Audio Processing. 10 (8),

Jelinek, F. (1999). *Statistical Methods for Speech Recognition.* MIT Press.

Jurafsky, D. & Martin, J. H. (2000). *Speech and Language Processing Upper* Saddle River: Prentice Hall.

Rabiner, L. & Juang, B.-H. (1993). *Fundamentals of Speech Recognition.* Prentice Hall.

O'Shaughnessy, D. (2000). *Speech Communication* (2. Auflage). IEEE Press.

W3C (2006) Standards for Voicedialogs like Voice Extensible Markup Language (VoiceXML 2.1) or Semantic Interpretation for Speech Recognition (SISR) Version 1.0 http://www.w3.org/Voice.

Wahlster, W. (1993). *Verbmobil: Foundations of Speech-to-Speech Translation. Artificial Intelligence.* Berlin, Heidelberg, New York; Springer Verlag.

A Speech Dialog System (SDS) as an Additional Communication Channel in Tourism – a Vision for the Destination of Innsbruck

Anita Zehrer
Tatjana Hobbhahn

School of Tourism and Leisure
Management Center Innsbruck (MCI), Austria
anita.zehrer@mci.edu
tatjana.hobbhahn@gmail.com

Abstract

IT in tourism helps to reduce information gaps among suppliers by providing information on market products, and among consumers by reducing the complexity of decision making. Mobile tourist information applications for in-trip information services are developed in different ways. Speech technology offers a similar in-trip information system in the form of a telephony speech dialog systems (SDS), which provides diverse information via a telephone voice interface in a dialog of question and answer. The idea of a destination speech dialog system so far solely exists in theory. The system can be reached by tourists via a (mobile) telephone in the destination where they receive information on sights, accommodation, opening hours, entrance fees, the weather, etc. The exploratory qualitative study adopts a supplier-centred approach, interviewing ten tourism suppliers and IT experts. Besides the study results on SDS, the paper gives insights into the structure and information content, image effects, marketing ideas, and directions for future research.

Keywords: telephony speech dialog system, speech technology, mobile information, suppliers' view.

1 Introduction

Speech technology ranks among artificial intelligence and facilitates the control of computer technology by using voice commands via a voice interface. It aims at enabling computers to recognise, understand, interpret and generate all forms of human speech (Anonymous, 2003). This definition implies that computers understand acoustic commands given by a person over telephone or microphone and, that computers like human beings provide information saved in a database to build a dialog with the caller. Therefore, these systems are called speech dialog systems or voice portals. Experts in speech technology forecast a wide range of usage in the future, even though the technology suffered a loss of image by employing poorly delivered applications in the past (Buhalis, 1996). But with the development of speech technology commercial applications are possible, promising advantages to both, consumers and suppliers. In the tourism industry, speech dialog systems can also be applied, giving the tourist the opportunity to ask for information over a voice user interface via (mobile) telephone anywhere and at any time. Most of today's' speech technology applications can be found in time–table and booking information for the railway, airport, traffic information, or weather reports. The vision of the destination dialog system is a further development of this traffic information. Information on the destination itself, accommodation, catering, attractions and sights, as well as information on opening hours of e.g. the tourist office, shops, or museums could be included in such a system, too. Moreover the system could dispose of information about up-coming events and congresses, information on public transport like time tables, or a navigation tool based on LBS for a better orientation in the city. It builds an opposite to the visual or multi-modal tourist guides that are being developed in many cities at present (i.e. solutions like DEEP Map, Ling Ware, CRUMPET, etc.).

At the moment, the vision of a tourism speech dialog system still is in its beginning and solely exists in theory. Hence, the purpose of the study is to examine the view of tourism suppliers in Innsbruck towards a destination voice portal. Besides studying the information supply to the tourists as a service, the marketing effects of a potential destination voice portal was a point of discussion. In this case, the voice portal can be seen as an additional communication channel in the tourism industry, delivering the required information to the tourists via a telephone voice interface anywhere and at any time, while simultaneously marketing the products of the destination.

2 Theoretical Background

Information is vital to the tourism industry which was already shown by Schertler in 1994, describing the tourism branch as an information industry (Schertler, 1994). The characteristics of heterogeneity (Roth, 2003) and intangibility (Kreilkamp, 1998) of the tourism product cause a high demand of information on the customer's side. Especially the intangibility involves that consumers can not test or touch the tourism product before they actually consume it. Thus, the consumer accepts a certain risk on the service performance by the tourism supplier (Cowell, 1992). This implies that the tourism product can be defined as a high-risk product that demands authentic and adequate information (Seaton & Bennett, 1996), while information can be classified into static information such as the furnishing of a hotel almost does not change during time, versus dynamic information that varies with capacity such as hotel rates during the seasons (Sheldon, 1997); and pre-trip information which is sought after by the guest before the trip, versus in-trip information which includes all kinds of information that the guest searches during his stay in the destination (Sheldon, 1997). For further decision making, information is needed by tourists before the journey as well as during their trip (Werthner, 2003). Especially the demand for in-trip information is growing, following the trend of getting information rather late, i.e. tourists search for information and choose a destination shortly before their vacation starts (Sheldon, 1997). Tourism suppliers have to provide information to consumers not only to fill the lack of information before and during the journey, but also to market their products (Sheldon, 1997). Simultaneously, suppliers need information about the consumers to meet their wishes and needs. If these parts do not fit together, information asymmetries arise on the market, which have to be reduced as much as possible by the use of different strategies (Schertler, 1994).

One possible strategy to reduce gaps between information supply and demand is the usage of information technology (IT). Especially companies or industries with a high need of accumulating, saving, converting and allocating data, are affected by the digitalisation (Clement, 2001). Tourism as an information industry is affected by the infiltration of IT (Corigliano & Baggio, 2004; Poon, 1993). The automatisation in the services industry has lead to a discussion on missing or bad personal services by using IT, especially due to the constant growth of the Internet. Retrospectively, the suspected apprehension of technology did not occur (Witt & Mountinho, 1989). Moreover, consumers accepted IT in tourism, and today online reservation and booking systems belong to the most frequently used internet applications in tourism (Schulz, Frank, & Seitz, 1996). With the development of the internet, an important tool for information search and product marketing was born. Witt and Moutinho (1989) realised at an early stage that the upcoming internet-based information systems are an excellent channel to market products efficiently and provide information to consumers. The further deployment of IT will determine the competition in (electronic) tourism in terms of artificial intelligence applications for tourism (Hair & Keep, 1997). Yet, artificial intelligence should not be understood as manlike robots that serve humans, but as applications such as intelligent user interfaces, animated web agents, and speech technology applications. Speech dialog systems consist of several components; the two most often named are a) the automatic speech recognizer (ARS) at the input level and b) the text-to-speech engine (TTS) at the output level.

Speech technology has already been deployed in the tourism industry in 1990, but is still named "audio text". Audio text was defined as "interactive online access to databases utilizing speech- or audio– recognition technology" (Schulz et al., 1996). The possibilities to transform text to speech was constituted as "very good", and the systems disposed of speaker-independent voice recognition with a vocabulary of approximately twenty words. The identified applications lay in the field of information, reservation, marketing and entertainment. The REISEfon for instance can be named as one of the earliest applications of voice technology in tourism that contained last minute offers (Schulz et al., 1996). Moreover, the Galaxy system holds information on flight plans, city maps and weather reports (Sheldon, 1997). Today, more up-to-date applications such as e.g. "Der sprechende Fahrplan" of the city of Salzburg for timetable information on public transport (www.salzburger-verkehrsverbung.at) or the "hotelofon", which provides accommodation information in the whole of Austria (www.hotelofon.at) exist.

Although the idea behind a tourism speech dialog system or voice portal is easy, the technological implementation presumably is sophisticated and time intensive. Yet, it can be stated that the acoustic destination guide provides information to tourists as an informative service over a (mobile) telephone interface, building a dialog with the caller. Furthermore, the marketing chances of a destination voice portal become apparent. By being represented in this tourism dialog system, the different tourism suppliers may easily market their products, as well as gather information on consumers' needs with the software recording the required information.

2.1 Advantages of Speech Technology

Especially, tourism information is depending on location (Malaka & Zipf, 2000). Tourists moving around in a destination need direct access to information over IT systems, that are easy to use and that can be carried around without major problems (Malaka & Zipf, 2000). Speech, as the most natural interface of human beings (Steimel & Klemann, 2004, [onl.]) is always available and also supports hand-free and eye-free interaction which can be the deciding factor for pedestrians or drivers (Malaka & Zipf, 2000). Moreover, input modalities of future PDAs and mobile phones will still be limited due to small keyboards. In other words speech input offers a good alternative (Erbach, 2000). Moreover, the possibility to offer access to information 24/7 is a big advantage as the "new tourist" is more experienced and expects a reliable day and night service (Vickery, 2005, [onl.]). Giving him the chance to ask for information in a kind of self-service system, he can feed his need of an individual and around the clock service (Corigliano & Baggio, 2004, [onl.]), instead of forming a queue in the tourist office or be placed on hold on the telephone.

2.2 Disadvantages of Speech Technology

Speech has a high variability, meaning that a person can express the same term in different ways (Mittendorfer, Niklfeld, & Winiwarter, 2001, [onl.]). Also dialects or accents may cause problems for speech recognition (Baum, Erbach, & Kommenda, 2001; Hitzenberger, 1999). Moreover, problems with background noise, particularly in mobile surroundings, may arise and influence the quality of speech recognition (Baum et al., 2001). Another problem might be a dialog logic related to the DTMF (Dual Tone Multi Frequency) which is developed on keyboard logic. However, speech dialog systems should be related more to a dialog lead by a call centre agent (Klemann & Steimel, 2004, [onl.]). Next to the technical challenges, there are also some psychological ones. First, there has to be referred to the missing personal contact of a speech dialog system. Although, anonymity and reduction of personal contact are sometimes welcome, especially when service quality highly depends on the education and attitude of the employees (Corigliano & Baggio, 2004; Scheuch, 1982). Simultaneously, a speech dialog system can have an own personality, speaking of 'himself' in the first person singular, having a certain humour or sex (Kotelly, 2003). Another psychological challenge is the anxiety of employees that they will be substituted by technology. But the application of a speech dialog system can not be planned under the aspect of complete automation. It has to be considered that there will always be inquiries the dialog system can not answer, e.g. due to the high complexity of a question. In this case, a transmission of these questions to a human being or call centre agent is still necessary. Therefore, a speech dialog system can be seen as a chance and as an additional instrument for answering standard questions of tourists while employees at the same time deal with more complex inquiries. Both will help the guest and contribute to improve consumer satisfaction (Sohn, 2005, [onl.]). Additionally, costs have to be considered. Costs of development and implementation are still high as there does not exist an out-of-the-box solution, although the average pay-pack period is said to be eight months (Steimel & Klemann, 2004, [onl.]). First, the number of daily calls to the speech dialog system has to be calculated. Second, the question arises whether a tourism speech dialog system shall be a free service or whether the caller will be liable to pay. On the one hand, the solution for this question depends on the funding of the speech dialog system in a destination (Flouri & Buhalis, 2004), which might be a challenge. A speech dialog system will be an overall destination project, requiring a high cooperation among the different stakeholders of the destination. On the other hand, the willingness to pay depends on the benefit of the service for the consumer: The higher the benefit, the more willingness to pay can be expected (Tascher, 2001). In the future, different mobile internet services will come up and provide information to tourists by visual and graphic interfaces. Yet, the question about cost allocation is not resolved, even if a former study revealed that the majority of people is willing to pay a similar fee as a call in a mobile net would cost for graphical or textual location-based services (Corigliano & Baggio, 2004; Ghandour & Buhalis, 2003). However, there still has to be considered that the navigation on mobile devices is complicated due to the small keyboards and displays, the access to mobile internet is still relatively limited (Schmidt-Belz, Zipf, Poslad, & Laamen, 2003) and not all internet pages support WAP technology (Ghandour & Buhalis, 2003).

3 Methodology

Authors carried out an exploratory study on the possible future implementation of a speech dialog system in the destination of Innsbruck (Austria) from the suppliers' point of view. The qualitative survey was conducted as ideas of an acoustic destination guide and voice technology are innovative and need explanation for most of the people. As interviewing technique a personal interview was chosen and authors spoke to ten experts of the tourism industry in the Tirol, most of them from the city of Innsbruck, with all experts either actively working in tourism – new media in tourism, local tourist organizations and hotel managers. The selection of experts was taken on the supposition that speech technology experts and enthusiasts may be prejudiced against and not critical enough towards the idea of an acoustic destination guide. The interviews were conducted between April 10th and April 24th 2006. A list of seven open questions was developed and divided into three major parts: part one included initial questions about the interviewer's personal knowledge and experience with dialog systems in general. The second part consisted of questions directly connected to the vision of a tourism speech dialog system in Innsbruck asking interviewees about what kind of information the system should contain, what kind of organisation could be the initiator of such a voice portal and what kind of advantages and disadvantages such a system could have. The last part of the questionnaire addressed marketing questions, i.e. dealing with the image effects of a voice portal and the choice of marketing activities to introduce the acoustic destination guide to the users.

All experts were first contacted via e-mail and informed about the objective of the study, including a short introduction into voice technology. Appointments were made without major problems. Except from three interviews which were held via a skype internet telephone connection, all interviews were conducted personally, recording all interviews with hot recorder software for further evaluation. The interviews lasted between 20 and 45 minutes and were analysed by means of the content analysis of Mayring (2000). Mayring's concept of qualitative content analysis was developed in the 1980s with the main idea "to preserve the advantages of quantitative content analysis as developed within communication science and to transfer and further develop them to qualitative-interpretative steps of analysis" (Mayring, 2000, p. 2).

4 Results

The majority of the interviewees have already heard about dialog systems and related them to DTFM systems, where the caller has to press buttons on the keyboard of his telephone to be forwarded to a certain person. But DTMF systems are still too complicated and sometimes the option the user needs is not available. Also, experiences with SDS have already been made by the interviewees and largely consisted of flight or timetable information. But in Europe SDS still not exist very often and experts concluded that the first contact with SDS is very important. For most consumers it can be surprising to talk to a computer all over a sudden. At the same time, it has to be made clear that one is talking to a computer, whereas most interviewees stated that they would still prefer personal attendance.

4.1 Personal Experiences with SDS

The missing personal contact has been named to be one of the main arguments against the implementation of a tourist SDS. Next to this the complexity of questions is stated as a problem for a SDS, which can only be answered by a person with adequate background. Nonetheless, interviewees stated what kinds of information a SDS should contain: information on tourism-related enterprises, location of the accommodation in the city, rates, furnishing, but also information on POI, architecture, events, theatre & cinema, museum & castles, sports & nature, public transport, weather, opening hours, car parks, etc. Interestingly the internet was seen as comparable medium which led to the conclusion that a destination SDS should include all information the internet offers. But it will be difficult acoustically to include that much information, as a caller will not listen to texts which are too long.

4.2 Information Provision of SDS

Reducing the information and choosing an adequate information depth is a very important aspect for SDS. Furthermore, the type of information has to be classified, into the following types: standard versus complex inquiries, static versus dynamic information, city tourism versus holiday tourism, and pure information versus booking option. Interestingly the first three information tpyes are seen as parallel topics: standard queries are allocated to static information and at the same time to city tourism, which implies that an answer can be given by a SDS without major problems. On the other hand, complex queries are seen related to dynamic, changing information and holiday tourism, where emotion and atmosphere has an important role and inquiries therefore can not be answered via SDS as it can not build up confidence and emotional connectedness. Next to this category there was also made a distinction between a SDS as a pure information service by telephone, equal to the category of standard inquiries and static information. But then there can also be included a booking option in a SDS, e.g. for accommodation facilities. This aspect was seen critical and not probable, as the internet was identified as a better tool. Therefore, interviewees suggested a transmission to the respective hotel as it is already done by the "hotelofon" (see www.hotelofon.at) to guarantee individual and personal attendance. Another argument against a booking interface in the SDS was that information in the home country is not critical for most travellers. Before deciding on a destination, consumers invest some time in information search, whereas the information in the destination is needed immediately. The most important kinds of information a SDS should provide according to the experts are the following.

Table 1. Information of SDS

Information on	Counts
• tourism service providers (4)	10
• sights/POI	5
• events	5
• architecture/history	5
• cultural events (theatre/music/cinema/museum)	4
• sports/nature/adventure	4
• maps of the destination	4
• catering (60 providers in the old town of Innsbruck)	3
• public transport, taxi, cityliner	3
• weather (weather forecast)	3
• opening hours	2
• cable cars	2
• peculiarities of the region	1
• car parks	1

4.3 Functionality and Organisation of SDS

Irrespective of the categorisation of information, the study revealed that a SDS can not answer all incoming questions, but a scenario and a method for resolution can be developed. First, all incoming questions at the different information agencies of the city of Innsbruck have to be recorded and analysed to unveil which questions are the most frequent ones. In a second step, an overall picture will result from the comparison among information agencies, which can be classified again in standard queries and complex queries. The last ones can be analysed again for feasibility of being answered by a SDS. In the third step there will always be questions that the system can not answer and have to be dealt with by a call centre agent. Moreover interviewees stated that a call centre agent can avert dissatisfaction of consumers that do not understand the system. These scenarios lead to an important question about the sponsorship to take over the costs of implementation, information analysis, up-dating of information, etc. On the one hand, there has to be a main sponsor, who interviewees identified in the local tourist organisation (LTO). Yet, the representative of the LTO argued that it is not a competence centre for speech technology while in the same moment the existing image of the city of Innsbruck was not conforming to a "high tech"-SDS. On the other hand, there was also seen a private organisation to be better qualified for this challenge as it has more competitive power, especially in terms of price and profitability. In the end, the solution seems to be an aggregation of the two approaches - a main sponsor such as the LTO offers the skeletal structure of the SDS, which was acknowledged under certain circumstances by the LTO. At the same time a private contraction by the different tourism stakeholders of the destination can provide the opportunity to develop an individual acoustical representation of their enterprise in the SDS depending from their individual marketing budget.

4.4 Identified Advantages of SDS

A SDS offers information access 24/7, which was identified as the most important advantage, next to the promptitude of service delivery. At the same time a SDS can answer several calls synchronically. Another advantage was the consistent cordiality that a SDS offers, meaning that it does not suffer from bad mood even if the same question is asked a hundred times. Moreover, the needed multilingualism in tourism can be offered by a SDS and was seen as positive, but also critical as there may be a lot of different accents and dialects on the side of the callers. Also literature determines dialect and accent issues to be one of the main problems of ARS (Baum et al., 2001; Hitzenberger, 1999). The kinds of languages depend on the marketing strategy of the destination - if the SDS reach international consumers implying a world-wide marketing campaign for the SDS, at least the most important world languages have to be represented in the system. Additionally, interviewees discussed the voice to be critical for a successful voice system, i.e. a Tyrolean accent that is not too intensive could authentically convey Tyrolean hospitality. Two other important advantages were named - the independence of the tourist from printed material of the destination, especially if the SDS is called from the own mobile phone. And secondly, the advantage of having answered standard questions while at the same time having more time available for personal service and care in case of complex inquiries.

4.5 Identified Disadvantages of SDS

One of the main disadvantages pointed out by the experts is the missing personal contact, followed by charging tourists' telephones for information services. Hence, it is assumed that the willingness to pay for the service equals the importance of the information to the guest. As far as the information depth is concerned, interviewees agreed that a SDS should contain the information of a printed city guide. Following this proposal, the SDS fee could amount to the price one would pay for a printed city guide. As a matter of fact, the willingness to pay depends on the individual time-benefit and cost–benefit relation. Independent from how this topic will be resolved, a demand for an international telephone number which is easy to remember exists. This number should be communicated via all printed information material with sound information on the SDS facility. At best, marketing activities shall inform the tourist about the SDS before he arrives in the destination.

4.6 Challenges of SDS

Besides advantages and disadvantages certain challenges were identified in the study.

- The density and up-dating of information in the SDS. A well-balanced information density is needed, as well as up-to-date information. A system can only be as good as the up-dating process of the system works.
- T‚ᴗ many advertisements. An option to fund a SDS is to include sponsored advertisements, similar to spots on the radio.
- Anxiety of employees to be substituted by the SDS. Internal marketing has to convey that SDS can not work without human backup.
- The implementation of a SDS will have influence on the image of Innsbruck. The majority of the interviewees agreed that SDS will be seen positive for the destination, whereas scepticism exists.

5 Conclusion and Further Research

The study tried to reveal the atmosphere among tourism suppliers towards the implementation of a voice portal in Innsbruck. The interviewees were chosen according to three groups: new media in tourism, local tourist organisations and hotels managers. In the first group a neutral to positive spirit predominated towards the idea of a tourism-based SDS, while at the same time the technical challenges were seen in implementing the system. The representatives of the LTO have been more sceptical due to the high complexity of inquiries in tourism that are made by telephone and the challenge to convince the different tourism stakeholders to participate in the project. The third group of experts clearly showed their positive attitude to successfully implementing such a system. To sum up, it can be concluded that there still exist a lot of challenges, i.e. the lacking experience of the population with an upcoming technology such as a speech dialog system. This question for instance will be answered by carrying out a follow-up survey among tourists in the destination of Innsbruck, where the tourists' perception of SDS is analysed.

References

Baum, M., Erbach, G. & Kommenda, M. (2001). Kommunikation mit Maschinen. *Funkschau* 1/2001: 26- 28.

Buhalis, D. (1996). Information and telecommunication technologies as a strategic tool for tourism enhancement at destination regions. In S. Klein, B. Schmid, A. Tjoa & H. Werthner (Eds.), Information and Communication technologies in tourism. ENTER 1996. Wien-NewYork: Springer Verlag.

Clement, M., Peters, K., & Preiß, F. J. (2001). Electronic Commerce. In S. Albers, M. Clement, & K. Peters (Eds.), *Marketing mit interaktiven Medien.* F.A.Z. - Institut für Management-, Markt- und Medieninformationen (56 – 70). Frankfurt am Main: Suhrkamp Verlag.

Corigliano, M., A. & Baggio, R. (2004). Tourism, technology, information and relationship with customers. In proceedings of the International Leisure Futures Conference. Bolzano, Italy. Retrieved February 3, 2006 from http://www.iby.it/turismo/baggio_leisfut02.pdf

Cowell, D. W. (1992). Marketing Services. In M.J. Baker(Ed.), The Marketing Book (456 – 466). Oxford: Butterworth Heinemann.

Erbach, G. (2000). Sprachdialogsysteme für Telefondienste, Stand der Technik und künftige Entwicklungen. In proceedings „Sprachtechnologie für eine dynamische Wirtschaft im Medienzeitalter“. Cologne, Germany. Retrieved March 20, 2006 from http://www.mcgreg.net/pub/ivsw00/ivsw2000-erbach.pdf

Flouri, E. & Buhalis, D. (2004). Wireless Technologies for tourism Destinations. In A. J. Frew (Eds.), International Conference on Information and Communication Technologies in Tourism (27– 38). Wien: Springer Verlag.

Ghandour, R. & Buhalis, G. (2003). Third Generation Mobile Services and the Need of mTravellers. In A. J. Frew, M. Hitz, & P. O'Conner (Eds.), Proceedings of the international Conference on Information and Communications Technologies in Tourism (222 –231). Wien – New York: Springer Verlag.

Hair, J. F., & Keep, W. W. (1997). Electronic Marketing, future possibilities. In R. A. Peterson (Eds.), Electronic Marketing and the consumer (163 – 173). Thousand Oaks – London - New Delhi: SAGE Publications.

Hitzenberger, L. (1999.) Spracherkennung: Grundlagen und Perspektiven. In F. Lehner, G. Braungart, & L. Hitzenberger (Eds.), Multimedia – Informationssysteme zwischen Bild und Sprache (109 – 116). Wiesbaden: Gabler Deutscher Universitätsverlag.

Klemann, J., & Steimel, B. (2004). Sprachanwendungen auf dem Vormarsch. Study on speech dialog systems in the enterprise market. Bad Homburg: m|i|n|d und Strateco GmbH. Retrieved April 4, 2006 from http://www.callnet.ch/CallNetSolution/

Kotelly, B. (2003). The Art and Business of Speech Recognition: Creating the noble voice. Boston: Pearson Education.

Kreilkamp, E. (1998). Produkt- und Preispolitik. In G. Haedrich, C. Kaspar, H. Kleinert, & K. Klemm (Eds.), Tourismus-Management – Tourismus-Marketing und Fremdenverkehrsplanung (325-356). Berlin: de Gruyter.

Malaka, R. & Zipf, A. (2000). DEEP MAP – Challenging IT research in the framework of a tourist information system. In D.R. Fesenmaier, D. Klein, & D. Buhalis (Ed.), International Conference on Information and Communication Technologies in Tourism 2000, ENTER (15-27). Wien: Springer Verlag.

Mayring, P. (2000). Qualitative content analysis [28 paragraphs]. Forum Qualitative Sozialforschung. *Qualitative Social Research*, 1(2): 1-10.

Mittendorfer, M., Niklfeld, G. & Winiwarter, W. (2001). Evaluation of Intelligent Component Technologies for Voice XML Applications. Retrieved February 2, 2006 from http://speech.ftw.at/download/EvalVoiceXML.pdf.

Poon, A. (1993). Tourism, technology and competitive strategies. Oxford: C.A.B. International.

Roth, P. (2003). Grundlagen des Touristikmarketing. In P. Roth, & Schrand, A. (Eds.), Touristikmarketing (31 – 147). Muenchen: Vahlen Verlag.

Seaton, A. & Bennett, M. M. (1996). Marketing Tourism Produkts – Concepts, Issues, Cases. London: International Thomson Business Press.

Sheldon, P. (1997). Tourism Information Technology. Oxford: Cab International.

Scheuch, F. (1982). Dienstleistungsmarketing. Muenchen: Verlag Franz Vahlen.

Schertler, W. (1994). Tourismus als Informationsgeschäft, Strategische Bedeutung neuer Informations- und Kommunikationstechnologien im Tourismus. Wien: Wirtschaftverlag Karl Ueberreuter.

Schmidt-Belz, B., Zipf, A., Poslad, S., Laamen, H. (2003). Location Based Tourist Services – first User Experiences, In A. J. Frew, M. Hitz, & P. O'Connor (Eds.) Information and Communications Technologies in Tourism, (115- 123). Wien, New York: Springer Verlag.

Schulz, A., Frank, K. & Seitz, E. (1996). Tourismus und EDV, Reservierungssysteme und Telematik. Muenchen: Verlag Franz Vahlen.

Sohn, G. (2005). Einsatz von Sprachcomputern immer noch umstritte. Retrieved January 5, 2006 from http://www.voiceaward.de/index.aspx?page=139

Steimel, B. & Klemann, J. (2004). Praxisreport, Sprachapplikationen auf dem Prüfstand, Studie- Executive Version. Düsseldorf, Bad Homburg: m|i|n|d und Strateco GmbH. Retrieved March 31, 2006 from http://www.competence-site.de/dienstleistung.nsf/C6A8A0566625D778C1257053002B3B53/$File/voice%20studie%20exec%20vers_1.0.pdf

Tascher, A. (2001). Interaktive Medien als Systemgut. In S. Albers et al. (Eds.), Marketing mit interaktiven Medien (83 – 99). Frankfurt am Main: F.A.Z.- Institut für Management-, Markt- und Medieninformationen.

Anonymous (2003). VDIVDE Lexikon, Retrieved August 30, 2006 from http://www.vdivde-it.de/euromap/info/glossar.html

Vickery, G. (2005). Digital Delivery of Travel and Tourism Services, OECD/Committee for Information, Computer and Communications policy. Retrieved April 23, 2006 from http://www.anet-network.at/files/DSTI_ICCP_IE(2005)7_ENG-Summary.pdf

Werthner, H. (2003). Intelligent Systems in Travel and Tourism. Retrieved April 18, 2006 from http://dietorecs.itc.it/Papers/ijcai2003werthner.pdf.

Witt, S. F. & Moutinho, L. (1989). Tourism Marketing and Management Handbook. New York - London: Prentice Hall International.

Connecting Destinations with an Ontology-Based e-Tourism Planner

Roopa Jakkilinki
Mladen Georgievski
Nalin Sharda
School of Computer Science and Mathematics
Victoria University, Melbourne
{roopa, mladeng}@csm.vu.edu.au
nalin.sharda@vu.edu.au

Abstract

This paper presents the underlying structure and operation of a semantic web based intelligent tour planning tool. The semantic web is the future of the web and it can support the development of a wide range of intelligent services. Ontologies form the core of the semantic web; they provide a common understanding of domains and allow people and machines to communicate effectively to develop intelligent applications. The proposed tour planner has inbuilt intelligence which allows it to generate travel plans by matching the traveller requirements and vendor offerings stored in conjunction with the travel ontology.

Keywords: Tour Planner, Semantic Web, Tourism Ontology.

1 Introduction

Tour planning is an essential part of a successful trip. Before the advent of Information & Communication Technologies (ICT), planning a holiday or a trip was a cumbersome process. A tourist was required to manually seek information from various tourism operators and travel agencies in order to make travel arrangements. Developments in ICT have revolutionised the way various businesses are conducted. Tourism has benefited from ICT with the adoption of online web services, making tourism information universally accessible to the common traveller. Current websites facilitate users to access tourism related information, where they can research information about the places they want to visit by looking at different websites, online images, and even downloading video clips.

Current tourism websites also provide facilities for users to make hotel reservations, hire cars, and book flight tickets. However, this is still a complex procedure as the user has to visit a number of websites to gather information and make such bookings. Even gathering information is a complicated process, as the information available on the Internet is fragmented, making it difficult to locate just the right information. There is a need for a tour planner that provides easy access to required information, and a streamlined process to plan and book the travel arrangements. We propose to develop an Ontology-Based e-Tourism Planner that provides a mechanism for planning trips using semantic web technologies. This system uses intuitive interfaces developed using rich Internet application programming techniques. It enables users to specify their travel preferences, vendors to advertise their products, and the tool matches the user's travel preferences with the vendor offerings to develop an itinerary. The user can easily plan their trip from start to end.

Section 2 describes the Australian Sustainable Tourism Ontology (AuSTO), section 3 gives an overview of the design for the tour planner, and section 4 presents details of the system development and interfaces. Section 5 presents the tour planner's implementation, while sections 6 and 7 respectively present future work and conclusions.

2 Australian Sustainable Tourism Ontology (AuSTO)

An ontology is a data model that represents a domain; it can be used to reason about the objects in that domain and the relations between them. Ontologies represent knowledge about the world or some part of it, they consist of: *classes* - collection of objects; *attributes* - properties an object can have and share; *relations* - represent the way the objects are related; and *individuals* - which are instances of the class (Chandrasekaran, Josephson, & Benjamins, 1999). To create a productive ontology a well defined methodology has to be followed. Methodology encompasses the tools, techniques and procedures followed to develop ontologies. There are a number of established methodologies such as Uschold and King Methodology, Gruninger and Fox Methodology, Berneras et al Methodology, Methontology, Sensus Methodology (Corcho, Lopez, & Perez, 2003). The methodology adopted to develop an Australian Sustainable Tourism Ontology (AuSTO) is similar to Uschold and King methodology and was previously applied to develop an ontology in the Multimedia Design and Planning Pyramid project (Jakkilinki, Sharda, & Georgievski, 2005).

This methodology involves *identifying the purpose behind ontology development* which involves analysing why the ontology is being built, what is its intended use, and who would be the end users. The next step is to capture knowledge into the ontology which involves *determining the scope of the ontology* and selecting an approach for ontology development, and transforming the concepts into the ontology. This is then followed by *coding the ontology* which requires representing the ontology in a formal language. Numerous ontology editors are available to create ontologies. Protégé is the editor used to create AuSTO, and OWL (Web Ontology Language) is the language used to represent the ontology. *Refinement* follows coding and during this stage the ontology is further rectified. Refinement consists of two stages: intra coding refinement and extra coding refinement. *Intra coding refinement* involves perfecting the ontology and eliminating errors during the programming phase. *Extra coding refinement* is conducted at the post coding phase; the implementation is tested and debugged for any defects. *Testing* takes place once the implementation is complete; and final debugging is performed to eliminate deficiencies. The last phase is maintenance, which is an ongoing process, and could be corrective, adaptive or perfective (Jakkilinki et al., 2005; Pressman, 1997).

The AuSTO ontology is a knowledge store for the tourism domain information. It consists of classes, which describe various activities in the tourism domain. Some of the important classes in AuSTO are *Involved Party* which represents a traveller, vendor or operator. *Traveller Requirements* class is used to store the requirements of a traveller for a trip, the *Offering* class stores information regarding the vendor offerings, *Resource* class stores information regarding tourism resources, *Traveller Preference* class stores information regarding traveller preferences, *TourismRelatedEvent* class stores information regarding tourism related events such as conference event, entertainment event etc. The *Traveller* class stores information about the traveller, and *Destination* class stores information regarding the travel destination.

3 AuSTO system design

Fig. 1 depicts the underlying system design of the AuSTO. It consists of three layers: the Ontology Layer (OL), the Business Logic Layer (BLL) and the Graphical User Interface layer (GUIL). The OL contains the tourism ontology; the BLL includes two common components, which are the Inference Engine (IE) and the Custom Logic (CL) and part of the tour planner. The GUIL layer includes the Graphical User Interface (GUI) components of the tour planner application.

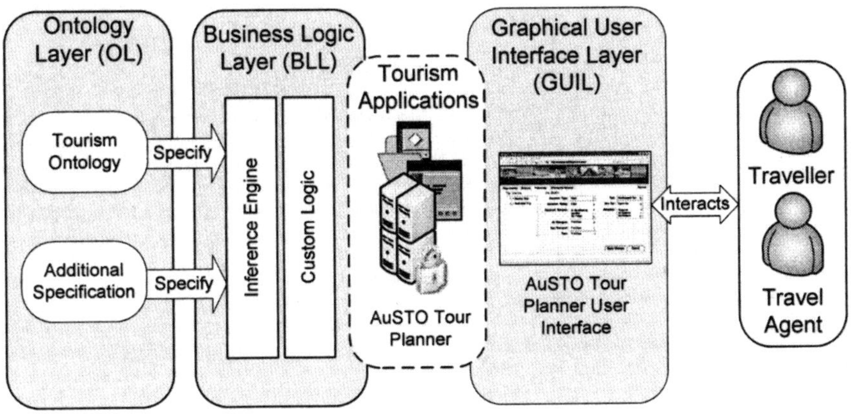

Fig. 1. AuSTO tour planner System Design

3.1 Ontology Layer

The Ontology Layer consists of the ontology which embodies knowledge about the domain and some additional specifications. This layer is the core of all semantic web systems. Creating the ontology involves delineating the concepts into a class hierarchy. The three important approaches to develop class hierarchies are top-down, bottom-up and a combination approach (Uschold & Gruninger, 1996). In the top-down approach the development process starts with the definition of the most general concepts in the domain, followed by specialised concepts. In the bottom-up approach the development process starts with the definition of the most specific classes, which form the leaves of the class hierarchy tree, with subsequent grouping of these classes into more general concepts. The combined approach uses a combination of top-down and bottom-up processes. The approach used to develop AuSTO is the bottom-up approach. This approach is usually driven by the need for having a workable vocabulary. AuSTO is an OWL (Web Ontology Language) ontology. The Ontology Layer (OL) acts as a knowledge store for the AuSTO system as it contains data regarding the tourism domain and the Business Logic Layer (BLL) acts upon this layer to generate itineraries.

3.2 Business Logic Layer

The Business Logic Layer (BLL) is the layer responsible for generating outcomes, it takes the user queries from the GUIL and matches them with the domain knowledge residing in the Ontology Layer and returns the results to the user via the GUIL. The BLL consists of a reasoner and custom logic, since the knowledge base is very large, inferencing mechanisms are needed to search through the knowledge base and deduce results in an organized manner. The BLL, which contains the reasoner, fulfils this need. The reasoner software applies axiomatic knowledge in the knowledge base to the task-specific data embodied for arriving at some conclusions (*Inference Engine*, n.d.). The Custom Logic is a mechanism which acts as a mediator between the reasoner, user interface and the ontology.

3.3 Graphical User Interface layer

The Graphical User Interface Layer (GUIL) comprises intuitive interfaces that allow the user to interact with the AuSTO tour planner tool. These interfaces allow users to enter travel requirements for a tour, including accommodation, transport facility, and venue booking. Other interfaces also available in this layer enable vendors to enter their offerings and services, such as hotels advertising their products. Once users have finalized their travel arrangement, their itinerary is produced by the system and then displayed to the user.

4 System Development and Interfaces

The user interface design for a system plays a crucial role in its success. Users want an easy to use and efficacious interface that takes them no more than ten minutes to learn. A user interface with these properties enhances the chances that users will return to use the system in the future (Nelson, 1987). User interface development involves design of the graphical elements on the computer screen which the user interacts with to complete required tasks. The first step in user interface design is to use task-modelling techniques to create a task model of the user interaction.

Task modelling technique is used to model the behaviour of a system from the user's perspective, thus enabling the requirements and actions of the system to be defined as a set of tasks. The behaviour of the system is modelled as a set of scenarios, where each scenario comprises a sequence of tasks. This allows the designers to improve the Human Computer Interaction (HCI) aspects when designing a systems operation (Georgievski & Sharda, 2003). Task models play an important role because they represent the logical activities that should support users in reaching their goals, thus knowing the tasks necessary for attaining their goal is fundamental to the design process.

CTTE (Concur Task Tree Environment) is a Java applet based tool developed by Human Computer Interaction Group-ISTI (Pisa) (*CTTE: Concur Task Trees Environment*, n.d.); it provides the ability to build task models from a visual perspective. Prior to the development of the AuSTO user interface we developed task models that modelled the behaviour of the system and the user interaction involved (Jakkilinki & Sharda, 2006). These task models have guided the development of AuSTO user interfaces.

This section presents the prototype user interface developed for the tour planner. The final system will be developed based on these prototype user interfaces. Fig. 2 shows the requirements screen, this allows the user to enter the trip requirements. The column to the left of the screen displays the trip overview. Towards the right of the screen are the trip details. This interface allows the user to enter the requirements of the trip such as trip name, accommodation, transport required and the attractions the user is planning to visit. This interface will also allow creating new trips, and adding trip Legs.

Moreover, Fig. 2 displays a snippet of OWL code for the AuSTO tourism ontology shown in the callout boxes. Line 12 to 15 in the OWL classes box shows the classes Trip, Attraction, Transport and Accommodation. Classes in an ontology have attributes or properties, the OWL Class properties box displays the property trip name which belongs to the class Trip.

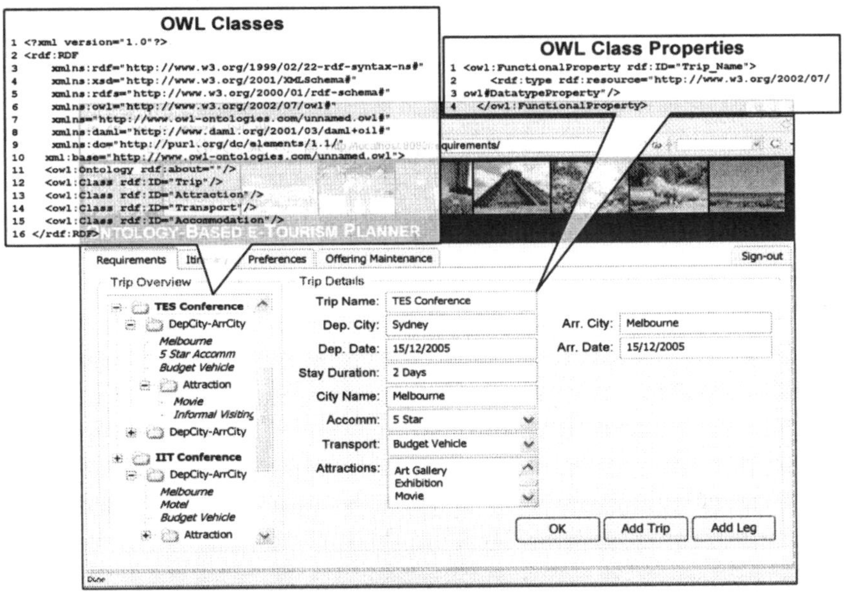

Fig. 2. AuSTO Tour planner requirements screen

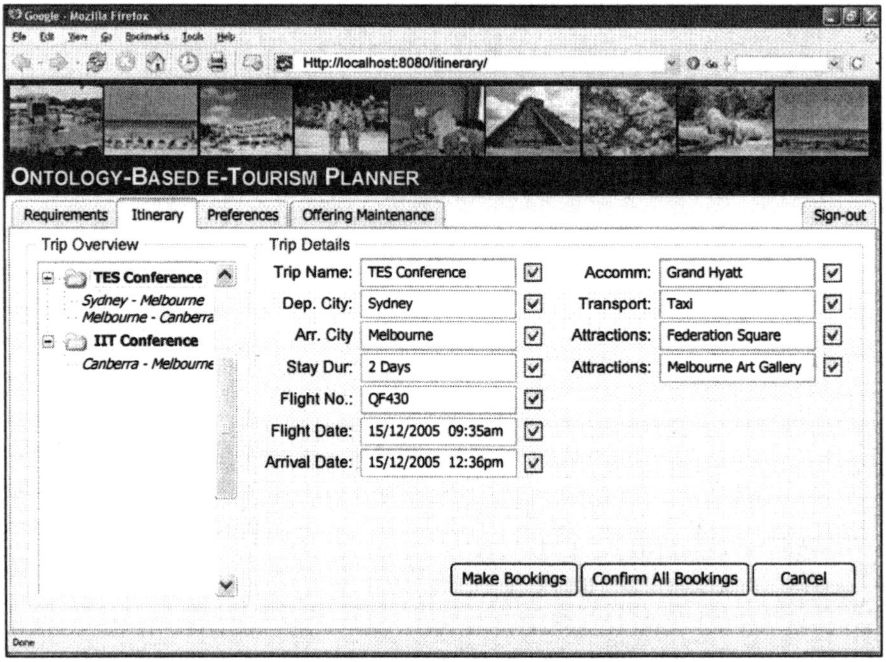

Fig. 3. AuSTO Tour planner itinerary screen

Fig. 3 shows the itinerary screen. The tour planner tool matches the user requirements with the vendor offerings and generates an itinerary, which is then displayed through this screen. Once the itinerary is created, the user can make bookings by selecting the make bookings button. Bookings can be confirmed by selecting the confirm bookings button.

Fig. 4 displays the *offering maintenance* screen; this screen displays the services being provided by tourism vendors such as hotels and transport providers. The user can browse these services, and then make a booking, by clicking the ‘Accept’ button.

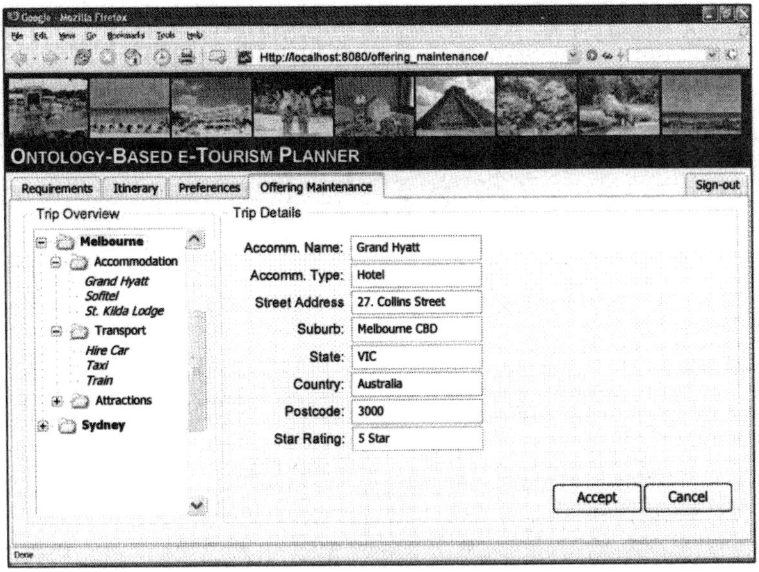

Fig. 4. AuSTO Tour planner offering maintenance screen

5 AuSTO System Implementation

The AuSTO system is deployed using the Semantic Web Application Model, as shown in Fig. 5. The system model employs the commonly used client-server model. The user interfaces that reside on the client-side are developed as Rich Interface Applications, using the Ajax development technique (Garrett, 2005). The server includes a combination of applications that form the structure of the AuSTO semantic web. This includes an Apache Web-Server that hosts the website; Jena Semantic Web Toolkit (*Jena: A semantic Web Framework for Java*, n.d.); and a Database Server using MySQL used for the Ontology repository. Further details of the different technologies used to implement the AuSTO system are presented in the following.

5.1 Semantic Web Application Model

The Semantic Web was thought up by Tim Berners-Lee as a mesh of information linked up in such a way so as to be easily processable by machines. Currently, the World Wide Web enables searching, sharing, and exchange of information, which identifies it as being the world's largest library. As the accessibility of information grows at an exponential rate, sourcing the 'right' information makes it cumbersome.

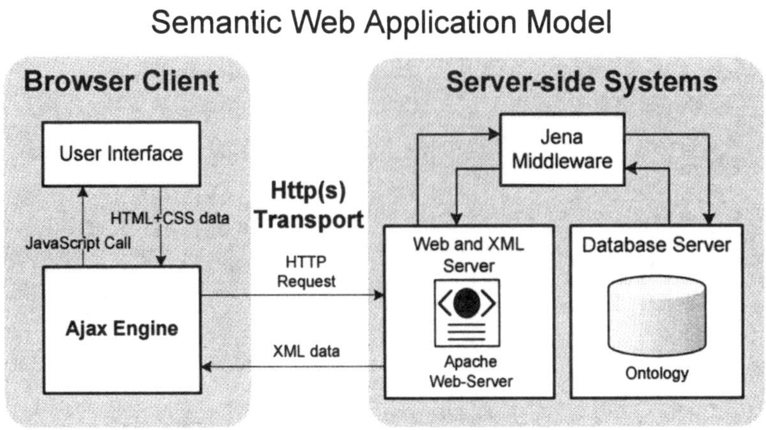

Fig. 5. Semantic Web Application Model for AuSTO

The semantic web (considered as the next generation web) helps overcome this problem by describing relationships between software such that machines can interpret (Palmer, 2001). Semantic web also provides a platform for the creation of so called intelligent applications; these intelligent applications are based on a bundle of semantic web technologies, and Ontologies lie at the core. These intelligent semantic web applications are superior to the existing web based applications as they are capable of reasoning, which means they can derive a conclusion based on a set of given facts. The AuSTO tour planner application is an intelligent application developed based on semantic web technologies. Fig. 5 describes the semantic web technologies that constitute the AuSTO tour planner.

The AuSTO system is based on various semantic web technologies. It can be viewed as a two tier architecture, comprising a browser client, and a server side system. The server side system contains the ontology which is the knowledge base, Jena middleware and the XML server. The browser client comprises the Ajax engine and the user interface. The client side operations formulate the user queries which are compiled by the user interfaces; these queries are converted into JavaScript and sent to the Ajax Engine. The Ajax Engine sends an HTTP request to the server, this request is received by an XML server, which forwards the request to the Jena middleware, the Jena middleware in-turn queries the ontology, the results are sent back from the server to the client and then displayed via the user interfaces. Details of these technologies are given in the following.

5.2 Ajax (Asynchronous JavaScript and XML)

Ajax is a combination of technologies which allows the development of interactive web applications. The present shortcoming of standard web applications is that each time the user places a request, an HTTP request is sent to the server, and when the server responds, the entire page is reloaded. Ajax overcomes this by adding an Ajax engine between the user and the server. The Ajax engine sends small parts of the data to the server rather than the entire content of the page. This eliminates the need for reloading the entire page each time the server responds to a request. The technologies that comprise Ajax are XHTML and CSS for marking up information, JavaScript to dynamically display information and the XMLHttpRequest object to exchange data asynchronously with the web server (Garrett, 2005).

5.3 Web and XML Server

An XML server is used to dynamically receive, interpret and generate XML documents. The XML documents generated will be used for the purpose of data interchange between applications. The XML server is a server-side component which can receive data via HTTP and generate output in XML format (*Dynamic XML Servers*, 1999). In the AuSTO application model the XML server receives the HTTP request in the form of a query from the browser, the query is processed and the result is forwarded back to the browser in the form of an XML document (*Dynamic XML Servers*, 1999; Bickel, n.d.).

5.4 Jena Middleware

Middleware is the software that connects the *reasoner*, the ontology and the user interface. Custom made middleware can be created for an application, but it is much easier to use existing middleware software such as Jena (*Jena: A semantic Web Framework for Java*, n.d.). Jena is a Java framework for building semantic web applications; it is open source and has been developed by HP Labs. Jena started as an RDF (Resource Description Framework) API (Application Programming Interface), and has extensive support for XML. It has been extended with an OWL-aware API and database connectivity and two forms of query languages, namely RDQL (RDF Query Language) and SPARQL (Simple Protocol and RDF Query Language). In Jena, all operations are completed by manipulating the Jena model. In order to manipulate an ontology it needs to be loaded into the Jena model first.

Jena has four subsystems: the query engine, database interface, reasoning engine and ontology management. Jena's architecture allows external reasoners to be plugged into the Jena models. The user queries are sent via a user interface to the Jena model, Java code converts these queries into SPARQL format, which can be read by Jena; and the result is sent back to the user. Fig. 6 presents an example of SPARQL code for performing a query on the AuSTO tourism ontology via the Jena middleware. This query retrieves Business Name and URL of all Apartment-Holiday Units in St Kilda with Five Star rating that have Swimming Pool and Air-conditioning facilities.

```
PREFIX Q: http://www.owl-ontologies.com/Accommodation.owl#
SELECT? BusinessName? URL
WHERE {?Accommodation  Q:hasCategory  Q:Apartment_HolidayUnit .
       ?Accommodation  Q:hasStarRating  Q:FiveStar .
       ?Accommodation  Q:hasDestination  Q:StKilda .
       ?Accommodation  Q:hasFacility  Q:SwimmingPool .
       ?Accommodation  Q:hasFacility  Q:Airconditioning .
       ?Accommodation  :hasBusinessName  ?BusinessName .
       ?Accommodation  :hasURL ?URL
```

Fig. 6. SPARQL query Example.

5.5 Database Server for Ontology

The AuSTO ontology is the knowledge base repository for storing information regarding the tourism domain, and is loaded into a database. MySQL is an open source RDBMS (Relational Database Management System) for processing data in the database. MySQL is commonly used in web applications. MySQL provides support to Jena libraries, which allows Jena to manipulate the ontology when loaded in the database.

6 Future work

The AuSTO tour planner acts as an itinerary planning tool, it relies on the AuSTO ontology as the source of tourism domain knowledge. Currently the tour planner is restricted to generating travel plans or itineraries; we intend to extend the functionality of the tour planner so that it can suggest places to visit based on the user preferences stored in the AuSTO ontology. Fig. 7 shows the long-term development plan for this research. Investigations are being conducted into deployment of AuSTO and the development of tools that will enable it to interoperate with the Harmonise ontology. We also are conducting research into using AuSTO for creating Visual Travel Recommender Systems. Usability studies of the AuSTO tour planner are being conducted at all phases of research and development to ensure that the system satisfies the requirements of a common traveller. Usability studies will be conducted at three levels: 1. Interface level, 2. System level, and 3. Service level (Sharda et al., 2005).

At the interface level, this will require conducting heuristic as well as empirical usability tests with real users, where they will be required to perform tour planning functions using the developed interfaces. Feedback will be gathered via pre-experiment and post-experiment questionnaires, which will evaluate the usability, efficiency, and effectiveness of the user interaction, interfaces and the system. Performance factors, such as error count and task completion times will be monitored to determine whether the user can complete given tasks within a certain error and completion time limit. At the system level, such investigations will involve determining whether the system provides sufficient response times, and feedback to the user that enhances their experience rather than making the system cumbersome to use. At the Service level, factors such as available bandwidth, delays, response times, and errors will be observed to ensure that the network can deliver the required traffic.

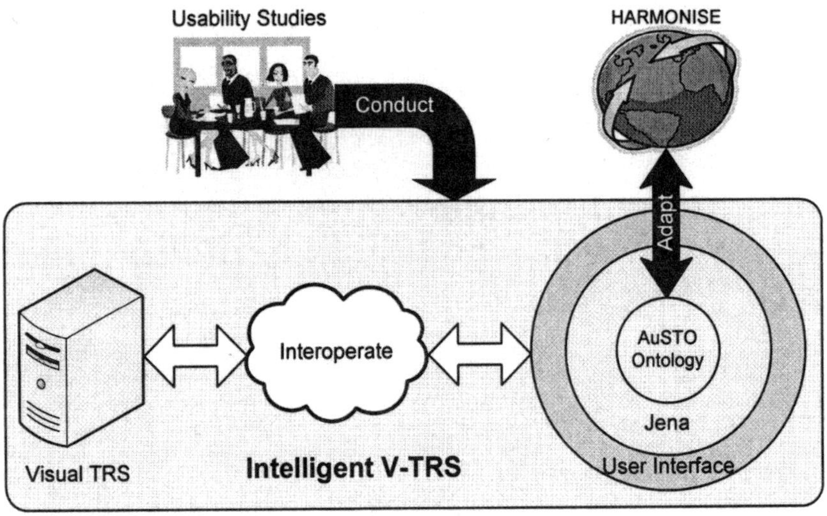

Fig. 7. Development plan for an Intelligent Visual Travel Recommender System

7 Conclusions

Tourism is one of the fastest developing sectors; information technology is playing an important role in accelerating this growth. Web based applications are being used for various activities to enhance tourism operations. AuSTO tour planner is one such effort to provide an all-rounder semantic web based tool for tourism. AuSTO tour planner is an intelligent tool that builds on semantic web technologies. This tool allows the users to input their travel requirements, tourism vendors can advertise their products via this tool and it automatically generates an itinerary or travel plan by matching the user requirements with the vendor offerings. AuSTO tour planner acts as a destination connector by allowing users to plan different parts of their trips.

References

Bickel, B. (n.d.). XML Integration Platforms. Retrieved August 29, 2006 from http://www.webtechniques.com/archives/1999/06/bickel/

Chandrasekaran, B., Josephson, J. R., & Benjamins, V. R. (1999). What are ontologies, and why do we need them? IEEE, 14(1), 20-26.

Corcho, O., Lopez, M. F., & Perez, A. G. (2003). Methodologies, Tools and Languages for Building Ontologies. Where is the Meeting Point? Data and Knowledge Engineering, 46(1), 41-64.

CTTE: Concur Task Trees Environment. (n.d.). Retrieved April 15, 2006 from http://giove.cnuce.cnr.it/ctte.html

Dynamic XML Servers. (1999). Retrieved August 29, 2006, from http://h21022.www2.hp.com/downloads/pdf/0599DynamicXMLServersWhitePaper.pdf #search=%22xml%20servers%22

Garrett, J. J. (2005). Ajax: A New Approach to Web Applications. Retrieved August 29, 2006, from http://www.adaptivepath.com/publications/essays/archives/000385.php

Georgievski, M., & Sharda, N. (2003). Task Modelling for a Holistic Quality of Service Model - TRAQS. Paper presented at the IEEE India Council Annual Convention and Exhibition, India.

Inference Engine. (n.d.). Retrieved May 15, 2006 from http://www.emclab.umr.edu/consortium/Whatis/node17.html

Jakkilinki, R., & Sharda, N. (2006). *A Framework for Creating Ontology-Based e-Tourism Applications.* Idea Group.

Jakkilinki, R., Sharda, N., & Georgievski, M. (2005). Developing an Ontology for Multimedia Design and Planning Pyramid. Paper presented at the International Symposium on Information and Communications Technologies, Petaling Jaya Malaysia.

Jena: A semantic Web Framework for Java. (n.d.). Retrieved April 15, 2006 from http://jena.sourceforge.net/

Nelson, T. (1987). *Computer Lib/Dream Machines.* Redmond, WA: Microsoft Press.

Palmer, S. B. (2001). The Semantic Web: An Introduction. Retrieved May 25, 2006 from http://infomesh.net/2001/swintro/

Pressman, R. S. (1997). *Software Engineering, A Practitioner's Approach* (4th ed.): McGraw-Hill.

Sharda, N., Georgievski, M., et al. (2005). Leading Edge Developments in Tourism ICT and Related Underlying Technologies: Key Findings and Future Directions. Project# 70153, Sustainable Tourism CRC, 2005. Retrieved November 5, 2005, from http://melba.vu.edu.au/STCRC/2004/2004FinalReport/STCRCReport2004V5.7.pdf.

Uschold, M., & Gruninger, M. (1996). Ontologies: Principles, Methods and Applications. *Knowledge Engineering Review,* 11(2).

A High Level Model for Developing Intelligent Visual Travel Recommender Systems

Mohan Ponnada
Nalin Sharda

School of Computer Science and Mathematics
Victoria University, Australia

Mohan.ponnada@ students.vu.edu.au
Nalin.sharda@vu.edu.au

Abstract

This paper presents the model of an Intelligent Visual Travel Recommender system (IV-TRS). IV-TRS is a system that makes use of visual information such as images and video, along with audio, to present a virtual tour of the destination. The IV-TRS model is divided into three layers, namely *Augmented Web*, *Application* and *Intelligence* layers. The IV-TRS makes use of the TRIPS (Tour Recommendation using Image-Based Planning with SCORM) concept to bring together relevant tourism data stored in the form of Sharable Content Objects (SCOs). The Augmented Web Layer consists of data stored as SCO's built on the SCORM standard with their location is resolved by CORDRA. SCORM (*Sharable Content Object Reference Model*) is a model that defines how information is to be stored, referenced and used by packaging data with metadata. CORDRA (*Content Object Repository Discovery and Registration/Resolution Architecture*) is a model that aims to locate and reference SCORM repositories over the web. The Intelligence Layer provides the reasoning engine of the system, and can be built on Semantic Web technology, Expert Systems technology, or Artificial Neural Networks. For this research, we focus on the Semantic Web technology for building the Intelligence Layer. The Application layer is made up of two components; namely, Search and Presentation. The Search component makes use of the CORDRA functionality to crawl and index the SCO's on the Internet. The Presentation component aims to provide a user interface that lets the user customize the presentation based on personal preferences. The IV-TRS system will provide the user a virtual experience to support better destination selection, and tour planning.

Keywords: Semantic Web, CORDRA, SCORM, SCOs, Intelligent Travel Recommender Systems.

1 Introduction

Tourism is one of the most successful and dynamic industries in the world, and is constantly evolving with support from continuous advancements in technologies, such as the Internet. One such advancement is the Travel Recommender System (TRS). Much research has been done on the topic of Intelligent Recommender systems. Burke (2000) presents the working and description of knowledge-based recommender systems; Mooney (1998) provides an example of book recommending using text categorisation. An example of a working TRS can be found at (crm.ittoolbox.com/pub/LK032002.pdf [Jan. 20, 2006]).

A TRS allows a traveller to obtain an informed recommendation for travel planning via an artificial intelligence system. However, current TRSs do not provide the traveller with the facility to visualise their complete holiday itinerary, integrating location, transportation, accommodation, attractions, and entertainment etc. For this one has to browse through individual web pages to build a mental picture of the planned trip. To overcome this limitation, there is a need for developing a system that not only provides visual presentations but is also intelligent. This paper presents a High-level model for developing an Intelligent Visual Travel Recommender System (IV-TRS).

2 Recommender Systems

Recommender systems are programs that attempt to predict what the user needs based on the information provided by the user. A formal definition of a recommender system is: "Recommender Systems are an attempt to mathematically model and technically reproduce the process of recommendations in the real world" (Berka & Plößnig, 2004).

Recommender systems are being used by many e-Commerce websites to make suggestions to their customers (Schafer 1999). Demographics, past buying behaviour and prediction of future buying behaviour are some of the factors based on which recommendations are made (Ricci, 2002). In the present competitive world, businesses can differentiate their offerings by providing better services to its customers. Customers are drawn towards fast, easy to use, hassle-free and efficient services. The same concept applies to businesses offering services in the tourism industry. Tourism Websites need to use new technologies to provide an enriching experience to the user.

3 Intelligent Visual Travel Recommender System

An Intelligent Visual Travel Recommender System (IV-TRS) is a recommender system that works on an Artificial-Intelligence based engine. IV-TRS combines audio and visual media to enhance the presentation quality of the recommendations made to the user. Though current systems can provide good recommendations to the user, there is a lack of standardisation for content storage; i.e., there is no universal standard for storing tourism data on the web. It will be easier to retrieve and modify data if it is stored in a standard format. There are some domain specific standards, such as the standard format used by the Australian Tourism Data Warehouse (ATDW) (http://www.atdw.com.au [Dec. 9, 2005]).

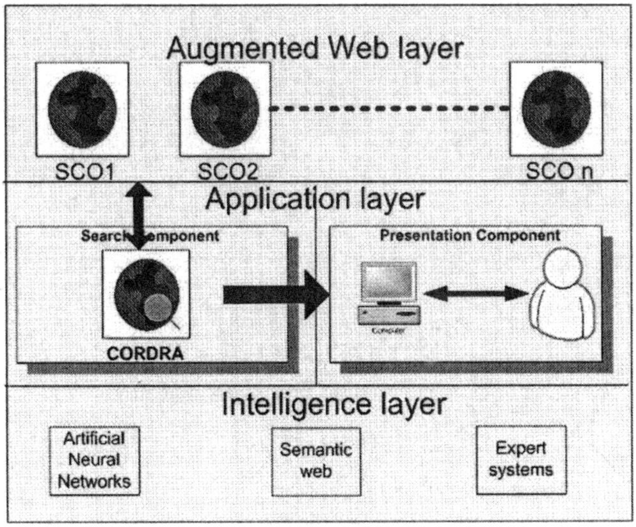

Fig.1. Conceptual model of in Intelligent Visual Travel Recommender System

Fig. 1 shows the overall conceptual model of in Intelligent Visual Travel Recommender System (IV-TRS). This system is divided into the following three layers.

- Augmented Web layer
- Application layer
- Intelligence layer

The Application layer is further divided into two components.

- Search component
- Presentation component

4 Augmented Web Layer

The Augmented Web layer comprises data in the form of Sharable Content Objects (SCOs). These SCOs can be referenced and resolved by the Content Object Repository Discovery and Registration/Resolution Architecture (CORDRA). The Augmented Web layer works on concept of Sharable Content Object Reference Model (SCORM). These standards were originally created for standardising content storage for e-Learning systems. Our aim is to use these standards for creating the IV-TRS, rather than develop another content standardisation method.

4.1 Understanding SCORM

The SCORM standard was proposed by The Department of Defence (DoD) and Advanced Distributed Learning (ADL) laboratories in 1997 to standardise the format of e-Learning content on the Web (www.adl.org [Dec. 9, 2005]). This model aims to improve performance and reduce costs for e-Learning systems. The motivation for developing SCORM is to build a standard that adheres to the following requirements (ADL 2005).

The main objectives of SCORM standards are to define reusable learning objects, develop content and assessment models, create models to sequence contents and finally create knowledge repositories. SCORM is thus an e-Learning standard that enables portability of learning contents for SCORM-compliant Learning Management System (LMS), thereby allowing content to be used across different courses.

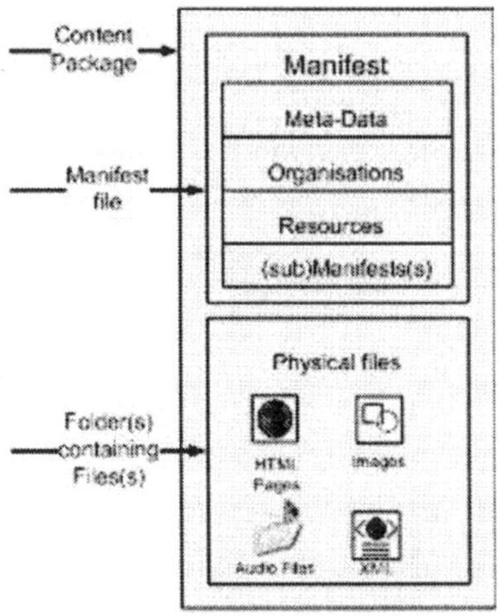

Fig. 2. Sharable Content Objects (SCOs)

SCORM is a collection of protocols and web based technologies that enable the sharing of different contents amongst diverse areas of learning management systems. SCORM makes use of eXtensible Markup Language (XML) and JavaScript to define protocols for developers who want to create data that can be shared between learning systems utilising various technologies and structures. The two key components of SCORM are the Content Aggregation Model (CAM) and the Runtime Environment (RTE). These two components enable exchange of SCOs (Lowman, 2004).

4.2 Sharable Content Objects (SCOs)

Fig. 2 shows the structure of an SCO. The SCO contains all contents for a particular unit of instruction. This can include sounds, text, images, videos or any other electronic media. The SCO can also include data related to other relevant SCOs. The Content Aggregation Model (CAM) is a set of standards for defining the data and content in a SCO using XML. CAM is also the standard for packaging the SCOs for the electronic delivery between systems. CAM consists of three components for defining and delivering SCOs: The Content Model, the Meta Data component, and specifications for Content Packaging. The Content Model makes use of XML to define all contents in the SCO; it also defines their relationship to other assets. The structure of various files contained in the SCO is also defined by the Content Model. The Meta Data component also makes use of XML to define nine categories of data used in SCOs. The Content Packaging component is a standard format for packaging the final SCO for its transfer. SCORM uses Package Interchange File (PIF) as a standard format to package the SCOs. This PIF file contains an XML file called "imsmanifest.xml" which describes all the contents of the PIF and how they can be accessed.

4.3 Runtime Environment

An Application Programming Interface (API) has been developed which helps developers by providing a common language for developing and using SCOs. This API allows the initialising and importing of the data from SCOs by the LMS. Through this API, the LMS is able to set and retrieve the data defined in the SCOs.

5 Application Layer

The Application Layer is the middle layer in the IV-TRS, where the referencing of various SCOs is done; it is the layer which handles the user interaction with the system. The Application Layer is made up of two components, namely, the Search and Presentation components. The Search component is built with the Content Object Repository Discovery and Registration/Resolution Architecture (CORDRA), which has been developed along with the SCORM standard. CORDRA enables the system to locate and resolve various SCOs in the Augmented Web layer.

The CORDRA model is also an undertaking of the Department of Defence (DoD) and Advanced Distributed Learning (ADL). CORDRA aims to extend the current SCORM standard. This model is being developed so that SCORM repositories can be located and referenced throughout the Internet. Fig. 3 presents a conceptual model of how CORDRA will achieve this.

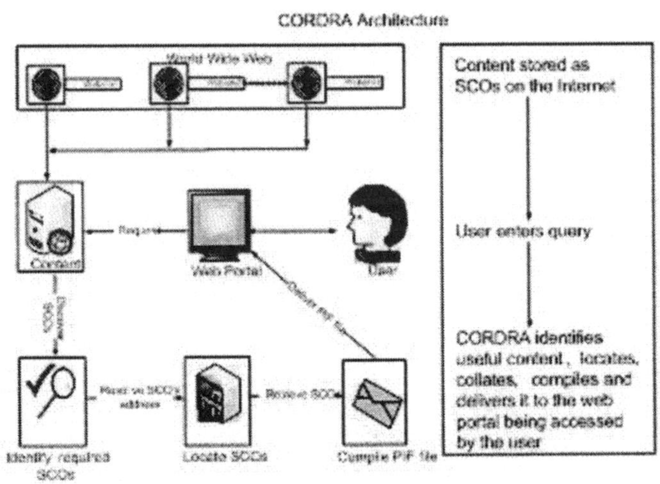

Fig.3. Finding and delivering content as SCO's

CORDRA searches the World Wide Web for the required resources. Once the resources are discovered, it resolves their location, making the resources accessible to the SCORM based systems as SCO's. Based on a user query, the CORDRA system can collate all related information (stored as SCOs) from the web. However, the information gathered should be then converted into presentations that the user can view in a controlled manner.

5.1 Presentation Component

The Presentation Component is another part of the IV-TRS Application layer. This component is responsible for the entire Human-Computer Interaction (HCI) process. It consists of an interface where the user can enter queries, make selections, or perform other available functions. It is important for any application to appear attractive, so as to entice the user to come back to it in the future. The Search component searches and locates the required SCOs in the Augmented Web Layer based on the user query entered through the User Interface offered by the presentation component. The retrieved data is then sent to the user device as a continuous video-like presentation.

6 Intelligence Layer

The Intelligence Layer of the IV-TRS provides the reasoning engine of the system. This layer enables the system to think, and learn. It makes the system learn from the previous recommendations made, to enhance the quality of current and future recommendations. There are many different ways of constructing an intelligent engine for this system. In the initial stages of this project, we explored three options. The Intelligence engine can be built on either of the following technologies.

- Expert Systems.
- Semantic Web Technology.
- Artificial Neural Networks.

In this research project, we decided to focus on the Semantic Web Technology, as these are considered the future of the Web. Further research can aim to explore the other technologies for application in the IV-TRS.

6.1 Application of Semantic Web in IV-TRS

The Semantic Web was introduced by Tim Berners-Lee as the conceptual model of an intelligent Web. As per Palmer (www.infomesh.net [Aug. 4, 2006]), "The Semantic Web is a mesh of information linked up in such a way as to be easily processable by machines, on a global scale. You can think of it as being an efficient way of representing data on the World Wide Web, or as a globally linked database."

Over the past few years several advancements have been made to improve, extend and standardize the Semantic Web systems. Many tools have been developed for this purpose. Even with this progress the Semantic Web technology still requires much research to make it fully operational, nonetheless its future appears to be bright. (Passin, 2004).

Data is being progressively added to the Internet everyday. One of the major problems with today's Eeb is that it is difficult for us to use this data effectively, because there is no standard throughout the Internet for publishing this data. The Semantic Web seems to be a promising technology for providing a solution to this problem. The IV-TRS system aims to incorporate the Semantic Web technologies for improved Web data integration while building on earlier research in creating image based tour planning systems (Kimber, Georgievski, & Sharda, 2006).

6.2 Tourism Recommendation using Image-Based Planning (TRIP)

Before booking a tour, most travellers would like to build a mental picture of the forthcoming experience of the trip. Travellers often have questions regarding matters such as how to organise the trip so as to spend their time effectively. Most of the time, it is difficult for the traveller to find the right details about all aspects of the trip. Often, one has to gather all that information by visiting various Websites, which is a time consuming process. The Tourism Recommendation using Image-Based Planning (TRIP) system aimed to overcome this drawback by presenting the details visually (Kimber et al., 2006). However, the problem of content standardisation remained. This problem can be overcome by using the SCORM standard, leading to the development of the Tour Recommendation using Image-Based Planning with SCORM (TRIPS) concept.

The proposed IV-TRS system, which builds on the TRIPS concept, will allow tourists to visualise their entire tour by bringing together content from various Websites. It uses the Sharable Content Object Reference Model (SCORM) to store all relevant tourism information on different Web servers. If all tourism related information is posted on the Augmented Web based on the SCORM standard, the IV-TRS could assemble the required multimedia content from different sites and present it to the user to create a virtual tour.

6.3 Creation of the Virtual Tour using TRIPS

Creating a virtual tour of the propose itinerary is a two step process: gathering relevant multimedia content from the Augmented Web, and combining it to make a complete visual presentation.

Once a traveller's destination is finalised, further travel options are often explored. The TRIPS system contains information about the tourist's destination and other preferences. Based on these preferences, it gathers the related SCOs from the Web. Once the destination activities are finalised, TRIPS creates an activity tree of the itinerary, and delivers the gathered SCOs related to these activities as a Package Interchange File (PIF). The PIF contains the imsmanifest.xml file, with all control files and resources referenced in the contents pages. The PIF therefore contains all the information about the activities available to the tourist, structured in a hierarchy.

Next, the IV-TRS makes use of the SMIL standard to convert the PIF file into a multimedia presentation. The Synchronized Multimedia Integration Language (SMIL) makes use of XML for creating descriptive multimedia presentations. It defines different mark-ups, layouts, animations, and visual transitions that can be rendered by any SMIL player. The playable SMIL file can be sent to any user device such as a Web browser on a computer, or on a portable device. A customisation program checks for parameters of the device, such as screen resolution / bandwidth, and customises the SMIL presentation using these system parameters. This process modifies the presentation to suit the viewers display, for example, a high resolution file can be sent to a desktop computer while only a low resolution file must be sent to a mobile phone.

7 Case Study

Though the recommender systems that exist today make quality recommendations, these are not very interactive. The recommendations displayed are in simple text, describing the different options available, but do not allow the user to get a feel of the planned tour. For the purpose of this case study, we have developed a website mock-up to demonstrate how the proposed system is going to work. We discuss this system and present screen shots of its user interface.

Fig. 4 displays the Requirements page where the user can enter requirements such as the arrival city, departure date, stay duration, transport type etc.

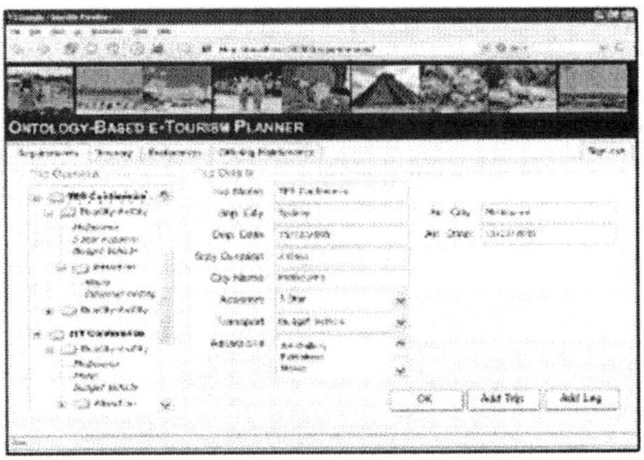

Fig. 4. Requirements page

Fig. 5 displays the itinerary page. After all the requirements have been entered in the requirements page, the system matches the user selections to the available SCOs and then populates the fields in the itinerary page. The user can then select most desirable options and then view their virtual tours.

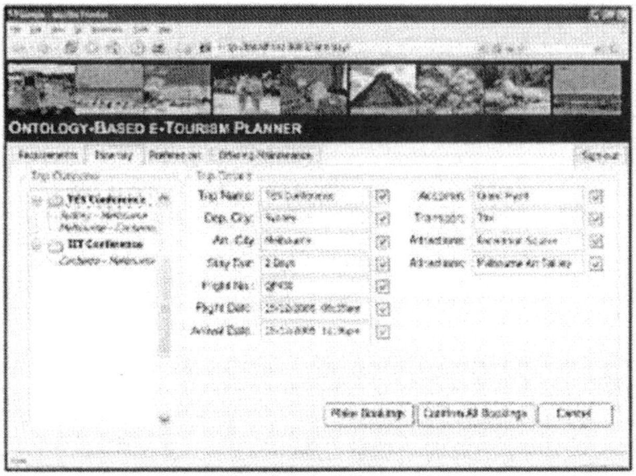

Fig. 5. Itinerary page

Fig. 6 displays the screen shot of the virtual tour display. It shows what the user will view after all the selections have been made. The virtual tour can be regenerated any number of times based on the selections made.

Fig. 6. Virtual tour generated by the IV-TRS

With this IV-TRS, the user can get virtual tours of the various tours recommended by the intelligence engine, and select the most appealing tour, with much greater confidence in the final selection before committing to all the bookings.

8 Future Work

The aim of the current research and its future extension is to use audio-visual media to create more appealing Travel Recommender Systems. Some of the ideas of communal decision making, as discussed by Hill (1995), could be used when a group of users is developing intertwined itineraries. An enhancement to the proposed IV-TRS is to add text descriptions of each image for better understanding, especially if the user is not able to play the audio in an office or other communal environment. For the proposed IV-TRS to work universally it will be essential to make all tourism websites SCORM and CORDRA compliant, and would require invitations into making current tourism web sites move towards these standards. Future Travel Recommender Systems should also provide tourists with an easy and effective method of planning their trip over the Internet by implementing the proposed IV-TRS as a Semantic Web service. This will make it not only available universally, but also be useable by other application, as Web service APIs.

9 Conclusions

Information technology is playing a major role in the incessant growth of the tourism industry. Even though the current Travel Recommender Systems make quality recommendations to the user, these recommendations are not presented in a way that lets the user visualise the entire tour. The proposed Intelligent Visual Travel Recommender system (IV-TRS) will make use of audio-visual media to provide a comprehensive view of the proposed tour. IV-TRS will aim to make the human-computer interaction more interesting by using audio and video in innovative ways. With the help of IV-TRS, tourists will have an easy and effective way of planning their personal or business travel. Overall, the proposed Intelligent Visual Travel Recommender System aims to provide a virtual travel experience to the user and give greater control over the difficult task of destination selection and tour planning.

References

Berka, T. & Plößnig M. (2004). Designing Recommender Systems for Tourism. In proceedings of *The Eleventh International Conference on Information Technology in Travel & Tourism*, ENTER 2004, Cairo, Egypt: January, 26-28, 2004.

Burke, R. (2000). Knowledge-based Recommender Systems. In A. Kent (ed.), Encyclopedia of Library and Information Science. 69 (32). New York: Marcel Dekker.

Ricci, F. (2002). Travel Recommender Systems. *IEEE Intelligent Systems*, 17 (6), 55-57.

Hill, W., Stead, L., Rosenstein, M., & Furnas, G. (1995). Recommending and Evaluating Choices in a Virtual Community of Use. In proceedings of the *SIGCHI conference on Human factors in computing systems*, CHI-95. Denver, USA: May, 7-11, 1995.

Kimber, J., Georgievski, M., & Sharda, N. (2006). Developing a Visualisation Tool for Tour Planning. In proceedings of the *IFITT Global Travel & Tourism Technology and eBusiness Conference,* ENTER 2006. Lausanne, Switzerland: January, 18-20, 2006.

Lowman, D. (2004). Sharable Content Object Reference Model. In B. Hoffman (Ed.), Encyclopedia of Educational Technology. San Diego.

Mooney, R., Bennett, P., & Roy, L. (1998). Book Recommending using Text Categorization with Extracted Information. In the proceedings of *Workshop on Learning for Text Categorization,* ICML-98. Madison, Wisconsin: July, 24-26, 1998. pp: 70-74.

Schafer, J. B., Konstan, J. A. & Riedl, J. (1999). Recommender Systems in Electronic Commerce. In the proceedings of the *ACM Conference on Electronic Commerce.* Denver, Colorado: November, 3-5, 1999.

Passin, T. B. (2004). *Explorer's Guide to the Semantic Web.* Greenwich, Connecticut: Manning Publications Co.

Developing a Conversational Travel Advisor with ADVISOR SUITE

Dietmar Jannach[a]
Markus Zanker[a]
Markus Jessenitschnig[a,b]
Oskar Seidler[c]

[a] Institute for Intelligent Systems and Business Informatics
University Klagenfurt, Austria
{dietmar,markus}@ifit.uni-klu.ac.at
[b] e-tourism competence center Austria (ECCA)
Innsbruck, Austria
markus.jessenitschnig@etourism-austria.at
[c] ThermenResort Warmbad-Villach
Villach, Austria, oskar.seidler@warmbad.at

Abstract

Due to the inherent complexity of building highly-interactive and personalized web applications, the development of a web-based travel advisory system can be a costly and time-consuming task. We see this as one of the major obstacles to a more widespread adoption of such systems in particular with respect to small and medium-sized companies and e-Tourism platforms. The goal of the ADVISOR SUITE project discussed in this paper is thus to provide an off-the-shelf framework and development environment that allows us to build intelligent and easy-to-maintain advisory applications in a cost-efficient way: The main pillars of the presented system are therefore an integrated graphical modelling-environment, the provision of different domain-independent recommendation algorithms, as well as model-based mechanisms to fully generate functional web applications based on declarative definitions in a central knowledge repository. The paper discusses the core concepts and main functionalities of the system by means of an example of an interactive travel advisor developed for an Austrian spa resort.

Keywords: Recommendation system, interactive travel advisory, consumer decision support systems.

1 Introduction

According to a variety of recent studies (e.g. European Travel Commission – ETC) at least in Western countries the Web is the primary source of information for people when searching for suitable travel destinations or planning a trip. In addition, these studies show that also the share of people that actually book their arrangements via the online channel is constantly increasing. In parallel, the number and variety of information offerings on the Web is also growing, which increases consumer confusion.

Thus, it is becoming increasingly important for platform providers to differentiate among each other and come up with value-adding (electronic) services to turn lookers into bookers. Recommender systems can be seen as one of these services as they have proven to be a valuable means to help online customers to overcome information overload and to support them in the decision-making process. Thus, such systems are supposed to play a vital role in current and future e-tourism (see, e.g. Werthner, 2003; Ricci & del Missier, 2004).

However, developing recommender applications and fielding them successfully is a challenging task, in particular w.r.t. small and medium-sized companies and platform providers: On the one hand, established collaborative-filtering based approaches can be quickly deployed but require the existence of a relatively large user community and suffer from cold-start problems. Conversational and knowledge-based approaches on the other hand typically help us to overcome and minimize these ramp-up problems as they base their recommendations - at least partially - on general domain knowledge. However, the development of such a knowledge-based system may induce significant costs for initial knowledge acquisition as well as for application maintenance. Furthermore, the development of a *conversational* user interface (Bridge, 2004; Carenini, Smith, & Poole, 2003; Thompson, Göker, & Langley, 2004) that aims at simulating the behaviour of an experienced sales agent or travel assistant by leading a personalized dialog with the customer is a cost-intensive task.

The ADVISOR SUITE system discussed in this paper has been designed with the goal of providing an off-the-shelf software system for the cost-efficient development of such advanced, conversational recommender systems. The key contributions lie in the provisioning of a graphical modelling environment for such knowledge-intensive applications, mechanisms for the automated generation of functional web applications, as well as in establishing a more comprehensive approach to product recommendation ('advisory'): The task of *virtual advisor* built with the system shall thus not be limited to retrieving a suitable set of products for a given set of customer requirements, it shall for instance also be able to elicit the real customer requirements in a personalized way, be capable of explaining the proposal, finding alternatives, explaining differences and similarities between products, or providing additional help and guidance depending on the user's background.

In the paper we will first give an overview of a deployed application in the e-tourism domain (a virtual advisor developed for an Austrian spa resort) and will subsequently discuss on the system's architecture and the design rationale behind selected components. The paper finishes with a discussion of experiences gained from several projects and gives an outlook on future work.

2 VIBE – The virtual spa advisor

The Warmbad-Villach resort is one of Austria's most renowned spas offering a variety of different tourism products that ranges from hotel accommodation in four and five-star categories, a variety of recreational and sporting facilities to health and beauty therapies. Being part of the resort's Web portal, the goal of the virtual advisor VIBE (signifying the name of an ancient goddess of fonts) in that context is to welcome online visitors and provide them a single point of contact for multi-lingual guidance and preference elicitation.

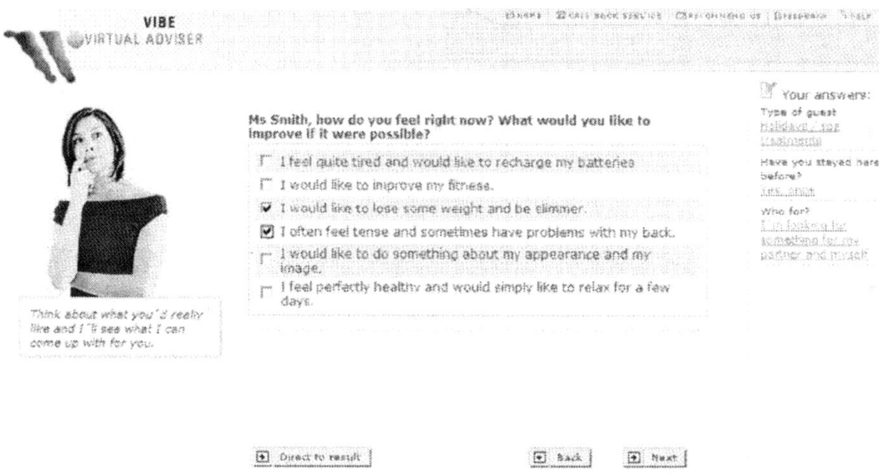

Fig. 1. Virtual advisor screenshot (http://www.warmbad.at)

Fig. 1 depicts an exemplary screenshot of the application and gives an impression of the basic question/answer communication style of ADVISOR SUITE: Rather than allowing free-text interaction or using static fill-out forms, the virtual advisor guides the online user through a personalized series of questions in which the customer preferences are incrementally elicited; depending on the current situation, the advisor will also provide additional explanations or give situation-dependent hints and tips.

At the end of the dialog or when the user decides to have provided enough details, VIBE comes up with suitable recommendations (Fig. 2) which also include a personalized list of supplementary add-on packages as well as additional information and explanations which are again based on the customer's preferences.

3 Application development with ADVISOR SUITE

In order to build an interactive, personalized advisory service like VIBE, background knowledge has to be elicited from domain experts and formalized in the system. Moreover, the development of a highly-adaptive and maintainable user interface, which reflects the underlying personalization knowledge, can also be a challenging task due to the typically strong interdependencies between recommendation-, personalization-, and presentation logic. ADVISOR SUITE's model-driven development process thus aims at minimizing the costs associated with the construction of such applications (Fig. 1). All of the required knowledge, i.e., both the recommendation- and personalization knowledge can be modeled and maintained with the help of a user-oriented, graphical modeling environment and are stored in a central, declarative knowledge base. A novel template-mechanism and a GUI-generation module are subsequently used to compile a working web application from these definitions; layout changes can be done by a Web developer whose typical task is to adapt the appearance of the application to be coherent with the layout of the e-Tourism platform· (For technical details of the implementation and underlying methodology and framework, see for instance (Jannach & Kreutler, 2004) and (Felfernig, Friedrich,, Jannach, & Zanker, 2006).

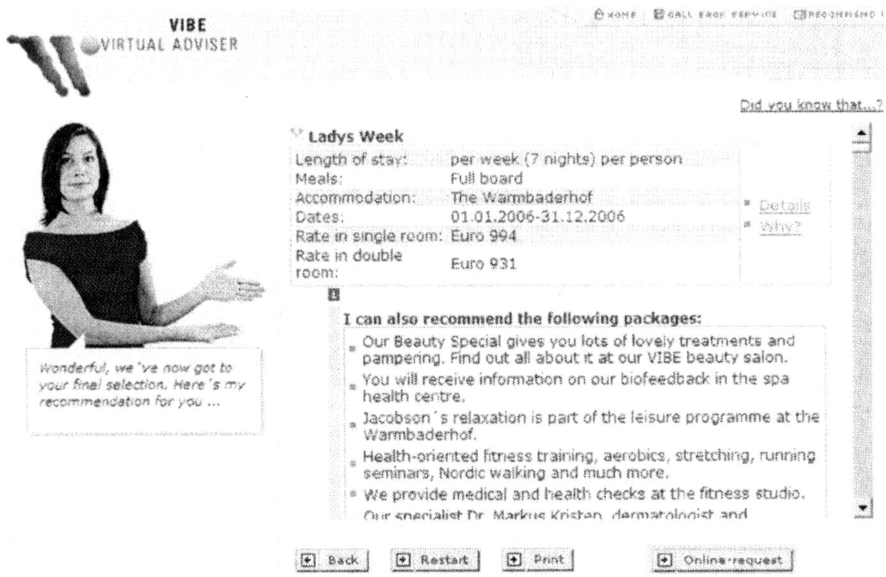

Fig. 2. Vibe's personalized recommendation

At run-time, an intelligent domain-independent personalization agent evaluates the content of the knowledge base and manages the interaction with the individual users accordingly. Personalization itself is implemented based on a rule-based approach as described for instance in (Ardissono, Felfernig, Friedrich, Goy, Jannach, Petrone, Schäfer, & Zanker, 2003); however, the scope of personalization is much broader here and allows for personalization in various dimensions: content, dialog, and presentation (Jannach & Kreutler, 2005).

Within the application-modelling phase, the following different pieces of knowledge (models) have to be designed: The *product model*, which is developed in the first phase, comprises the characteristics of the offered products and services. In the tourism domain, the product model typically comprises a service identifier, prices, availability dates, and so forth. Note that this initial phase is in most cases straight forward, as data about products and services already exists in some electronic form. Developing a *customer model* in the next phase is not that easy anymore, as the domain expert already has to bear in mind, which customer characteristics are of relevance for computation of recommendations and, in addition, which questions need to be posed in order to elicit these potentially latent preferences. The *recommendation model*, in which the logic for generating actual proposals is represented, consists of two separate sub-models: In the *preference-and-filter* model the relationship between customer properties and desired product features can be expressed in terms of *if-then*-style recommendation rules like *"If the customer is interested in a family vacation with children, prefer packages that include a childcare service or a petting zoo"*. It is important to note that with the help of these rules we can also devise a more customer-oriented interaction style, i.e., the virtual advisor will rather ask the customer about preferences and desires rather than on product or service features.

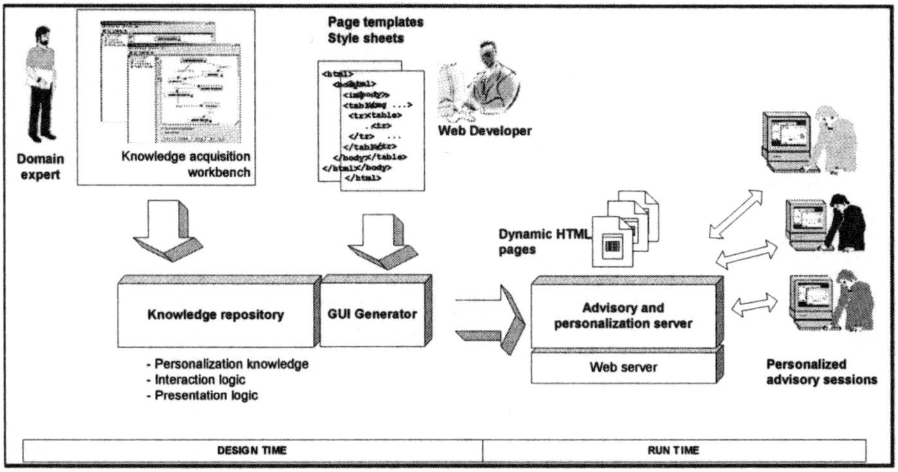

Fig. 3. Process overview (Jannach and Kreutler, 2004)

At run-time, the system will then – based on a new matching and relaxation procedure (Jannach, 2006) – determine those offerings that fulfil as many of the requirements as possible; this particular techniques are also used to derive human-readable explanations that can be presented to the user. In the *utility model*, finally, one can define the rules, according to which the remaining products shall be ranked: In ADVISOR SUITE, the ranking of products is also personalized, i.e., it depends on the user's preferences and is based on the Multi-Attribute-Utility Theory (for more details, see e.g., Felfernig et al., 2006).

One of the major differences between the ADVISOR SUITE system and other content- and knowledge-based approaches to product recommendation lies in the existence of a *dialog and preference-elicitation* model. In this particular modelling view, the domain expert can define how the conversation between the system and the customer shall proceed: Here, the expert can for instance define which questions should be asked in which order or under which circumstances additional hints and explanations should be given to the customer. Like all other modelling views implemented by the system, the dialog is designed on a graphical level, in that case with the help of a sort of flowgraph-based representation. Compared with a natural-language interaction style, the number of conversational paths is of course more restricted. On the other hand, this restriction allows us to keep the modelling complexity at a level, which is still manageable by a domain expert. Furthermore, this rather simple approach of dialog modelling allows us to develop interactive recommenders whose functionality goes far beyond what is available in current web-based recommender applications on the Web.

4 Experiences and Further Directions

Experiences: Up to now, we have developed more than two dozen commercial advisory applications for different domains with the now-commercialized ADVISOR SUITE system. The broad spectrum of application domains besides e-tourism (from consumer electronics over financial services to fine wine and cigars) indicates that on the one hand our overall system design and the implemented algorithms are domain-independent and sufficiently general; on the other hand, the framework has also proven to be flexible and extensible enough such that domain-specific extensions and characteristics can be easily taken into account. From the perspective of time and costs required for developing a virtual advisor and keeping it up to date, the benefits of using the presented off-the-shelf system as opposed to creating a new solution from scratch have also met our expectations: Quite interestingly, in most cases, the initial sketch of the knowledge base including product data, questions, basic recommendation rules, and a first dialog model can be already drafted already within a first full-day workshop assuming lively participation of stakeholders. In this first project phase, the ability to quickly generate functional prototype applications proved to be specifically advantageous: This feature helped us on the one hand to establish a common understanding of the projected project outcomes in the early project phases; on the other hand, it also increased the stakeholders' involvement as they see their suggestions and ideas to be immediately taken into account. In addition, we noticed that the number of core recommendation rules in most domains (and also in the travelling domain) remains at a manageable size of a few dozens; the overall costs are mainly determined by the amount of additional information to be provided by the system, the fine-tuning of the different personalization rules, as well as the amount of development times required for setting up the layout or integrating external data sources.

The design of ADVISOR SUITE's user-oriented conceptualisations and graphical modelling tools is driven by the idea that the domain expert herself shall be able to formalize her expert knowledge into the system. However, in most projects up to now, the help of a knowledge engineer was required at least in the early phases or for designing more complex business rules. After that initial phase, however, many of the domain experts were – supported by a comprehensive test and debugging environment (Felfernig et al., 2006) – capable to modify and update the system's knowledge base by themselves. Although these experiences are basically encouraging, further improvements in that direction are required and are part of our future work.

In detail, this specific e-tourism application is characterized as follows: About thirty possible questions have been modelled, out of which always only a personalized subset is asked in order to keep dialog lengths at a size which is acceptable by end users. About the same number of rules has been designed, which – together with a specific relaxation rule for searching for suitable arrival and departure dates – were sufficient to generate personalized recommendations. Overall, one particularity of the domain lies in the limited number of available 'products': In the consumer electronics domain, for instance, sometimes hundreds of different products are available, whereas typical in this domain only a smaller number of packages is available. These limitations could be overcome by using the relaxation mechanism described above ('near matches') together with a possibility to propose 'bundles' consisting of a basic package and a personalized set of add-on activities and side-offers. However, a detailed evaluation of the interaction data of currently several thousands of online users having successfully completed the advisory dialogues has not been done yet; an analysis in the line of (Zanker, Aschinger, & Jessenitschnig, 2006) is part of our current work.

Future directions: In the particular context of e-tourism applications, we see the following extensions to our system to be highly relevant for future applications:

a) *Intelligent bundling*: In the current implementation of VIBE, the products to be recommended are already bundled packages consisting of hotel accommodation, a set of therapies and so forth. In addition to each package, VIBE also proposes a suitable set of individual add-on services (Fig. 2), whose selection is based on rather simple business rules. However, current trends suggest that in the future the demand for individualized touristic arrangements will be further increasing. Thus, we are currently implementing mechanisms that shall allow us to 'configure' and ensure the validity of such individual combinations (Zanker et al., 2006b). As a basic mechanism we employ a constraint-based configuration approach (see, e.g., Mailharro, 1998), which supports more complex dependencies and bundling rules.

b) *Mobile applications*: VIBE is a pre-trip information and decision support tool. However, travel advisory and recommendation could also be an added value for the customer during and even after his or her journey: The etPlanner project (Höpken et al., 2006), which is partially based on the ADVISOR SUITE technology, is an approach towards more comprehensive electronic service support, which addresses issues of 'context' in the recommendation process as well as content adaptation for mobile devices. Integration of geographical information systems will thus greatly improve the perceived utility und quality of recommendations.

c) *Data analysis:* The ADVISOR SUITE system comprises a built-in logging component which can be configured to record the full history of interactions of each individual user, which means that ADVISOR SUITE's interaction logs are much more detailed and structured than standard Web server logs. Thus, from such logs important types of information about the customer and his preferences can be obtained. One can, for instance, analyse whether there are typical customer profiles or combinations of services which are requested by customers but are not part of any package. This additional knowledge could be subsequently used to adapt the range of offered services accordingly. A second type of information contained in the logs is related to the advisory service itself and pertains to the effectiveness of the application: Typical questions in that context are, e.g., whether the virtual advisor is a) accepted and used by customers and b) whether the system is actually capable of influencing the buying behaviour, which is of particular importance for determining the business value of providing such an add-on service. Although ADVISOR SUITE in its current state already comprises a 'statistics' module which documents the distribution of user answers to specific questions or the ratio of successfully completed user sessions, both further engineering as well as research are still required and part of our current work: On the engineering side, we currently aim at integrating a data mining component with which we can for instance detect hidden correlations between user preferences. On the research side, we are both interested in new metrics that allow us to, e.g., measure changes in actual sales when using such a system and on the other hand on finding basic concepts and guiding principles that are capable of allowing recommender systems to become an even more persuasive type of technology (Zanker et al., 2006).

d) *Self-adaptation and learning:* One shortcoming of the described system compared with other approaches to recommendation lies in the *static* nature of the system's behaviour: While for instance in systems based on collaborative filtering or case-based reasoning recommendations continuously improve over time, there is up to now no means in our system that resembles such a learning behaviour. In the context of our system, such an improvement has to be based on advanced analysis capabilities as described above. Currently, we work on extending our framework to accommodate such learning behaviour by taking community ratings into account when generating proposals. The question of how such hybrid system can be fine-tuned (e.g., balancing the weight of a community rating vs. an expert opinion) is still in the scope of further research.

5 Conclusions

The cost-efficient development of an interactive travel recommendation service can be a challenging task, in particular for small and medium-sized e-tourism platforms or service providers as standard collaborative approaches do not work well when there is no broad user-community and on the other hand the costs and complexity of building conversational, knowledge-based systems are comparably high.

The ADVISOR SUITE presented in this paper is thus an approach to providing an off-the-shelf software framework for the rapid and cost-efficient development of an online pre-trip travel advisory service, the main novelties being the model-driven development approach and the support for the automatic generation of functional web applications. By using an example of a commercially deployed travel advisory application for an Austrian spa resort, we have shown how the development process is supported by the tool and how the typical knowledge-acquisition bottleneck of knowledge-based approaches can be overcome, when adequate modelling environments and user-oriented conceptualisations are provided.

Further work primarily aims at developing general methods and algorithms, with which the information in the detailed interaction logs can be further exploited, both for learning more about the customers as well as for improving the effectiveness of the advisory application itself.

References

Ardissono, L., Felfernig, A., Friedrich, G., Goy, A., Jannach, D., Petrone, G., Schäfer, R. & Zanker, M. (2003). A Framework for the Development of Personalized, Distributed Web-Based Configuration Systems. *AI Magazine*, 24 (3) 93-110.

Bridge, D., (2002). Towards Conversational Recommender Systems: A Dialogue Grammar Approach. *In proceedings of the Workshop in Mixed-Initiative Case-Based Reasoning, Workshop Programme at the Sixth European Conference in Case-Based Reasoning*, (pp. 9-22), 2002.

Carenini, G., Smith, J., & Poole, D. (2003). Towards more Conversational and Collaborative Recommender Systems, In *proceedings of the 8th international conference on Intelligent user Interfaces*, Miami, Florida, 12-18.

Ricci, F. & Del Missier, F. (2004). Supporting Travel Decision Making through Personalized Recommendation. In Clare-Marie Karat, Jan Blom, and John Karat (Eds.), *Designing Personalized User Experiences for eCommerce* (pp. 221-251), Kluwer Academic Publisher.

Felfernig, A., Friedrich, G., Jannach, D. & Zanker, M. (2006). An Integrated Environment for the Development of Knowledge-Based Recommender Applications. *International Journal of Electronic Commerce, Special issue on Recommender Systems,* to appear.

Höpken, W. et al. (2006). etPlanner: An IT framework for comprehensive and integrative travel guidance, in: Hitz, M. et al. (Eds.) *Information and Communication Technologies in Tourism, ENTER 2006* (pp. 125-134), Springer Wien/New York.

Jannach, D., & Kreutler, G. (2004). A Knowledge-Based Framework for the Rapid Development of Conversational Recommenders. In: X. Zhou, S. Su, M. Papazoglou, M. Orlowska, K. Jeffery (Eds.), *Web Information Systems* - WISE 2004, (pp. 390-402). Springer New York, LNCS 3306.

Jannach, D., & Kreutler G.. (2005). Personalized User Preference Elicitation for e-Services. In: Cheung W., Hsu J. (Eds.): IEEE International conference on e-Technology, e-Commerce and e-Service, Hong Kong, IEEE Computer Society, 604-611.

Jannach D. (2006). Finding Preferred Query Relaxations in Content-based Recommenders. *Proceedings of IEEE Intelligent Systems Conference IS'2006*, (pp. 355-360) Westminster, UK, IEEE Press, 2006.

Mailharro, D. (1998). A classification and constraint-based framework for configuration. *AI in Engineering. Design and Manucturing*, 12, 383–397.

Thompson, C.A., Göker, M.H. & Langley, P. (2004). A Personalized System for Conversational Recommendations. *Journal of Artificial Intelligence Research*, 21, 393-428.

Werthner, H. (2003). Intelligent Systems in Travel and Tourism. *Proceeding of the 18th International Joint Conference on Artificial Intelligence, IJCAI-03*, Acapulco, Mexico, 2003.

Zanker, M., Bricman, M., Gordea, S., Jannach, D. & Jessenitschnig, M. (2006). Persuasive online-selling in quality & taste domains, *Proceedings of 7th International Conference on Electronic Commerce and Web Technologies - EC-Web '06*, (pp. 51-60). Krakow, Poland.

Zanker, M., Aschinger, M. & Jessenitschnig, M. (2006b). Knowledge-based composition of Recommendations, Extended Abstract, *Workshop Notes of the Configuration Workshop held in conjunction with the European Conference on Artificial Intelligence* (ECAI-06), Riva del Garda, Italy.

Web-based Recommenders for Personalized City Tours: A Usage Analysis

Ronny Kramer[a]
Marko Modsching[a]
Klaus ten Hagen[a]
Ulrike Gretzel[b]

[a] Department of Computer Science
University of Applied Sciences Zittau/Görlitz, Germany
{K.tenHagen, MModsching, RKramer}@HS-ZiGr.de
[b] Laboratory for Intelligent Systems in Tourism
Texas A&M University
ugretzel@tamu.edu

Abstract

The World Wide Web provides information for most tourist locations and thus has enormous influence on tourists' decisions. However, Web applications rarely support all phases of tour planning. The city of Görlitz offers website visitors an opportunity to plan individual city tours in advance by specifying personal interests and tour preferences. Using this information, the system creates a personalized tour plan with content and navigational information displayed online or sent per email as a PDF document. Analyses of the usage data indicate that most of the average use time of 9 minutes is spent looking at the recommended tour, which suggests that users had a general interest in the recommendations made. Based on the overall use behavior, two kinds of users were identified: concrete planners and destination explorers. A comparison of the web-based application with the mobile version suggests the Web a more user-friendly environment than mobile devices.

Keywords: destination marketing, trip planning, semantic matching, ontology, tour recommendation, personalized city tour, web services.

1 Introduction

The web has become an important part of everyday life. Online banking or product sales via online shops are only some examples of ordinary processes that have been shifted to the web. Similarly, the tourism industry has taken advantage of the web's permanent availability and widespread distribution. Having been considered as a threat first, the web is now widely recognized as a gain for any destination. Beside attractive pictures and written text, there are additional possibilities like audio and video to draw tourists' attention to certain destinations. This provides better chances to reach and persuade tourists, especially for smaller destinations. The challenge for any destination is thus to present itself effectively via web pages. The more imaginative, individual and professional the offers are, the more interested the tourists will be in a destination.

Recent research (Schmidt-Belz, 2003) indicates that the web is the most important information source for trip preparations, far ahead of books and maps. Han and Oh (2006) analyzed online travel behavior and found out that consumers with high levels of income and education and those with previous online purchase experience search and book more on the web. But online tourism information is often unstructured and thus hard to find. Users typically have to manually go through many web pages to find and combine information they need. It is highly unsatisfactory for tourists to look for interesting sights on certain websites, to find addresses on other sites, and to have to combine these sights into a tour using the help of a routing system. Thus, there is clearly a need for services provided over the web that unite diverse information while considering personal needs and preferences. The city of Görlitz in Germany adapted the concept of a mobile dynamic tour guide to the web in order to provide their visitors with the opportunity to plan their city tour in advance (http://www.Goerlitz.de/dtg/). Based on personal interests and constraints, like available time, start- and endpoint and an optional integration of a café or restaurant, an individual tour is computed and illustrated with a map, pictures and text for each attraction as well as directions from one attraction to the next. Hopefully these kinds of services help to make destinations more attractive for tourists by supporting actual visits and to make online offerings more persuasive by individualizing content.

The goal of this paper is to present the specific web application designed for the city of Görlitz as an innovative trip planning aid providing personalized tour recommendations. The main focus is on evaluating the tour planner for Görlitz using logged user data. Selection behavior and selected interests are then compared to usage in mobile context. Implications for online destination marketing are provided.

2 Related work

Common ways of trip planning involve the use of route planners like Map24 when traveling by car, or railway homepages when traveling by train. Travelers have to specify their start- or arrival time and place and have the option to add stopovers. An algorithm then determines the fastest or cheapest route. These recommendations are based on time/cost constraints only and involve the calculation and display of travel routes from one place to another. In contrast, recommendations for tourist activities like museum visits, adventure holidays or city tours should also consider the personal preferences of tourists.

Applications for travel or trip planning have only emerged very recently. First approaches taking user specific characteristics into account are the following: In Spain, data warehouse technology and a decision support system are applied to select appropriate routes for soaring (paragliding, sailplane, hang gliding and others) (Araque, Salguero, & Abad, 2006). Travel agencies can use the system when suggesting areas and routes to perform soaring, considering former flights for a skill classification and the weather forecast to be able to find the right conditions for a flight. Ricci (2002) describes an interactive web system called Trip@dvice that helps tourists to build a personalized travel itinerary by means of content-based and collaborative filtering. The user has to specify initial constraints like companions, budget and transportation and can then search for products like destinations, accommodation or attractions. The system provides suggestions to reformulate the query to find a suitable number of products. It was lately integrated into www.visiteurope.com. Often there is also the problem that tourists planning a trip are forced to gather information on various web pages. The Australian System Data Warehouse (Kimber, Georgievski, & Sharda, 2006) tries to alleviate this by combining the content of single web pages with a system called TRIP. As the tour planning experience is a very important factor, there is a strong need for a significant enhancement such as a visualization of the whole tour. The DTG@Web combines both features of personalisation and holistic trip planning.

Several cities provide guided tours via mobile devices (e.g. Athens, Berlin, Rome, London, Munich, Weimar, and Dresden (Enarro, 2006; ITour, 2006)) with a certain amount of attractions following a predetermined route and affording no preparation. Other systems like INTRIGUE (Ardissono, 2003) which is available for handhelds and desktops provide a tour schedule by selecting attractions and defining constraints. But,tour planners on the web to support the preparation phase of a trip are still very scarce, though one might reason that a planning phase is much more intense at home than on location due to stress. The presented project called DTG@Web (a mobile Dynamic Tour Guide application adapted to the web environment) aims to improve the planning/preparation component of a tour by visualizing the itinerary in a map. It also provides photos of each sight to support tourists in picturing a destination in their mind and to help them form clear expectations regarding the destination.

To find out how the application is used and by what kind of users, the evaluation is based on de Certeau's appropriation theory (1974) which examines what people actually do with a product in daily usage. Therefore questionnaires are inefficient means as there are often discrepancies between what users say and do. Also due to the large number of participants, the only way to analyse real usage is logging and evaluating the interactions of users quantitatively and automatically. As the original web server logs are of low quality they need to be enhanced by additional logs safely distinguishing between users (Spiliopoulou, 2000). This is reached by sessions.

3 The web application DTG@Web

Based on an existing concept and prototype of a mobile application for a dynamic tour guide for Görlitz (ten Hagen, 2004), a web application providing the main tour recommendation and planning functionality was programmed. The tourist has to input his/her personal interests, the desired start and end in time and place (offered are central places, like parking lots and train stations). Additionally, a restaurant or café may be included, demanding the specification of the desired time span, nationality and price class as well as the decision if it should provide a terrace and/or vegetarian food. This information is combined to an optimal tour, including as many preference-specific attractions as possible within the given tour duration. In addition to simply viewing the recommended tour, users can print or email the tour as a PDF file. The printed document supports the tour execution by providing directions, though not dynamically based on the contextual situation. Furthermore the document with photos and information can serve as a souvenir and memory aide after the trip. Users can also modify the tour if it does not meet their expectations.

3.1 Components

The project consists of four main components:

ASPX web application running on an IIS (web server) and creating html output for the browsers
.NET web services executing the semantic matching and tour computations
Content database providing pictures and text for each attraction
Commercial routing web service (PTV) calculating the path segments between attractions and generating the map

3.2 Functionality

The web application consists of several forms for specifying the necessary data to compute a tour, to show the results and to do manual modifications. Each form is introduced by name and short explanation as the later evaluations refer to these forms:

Start – Welcome page to start the application
Demographics – Asks for the user's gender, age and computer literacy
Interest specification – The user has to select his/her general interests by one of three methods (displayed left to right in Figure 1)

- Tree view – Interests are structured hierarchically in a tree (3 levels of subcategories) and can be selected by checkboxes
- Image buttons – Similar to the tree view: interests and subcategories are displayed by icons or image buttons
- Main categories – Only five main categories (landmarks, architecture, culture & leisure, nature and celebrities) can be rated with up to 5 stars

Tour specification – The user must select date, duration, start- and endpoint of the tour and can additionally include a restaurant
Tour computation – Waiting screen while the tour is computed
Tour visualization – Displays the computed tour in a map, and pictures and textual information for each tour item
Email – An email with the attached tour as a PDF document is sent to the user's address
Tour modification – The user can modify the tour by adding or deleting tour items

The three different interest elicitation methods shown in Figure 1 and explained above are to be analysed in more detail to find out which concept is best suited for the web.

Fig. 1. Screen cuttings of interest elicitation methods on the web

4 Usage Analysis

For evaluation purposes the web logs automatically created by the IIS as well as user interaction and input recordings which were stored in an MS SQL database were used. The sample consists of 502 entries gathered from May to July 2006, the first two months after DTG@Web went online. To make sure only external users were taken into account; all internal entries were filtered out. Two marketing initiatives, first a newsletter and second a pop-up hint for all visitors of the Görlitz homepage (2006) were used to raise the number of visitors. Weekdays showed a much higher usage than the weekend, indicating that tourists are more likely to plan their trips for the weekends during the week. The mean age of the participants is 43 years, just a little bit higher than the average age in Germany of 41 years (EuroStat). The majority of participants also indicated that they use PCs and the Internet on a daily basis.

Figure 2 shows the possible workflow through the application, each path is numbered with the amount of visitations for each screen. After completing a demographic profile, users are assigned to one of the three preference elicitation methods. 25% of users quit during these dialogues. As the loss rate is similar for the three methods some tourists may not be willing to specify their interests at all. The next dialogue reunites the users by specifying, computing and visualizing the tour. 374 users reached the screen to compute a tour (75%), while 342 tours were displayed. Most users quit the application after having seen the tour; these are 50% of all users who started and 90% of those who reached this screen. Only few take the possibility to receive the tour via email or to modify it. Most likely the rendering of the tour in the browser is sufficient and a PDF document is not necessary to guide the actual walk through the city.

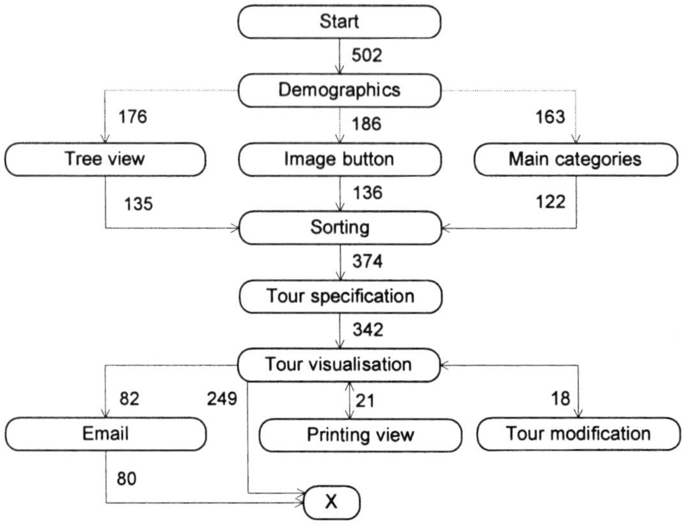

Fig. 2. Flow chart

Tourists used on average 32 clicks and spent almost 9 minutes interacting with DTG@Web. Although the median value is only 6 minutes there is a strong indication that many users really intend to plan a trip by investing this much time. Interaction metrics for individual screens are presented in Table 1. What can be seen in Table 1 is that most of this time is spent analyzing the computed tour looking at the pictures and information about it. This is the only page which needs to be scrolled down as it may contain a lot of sights depending on the tour length. The time spent for the interest specification is relatively short with about a minute on average. The main category method shows the highest value.

Table 1. Clicks and time per screen

Screen	*Clicks*			*Time [seconds]*		
	Mean	*Median*	*Std. dev.*	*Mean*	*Median*	*Std. dev.*
Start	1	1	0	25	16	36
Demographics	5.8	6	2.2	42	34	57
Interests						
- tree view	8.6	6	7.8	84	60	73
- image button	6.5	5	6.3	34	23	37
- main categories	12.9	16	5.8	74	61	64
Tour specification	11.5	11	5.1	77	67	52
Tour computation	-	-	-	35	27	29
Tour visualization	1.4	1	0.7	200	109	248
Email	2.4	2	0.8	34	23	59
Tour modification	5.9	3	4.6	65	44	66

The visitors to DTG@Web were assigned to one of three preference elicitation methods. The usage analysis shows that there is a big difference between the three methods in terms of the interests selected. Tourists using the main categories specify diverse values for the five interest categories. The most rated category is architecture, which is no surprise since Görlitz offers unique architectural ensembles from Medieval to Wihelmian styles. For the image button method the selected interests are the least diverse and users hardly reach levels deeper than the top level.

One might now reason that tourists have no specialized interests but the tree view usage pattern shows that more than 50% of the interest selections are placed in detailed levels. Figure 3 visualizes this distribution. This might indicate that the creation of a mental model to traverse a tree by clicking on images representing the nodes has not been supported sufficiently whereas a text-based tree view is familiar and, thus, used.

The default value for the intended travel date was "Same Day", which was chosen by 68%. One third of the remaining visitors planned for the next three days and another third planned for more than 2 weeks ahead. The last third lies in between. When specifying the tour, the tourists could also enter the number of participants for that tour. About 50% of the tours were calculated for an individual traveler, the other half for couples and bigger groups. Again, one person was the default level and it can be assumed that many users did not change it.

Although individual tours dominate, the number of tours calculated represents a much larger number of tourists (Figure 4).

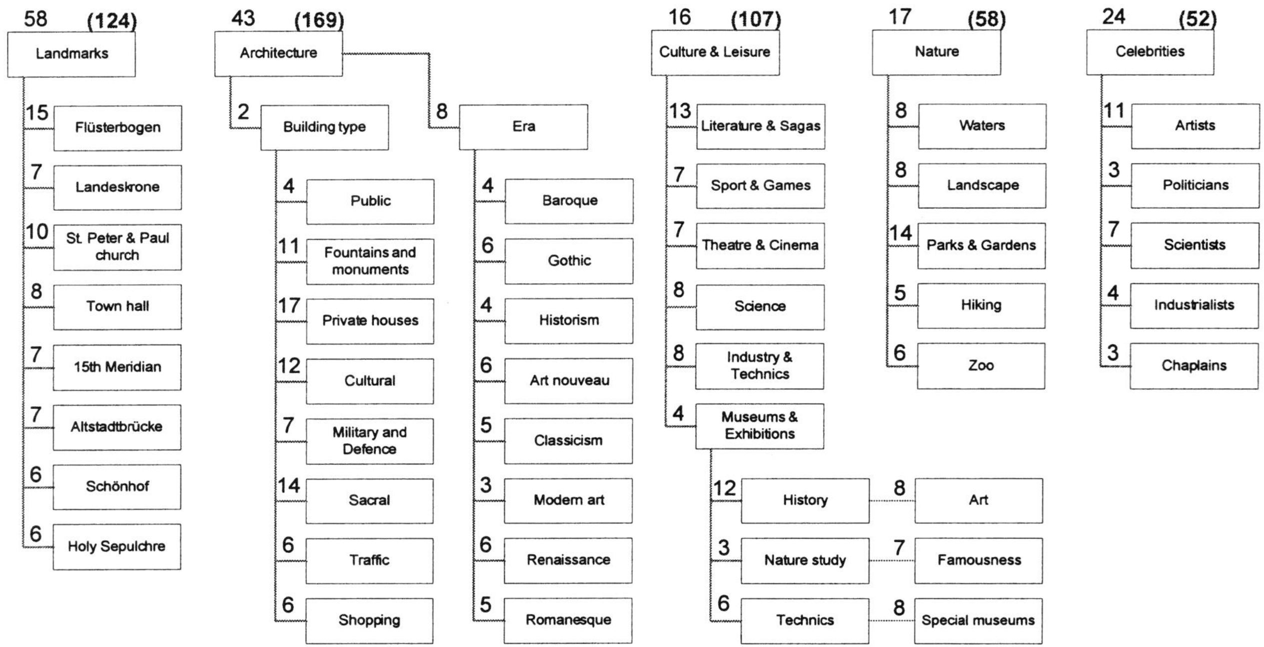

Fig. 3. Distribution of selections in interest tree view

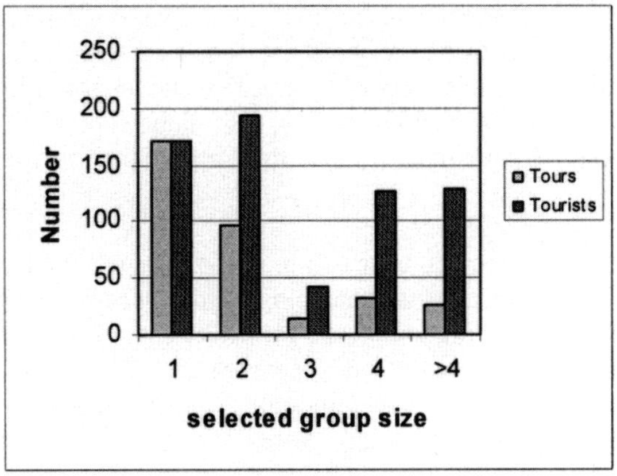

Fig. 4. Number of tours and tourists for different group sizes

Figure 5 shows the distribution of specified tour lengths. The mean and median value for a tour is 7 hours. Most tourists chose 9 or 10 a.m. as the start time and 4 p.m. as the end time of their tour. The question is if they really intend to walk up to 7 hours, or if they only wanted to create a tour with a lot of content to obtain more information about the destination. In 58% of the cases, the selected start- and endpoint were the same. The most frequently chosen places are a bridge connecting the German and Polish part of the city, the train station for tourists traveling by train and a central place with a car park.

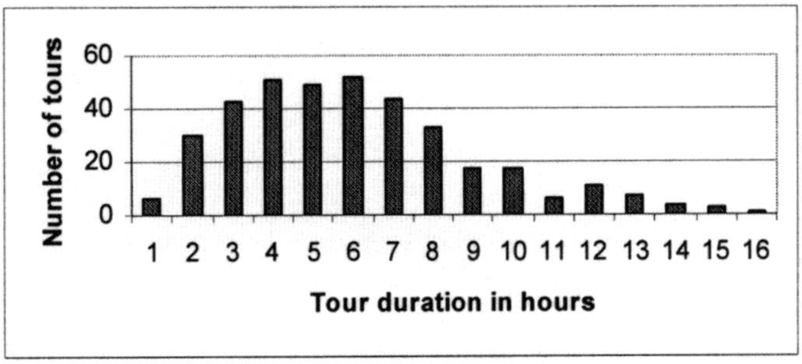

Fig. 5. Tour durations

The mean amount of sights included in a tour is 28. As a mean tour is computed for 7 hours, a tourist would visit 4 attractions per hour, which is a realistic scenario. The tour planner uses an estimated staying time of 7 minutes for each sight and a walking speed of 3 km per hour for the tourists. A simple monument or fountain may not attract tourists for so long, but they may stay much longer in parks or churches. Also, the sights in Görlitz are located very close to each other so that there is very little walking time between two tour items.

A mobile field trial in Görlitz (Modsching Kramer, ten Hagen, & Gretzel, 2006) identified restaurants as the most frequently visited attractions in a city. The fact that

60% of the tours planned on the web include either a café or a restaurant underlines this. In particular, only 40% of the tours are specified without a restaurant, 35% contain a restaurant for lunch and 25% a café. The opportunity to modify the automatically created tour was only used by 5% of the tourists. That might either mean the tourists did not take note of the button or they trust the device in choosing the optimal tour.

All together DTG@Web seems to have two modes of usage: (1) Concrete planning of a tour for a scheduled trip and (2) imagining of the experience at the destination during the selection of a destination. In the former case the inclusion of a restaurant, detailed timing and routing is important, whereas in the latter adding many interesting attractions independent of any date and duration seems to be the goal. This indicates that future tour planning systems should provide functionality for both usage modes, e.g. creating a tour step by step based on a general overview.

5 Comparison Web and Mobile Context

A field study in the summer of 2005 evaluated different methods for preference elicitation in a mobile context (Kramer, Modsching, Gretzel, & ten Hagen, 2006). The DTG@Web application provides the same methods in a web environment with the advantages that elements appear larger, scrolling isn't necessary anymore and more detailed explanations are provided. For comparison purposes the underlying concepts remained the same. Table 2 shows clicks and durations for the elicitation of interests for all three methods, comparing both contexts.

Table 2. Median clicks and duration comparison for mobile and web context

	Method	*Mobile*	*Web*
Tree view	Clicks (deviation)	12 (16)	6 (8)
	Duration [min] (deviation)	1.44 (1.30)	1.00 (1.13)
Image button	Clicks	13.5 (42)	5 (6)
	Duration [min]	1.28 (2.30)	0.23 (0.37)
Main categories	Clicks (deviation)	19 (12)	16 (6)
	Duration [min] (deviation)	1.50 (1.02)	1.01 (1.04)

It took the users many more clicks and more time to select their interests in the mobile context. At present people are much more familiar with the web than with mobile devices, screens are 25 times bigger and handling a mouse poses a much smaller challenge to hand-eye coordination. Another fact is that on the mobile device scrolling was necessary as all elements could not be displayed on a single screen. This was not the case for the web browser version. Some users even needed multiple tries to hit the right element on the small mobile display. Also, users were unobserved when using the web application and the interaction took place in their familiar environment. These conditions may have helped them working through the dialogs much faster.

6 Future Research

A large majority of the individual tourists travels in small groups. Therefore, an important research area for the future is group support. The tour computation has to be able to compromise between different interests, and in a mobile context the context driven interpretation has to be synchronized for multiple devices. Another research opportunity to be explored is giving the tourist the option to plan an entire trip of a couple of days by including transportation, accommodation and tours at indoor locations. Preference elicitation by presenting images of iconic examples of a category has many advantages, but traversal of a tree by clicking on images representing nodes is an unfamiliar concept. Future research needs to focus on how to best provide visual cues to support the creation of a mental model that supports traversal. Last, tourism consists of three important components: plan, action and memory. The planning component is covered by the presented system. The mobile DTG will implement the action component. To provide the memory effect, a tour diary might be logged on the mobile device and converted to a website later.

7 Conclusion

DTG@Web provides visitors with the chance to prepare an individual tour in advance via the web and have a PDF document created and printed that will support the actual visit. The usage analysis shows that many tourists have already taken advantage of the possibility to receive an impression of their destination compressed within a single application. Others used it to plan a concrete tour. A comparison of the application in a mobile and a web environment has revealed that interacting with a web application is much faster, probably due to much greater familiarity. These findings indicate the usefulness of such an application and its great potential to persuasively communicate the many attractions offered at a destination. However, the results also show the need to further improve the system in order to fully support advance tour planning. Last, integrating Web and mobile applications seems to be an important next step in developing recommenders for personalized city tours.

References

Araque, F., Salguero, A. & Abad, M. (2006): Application of data warehouse and Decision Support System in soaring site recommendation. In M. Hitz, M. Sigala, & J. Murphy (Eds.), *Information and Communication Technologies in Tourism*. Wien-NewYork: Springer Verlag.

Ardissono, L., Goy, A., Petrone, G., Segnan, M., Torasso, P. (2003): Intrigue: Personalized Recommendation of Tourist Attrcations for Desktop and Handset Devices. Applied Artificial Intelligence: Special Issue on Artificial Intelligence for Cultural Heritage and Digital Libraries 17(8-9), 678-714.

De Certeau, M. (1974) L'invention au quotidien. 1. Arts de faire. Paris: Gallimard.

Enarro (2006): www.enarro.com

Görlitz (2006): www.goerlitz.de

Kimber, J., Georgievski, M., & Sharda, N. (2006) Developing a Visualisation Tool for Tour Planning. In M. Hitz, M. Sigala, & J. Murphy (Eds.), *Information and Communication Technologies in Tourism*. Wien-NewYork: Springer Verlag.

Kramer, R., Modsching, M. Gretzel, U. & ten Hagen, K. (2006): A Field Trial to Elicit Individual Preferences in the Context of a Mobile Dynamic Tour Guide. In M. Hitz, M. Sigala, & J. Murphy (Eds.), *Information and Communication Technologies in Tourism*. Wien-NewYork: Springer Verlag.

Han, J. and Oh, K. (2006): The Trend of Online Travel Behaviours: Cohort Analysis of 2000 and 2002. In M. Hitz, M. Sigala, & J. Murphy (Eds.), *Information and Communication Technologies in Tourism*. Wien-NewYork: Springer Verlag.

ITour (2006): http://de.itour.de/cnt/311004232955.htm

Modsching, M., Kramer, R., ten Hagen, K., & Gretzel, U. (2006): Capturing the Beaten Paths: A Novel Method for Analysing Tourists' Spatial Behaviour at an Urban Destination In M. Hitz, M. Sigala, & J. Murphy (Eds.), *Information and Communication Technologies in Tourism*. Wien-NewYork: Springer Verlag.

Ricci, F., Arslan, B., Mirzadeh, N. & Venturini, A. (2002): ITR: a case-based travel advisory system. In S. Craw & A. Preece (Eds.), 6th European Conference on Case Based Reasoning, ECCBR 2002, Springer Verlag, 613–627.

Schmidt-Belz, B.; Posland, S. (2003). User Validation of a mobile Tourism Service. Workshop HCI mobile Guides, Udine (Italy).

Spiliopoulou, M. (2000). Web usage mining for Web site evaluation. *Communications of the ACM, 43*(8).

Tjostheim, I. and Lous, J. (2006). Attracting visitors – Using Computer Games Technology to Build a VR-Museum In M. Hitz, M. Sigala, & J. Murphy (Eds.), *Information and Communication Technologies in Tourism*. Wien-NewYork: Springer Verlag.

Ten Hagen, K., Kramer, R, Müller, P., Schumann, B., Hermkes, M. (2004): Semantic Matching and Heuristic Search for a Dynamic Tour Guide. In A. Frew (Ed.), *Information and Communication Technologies in Tourism*. Wien-NewYork: Springer Verlag.

Consumer Behaviour in e-Tourism

Annette Steinbauer
Hannes Werthner
Department for Information Systems/ e-tourism
Leopold-Franzens-University, Austria
annette.steinbauer@gmx.net

Abstract

During the last decades Tourism as an information intensive business has been strongly affected by the rapid changes in technology, especially the Internet,. One of the major results is the changing in traveller's behaviour. Therefore the challenge of identifying, attracting and retaining customers in the online market as well as the issue of understanding consumer's perceptions is becoming a critical success factor. The aim of this paper is to identify the determinants that influence potential travellers to use the Internet for travel planning and to show their interrelations. A major result of these findings is a causal model of e-tourism usage. Constructs such as Internet affinity, attitudes and self-efficacy prove to have a major impact on the actual use of the Internet for travel planning, whereas moderating variables such as gender or customer involvement prove to be important as well.

Keywords: e-tourism; online travel planning; consumer behaviour; travel websites.

1 Introduction

Travel and Tourism as one of the world's highest priority industries has an important economic impact on the global as well as on the local level (Werthner & Klein, 1999). Information is the crucial factor for tourists while planning, booking and being on vacation as well as after their trips. The nature of tourism and its products makes tourism an information intensive business (Werthner & Klein, 1999). These issues lead to the insight that tourism belongs to the industries most affected by the rapid changes in technology during the last decades. The role of information explains the importance of Information Technology (IT) applications in tourism. The Internet can be seen as one of the most influential technologies that change traveller's behaviour. While the number of Internet users increases and is reported to have reached 957 million (IWS, 2005), the diffusion of IT has improved the travel service supply in efficiency, quality and flexibility (Jung & Baker, 1998; Werthner & Klein, 1999). According to these facts, the European Online Travel Market is estimated to generate € 41 bn in 2006, and 15-20% of all travel expenses are forecasted to be made via the Internet in 2006 (PhoCusWright, 2004). Even though the Internet is an important tool for information search and purchase of products, most consumers are using multiple channels in their decision making process. 60% of online information searchers are finally buying offline (Fittkau & Maass, 2005). And in the travel industry 68% of online travel buyers are not only purchasing via the Internet, but use multiple channels for purchasing their travel products (PhoCusWright, 2005).

The aim of this study is to identify the determinants that influence potential travellers to use the Internet for travel planning and to show their interrelationships. The result of these findings is a causal model of e-tourism usage (e-tourism within this context is defined as the process of potential travellers using the Internet for travel planning). Special focus is also on differences in model structure for exclusive information searching travellers compared to online booking travellers as well as business versus private travellers. Based on the results from the e-Tourism Usage Model, the study is also going to identify current barriers and problems of potential travellers in using the Internet for travel planning.

The paper is starting with presenting theoretical considerations and the literature background for developing the research model. The literature overview is followed by the presentation of the theoretically derived "e-Tourism Usage Model". Furthermore, the applied methodology as well as empirical results concerning the overall model structure and the moderating effects of the e-Tourism Usage Model are introduced and discussed.

2 Theoretical Background and the e-Tourism Usage Model

Starting with a theoretical evaluation of determinants influencing the use of the Internet for travel planning, the e-Tourism Usage Model was derived on the basis of previous models concerning relevant fields of research. The following three fields of research proved to be interesting and relevant for deriving the model: i) theories of consumer behaviour, ii) models of decision making in tourism and iii) theories of e-shopping acceptance including the subject of website evaluation. In the following a short overview of existing theories within these fields of interest will be provided. Based upon these theoretical considerations the "e-Tourism Usage Model" will be introduced.

Theories in consumer behaviour are generally developed to better understand and explain consumer decisions and behaviour. These studies aim to find principles in consumer behaviour to be able to derive practical implications and advices to predict and to influence consumer decisions (Kroeber-Riel & Weinberg, 1999; Gröppel-Klein, 2001). The consumer behaviour research shows two different views in looking at the consumer decision process: the behaviouristic and the neobehaviouristic view of research. While behaviourists are focusing on the observable constructs of stimulating aspects and responses within the consumer decision process, neobehaviourists expand their research on the theoretical and hypothetical constructs interceding between stimuli and responses (Kroeber-Riel, 1996). The present study is following the neobehaviouristic research tradition in building upon a three-step structure of consumer behaviour (Freter, 1983). This structure was also adopted from (Middleton, 1994; Swarbrooke & Horner, 1999) to explain tourists' behaviour during the decision making process. Stimuli within this context consist of endogenous and exogenous factors showing decision relevant characteristics of the consumer. These include consumer's usage of new technologies as well as variables describing his social and economic environment. The responses show the consumer's reaction on these stimuli, meaning purchase of a special product or brand, choice of distribution channel or intensity of usage. Following the neobehaviouristic research tradition, the process of stimuli leading to responses is explained by viewing the constructs in between. Those interceding constructs appear as cognitive, activating and combined aspects. Cognitive aspects can be described as buying intention and preferences, activating constructs include emotions, attitudes and motivations. Combining those aspects involvement and trust are also seen as interceding constructs.

Tourism research mainly views travel planning as a complex and multi-faceted decision making process (Fesenmaier & Jeng, 2000). Therefore, **theories of decision making in tourism** commonly focus on identifying the various aspects of a tourist's decision. While (Swarbrooke & Horner, 1999; Wahab, Crompton, & Rothfield, 1976) developed the first research papers and models of decision making in tourism in the 70ies, researchers like (Mathieson & Wall, 1982; Moutinho, 1987; Swarbrooke & Horner, 1999) enhanced their findings in formulating further theories in identifying determinants and describing phases of the decision making process. Those classical theories of decision making in tourism were facing some criticism in having difficulties in meeting fast moving changes within the tourism as well as the communication and technology industry. Therefore, current theories describing tourist's behaviour within the age of new technology and Internet environment also needed to be reviewed and considered for deriving a model of decision making in e-tourism. (Woodside & MacDonald, 1994) published their "Tourism Service Decision Process Model" by describing the tourist's decision making process determined by eight aspects contributing to the final decision. Situational factors like traveller's characteristics as well as marketing activities affect the individual information search behaviour within this research. (Fesenmaier & Jeng, 2000) also build their "Decision Net Model" on the assumption of viewing the tourist's decision as a complex decision consisting of various sub-decisions. The decision process is described as having a hierarchical overall structure, where some decisions are contingent upon other decisions that have already been made. Forming a net structure based on the assumption that every aspect of each decision affects and is being affected by other sub-decisions, the final travel decision is hypothesised to consist of core, secondary, and en route sub-decisions.

Consumer's use of the Internet at any stage of the decision making process has become a major subject within the consumer behaviour research during the last decade (**e-shopping acceptance**). The present study will contribute to research in the field of tourists' behaviour by looking at their behaviour while using the Internet as information and/or booking channel. Therefore, theories describing the acceptance of technology and satisfaction of consumers with using the Internet were an interesting subject in deriving the "Model of e-Tourism Usage". Most common theories in explaining the acceptance of new technologies are the "Innovation Diffusion Theory" (IDT), "Theory of Reasoned Action" (TRA), "Theory of Planned Behaviour" (TPB) and the "Technology Acceptance Model" (TAM). The IDT describes the process of technology acceptance by five characteristics of the technology influencing the consumer's attitude leading to adopting or refusing the technology (Rogers, 1995). These crucial characteristics include relative advantage, compatibility, complexity, trialability and observability. The TRA points at the attitude as a critical construct towards adopting or refusing the use of a certain technology. While individual attitudes and subjective norms form a person's behavioural intention, an individual's actual behaviour is the natural consequence (Fishbein & Ajzen, 1975). Introducing perceived behavioural control as an additional determinant of behavioural intention, the TPB was built upon the TRA (Ajzen & Madden, 1986). The most common and most adopted theory of accepting a new technology is the TAM (Davis, 1989; Davis, Bagozzi, & Warshaw, 1989)The TAM states attitude as the central construct influencing the behavioural intention and thereby the actual use or non-adoption of the technology. This theory explains a person's attitude towards using a certain technology by three determinants: perceived ease of use, perceived usefulness and perceived enjoyment.

Theories addressing the issue of accepting the Internet as information and/or booking channel focus rather on the consumer's evaluation of the system than on the process of adoption. Highly acquainted and effective in this field of research was the "Information System Success Model" (IS Success Model) introduced by (DeLone & McLean, 2003). The theory introduces six constructs to quantify the success of an information system in the e-commerce environment: system quality, information quality, service quality, usage, user's satisfaction and net benefits. Assigning these theories to the subject of tourism a couple of highly useful empirically proved models have been published focusing on travel website quality (Mills & Morrison, 2003; Sigala & Sakellaridis, 2004; DeLone & McLean, 2003) and usability (Essawy, 2005; DeLone & McLean, 2004; Kao, Louvieris, Powell-Perry, & Buhalis, 2005). Based upon these theoretical considerations the "e-Tourism Usage Model" (eTUM) was derived. Fig 1. shows the simplified version of the determinants hypothetically contributing to the attitude towards using and actual use of the Internet for travel planning.

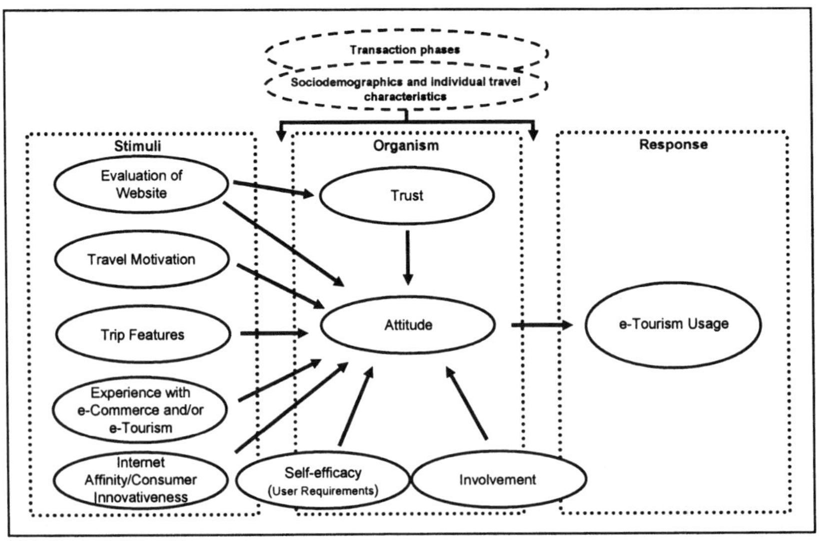

Fig. 1. The e-Tourism Usage Model (eTUM)

The objective of the eTUM is to identify determinants of using the Internet for travel planning, to elaborate the model structure as well as to quantify the effects between the identified determinants. By showing quantitative differences in the model structure between different types of travellers the model is contributing to identifying problems and barriers in using the Internet for travel planning.

The e-Tourism Usage Model is built upon a three-step structure of consumer behaviour classifying the hypothesised constructs as being stimulating, interceding, responding and moderating. The discovered constructs influencing consumer's choice to use the Internet as travel planning channel are as follows: evaluation of the website, travel motivation, trip features, experience with e-commerce and/or e-tourism, Internet affinity, self-efficacy, involvement and trust. The attitude towards using the Internet for travel planning is hypothesised to be the central concept in affecting the decision to actually use the Internet as information and/or booking channel. The attitude therefore is a central interceding – combining active and cognitive aspects – determinant of the actual use of online travel planning (Davis, 1989; Davis et al., 1989; Delago-Ballester, 2003; DeLone & McLean, 2004; Fishbein & Ajzen, 1975; Heinemann, 1974; Jung & Butler, 2000; Kuß & Tomczak, 2000; Nieschlag, Dichtl, & Hörschgen, 2002; Schramm-Klein, 2005; Wolff, 2005). The exogenous and endogenous determinants are indirectly influencing the actual use via having a direct impact on the attitude toward using the Internet. Exogenous and endogenous stimuli within this context are represented by evaluation of the website, travel motivation, trip features, experience and Internet affinity. The traveller's reaction to these stimuli within his channel choice process is defined as the actual use of the Internet for travel planning. In contrast to stimuli and reaction the interceding determinants are not observable. The formulated interceding constructs are trust, self-efficacy, involvement and attitude. Moderating influences are expected from the stage of transaction process as well as travel specific and demographic characteristics of the potential tourist. These moderating variables are hypothesised to influence the interrelations between the introduced constructs but not to have a determining impact on the constructs itself.

3 Methodology

3.1 Study Design

To validate the theoretical model described above an online questionnaire for potential travellers was designed. The data were collected on four different travel websites, which were selected by their range of supply and the available transaction phases they offer with their services. The websites should on the one hand be able to offer all phases of the customer buying process from information gathering to buying the travel product online. On the other hand they should represent different supply ranges from offering only individual travel products to offering individual products as well as complete travel packages. The Tiscover AG, Thomas Cook Touristik GmbH, Travel Scout 24 and Nix-wie-weg.de supported the study by placing a link to the questionnaire on their website and/or in their newsletter(s). The questionnaire was formulated in German, so only German-speaking travellers were addressed to take part in the study. The questionnaire was placed on the website of the Institute of Information Systems/Department for e-Tourism at the University of Innsbruck. To encourage persons who were visiting these websites, to take part in the study, travel vouchers were promised to be raffled as incentives for participants.

3.2 Sample Characteristics

1.458 users took part in the study by filling out the online questionnaire. The gender distribution was nearly equal. 53% of the participants were female and 47% male. With more than one third the survey's age peak was between 41 and 50 years. Rather surprising is that 25% of all respondents announced to be older than 50 years. All groups of income were represented in the study. On average the interviewed persons are traveling three times a year. Most of these people mainly travel for private purpose, but there are still 21% that are doing at least a quarter of their journeys for business reason. And 71% of these potential travellers declared to have already booked a travel product online. The people that were interviewed while surfing on one of the four travel websites showed to be rather Internet affine. More than one third has seven or more years of Internet experience and over 50% of the interviewed persons use the Internet at least 10 hours per week. The sample was dominated by travellers searching for information on the homepage of Tiscover. 79% of the participants took part in the survey via Tiscover, 14% via Travel Scout 24 while 24,5% were generated by nix-wie-weg.de and 2% by Thomas Cook.

3.3 Constructs Used and their Reliability

Eight determinants were theoretically hypothesised to have an influence on the attitude towards using the Internet for travel planning as well as on the actual choice to use the online channel for gathering travel information and/or booking. Demographics as well as individual traveller's characteristics and the actual transaction phase were hypothesised to be moderating variables. As mentioned above the theoretical determinants were evaluation of the website, trip features, experience, Internet affinity, self-efficacy, involvement and trust. These determinants where operationalised by using single statements. The items used for operationalising the constructs were adopted from established and reliability proved scales (Bieger, Beritelli, Weinert, & Wittmer, 2005; DeLone & McLean, 2004; Fesenmaier & Johnson, 1989; Fishbein & Ajzen, 1975; Gretzel, Mitsche, Hwang, Fesenmaier, 2004; Gursoy & McCleary 2004; Jung & Butler, 2000; Kroeber-Riel & Weinberg 1996; Li & Buhalis, 2005; Luo, Feng, Cai, 2004; Mills & Morrison, 2003a; Morrison, Jing, O`Leary, & Lipping, 2001; Scharlet al., 2004; Schmidt, Schögel, & Tomczak, 2003; Sigala & Sakellaridis, 2004; Schramm-Klein, 2003; Wolff, 2005). All of these measurement items were subject to a 6-point Likert-Scale (if not specified otherwise). Those items were tested for reliability and optimised by indicator and factor reliability criteria as well as using confirmatory factor analysis. In cases with less than three items remaining the Cronbachs alpha was regarded as the final decision criteria. **Table 1** shows the number of items remaining and the fulfillment of reliability criteria for each of the hypothesised constructs.

Table 1. Constructs used and their reliability

Constructs		Nr. of Items	Reliability (Cronbach's Alpha)
Website Evaluation	Ease of Use	3	0.90
	Usefulness	3	0.86
Trip Features		2	0.74
Experience		2	0.87
Internet Affinity/DSI		2	0.62
Self-efficacy	Information Search	2	0.79
	Online Booking	3	0.79
Involvement		2	0.62
Trust		3	0.80
Attitude	Information Search	2	0.69
	Booking	3	0.88
Usage	Intensity	2	0.70
	Loyalty	2	0.78

4 Explaining e-Tourism Usage

4.1 Overall Structural Model

After performing the analysis of missing values 533 completed questionnaires were evaluated to be representative for the sample. With this sample of 533 cases it was aimed to fit a model using structural equation techniques with latent variables (using AMOS 5.0-Software). The exogenously influencing as well as the endogenous constructs and their operationalisation were described in the previous chapter. After some modifications the e-Tourism Usage Model was accepted with the following parameters: df = 228, Cmin/df = 2.164, SRMR = .043, GFI = .931, AGFI = .909, CFI = .956, RMSEA = .047. 1 Fig 1. shows the validated model displaying solely arrows with significant causal correlations. The standardized direct effects are illustrated in the figure.

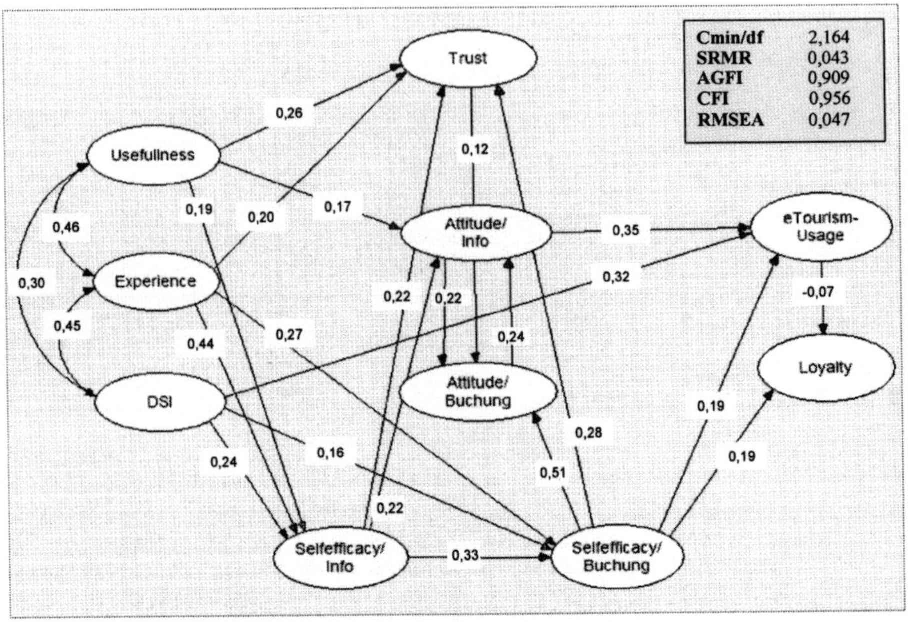

Fig. 2. Validated structural model for explaining e-tourism usage

To quantify the influences the total effects were considered. Total effects result as the sum of direct and indirect causal effects one latent construct has on another construct. Indirect effects are obtained if a construct influences another construct via intermediary constructs. W hile analysing and modifying the theoretically derived model the constructs ease of use of the website, trip features, motivation and involvement did not prove to have any significant causal interdependencies with the other mentioned constructs. Involvement still showed significant correlations with all other constructs so this latent variable was later on analysed for having a moderating impact on the model. The actual use of the Internet for travel planning is mainly driven by the traveller's Internet-affinity (tot.eff = .40). The more someone is Internet literate the more he is likely to use the Internet when planning a journey. Following psychological-behavioural theories, the attitude towards using the Internet for travel-information search plays also a major role for the actual use of e-tourism (tot.eff. = .37). The importance of someone's attitude towards performing a behaviour for the actual behaviour has been discussed in many empirical studies and is also confirmed in this study. Rather surprising is the finding that in this study the attitude towards booking a travel product online does not have a direct impact on the actual use of e-tourism (tot.eff. = .09). This cognition leads to the insight that a positive attitude towards using the Internet as an information channel is a precedent condition for the traveller's consideration to increase his usage of the Internet as a booking channel as well. The potential traveller's self-efficacy towards booking a travel product online is the last of the three constructs having a direct impact on the actual use of e-tourism (tot.eff. = .23). The more a person is confident in knowing how to book a travel product online the more he will consider the Internet as a useful channel for planning the journey.

After showing its importance for the actual use of e-tourism it is interesting to look at the determinants of someone's attitude towards using the Internet for travel planning. The attitude towards using the Internet for travel information search is mainly driven by someone's self-efficacy (tot.eff. = .28). Similar impact on the attitude towards using the Internet for travel information gathering shows the attitude towards booking as well as the evaluation of the website's usefulness (both tot.eff. = .25). The two facets of attitude, information search and booking, are influencing each other by showing significant positive causal correlations in between them (tot.eff. = .25/ .23). Experience and self-efficacy towards booking online have rather little and only indirect influence on the attitude towards information search (tot.eff. = .17/ .14). Attitude towards booking a travel product online is mainly dependent on the self-efficacy towards booking online (tot.eff. = .58). The potential traveller's attitude towards booking is thus the more positive the more the person feels capable of proceeding with the online booking transaction. Experience and self-efficacy towards information search are also pushing the attitude towards booking a travel product online (tot.eff. = .30/ .27). The construct of trust plays surprisingly a rather small role within the e-tourism usage model but is having its main impact on the attitude towards booking (tot.eff. = .13). Trust itself is mainly causally influenced by experience (tot.eff. = .42). Self-efficacy towards booking and the evaluation of the website's usefulness are also strengthening a potential traveller's trust (tot.eff. = .28/ .32). Interesting is also the finding that loyalty towards a travel website is mainly driven by the self-efficacy towards the capability of booking a travel product at the specific travel website. The more a person is confident of his own abilities to proceed with the online booking process the rather he will be loyal and using the same website again for the next travel planning. The more a potential traveller is using the Internet for travel planning the less he is loyal to a specific website. This negative impact of actual e-tourism usage on loyalty is rather minor (tot.eff. = -.07). As also shown by the descriptive analysis the online travel brand loyalty seems to be rather low. The large variety of travel offerings all over the World Wide Web seems to cause a rather small emotional commitment to specific websites of travellers planning their journey online.

4.2 Moderating Variables

After analysing the overall model structures, the additional variables that were hypothesised to have a moderating effect on the interdependencies between the analysed constructs were examined. Gender, individual traveller's characteristics, transaction phase and involvement were hypothesised to be moderating variables for the structural model. Focusing on the most interesting effects resulting from the construct of involvement, its moderating effects will be discussed in detail as follows. The construct of involvement was former hypothesised to be one of the determinants having direct influence on the attitude and actual use of e-tourism but analysing the structural model showed no causal influences of involvement. Nevertheless, involvement proved to have significant correlations with the other determinants, so this construct was tested to have a moderating impact. People with low involvement seem to be far more influenced by the website's perceived usefulness than highly involved people. Low-involved people also perceive the usefulness of the website and ease of use significantly less positive than people with high involvement. While highly involved people have a more positive attitude towards using the Internet for travel planning, low-involved people show significant less trust into travel websites. They also have less experience and seem to be less Internet-affine than people being highly involved in their travel plans. Recapitulating the hypotheses about the variables gender, type of traveller, online booking experience and involvement having moderating influences on the validated structural model could be corroborated.

5 Discussion and Implications

The aim of this study was to develop an empirically validated model of e-tourism usage that identifies the relevant factors influencing customer's choice of using the Internet for travel planning. The model analyses the weight of each factor on the attitude of using the online channel. The research furthermore shows differences in model structure (i.e. different weighting of individual influencing factors) for different types of travellers. The empirical analysis of the study has brought up the following findings. The actual use of the Internet for travel planning is mainly influenced by the attitude towards using the Internet as an information gathering channel, Internet familiarity and self-efficacy towards booking the travel product online. Moreover, regarding the potential traveller's attitude it is obviously determining to differentiate between attitude towards using the Internet for information search and towards using it as a booking channel. These aspects have to be viewed separately for these constructs show clearly different profiles concerning their impacts, although they are strongly affecting each other. While attitude towards using the Internet as an information channel is mainly influenced by evaluating the website's usefulness, attitude towards using the Internet as a booking channel strongly depends on the traveller's self-efficacy mainly regarding online booking but as well information searching. Also important for the traveller's attitude towards online booking are experiences the traveller has made with travel websites and e-commerce in the past as well as his trust into travel websites in general and the Internet affinity of the user. Trust on the other hand strongly depends on the users' past experiences with using the Internet. But also usefulness of the website and self-efficacy towards information search and booking via the Internet have an important impact on the potential traveller's trust. The structural model also proves to be strongly affected by moderating variables. Therefore demographics, type of traveller (business vs. private), online booking experience (booker vs. looker) as well as involvement were validated to have a strongly influencing effect on the causal correlations between the constructs of the empirically proved e-Tourism Usage Model.

While the supply of online travel information sources and booking facilities in the Internet is permanently increasing, the issue of consumer and customer relations is becoming even more important for tourism market players. An enhanced understanding of the customer and his specific needs, perceptions and motives in the decision making process is the critical success factor in providing a successful and profitable online customer relationship. The Internet's key attraction as a marketing tool lies in the level of interactivity that can be developed between suppliers and consumers. The findings and results of this study show perceptions, motives and barriers of online travelers. Thus, the study intends to contribute to developing advanced effective online marketing strategies to attract tourists to use the online channel for travel planning. The study was constructed on the assumption of addressing only middle European and German-speaking countries. The cultural dimension was hence excluded to be influencing in this context. Therefore the construct of culture is recommended to be included in further analysis.

References

Ajzen, I. & Madden, T. (1986). Prediction of goal-Directed behaviour: Attitudes, Intentions, and Perceived behavioural Control. *Journal of Experimental Social Psychology*, 22 (4), 453-474.

Bieger, T., Beritelli, P., Weinert, R., Wittmer, A. (2005). Building Trust and Identity on the Web – New IT Transaction Platforms to Overcome Psychological Barrier to Rent. In A. Frew (Eds.). *Information and Communication Technologies in Tourism 2005 – Proceedings of the International Conference in Innsbruck.* Wien.

Davis, F. (1989). Perceived Usefulness, Perceived Ease of Use, and User Acceptance of Information Technology. *MIS Quarterly*, 13, 319-340.

Davis, F. D., Bagozzi, R. P., Warshaw, P. R. (1989). *User Acceptance of Computer Technology: A Comparison of two Theoretical Models.*Maryland.

Delago-Ballester, E. (2003). Development and Validation of a Brand Trust Scale. *International Journal of Market Research*, 45(1), 35-54.

DeLone, W. H., & McLean, E. R. (2003). The DeLone and McLean Model of Information Systems Success: A Ten-Year Update. *Journal of Management Information Systems*, 19(4), 9-30.

DeLone, W. H., & McLean, E. R. (2004). Applying the DeLone&McLean Information Systems Success Model. *International Journal of Electronic Commerce,* 9(1), 31-47.

Essawy, M. (2005). *Testing the Usability of Hotel Websites: The Springboard for Customer Relationship Building*. Leeds.

Fesenmaier, D. & Jeng, J. (2000). Assessing structure in the pleasure trip planning process. *Tourism Analysis*, 5, 13-27.

Fesenmaier, D., & Johnson, B. (1989). Involvement-based segmentation: implications for travel marketing in Texas. *Tourism Management*, 10, 293-300.

Fesenmaier, D., Pan, B., Gretzel, U., Hwang, Y., Grabler, K., Zins, A., & Mazanec, J. (2002). Tourist Decision Model Report. *Project DieToRecs on Intelligent Recommendation for Tourist Destination Decision Making.*

Fishbein, M., & Ajzen, I. (1975). *Belief, Attitude, Intention and Behavior.* London.

Fishbein, M., Ajzen, J. (1980). *Understanding Attitudes and Predicting Social Behaviour.* London.

Freter, H. (1983). *Marktsegmentierung*. Stuttgart.

Frew,A. J. (Ed.) (2005). Information and Communication Technologies in Tourism 2005. *Proceedings of the International Conference in Innsbruck.* Vienna.

Gretzel, U., Mitsche, N., Hwang, Y.-H., Fesenmaier, D. (2004). Tell me who you are and I will tell you where to go – Use of Travel Personalities in Destination Recommendation Systems. *Information Technology & Tourism*, 7(1), 3-12.

Gröppel-Klein, A. (2001). Kons umentenverhaltensforschung. In M. Bruhn & C. Homburg (Eds.): *Gabler Marketing Lexikon.* 325-328. Wiesbaden.

Gursoy, D. & McCleary, K. (2004). An Integrative Model of Tourists' Information Search Behaviour. *Annals of Tourism Research*, 31(2), 353-373.

Heinemann, M. (1974). *Einkaufsstättenwahl und Firmentreue des Konsumenten.* Münster.

Hildebrandt, L.; Homburg, C. (1998). *Die Kausalanalyse – Ein Instrument der empirischen betriebswirtschaftlichen Forschung.* Stuttgart.

Kao, Y., Louvieris, P., Powell-Perry, J., Buhalis, D. (2005). E-Satisfaction of NTO's Website Case Study: Singapore Tourism Board's Taiwan Website. In A. Frew (Ed.) *Information and Communication Technologies in Tourism* 2005 – Proceedings of the International Conference in Innsbruck. 227-237. Wien.

Kroeber-Riel, W. & Weinberg, P. (1996). *Konsumentenverhalten.* München.

Kroeber-Riel, W. & Weinberg, P. (1999). *Konsumentenverhalten*, 7.Aufl.. München.

Kuß, A. & Tomczak, T. (2000). *Käuferverhalten: Eine marketingorientierte Einführung*, Stuttgart.

Li, L. & Buhalis, D. (2005). Predicting Internet Usage for Travel Bookings in China. *Information and Communication Technologies in Tourism 2005* – Proceedings of the International Conference in Innsbruck.429-439.Wien.

Luo, M. & Feng, R., Cai, L. (2004). Information Search Behavior and Tourist Characteristics: The Internet vis-à-vis Other Information Sources. *Handbook of Consumer Behavior, Tourism, and the Internet*. Harworth. 15-25.

Jung, H. & Baker, M. (1998). Assessing the Market Effectiveness of the World-Wide-Web in National Tourism Offices. Buhalis, D.; Jafar, J.; Toja, A. (eds.). *Information and Communication Technologies in Tourism*. 95-102. Wien.

Jung, T. & Butler, R. (2000). The Measurement of the Marketing Effectiveness of the Internet in the Tourism and Hospitality Industry. In D. Fesenmaier, S. Klein, D. Buhalis (Eds.) *Information and Communication Technologies in Tourism 2000* – Proceedings of the International Conference in Barcelona. Wien. 461-471.

Mathieson, K. & Wall, G. (1982). *Tourism: Economic, Physical and Social Impacts*, Harlow.

McDonald, M.& Wilson, H. (2002). *The New Marketing: Transforming the corporate future*. Oxford.

Middleton, V. (1994). *Marketing for Travel and Tourism*, 2.Aufl.. London.

Mills, J. & Law, R. (Ed.) (2005). *Handbook of Consumer Behaviour, Tourism and the Internet*. Harworth.

Mills, J. E. & Morrison, A. M. (2003a). Measuring Customer Satisfaction with Online Travel. *International Federation of Information and Communication Technologies in Tourism 2003 Conference Proceedings*. Helsinki.

Mills, J. E; Morrison, A. M. (2003b). Expanding and Re-Testing E-SAT: An Instrument and structural model for measuring customer satisfaction with travel websites. *Travel and Tourism Research Association Conference*. St.Louis.

Moutinho, L. (1987). Consumer Behaviour in tourism, in: *European Journal of Marketing*, 21 (10), 3-44.

Morrison, A. M., Jing, S., O`Leary, J. T., & Lipping, A. C. (2001). Predicting Usage of the Internet for travel bookings: an exploratory study. *Information Technology & Tourism*, 4, 15-30.

Nieschlag, R., Dichtl, E., & Hörschgen, H. (2002). *Marketing*. Berlin.

Rogers, E. M. (1995). *The Diffusion of Innovations* (4th ed). New York.

Scharl, A., Wöber, K., & Bauer, C. (2004). An Integrated Approach to Measure Web Site Effectiveness in the European Hotel Industry. *Information Technology & Tourism*, 2004,.6, 257-271.

Schmidt, I., Schögel, M., & Tomczak, T. (2003). Nutzung von Distributionskanälen aus Kundensicht: Eine explorative Analyse der Reisebranche. In C. Belz, T. Tomczak, T. Rudolph (Eds.). *Thexis – Fachbericht für Marketing*. St.Gallen.

Schmoll, G. A. (1977). *Tourism Promotion. marketing background, promotion techniques and promotion planning methods*. London.

Schramm-Klein, H. (2003). *Multi-Channel-Retailing – Verhaltenswissenschaftliche Analyse der Wirkung von Mehrkanalsystemen im Handel*. Wiesbaden.

Sigala, M.; Sakellaridis, O. (2004). Web User`s Cultural Profiles and e-Service Quality: Internationalisation implications for Tourism Websites. *Information Technology & Tourism*, 7, 13-21.

Swarbrooke J.; Horner, S. (1999). *Consumer Behaviour in Tourism*. Oxford.

Venkatesh, V.; Morris, M.; Davis, G.; Davis, F. (2003). User Acceptance of Information Technology: Towards a Unified View. *MIS Quarterly*, 27 (3), 425-478.

Wahab, S.; Crompton, L.; Rothfield, L. (1976). *Tourism Marketing*. London.

Werthner, H. & S. Klein (1999). *Information Technology and Tourism - A Challenging Relationship*. New York/Vienna.

Wolff, M. (2005). *Determinanten und Beeinflussungsstrategien des Kundenadoptions- und -nutzungsverhaltens von Distributionskanälen* - Eine absatzabschlussfokussierte Analyse aus der Kundenperspektive, Inaugural-Dissertation an der Ludwig-Maximilians-Universität München. München

Woodside, A. & MacDonald, R. (1994). General system framework of customer choice processes of tourism services. In R. Gasser & K. Weiermair (Eds.) *Spoilt for choice. Decision making processes and preference change of tourist: Intertemporal and intercountry perspectives*. 30-59. Thaur.

Similarities in Information Search of City Break Travelers – A Web Usage Mining Exercise

Karl Wöber

Institute for Tourism and Leisure Studies
Vienna University of Economics and Business Administration, Austria
karl.woeber@wu-wien.ac.at

Abstract

This paper focuses on understanding the competitive situation in European city tourism based on log file analysis of keywords entered by users on www.visiteuropeancities.info. It applies various text analysis steps in order to extract significant patterns from the queries made by the users. Multi-dimensional scaling (MDS) is used for constructing a map of similarities based on the unaided responses gained from the users' information requests. Multiple regression analysis between the most frequently used terms entered by the users and the geometrical representation generated by the MDS provides additional insights in the semantics defining competitive differences between 32 city break destinations in Europe. Findings comprise information on cities that can be considered as rivals in regard to the information demanded by the users of the web portal. As it becomes clear in which areas cities are perceived as similar, this findings can be used by city (tourism) managers in order to revise their communication plan regarding their own city if desired.

Keywords: Web usage mining, log file analysis, data mining; city tourism; information search behavior; domain specific search portal.

1 Introduction

Competitor identification is a major component of any approach to formulating marketing strategy. Managers who are marketing a tourism region have to take long-range decisions on which products they want to offer to which segments of international tourism demand. Thus, tourism managers must accomplish a planning approach equivalent to product positioning and market segmentation in general consumer marketing. On the simplest level of strategic planning, tourism managers acknowledge the region as a whole as their 'product' and the tourism generating countries as their potential market segments (Gunn, 1994; Mazanec, 1994). Analysis of the competitive situation among several tourism regions is therefore a pre-requisite for many tourism managers before they can start with the actual strategic planning process. This task, which is not a trivial problem, has gained considerable attention in the marketing literature (Heath & Wall, 1992; Kozak, 2003; Kozak & Rimmington, 1999; Ritchie & Crouch, 2000, 2003; Wöber, 2002).

There are many approaches to define competition regarding tourism in general (Ritchie and Crouch, 2000, 2003), and city tourism in particular (Mazanec, 1997). Probably the most intuitive approach is to compare the tourism specific infrastructure and the number and type of attractions that cities are offering. In addition, it would be possible to compare statistics about the market power of cities through the volume and guest mix structure of their visitors or other measures like, for instance, the number of tourists visiting different types of sights (Grabler, Mazanec & Wöber, 1996). A different approach could be to ask tourists of their opinions regarding specific cities and derive similarities from their responses (Grabler, 1997a; Mazanec, 1995). A further method is to exploit the knowledge of experts in the field of European city tourism (Grabler, 1997b; Wöber, 2001). Of course, each of this methods and approaches has its strengths and weaknesses.

For competitive analysis, the notion of understanding competitors is an important area of study in order for understanding market structures and boundaries that are required for any strategic planning procedure (Chen, 1996). Research on the objective market structure that characterizes industries has pursued two principle approaches to competitor identification. The first is what we call the supply-based approach, which classifies competitors based on attributes of the competing firm (Thomas & Venkatraman, 1988). This approach identifies competitors based on how similar firms are in terms of technology, strategy employed, products offered, and so forth. The second approach is what we call the demand-based approach, which classifies competitors based on the attributes of customers. This approach identifies competitors based on customer attitudes and behaviours and has been an important research area in marketing (Day, Shocker & Srivastava, 1979). Firms are competitors when customers perceive offerings as similar, whether through direct judgements of similarity, similarity in attributes toward competing offerings, or behaviour in the form of brand purchase patterns. Marketing has a rich tradition of examining markets from a customer perspective through attempts to identify product market boundaries or competitive market structure (Cooper & Inoue, 1979).

Compared with these two streams, relatively little information is available on how managers identify competitors in practice. Clark and Montgomery (1999) propose a cognitive framework for managerial identification of competitors; Wöber (2001) suggests a collaborative management information system in order to study competitive structures among Austrian tourism destinations.

For this study, the author decided to use an unobtrusive method of measuring customers' information search behaviour. Through that, the customer must not provide his opinion and he cannot adulterate the results on purpose, as he does not know that he is actually part of the study.

The paper suggests using log file analysis of keywords entered by the users on a tourism-specific web portal when they search for information for planning a trip. The portal used in this study provides access to information from multiple destination management organizations' websites (www.visiteuropeancities.info) and functions like a domain specific search engine (Wöber, 2006). The system keeps track of the keywords that people use when they are searching information about a particular city. This form of observation is similar to the significant and symbolic information a city and its various information providers transmit, as people often look for things that they know about a city or that they have heard about (Um & Crompton, 1990:432).

Next, the paper introduces the design of the portal and the technology that automatically produces the content. The paper then explains how to apply various text analysis procedures in order to extract significant patterns from the queries made by the users. The author demonstrates how multi-dimensional scaling (MDS) and multiple regression analysis allows for analyzing the competitive differences between 32 city break destinations in Europe. Findings include a map that describes the similarities of cities based on the information requests made by the visitors to the portal. The final discussion includes various implications for tourism management.

2 The European Cities Tourism Web Portal

The European Cities Tourism (ECT) web portal (www.visiteuropeancities.info) is a domain-specific search engine that serves not only tourists to find their most preferred city break destination in Europe, but also tourism managers for understanding information needs of potential visitors. The ECT web portal allows access to a data-base of tourist relevant information which is automatically updated by a web crawler (web robot) regularly visiting more than 200 official tourist offices' web sites (a full description of the system is provided by Wöber, 2006).

The appearance of the ECT web portal's homepage is very simple (see Figure 1). The basic query feature requires the user either to enter a keyword (or phrase), or to select a city from a list, or both (top figure). Users can search documents using keywords together with appropriate Boolean operators thanks to a query processor, which generates a reasonable database query from the user input. If the keyword or phrase specified by the user is available on one of the cities' web sites, the system will retrieve and present all available web pages ranked by its relevance (bottom figure). Responsible for the ranking is a scoring module, which processes each result before sending the result to the user interface for display. Each search result features a page link, the name of the city the page is associated with, a rating that indicates the relative number of times the term was found on the page (compared to the number of other terms that appear on the page), as well as an abstract. Using the ECT web portal is similarly easy as using any of the main, well-known, global search engines (Google, MSN Search, and Yahoo).

Fig. 1. The www.visiteuropeancities.info Web Portal.

The portal monitors all user activities in a user log file including the text and/or city the user has selected or entered into the system. In case the user has specified a keyword which is unknown by the system, the word will also be stored in the user log file. Whereas automated web site analyzing tools can be used to obtain information about navigation, interactivity, layout and textual features (Scharl, Wöber, & Bauer, 2004), analysis of the user log file helps to identify highly interesting key-indicators that support managers in understanding the information needs of their consumers. Moreover, combining web content and web usage mining technology can be used for benchmarking the performance of web sites. The strengths of this computer supported type of evaluation lies in the inclusion of unobtrusively observed measures, which reduces the biases that frequently result from the intrusion of the measurement instrument.

Keywords and phrases extracted from the user log file can help to reveal the image of a particular city relative to other city break destinations. Information, which describes the users' interests, is available from the text he/she enters in the fields 'keyword' and 'city'. Information collected here is comparable to the unaided response frequently applied in travel surveys that ask customers where they want to spend their vacation and/or what they are actually interested in or during their stay. A great number of valuable information can be generated, which, for instance, includes the most frequently asked keywords and cities. Even more interesting are relative measures for each participating city. The analysis of these city bundles, i.e. groups of cities with similar information requests by the users, is a precondition for developing effective city tourism management collaborations, and therefore highly interesting information from a managerial point of view.

3 Methodology

The underlying competitive structure is best analysed by one of the very widely used methods in marketing science. Based on the keyword profiles the multidimensional scaling (MDS) method can construct a map that displays the cities geometrically. One of the advantages of the MDS procedure is its ability to extract and to visualize an inherent underlying competitive structure. The MDS will provide similar configurations for cities where users have similar information requests. Thus, MDS renders the data more manageable and strategically meaningful. MDS uses proximities as input data. A proximity value indicates how similar or how dissimilar two objects are. For n objects to be scaled there are n(n-1)/2 pairs. Each pair of cities is characterized by a (dis)similarity value. To analyse the competitive relationship between two cities, the keywords entered by the visitors to the ECT web portal have to be filtered by selecting all entries where the users have entered at least one English keyword or phrase in one particular city (i.e., search queries for all cities are not subject of this investigation). City-specific search words (e.g. Louvre-Paris; Prado-Madrid; Porsche-Stuttgart; Grand Place-Brussels, etc.) found by calculating standard deviations for all keywords were eliminated from the analysis. The data have to be further pre-processed in order to remove double entries and typos as well as to account for the problem of semantically similar but character-wise different words. Words that appear in documents or in queries often have many morphological variants. Thus, it is difficult to recognize pairs of terms such as *hotels* and *hotel* (or *relaxing* and *relaxation*) as equivalent without some form of natural language processing (NLP).

Martin Porter's stemming algorithm (or Porter stemmer) is the most commonly used process for removing the common morphological and inflexional endings from words in English (Porter, 1980). One disadvantage of the Porter stemmer is that when not used in combination with a lexicon, it can produce unsatisfactory results. For instance, the program will also truncate words that are proper names of attractions, restaurants, destinations etc. (e.g. paris -> pari) and frequently also mutilate other words until they become almost unrecognizable (e.g. apartment -> apart, airline -> airlin, bus -> bu). Since users of www.visiteuropeancities.info commonly enter proper words, and the costs of extending the Porter stemmer was considered as too high, this study was looking for alternative approaches to group words with a similar stem. One of most frequently used algorithms for comparing strings in text analysis is the Levenshtein distance measure named after the Russian scientist Vladimir Levenshtein (Levenshtein, 1965). The Levenshtein distance (LD) is a measure of the similarity between two strings, which is defined by the minimum number of operations (insertion, deletion, or substitution of a single character), needed to transform one string into the other. The measure frequently used for spell checking, speech recognition, and plagiarism detection, was embedded in a procedure that not only compares the similarity of keywords but also considers the stem of two strings. This new 'Levenshtein Stemmer' sorts words of a given data set alphabetically and then condenses two words that are located next to each other and have a Levenshtein distance, which is below, or equal a certain threshold decided by analyst.

In the present study two keywords (w_1, w_2) have been defined as similar when LD ≤ 2. In the case that similarity was detected, one of the two possible transformations, $w_1 = w_2$ or $w_2 = w_1$ has been performed by considering the frequency the words have been entered by the users (if $f(w_1) > f(w_2)$ then $w_1 = w_2$ otherwise $w_2 = w_1$). After replacing all words in the list, the list is resorted and the program starts again. The procedure terminates when no further similarities between words is found. The full algorithm, illustrated in Figure 2, delivered excellent results for the present study. The strength of the algorithm is its applicability as a universal stemmer for a large number of languages and that it is adjustable by means of the LD parameter. Although it does not require a dictionary, the collaborative characteristic of the algorithm to consider other users' frequency entering a particular word, allows detecting and removing typos from the dataset, except when typos are located in the very beginning of a word. Finally, it is a fast algorithm, which is capable to handle large data sets.

```
while (1)
    sort n keywords k alphabetically
    where k_i(f) is the number of times
    the i-th keyword appears in the text/logfile
    c = 0
    For i = 1; i <= N; i++
        if LD(k_i, k_i+1) <= 3
            if (k_i+1(f) > k_i(f))
              k_i+1 = k_i
              k_i+1(f) = k_i(f) + k_i+1(f)
            else
              k_i = k_i+1
              k_i(f) = k_i+1(f) + k_i(f)
            endif
            c++
        endif
    endfor
    if c = 0
        last
    endif
endwhile
```

Fig.2. The Levenshtein Stemmer.

Between July 2003 and May 2006, www.visiteuropeancities.info has experienced 1,5mn log file entries, but only 42,000 city-keyword pairs (5,550 unique keywords for 186 different cities entered by 24,400 different visitors) remained after the data pre-processing steps outlined before. The dataset need to be further condensed in order to account for the sparseness of entries that occurs when the 42,000 observations spread on a matrix of 5,550 unique keywords and 186 cities. In addition, the top 100 keywords represent 75% of all search queries. Knowledge on these keywords can assist managers to optimize the design of their web site. Following 20 keywords (28% of all words) were finally selected for the analysis of the competitive structure: shopping, events, guided tours, attractions, opera, art, museum, camping, restaurants, youth hostels, gay, festival, monuments, church, exhibitions, culture, nightlife, golf, music, and theatre. Cities with less than 300 entries for any of these keywords were excluded from the analysis, which finally provided a list of 32 cities, which were considered for the MDS study. The raw data transformed into vectors of keyword percentages and arranged in tabular form. The rows of this table correspond to the cities; the columns represent the shares of the 20 selected keywords. Each row stands for a city profile in terms of the ECT web portal users' information needs. The usual way to derive proximities from a set of profile data is to compute correlations, contingency or distance measures (Euclidian, City Block, or more general Minkowski distances). Squared Euclidian distances were chosen for computing the dissimilarity coefficients of the 496 city pairs (32*(32-1)/2). Commandeur and Heiser (1993) provide a detailed mathematical derivation of the SPSS PROXSCAL algorithm used in this study. The MDS algorithm typically outputs a two- or higher-dimensional 'map' with a configuration of points. In advance, the number of adequate dimensions is unknown. The number depends on how well the distances in the map reflect the observed proximities, which derives the space. Kruskal's stress formula measures the goodness of fit (Kruskal & Wish, 1976: 29). In addition, the r^2 value indicates the proportion of the variance of the observed proximities accounted for by their corresponding differences. For the two-dimensional solution, the stress indicator calculates an acceptable 0.12, and the r^2 value with .96 is highly satisfactory.

4 Results and Implications

Figure 3 visualises the findings of this study. The most common way of interpreting the geometrical representation is to examine the dimensions in the space and the co-ordinates of the stimuli. A hint for interpreting the map may appear when if the city points projected on to an axis at opposite extremes differ from each other in some discernible and systematic manner. Optimal rotation and labelling of the axes can be handled more objectively with multiple regression analysis. This is particularly useful if additional variables (properties) are associated with the competitive space positions of the cities. With no additional properties at hand, multiple regression analysis was used to exploit the same data input matrix, which was used for generating the information space before. Which are the keywords where the keyword space dimensions contribute significantly to explaining the cities locations on the map? According to the explanations offered by a stepwise regression analysis, guided tours (Dim 1: $\beta = -.742$, Dim 2: $\beta = .124$), attractions (Dim 1: $\beta = -.417$, Dim 2: $\beta = -.400$), shopping (Dim 2: $\beta = -.669$), opera (Dim 2: $\beta = .434$), museum (Dim 1: $\beta = .383$), art

(Dim 1: β = .147), and events (Dim 1: β = -.136) are the most discriminating keywords for the cities under evaluation. Keywords with β-values for dimension 1 explain 98.5% of the variance in the horizontal presentation of the cities; keywords with β-values for dimension 2 even explain 99.1% of all vertical positions.

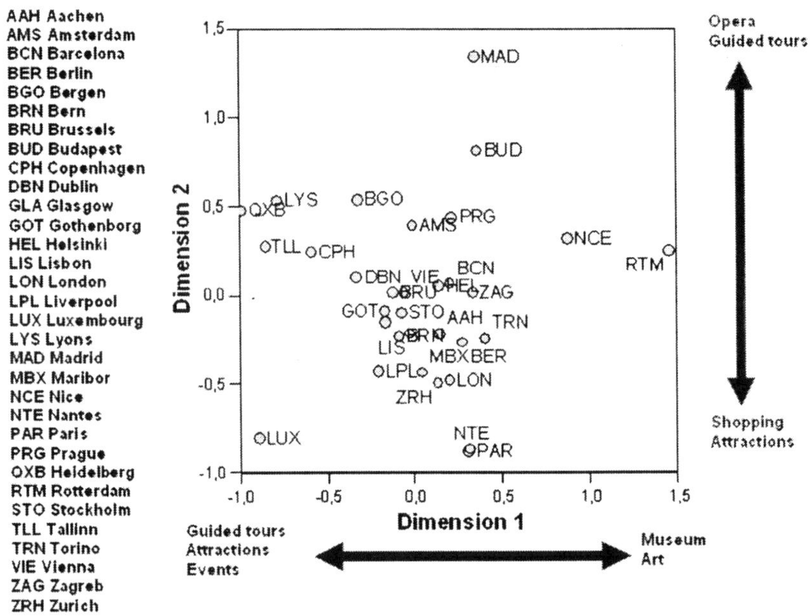

Fig. 3. Multi-dimensional Scaling (MDS) based on similarities of information queries made for 32 European cities by Internet users of www.visiteuropeancities.info.

Visual inspection of the information space in Figure 3 suggests a subdivision into one main group of competitors and three smaller groups of cities with very specific information requests by the www.visiteuropeancities.info users. The first group, located in the northeastern hemisphere of the spatial configuration, consists of five cities where users have specifically expressed information needs for guided tours, operas, museum and art (Madrid, Budapest, Prague, Nice and Rotterdam). The western to north-western part of the information space is populated by a group of seven European cities with substantial user interests in guided tours, attractions and events (Heidelberg, Lyons, Tallinn, Bergen, Copenhagen, and Amsterdam). The third group, located in the southern hemisphere of the spatial configuration, consists of only three cities specifically interested in shopping (Paris, Nantes, and Luxembourg). Finally, the largest subgroup with eighteen competing European cities is located in the central sector of the space. For those cities ECT web portal users are not particularly focused on any of the identified most discriminating keywords (Aachen, Barcelona, Berlin, Bern, Brussels, Dublin, Glasgow, Gothenburg, Helsinki, Lisbon, London, Liverpool, Maribor, Stockholm, Torino, Vienna, Zagreb, and Zurich).

5 Conclusion and Future Work

For tourism managers it is important to understand the perceptions of consumers concerning their city in order develop more effective marketing campaigns. The aim of the following exercise was to find out which cities are rivals in regard to the information demanded by the users of the web portal.

This paper introduced a new stemming algorithm that uses pattern recognition rather than language dependent characteristics in order to aggregate keywords that users are using when they search information on the Internet. This new algorithm has several advantages compared to the traditional forms of stemming and has produced excellent results in the present study. Nevertheless, evaluations that are more systematic will be required in order to understand the power and the limitations of the algorithm in more detail. The analysis demonstrates how MDS establishes a pattern of the 32 European cities competing for visitors. Instead of physical characteristics commonly used in competitive studies of tourism destinations, this approach considers the perception of consumers and their information needs when they plan to go on a city trip. Even more importantly, the evaluation of the Internet users search behaviour reaches the consumer in a very early phase of the consumer's decision-making process, where knowledge on consumers' preferences is particularly important for developing persuasive marketing strategies. Comparing the findings of this type of study with other forms of competitive assessment is an important area of future research.

References

Chen, M. J. (1996). Competitor Analysis and Interfirm Rivalry: Toward a Theoretical Integration. *Academy of Management Review*, 21(1), 100-134.

Clark, B. H. & Montgomery, D. B. (1999). Managerial Identification of Competitors. *Journal of Marketing*, 63 (July), 67-83.

Cooper, L. G. & Inoue, A. (1979). Building Market Structures from Consumer Preferences. *Journal of Marketing Research*, XXXIII (August, 1996), 293-306.

Commandeur, J. J. F. & Heiser, W. J. (1993). Mathematical Derivations in the Proximity Scaling (PROXSCAL) of Symmetric Data Matrices (Tech. Rep. No. RR-93-03). Leiden, The Netherlands: Department of Data Theory, Leiden University.

Day, G. S., Shocker, A. D. & Srivastava, R. K. (1979). Customer-Oriented Approaches to Identifying Product-Markets. *Journal of Marketing*, 43 (Fall), 8-19.

Grabler, K. (1997a). The Managerial Perspective. In J. A. Mazanec (ed.) International City Tourism. London: Cassell, 147-166.

Grabler, K. (1997b). Perceptual Mapping and Positioning of Tourist Cities. In J. A. Mazanec (Ed.) International City Tourism. London: Cassell, 101-113.

Grabler, K., Mazanec, J. A. & Wöber, K. W. (1996). Strategic Marketing for Urban Tourism. Analyzing Competition Among European Tourist Cities. In C. M. Law (Ed.) Tourism in Major Cities. London: Routledge, 23-51.

Gunn, C. A. (1994). Tourism Planning: Basics, Concepts, Cases (3rd ed.) Washington: Taylor & Frances.

Heath, E., & Wall, G. (1992). Marketing Tourism Destinations: A Strategic Planning Approach. New York: Wiley.

Kozak, M. (2003). Destination Benchmarking: Concepts, Practices and Operations, Wallingford: CABI.

Kozak, M. & Rimmington, M. (1999). Measuring Tourist Destination Competitiveness: Conceptual Considerations and Empirical Findings. *Hospitality Management*, 18, 273-283.

Kruskal, J.B. & Wish, M. (1976). Multidimensional Scaling. In J. L. Sullivan & R. G. Niemi, (Eds.) Quantitative Applications in the Social Sciences. Beverly Hills, CA: Sage.

Levenshtein, V. I. (1965). Binary Codes Capable of Correcting Deletions, Insertions, and Reversals. In: Doklady Akademii Nauk SSSR, 163 (4), 845-848, (Russian); English translation available in: Soviet Physics Doklady, 10 (8), 707-710.

Mazanec, J. A. (1994). International Tourism Marketing. Adapting the Growth-share Matrix. In J. Montana (Ed.) Marketing in Europe. Case Studies. London: Sage.

Mazanec, J. A. (1995). Competition among European Tourist Cities: A Comparative Analysis with Multidimensional Scaling and Self-organizing Maps. *Tourism Economics*, 1, 283-302.

Mazanec, J. A. (1997). International City Tourism. Analysis and Strategy. London: Cassell.

Porter, M. F. (1980). An Algorithm for Suffix Stripping. *Program*, 14 (3), 130−137.

Ritchie, J. R. B. & Crouch, G. (2000). The Competitive Destination: A Sustainability Perspective. *Tourism Management*, 21 (1), 1-7.

Ritchie, J. R. B. & Crouch, G. (2003). The Competitive Destination: A Sustainable Tourism Perspective, Wallingford: CABI.

Scharl, A., Wöber, K. W. & Bauer, C. (2004). An Integrated Approach to Measure Web Site Effectiveness in the European Hotel Industry. *Information Technology and Tourism*, 6 (4), 257-272.

Thomas, H. & Venkatraman, N. (1988). Research on Strategic Groups: Progress and Prognosis. *Journal of Management Studies*, 25 (6), 537-555.

Um, S. & Crompton, J. (1990). Attitude Determinants in Tourism Destination Choice. *Annals of Tourism Research*, 17, 432-448.

Wöber, K. W. (2001). Identifying Competing Tourism Destinations Using Group Decision Support Systems. In P. Sheldon, K. W. Wöber, & D. R. Fesenmaier (Eds.) Information and Communication Technologies in Tourism. ENTER 2001. Proceedings of the International Conference in Montreal, Canada, Vienna-New York: Springer, 1-12.

Wöber, K. W. (2002). Benchmarking in Tourism and Hospitality Industries. The Selection of Benchmarking Partners, Wallingford: CABI.

Wöber, K. W. (2006). Domain-Specific Search Engines. In D. R. Fesenmaier, H. Werthner, K. W. Werthner (Eds.) Destination Recommendation Systems. Behavioural Foundations and Applications. Wallingford: CABI, pp 147-166.

Quo Vadis Homo Turisticus?
Towards a Picture-based Tourist Profiler

Helmut Berger[a]
Michaela Denk[a]
Michael Dittenbach[a]
Dieter Merkl[b]
Andreas Pesenhofer[a]

[a] E-Commerce Competence Center - EC3
Wien, Austria
{firstname.lastname}@ec3.at
[b] Institut für Rechnergestützte Automation,
TU Wien, Austria

Abstract

The World Wide Web has become an important source of information for tourists planning their vacation. So, destination recommendation systems supporting users in their decision making process by suggesting suitable holiday destinations or packages based on user profiles are a vivid area of research. Considering the complex and often tedious task to obtain such profiles we are exploring a new direction to manufacture user profiles. Having in mind that a picture paints a thousand words we conducted an online survey that allows investigating the relationship between tourism-related photographs and tourist types. In a nutshell, our findings show a significant relationship between different tourist types and the preference for particular visual impressions conveyed by photographs. Thus, tourist types can be determined by representative photos without necessarily requesting users to provide additional information.

Keywords: Tourism habits; user profiles; visual preferences; destination recommendation

1 Introduction

The importance of the Internet as an influencing factor for the tourism business is marked by the steadily increasing number of online travel sales worldwide. This makes tourism the leading application in business-to-consumer e-Commerce (Werthner & Ricci, 2004). Besides this economic perspective of e-Tourism, from which users increasingly act as their own travel agents, the Internet has become much more than an additional sales channel or a platform for conducting business transactions. It is an important source of information supporting the pre-trip search as well as the decision making process of tourists. Personalization plays an important role in such information systems, because personal preferences can be used to adapt the user's environment to her needs. Intelligent services such as destination recommendation systems heavily rely on personal profiles for the recommendation algorithms. Destination recommendation systems support the decision making process of tourists and transcend pure information provision and exchange (Staab, Werthner, Ricci, Zipf, Gretzel, Fesenmaier, Paris, & Knoblock, 2002; Fesenmaier, Ricci, Schaumlechner, Wöber, & Zanella, 2003). The focus of recommender systems in tourism is on destination selection and offering product bundles tailored to the user's needs (Ricci & Werthner, 2002). In addition to explicitly expressed needs and constraints, a vital piece of information is the user profile. However, the process of creating such profiles can be a rather annoying, time-consuming and cumbersome task (Gretzel, Mitsche, Hwang, & Fesenmaier, 2004). This may result in poorly maintained user profiles reducing the quality of recommendations, and consequently, the acceptance and, thus, the success of destination recommender systems.

Vogt and Fesenmaier (1998) have proposed a model of tourists' information needs forming a categorization of different types of needs. A substantial part of this model is composed of hedonic as well as aesthetic needs. This highlights the importance of communicating emotion in the tourism business in addition to hard facts that usually answer functional and innovation needs. Gretzel & Fesenmaier (2003) argue that more than audiovisual content needs to be communicated in the future to improve tourism marketing strategies. It has been shown that sensory information such as colour, scent and sound plays an important role for tourists when imagining how a holiday destination might be. This finding is backed by Govers & Go (2004), who have analyzed text and images on Web sites related to tourism in Dubai. They draw the conclusion that the use of photographs to design effective tourism experiences is limited and more creativity is needed to effectively use the Internet for marketing purposes in the tourism business. However, besides videos, 360 degree panoramas or virtual tours, photographs still remain the most important instrument for communicating emotion on tourism Web sites. In this paper, we present the findings of an online survey conducted to investigate whether tourist's habits can be derived from tourism-related photographs in order to facilitate the process of user profile creation. The findings will be used in the 3D e-Tourism environment "itchy feet" that we are currently developing (Berger, Dittenbach, & Merkl, 2006). In particular, in a welcome area for newbies and first-time users, they will be able to select from an expressive set of visual impressions by simply navigating through the environment. Depending on their choices initial user profiles will be manufactured.

2 Questionnaire Design

The instrument of our survey was an online questionnaire that was created with the *Infovalidator* tool by MindTake (www.mindtake.com). It was made public in July 2006 on a Web portal. This questionnaire consisted of three parts whereof the first part aimed at obtaining personal and demographic data of the participants. These were age group, gender, marital status, number of children, highest level of education, and whether they live in a city or town. The second part of the questionnaire was created to capture the personal tourism habits of the participants. To this end, a set of 17 tourist types based on the work by Yiannakis & Gibson (1992) was chosen. The tourist types were described in terms of statements such as *"interested in relaxing and sunbathing in warm places with lots of sun, sand and ocean"* or *"mostly interested in meeting the local people, trying the food and speaking the language"* whereof the first description corresponds to the tourist type referred to as the *Sun Lover* and the latter to the *Anthropologist*. Note that we refrained from providing the actual labels of the tourist types presuming that participants might be biased by these. Additionally, we have defined four age groups, viz. less than 20, 21 to 40, 41 to 60, and over 60.

Each participant was asked to select those tourist types which she has belonged to in earlier periods of her life, or currently belongs to. For example, a participant aged 47 was requested to select her personal tourism habits when she was younger than 20, between 21 and 40 as well as her current preferences. The third part of the questionnaire comprised ten pages, each of which containing six photos of different tourism-related situations, i.e. a set of 60 photos. Participants were asked to identify those photos that best represent their past and present personal tourism habits. The set of photos was manually compiled with the goal in mind to provide a representative sample for each tourist type. We explicitly asked the participants to abstract from the specific situation shown on the photo and to completely disregard its aesthetics, i.e. its photographic quality.

3 Discussion of Survey Results

The survey was completed by 476 respondents in about eight minutes on average. Some of the respondents provided incomplete data resulting in the removal of 50 respondents' answers. Thus, we removed i) seven that provided no information about their past or present tourist types, ii) two that did not select any photo, iii) age group "less than 20" which just contained eight individuals and iv) 33 individuals who seemingly misunderstood the third part of the questionnaire. They restricted themselves to select exactly one photo per photo page. The demographic composition of the sample is shown in Table 2.

Table 2. Personal and demographic characteristics of survey sample (n=426).

Gender	Female - **208**; Male - **218**
Age group	21 to 40 - **200**; 41 to 60 - **187**; 61 and above – **39**
Education	Primary - **148**; Secondary - **156**; University – **122**
Marital status	Single/separated - **115**; married/living with long term partner - **311**
Kids	no kids - **189**; one or more kids – **237**
Resident of a	city - **188**; village/town – **238**

The 17 tourist types are given in Table 3. Additionally, the descriptions provided in the questionnaire as well as the absolute and relative frequencies of the respondents' current tourism habits are shown. Please note that the sum of the percentages exceeds 100%, because most respondents obviously belong to multiple tourist types. The rank order of tourist types in this table significantly correlates (Pearson's $r = 0.895$, $\alpha = 0.001$) with the results presented in Gibson & Yiannakis (2002).

We evaluated the dependencies between tourist types and demographic features with a chi-squared test. The results given in Table 4 an 5 provide the p-values with significant entries ($\alpha = 0.05$) being identified with an asterisk. In those cases the direction of the dependency is shown as well. Consider, for example, the first row in Table 4 describing the dependencies of the tourist type *Action Seeker*. This type depends on the age group, with a dominance of age group II (28% of the respondents of this age group described themselves as *Action Seekers*), over age group IV (25.6%) and age group III (10.7%). Regarding the marital status, single *Action Seekers* (28.7%) dominate those that are currently in a relationship (17%). Finally, the group of *Action Seekers* without children (27.5%) dominate those with children (14.3%).

Table 3. Tourist types, their descriptions and distributions statistics

Tourist type	Description	Freq.	%
Anthropologist	Mostly interested in meeting the local people, trying the food and speaking the language	334	78.40
Escapist I	Enjoys taking it easy away from the stresses and pressures of home environment	320	75.12
Archaeologist	Primarily interested in archaeological sites and ruins; enjoys studying history of ancient civilizations	265	62.21
Sun Lover	Interested in relaxing and sunbathing in warm places with lots of sun, sand and ocean	263	61.74
Independent Mass Tourist I, (IMT I)	Visits regular tourist attractions but avoids packaged vacations and organized tours	223	52.35
High Class	Travels first class, stays in the best hotels, goes to shows and enjoys fine dining	207	48.59
Independent Mass Tourist II, (IMT II)	Plans own destination and hotel reservations and often plays it by ear (spontaneous)	196	46.01
Escapist II	Gets away from it all by escaping to peaceful, deserted or out of the way places	174	40.85
Organized Mass Tourist, (OMT)	Mostly interested in organized vacations, packaged tours, taking pictures/buying lots of souvenirs	163	38.26
Active Sports	Primary emphasis while on vacation is to remain active engaging in favourite sports	158	37.09
Seeker	Seeker of spiritual and/or personal knowledge to better understand self and meaning of life	136	31.92
Explorer	Prefers adventure travel, exploring out of the way places and enjoys challenge in getting there	132	30.99
Educational Tourist, (Edu-Tourist)	Participates in planned study tours and seminars to acquire new skills and knowledge	127	29.81
Jet Setter	Vacations in elite, world class resorts, goes to exclusive night clubs, and socializes with celebrities	104	24.41
Action Seeker	Mostly interested in partying, going to night clubs and meeting people for uncomplicated romantic experiences	86	20.19
Thrill Seeker	Interested in risky, exhilarating activities which provide emotional highs for the participant	61	14.32
Drifter	Drifts from place to place living a hippie-style existence	55	12.91

Table 4. Dependencies between tourist type, age group, marital status and children

Tourist type	Age group II: 21-40, III: 41-60, IV: > 60		Marital status S: Single, R: Relationship		Children N: No, Y: Yes	
Action Seeker	0.000*	II (28.0) > IV (25.6) > III (10.7)	0.008*	S (28.7) > R (17.0)	0.001*	N (27.5) > Y (14.3)
Drifter	0.494	-	0.094	-	0.005*	N (18.0) > Y (8.9)
Escapist I	0.000*	II (86.0) > III (67.9) > IV (53.8)	0.156	-	0.007*	N (81.5) > Y (70.0)
Escapist II	0.000*	II (49.5) > III (36.4) > IV (17.9)	0.119	-	0.081	-
Explorer	0.002*	II (39.5) > IV (25.6) > III (23.0)	0.027*	S (39.1) > R (28.0)	0.005*	N (38.1) > Y (25.3)
High Class	0.587	-	0.002*	R (53.1) > S (36.5)	0.034*	Y (53.2) > N (42.9)
IMT I	0.020*	II (59.5) > III (46.5) > IV (43.6)	0.965	-	0.115	-
IMT II	0.002*	II (55.0) > III (39.0) > IV (33.3)	0.770	-	0.018*	N (52.4) > Y (40.9)
OMT	0.008*	II (46.0) > IV (33.3) > III (31.0)	0.823	-	0.949	-
Seeker	0.007*	II (39.0) > III (27.3) > IV (17.9)	0.216	-	0.163	-
Sun Lover	0.000*	II (71.5) > III (54.0) > IV (48.7)	0.653	-	0.023*	N (67.7) > Y (57.9)
Thrill Seeker	0.001*	IV (20.5) > II (20.0) > III (7.0)	0.001*	S (23.5) > R (10.9)	0.002*	N (20.1) > Y (9.7)

Table 5. Dependencies between tourist type, gender, residence and education

Tourist type	Gender differences F: Female, M: Male		Living in T: Town, C: City		Education P: Primary, S: Secondary, U: University	
Edu-Tourist	0.001*	F (36.5) > M (23.4)	0.086	-	0.658	-
High Class	0.446	-	0.009*	T (54.2) > C (41.5)	0.073	-
Jet Setter	0.239	-	0.043*	T (28.2) > C (19.7)	0.110	-
OMT	0.934	-	0.556	-	0.015*	P (46.6) > S (37.2) > U (29.5)
Seeker	0.028*	F (37.0) > M (27.1)	0.997	-	0.774	-
Sun Lover	0.360	-	0.005*	C (69.1) > T (55.9)	0.990	-

Please note that Tables 4 and 5 show only those tourist types that are significantly depending on at least one demographic feature.

Due to space restrictions in this paper, we cannot elaborate on the results given in Table 4 and 5 in full detail. We rather concentrate on a small number of findings. As might have been expected, the age group of the respondent plays a major role with 10 out of 17 tourist types depending significantly on the age group. Interestingly, the fact of having children shows comparable influence. For instance, the *Explorer* – the one that travels uncharted territory (we exaggerate, of course) – is most likely to be young without kids. Gender seems to influence only the *Educational Tourist* and the *Seeker*. In both cases, the number of females dominates the number of males. Finally, the degree of education just influences the *Organized Mass Tourist* in a significant way.

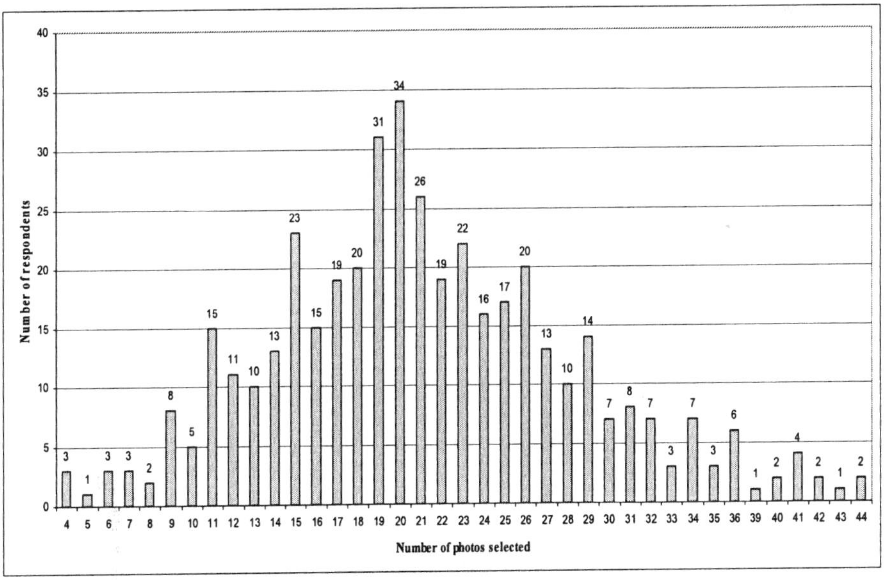

Fig. 1. Frequency distributions of photographs

In Fig. 1 the frequency distribution of photo selections is shown. For example, 34 respondents have selected 20 photographs to illustrate their tourism habits and on average 21 photos were selected. Additionally, we performed a frequency analysis of the tourist types per respondent. The peak was five which correlates with the maximum obtained for the frequency analysis of photo selections when taking intoaccount that we selected roughly four photographs per tourist type.

A thumbnail of each photo and its corresponding frequency of selection is provided in Table 6. In this sense, the most popular photo in our survey was photo 44 (a quite alpine region) with a total of 332 selections and the least popular one was photo 30 (audience with an Indian Bhagwan) with just 11 clicks.

Table 6. Photos used in the survey; for details see http://ispaces.ec3.at/tourismsurvey/

photo 01 (147)	photo 02 (210)	photo 03 (86)	photo 04 (84)	photo 05 (75)	photo 06 (222)
photo 07 (124)	photo 08 (243)	photo 09 (155)	photo 10 (152)	photo 11 (60)	photo 12 (121)
photo 13 (296)	photo 14 (58)	photo 15 (293)	photo 16 (104)	photo 17 (104)	photo 18(119)
photo 19 (363)	photo 20 (213)	photo 21 (45)	photo 22 (133)	photo 23 (60)	photo 24 (155)
photo 25 (295)	photo 26 (301)	photo 27 (26)	photo 28 (207)	photo 29 (71)	photo 30 (11)
photo 31 (74)	photo 32 (275)	photo 33 (42)	photo 34 (268)	photo 35 (262)	photo 36 (283)
photo 37 (165)	photo 38 (163)	photo 39 (195)	photo 40 (226)	photo 41 (209)	photo 42 (138)
photo 43 (154)	photo 44 (332)	photo 45 (54)	photo 46 (110)	photo 47 (29)	photo 48 (142)
photo 49 (39)	photo 50 (299)	photo 51 (166)	photo 52 (66)	photo 53 (196)	photo 54 (53)
photo 55 (120)	photo 56 (27)	photo 57 (161)	photo 58 (62)	photo 59 (92)	photo 60 (79)

Correspondence analysis was used to produce a map of the relationships between tourist types and the photographs. Starting from a cross tabulation of photo click frequencies by tourist type, we obtained the correspondence analysis map depicted in Fig. 2. The numbers in the figure correspond to the photographs as presented in Table 6. The results show that the relationship between tourist type and photo can be mapped onto two dimensions that account for 56.44% of the inertia, i.e. a large amount of the total variance is explained by the first two principal axes. In particular, the x-axis (35.7% of the inertia) can be referred to as the *Pack Factor* and the y-axis (20.74% of the inertia) represents the *Kick Factor*. The *Pack Factor* identifies the "level of collectivity" one might associate with a particular tourist type. Consider, for example, the *Explorer*, which is the left-most tourist type, and the *Organized Mass Tourist*, the right-most tourist type along the x-axis. The *Explorer* might be identified as a rather solitary individual compared to an *Organized Mass Tourist,* who is generally accompanied by a larger number of like-minded tourists. Interestingly, this dimension corresponds to the findings of a study in which tourist experiences have been identified to vary along a continuum of individualistic/collectivistic orientation (Mehmetoglu, 2004). The *Kick Factor* identifies the "level of excitement" one might associate with a particular tourist activity. The *Thrill Seeker*, for instance, is per definition interested in risky, exhilarating activities that provide emotional highs. Contrary, the *Escapist I* enjoys taking it easy, far away from the stresses and pressures of the home environment. The generated layout of photos is to a high degree in-line with the alignment of the tourist types. For example, photos 22 (alpine ski touring) and 37 (alpine skiing) are highly associated with *Active Sports* whereas photos 46 (whitewater rafting), 52 (sky diving), 56 (bungee jumping) and 59 (windsurfing) correspond to the *Thrill Seeker*. The *Action Seeker,* however, is represented by photos such as 3, 21 and 29 all of which are party *sujets*. The photo layout also reflects the criteria defined by each axis. For example, photo 27 shows the highest level of individualism – in fact it depicts a solitary hitch hiker. Contrary, photo 14 represents a typical packaged tour enjoyed by a group of bus tourists. In terms of the *Kick Factor*, photos 1 (car rental area in airport) and 55 (rainy; group listening to tour guide) identify a moderate level of excitement whereas photos 52 and 56 depict risky and exhilarating activities. Interesting findings can be derived from the actual position of each particular tourist type in the map. The lower left quadrant, for example, corresponds to a high level of individualism and rather tranquil activities. As a result, this quadrant contains tourist types such as the *Anthropologist*, *Archaeologist* as well as the *Escapist I* that were quite frequently chosen by the respondents (with a total of 1,589 assignments). Note that these figures include the respondents' past and present tourist type assignments. Thus, these numbers exceed the ones given in Table 3. The rather compact arrangement of these tourist types reflects their very close relationship and explains the difficulty to distinguish between them. The upper-left quadrant comprises the *Explorer*, *Active Sports* and *Drifter* tourist types, which show a rather high level of individualism as well as excitement. These rather specific tourist types account for 679 assignments.

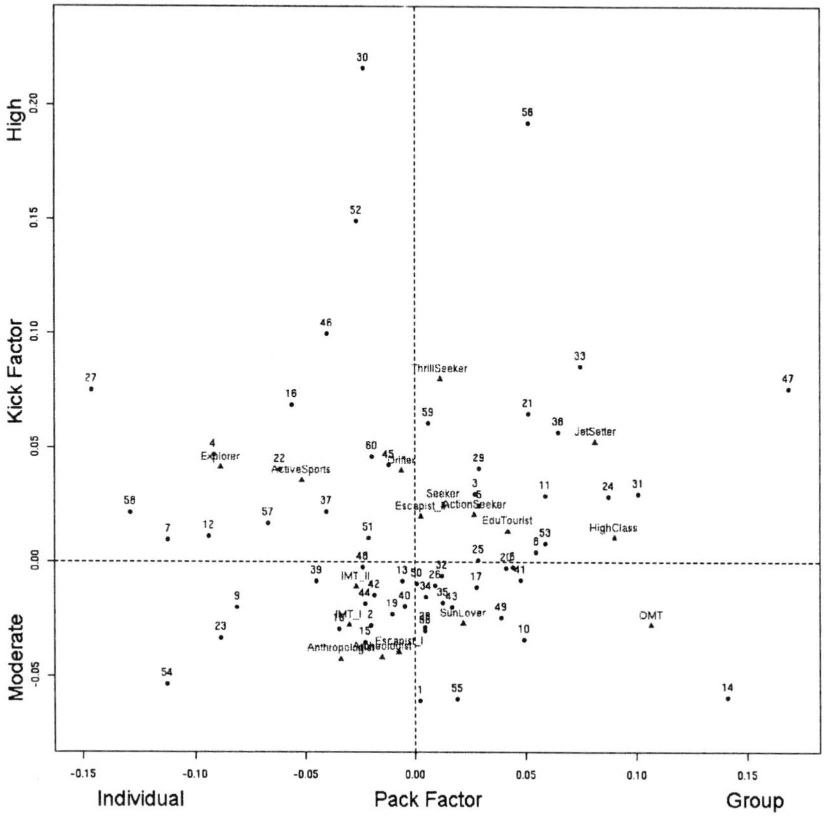

Fig. 2. Correspondence map of the relationship between tourist types and photos

A large number of tourist types can be found in the upper-right quadrant of the map comprising 1,368 assignments. The types range from the *Thrill Seeker*, over the *Jet Setter* and *High Class* to the *Action Seeker*. We may conclude that the higher the *Kick Factor* of a particular tourist type is the less frequently it is chosen. However, the differences between some of these types seem to be rather small taking their close position in the map into account. A possible interpretation is, that for instance the *Seeker* ("... searching for spiritual and/or personal knowledge...") and the *Educational Tourist* ("... searching for new skills and knowledge...") share some common ground or are performed in a sense simultaneously. The lower-right quadrant contains two tourist types, namely the *Sun Lover* and the *Organized Mass Tourist*. With these groups this quadrant accounts for 556 assignments. The degree of individuality attributed to these two tourist types is rather low since packaged tours and all-inclusive offers can be regarded as the dominating characteristic of these tourist types. Nevertheless, there seems to be a not negligible difference in terms of individuality between the *Sun Lover* and the *Organized Mass Tourist* taking the distance of their alignment in the map into account. The *Kick Factor* associated with these tourist types is rather moderate highlighting the desire for relaxation and hassle-free tourism experiences. The importance of individual photos to distinguish between tourist types is analyzed by means of logistic regression. In particular, the photos with positive and significant coefficients in the regression model are regarded as positive examples for a particular tourist type. Conversely, photos with negative and significant coefficients are counter examples. Following this approach, we obtain the mapping of photos to tourist types as given in Table 7. We indicate the significance levels with asterisks *** (α=0.001) and ** (α=0.01). Regarding the positive examples, we obtain impressive results for characterizing the following tourist types: *Anthropologist* (photo 02 – a group of indigenous musicians), *Archaeologist* (photo 34 – the remnants of an ancient Greek temple), *Sun Lover* (photo 25 – a beach), *High Class* (photo 24 – the entrance hall of an elegant hotel; photo 31 – a posh bar), *Organized Mass Tourist* (photo 14 – group of bus tourists), *Active Sports* (photo 39 – cyclists), *Action Seeker* (photo 29 – a party), and *Thrill Seeker* (photo 46 – whitewater rafting; photo 52 – sky diving). However, we also recognized the rather unexpected phenomenon that photo 38, showing the Burj al-Arab hotel in Dubai, can be found as representative for six tourist types. Moreover, 163 participants of the survey selected this particular photo. As a first guess to explain this phenomenon, we tend to conclude that a fairly large number of participants used photo 38 as the emblem of their vacation dreams rather than their vacation practice.Regarding the negative examples, we want to refer to photo 54 depicting a street musician. Selection of this photo significantly excludes membership to the *Archaeologist*. Photo 13, showing a tranquil scenery with boat, is a perfect example against the typical *Active Sports* tourist. We also want to mention the photographs that showed no significance, neither positive nor negative: photo 06 (devoid golf course), photo 33 (posh party), photo 35 (street café), photo 36 (the Eiffel tower), photo 41 (holiday resort with pool), photo 45 (group performing Tai Chi), photo 47 (celebrities on red carpet), photo 55 (rainy; group listening to tour guide), and photo 58 (hippie-style Volkswagen bus). Please note that only for a small number of tourist types we were unable to identify important photos, i.e. *Seeker*, *Explorer* and *Drifter*.

Table 7. Important photos to visually represent a tourist type

Tourist type	Positive Examples	Negative Examples
Anthropologist	photo 02**	
Escapist I	photo 38**	
Archaeologist	photo 34***	photo 54***
Sun Lover	photo 25***	
IMT I	photo 02**, photo 05**	
High Class	photo 24***, photo 38***, photo 31**	photo 15**
IMT II	photo 38***, photo 39***	
Escapist II	photo 05**	
OMT	photo 14***, photo 38**	photo 15***
Active Sports	photo 39**	photo 13**
Edu-Tourist	photo 38**	
Jet Setter	photo 38**	photo 15**
Action Seeker	photo 29**	
Thrill Seeker	photo 46**, photo 52**	

4 Conclusion

In this paper, we presented the findings of an online survey conducted to investigate whether tourist's habits can be derived from tourism-related photographs in order to facilitate the process of user profile creation. The results of this survey show a significant relationship between different tourist types and the preference for particular visual impressions conveyed by photographs. For most tourist types, we have determined representative photos, which, in turn, allow the assignment of tourist types to persons based on their selection of a set of photos. Considering the relationship of tourist types and tourist activities stated by Gretzel et al. (2004), we arrive at a mapping between tourism-related photographs and tourist activities. It is now possible to make the traditional process of registration and profile generation more fun by letting the user select from a couple of photos that reflect her tourism habits, and then infer her according tourist types.

References

Berger, H., Dittenbach, M., & Merkl, D. (2006). Let's Get Social in e-Tourism: The "itchy feet" Way. In *Proceedings of the 7th Asia-Pacific Conference on Computer-Human Interaction (APCHI'06)*, Taipei, Taiwan.

Fesenmaier, D.R., Ricci, F., Schaumlechner, E., Wöber, K., & Zanella, C. (2003). DIETORECS: Travel Advisory for Multiple Decision Styles. *Proceedings of the 10th International Conference on Information Technologies in Tourism (ENTER 03)*, A.J. Frew, M. Hitz, and P. O'Connor, pp. 232-241, Helsinki, Finland, January 29-31 Springer-Verlag.

Gibson, H., & Yiannakis, A. (2002). Tourist Roles - Needs and the Lifecourse. *Annals of Tourism Research*, 29(2),358-383.

Govers, R., & Go, F.M. (2004). Projected destination image online: Website content analysis of pictures and text. *Information Technology and Tourism*, 7(2), 73-89.

Gretzel, U., & Fesenmaier, D.R. (2003). Experience-based Internet Marketing: An Exploratory Study of Sensory Experiences Associated with Pleasure Travel to the Midwest United States. *Proceedings of the 10th International Conference on Information Technologies in Tourism (ENTER 03)*, A.J. Frew, M. Hitz, and P. O Connor, pp. 49-57, Helsinki, Finland, January 29-31. Springer-Verlag.

Gretzel, U., Mitsche, N., Hwang, Y.-H., & Fesenmaier, D.R. (2004). Tell me who you are and I will tell you where to go: Use of Travel Personalities in Destination Recommendation Systems. *Information Technology and Tourism*, 7(1),3-12.

Mehmetoglu, M. (2004). A typology of tourists from a different angle. *International Journal of Hospitality & Tourism Administration*, 5(3), 69-90.

Ricci, F., & Werthner, H. (2002). Case based Reasoning for Travel Planning Recommendation. *Information Technology and Tourism*, 4(3-4), 215-226.

Staab, S., Werthner, H., Ricci, F., Zipf, A., Gretzel, U., Fesenmaier, D.R., Paris, C., & Knoblock, C. (2002). Intelligent Systems for Tourism. *IEEE Intelligent Systems*, 17(6), 53-64

Vogt, C.A. & Fesenmaier, D.R. (1998). Expanding the Functional Information Search Model. *Annals of Tourism Research*, 25(3), 551-578.

Werthner, H., & Ricci, F. (2004). E-Commerce and Tourism. *Communications of the ACM*, 47(12), 101-105.

Yiannakis, A., & Gibson, H. (1992). Roles Tourists Play. *Annals of Tourism Research*, 19(2), 287-303.

Adaptation of Storytelling to Mobile Entertainment Service for Site-Specific Cultural and Historical Tour

HyunJeong Kim[a]
John Schliesser[b]

[a] Graduate School of Digital Design
kimhj@star.ks.ac.kr
[b] Kyungsung University, South Korea
j_schliesser@yahoo.com

Abstract

This study emerged from the question of how mobile handsets can change the nature of cultural and historical tourism in ubiquitous city environments. The paper describes the development of a new and entertaining type of mobile tour guide system that positions the mobile handset as a key delivery system for site-specific cultural and historical information. The central objective of the project was to organize a cultural and historical walking tour around the mobile handset and its unique advantages (i.e. portability, multi-media capacity, access to wireless internet, and location-aware potential) and then integrate this tour with a historical story and role-playing game that would deepen the mobile user's interest in the sites being visited, and enhance his or her overall experience of the area. After prototyping and user testing, new strategies for developing mobile 'edutainment content' to deliver cultural historical content of location were considered.

Keywords: digital storytelling, mobile content, virtual tour guide, cultural heritage tour, historical story, quest game.

1 Introduction

How can the mobile device be brought to bear on cultural and historical tourism in such a way that it creates a new and dynamic travel experience in ubiquitous wireless city environments? According to William Norman, President of the Travel Industry Association of America, "history and culture continue to be a significant part of the travel experience." In 2002, for example, four in ten (or eighty five million) U.S. adults cited at least one historic activity or event while they travelled. As interest in cultural and historical tourism increases worldwide, the mobile device, with its portable size, and unique multi-media and location-aware features, can both lead and expose mobile equipped tourists to sites of cultural and historical significance. The successful application of mobile to cultural and historical tourism can shed light on interesting attractions by re-animating them through the virtual means available to mobile devices. With its 3G Wireless Networks and high penetration rate of mobile users, the Republic of Korea is arguably the World's most advanced mobile environment. In Korea, some tourist information services are already being offered over the country's Wireless Internet and Telematics systems (on Jeju Island, for example); and in certain cities, like Taegu, civic governments make PDAs with free tourist information available for rental. But most of these mobile tourist information services are limited to practical content (i.e. train schedules, local hotels and restaurants, and so forth).

The challenge for the *Time Treks* project was how best to exploit the mobile handset as a device to draw mobile equipped travellers to a culturally and historically potent area, and then compel them on a rewarding site specific tour of this area. The main goal of Time Treks was to use the unique multi-media and location properties of the mobile handset to illuminate neighbourhoods rich in cultural and historical heritage. Because of the universal appeal of story, and the present popularity of story-based on-line and mobile games in Korea, a role-playing scenario and storyline was created to deepen the user's involvement, and enhance his or her enjoyment of the area being toured. Major factors to be considered were: the composition of walking tour for this new style of tourism service; the integration of entertainment features (story and game components) with standard historical and cultural information to create the right attractant; effective user interface design and deployment of mobile location-based services.

2 State of the Art

As previously noted, most mobile tourism services remain at a basic information level. In Korea, the advanced 3G Mobile Network and high user penetration rate are driving the domestic development of mobile travel services, and this is also true of other regions around the globe. A location-based tourist information service (using the GPS feature in mobile handsets to cue relevant tourist information based on a mobile users' location) has recently been developed by the Korea National Tourism Organization. U-Kangnam, another developing state of the art city information program that highlights Seoul's Kangnam district, uses location-based services to present practical information about this neighborhood's government offices and services. In Japan, NTT DoCoMo has recently developed "I-Area", an area specific information service that can be accessed by travelers in nearly four hundred zones throughout Japan, but like many of the LBS tourism services in Korea, the content here tends to present practical sorts of tourist information. CRUMPET, an EU-funded project for the 'creation of user-friendly mobile services personalized for tourism' has focused on location-based services for tourists, and has developed functional prototypes for testing in cities such as Heidelberg, Helsinki, London, and Aveiro, Portugal, and features predominantly practical tourist information. The European Media Laboratory's DEEP MAP combines LBS with a natural language user interface in an attempt to improve user interaction with basic tourist information.

Some cultural and historical mobile travel information services are presently in existence, either at the prototype or commercial product phase. In Europe, PEACH (which stands for 'personal experience with active cultural heritage') has experimented with an array of advanced technologies to "significantly increase the quality of cultural heritage appreciation." In Korea, the Seoul City Master Plan will offer detailed historical information about Seoul via mobile that is stored on RFID chips, and is scheduled for completion in 2006. In the U.S., IST (Intelligent Spatial Technologies) has recently been developing its I-Pointer digital tour guide with the U.S. National Parks Service to provide object-based cultural and historical information for travellers. The company Mobile Adventures has commercially serviced a site-specific voice-centric walking tour to mobile that offers cultural and historical information on areas in Hong Kong, Macao, and Singapore through an entertaining anecdotal presentation format. The American company Talking Street offers similar audio-based cultural and historical tours serviced to mobile handsets in New York City, and for Boston's Freedom Trail. France Telecom's *Geoquest* provides an example of a location-aware mobile service that used an entertaining store premise and role-playing scenario to attract mobile users to explore interesting sites in the city of Marseilles through their mobile devices.

It can be generally seen from the global state of the art that the tendency has been to create a) a highly technical application (with LBS for example) for the most basic tourism content or b) a low level technical approach (simple audio guide serviced to mobile handsets) for interesting and rich site-specific cultural and historical information. The Seoul City's Master Plan provides an example of a state of the art technical solution to historical information for tourists, but its presentation renders this information generic, and hence bland. France Telecom's *Geoquest* offers a fun mystery story line to attract users to historical areas, but then does not offer anything in the way of substantial historical information, only the basic sensation of a return to the past. Based on existing mobile tourism platforms, *Time Treks* sought to apply a higher technical and design standard to mobile-delivered cultural and historical tourism information, and to attract users to this information through an engaging and related story line.

3 Time Treks Project

3.1 Service Concept

Time Treks combined a story-based game with rich cultural and historical information to create a highly satisfying mobile tour. As shown in Fig.1, it has both tour mode and game mode, which can be selected according to the user's preference. The tour has been rendered in both Korean and English.

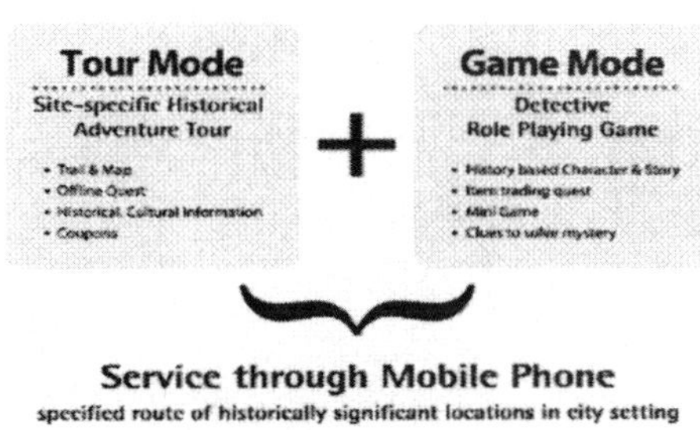

Fig. 1. Service concept

At a basic level, the mobile device is used to navigate and find selected locations. The modality of the first Time Treks prototype was designed with the future inclusion of LBS (GPS or Zone-based) in mind; however, Time Treks is not presently serviced with LBS. Mini-maps and text instructions were provided for users to get from site to site. There is also a function in which the user must identify an aspect of each location to confirm that he or she is actually there. For its technical platform, Time Treks used SKVM (SK Telecom's Virtual Machine). The application can be downloaded through SK Telecom's Wireless Internet to the user's mobile phone. During the tour, the user can access the server to receive additional cultural and historical information.

3.2 Location & Tour Trail

Locations were selected for their historical and cultural interest, proximity to one another (ease of access for user), and relation to the story and quest objectives. The overall tour trail consists of twelve locations. At each of these locations, the end user can access nuanced cultural and historical information (in the form of text, old photos, and in some cases audio) about the site through his or her mobile handset. He or she will also come into contact with important characters, both real and fictional, from the time period. This is the story foundation of the tour, and will be discussed in the next section. The overall tour encompasses the area around Young-do Mountain Park and the Nampodong district of Pusan as shown in Fig.2. Completing the tour trail of twelve locations by walking takes about three hours, and other optional points of interest between the main sites are also noted by the end user's mobile device.

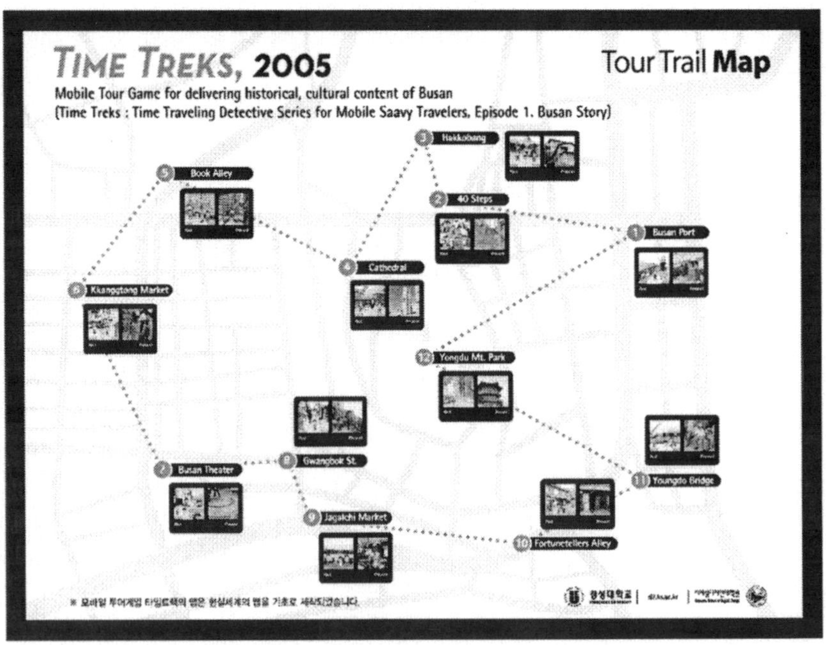

Fig. 2. Tour trail map

3.3 Adaptation of storytelling element

Story Approach

As Seymour Chatman points out, story is a universally appealing way of organizing and presenting information. People are largely attracted to stories because they provide "pleasure" and, at their best, prove "absorbing." Hence, story is "one of the best--and certainly one of the most enjoyable--routes to an understanding of the astonishing variety of people and events in the world (not to mention other conceivable worlds)". Time Treks sought to create a compelling story line that could be integrated with rich cultural and historical information (in the manner of a period movie or historical novel) so as to yield a uniquely pleasurable and absorbing mobile tour. The original *Time Treks* story premise is directly related to the historically relevant locations the end user tours using the mobile device. The story is structured like a classical mystery, but with a twist: the end user plays a time-traveling detective capable of returning to the past and solving mysteries that can change the course of history. The story setting is Pusan during the Korean War (circa 1950), when this city was the provisional capital, the last line of defense against the North Korean Army, and a city swelling with refugees displaced by the war. The mobile end user (as detective) is assigned the task of finding a woman who went missing during this time. He or she follows her 'trail', which is also the tour trail of significant historical locations, with the ostensible goal of uncovering this character's whereabouts. The quest for the missing woman character and solving the mystery of her disappearance requires that the end user also visit each location and learn something about its significance.

Fig. 3. Fictional characters vs. Real historical figures

Fictional characters vs. Real historical figures

In pursuit of the missing woman, the end-user/time-traveling detective also comes into contact with *real* historical figures that inhabited Busan during the period, and have gone on to prominence in Korean culture, for example, the Korean writer Kim Dong-Lee, painter Yi Joong-Sup, Korean film director, Im Kwon-Taek. Other minor characters of early 1950s Pusan, such as a dockworker, a nun, a fortuneteller, and a war refugee also appear to the end user to evoke the aura of life in early 1950s Pusan. Character design is shown in Fig. 3 above.

Relation between story setting and actual locations

The story follows the 'investigation' structure of a classical detective story, but with a twist. Playing the role of time-traveling detective, the mobile end user picks up clues and follows the trail of the missing woman from location to location, but does this in real physical space. Each actual physical location in the tour is culturally and historically significant, but also corresponds to a story scene in which the mobile user/detective will encounter a character or clue. Each location/scene will bring the end user a step closer to uncovering the mystery of what happened to the woman, and will also put the end user in contact with other interesting historical characters and events of this time. Photographic images of the locations from the era were used as a background image to enhance the historical atmosphere. By viewing this background, the end user can gain a better sense of the historical story setting, as well as compare images of the past with those of the present.

3.4 Adaptation of Tourist Information Element

Trail & Map

The mobile handset functions as a guidance mechanism by supplying maps to help the user navigate a series of real physical urban locations that all have some historical or cultural value. In the middle of the trail, the end user may access some touri st information such as old traditional restaurants, museums and street that are nearby. The example screen shot is shown in Fig.4.

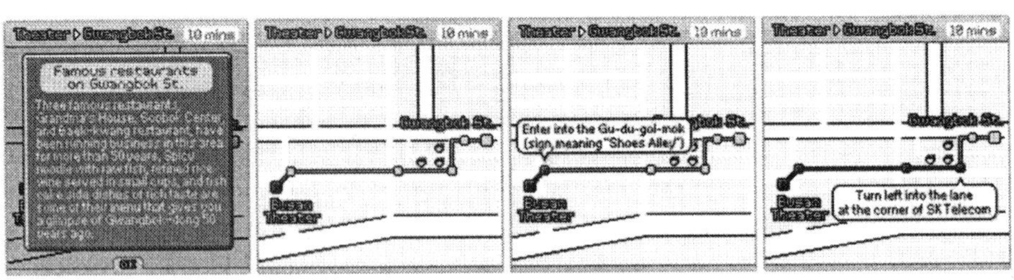

Fig. 4. Example of map

Offline Quest

At each of the twelve designated locations, the end user must identify a particular item or object that he or she can only observe by having actually visited the site. This ensures that the end users actually visit and explore each important site, and acquire some knowledge about this place through the answering process for the quest. It also confirms to the end user that he or she is at the next site on the tour trail, and in the next 'scene' in the story. Figure 8 provides an example of this identification process: the end user must select which of the masks actually appears in this particular location to continue with the tour and story. The example screen shot is shown in Fig.5.

Fig. 5. Example of offline quest

Historical, Cultural Information

Characters external to the *Time Treks* story world (like Im Kwon Taek and the 'Sage' character) function to provide local historical information and film location information. By selecting one of these characters in a particular location, the end user may access several layers of historical and cultural information delivered in a multi-media format that includes text, images, and even audio that features period music, and famous songs about the area during the setting's era. The example screen shot is shown in Fig.6.

Fig. 6. Example of historical information: past images of Pusan Customs Building

Coupons

The End User can receive coupons for nearby restaurants or shops throughout the tour. The coupon featured in the example below gives the end user a discount to a well-known area restaurant.

3.5 Adaptation of Game Elements

Item Trading Quest and Mini Game

An item-trading and mini game element was included in Time Treks to attract younger mobile users who enjoy item-trading games. As the detective, the end user should buy or obtain items to give to certain characters in return for information about the missing woman. Some items are particular to the period being evoked by *Time Treks*, and so also enhance historical and cultural knowledge. The example screen shot is shown in Fig.7.

Fig 7. Example of item trading quest game screen

The content of the mini-games games relates directly to a favorite activity in Pusan (feeding the seagulls), and thus reinforces an element of Pusan culture. In the mini game featured below, the end user scores points by feeding as many seagulls as he or she can. The example screen shot is shown in Fig.8.

Fig. 8. Mini game screen

Clues to Solve Mystery

Playing the role of detective, the end user should collect all 6 clues to solve the case. If the end user finds all the clues, he or she will have a chance to know the final destination of the missing woman, and can thereby reunite her and the client before they will be separated by time. The example screen shot is shown in Fig.9.

Fig. 9. Screen design for collecting clues and solving mystery

4 Prototype Evaluation

4.1 Introduction of End User Test to Prototype

The first Time Treks prototype was tested at the Tenth Annual Pusan International Film Festival (PIFF), in October, 2005. This event was selected for the initial test because it is a prestigious international arts event that takes place in the Nampodong area where the tour is set. From a booth near the Pusan Film Theater, mobile phones with Time Treks pre-downloaded were loaned to those who wanted to take the tour. 34 people (24 teams) tested the prototype, and were interviewed after the tour. The survey for test subjects was made up of the following eight categories and questions: Demographic: age, gender, address, experience with wireless internet and/or mobile games

1. How many locations were visited?
2. How many places did the end user check additional local historical and cultural information?
3. Did the end user use coupons? How many?
4. How many clues did the end user find for the game element?
5. What did the end user like best about Time Treks?
6. Like least?
7. What was its most memorable aspect?

4.2 Test Result

The Analysis of testers' profile is shown in Table 1.

Table 1. Testers' profile

<table>
<tr><td rowspan="2">Gender</td><td colspan="2">Male</td><td colspan="2">Female</td></tr>
<tr><td colspan="2">17</td><td colspan="2">17</td></tr>
<tr><td rowspan="2">Age, Position</td><td>Students with parents (pre-teen)</td><td>Middle school students (teens)</td><td>College or graduate students (20s)</td><td>Non-student (young professionals) (Early 30s)</td></tr>
<tr><td>1</td><td>3</td><td>22</td><td>8</td></tr>
<tr><td rowspan="2">Tourist or not</td><td colspan="2">Tourist (domestic/foreign)</td><td colspan="2">Local Citizen</td></tr>
<tr><td colspan="2">18/6</td><td colspan="2">16</td></tr>
<tr><td rowspan="2">Mobile experienced or not</td><td colspan="2">Yes</td><td colspan="2">No</td></tr>
<tr><td colspan="2">28</td><td colspan="2">6</td></tr>
</table>

Table 2. Extent of testers' progress

Did tour and tried game mode				Only played game mode
Completed tour and game	**Completed tour but did not finish game**	**Did not finish tour but finished game**	**Completed part of tour and part of game**	**No tour + only played game**
3teams (5people)	1 team (2 people)	1 team (3 people)	17 teams (20 people)	2teams (4people)
22teams (30 people)				2team (4people)

Table 3. Testers' positive & Negative feedback

	Positive	Negative
Historical and Cultural Tourist Information	• Historical and cultural information for spaces very interesting—new information (local citizens) • Historical sites were made much more interesting through presentation • Movie location information very interesting (tourists from Seoul for PIFF)	• Too much text too read • Text too small • Text too hard for young demographic to read
Trail and Map	• Tour effective way to learn about Pusan history and culture for foreigners & tourists • Maps effective at helping guide end users to from location to location	• End users wanted more freedom to visit sites in non-sequential order • End users wanted a better technical feature like LBS to make the mapping more accurate and easier • Walking tour too long and physically tiring
Game Element	• Story/Game element provided objective and a motive to finish the tour • The combination of tour, story, and game was a fresh concept • The off-line quest was very interesting and challenging • Gathering clues and solving the mystery was interesting	• Not really a mobile game, but more of an information service • Wanted more mini-games • There was little or no character movement • There was no repeatable play • The ending was too short and unsatisfying • Needs more sound effects • Would be better in a multi-player format
Coupons and Restaurant Information	• Really liked this element	• Thought there should be more coupons offered during tour
User Interface	• Not Difficult (experienced end users)	• Difficult (inexperienced end users)

4.3 Analysis

Time Treks' story-based game element was seen to have enhanced its historical and cultural walking tour by giving end users a focused objective, and a more personal stake in learning the history of the area. The story element also had the effect of transmitting historical and cultural knowledge to end users indirectly, in the manner of a historical novel or fiction film, and all those who tested the prototype found elements of this approach unique, enriching, and ultimately satisfying. H owever, because *Time Treks* was positioned as mobile game, it appealed primarily young people, even though it had great deal of cultural historical information for all generations of tourists. Also, those who tested the prototype expecting a new type of state of the art mobile game had to lower their expectations. Since Time Treks was subjected to the rigorous standards of the advanced gaming environment in Korea, it is perhaps not surprising that gamers did not embrace the prototype as a 'stand-alone' game. But, in less evolved gaming environments, this reaction might be different. Still, it does indicate that Time Treks should be positioned not as a mobile game with edutainment value, but as a new mobile tourist product with entertainment facets. The historical and cultural contents, combined with an efficient walking route, make for an overall good mobile tour guide system, and proved especially strong for foreign tourists who are unfamiliar with the location. It was convenient and satisfying for tourists to receive site specific and situation based information through the predetermined trail. However, there was a sense that the tour course was too long and also restricted end user options for visiting sites out of sequence and/or in effect modifying the walking tour to suit their own interests, needs, or constraints. Past images of featured sites were satisfying, and reinforced the 'time travel' theme of the prototype, especially when they are rare and not widely known. However, the text aspect of the historical and cultural presentation proved overly long and for some hard to read. This aspect of the project could be modified effectively into an audio segment, though at the moment audio requires a large data size that would pose an economical challenge to end users.

5 Conclusion and Further Work

Mobile devices offer opportunities to redefine tourism, as we know it. They allow the independent traveler a new mode of access and navigation in rich cultural and historic areas. Because the mobile device is quickly being coded as an entertainment medium, it also provides a new way to deliver edutainment content that integrates site-specific cultural and historical information with story and game scenario formats. The intended effect of combining a site-specific walking tour with an entertaining fictional historical story and off-line quest game was to make mobile users more interested and involved in the area they were touring. It also provided a way to organize this information in an accessible format for mobile. Further consideration for the *Time Treks* project requires modifications in the prototype at a number of levels based on user tests and the resulting target segmentation. The target can be segmented along an axis of mobile gamers and tourists. Although originally Time Treks was targeted at gamers and tourists, its platform can easily be adapted for tourists and non-gamers by minimizing the game element, and emphasizing its basic level functions. A simpler interface, and the inclusion of LBS would make the prototype easier to use. The replacement of text with audio would make the prototype more elegant and memorable. The prototype should also be refined to reflect its nature as a new tourism product rather than a stand-alone mobile game. Further development strategy according to target segmentation is integrated in the Fig. 10. As cultural and historical tourism grows, it is important to adapt the mobile device to this purpose, and work toward setting a new standard for it. The mobile device offers a variety of new opportunities for personalized edutainment medium that can drive a new style of tourism.

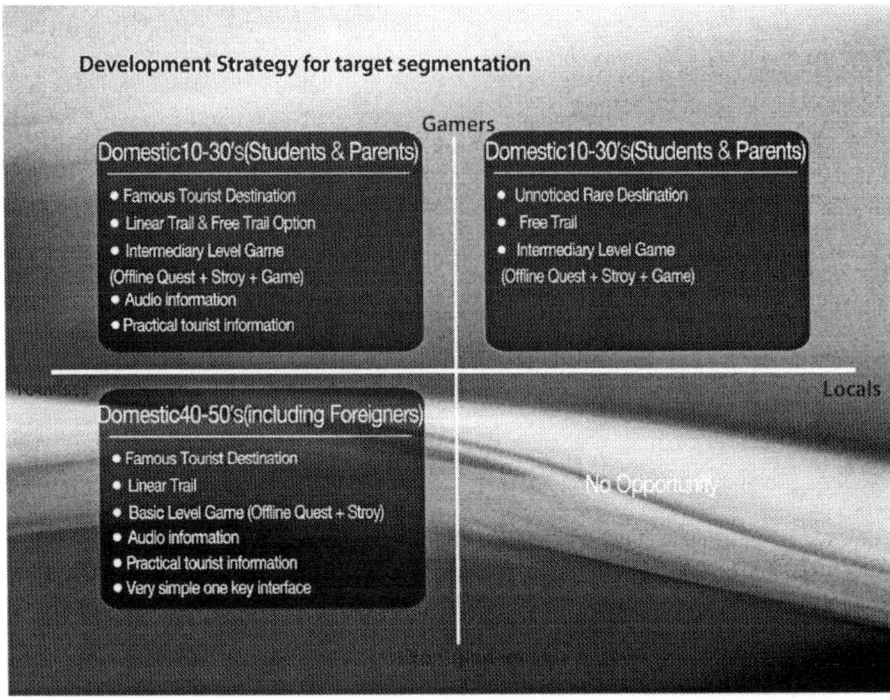

Fig. 10. Development strategy of mobile tour game for different target segmentations

References

Keronen, A. Myllyaho, M. Alatalo, P., Oivo, M., Antikainen, H. & Rusanen, J. (2004). Experimental Development of a Prototype for Mobile Environmental Information Systems (MEIS). In F. Bomarius & H. Iida (Eds.), *PROFES 2004*, LNCS 3009 (pp. 442-456), Springer-Verlag.

Bellows, M. (2001). *Location-Based Gaming in France. WGamer* http://wgamer.com/articles/francetelecom092801.php [Oct. 20, 2006].

Chatman, S. (1993). *Reading Narrative Fiction*, MacMillian.

Miller, C. H. (2001). *Digital Storytelling,* Elsevier Inc.

Norman, W. (2003). *Travelers Desire to Experience History and Culture Stronger Than Ever.* Travel Industry Association of America Annual Forum.

Yim, Y. (2004). *LBS mobile content using location information.* Digital Content (pp 121-125), Seoul, Digital Content Organization.

http://www.jejutelematics.com/JejuWeb/jsp/kor_ver02 [Oct. 20 2006] .

http://www.seoul.go.kr/info/organ/subhomepage/info/electronic_government/master_plan/1224324_13302.html [Oct. 20 2006]

http://minne.oulu.fi/projects.html [Oct. 20 2006]

http://www.walkthetalk.hk/main.php [Oct. 20 2006]

http://peach.itc.it/home.html [Oct. 20 2006]

http://tour.daegu.go.kr/guide/guide_pda_01.php [Oct. 20 2006]

http://www.cbtour.net/cb_web/cb_tour/kw_wireless[Oct. 20 2006]

Behavioural Impacts of Mobile Tour Guides

Ronny Kramer[a]
Marko Modsching[a]
Klaus ten Hagen[a]
Ulrike Gretzel[b]

[a] Department of Computer Science
University of Applied Sciences Zittau/Görlitz, Germany
{K.tenHagen, MModsching, RKramer}@HS-ZiGr.de
[b] Laboratory for Intelligent Systems in Tourism
Texas A&M University
ugretzel@tamu.edu

Abstract

Electronic tour guides have been developed to personalise guided tours. Also, in contrast to traditional tours, electronic tour guides allow their users to abandon or modify tours at any time. Research as to whether users take advantage of these added capabilities is currently not available. A field trial was conducted comparing the behaviour of tourists as they were using a Planner providing a personalized guided tour and an Explorer displaying the current location in a map and supplying information about sights on request. The results indicate that users differ significantly in the way and extent to which they take advantage of both mobile applications. It seems that the Planner satisfies the demand for guided tours additionally leaving much needed room for spontaneous deviations. Surprisingly, tour duration, walking distances and number of sights visited using these different mobile applications were similar to traditional guided tours.

Keywords: Personalized tour, mobile tour guide, user perceptions, tour adaptation, tour modification, field trial.

1 Introduction

Intelligent mobile devices featuring dynamic tours promise tourists the opportunity to enhance the experience of a destination by providing relevant and personalized information anytime and anyplace. However, the term "tour" typically relates to a paradigm of tourists following a fixed schedule and visiting the most popular attractions at a destination. One can expect that these perceptions can carry over to a tool which includes "tour" in its name. Thus, a mobile tour guide might be expected to provide a traditional tour guided by an electronic device rather than a human being, but otherwise following the same structure. If this is the case, users who feel comfortable with guided tours and like to adhere to the guidance of a tour guide will be more likely to execute suggestions received from a mobile tour guide. On the other hand, users who would like to freely explore the destination might not realize that a mobile tour guide can also support this kind of tourist behaviour, especially when it has the capabilities to dynamically adapt to users signalling less or increased interest.

The Dynamic Tour Guide (DTG) is a mobile application which, in its "Planner mode", is able to create personalised tours based on tourists' generic preferences and context based constraints such as tour duration, starting time and location. A previous field trial (Kramer, Modsching, Gretzel, & ten Hagen, 2006) showed its ability to elicit generic interests in the mobile context, to select attractions and to combine them into an appropriate tour. The DTG also offers an "Explorer mode" that computes no tour plan but provides context-based information whenever requested. Tourists can follow their own position on a map and see a list of available attractions in their close vicinity. Either manually selecting or staying at a certain sight will trigger context-driven interpretation. The two modes represent very different paradigms of a mobile information system and raise the question whether they lead to differences in user acceptance of the tool, use of its features, and, ultimately, impacts on tourist behaviour.

2 Related work

Developing tools which can provide personalized tours is a complex task and has become a central issue in current research. The main projects regarding mobile tour guides are C yberguide (Abowd, 1997), GUIDE (Cheverst, 2000), the Deep Map (Malaka, 2001) and Crumpet (Schmidt-Belz, 2003). Unfortunately, evaluations of mobile recommenders by the intended user groups are rare and typically conducted using very small samples. Also, a review of previous studies clearly shows the methodological shortcomings of existing evaluation approaches. For instance, GUIDE is a mobile tour guide that computes a route based on selections of concrete sights by the tourist him/herself. Reaching a sight, context-sensitive information is provided. In a field trial over 4 weeks 60 tourists were asked to use a mobile device with the GUIDE prototype. Time stamped interaction logs, audio recording protocols and personal interviews delivered data for later evaluation with the objective to validate system requirements. Although audio recordings provide insights into user problems, they are not tied to a specific location and their analysis is time-intense. Another example is the Crumpet project, which developed a personalized, location-aware multi-agent system. It recommends and informs about tourist attractions, and provides interactive maps displaying the user's position as well as points of interest (PoIs). A usability evaluation at four different trial sites served to find out if the system was useful and provided benefits compared to currently available media. Users had to perform typical tourist tasks while being observed, and later completed a questionnaire. However, observing subjects is not only extremely intrusive and might cause changes in behaviour but is also very personnel- and time-consuming. GPS-based log approaches can help overcome some of these problems. Ashbrook and Straner (2003) collected data of 5 subjects over 7 months using this methodology. Such GPS-based approaches are not only important for system evaluations but also provide general insights into travel behaviour. According to Brown and Chalmers (2003), previous studies on tourist behaviour lack detailed observations of tourists in practice. Most are questionnaire-based like the study of Freytag (2003) and thus are static and dependent on tourists' memory and perceptions.

March and Woodside (2005) argue that planned and realized tourist behaviour differ substantially and consumer decisions can be greatly influenced by product information at the destination. Similarly, Pearce (2005) outlines the often substantial effect of interpretation on on-site experiences and behaviours. By providing recommendations and interpretation of sights, mobile tour guides are expected to have great influence on tourist behaviour. Consequently, a methodology is needed which can capture tourist behaviour in a spatial context and at the same time minimizes the influence of the research methodology on the behaviour studied.

3 Methodology

In August 2006 a field trial was conducted in Görlitz, Germany to examine the behaviour of tourists resulting from the use of the mobile recommender system DTG. The main objective was to study the differences of the Planner and Explorer modes in terms of their impact on tourist behaviours. A total of 20 mobile devices (MDA III or VPA III) connected to a Bluetooth GPS receiver and equipped with the mobile DTG application were utilized. Respectively 10 devices configured as operating in the Planner or in the Explorer mode were handed to the tourists each day in the morning and received back in the afternoon. The devices were dispersed at several places throughout the city and could either be brought back to a central collection station or deposited at any restaurant or hotel in the city. The tourists were also asked to fill out a questionnaire and received a DVD of the city Görlitz as an incentive for participating.

Instead of observing the users directly which inevitably runs the risk of taking influence on their decisions, the software was equipped with an instrumentation mechanism in the background. Also, rather than defining tasks for the field trial which would constrain actual tourist behaviour, tourists were asked to use the mobile devices to support their exploration of the destination. Letting the tourist use the mobile device unobserved provided them with the choice to abandon the use at any time if the effort necessary to interact with it exceeded the perceived value.

Different types of data were used to evaluate different research targets:

- XML files containing all user interactions (inputs, clicks) and application events (automatic information presentation, tour adaptation) and results (computed tour)
  → Specified interests and tour constraints for tour computation
  → Planned duration, distance and specific attractions
  → Manual modifications (add or remove attractions) of the tour plan
  → Interactions during the tour and conditional on the tour progress
- GPS log file containing NMEA values delivered by the GPS receiver
  → Actually covered distance based on coordinates
  → Actual tour duration based on timestamps
  → Actually visited locations by comparison to their coordinate referenced areas
  → Actual visit durations based on hardly varying coordinates for longer time spans
- Supplementary questionnaire asking for demographic data (age, gender) and tour relevant facts (information sources, difficulties)

Despite its advantages over methodologies used in previous studies, this methodology is limited for the following reasons: The evaluation relies on automated data that reveal user decisions but give no insight regarding their intentions or reasons. In addition, all behavioural decisions are assumed to be triggered by the tourists or their mobile device without taking into account external influences like companions, traffic, weather or else. Furthermore tourists are assumed to have recognised certain attractions based on predefined staying times though they may not have seen the attraction as such. Last but not least, GPS accuracy in towns like Görlitz is limited (ten Hagen, 2005). This affects the anticipated locations on one hand and causes navigation problems on the other. The DTG application integrates the commercial navigation software Navigon (2006). Detailed studies during the beta phase indicated that around half of the navigation instructions were either plainly wrong or at least misleading, e.g. to "turn right" after one has already passed the turning point. The tourists were advised that the directives may be inexact and should not be followed blindly. Indeed, the survey results show that the DTG Planner was only ranked fifth (15%) as the most trustful orientation help. Tourists preferred city maps (22%), road signs (18%), distinctive buildings (16%) and information signs (15%).

4 Results

Throughout August 2006, 274 tourists (132 using the Planner mode and 142 the Explorer mode) took part in the field trial. The majority (56%) of the participants had never been in Görlitz before. The mean age was 47 years and 68% of the participants were male. Only 13% of the tourists were travelling alone, the average size of a travel group was 3 persons. The majority of the participants felt comfortable handling the application, though 85% rated their capabilities with such mobile devices as very low or low, 79% stated zero years of usage and 81% stated zero hours of usage per week. Nevertheless, less than one fourth complained about difficulties regarding the handling of the device.

Use and Influences of the DTG Planner Mode

Only few tourists who used the Planner mode of the DTG engaged in detailed interest specification; most weighted a small number of main interest categories. After all constraints were specified the DTG Planner computed a tour. The median planned tour had a duration of 2.4 hours and included 12 attractions. Tourists can manually add or remove attractions which results in a recalculation to optimise the tour with the new constraints; however, 65% of the tourists did not make use of this option and performed the tour as it was proposed. This might indicate that most tourists like to have a tour plan and trust the recommendation. Tourists who modified their tours did it twice per tour. They more often added than removed attractions, suggesting that tourists must be well informed about what is worth seeing in Görlitz. Tourists who removed attractions might have already visited them. Fig. 1 displays the distribution of tour modifications during the tour. A high percentage of modifications occurred during the planning phase but tourists also modified their tour in the second half. By reaching special sights along their way tourists might try to include those to expand the tour. Closer to the end they might feel tired of walking and try to finish the tour earlier by shortening it.

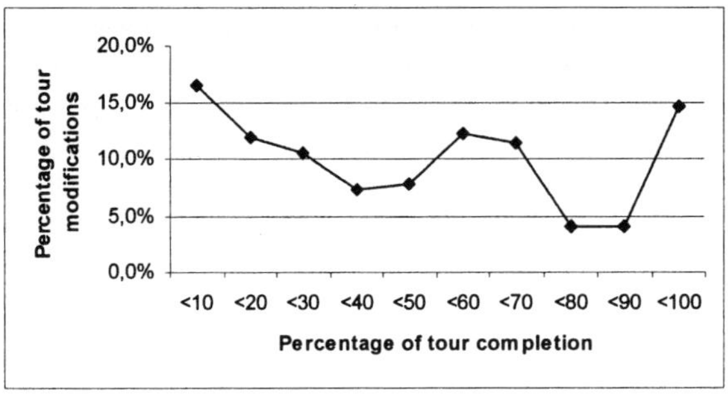

Fig. 1. Distribution of modifications during tours

Table 1 compares the actual tour with the original tour plan. On average the tourists visited 50% (6 out of 12) of the attractions proposed by the DTG Planner (the distribution of the tour completions according to the tour plan is displayed in Fig. 2). Thus, the actual duration and length of the tours are smaller than planned. Fig. 3 visualizes the amount of sights of the original plan that are being visited or skipped during the tour execution. Most tour building blocks (TBBs) that were skipped were scheduled at the end of the tour. This is a strong indication that tourists often finish their tours earlier and abandon the last part maybe due to tiredness. However, the last TBB is almost always visited as it is the desired endpoint of the tour.

Table 1. Comparison of planned and actual tours (median values)

	Planned	***Actual***
Tour duration [min.]	142	76
Number of sights in tour	12	11
→ actual visits of those originally planned		6
Percentage of planned visits	100%	55%
Percentage of unplanned visits	0%	45%

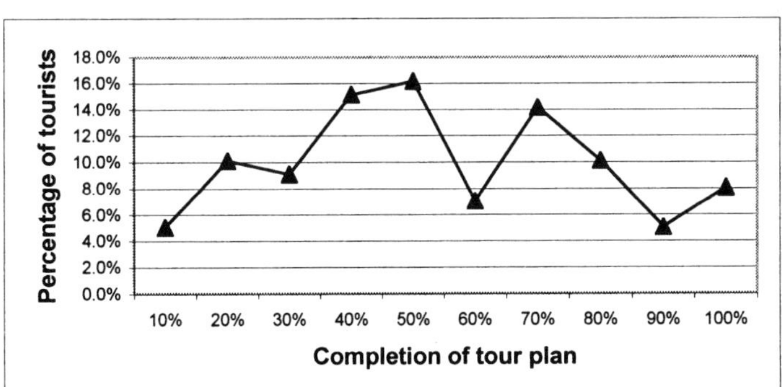

Fig. 2. Percentage of tour completion according to plan

The results also indicate that tourists visit a lot of unplanned attractions, likely for two reasons: they stop at additional attractions when passing by along their normal route or they explicitly deviate from the given itinerary to visit a certain attraction they saw from afar. The median duration of an actual tour is 1.3 hours which approximately equals the duration of common guided tours. That might mean tourists are not willing or simply not used to perform longer tours. And it underlines the fact that tourists only used the DTG Planner for one activity, a tour, and, thus, for just a small segment of their stay in Görlitz.

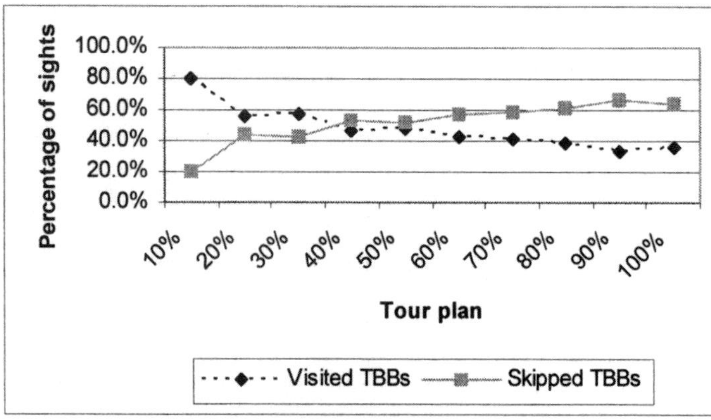

Fig. 3. Percentage of visited and skipped sights according to tour plan

Fig. 4 shows the distribution of actual and planned tour duration. It seems tourists were a bit too optimistic when planning their tour as their actual walking time is much shorter. This diagram again underlines the findings of Table 1.

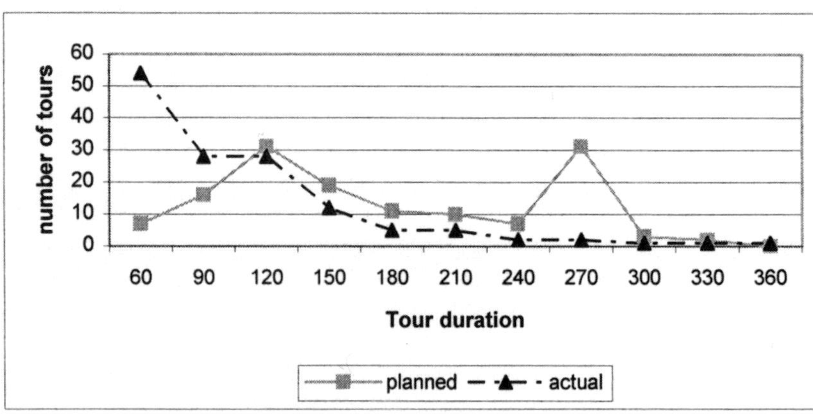

Fig. 4. Distribution of planned and actual tour duration

A total of 55% of the tourists got distracted during their tour at least once. A distraction is defined as three deviations of more than 100 metres from the proposed itinerary. In 89% of the cases another sight was the reason for leaving the recommended route. In other cases tourists got lost, probably because of misleading directives of the mobile navigator due to bad GPS accuracy within the Old Town of Görlitz. What becomes clear is that tourists really try to execute the plan as it is proposed. Deviations are pretty rare considered the covered distances and always lead the tourists back to the planned route.

The DTG Planner tracks the execution of the tour plan. If the plan and the actual execution deviate by more than ½ hour the DTG suggests adapting the tour to account for the accumulated changes. If the tourist agrees a new plan is computed for the remaining amount of time. The tourist can also choose to continue the tour with the acceptance of later or earlier arrival. The need for adaptation arises since some tourist might walk faster or slower or tourists might stay longer at a sight than anticipated. Furthermore a tourist might simply get distracted by an attraction or a souvenir shop along the way and ignore the execution of the tour plan. Last but not least a tourist might simply get lost. Of the 132 planned tours only 9% were adapted, though 17% of the tours were recommended to be adapted. This means that almost half of the tourists who were provided with an adaptation suggestion by the DTG Planner did not agree to an adaptation and continued with their tour as it was planned. Anyhow, those few adaptations took place during the last 10% of the tour for 47% of the cases. The reason for adaptation is a time deficit in 78% of the cases, which entails a shortening of the tour, and a time surplus in 22% of the cases, which in contrast entails an expansion of the tour. These results show that in practice for such short tours around 1.5 hours the predefined deviation time of ½ hour might be too long and needs to be reduced.

The DTG Planner also allows for integrating restaurant stops into the plan. The mean time spent at restaurants was 27 minutes, with most tourists choosing a café. But in 69% of the cases the tourists who had planned a restaurant decided not to visit them. Reasons for that, according to the questionnaire data, are that 62% decided not to visit a restaurant at all and 27% spontaneously visited a different restaurant along the way, sometimes just a bakery. Other reasons trace back to the short duration of the tours and the mind set associated with a "Guided Tour", which generally does not have a restaurant break. The DTG Planner data suggests that tourists first finish the tour, return the mobile device and start another activity like having lunch or coffee. The planner mode provides a Guided Tour, which is a well-known model. Tour adaptation and the inclusion of a restaurant visit are abilities of a "Day Planner", which is an entirely new mental model lacking a traditional analogue.

Comparison of Planner and Explorer Mode

The results of the previous section show that the tour plan is helpful as half of it was performed in the recommended manner. Nevertheless tourists took the opportunity to enrich the tour plan by attractions along the way. This suggests that even the DTG Planner provides a level of independence guided tours performed within a group can not offer. In contrast to the still very structured tours resulting from interactions with the Planner version, use of the Explorer mode is not based on a tour plan but entirely driven by spontaneous user decisions.

Table 2. Clicks and time for different actions with the Planner (median values)

	Clicks	*Time [min.]*
Interest specification	25	2.3
Tour specification	6	2.3
Navigation mode	37	29
Total interaction	**93**	**85**

Table 2 shows the interaction data for the DTG Planner. In a preceding field trial (Kramer, 2006) the elicitation of interests took about 2 minutes and less than 20 clicks. This year the values are slightly higher as the tourists had the opportunity to perform the tour afterwards and seemed to invest more effort into planning. No interest specification is necessary for the Explorer mode. Fig. 5 shows the amount of interactions with both applications during the duration of the tour. The Planner demands much more clicks in the beginning as the tour must be specified. The Explorer shows a more even dispersion of clicks over time as there are only two interaction schemes: orientation by a map and requesting information, which is equal throughout the whole tour. Fewer clicks in the end may mean that tourists request less information as they become tired or return to places they have already been at and heard about. However in both cases the average interaction frequency is 1.1 click/min.

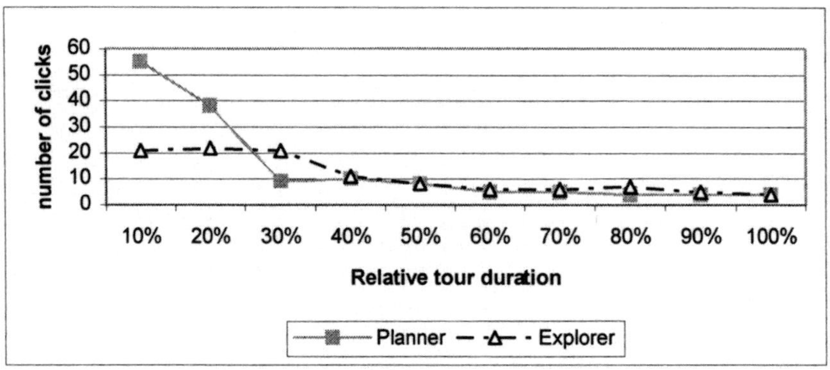

Fig. 5. Distribution of clicks

Table 3 compares both versions considering distance, duration and number of visited sights. The observed behaviours are, first, very similar for the two different modes and, second, pretty close to what one would assume to be the case for traditional tours without the use of a mobile tour guide. Either the "tour paradigm" is so engrained that it determines the behaviour of the tourists or it reflects more fundamental human constants like attention span, distance willing to walk or amount of information that can be processed. These experiences derive the need for a combination of both modes for a practical adoption. As the tourists pass additional sights during their planned tour they may want to receive appropriate information as it is provided by the Explorer mode.

Table 3. Comparison of performed tours (median values)

	Planner	***Explorer***
Tour distance [km]	3.4	4.2
Tour duration [h]	1.3	1.7
Number of visited sights	11	14
Time per sight [min]	7.1	7.1
Sights per distance [1/km]	3.2	3.3

5 Future research

Results of the questionnaire data indicate that only 10% of all tourists are walking by themselves. Most are couples, families or groups. As proposed for online planning systems by Franke (2002) the concept of the DTG needs to be extended to serve groups of tourists jointly discovering a destination. Especially an interest profile for the whole group has to be synthesised from the individual ones as described by Masthoff (2004) who combines multiple preferences for a common television programme. In general, the findings indicate that the methodology employed was appropriate. However, detailed insights into the reasons for behaviour changes could not be derived. A study design with prompts by the system asking the user to indicate why a certain behaviour was triggered should be explored for future studies. It was found that the Planner mode is used for a single activity, a tour, and this tour may only be the first one with others to follow. For these subsequent tours the "tour guide" paradigm needs to be reframed to a mobile information system. Such a mobile information system will remember the sights visited at this destination as part of an earlier guided tour or during self-guided exploration to propose an additional tour that helps the tourist discover the not so obvious beyond the beaten paths. This requires more research on users' conceptual model of mobile tour guides as well as on effective ways to communicate different paradigms to a user so that impacts on behaviour can be realized.

6 Conclusion

The presented results indicate that tourists are accepting the guided tour model. However they seem to enjoy with relish the ability to ignore the plan, since they are just executing 50% of the planned sights, adding sights along the way and dropping sights at the end of the plan. This additional level of independence is a unique differentiation of the mobile tour guide versus traditional guided tours in a larger group. However advanced features like the inclusion of a restaurant or the adaptation of the tour plan were rarely used. These are features of a Day Planner with a planning horizon beyond a single guided tour and –unfortunately- without such a strong traditional analogue. The Explorer as an entirely passive mobile application was used for tours a little bit longer enabling the discovery of proportionally more sights. However the Explorer relies on traditional means, e.g. signs, to guide the tourist. In this field study pretty much all tours were initial tours and hence they covered the highlights in the mediaeval town centre. A planner remembering the sights visited before can devise a plan that leads to entire different areas of the city that an exclusive user of the Explorer might have trouble finding. Despite the fundamental differences between the Planner and Explorer application the distances, durations and number of sights visited were similar and close to traditional guided tours potentially indicating fundamental constraints about the will of a tourist to walk, focus on one activity and process information about sights.

References

Abowd, G. D., Atkeson C. G., Hong, J., Long, S., Kooper, R. & Pinkerton, M. (1997). Cyberguide – a mobile context-aware tour guide, Baltzer/ACM Wireless Networks.

Ashbrook, D. & Straner, T. (2003). Using GPS to learn significant locations and predict movement across multiple users. *Personal Ubiquitous Computing*, Springer-Verlag London Limited 2003.

Brown, B. & Chalmers, M. (2003). Tourism and mobile technology. In K. Kuutti & E. H. Karsten (Eds.) *Proeceedings of the Eighth European Conference on Computer Supported Cooperative Work*, Helsinki, Finland, 14-18 September 2003., Kluwer Academic Press.

Cheverst, K., Davies, N., Mitchell, K., Friday, A., & Efstratiou, C. (2000). Developing a Context-aware Electronic Tourist Guide: Some Issues and Experiences, Distributed Multimedia Research Group, Lancaster University, UK.

Franke, T. (2002). Integration of Group Support Tools into an Online Tourism Advising System. *Workshop on User Modeling and Decision Making in Travel and Tourism Emergent Systems*, Trento, April 9-10. Retrieved September 6, 2005 from http://ectrl.itc.it/home/umtts/program.htm

Freytag, T. (2003). *Städtetourismus in Heidleberg – Ergebnisbericht zur Gästebefragung 2003.* Geographisches Institut der Universität Heidelberg.

Kramer, R., Modsching, M., Gretzel, U., & ten Hagen, K. (2006). A Field Trial to Elicit Individual Preferences in the Context of a Mobile Dynamic Tour Guide. In M. Hitz, M. Sigala & J. Murphy (Eds.), *Information and Communication Technologies in Tourism 2006*. p.100. Vienna, Austria: Springer Computer Science.

Malaka, R. (2001). Deep Map – The Multilingual Tourist Guide, European Media Laboratory, Heidelberg, Germany.

March, R. & Woodside, A. G. (2005). *Tourism behaviour: travellers' decisions and actions.* Cambridge, MA: CABI Publishing.

Masthoff, J. (2004). Group modeling: Selecting a sequence of television items to suit a group of viewers. *User Modeling and User Adapted Interaction*, 14, 37-85.

Navigon (2004): http://www.navigon.de

Pearce, P. L. (2005). *Tourist Behaviour: Themes and Conceptual Schemes*. Clevedon, UK: Channel View Publications.

Schmidt-Belz, B., Laamanen, H., Posland, S, & Zipf, A. (2003). Location-based mobile tourist service – first user experiences. In A. Frew, M. Hizt & P. O'Connor (Eds.), Information and Communication Technologies in Tourism 2003, 115-123. Vienna, Austria: Springer Computer Science.

Ten Hagen, K., Kramer, R., Müller, P., Schumann, B., & Hermkes, M. (2004). Semantic Matching and Heuristic Search for a Dynamic Tour Guide. In A. Frew, M. Hiztz & P. O'Connor (Eds.), *Information and Communication Technologies in Tourism 2005.* Vienna, Austria: Springer Computer Science.

Acknowledgements

This project is part of VESUV in cooperation with Siemens AG, Microsoft's European Innovation Center (EMIC) and Fraunhofer Institute IGD. VESUV is supported by the Federal Ministry for Economics and Labour (BMWA).

Mobile Positioning Data in Tourism Studies and Monitoring: Case Study in Tartu, Estonia

Rein Ahas[a]
Anto Aasa[a]
Siiri Silm[a]
Margus Tiru[b]

[a]Institute of Geography
University of, Tartu
rein.ahas@ut.ee [a]
[b] IPositium ICT
Niine 11, Tallinn, Estonia
margus.tiru@@positium.ee

Abstract

We introduce mobile positioning based data sources in tourism studies using the case study of tourism in Tartu, Estonia. Mobile positioning data is a promising source for tourism geography as it is one easiest and most cost effective sources for investigating the flows of tourists with relatively good spatial and temporal coverage. Mobile positioning data allows one to link the digital track of visitors with visited events and locations retrospectively. The data also has potential for the development of real-time monitoring tools for tourism planning and management, as it has been tested in Estonia with "Positium Tourism Barometer". The biggest problem with positioning data is privacy and surveillance, and those issues needs to be addressed and discussed very carefully.

Keywords: mobile phone positioning, LBS, social positioning method, roaming, space-time behaviour, real-time mapping, Estonia.

1 Introduction

In this paper we introduce some methodological aspects and a case study in Tartu, Estonia using mobile telephone positioning data in the researching of tourism. Thus far, border crossing and accommodations statistics have been the primary sources of quantitative statistics used in tourism studies. Nowadays, in conditions in which Europe's borders have been opened, the comprehensiveness of this approach has continually declined and at the moment, one of the main indicators describing the flow of tourists is the number of visitors and overnight stays at accommodation establishments.

The Institute of Geography, the University of Tartu and Positium ICT have experience studying and monitoring tourism using the passive mobile positioning dataset of roaming clients of EMT – the biggest mobile operator in Estonia. They developed a data-gathering method that uses the passive mobile positioning data of roaming calls in Estonia (Ahas, Aasa, Mark, Pae, & Kull, 2006; Ahas, Aasa, Roose,

& Silm, Submitted). The anonymous database contains the country of origin, location and time of the call activities of foreign phones in Estonia. This data has some perspectives for tourism research, due to its better space-time coverage and the possibility for real-time tourism monitoring (Ratti, 2005).

2 Mobile Positioning

Mobile positioning means the tracing of the location coordinates of handsets in the cellular network. There are different ways to locate a phone in the network – using the reference of antennae/cells or through GPS signals. The easiest and cheapest method is *Cell ID* – every network cell in a mobile phone network has a unique ID, and the location of a phone in the cell can be determined easily for every call activity. The geography of the cell is usually determined through base station (antenna) radio coverage. The positioning data can be defined as active and passive. *Active mobile positioning data* is collected using mobile tracing, and the location of a mobile phone is determined with a special query using radio waves (Positium, 2006).

Passive mobile positioning data – location data that is stored automatically in the databases of mobile operators when a person uses a mobile phone (call activity). This can be log files or the billing memory of an operator such as the Home Location Register in the Ericsson software used in the EMT network in Estonia (Ahas et al., 2006; Ahas et al., Submitted). The use of mobile positioning data in the investigation of space-time behaviour has been proposed by several authors (Mountain & Raper 2001), and this is called the social positioning method (SPM) in Estonia (Ahas & Mark, 2005). SPM analyses space-time behaviour with a combination of the location coordinates of mobile phones (tracing or passive data) and the social features of the phone's owners.

In this research project we used passive mobile positioning data recorded at EMT, the largest network operator in Estonia (EMT 2006). This data was recorded for all call activities made by foreign phones in the EMT network (roaming) with the precision of Cell ID. Call activities mean any active use of a mobile phone in networks: calling out and in; SMS out and in; Internet or GPRS services; location-based services. The network cell is not a fixed area; the phone normally switches to the closest or strongest radio coverage antenna. If the network is crowded, phones can be switched not to the nearest station but to any other in the neighbourhood.

3 Data

The database is unpersonalised, all respondents (foreign phone identities) remained anonymous, and the operator provided generalised data: the country identification and the cell coordinates where the phone was used. The data use conforms to the principles of confidentiality of information in Estonia and the EU regulation on the use of electronic databases (DIRECTIVE 2002/58/EC). Only the information on nationality (the country in which the phone is registered) is recorded. Every respondent is given a unique random ID number (for example: Finn No. 43204) that makes it possible to recognise the same tourist during a long trip or several visits to Estonia. An excerpt from the passive positioning database is offered in Table 1.

Table 1. Example from the mobile positioning database.

Time	Rand. ID	Country	E	N
01/04/2004 00:00:04	43204	FIN	E24-45-34.00	N59-26-36.00
01/04/2004 00:00:23	55861	FIN	E24-44-37.00	N59-25-49.00
01/04/2004 00:00:24	770841	RU	E27-44-38.00	N57-52-12.00
01/04/2004 00:00:31	505262	LAT	E24-45-34.00	N59-26-36.00
01/04/2004 00:00:35	49104	FIN	E24-44-41.00	N59-25-27.00
01/04/2004 00:00:36	586313	UK	E24-43-53.00	N59-26-06.00
01/04/2004 00:00:39	585543	UK	E24-44-37.00	N59-25-49.00

During the interval from 1 April 2004 to 31 July 2006, the database consists of approximately 21 million roaming call activities from more than 110 nationalities. On average, one tourist performed 10 call activities in Estonia. The highest number of call activities per ID were for Latvians, Danes and Norwegians – up to 20; and the smallest numbers were for Spanish, Italian and Austrian visitors, 5–7 calls per ID. The number of call activities during the study period is presented in Figure 1. The figure confirms the knowledge that tourism in Estonia is seasonal (Ahas et al., 2006). The rhythm of the weeks is another important aspect that can be seen in the figure. It indicates that there are more tourists on business days, with a maximum on Fridays and fewer on Sundays.

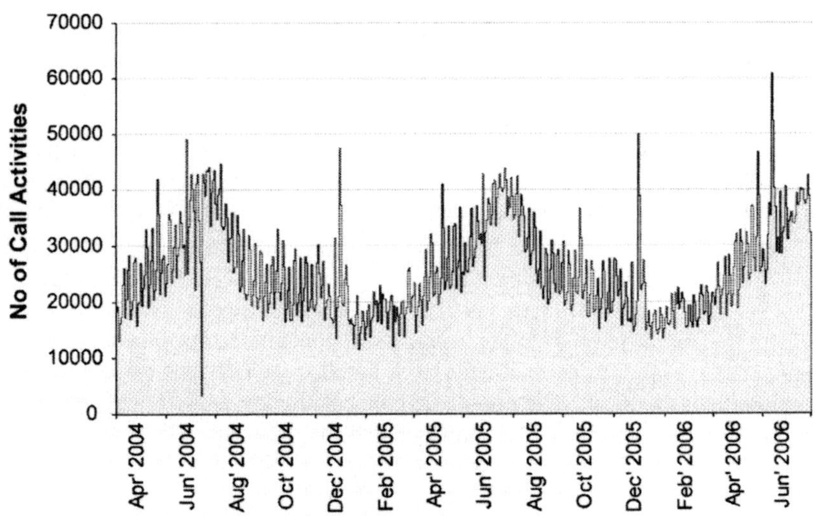

Fig. 1. Distribution of mobile positioning database entries (call activities per day) from 1 April 2004 to 31 July 2006, illustrating seasonal and weekly rhythms.

The national distribution of call activities in Estonia is similar to accommodation statistics (Table 2). It has been determined (Ahas et al., 2006) that Estonia's closest neighbours, the Finns, Latvians, Russians and Lithuanians, have proportionally more records in mobile positioning data (both call activities and IDs) than the number of nights they spend in Estonia. This is related to the large share of one-day visits of these neighbours who do not stay overnight in Estonia. Visitors from farther destinations such as Western Europe stay much longer in Estonia, and the difference between call activities and accommodation nights is smaller.

Table 2. Number of tourists in mobile positioning and accommodation data of top 12 nations for period 1.04.2004 – 31.08.2005.

Country	Mobile call activities %	Nights accommodation
Finland	51.5%	45.1%
Latvia	8.0%	2.4%
Russia	6.4%	2.3%
Sweden	6.1%	5.4%
Lithuania	4.9%	1.2%
Norway	4.2%	2.0%
Germany	3.9%	5.9%
UK	2.8%	2.7%
Poland	2.0%	0.7%
Denmark	1.5%	0.8%
Italy	1.5%	1.6%
Netherlands	0.9%	0.7%

4 Tourists in Tartu: Mobile Positioning Case Study

The objective of the study was to provide an overview of the regular patterns of foreign tourists visiting Tartu, using mobile positioning data. The results of this research were used as one source in the development of Tartu's tourism strategy, and therefore we selected 1 April 2004 - 31 March 2005 as the first reference period for the study. During this period in the city of Tartu, 37,941 people of 61 nationalities (IDs) executed call events in the EMT network, and 346,896 call events were made. During the period of the study, the following nationalities were predominant in Tartu: Finns 45%, Latvians 10%, Germans 7%, Russians 7%, Swedes 6% and Lithuanians 5%. Tartu tourism differed from the average in Estonia in terms of the smaller number of Finns (11% less) and the relatively large numbers of Latvians (6%) and Germans (3%) more than the mean. The comparison of positioning data of Tartu tourists with accommodation data (ESA 2006) indicates that the differences between the two sets of data are minimal. It is logical that Latvian, Lithuanian, Russian and Polish neighbours stay overnight somewhat less often than indicated by mobile positioning. Finns and Germans, on the other hand, stay overnight more often than indicated by positioning.

4.1 The temporal dimension of visits to Tartu.

Compared to Estonia's tourist regions, Tartu's tourism is not particularly seasonal. The presence of tourists is relatively stable throughout the year. An increase in the number of tourists is noticeable in the summer, with the maximum in July and the minimum in February. The most seasonal visitation of Tartu, which is concentrated in the summer, is that of the Germans, Icelanders and Swiss. The centre of Tartu, which has many sights, service establishments and hotels, is mainly notable for its summertime maximum and seasonal tourist pattern. In other parts of the city, seasonality in tourism is not as noticeable. The winter tourism peak in the Tartu region is associated with the large numbers of Latvian ice fishermen who visit the north-eastern area of Tartu County on Lake Peipsi. The number of Latvians who stay by the lake and travel through the city of Tartu on their way there significantly exceeds the relative importance of other winter tourists.

Another component of Tartu tourism which has a clear rhythm is weekends, which apply primarily to the nearby neighbours: Latvians, Finns, Lithuanians and Russians. In the city, this is associated with transit highways. The component of the number of tourists in the weekly rhythm is also associated with major highways (including transit) and the city of Tallinn in Estonia as a whole (Ahas et al., 2006). The weekly rhythm of visitors to Tartu is divided into two groups: a) the weekend majority of vacationers, which includes Finns and Russians; b) the maximum of business days with Latvians, Swedes, Germans and Britons. This kind of regularity is quite an important indicator of the travel destinations of tourists.

The duration of tourist visits differs from the Estonian average. More tourists make prolonged stays in Tartu than in Estonia as a whole. A total of 55% of tourists visit Tartu for 1 day, 24% of tourists visit for 2-3 days, 9% for 4-30 days and 14% for over 30 days. The number of visitors staying for relatively long periods is greater than the Estonian average. Among them, foreigners from Finland, Latvia, Russia and Sweden predominate. Many are presumably connected with study or work at the university.

4.2 The geography of the distribution of tourists in Tartu.

The distribution of tourists is very different within the city of Tartu. The city centre and the surrounding area predominate. Tourists are found in those areas on all days of the week, and the seasonal peak occurs in the summer. Naturally, Finns, who also predominate elsewhere in Estonia, make up its seasonal maximum. Nevertheless, there are proportionally more Central European tourists in the city centre in the summer months: especially representatives of Germany, Switzerland and the Netherlands (Figures 2 and 3). The proportion of Latvian, Lithuanian, Polish and Russian tourists is greater in the western part of the city, which is affected by the transit highways that pass through Tartu. The relative importance of Russians is greater in the eastern and south-eastern part of the city (Annelinn and Ihaste).

Events taking place on the outskirts of the city can also significantly affect the distribution of tourists within the city. For example, an international festival of motorcyclists in late July 50 km north of Tartu, which had a large proportion of Finns, significantly affects the numbers of tourists in the Ülejõe area (District 1 in Figure 3).

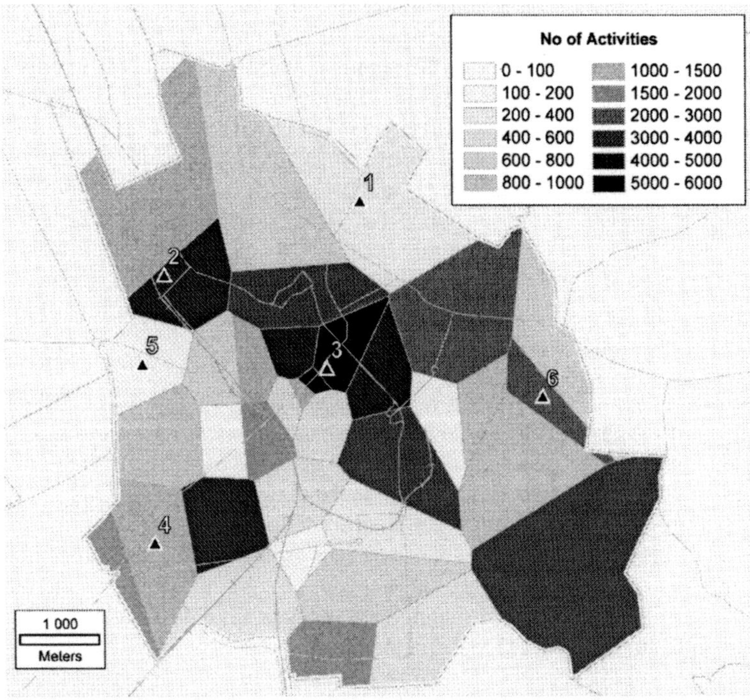

Fig. 2. The distribution of call activity in Tartu in July 2004. Districts in the city of Tartu denote the relative importance of tourists: 1-Ülejõe; 2- City Centre; 3-Supilinn; 4-Veeriku; 5-Tammelinn and FI; 6-Annelinn.

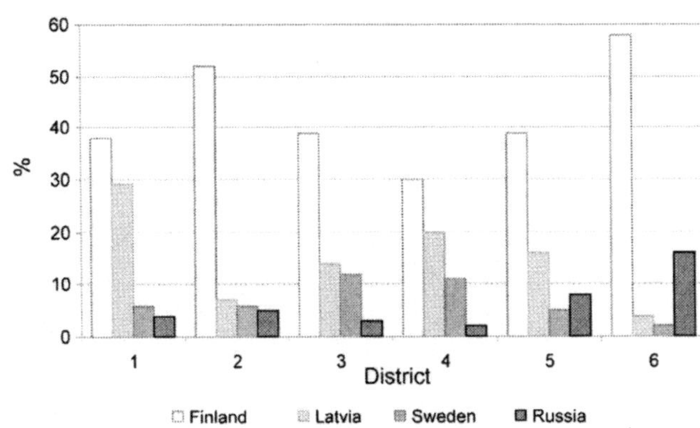

Fig. 3. The relative importance of visitors from Finland, Latvia, Sweden and Russia in districts 1-6 of the city of Tartu.

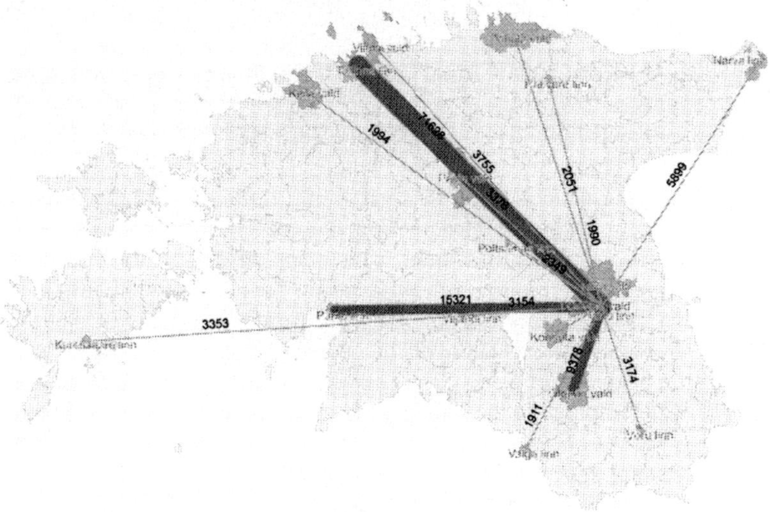

Fig. 4. The 10 most popular places in Estonia among tourists who visited Tartu, and the number of visits

We also analysed the other locations in Estonia that were visited by tourists who had visited Tartu. This information is important in marketing and developing cooperation between tourism regions in the country. The 10 most important municipalities that were associated with tourists who had visited Tartu are presented in Figure 4 above.

4.3 Monitoring tourism events

In addition to geographical aspects, mobile positioning enables the very effective analysis of the temporal distributions and space-time dynamics of events. Ordinary tourism data often does not make it possible to determine the extent and meaning of various kinds of large-scale events, because there are not enough hotel vacancies during large-scale events, and people stay at alternative places of accommodation. The organisers and supporters of such events, however, wish to trace the effect thoroughly for many reasons.

We observed events in Tartu more broadly. The effect of agricultural fairs taking place in Tartu was very great. Tartu has historically been an important agricultural centre in southern Estonia. The effect of several international events was also great. Here we present the peaks of 2004 and 2005. There was an average of 896 call events by foreigners per day in the city of Tartu during the study period.

- - 16 April 2004 – Rural Fair 2004 - 1895 call events
- 21 May 2004 – Vanemuise Cultural Street Festival 21 May; Tartu 14th French Horn Festival. – 1375 call events.

- 30 July 2004 – Tammeka Cup International Soccer Tournament 2004; Jõgeva TREF Motorcyclists' Festival – 2039 call events
- 31 December 2004 – 1 January 2005 – New Year's Eve – 1558 call events
- 21 - 22 April 2005 – Rural Fair; 4th Tartu Souptown Festival. – 2225 call events
- 30 June- 3 July – Hanseatic League Festival – 1071 call events

The International Hanseatic League Festival from 30 June – 3 July 2005 was the biggest event in Tartu in the summer of 2005 (Figure 5). Preparations for this event took place over several years and there were many visitors from both home and abroad (including delegations from other Hanseatic towns). We studied the effect of the Hanseatic Festival on local tourism using SPM data. It turned out that a total of over 10,000 call events were made over the course of the festival. There were 3000 call events on the peak day of 1 July. The call activities of tourists in Tartu during the Hanseatic Festival compared to the same period in 2004 are illustrated in Figure 5.

It is very interesting to discover an even larger tourist event that followed the Hanseatic Festival, the top event in Tartu: the EOS Peugeot Rally 2005. The rally took place on 22–23 July 2005. The driving took place in Tartu on the first of these days and in Otepää on the second day. Many of the top rally performers in the world participated. The number of foreigners who participated in the rally that briefly visited Tartu and the amount of call activity substantially surpassed that of the Hanseatic Festival, which was organised with great care, effort and costs (Figure 5). The amount of different people who used cellular phones (cellular phone ID numbers) on the peak day of the Hanseatic Festival on 1 July 2005 was 910, but this number was 1125 on the Tartu day of the EOS rally on 22 July 2005. Neighbours from nearby countries, mainly from Latvia and Lithuania, predominated at the rally. The Hanseatic Festival, however, attracted many visitors from Central Europe. Thus the relative importance of German representatives (and those from other countries of the Hanseatic League) was unprecedented, and was the largest in Tartu (Figure 6).

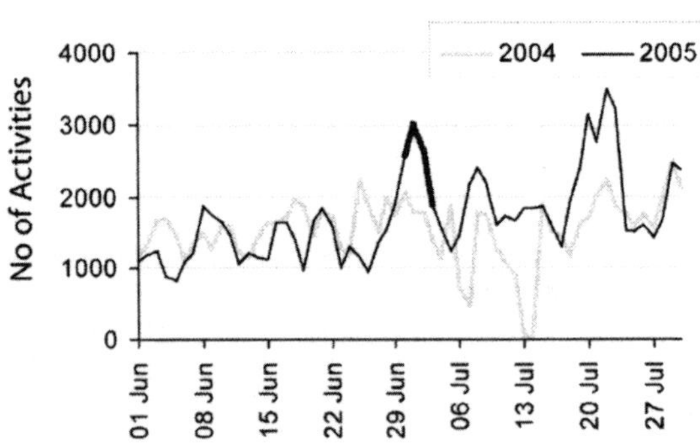

Fig. 5. The dynamics of call events in 2004 and 2005 as a comparison during the period of the Hanseatic Festival from 30 June- 1 July

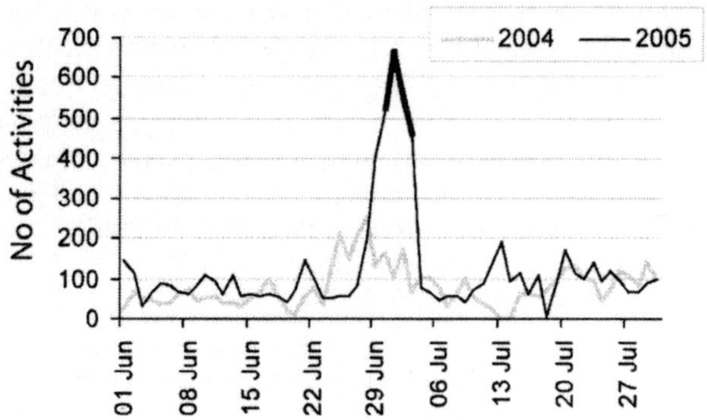

Fig. 6. Call activities by Germans in Tartu in June and July of 2004 and 2005.

5 Conclusion

As our data description and case study demonstrated, mobile positioning is a promising source of information for the investigation and management of tourism. The cost of data units of passive positioning dataset is relatively low and the quantity of data entries high. The limiting aspect is that positioning data is quantitative; there are relatively few parameters concerning the call activity in the database: the time, location and country of origin. This quantitative data allows one to analyze tourist flows to some extent, but does not answer many important questions in contemporary tourism research, such as why, how and who? Our preliminary studies proved the relevance of positioning dataset as correlations with conventional accommodation statistics in Estonia were up to 0.99 in the most visited tourist regions. Regions with less infrastructure and tourists, had much lower correlations (0.65) because of the high number of transit tourists on the highways. Cost of roaming calls and different income rates in home country may influence use of phones in destination country. This impacts needs further study.

Nevertheless, passive mobile positioning data has several advantages, which can substantiate its use and even open up new perspectives in tourism studies and management tools. This data has better spatial and temporal precision than regular tourism statistics. The precision of antennae offers more perspectives of research than accommodation statistics. Digital records of a tourist's movements make it possible to analyse space-time movement. This allows the linking of routes used by tourists with the places they visited; the connecting of sites of interest with points of entry or with final destinations in the country etc. Space-time precision enables the investigation of single events and their geography much better than had previously been possible. This allows one to study the extent and impacts of events such as fairs, concerts, sports events and also to manage crowds of visitors. Positioning data is excellent for the studying of tourism in less visited natural areas where it is difficult to use other methods such as accommodation statistics or questionnaires.

One of the biggest advantages of positioning data is the possibility of monitoring tourism in real time. The data can be gathered regularly and visualised in a real-time environment. Positium ICT have developed a real-time tourism monitoring environment on the Internet for research purposes, and this is partly used by tourism managers from Enterprise Estonia and several municipalities. This system is called the Positium Tourism Barometer, and it helps to monitor short and long term changes in tourism and to evaluate the successfulness of marketing strategies, single campaigns or investments in certain locations. Real-time maps or live maps of tourism are also interesting data sources for researchers.

There are also problems with data, such as surveillance and privacy issues, which need to be addressed properly during studies and the development of new methodologies. Mobile positioning data is very sensitive to infringed privacy borders.

References

Ahas, R., Aasa, A., Mark, Ü., Pae, T., & Kull, T. (2006). Seasonal tourism spaces in Estonia: case study with mobile positioning data. *Tourism Management* (published online in July 2006).

Ahas, R. Aasa, A., Roose, A., & Silm, S. (Submitted). Mobile positioning as a new data source and method for tourism surveys: an Estonian Case Study. *Tourism Management*.

Ahas, R. & Mark, Ü. (2005). Location based services – new challenges for planning and public administration? *Futures*, 37(6): 547-561.

Casino, V. J. D. & Hanna, S. P. (2000). Representations and identities in tourism map spaces. *Progress in Human Geography*, 24(1): 23-46.

DIRECTIVE 2002/58/EC: Directive on privacy and electronic communications of the European Parliament and of the Council of 12 July 2002 concerning the processing of personal data and the protection of privacy in the electronic communications sector. http://europa.eu.int/eur-lex/pri/en/oj/dat/2002/l_201/l_20120020731en00370047.pdf [8. Sep 2006]

EMT (2006). EMT homepage www.emt.ee.[Aug. 12, 2006]

ESA (2006). Estonian Statistical Board homepage. http://www.stat.ee. Accommodation statistics. [May 11,2006]

Hall, C. M., Page, S. (2006). *The geography of tourism and recreation. Environment place and space*. Routledge.

Kwan, M. P. (2000). Interactive Geovisualization of Activity-travel Patterns Using Three-dimensional Geographical Information Systems: Methodological Exploration with a Large Data Set. *Transportation Research C*, 8: 185-203.

Mountain, D. & Raper, J. (2001). Modelling human spatio-temporal behaviour: a challenge for location-based services. in *Proc. of the 6th Internat. Conference on GeoComputation* Eds (University of Queensland, Brisbane, Australia).

Positium (2006). Web-site of Positium ICT www.positium.ee [Sept. 5, 2006].

Ratti, C. (2005). Mobile Landscape - Graz in real time. *Proceedings of 3rd Symposium on LBS & TeleCartography*, Vienna University of Technology, 28-30. November 2005.

CAIPS: A Context-Aware Information Push Service in Tourism

Thomas Beer[a]
Matthias Fuchs[a]
Wolfram Höpken[a]
Jörg Rasinger[a]
Hannes Werthner[b]

[a] Etourism Competence Center Austria (ECCA)
{firstname.lastname}@etourism-austria.at
[b] Institute for Software technology and Interactive Systems
Vienna University of Technology, Austria
hannes.werthner@ec.tuwien.ac.at

Abstract

A context-aware information push service provides the user with tailored information regarding her/his actual situation (the *actual situation* is also referred as *context*). This paper motivates and discusses the development of a context-aware information push service. A survey is presented motivating the implementation of such a system. Further, key requirements are identified leading to a description of the system architecture, thereby giving insight into how the requirements are tackled. Finally, the rule language which is used to formally declare push processes and the inference engine translating such rules into concrete push messages is explained in detail. The push service presented in this paper is part of the overall $_{et}$Planner system, a framework for mobile tourist guides (Höpken, Fuchs, Zanker, Beer, Eybl, Flores, Gordea, Jessenitschnig, Kerner, Linke, Rasinger, & Schnabl, 2006a).

Keywords: context-awareness, push, production rule, proactive systems, ambient intelligence

1 Introduction

Tourism services are characterized by a strong need for information. Both on the consumer (i.e. tourist) as well as on the supplier side the sale, purchase, production, and consumption of a tourism product claims high effort in terms of information effort. Tourism experts therefore describe a main challenge of the tourism industry as the seamless integration of information and physical services, as well as a flexible configuration of the physical and the informational parts (Werthner, 1999). In this way intelligent information services are required in order to reduce the information retrieval effort and a possible information overload for the consumers (Höpken, et al., 2006a). The CAIPS (*Context Aware Information Push Service*) is a service designed to meet these requirements, by offering an intelligent mechanism for actively providing personalized information to tourists depending on their context. Similarly, Hinze (2003) proposed a notification system where tourists are informed about events or places in their domain of interest based on their location, profile and the actual time. Further, Cheverst, Davies, and Mitchell (2002) propose and implement both, a pull- and push-based mobile information service for the trourism domain (GUIDE). However, existing approaches are not suitable for completely coping with the requirements of CAIPS. The following scenario gives examples of possible use cases of CAIPS.

1.1 Scenario

A tourist plans to spend a weekend in Innsbruck. It is assumed that s/he has already used $_{et}$Planner during her/his trip to Vienna three month ago. Therefore s/he is already registered and known to the system by means of a user-profile. S/he has stayed in Vienna for two days and visited among other things “Schönbrunn Palace”. Two weeks before departure s/he interacts with an online booking platform to plan her/his trip to Innsbruck. In first step s/he books a room in the “Innsbruck Inn” hotel. The $_{et}$Planner system is now able to infer where s/he wants to go to and how long s/he is planning to stay. In the next step, the system queries personal information to complete her/his user profile with the necessary information for the specified region, e.g. information on activities s/he is planning to conduct. S/he loves skiing and therefore searches skiing-regions near Innsbruck. The “Axamer Lizum” seems convincing and s/he therefore schedules the activity "Skiing in the Axamer Lizum" on Saturday. Two weeks later, on Friday night, s/he arrives in Innsbruck. During night there is a spontaneous and disadvantageous weather change – strong wind comes up and it will be snowing, soon. At breakfast time a message is sent to her/his mobile device, that there will be a blizzard in “Axamer Lizum” and it is not recommendable to go skiing on that day. Additionally the message includes a number of alternative suggestions for bad-weather activities based on her/his user profile. Amongst them, the user is welcomed to visit the “Hofburg” in Innsbruck (because s/he has shown interest in similar buildings in the past) and at the same time a 10% rebate on the entry fee is offered. After her/his visit of the “Hofburg” the system pushes a SMS to her/his mobile device informing her/him that Pizza Gino offers a special lunch menu (20% off) for all visitors of the “Hofburg”. Both push information messages are triggered by business rules that have been defined by tourism-experts from the city of Innsbruck.

2 Push Services in Tourism

Prior to the design of the system described in this paper, a survey was conducted for determining the attitude towards such a system and the expected behavioural intention of potential users. Before presenting the empirical results the most promising functionalities of mobile information systems as suggested in the literature are sketched. In particular, for tourism related mobile information services the latter can be described as search & browse functionalities (Gretzel & Wöber, 2004), value adding functionalities, such as context-aware recommendation and push-functionalities, respectively (Ricci & Werthner, 2001; O'Grady & O'Hare, 2002), mCommerce functionalities (e.g. reservation, booking, ticketing, paying, etc.) as well as feedback functionalities (Forum, 2005). The aim of the briefly presented study was to identify most attractive mobile information services adequate to support tourists during their destination stay. In addition, the particular significance of the above stated functionalities has been evaluated by potential final users (i.e. tourists).

2.1 Study design

The first determination of potentially successful information services was derived from questions typically posed by tourists at prominent information points within a destination (e.g. tourist information points, welcome centres, taxi, airport, etc.). Thus, 15 qualitative interviews have been conducted in Innsbruck (Austria) during September 2005 (Rasinger, Fuchs, Höpken, & Tuta, 2006). Doing so, a total of 290 typical information requests along the destination value-chain could be identified (Bieger, 2005). In addition, focus interviews took place in fall 2005 with 17 individuals from different European countries (i.e. Italy, Germany and Austria). The obtained results led to a list comprising a total of 15 potentially successful mobile information services to be used by tourists during destination stay. Described by their functionalities and usability potentials they have been evaluated in Tyrol (Austria) in fall 2005 by tourists on the base of a quantitative pilot-study (N = 100) (Rasinger et al. 2006, p. 40). In descending order of importance six mobile information services have been rated as attractive by tourists, namely: (1) Transport & navigation (2) security assistant, (3) news & weather, (4) event information, (5) gastronomy & night-life and (6) sightseeing & shopping. Subsequently, in January 2006 data collection took place in Tyrol by interviewing a tourist sample totalling 705 individuals with respect to their perceived significance of the various functionalities for mobile information services. More precise, according to the Technology Acceptance Model (TAM) the 'intention to use' a specific mobile information service acted as dependent variable whereas the 'intention to use' the various functionalities served as independent variables (Venkatesh, Morris, Davis & Davis, 2003). Agreement measurement took place on a 6-point Likert scale.

2.2 Study results

The average age of the participants was 33.6 years with a range from 9 to 64 years, 40% were female and 60% male. The majority (i.e. 92%) of the respondents declared skiing and other sports activities as the main purpose of their current destination stay, 3% were present for business reasons. 40% of the respondents were holding a high school-, 32% a college-, and 28% a university degree. 54.9% of the respondents visited Tyrol for 3 days or less and 21.2% booked at least one tourism service via the internet. Generally spoken, the results of the pilot-study (N= 100) have been confirmed as the same mobile information services proved to be attractive for destination usage. The following sub-section displays the obtained regression results for each of the six examined mobile information services with specific consideration of the 'context-aware push-functionality'.

Table 1. Use-Intention of Mobile Information Services determined by Functionalities

Information services	Functionalities	Beta	Description
1. Transport & Navigation	*Search & Browse*	.203**	Route and transport mean, actual and target position
	Recommendation	n.s.	
	Context-aware P.	.276**	Event-based (e.g. congestion) actively proposes routes
	mCommerce	.161*	Ticketing and reservation forpublic transport
	Feedback	n.s.	
F-value: 72.87 Sig. of F = .001 Adj. R^2 = .41			
2. Security Assistant	*Search & Browse*	.360**	Search for risks per region and tourism activity
	Recommendation	n.s.	
	Context-aware P.	.442**	Active warning (e.g. storm, avalanche, etc.)
	mCommerce	n.s.	
	Feedback	n.s.	
F-value: 128.18 Sig. of F = .000 Adj. R^2 = .62			
3. News & Weather	*Search & Browse*	.363**	Actual news and weather forecasts for various regions
	Recommendation	.189*	Location and preference specific information filter
	Context-aware P.	.484**	Location-, activity- & preference-based actively informs
	mCommerce	n.s.	
	Feedback	n.s.	
F-value: 93.88 Sig. of F = .000 Adj. R^2 = .54			
4. Event Guide	*Search & Browse*	.261**	Simple and category-based search
	Recommendation	.313**	Filter for local/regional events during stay period
	Context-aware P.	n.s.	
	mCommerce	n.s.	
	Feedback	.108*	Evaluating and reading customer evaluations
F-value: 49.59 Sig. of F = .001 Adj. R^2 = .56			
5. Gastronomy & Nightlife	*Search & Browse*	.435**	Simple and category-based search
	Recommendation	n.s.	
	Context-aware P.	n.s.	
	mCommerce	.181*	Checking occupancies and making reservations
	Feedback	.163*	Evaluating and reading customer evaluations
F-value: 92.21 Sig. of F = .000 Adj. R^2 = .61			

			Continued …
6. Sightseeing & Shopping	*Search & Browse*	.373**	Simple and category-based search
	Recommendation	n.s.	
	Context-aware Push	.184*	Act. recommends sights/marts while moving in destination
	mCommerce	.199*	Ticketing (e.g. museums, etc.)
	Feedback	n.s.	
F-value: 42.63 Sig. of F = .001 Adj. $R^2 = 0.51$			
Dependent variable: Intention to Use **Sig. of (std.) Beta**: ** < 1% * <5% not sig.: n. s.			

First of all, the employed approach to statistically 'explain' the (i.e. dependent) TAM-variable 'intention to use' a specific information service by its typical functionalities proved to be adequate as for all the six examined mobile services the corresponding regression model showed significant F-values as well as relatively high adjusted R^2 values (i.e. ranging between .41 and .62). Secondly, the search & browse functionality can typically be classified as 'base-functionality' as it proved to be (i.e. significantly) relevant for all the six examined mobile information services. Interesting enough, for a total of four information services the context-aware Push functionality seems to play a significant role in determining the 'intention to use' the mobile tourist guide during the destination stay. More precise, for the three most attractive services in the eyes of the customers, namely (1) Transport & navigation, (2) the security assistant and (3) news & weather the corresponding context-aware Push functions are acting as the most prominent functionalities what can be seen from the high and strongly significant (i.e. standardized) regression coefficients (Hair, Black, Babin, Anderson, & Tatham, 2005). In addition, Push functionalities (significantly) support also the intention to use a mobile information service supporting (6) sightseeing & shopping activities in the destination (see Table 1). To summarize, in the eyes of the final users (i.e. tourists), the following context-aware Push functionalities emerged as highly relevant for mobile tourist guides to be used during destination stay (Table 2).

Table 2. Most relevant Push functionalities for mobile information services in tourism

Mobile Service	**Context based Push Functionality description**
Transport & Navigation	In the case of transport-related events (e.g. postponements, congestion, detours, etc.) the system actively informs about delays and proposes alternative routes (e.g. connection flights, busses, etc.)
Security Assistant	While moving within the destination and depending on the individual location the system actively informs about risks (e.g. storm, avalanche, etc.)
News & Weather	Based on location, individual preferences (i.e. areas of interests), and actual (e.g. tourism) activities the system actively informs about the various destination offers and weather conditions/forecasts.
Sightseeing & Shopping	While moving within destination and depending on the location and individual preferences the system actively recommends sights and shopping opportunities

After having empirically shown that context-aware *Push functionalities* play a significant role in altering the acceptance rate for mobile information services in tourism, the following sections introduce the context-aware push system (*CAIPS*).

3 Context Awareness

To have a better understanding of the proposed system it is important to know how the term *context* is used within CAIPS. One of the most often cited context definition is "Context is any information that can be used to characterize the situation of an entity. An entity is a person, place, or object that is considered relevant to the interaction between a user and an application, including the user and applications themselves." Dey and Abowd (Dey, 2000) emphasized the importance of creating "context categories". Based on the categorisations from (Dey & Abowd, 2000), (Schilit, 1994), (Schmidt & Beigl 1999), (Ryan, 1997], (Brekop & Burnett, 2003) and (Hofer, 2003) the following *context categories* were identified (see **Table**).

Table 3. Context Categories of CAIPS

Context Category	Example Instances
User	the user's demographic data or current location
Environment	actual weather
Time	time of day, or time of year
Travel	flight information
Computing	used mobile device, display size

The instances of these context-categories applied in CAIPS are used for realising the following context-aware system features:

Context-triggered message dissemination (cf. 4.3 and 4.4)
Context-driven content generation (cf. 4.3 and 4.4)
Context-driven presentation adaptation (computing context)

4 The CAIPS System

CAIPS is based on a client-server architecture, which is in the field of context-aware systems also known as the "Context-Server" approach (cf. http://www.infosys.tuwien.ac.at/Staff/sd/papers/TUV-1841-2004-24.pdf [Sep. 9, 2006]). One advantage of this approach is that the client is relieved of resource intensive operations (cf. requirement 2).

4.1 Requirements

A set of requirements for building the context-aware information push service were identified. The key requirements are:

R1: The system provider can define the sending time, the (abstract) content of a push message (PM) and the potential recipients in a declarative way compliant to the user's actual situation (context), cf. ease-of-use of the system.

R2: The system does not require additional hardware on the client side (tourist)

R3: The end-user must be able to expressively specify her/his information needs (cf. "expressive notification selection" in Mühl, 2002:3)

R4: Extendibility: The context data sources (cf. mediator and context triggers in section 4.4) should not be restricted to predefined context data sources. The CAIPS architecture must allow to further add context data sources and to easily embed them in the overall architecture.

4.2 Methodology

One of the key requirements of the proposed system is "ease of use" for the system provider (cf. *R1*), i.e. that s/he can straightforwardly define *when* to send *what* to *whom*. The proposed approach to tackle the requirement is to define push-processes through *rules*. Rules are a well known technique in the field of knowledge representation (Sowa, 2000; Brachman & Levesque, 2004). They provide an excellent trade-off between readability (i.e. understand-ability) of the knowledge representation and formal requirements. Conditional clauses (i.e. "if *condition* then *action*" clauses) were already used in pre-Christian times to express activity-instructions (cf. Jaynes, 1976). It therefore can be assumed that rules are well known for the user. Using rules addresses one of the prior objectives when designing a knowledge based system, namely the similarity to human thinking and the consequently improvement of usability (Baierle & Kern-Isberner, 2003). One of the key ideas when building CAIPS was therefore the design of a *rule-language* (see 4.3) which enables the SP controlling the push process in general. The system provider uses the language to write (production) rules which declare the sending time, the target group, and the push message's content. The content of the PM is thereby merely predefined in an abstract style, i.e. the system provider specifies the *type* of tourism service or type of additional information (respectively an aggregation of these types). The term *type* is employed similar to the term *class* known from object-oriented programming languages or *field* as referred to in the area of ontology languages (Antoniou & van Harmelen, 2004). The predefined abstract content is refined using a recommender system (cf. Beer, Höpken, Zanker, Rasinger, Jessenitschnig, Fuchs, & Werthner,, 2006), i.e. the recommender system determines the appropriate *instances* of the tourism services for every potential recipient, i.e. tourist. *Instances* in this context can be interpreted as *objects* or *individuals* as referred to in the field of object-oriented programming or ontology web languages, respectively. Using a rule language therefore addresses requirement 1. The approach to address requirement 3 is as follows. First, the user can set her/his preferences regarding a tourism service. Secondly s/he can specify her/his *information preferences* regarding a *category* of a push message. The SP is enabled to create different PM *categories* where each in turn can include several tourism services. The evaluation of these information preferences is automatically executed when the condition is checked (see 4.4). This approach stands in contrast to conventional *publish-subscribe systems* (Mühl, 2002) where the message is produced and subsequently the content is matched to the preferences of the potential recipients. The CAIPS approach instead produces tailored messages *on demand.*

4.3 Push Rule Language

Similar to active database systems (Dayal, Hanson, & Widom, 1994; Paton & Díaz, 1999) CAIPS uses an extended version of standard production rules (Brachman and Levesque, 2004), so-called E-C-A rules (*Event-Condition-Action* rules). This allows rules to be triggered by external events (see section 4.4) such as *Location*, *Weather*, or *Time* events. When the triggering event occurs the condition statement is evaluated against the connected data sources (cf. *Mediator* in section 4.4) and if the condition is satisfied the appropriate action is executed. A typical E-C-A rule applied in CAIPS for example is:

Event:	[WeatherEvent (statechange=blizzard)]
Condition:	[User.bookedEvent = outdoor AND User.bookedEvent.location = weather.location]
Action:	[Recommendation(Event)]

Because of comprehension purpose the notion of the rule syntax is in informal "pseudo code" only. The meaning of the rule is that when a weather-change occurs (e.g. a blizzard rises) an appropriate *Event* is triggered which in turn activates the condition evaluation. If there is one or more users fulfilling the condition (i.e. who booked an outdoor event today) they will be informed about a suitable indoor event. The condition statement is designed similar to the *where* clause of a SQL select statement. The result of its evaluation is a set of users (i.e. tourists) satisfying the condition. The content of the push message is generated using the recommender system and the template engine (see *Message Generator* in section 4.4) when the action is executed. As the recommender system in general takes into account the current weather conditions as part of the context it will select indoor events, only. The underlying inference process presumes *negation as failure* and is based on the *closed-world assumption* (cf. Russel & Norvig, 2003).

4.4 System Architecture

An overview of the architecture of CAIPS is illustrated in figure 1. One focus of this article is to explain the rule-based concept CAIPS is based on. The *Inference Engine* is therefore explained in more detail. The other components are briefly described as follows.

Web-Application: The frontend for the *Registration & Subscription Service* is realised as a web-application using *Cocoon* (http://cocoon.apache.org [Sep. 9, 2006]), as described in Höpken et al. 2006a.
Message Gateway: Responsible for delivery of the PMs. Beside traditional communication channels such as SMS or email a new communication channel is introduced, namely the *PP* channel (*Push→Pull*).
Rule-Editor: To assist the tourism service suppliers in creating push rules a graphical editor is developed. The tourism experts are supported in writing rules by means of a high-level interface using wizards and graphical, context sensitive editors.
Registration & Subscription Service: To provide the tourist with tailored PMs it is fundamental for the system to "know" its user. This service enables the user to specify

her/his demographic data, information preferences (cf. requirement 3), preferences concerning tourism services, or to access her/his travel-profile.

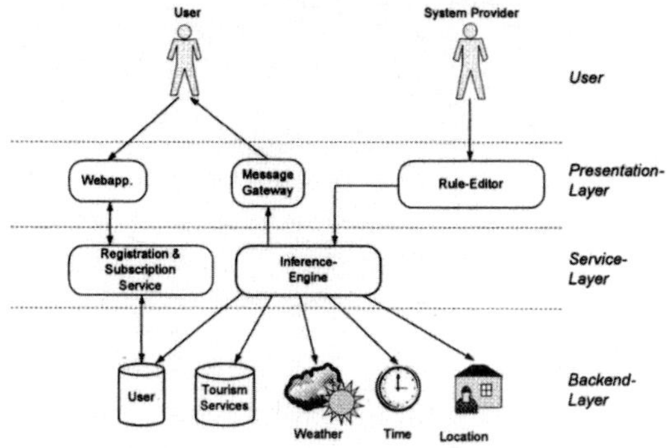

Fig. 1. CAIPS: System Architecture

4.5 Inference Engine (IE)

The IE evaluates the push rules, i.e. it transforms the rules into "real" actions. It is based on four elementary components, namely the *Event-Trigger*, the *Event-Handler*, the *Mediator* and the *Message Generator*. The concept of an abstract *Event-Trigger* enables the "plug-in" of different concrete *Event-Triggers* (cf. requirement 5) such as Time-, Location-, or Weather-Trigger. Depending on its configuration parameters (e.g. an event should be triggered if any user reaches location *y*) it triggers the occurrence of the configured event (e.g. Location *y* reached by user *u*). Context-aware applications have to deal with a huge amount of low level context data (i.e. sensor data). Tracking these fine-granular sensor data and mapping it to higher level context information (semantic or representational level) is encapsulated within the concrete Event-Triggers (cf. Christopoulou, Goumopoulos, & Kameas, 2005; Strang, 2003). The user is therefore enabled to use labels (which are mapped to a location defined via GPS coordinates) instead of using the GPS coordinates directly. The *Event-Handler* is responsible for interpreting occurring events i.e. it determines which condition is linked to the occurred event. The condition is evaluated using the *Mediator* (cf. Power, Lewis, O'Sullivan, Conlan, & Wade, 2004). To state expressive condition statements several heterogeneous data sources must be accessed, e.g. a database storing the user profile and a web-service for retrieving the user's actual location or the actual weather. The Mediator translates the condition statement (which is compliant to the shared schema) to the underlying query languages, retrieves the result and returns the result compliant to the shared schema (cf. Wiederhold, 1992; Kärger, Melis, & Ullrich, 2006; HERMES. http://www.cs.umd.edu/projects/hermes/publications/abstracts/hermes.html [Sep. 9, 2006]). The *Message Generator* uses the *Hybrid-Recommendation-Service* (as described in Beer et al. 2006; Höpken et al. 2006b) and the *Velocity* template engine (http://jakarta.apache.org/velocity/ [Sep. 9, 2006]) for generating personalised messages.

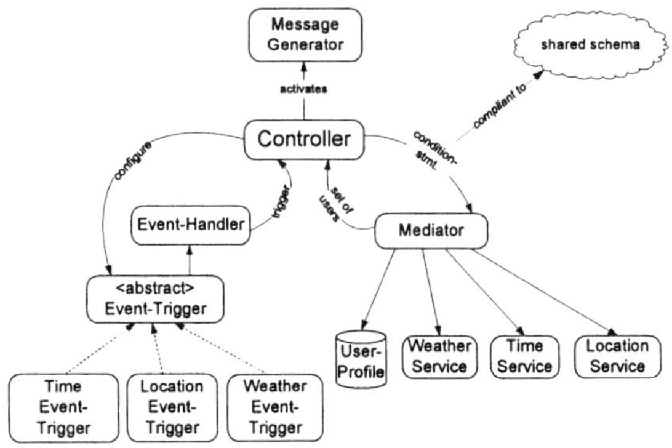

Fig. 2. CAIPS: Inference Engine

5 Conclusion and Future Work

Based on a large scale survey, push services were proved to enhance the overall intention to use mobile information systems in tourism. The proposed scenario illustrates the usefulness of such a system from the tourists' point of view. In addition, push services may leverage B2C communication by opening a new smart channel to tourists. Further, the paper explained why a rule language is well suited to control a context-aware information push service. It presented the architecture of a *context-aware information push service.* As part of the etPlanner application a first version of the CAIPS system was already implemented. A first field trial within the destination of Innsbruck took place in the autumn of 2006. The construction of the push rules applied in the field trial was based on interviews with domain experts. Future research will include an evaluation whether learning techniques are suitable for constructing useful rules.

References

Antoniou, G., & van Harmelen, F. (2004). Web Ontology Language: OWL. In S. Staab & R. Studer (Eds.), *Handbook On Ontologies*. Karlsruhe: Springer.

Beer, T., Höpken, W. R., Zanker, M., Rasinger, J., Jessenitschnig, M., Fuchs, M., & Werthner, H. (2006). An Intelligent Information Push Service for the Tourist Domain. Paper presented at the European Conference on Artificial Intelligence (Workshop on Recommender Systems), Riva del Garda.

Beierle, C., & Kern-Isberner, G. (2003). *Methoden wissensbasierter Systeme.* Hagen: Vieweg.

Bieger, T. (2005). *Management von Destinationen, 6. Auflage*. München, Wien: Oldenbourg

Brachman, R. J., & Levesque, H. J. (2004). *Knowledge Representation and Reasoning.* San Francisco: Morgan Kaufmann.

Prekop, P., & Burnett, M. (2003). Activities, context and ubiquitous computing. *Computer Communications* 26(11), 1168-1176.

Cheverst, K., Davies, N., & Mitchell, K. (2002). Exploring context-aware information push. *Personal and Ubiquitous Computing*, 6, 276–281.

Christopoulou, E., Goumopoulos, C., & Kameas, A. (2005). An ontology-based context management and reasoning process for UbiComp applications. Paper presented at the Joint conference on Smart objects and ambient intelligence, Grenoble, France.

Dayal, U., Hanson, E. N., & Widom, J. (1994). Active Database Systems. In W. Kim (Ed.), *Modern Database Systems: The Object Model, Interoperability and Beyond.* Reading/Massachusetts: Addison Wesley.

Dey, A., & Abowd, G. D. (2000). Towards a Better Understanding of Context and Context Awareness (No. GIT-GVU-99-22): Georgia Institute of Technology.

Forum, UMTS. (2005). *Magic Mobile Future.* London.

Gretzel, U. & Wöber, K. (2004). *Intelligent Search Support: Building Search Term Associations for Tourism specific Search Engines.* Information and Communication Technologies in Tourism.

Hair, J.F., Black, B., Babin B., Anderson, R.E. & Tatham, R.L. (2005). *Multivariate Data Analysis.* 6th edition, Upper Saddle River, NJ: Prentice-Hall

Hinze, A., & Voisard, A. (2003). Locations- and Time-Based Information Delivery in Tourism. Paper presented at the Advances in Spatial and Temporal Databases, 8th International Symposium. Retrieved.

Hofer, T., Schwinger, W., Pichler, M., Leonhartsberger, G., & Altmann, J. (2003). Context-Awareness on Mobile Devices - the Hydrogen Approach. Paper presented at the 36th Annual Hawaii International Conference on System Sciences, Hawaii.

Höpken, W., Fuchs, M., Zanker, M., Beer, T., Eybl, A., Flores, S., Gordea, S., Jessenitschnig, M., Kerner, T., Linke, D., Rasinger, J., & Schnabl, M. (2006a). $_{et}$Planner: An IT framework for comprehensive and integrative travel guidance. In: Hitz, M., Sigala, M., Murphy, J. (Eds.): Information and Communication Technologies in Tourism 2006, Wien, Springer-Verlag, pp.125-134.

Höpken, W., Fuchs, M., Beer, T., Linke, D., Zanker, M., Aschinger, M., & Jessenitschnig, M. (2006b). Context awareness within mobile services. Paper presented at the MobileHCI (IMAC Workshop - Innovative Mobile Applications of Context), Espoo, Finland.

Jaynes, J. (1976). *The Origins of Consciousness in the Breakdown of the Bicameral Mind.* Princeton.

Kärger, P., Melis, E., & Ullrich, C. (2006). Querying Heterogeneous and Distributed Learning Object Repositories via Ontology-Based Mediation. Paper presented at the 6th IEEE International Conference on Advanced Learning Technologies, ICALT 2006, Kerkrade, The Netherlands.

Liang, T.-P. & Wei, C.-P. (2004). Introduction to the Special Issue: Mobile Commerce Applications. *International Journal of Electronic Commerce* 8(3), 7-17.

Mühl, G. (2002). *Large-Scale Content-Based publish subscribe systems.* Technische Universität, Darmstadt.

O'Grady, M. J. & O'Hare, G. M. P. (2005). Mobile Devices & Intelligent Agents - Towards a New Generation of Applications and Services. *Journal of Information Sciences* 171(4), 335-353.

Paton, N. W., & Díaz, O. (1999). Active Database Systems. *ACM Computing Surveys*, 31(1).

Power, R., Lewis, D., O'Sullivan, D., Conlan, O., & Wade, V. (2004). A Context Information Service using Ontology-Based Queries. Paper presented at the Sixth International Conference on Ubiquitous Computing (Ubicomp'04), Nottingham, England.

Rasinger, J., Fuchs, M., Höpken, W. & Tuta, M. (2006) A Customer Based Approach to discover Accepted Mobile Information Services in Tourism. In Research@EyeforTravel, London, 5-6 June, pp. 31-46.

Ricci, F. & Werthner, H. (2001). Case Base Querying for Travel Planning Recommendation. *Information Technology & Tourism* 4(3-4), 215-226.

Russel, S. J., & Norvig, P. (2003). *Artificial Intelligence: A modern approach.* Upper Saddle River: Prentice Hall Series in Artificial Intelligence.

Ryan, N., Pascoe, J., & Morse, D. (1997). Enhanced Reality Fieldwork: the Context Aware Archaeological Assistant.

Schilit, B. N., Adams, N., & Want, R. (1994, December 8. - 9. 1994). Context-Aware Computing Applications. Paper presented at the IEEE Workshop on Mobile Computing Systems and Applications.

Schmidt, A., Beigl, M., & Gellersen, H.-W. (1999). There is more to context than location. Paper presented at the IMC'98.

Sowa, J. F. (2000). *Knowledge Representation: Logical, Philosophical, and Computational Foundations.* Pacific Grove, CA: Brooks Cole Publishing.

Strang, T. (2003). *Service-Interoperabilität in Ubiquitous Computing Umgebungen.* Ludwig-Maximilians-Universität München, München.

Venkatesh V., Morris M., Davis G. & Davis, F. (2003). User Acceptance of Information Technology: Toward a Unified View. *MIS Quarterly* 27(3), 425-478.

Wiederhold, G. (1992). Mediators in the architecture of future information systems. Computer, 25(3), 38-49.

Werthner, H. & Klein, S. (1999). *Information Technology and Tourism - A challenging relationship*. New York: Springer.

Exploring Tourist Satisfaction with Mobile Technology

JungKook Lee[a]
Juline E. Mills[b]

[a]Department of Consumer Science & Retailing

[b]Department of Hospitality and Tourism Management
Purdue University, U.S.A.
{lee205; millsje}@purdue.edu

Abstract

Wireless access with handled devices is a promising addition to the WWW and traditional electronic business. Handheld devices provide convenience, portable access, and large amounts of information to travelers. Many mobile commerce application models have been developed, however, limited research exists on mobile users' perspectives with regard to satisfaction towards mobile technology. There is a need to develop an understanding of travelers' satisfaction with mobile commerce in order to gain optimum competitive advantage. In this paper, we adapted and developed the American Customer Satisfaction Model (ACSM) to m-commerce in the tourism industry. The results of this study suggest that the degree of perception and perceived value are key factors affecting mobile travelers' satisfaction with mobile experiences. Satisfaction, in turn, influences the extent of intention to continue to use mobile devices during travel.

Keywords: Mobile commerce, customer satisfaction, the American Customer Satisfaction Model (ACSM), mobile technology

1 Introduction

In recent years, there has been significant growth in the use of mobile devices such as hand-phones, personal digital assistants (PDAs), and handheld computers. Mobile commerce is expected to grow to $250 billion worldwide by 2006 (Kumar & Zahn, 2003; Vogt, Gartner, & Pagnia, 2003). Mobile technology not only extends the reach of wired networks, but also serves as an alternative information channel providing a new range of opportunities to travelers as well as changing the way certain information-related activities are conducted. In the past, mobile devices were regarded as a luxury for individuals. However, mobile commerce (m-commerce) now offers great flexibility for the tourism industry both to suppliers and travelers. Users can surf the web, check e-mail, read news, pay transaction and quote stock prices using these hand held devices. From the supplier's perspective, the promotional message can be changed much more quickly than through the use of traditional media. M-commerce is now becoming the standard in handling travel yields effectively (Eriksson, 2002). Ninety percent of households in Japan, South Korea and urban China now own cell phones, as do 80% of households in Western Europe, 60% in Canada, and three out of four households in the U.S. (CNET News, 2006). With this skyrocketing rate of ownership of mobile devices (Fernadez, 2000; Bughin, Lind, Stenius, & Wilshire, 2001), considerable research efforts are now being devoted to understanding how mobile technology could support the information needs of travelers, ranging from touring in museums (Yang, & Jun, 2003; Oppermann & Specht, 1999), transportation and parking information (Rodseth, Jenssen, Moen, & Asmundvaag, 2001), location identification (Eriksson, 2002), to tracking and navigation (Corona & Winter, 2001). The findings of these research efforts imply that travelers are interested in new ways to carry out their travel plans. However, limited research exits on traveler's satisfaction with mobile technology and mobile devices. The purpose of this study, therefore, is to develop a conceptual framework that examines and explains the factors influencing mobile users' satisfaction and purchase intention. The study is organized as follows: first, the background of the study is described; second a tourist satisfaction model for mobile devices is proposed with corresponding hypotheses; third, the proposed model was tested using confirmatory factor analysis and structural equation modeling. The study ends by presenting conclusions and discussing study implications.

2 Study Background

2.1 M-commerce

M-commerce, in this study, is defined as a transaction that takes place via wireless Internet-enabled technology (through handheld computers, cellular phones, personal digital assistants (PDAs), or palmtop computers) while allowing for freedom of movement for the end user (Wei & Ozok, 2005). Wireless Fidelity (Wi-Fi), the transmission of short-ranged radio signals between a fixed-based station and an end-user's mobile device, is the driving technology that facilitates m-commerce (Wei & Ozok, 2005). M-commerce can also be defined as any transaction with a monetary value either direct or indirect that is conducted over a wireless telecommunication network (Clarke, 2001). M-commerce is about the explosion of applications and services that are becoming accessible from Internet-enabled mobile devices involving new technologies, services, and business models. Mobile phones or PDAs impose very different constraints from desktop computers traditionally used in e-commerce transactions opening the door for the entry of a slew of new applications and services. These new devices and applications makes it possible for the user to access the Internet while walking down the street with friends and family or while driving, looking for a nearby restaurant or gas station.

There are many advantages to mobile services including: high availability, the ability to enjoy e-commerce services regardless of time or location, as well as portability and location awareness capabilities (Siau, Lim, & Shen, 2001; Varshney & Vetter, 2002). The nature of mobile technology is summarized as follows: *Ubiquity* - services and applications provided via wireless Internet will be available anywhere and at anytime (Tsalagidou, Veijalainen, & Pitoura, 2000; Anckar & D'Incau, 2002). Thus, travelers will have larger flexibility to access and receive information and services from different physical locations; *Localization awareness* - Users can obtain their physical location at any particular moment via the mobile network operator or Global Positioning System (GPS). Users are able to track personal belongings for security or request emergency services (Tsalagidou et al., 2000); *Immediacy* - users are given the capability to react in time critical situations, this capability also allows users to make spontaneous decision (Anckar & D'Incau, 2002); *Personalization* - this feature is also called customization. Since user can receive personalized service, they may gain unique experience, distinct from other existing technologies (Advani & Choudhury, 2001). Personalization is a means of meeting the customer's needs more effectively and efficiently, making interactions faster and easier, and increasing customer satisfaction and the likelihood of repeat visits; *Broadcasting* - mobile technology provides an efficient means to disseminate information to a larger population, wherein users can use this features to share information of common interest with others such as picture taking while on vacation; *Portability* – is the functionality pertaining to the fixed and mobile networks which allows a telephone customer in the U.S., for example, to retain their local phone number if they switch to another local telephone service provider; *Identification* - SIM-cards can be used as electronic signature, making the individual identity always recognizable. Electronic payment with mobile devices thus becomes a reality.

2.2 Mobile Technology and Tourism

M-commerce is a new and exciting field in tourism as such the literature about tourist satisfaction with M-commerce is limited. Unlike other industries that will embrace mobile communication as an added convenience to consumers, the tourism industry view m-commerce as an integral part of their customers' overall travel experiences (Eriksson, 2002; Schmidt-Belz et al., 2003). M-commerce not only extends the benefits of the Web, but also allows for unique services enabled by the convergence of the Internet with mobile technologies. Travel service providers are finding new ways to increase customer loyalty, generate supplemental revenue streams, and reduce operating costs using m-commerce. Similarly, the costs of obtaining information are reduced for customers and suppliers with a wide diversity of information being represented on one mobile device terminal, which further reduces the information search costs for potential tourists (Kumar & Zahn, 2003; Vogt, Gartner, & Pagnia, 2003).

2.3 The American Customer Satisfaction Model

Customer satisfaction generally means the customer's reaction to the state of fulfillment, and customer judgment of the fulfilled state (Oliver, 1997). Normally, the main factor determining customer satisfaction is the customers' own perception toward the quality of the product or service. Several mobile device studies attempted to explore the antecedents of customer satisfaction (Gerpott, Rams, & Schindler, 2001; Kim, Park, & Jeong, 2004). These studies build on the notion that retention measurement and analysis of factors affecting it are vital for business success. However, variables such as loyalty and intention were examined as one concept. The American Customer Satisfaction Model (ACSM) is a general, cross-industry model that provides market-based performance measures for firms, industries, sectors and nations (Turel & Serenko, 2006). The original ASCM measures the quality of goods and services as experienced by consumers (Fornell, Johnson, Anderson, Cha, & Bryant, 1996) and gauges their actual and anticipated consumption experiences. According to ACSM, there are positive associations between perceived expectation and perceived value, and perceived value and satisfaction. In turn, satisfaction has a positive association with repurchase likelihood. The model also demonstrates high predictive capabilities. The ACSM and its adaptations have been utilized in many studies in various industries such as banking services (Mukherjee, Nath, & Pal, 2003), conferences (Gorst, Wallace, & Kanji, 1999), and retailing industries (Arnett, Laverie, & Meiers, 2003). In this study, the ACSM was used to measure the relationship among mobile travelers' satisfaction and other constructs. The original ACSM was modified for the characteristics of both tourism industry and mobile travelers. The model is shown in Figure 1.

3 Research Hypotheses

Consistent with previous studies that employed ACSM, a number of hypotheses are suggested. Researchers acknowledge that the satisfaction level can be influenced by such factors as the perception and experiences (Turel & Serenko, 2006). Kim et al. (2005) also argued that perceived value has an effect on users' satisfaction. It can be also assumed that satisfaction positively influences the intention. Therefore, it is proposed in this study that experience and perceptions are antecedents that influence the two determinants of satisfaction and intension to use mobile devices. Thus, the following hypotheses were developed and tested.

H1: Reliability towards m-technology is a significant predictor of satisfaction and intention to use M-technology;

H2: Reliability toward m-technology is positively related to perception and perceived value of m-commerce usage;

H3: Travelers' m-commerce technology experiences are significant predictors of satisfaction and intention to use M-technology;

H4: Travelers' technology experiences are positively related to perceptions and perceived value of M-commerce usage;

H5: Perception and perceived value are positively related to users' satisfaction with m-technology;

H6: Users' satisfaction with m-technology positively influences the intention to use mobile devices for travel.

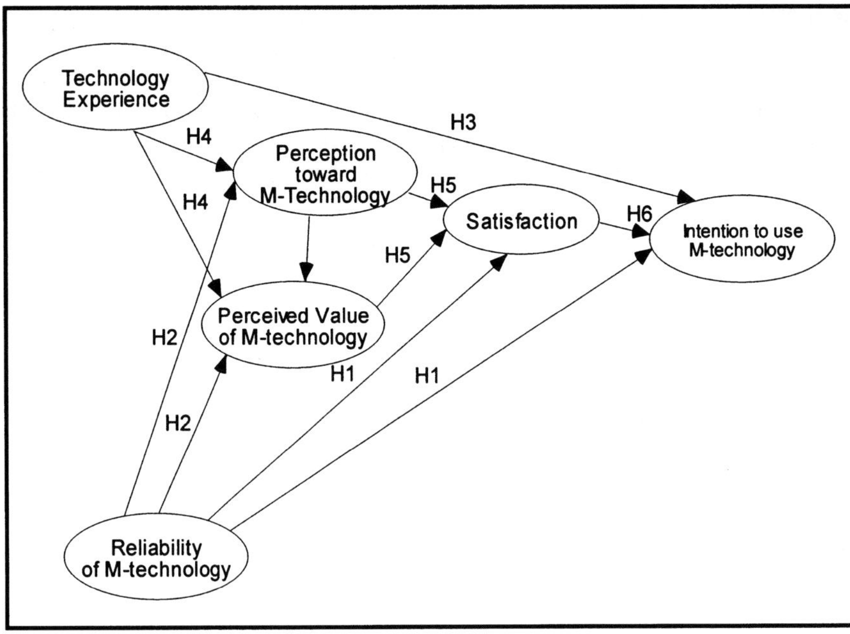

Fig. 1. Hypothesized Model of Tourist Satisfaction with Mobile Technology

4 Methodology

The study employed an online data collection process. For the online survey, the data was purchased through E-reward. The sample was screened as the mobile users who had prior travel experience. E-Reward provides one of the highest quality means of conducting primary online market research and gauging consumer interest. An e-mail message was distributed to the E-reward.com members along with a cover letter and the Website questionnaire's address. The survey comprised of 54 questions focusing largely on travelers' responses on: (a) trip experiences; (b) general attitudes toward the use of wireless devices; (c) technology experiences; (d) the constructs that directly influence behavioral intention in the model; and (e) demographic information. The items for the five constructs uses a seven-point Likert scale (1 = strongly disagree; 7 = strongly agree).

A list of the survey items and the constructs they represent is shown in Table 2. The respondents were assured that all responses were kept strictly confidential and no unsolicited marketing material would be directed to the as a result of the survey. Also respondents were not allowed to submit more than one entry using blocking IP number process. The survey was conducted over a one-month period from April 1 to May 1, 2005. A follow-up reminder e-mail was sent out to maximize the return rate. In total, 332 members of the E-reward.com Panel were contacted, and this effort resulted in 241 qualified completed responses for a 72.6% response rate.

5 Results

5.1 Profile of Respondents

First, the demographic profile of respondents in the survey was identified through frequency analysis. Table 1 provides a profile of the respondents. Among the 241 survey respondents, there are slightly more females than males, while over 50% of the respondents were in the 30-49 age range. Another 25% of the mobile users were over 50 years of age. One notable characteristic of the respondents was that a large majority (91%) of the respondents were highly educated (some college education or higher), and about 60% of the respondents' household incomes were over $60,000. This is consistent with the previous findings that online respondents are more likely to be professionals, and report higher incomes and education (McDonald & Adam, 2003). In terms of mobile experience, approximately 84% of the respondents had used mobile devices for more than three years. With regard to Internet experience, over 90% of the respondents had used the Internet for more than four years, and over 50% of the respondents surfed the Web more than 10 hours per week.

Table 1. Profile of Respondents

Characteristic	*f*	%	Characteristic	*f*	%
Gender			How long using mobile devices		
Male	137	55.6	Less than 1 year	16	6.6
Female	107	44.4	1 to 2 years	25	10.4
Age			3 to 4 years	88	36.5
Under 20	1	0.4	4 to 6 years	54	22.4
21 to 30	49	20.3	More than 6 years	58	24.1
31 to 40	71	29.5	How long using the Internet		
41 to 50	58	24.1	Less than 1 year	2	0.8
51 to 60	44	18.3	1 to 2 years	4	1.7
Over 69	18	7.4	3 to 4 years	14	5.8
Education			4 to 6 years	47	19.5
High School	22	9.1	More than 6 years	174	72.2
Some College	68	28.2	Web surfing hours in a week		
College graduate	95	39.4	Less than 1 hour	9	3.7
Post graduate	56	23.2	2 to 5 hours	33	13.7
Household income			6 to 10 hours	65	27.0
Less than 24,999	18	7.5	11 to 20 hours	60	24.9
25,000 to 39,999	34	14.1	Over 20 hours	74	30.7
40,000 to 59,999	47	19.5			
60,000 to 79,999	46	19.1			
80,000 to 99,999	28	11.6			
Over 100,000	68	28.2			

5.2 Measurement Model

Confirmatory factor analysis (CFA), using AMOS 4.0, was performed to analyze the underlying factor structure of the proposed constructs (Schumacker & Lomax, 1996; Byrne, 2001). Key statistics (item means, confirmation factor loadings, and reliability tests) for all variables considered in this study are shown in Table 2. Each scale was assessed for construct validity by examining the standardized CFA factor loading of items. Scale reliabilities were estimated and all six constructs exceeded the standard acceptance norm of 0.70 (Landis & Koch, 1977). Three items did not meet the standard of construct validity and were eliminated.

Table 2. The result of Confirmatory Factor Analysis

Latent variables	Observed variables of items	Mean	CFA Loadings	Construct Reliability
Mobile Experience				0.79
	Mobile devices enhance the quality of my travels	5.84	0.77**	
	Mobile devices enable me to have more convenient travels	5.47	0.76**	
	Using mobile devices enhances the effectiveness on my travels	5.53	0.94**	
	I have the knowledge necessary to use mobile devices while I am traveling	5.58	0.87**	
Perceived Value of M-technology				0.74
	Using mobile devices increases my travel productivity	5.28	0.83**	
	Using mobile devices during my travel fits into my travel style	5.48	0.77**	
	Learning to operate mobile devices would be easy for me	5.59	0.60**	
Perception towards M-technology				0.82
	Mobile technology can't be trusted because there are many technical problems	5.09	0.94**	
	In general, I can't rely on mobile technology for communication	4.74	0.87**	
	Mobile technology is useful when I consider the cost	4.77	0.70**	
	Mobile technology is valuable when I consider the cost	4.72	0.73**	
Satisfaction towards M-technology				0.84
	Overall, I am satisfied with mobile devices	5.11	0.91**	
	Overall, I am satisfied with my travels with mobile devices	5.16	0.89**	
Intention to use M-technology				0.75
	I predict I would use mobile devices for my "future travels"	5.54	0.92**	
	I intend to use mobile devices for my "next travel"	5.52	0.94**	
	I intend to use mobile devices at hotels for my "future travels"	5.30	0.85**	

5.3 Structural Equation Model

A separate set of structural equation model (SEMs) was run to assess the associations between the dimensions of each variable. SEM was used here because of its capacity to measure the causal relationship between sets of unobserved (latent) variables.

The analyses are presented in the Figure 1, which shows the path diagrams and relevant results. The chi-square statistics for the analysis was statistically significant. The model had a somewhat satisfactory goodness-of-fit statistics. The overall fit indices for the structural model indicate a chi-square (χ^2) of 158.6 with 128 degrees of freedom ($p = 0.00$).

As shown in Table 3, a number of additional factors were taken into consideration in assessing the model fit (Hair et al, 1998). The results indicate that all hypothesized paths are supported. As hypothesized, dimensions of personalization are positively and directly related to attitude, the latter in turn positively influence purchase intention. The same pattern applies to privacy dimensions as well. That is, dimensions of privacy are positively related to attitude towards privacy, which, in turn, exerts positive influence on purchase intention. The model also shows that attitudes influence purchase intention. Consequently, in summary we can say that higher privacy and personalization levels can potentially lead to higher product purchase intention online. [chi-square =158.6, Normed chi-square, p=0.00, GFI=0.96, NFI=0.92, CFI=0.96, RMSEA=0.06]

Table 3. Goodness of fit indices

	Values obtained
Absolute fit measures	
Chi-square	158.600
p-level	0.000
Non-centrality parameter (NCP)	979.93
Goodness of fit index (GFI)	0.96
Root mean square residual (RMSR)	0.09
Root mean square error of approximation (RMSEA)	0.06
Expected cross validation index (ECVI)	1.64
Incremental fit measures	
Adjusted goodness of fit index (AGFI)	0.91
Tucker Lewis index (TLI)	0.95
Normed fit index (NFI)	0.92
Comparative fit index (CFI)	0.96
Parsimonious fit measures	
Normed chi-square	2.23
Akaike information criterion (AIC)	226.62

The path diagram for the SEM model (Figure 1) represents the direction and magnitude of the direct impact through the positive and negative signs of the path coefficients and the absolute value of the standardized coefficients. The results of the path coefficients supported all of the hypotheses except for H1 and H2. The results indicated that the direct relationship between technology experience to perception (0.74) and perceived value (0.82) which were positive at $p < 0.01$ level. This supports the third research hypothesis. Both perception (0.76) and perceived value (0.87) were positively related to users' satisfaction (H5). This also indicates that perceived value has more influence on users' satisfaction. Finally, users' satisfaction was highly related to intention to use mobile devices (H6). However, the first two hypotheses were rejected at $p < 0.01$ level. The final SEM Model result is shown in Figure 2.

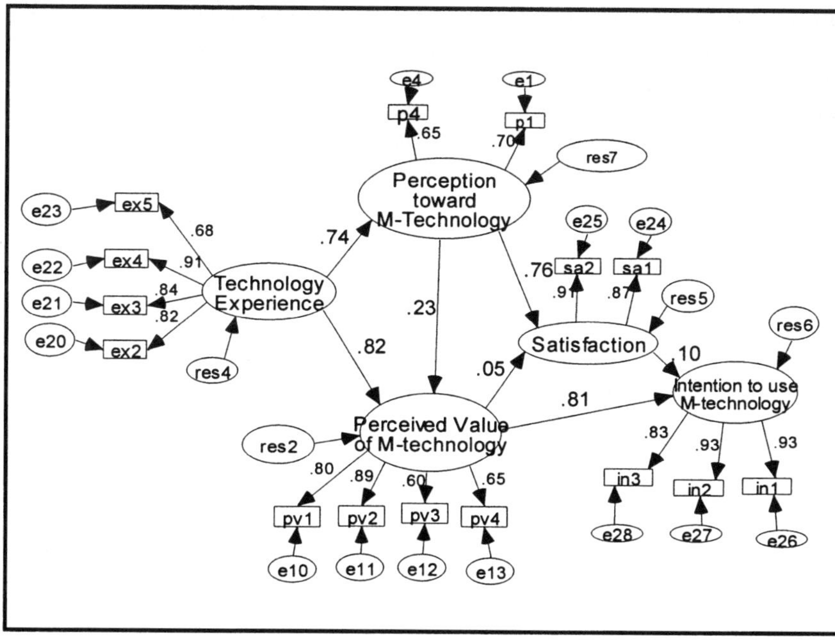

[Model fit stat; chi-square =158.6, p=0.00, GFI=0.96, NFI=0.92, CFI=0.96, RMSEA=0.06]

Fig. 2. Final Model of Tourist Satisfaction of Mobile Technology

6 Conclusions and Implications

The purpose of the study was to apply an adaptation of the ACSM to mobile travelers. This measure of satisfaction is suggested to be an important performance indicator for the tourism industry. The study demonstrates that the adaptation of the ACSM adequately describes the relationship between perceptions and experience to satisfaction of mobile travelers. Particularly, the study suggests that the degree of perception and perceived value are key factors affecting mobile travelers' satisfaction with their mobile experiences. The finding of this research also indicates that developing positive travelers' perception and perceived value is crucial to their satisfaction. Satisfaction, in turn, influences the extent of intention to continue to use mobile technology. As such, highly satisfied customers tend to demonstrate a high likelihood of repurchasing mobile technology devices.

There are some limitations in this study. The variables were limited in perception and perceived value and some variables in both perception and perceived value were overlapped. Future studies should examine those variables and should make sure about that. Another limitation is the generalizability of sample in the study. This research drew from a sample from E-reward.com Panel. Therefore, it cannot be assumes that the respondents were a representative sample of the population of all travelers in the U.S. Mobile commerce is set to become one of the most promising and lucrative growth markets. Understanding consumers' perception and satisfaction is very important in tourism industry.

Directions for future research on satisfaction, perception, perceived values, and experience of mobile travelers in travel industry are as follow: First, our analysis relies on cross-sectional data, thus, to provide an even more convincing case for causal interpretations of variable correlations, additional longitudinal research is needed in which exogenous factors are captured before data on endogenous criteria are collected. Second, the constructs in this study were measured by questionnaire items asking for respondents' attitudinal opinions. New research can help by explaining this measurement approach to include indicators of actual customer usage behaviors. Our work did not take into consideration views from the industry perspectives. Empirical research exploring determinants of the constructs from the industry perspectives would be beneficial and aid with greater generalization. Third, there are other factors influencing users' satisfaction. These must be structurally analyzed for their effects on travelers' satisfaction. In particular, an importance research task is to examine whether these factors function as an adjusting variables in the existing interaction. Our study on mobile users' satisfaction is an initial step toward understanding customer behavior in M-commerce. A major contribution we believe is that this study addresses the gap in the literature by developing a model that explores specific characteristics of tourist satisfaction with mobile device usage. We hope our findings will encourage further research and more in-depth and extensive analyses to demystify the driving forces of mobile commerce.

References

Advani, R. & Choudhury, K. (2001). Making the most of B2C wireless. *Business Strategy Review*, 12 (2), 39-49.

Anckar, B. & D'Incau, D. (2002). Value-added services in mobile commerce: An analytical framework and empirical findings from a national consumer survey. In Proceedings of the *35th Hawaii International Conference on System Science*, Hawaii, USA, 2004.

Arnett, D. B., Laverie, D. A. & Meiers, A. (2003). Developing parsimonious retailer equity indexes using partial least squares analysis: A method and applications. *Journal of Retailing*, 79 (3), 161-170.

Buhalis, D. & Licata, M.C. (2002). The future of e-tourism intermediaries, *Tourism Management*, 23 (3), 207-20.

Bughin, J., Lind, F., Stenius, P. & Wilshire, M. (2001). Mobile portals: mobile for scale. *The McKinsey Quarterly*, 38 (2), 118-127.

Byrne, B.M. (2001). *Structural Equation Modeling with AMOS: Basic Concepts, Applications and Programming*, Lawrence Erlbaum Associates, Mahwah, NJ.

Christian, R. (2001). Developing an online access strategy: issues facing small- to medium-sized tourism and hospitality enterprises. *Journal of Vacation Marketing*, 7, 2, 170-178.

Chetwynd, C. (1999). The exhibitionists. *Marketing Week*, 21 (43), 33 -41.

Clarke, I. (2001). Emerging value propositions for m-commerce. *Journal of Business Strategies*, 18 (2), 133-148.

CNET News (April, 2006). Mobile browsing becoming mainstream. 14.

Corona, B. & Winter, S., (2001). Navigation information for pedestrians for city maps. In Konecny, M., Friedmannova, L, Golan, J., Kolar, M. (Eds.), *GI in Europe: Integrative – Interoperable – Interactive. Proceedings of the 4th AGILE Conference on Geographic Information Science (*pp. 189-197). Masaryk University Brono.

Cravens, D.W, Shipp, S. H., & Cravens, K. S. (1993), Analysis of co-operative interorganizational relationships, strategic alliance formation and strategic alliance effectiveness. *Journal of Strategic Marketing*, 55-70.

Eriksson, O. (2002). Location Based Destination Information for the Mobile Tourist. *In* Wöber K.W., Frew A. J. & Hitz M. (Eds.) *Information and Communication Technologies in Tourism*, , Springer-Verlag Wien, Innsbruck, 22 – 25, Jan 2002.

Fernadez, A. (2000). The future of mobile telephony. *Presentation to Mobile Telephony and Communications*. Madrid, Spain, 22-23 May.

Fornell, C., Johnson, M. D., Anderson, E. W., Cha, J. & Bryant, B. E. (1996). The American customer satisfaction index: nature, purpose, and finding. *Journal of Marketing*, 60 (4), 7-18.

Gerpott, T. J., Rams, W. & Schindler, A. (2001). Customer retention, loyalty, and satisfaction in the German mobile cellular telecommunications market. *Telecommunications Policy*, 25 (4), 249-269.

Gorst, J. K., Wallace, W. & Kanji, G. K. (1999). Customer satisfaction at the Sheffield World Congress. *Total Quality Management*, 10 (4), 561-568.

Kim, M. K., Park, M. C. & Jeong, D. H. (2004). The effects of customer satisfaction and switching barriers on customer loyalty in Korean mobile telecommunication services. *Telecommunication Policy*, 28 (2), 145-159.

Kumar, S. & Zahn, C. (2003). Mobile communications: evolution and impact on business operations. *Technovation*, 23 (6), 515-520.

Landis, J. R. & Koch, G. G. (1977). The measurement of observer agreement for categorical data. *Biometrics*, 33, 159-174.

Mukherjee, A., Nath, P. & Pal, M. (2003). Resource, service quality and performance triad: A framework for measuring efficiency of banking services. *Journal of the Operational Research Society*, 54 (7), 723-735.

Oliver, R. L. (1997). *Satisfaction: A behavioral perspective on the customer*. Boston: Irwin McGraw-Hill.

Oppermann, R. & Specht, M. (1999). A Nomadic Information System for Adaptive Exhibition Guidance. In the *Proceedings of the International Conference on Hypermedia and Interactivity in Museums (ICHIM 99)*. Washington, USA, 23 – 25 September 1999.

Poon, A. (2001), The future of travel agents. *Travel & Tourism Analyst*, 3, 57-80.

Schumacker, R.E. & Lomax, R.G. (1996), *A Beginner's Guide to Structural Equation Modeling*, Lawrence Erlbaum Associates, Mahwah, NJ.

Siau, K., Lim, E. & Shen, Z. (2001). Mobile commerce: promise, challenges, and research agenda. *Journal of Database Management*, 12, 3, 112-120.

Sussmann, S. & Baker, M. (1996). Responding to the electronic marketplace: lessons from destination management systems, *International Journal of Hospitality Management*, 15 (2), 99-112.

Turel, O. & Serenko, A. (2006). Satisfaction with mobile services in Canada: An empirical investigation. *Telecommunication Policy*, 30(4), 314-331.

Rodseth, J., Jenssen, G. D., Moen, T. & Asmundvaag, B. (2001). ICT in road traffic. *In proceedings of the Eight World Congress on Intelligent Transport Systems*, 30 Sep. – 4 Oct., Sydney, Australia.

Tsalagidou, A. Veijalainen, J. & Pitoura, E. (2000). Challenges in Mobile Electronic Commerce, *In Proceedings of IeC2000. 3rd International Conference on Innovation Through E-Commerce*. Manchester UK, Nov. 14th-16th.

Varshney, U. & Vetter, R. (2002). Mobile commerce: framework ,applications and networking support. *Mobile Network and Applications,* 7 (3), 185-198.

Vogt, H., Gartner, F. C., & Pagnia, H. (2003). Surpporting fair exchange in mobile environments. *Mobile Network and Applications*, 8 (2), 127-136.

Wei, J. & Ozok, A. (2005). Development of a web-based mobile airline ticketing model with usability features. Industrial Management & Data Systems, 105 (9), 1261-1277.

Will, G. (2004). *Upstart airline shows direction of industry*. The Chicago Sun Times, Chicago Sun Times Inc., Chicago, IL, available at: http://web.lexis-nexis.com

Wireless Computing (2003). All about Wi-Fi. *Computer Reports*, 68 (9), 20-32.

Yang, M. C., Wang, G.C. & Tsai, P. S. (2003). The design of the PDA-based museum guiding system

Combination of Information Sources in Travel Planning A Cross-national Study

Ingvar Tjostheim[a]
Iis P. Tussyadiah[a]
Sigrid Oterholm Hoem[b]

[a]Temple University
{ingvar, iist}@temple.edu
[b]Innovation, Norway
Sigrid.Oterholm.Hoem@invanor.no

Abstract

This paper presents results from a study about the Internet as an information source for travel planning based on interviews with travelers in 13 countries in 2005. In 1997, a similar large scale survey was carried out in 15 European countries. The study shows a dramatic but well known change in information sources used by travelers since 1997. The Internet has become the most preferred information source by approximately 50% of the travelers. Travelers using the Internet as their primary source of information mostly combine it with other sources such as friends and relatives, brochures, guidebooks, and travel agents. A logistic regression analysis was performed in order to study the significance of demographics and countries on the preference of Internet as the first information source.

Keywords: Internet, information source, information search, travel planning, consumer behavior, cross-national study.

1 Introduction

The Internet is one of the most important marketing and distribution channels in the travel and tourism industry. Many travelers are using the Internet to seek information and purchase tourism-related products. The Internet has been widely used as a source of information as it saves cost and time invested for information searching process (e.g. for transportation, phone calls, etc). Another reason is that the internet can provide highly tailored content to users according to their preferences because it can be customized to a great extent (Newhagen & Rafaeli ,1996).

Consumer behavior research on information search has been going on quite extensively since the early 1970s (Arndt, 1986). There are a number of studies focusing on different aspect related to this topic in the field of travel and tourism (Schul & Crompton, 1983; van Raaij, 1986; Schmidt & Sprend, 1996: Fodness & Murray, 1997; 1999; Vogt & Fesenmaier, 1998; Gursoy & Umbreit, 2004). Travelers may need different information; the content of information that the travelers seek depends on a number of factors. For instance, extensive information acquisition may be expected for unknown destination and for expenditures involving large financial outlays (van Raaij, 1986).

Information is used in deciding among different alternatives such as destinations, holiday activities, transportation modes, accommodation, departure date and duration of a trip. Dellaert et al. (1998) presents a conceptual framework for travel decisions in which information search precede each of these choices. It is also possible to look at information from a different perspective. An example is Snepenger & Snepenger (1993: 830) who write: "For many vacationers, gathering, processing, and evaluating information is an integral part of the travel experience." Not all travelers are spending a lot of time on information search, but it seems that on most occasions the tourists are using a relatively long time on this activity before a trip (Dellaert, 1999).

Information search process can be divided into internal and external search. Initially, information search takes place internally when people use their long-term memory for relevant product knowledge as a basis to make decisions in traveling (Fodness & Murray, 1997; Vogt & Fesenmaier, 1998). When internal search cannot provide sufficient information, people turn to external sources, which can be marketing dominated such as brochures from tour operators, guidebooks, advertising and commercials, etc, or non-marketing dominated sources such as friends, relatives, and personal experiences (Engel, Blackwell & Miniard, 1990; Pan & Fesenmaier, 2006).

Information sources for travelers and tourists can be classified in different ways. Fodness and Murray (1997: 507) divide between source of information (commercial or noncommercial) and type of information (impersonal or personal) in their classification. Fodness and Murray (1997) state that: "Leisure tourists differ in their information search behavior such that homogenous groups can be formed on the direction of their search, defined by the specific source(s) used." Vogt and Fesenmaier (1998) distinguish the information sources into several categories: social, personal, marketing, and editorial. The Internet, as a form of information source, can fall into different categories. A travel portal and tourism board websites belong to the marketing category even though their contents are normally not labeled as marketing. Some travelers might have their private websites where they share their travel experiences. These personal websites as well as commercial websites also contain recommendations from/to travelers (Dellaert, 1999). The Internet is an interactive medium and communication between travelers in the Internet is quite common. Newspapers, magazines and other publishers are also using the web as a medium to publish travel stories or what can be labeled as editorial content. Hence, the Internet can also belong to the other categories.

In this paper, a cross national survey of experienced travelers is used in order to study information sources in a travel planning context. The following research questions are explored:

- How important has Internet become compared to other information sources,
- What are the differences and similarities pertaining travelers from the 13 countries,
- Based on a logistic regression analysis, are demographic and nationality variables associated with the preference for Internet as the most important information-source?

2 Method

In 2005, the Norway national tourist board, called "Innovation Norway," commissioned a trans-national survey from the market research company, MMI Synovate in Norway and companies in the Synnovate group in the other countries. This survey (named the 2005 survey) was targeted to travelers that had taken a vacation abroad in the last three years; a vacation that lasted more than four days and was not paid by an employer. Even though Norway also has short term visitors, the national tourist board chose not to target this segment for this survey. First, approximately 1000 telephone (CATI) interviews were carried out in each of the 13 countries: Denmark, Finland, Sweden, Germany, Spain, France, Italy, the Netherlands, UK, Norway, Russia, USA, and Poland. These countries represent the main markets for incoming tourism to Norway.

The purpose at this stage was to use a probability sample to estimate the travel population and the targeted market segments for the tourist board. To be included in the targeted population, an individual needs to have preference for an activity, such as nature-oriented vacation. Individuals who were interested in a typical package holiday to a destination in the Mediterranean region, for example, were excluded from the web-based survey. Secondly, a web-based survey was used for a follow up study targeted at individuals with the Internet access and relevant travel profiles, i.e. individuals that meet the above mentioned criteria. In this follow-up survey, the respondents were asked questions regarding what type of vacation they prefer, which could be nature and scenery oriented, out-door activities, culture, etc.

A number of useful studiės have used convenience samples. However, when the purpose of a study is to make estimates about market size or to describe a current trend, it is important to collect data with good validity. The data set presented in this paper should not be regarded as a random sample in the strict sense of the term (e.g. with very low or no non-response), but it is a good quality data set in particular compared to most convenience samples or self-recruited samples.

Table 1 presents the results of the two surveys: (1) a telephone survey used to estimate size of potential markets and (2) a web based survey used for a follow-up study in topics related to travel behavior, information sources, motivation for travel, destinations of interest, etc. Column (2) and (3) of Table 1 present the total population in each country with 18+ years of age and the percentage of the population who use Internet frequently. Column (4) and (5) present the number of targeted population for the web survey in each country (individuals that meet the criteria) and the percentage of frequent internet users in the targeted population. Based on the figures in column (4) and (5), even though not all respondents that had been on a vacation abroad the last three years were Internet users, they comprise a high percentage. It is important to notice that a high percentage of the respondents in the web-base survey were frequent Internet users. Hence, it is possible to argue that the survey is somewhat biased toward Internet and Internet usage.

Table 1. Total population and Internet/population (CATI survey) and targeted populations (web-based survey)

Countries (1)	Population 18+ yrs of age (2)	Internet-population in % of total population (3)	Targeted population, travelers, web survey (4)	% frequent internet users / targeted population (5)
(Countries in both surveys)				
Denmark	4.2m	76%	2.9m	78%
Finland	3.9m	69%	2.6m	74%
Sweden	7.1m	80%	5.5m	85%
Germany	67.3m	56%	36.7m	64%
Spain	35.7m	48%	16.5m	65%
France	45.8m	51%	20.3m	62%
Italy	47.2m	43%	21.3m	62%
Netherlands	12.2m	83%	8.6m	86%
UK	44.8m	63%	23.7m	68%
(Additional countries, 2005 survey)				
Norway	3.5m	75%	2.5m	78%
Russia	143m	36%	8.3m	60%
USA	218m	80%	122.9m	85%
Poland	30m	51%	15.9m	73%
Total Respondents	N=13001	N=13001	N=13668	N=13668

Table 2 presents the most important source of information for vacation planning according to the respondents, i.e. the primary source they used in the information search process. It is important to keep in mind that only Internet users can answer a web-based questionnaire. It is possible to present the Internet as an alternative information source to non-Internet users, but it is given that a non-Internet user will not prefer this information source.

According to the figures in Table 2, the Internet is chosen as the primary information source by respondents from all countries (Poland by 37%, and all other countries by more than 40% of the respondents). Additionally, the Internet is more than three times as popular as the second most preferred alternative for most countries. The facts show that the Internet has widely become the most important source to seek information in travel planning context. This is a key finding in this study.

Table 2a. Primary information sources (web survey)

Information Sources	Total Targeted Population	1	2	3	4	5	6
Internet	47%	41%	45%	49%	52%	42%	43%
Guidebooks	13%	13%	12%	15%	9%	13%	14%
Friends and family	12%	19%	16%	9%	8%	11%	12%
Travel agent	10%	6%	5%	10%	4%	13%	8%
Brochures from tour operator	4%	7%	6%	1%	18%	6%	5%
TV documentaries	3%	4%	4%	1%	3%	6%	4%
Local tourist office	2%	2%	1%	2%	0%	1%	1%
Magazines	2%	1%	2%	1%	1%	1%	1%
Travel fair	1%	0%	1%	1%	1%	1%	1%
Advertisement	1%	1%	1%	1%	1%	1%	0%
Newspapers	0%	3%	3%	4%	2%	0%	1%
Radio	0%	0%	0%	0%	0%	0%	0%
TV commercial	0%	0%	0%	0%	0%	0%	0%
Other	3%	2%	2%	4%	3%	3%	6%
None	3%	1%	1%	1%	0%	2%	3%
	N=13668	N= 1433	N= 1475	N= 1137	N= 643	N= 1000	N= 1000

Countries: 1 = Sweden, 2 = Norway, 3 = Denmark, 4 = Finland, 5 = Germany, 6 = Netherlands

Table 2b. Primary information sources (web survey)

Information Sources	7	8	9	10	11	12	13
Internet	48%	48%	45%	45%	37%	45%	51%
Guidebooks	9%	11%	14%	13%	18%	5%	13%
Friends and family	13%	13%	7%	10%	14%	22%	12%
Travel agent	7%	7%	13%	15%	9%	8%	9%
Brochures from tour operator	9%	10%	7%	4%	5%	2%	1%
TV documentaries	3%	2%	3%	3%	3%	5%	3%
Local tourist office	2%	2%	2%	2%	2%	1%	1%
Magazines	1%	2%	3%	2%	2%	3%	2%
Travel fair	0%	1%	1%	1%	0%	1%	1%
Advertisement	1%	1%	0%	0%	1%	1%	1%
Newspapers	1%	0%	0%	0%	0%	1%	0%
Radio	0%	0%	0%	0%	0%	0%	0%
TV commercial	0%	0%	0%	1%	1%	0%	0%
Other	3%	1%	2%	3%	4%	7%	2%
None	2%	2%	2%	2%	5%	2%	4%
	N= 1000	N= 1000	N= 1000	N= 1000	N= 1000	N= 1000	N= 1000

Countries: 7 = UK, 8= France, 9 = Italy, 10 = Spain, 11 = Poland, 12 = Russia, 13 = USA

Travelers are using more than one kind of information source (Tjostheim 2002; Gursoy & Umbreit 2004). Hence, it is important to look at the combination of sources used by potential travelers. Table 3 presents the additional information sources used by the respondents in combination with the Internet (the respondents could chosen more than one sources). Four sources that are mostly used as additional sources in combination with the Internet are friends and relatives, brochures, guidebooks, and travel agents. The importance of friends and relatives as information sources is highlighted in previous studies (Fodness & Murray 1999; Bieger & Laesser 2004). Bieger and Laesser (2004) point out that informal information from friends and relatives is important in travel planning, and is even more important and discriminates travel behavior after a definite trip decision. Travel programs and documentaries in television rank high utility as information sources. In five out of 13 countries (i.e. UK, France, Italy, Russia, and USA), TV documentaries are the second largest additional information sources used by those using Internet as the primary source. Tourists are likely to refer to multiple publications by tour operators (such as brochures) for more detailed information on specific activities or attractions in the destination. Travel agents are often used as information source by those who want to reduce risks (Bieger & Laesser 2004).

Table 3a. Additional information sources used in combination with the Internet

Information Sources	**All 13 countries**	**1**	**2**	**3**	**4**	**5**	**6**
Friends and family	50%	59%	62%	57%	40%	35%	50%
Guidebooks	49%	54%	53%	54%	49%	52%	48%
Travel agent	37%	32%	31%	42%	43%	36%	34%
Brochures	49%	55%	60%	57%	52%	43%	47%
TV documentaries	26%	35%	35%	15%	39%	27%	28%
Newspapers	18%			30%	30%		
Magazines	31%					28%	25%

Countries: 1 = Sweden, 2 = Norway, 3 = Denmark, 4 = Finland, 5 = Germany, 6 = Netherlands

Table 3b. Additional information sources used in combination with the Internet

	7	8	9	10	11	12	13
Friends and family	38%	26%	40%	35%	50%	38%	26%
Guidebooks	38%	43%	49%	52%	48%	38%	43%
Travel agent	34%	40%	43%	36%	34%	34%	40%
Brochures	54%	46%	52%	43%	47%	54%	46%
TV documentaries	20%	22%	39%	27%	28%	20%	22%
Newspapers			30%				
Magazines	29%	34%		28%	25%	29%	34%

Countries: 7 = UK, 8 = France, 9 = Italy, 10 = Spain, 11 = Poland, 12 = Russia, 13 = USA

3 A Regression Analysis on Demographics and Nationality

Stepwise logistic regression can be used in the exploratory phase of research task (Menard, 2002). Gursoy and Umbreit (2004) argue that culture, represented by countries in their analysis, is one of the most important factors to influence which source(s) of information travelers utilize to make travel decision. This study seeks to find other important factors that would likely to influence the choice of information source(s) other than cultural background. Demographics variables were chosen as the independent variables additionally to countries (nationalities). In this study, a forward stepwise logistic regression analysis (5 steps) was performed to find out variables that predict respondent's choice on primary information source, i.e. the internet or others. A binary dependent variable can be made by coding "Internet as the preferred information source" as one (1) and "others (not Internet) as the preferred information source" as zero (0). The first output of the logistic regression is presented in table 4. The results show that a number of independent variables are significant in predicting the model (i.e. with p-value less than the critical point 0.05). However, it is important to present more output results before the model can be accepted as good.

Table 4. Variables in the Equation

		B	S.E.	Wald	df	Sig.	Exp(B)
Step 5	Denmark			101.037	12	.000	
	Finland	-.019	.090	.044	1	.834	.981
	France	.148	.106	1.969	1	.161	1.160
	Italy	-.106	.092	1.318	1	.251	.899
	Netherlands	-.252	.097	6.808	1	.009	.777
	Norway	-.135	.094	2.056	1	.152	.874
	Poland	-.241	.085	8.013	1	.005	.786
	Russia	-.550	.094	34.323	1	.000	.577
	Spain	-.347	.091	14.476	1	.000	.707
	Sweden	-.381	.092	16.977	1	.000	.683
	Germany	-.383	.087	19.310	1	.000	.682
	UK	-.286	.096	8.795	1	.003	.751
	USA	-.025	.092	.072	1	.789	.976
	Age 18-29 yrs old			237.973	4	.000	
	Age: 30-39	.940	.072	168.965	1	.000	2.560
	Age 40-49	.898	.072	156.704	1	.000	2.455
	Age 50-59	.601	.072	69.860	1	.000	1.823
	Age 60+	.444	.072	37.505	1	.000	1.559
	Gender male/female	.272	.036	58.724	1	.000	1.313
	Education: low			29.864	2	.000	
	Education: medium	-.328	.063	27.062	1	.000	.721
	Education: high	-.134	.041	10.998	1	.001	.874
	Income: low			16.835	3	.001	
	Income: medium	-.019	.058	.109	1	.741	.981
	Income: high	.112	.053	4.460	1	.035	1.119
	Income: unwilling to answer	.179	.060	8.910	1	.003	1.196
	Constant	-.786	.100	61.756	1	.000	.456

The Hosmer and Lemeshow Goodness-of-Fit Test divides subjects into deciles based on predicted probabilities and then computes a chi-square from observed and expected frequencies. If the Hosmer and Lemeshow Goodness-of-Fit test statistic is 0.05 or less, then the null hypothesis is rejected, i.e. no difference between the observed and predicted values of the dependent implying that the model's estimates fit the data at an acceptable level. The classification table is a 2 x 2 table which tallies correct and incorrect estimates for the null model with only the constant. The columns are the two predicted values of the dependent, while the rows are the two observed (actual) values of the dependent. In the logistic regression model, a classification table compares the predicted values for the dependent variable with the observed values in the data. A high percentage means that the chosen regression equation (with the chosen independent variables) predicts correctly most of the time. The outputs for these two tests are presented in the table 5 and 6.

Table 5. The Hosmer and Lemeshow test

Step	Chi-square	Df	Sig.
1	.000	3	1.000
2	6.628	8	.577
3	4.465	8	.813
4	8.442	8	.392
5	4.233	8	.835

Table 6. Classification table

Observed	Predicted		
	Others 0	Internet 1	Percentage correct
Others 0	5675	1857	75.3
Internet 1	3823	2323	37.8
Overall percentage			58.5

According to table 5 one should not imply that the model estimates fit the data at an acceptable level. Moreover, the overall percentage is not high enough; only 58.5% of the data set can be explained by the model. Hence, nationality and demographic variables are not appropriate enough to predict the behavior of information source choice, i.e. associated with the question of who prefers and does not prefer the Internet as the most important information source. However, the finding can be a useful input for those who will perform similar surveys. There are many sub-categories in the internet, but the Internet is only considered as one category in this survey. As many travelers seek information on various types of websites, future survey should consider distinguishing many sub-categories of internet as information source. The choice of information sources in travel planning can also be influenced by other factors shaping travelers segmentation in a different way; i.e. not by nationalities and demographics but by interests and types of information sought. Hence, future surveys should emphasize on e.g. motivational statements of the respondents, expectations of the future vacation, and types of information they are trying to search specifically on destinations, accommodations, activities, etc. These variables are likely to have influences on type of information source that the travelers will use in planning their travel.

4 Discussion and Concluding Remarks

The respondents in this survey are individuals who are more experienced in traveling than the average citizen of the country. For the travel and tourism industry, the "non-travelers" and those who do not travel abroad are not as important as the more frequent travelers. Additionally, from the point of view of a national tourism board, knowing the behavior of international travelers is particularly important. Gursoy & Umbriet (2004) studied information sources on a transnational survey that has many similarities with the one presented in this paper. Nine of the countries were the same in both surveys and both focused on the use of information sources by travelers in planning a vacation. As expected, the Internet has become much more important since 1997 when this survey was performed. It is likely that the Internet will be even more important in the future.

Gursoy and Umbriet conclude, based on their analysis for EU travelers in 1997, that the national-culture of travelers is likely to influence their information search behavior. A key finding from the 1997 study is that travel agents are the most frequently utilized external information source by international travelers from almost all EU member states vacationing in other European countries. Moreover, in the study they identified five traveler segments and only in one of these segments Internet is an important (distinct) information sources. It is important to notice that the respondents in the 1997 were not asked to choose the most important information source as in the 2005 survey, only which ones they are using. However, an important change has taken place. Brochures from travel agents were the most frequently used information sources in 1997. While 45% answered that Internet was the most important information source, only 14% (all 13 countries) answered brochures from tour operator or travel agents (e.g. telephone conversation, meeting at travel agents office) in 2001. There are some differences between the 13 countries in the 2005 survey; nevertheless Internet is in a division by itself. A significant change has taken place; Internet has become the most important information source for many travelers. According to the 2005 study, around 47% chose Internet as number one. In addition, 73% of those that chose another information source as their primary source also use Internet as an additional source. It means that approximately 85% of all the respondents did use Internet when planning a vacation. There was no distinction between package holiday and individual travel in the 1997 survey, and in the 2005 survey, potential respondents who were only interested in package holiday were excluded from the sample. A study by Tjostheim (2002) based on a survey in 2001 showed that individuals planning a package holiday chose brochures as the most important information source while Internet was chosen as the most important information source by individual travelers. There are limitations to the 2005 survey and to the analysis presented in this paper. It is a weakness of this study (as in the 1997 survey) that Internet is considered as one category of information source and is not divided into a number of different sources. It is necessary and appropriate to distinguish between sub-categories of Internet (Tjostheim, 2002). Information sources for travel planning can be a website of a national tourism board, travel agent or other intermediaries, personal websites, etc. A survey on the use of each subcategory of internet can be valuable to draw implications on designing travel websites and providing customized information to travelers in different countries. The model fit with demographics and nationalities is not acceptable in this paper. Nevertheless there are some implications for further studies on travelers' choice of information sources for travel planning. Despite using demographics and nationalities, further studies can emphasize on characteristics of travelers/respondents such as their travel motivation and types of information sought. It is likely that Internet will become even more important in the future for travelers. This study focuses on the pre-travel phase; the planning phase. As the use of the mobile Internet (wireless phones and PDAs) increases and more and more hot spots are built, Internet will also become very important as information source in the travel phase for travelers on the move. The trend will broaden research potentials on internet as a primary information source in tourism and travel planning context in the future.

References

Arndt. J. (1986). Paradigms in Consumer Research: A Review of Perspectives and Approaches. *European Journal of Marketing* 20(8), 23-40.

Bieger, T., & Laesser, C. (2004). Information Sources for Travel Decisions: Toward a Source Process Model. *Journal of Travel Research* 42(4), 357-371

Dellaert. B. G. C. (1999). The Tourist as Value Creator on the Internet. In *Information and Communication Technologies in Tourism* 1999 (pp. 66-76). Innsbruck: Springer Wien New York.

Dellaert. B. G. C et al. (1998). Multi-faceted tourist travel decisions: a constrain-based conceptual framework to describe tourists' sequential choices of travel components. *Tourism Management* 19(4), 313-320.

Engel, J. F.; Blackwell, R. D. & Miniard, P. W. 1990. Consumer behavior 6th ed. Fort Worth, Texas: The Dryden Press.

Fodness. D. & B. Murray (1997). Tourist Information Search. *Annals of Tourism Research,* 24(3), 503-523.

Fodness. D. & B. Murray (1999). A Model of Tourist Information Search Behavior. *Journal of Travel Research,* 37(February), 220-230.

Gursoy. D & Umbriet, W. (2004) Tourist Information Search Behaviour: Cross Cultural Comparison of European Member States. *International Journal of Hospitality Management,* 23, 55-70

Menard. S. (2002) Applied Logistic Regression Analysis. 2nd Edition. Thousand Oaks, CA: Sage Publications. Series: Quantitative Applications in the Social Sciences, No. 106. First ed., 1995.

Newhagen, J. E., & Rafaeli, S. (1996). Why communication researchers should study the Internet: A dialogue. *Journal of Communication,* 46, 4-13.

Pan, B., & Fesenmaier, D.R. (2006). Online information search and vacation planning process. *Annals of Tourism Research,* 33(3), 809-832.

Schmidt. J. B. & Spreng R. A. (1996). A Proposed Model of External Consumer Information Search. *Journal of the Academy of Marketing Science,* 24(3), 246-256.

Schul. P. and Crompton J. L. (1983). Search Behavior of International Vacationers: Travel-Specific Lifestyle and Sociodemographic Variables. *Journal of Travel Research* 22(3), 25-30.

Snepenger, D. & Snepenger, M. (1993). Information Search by Pleasure Travelers. in *VNR'S Encyclopedia of Hospitality and Tourism.* New York. Van Nostrand Reinhold. 830-835.

Tjøstheim. I. (2002). The Internet in Competition with the Traditional Information Sources: A study of Vacation Planning for Package vs. Non-Package Travel. In *Information and Communication Technologies in Tourism 2002* (pp. 166-176). NewYork: Innsbruck Springer Wien

van Raaij. W. F. (1986). Consumer Research on Tourism. Mental and Behavioral Constructs. *Annals of Tourism Research* 13, 1-9.

Vogt. C. A. & Fesenmaier, D. R. (1998). Expanding the Functional Information Search Model. *Annals of Tourism Research* 25(3), 551-578.

Virtual Travel Communities: Self-Reported Experiences and Satisfaction

Svetlana Stepchenkova[a]
Juline E. Mills[a]
Hua Jiang[a]

[a] Department of Hospitality and Tourism Management
Purdue University, USA
{svetlana, millsje, jiang5}@purdue.edu

Abstract

Virtual communities have revolutionized the way people interact and have important marketing implications as a viable business model, particularly in the tourism industry. Virtual travel communities (VTCs) in general provide service benefits sought by community members along with pleasurable VTC experiences. This is a challenging task, since multiple factors, social, psychological, and technology used, contribute to end users' satisfaction with VTCs. This study examined experiences related by VTC members at different satisfaction levels in seven VTCs using CATPAC content analysis software. Implications for technology designers and virtual community managers are discussed.

Keywords: Virtual Travel Communities, Satisfaction, Experiences, CATPAC.

1 Introduction

Entirely new social environments and mechanisms, such as virtual communities, forums, blogs, wikis, and role playing games, have emerged in the last 10-15 years with the growth of the Internet (Nabeth, 2005). Virtual communities revolutionized the way people socialize, exchange information, access resources, and perform transactions. These virtual environments are becoming a viable business model for companies and organizations, as they bring together people of similar interests (Hagel & Armstrong, 1997; Kozinets, 1998). The travel industry, one of the first industries to go online, has long recognized the potential of virtual travel communities (VTCs) for destination and product promotion. VTCs make it easier for people to obtain information, maintain connections, develop relationships and, eventually, make travel-related decisions. However, the successful operation of a virtual community requires a thorough understanding of what brings people there in the first place, what their underlying needs are, what social laws govern members' conduct, and what technology it should implement to support its functions (Wang, Yu, & Fesenmaier, 2002). Effectively designed and managed VTCs contribute to stronger customer satisfaction, which can result in higher spending on travel-related products and services, customer retention, and, given the information-intensive nature of tourism products, decrease in promotional costs, providing economic gains to both VTC organizers and members (Buhalis, 1998; Rothaermel & Sugiyama, 2001). This study analyzed experiences of VTCs members provided in the form of qualitative responses to the "Digital Identity Management in VTCs" survey (Jiang, 2005) in order to understand what issues contributed to lower satisfaction level with VTCs. The paper concludes with implications of the study findings for VTC designers and management.

2 Study Background

The most often sited definition of a virtual community, first given by Rheingold (1994, p.57-58), is that of "social aggregations that emerge from the Net when enough people carry on public discussions long enough, with sufficient human feelings, to form webs of personal relationships in cyberspace. A virtual community is a group of people who may or may not meet one another face to face, and who exchange words and ideas through the mediation of computer bulletin boards and networks." Rothaermel and Sugiyama (2001) points out that a virtual community has common aspects with a community of mind described by Tonnies (1967), but without the bounding influence of space and time. Virtual communities are also similar to an organizational community defined by Lawrence (1995), where in the process of social interaction community members follow a certain behavioural code accepted by the community. Preece (2000) states that a virtual community generally include four elements: (1) people who communicate with one another as they attempt to satisfy their needs or perform particular roles; (2) a shared purpose on which the community is based – whether it be a common interest, special need, or information exchange; (3) guiding rules of communication within the community, or communication policy; and (4) implemented technology which supports, mediates, and facilitates the communication process in the community.

As the travel industry experiences strong growth, travel planning and booking are among the most popular online activities. In the U.S., currently nine out of ten consumers used the Web in the summer of 2005 to plan trips or purchase travel (www.etcnewmedia.com [March 25, 2006]). VTCs can provide tourism organizations with a more effective method for communicating products and services with the result being increased brand awareness and strengthened brand associations. To build a strong VTC that facilitates communication, information exchange, and, ultimately, transactions, an effective system of interrelated technology solutions must be in place. For example, the system implemented by virtualtourist.com administers end user authentication, access rights and restrictions, account profiles, passwords, and other attributes. This system is enforced by moderators and also regulates the style of communication among participants, accepted conduct, privacy and security policies, and repercussions for non-compliance with community rules (Wang et al. 2002). Dealing with all these concerns in virtual communities is a complex task as it involves not only technical but also social and psychological aspects (Wellman & Gulia, 1999). If end users are not satisfied with how the community functions, is managed or are unable to effectively use the technology, the successful application of VTCs may be at risk resulting in loss of members (Allison, Currall, Moss, & Stuart, 2004).

Customer satisfaction is viewed by scholars as a principal factor to the success of organizational profitability (Anderson & Srinivasan, 2003). Satisfaction is best understood as ongoing comparative evaluations of what was expected prior to the consumption experience and the actual level of product/service acquisition (Oliver, 1997). Research on the loyalty of Internet retail customers placed e-satisfaction as central to understanding intended behavior of Internet-channel customers (Winer, 2001; Mills & Morrison, 2003). Consumer satisfaction in an online environment is viewed as an important predictor of customer loyalty, which, in turn, leads to a firm's successful performance and economic vitality (Winer, 2001; Anderson & Srinivasan, 2003). Extending Oliver's (1997) definition to the VTC context, end users' satisfaction can be termed as an evaluative response to the overall performance of the virtual community. While the expectancy-disconfirmation theory considers satisfaction as primarily a cognitive process, a number of studies indicate that not only expectations and overall judgments but also affective evaluations contribute considerably to customer satisfaction response (Westbrook & Oliver, 1991). In this research the expectancy-disconfirmation paradigm, as well as affective component of satisfaction, are taken into account when evaluating consumer experiences. Analysis of positive and negative experiences related by VTC members shed light on what aspects of VTC performance can affect members' satisfaction scores.

3 Methodology

3.1 Data collection

Textual data used in this research was obtained from the "Digital Identity Management in VTCs" study conducted as part of the "Design and Use of Digital Identity" project funded by the National Science Foundation (NSF) in September 2005. The items selected for use in this study were: the three items that measured satisfaction with VTC on a 1-5 Likert-type scale (1 being the lowest and 5 being the highest satisfaction response), the item asking for a free-elicitation response on personal experience with VTCs, five items on demographic information, and one item on the frequency of Internet usage. The choice of components to measure satisfaction response included measurement of the expectation component "So far, how has your experience met your expectation in this community" (Q1), affective component "I consider my choice to participate in this community a good one" (Q2), and overall judgment "Based on all of your own experience, how satisfied overall are you when you communicate with other members in this community" (Q3). The open-ended Experience question was: "Briefly describe your experience with members in this community" (Q4). In total, 206 responses were obtained over the fifteen-day publication period of the survey questionnaire. The total number of hits was 712 and 206 respondents completed the questionnaire, generating a 28.93% response or cooperation rate. The data was screened for irregularities such as missing data and duplicate entries. The missing data rate was low for scale items and relatively high for the open-ended question (Q4), which had 61 missing entries out of 206 (29.6%). No abnormalities in data distribution were detected and no multicollinearity was found between the items. The data was judged adequate for further analysis.

3.2 Content analysis technique

Content analysis examines textual data for patterns and structures, develops categories, and aggregates them into perceptible constructs. Content analysis is capable of capturing a richer sense of concepts within the data due to its qualitative basis which, at the same time, can also be subjected to quantitative data analysis techniques (Roberts, 2000). A central idea of quantitative content analysis is that "many words of text can be classified into much fewer content categories" (Weber 1985, p.7). Despite critique that the method disregards the semantic structure of the language, which occasionally inflates the theme count, and is not sensitive enough to reveal what meaning the speaker had intended for the identified themes the method has long been employed in social studies due to its clear methodological reasoning based on the assumption that the most frequent theme in the text is most important. This study used CATPAC software that has long been employed in the content analysis of political speeches, focus groups interviews, marketing, and tourism-related research to identify the prevalent themes in textual comments of respondents to Q4. As stated by Woelfel (1998, p.11) in the manual, "CATPAC is a self-organizing artificial neural network that has been optimized for reading text. CATPAC is able to identify the most important words in a text and determine patterns of similarity based on the way they are used in text."

4 Results

4.1 Group comparisons

The majority of the survey participants were single, under 35 years of age, with Bachelor or higher degrees, income above 40K, and who use the Internet more than 5 hours per week. Two groups of respondents were identified based on their satisfaction scores. Among 206 respondents to the survey, 42 reported low or neutral levels of satisfaction (Strongly disagree, Disagree, or Neutral) for items Q2 or Q3 or disconfirmed expectations (Much worse than expected, Worse than expected) for item Q1. This group was labelled Negatives. The remaining 164 respondents were labelled Positives. The overall satisfaction score was calculated for every member of the two groups as the average of the three satisfaction scores (Q1, Q2, and Q3). Mean satisfaction score and standard deviation along with the number of textual responses for the two groups, Positives and Negatives, are given in Table 1.

Table 1. Positives and Negatives: Textual comments and satisfaction scores

Satisfaction Level	Textual Comment	Textual Comment (%)	No Comment	No Comment (%)	Mean Sat Score	SD
Negatives (42)	23	54.76%	19	45.24%	3.37	0.40
Positives (164)	122	74.39%	42	25.61%	4.47	0.47
Total (206)	145		61		4.25	0.61

The two groups, Positives and Negatives, were found statistically different with regard to their satisfaction level (Table 2). No significant differences at 0.05 level were detected between the groups on demographic and the Internet usage variables. At 0.10 level the groups differed on the Education variable with chi-square and p-value of 13.114 and 0.069 respectively, the Positives group being more educated.

Table 2. T-test results for the Positives and Negatives groups

			Levene's Test for Equality of Variances		t-test for Equality of Means		
Satisfaction Level	**N**	**Mean**	**F**	**Sig.**	**t**	**df**	**p-value**
Negatives	42	3.373	0.279	0.598	15.331	204	0.000
Positives	164	4.474					

4.2 Content categories of textual responses

Textual responses of the Positives and Negatives groups were pooled into two files and analysed by CATPAC. Words like "members" and "member," "communities" and "community" were combined. The forty most frequent meaningful words were identified, with the cut off line at the frequency of 2 occurrences. All topics mentioned in the pooled qualitative responses can be divided into seven broad categories: Members, Experiences, Community, Travel, Information, Site Issues, and Global Perspective. The categorization was based on the frequency analysis conducted with CATPAC and qualitative interpretations of the researchers. The identified categories are described below with total frequencies given in parentheses:

4.2.1 Experiences (Freq=111).

This category included the combined frequencies of the following words: "experiences"/"experience,""friendships"/"friends"/"friend," "help"/"helpers"/"helper," "met"/"meetings"/"meet-ups," and "life." The typical responses were: "very pleased with the experience," "some wonderful friendships have come out of it," "I signed up to be a travel helper," "I have met in person quite a few members," and "it's like the opening of a new and exciting chapter in my life." Most often, members described their experiences as being overall great, good, or, in come cases, negative. Members mentioned becoming friends with other members, higher involvement in community life by assuming the responsibilities of a moderator or event coordinator, and meeting in person with other members. Responses from this category were often classified into the Members, Community, and Travel categories.

4.2.2 Members (Freq=110).

This category included the combined frequencies of the words: "members"/"member," and "people." Responses in this category referred to personal characteristics of community members, e.g., "the members are very knowledgeable and nice" as well as group characteristics, e.g., "I feel like many of the people on this site are very much like me a rare thing these days." A number of responses in this category was about the relationships with other members, e.g., "I have met some of the members after getting to know them on line and would consider them as friends," or communication issues, e.g., "I have a great rapport with several members on this site." Responses from this category were often classified into the Experiences, Community, Travel, and Information categories.

4.2.3 Community (Freq=59).

This category included the combined frequencies of the word "community"/"communities." The typical responses were: "this particular site IS a community," "the community has grown larger," and "there are rude people as in any community." Responses from this category were often classified into the Members, Experience, and Travel categories.

4.2.4 Information (Freq=56).

This category included the combined frequencies of the words "information"/"info," "questions," and "advice." Examples of responses include "offers great information," "trading travel advice," and "some people do not provide relevant information." Responses from this category were often classified into the Members and Travel categories.

4.2.5 Travel (Freq=55).

This category included the combined frequencies of the word "travel"/"traveling"/"travels." Some of the responses were "I have been able to exchange travel information about very specific destinations and experiences," "good info on travel," "it has greatly helped me on my travels and in general," and "it provides me with a link to a life of traveling that for me is on hold due to being at uni[versity]." Responses from this category were often classified into Members, Experience, and Information categories.

4.2.6 Website Issues (Freq=49).

This category included the combined frequencies of the words "site"/"website," "[message] boards," "posts"/"postings," "forums"/"forum," and "moderators"/"moderator." Members referred to concerns with the Website or technology implemented in their VTCs. Some of the responses were "this site is extremely well run," "this website is a friendly place," "moderators of the website do a fantastic job," "the layout of the site is of the highest quality," and "the team that manage the site respond immediately if anything dodgy comes up which makes me feel safe."

4.2.7 Global Perspective (Freq=19).

This category included frequencies of the word "world." Examples: "people from all over the world," "knowledgeable about the world," and "many have clouded idea of the world."

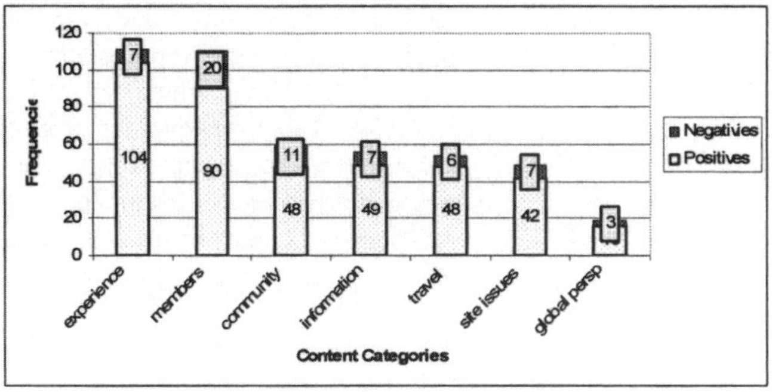

Fig. 1. Absolute frequencies of content categories

As can be seen from the provided examples, one response can be counted in several categories, e.g., "Members quickly become friends and you truly feel like part of a travel community." The absolute frequencies of topic categories for the Positives and Negatives groups are shown in Figure 1. Frequencies of content categories relative to the number of textual responses submitted in each group are shown on the radar diagram in Figure 2. Respondents from the Positives group most often mentioned their experiences and issues in connection to other community members in their textual comments. Responses from the Negatives group were most often classified into the Members category and much less into the Experience category. The second most frequent category for Negatives was Community.

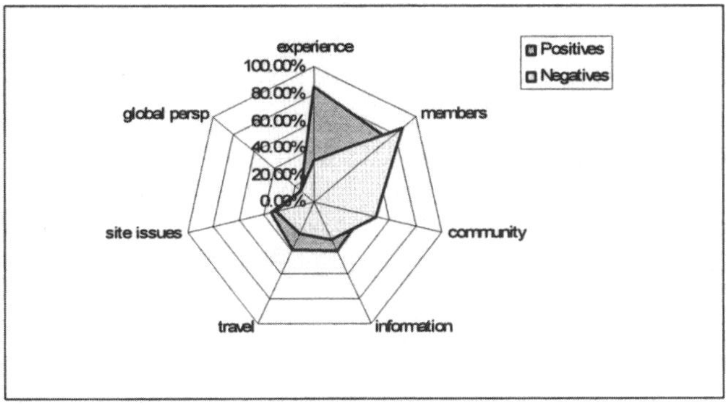

Fig. 2. Relative frequencies of content categories

4.3 Negative experiences

Analysis of negative comments was conducted "manually" in order to get a more detailed picture of concerns relevant to being unsatisfied with their VTCs. All negative comments were classified into the following four categories: Communication Style, Cliques, Irrelevant/Lack of Information, and Negative Website Dynamics. Each response was coded 0/1 in every category. For example, the response "Like most communities, a small core contributor base soon emerges, slowly changing membership over time. This base actively engages in a creative and generally objective fashion on interesting and relevant topics. Unfortunately, again, like most communities, much of the interaction is casual and off topic or trivial, and much filtering is needed by the serious contributor" was coded as "1" for Cliques, Irrelevant/Lack of Information, and Negative Website Dynamics categories. Not all textual responses from the Negatives group contained negative comments, e.g., "The members in this community seem honest with their questions and answers." Figure 3 shows absolute frequencies of negative responses in each of the four categories.

4.3.1 Communication Style.

Responses in this category referred mostly to communication style of community members and included such words like "curt," "judgmental," and "too critical," e.g., "I am surprised at how judgmental and condemning people in the community are." However, respondents from the Positives group emphasized that people with not so nice communication style can be expected in any community, e.g., "There are a few people who have a rather rough way of expressing their opinions (that is condescending) but that is to be expected in any group."

4.3.2 Cliques.

Responses in this category referred to exclusiveness of some of the groups formed within the community, e.g., "small core contributor base soon emerges" or "in general I have found the group overburdened with topics not relevant to travel in Europe and often dominated by a few regular contributors passing messages amongst themselves."

4.3.3 Irrelevant/Lack of Information.

In this category members commented about the large amount of irrelevant information with not enough feedback given on their postings. Typical responses include "not enough feedback on certain subjects" and "I may not always get the info I need, but I always get support and referrals if nothing else."

4.3.4 Negative Website Dynamics.

In this category respondents commented that things were changing for the worse or had slowed in the community, e.g., "it is not the same travel board I signed up for in the beginning" or "it is not a very active community."

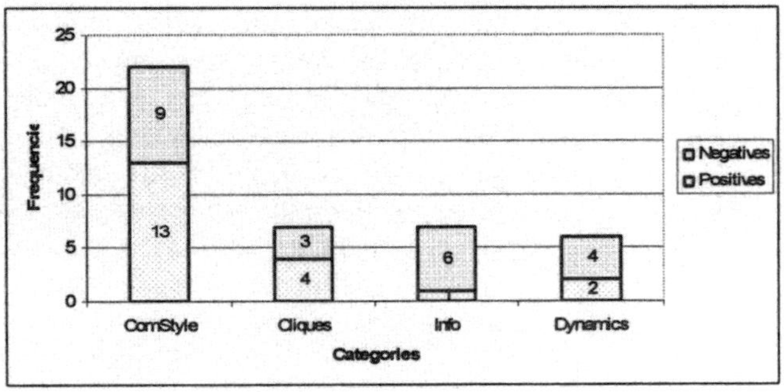

Fig. 3. Negative comments: Frequencies of categories

5 Conclusion

5.1 Implications for managers

The results of this study offer important implications for the development and maintenance of VTCs. The study found two groups of respondents with different satisfaction levels – Positives and Negatives. These two groups did not differ in demographics or in their level of technology competence. Thus, we suggest that differing satisfaction levels can be attributed, at least partially, to the experiences of end users with their VTCs. Among identified content categories, Members, Community, and Experience categories conveyed information about members' characteristics and respondents' relationships and experiences with other members. These findings highlight the social aspect of VTCs and the need of members to form meaningful relationships with like-minded individuals. This study found that for the Negatives group, the relationship with other members and a "community feeling" were highly important for personal satisfaction. Negatives often sited poor communication style of other members, e.g., "I have had very unsatisfactory relationships with a few members of the community where negative comments/judgments were directed towards me." This finding suggests to VTC management that the moderator's work is extremely important for members' satisfaction and should focus on upholding positive communication styles within the VTCs. The formation of exclusive groups within VTCs indicates that along with general forums where everyone can participate there should be mechanisms which allow members to form groups on certain topics of interest. However, these smaller groups should not lead or promote the ostracism of other members.

Content categories Travel and Information are also theoretically justified findings of this research. As Preece (2000) contended, one of the features of a virtual community is a common interest, or shared purpose. Since obtaining travel-related information is one of the reasons why people join VTCs in the first place, the quality of information is of utmost importance. Negative comments that a particular VTC contains irrelevant information or that "much filtering is needed by the serious contributor" indicates that the organization of information in a VTC is a serious designer task. Forums and discussion boards should be set up within the community so that different streams of information can be separated and easily found. End users experiences are often affected by technology implemented in a VTC. Respondents mentioned site management, "this site is extremely well run and cared for"; the quality of message boards, "any questions I've had have been answered unlike on other travel boards where you can post questions that just get lost and unanswered"; and the jobs done by moderators, "moderators of the web site do a fantastic job of monitoring any potential situations and keeping adverts/spam to a minimum". This is a direct indicator that technology implemented in a VTC along with community management is reflected on members' experiences. A few comments in this category mentioned slow website activity or negative changes (see Fig. 3). This finding suggests that if a VTC is considered as a business model for a travel organization, resources for its management should be carefully and consistently allocated. Careful virtual community management, either done professionally or on a volunteer basic, should ensure that interactions do not change for the worse overtime.

As shown in Fig. 3, some negative issues were mentioned by just a few respondents. However, it must be noted that people with lower satisfaction levels were less likely to relate their negative experiences: 45% of Negatives did not care to leave a comment, while only 25% of Positives did not give an answer to Q4 (see Table 1). We can further suggest that for end users who reported low or neutral satisfaction there were still benefits experienced and valued in being a VTC member, for example, "I can find useful information in this community." However, keeping members with low satisfaction scores in a community might be a challenging task for a management team as it requires a deep understanding of what experiences make members satisfied/dissatisfied with the virtual community in the first place. The identifying of some of these issues is the contribution of this study to the e-satisfaction body of research on virtual travel communities.

5.2 Further research

Three limitations of this study were noted. First, the sample of the "Digital Identity Management in VTCs" survey was limited to VTC members. Future research, surveying online communities of different types, can reveal other experience concerns and their relative "weight" in the overall structure of important content categories. Second, modern virtual communities are complicated environments which incorporate many advanced technology features. Layouts of websites integrating all these features can be quite complex, so that novice Internet and/or virtual community users might easily get frustrated and report a lower level of satisfaction with their VTC experience. Unfortunately, for this study, the level of technology competence was assessed by only one variable, Internet usage, which was operationalized as how many hours per week a respondent spent using the Internet. Such information as when a person started to use the Internet, how many communities he/she is a member of, or how long they have been a member of a particular community were not collected in the survey and thus were not available in this study. Third, the study examined community members' experiences with one VTC and not their general or overall VTC experiences. Future studies could consider asking respondents if they were members of more than one VTC and exploring their general satisfaction with virtual communities.

In closing, this study provides valuable consumer-delivered information for travel organizations and companies that are considering the use of VTCs as one of their marketing strategies. The study is also useful to technology designers and management teams of online communities that work on the creation and maintenance of successful network systems for end users in virtual communities in order to retain members who are satisfied. Further investigation into the complex process of satisfaction with the overall quality of virtual communities will be beneficial for a better understanding of the needs and concerns of virtual community members and could ultimately assists in perfecting the business models of e-marketers.

References

Allison, A., Currall, J. Moss, M. & Stuart, S. (2005). Digital Identity Matters. *Journal of the American Society for Information Science and Technology,* 56(4), 364-372.

Anderson, R. E., & Srinivasan, S. S. (2003). E-satisfaction and e-loyalty: a contingency framework. *Psychology and Marketing*, 20(2), 123-138.

Buhalis, D. (1998). Strategic use of information technologies in the tourism industry. *Tourism Management*, 19(5), 409-421.

Hagel, J., & Armstrong, A. (1997). *Net gain: Expanding Markets through Virtual Communities*, MA: Harvard Business School Press.

Jiang, H. (2005). An investigation of end users perception, attitude, trust and satisfaction with digital identity management in VTCs. Unpublished Master Thesis, Purdue University.

Kozinets, R. V. (1998). On netnography: initial reflections on consumer research investigations of cyberculture. *Advances in Consumer Research*, 25, 336-371.

Lawrence, T. B. (1995). Power and resources in an organizational community. *Academy of Management Best Papers Proceedings*, 251-255.

Mills, J. E., & Morrison, A. M. (2003). Measuring customer satisfaction with online travel. In proceedings of the *International Federation of Information and Communications Technologies in Tourism 2003.* Helsinki, Finland, January 27-February 1, 2003.

Nabeth, T. Understanding the Identity Concept in the Context of Digital Social Environments. INSEAD CALT - FIDIS working paper. http://www.calt.insead.edu/project/Fidis/. [Accessed on March 23, 2006]

Oliver, R. (1997). *Satisfaction: A Behavioral Perspective on the Consumer.* NY: McGraw-Hill.

Preece, J. (2000). *Online Communities: Designing Usability, Supporting Sociability.* Chichester: Wiley.

Rheingold, H. (1993). *The Virtual Community: Homesteading on the Electronic Frontier.* Reading, MA: Addison-Wesley Pub. Co.

Roberts, C. W. (2000). A conceptual framework for quantitative text analysis. *Quality and Quantity*, 34, 259-274.

Rothaermel, F. T., & Sugiyama, S. (2001). Virtual Internet communities and commercial success: individual and community-level theory grounded in the atypical case of TimeZone.com. *Journal of Management,* 27, 297-312.

Tonnies, F. (1967). Gemeinschaft and Gesellschaft. In C. Bell & H. Newby (eds.), *The Sociology of Community*, London: Frank Cass and Co. Ltd, 7-12.

Wang, Y., Yu, Q., & Fesenmaier, R. D. (2002). Defining the virtual tourist community: implications for tourism marketing. *Tourism Management*, 23, 407-417.

Weber, R. P. (1985). Basic content analysis. Beverly Hills, CA: Sage.

Wellman, B., & Gulia, M. (1999). Net surfers don't ride alone: Virtual communities as communities. In P. Kollock, & M. Smith (Eds.), *Communities and Cyberspace.* New-York: Routledge.

Westbrook, R. A., & Oliver, R. L. (1991). The dimensionality of consumption emotion patterns and consumer satisfaction. Journal of Consumer Research, 18(1), 84-91.

Winer, R. S. (2001). A framework for customer relationship management. California Management Review, 43(4), 89-108.

Woelfel, J. K. (1998). CATPAC: Users guide. New York, N.Y.: RAH Press.

Acknowledgements

The authors would like to thank the National Science Foundation (NSF), the Center for Education and Research in Information Assurance and Security (CERIAS) at Purdue University for financial support of this work (Funding Number: NSF0428554, Design and Use of Digital Identity).

Virtual Tourism Content Network TANDEM - A Prototype for the Austrian Tourism Industry

Roman Egger[a]
Jakob Hörl[a]
Brigitte Jellinek[b]
Mario Jooss[a]

[a] Forschung Urstein - Center for Futures Studies,
Salzburg, Austria
{roman.egger, jakob.hoerl, mario.jooss}@fh-salzburg.ac.at
[b] Department of MultiMedia Art
Salzburg University of Applied Sciences, Austria
brigitte.jellinek@fh-salzburg.ac.at

Abstract

Tourism is considered to be a highly information-intensive business, and there can be no doubt that information and communications technologies (ICTs) have made an impressive contribution in recent years by influencing and forming the market in an innovative way at both the process and product levels. The use of the Internet, in particular, has made destinations and their service providers aware of numerous possibilities and chances to optimise their performance and competitiveness. Virtual networks can assist small structures in saving time and money and increasing flexibility and quality while boosting receptiveness to innovation. This paper pursues two basic objectives. First, it discusses the significance of participating in a Virtual Tourism Network System for Small and Medium Sized Tourism Enterprises (SMTEs). Second, it introduces a prototype designed for the Austrian tourism industry that is based on these assumptions.

Keywords: virtual tourism networks, business webs, SMTEs, collaboration, business model.

1 Introduction

With respect to both revenue and arrivals, Austria ranks among the top 10 tourist destinations (UNWTO, 2006). As such, tourism plays a crucial role in the Austrian national economy. Added revenue stemming directly from tourism is 6.2% of the GDP - almost double that of the international average. Even the number of persons employed in the tourism industry clearly demonstrates its importance. Around 500,000 persons work in approximately 90,000 businesses linked to this economic sector (Statistik Austria, 2006). This fact alone reveals that tourism in Austria is shaped primarily by small and micro-sized businesses and naturally has a highly heterogeneous structure because of this. In addition to their size, SMTEs are also characterised by their independence, flexibility, seasonality, family ownership and management (Buhalis, 2002), and frequently by their geographical isolation. This often amounts to traditional management practices which are characterised by short-term perspectives, a lack of willingness to cooperate and an aversion to ICTs. For a number of years, the trend towards quality tourism has been growing strongly in Austria. Succeeding in this increasingly competitive market has become essential. These developments are the result of a variety of trends in the tourist industry. The establishment of low-cost carriers, for example, makes it possible to travel on short notice and on a low budget while at the same time allowing a broader selection of destinations. The opening of the Eastern markets, the trend towards short holiday breaks and the continuously declining proportion of loyal customers have increased competitive pressure. A push for service and quality in an information-intense business such as tourism is dependent upon the quality of information available. A market such as this, which is characterised by smaller structures in particular, requires increased networking of its participants in order to compete with differentiated offerings at the highest international levels.

On the demand side, German tourists, comprising around 66 percent of all guests, represent the most important country of origin for Austrian tourism. Domestic guests, with over 30 million overnight stays, come in second, followed by the Dutch. The top 5 countries of origin also have some of the highest Internet usage rates in Europe. As such, it is no surprise that, according to Tourismus Monitor Austria, 25 percent of the tourists visiting Austria exclusively use the Internet for obtaining information for their travel planning (Michl, 2006). According to a study by Overture and comScore, among the German tourists, the strongest Austrian guest group, over 90 percent use the Internet in order to gather information for their upcoming trip. Incidentally, these figures also correspond to the results of the Austrian online guest analysis (Egger , Filipp, Hörl, & Jooss, 2006). Search engines are among the most widely used sources for conducting research, followed by travel agencies and travel web sites. In addition to destination web sites, guests search primarily for accommodation. Three fourths of the Austrian accommodation and lodging businesses (77 percent) have their own web site and are among the many others involved in the struggle to gain potential visitors on the World Wide Web (Michl, 2006). The motivation for developing a virtual network prototype can be seen through the need to integrate and cross-link tourism enterprises in order to raise sustainable competitiveness for the whole destination.

2 Theoretical Background

2.1 Lack of Information and Need for Networking at the Destination Level

Principally, destinations can be seen as a conglomerate of services within a certain geographical area. Whenever a guest uses the Internet, a medium that has now become the primary method of travel planning, the search for suitable accommodation represents an important part of travel preparations. However, the real reason individuals spend their holiday in any given destination is generally not the hotel itself. People travel to experience the landscape, the culture and points of interest, sports offerings and attractions. This is because the real motivation for travel is to satisfy individual needs. If an Internet user seeks travel and hotel information, he or she searches for key words within the context of the destination. Studies clearly show that accommodation and destination information are at the beginning of the search (e.g. Favier, 2006; Mitsche, 2005). The tourist service provider is therefore compelled to acquire in-depth understanding of the destination in order to make use of the appropriate Search Engine Optimisation (SEO). To this effect, Starkov (2005) stresses, "a destination-focused search engine strategy requires in-depth knowledge of the travel and hospitality industry, extensive destination research, destination target keyword analysis, and destination search behaviour." Therefore, in more ways than one, it is necessary for detailed destination information to be integrated into hotel web sites. First, the potential guest expects interesting information about the destination (leisure and cultural offerings, sightseeing and sport offerings, etc.) in addition to information purely about the hotel. Secondly, search-engine optimised, destination-relevant content is a deciding factor in obtaining an adequate ranking with the search engines. However, hotel web sites rarely offer this information in the necessary scope and quality. The required data are usually adopted at the time of web site creation from the sites of the individual stakeholders or from a destination web site. As a result, information available on hotel web sites is often incomplete, out of date or poorly presented. As long as data cannot be exchanged mutually and dynamically for lack of a virtual network, all parties involved (attractions, activities, hotel owners, destinations and guests) will continue to suffer from the deficit of information. The result from a lack of information networking is demonstrated in Table 1.

Table 1. Result from a lack of information networking

Main stakeholders	Disadvantages due to existing information deficits
Attractions & Activities	Marketing takes place solely through the SMTE's own web site and/or the DMO web site. Guests are unaware of most attractions and activities before commencing their journey. As such, the search process takes place only within the context of the destination. A desperate struggle for attention on the web ensues; multiplier web sites are lacking. Economies of Scale and Economies of Scope are non-existent.
Accommodation	Marketing takes place solely through the SMTE's own web site and/or the DMO web site. Destination-specific content that can be optimised for search engines is missing. Existing information lacks quality and topicality. Economies of Scale and Economies of Scope are non-existent.
Tourist	The guest wants to be able to find all of the necessary information on a single page. Information on hotel web sites, however, is usually incomplete; topicality can rarely be guaranteed.
DMO	Destination Management Organisations are often subject to political and geographical boundaries. This, however, is not what the guest, who observes the destination according to topographical, cultural, linguistic, etc. conditions, perceives. Employees in tourist organisations often do not have the most current information on a destination, thereby demonstrating significant deficits during informational discussions and consultations.

2.2 Virtual Tourism Networks

In general, tourism services are immaterial and are subject to the *uno actu* principle. The guest does not purchase the actual service, but the right to receive this service. Furthermore, tourism is unique in that the service the customer perceives is usually comprised of a sum of partial services from various providers. Sheldon (1997) commented appropriately on this: "Information is the lifeblood of tourism." The need for information, along with a high level of topicality and quality of data, is particularly relevant when large numbers of providers are involved in creating the total service. For this reason, the concept of networking has always been more of a necessity than an innovation in tourism.

Through the use of ICT, new networking opportunities surface both at the informational and transactional level. Numerous processes in the tourism value chain can be performed virtually with the help of Internet, intranet or extranet solutions. The virtual value chain therefore no longer consists of sub processes conducted in a linear fashion. Rather, it represents a freely-configurable matrix with a number of starting points (Morris & Morris, 2002). Among the numerous descriptions and definitions to be found in literature, the following is especially suited to this paper: "A tourism network system is the one that compromises a multiplicity of autonomous, interdependent, enterprises without physical borders of separation from the environment, that rely on the Internet infrastructure to integrate and exchange value" (Ndou & Passiante 2005, p. 440-451).

The primary objective of a Virtual Tourism Network should lie in the creation of a sustainable win-win partnership (Hakolahti, 2006), whereby the involved partners can interact dynamically, creatively and proactively. Such networks are characterised by a healthy blend of cooperation and competition in which the provision of current relevant content plays an essential role. However, the desired common use of information can only be efficient and available on a wide basis when all enterprises can participate in the network with the least amount of expenditure and cost. This requires an innovative, yet easy-to-use system. In this context, a trend toward open platforms and standards can be observed (Ndou & Passiante, 2005). As a prerequisite for the implementation of an innovative and successful VTN, a radical change in thinking and acting of organisations is necessary, along with the establishment of new business models (Ndou & Petti, 2004). Increasing integration tendencies ensure that even SMEs can no longer cut themselves off from these developments. The European Commission indicated as early as 2003 that SMTEs must prepare themselves mentally and technologically for participation in virtual networks (European Commission, 2003).

Particularly organisations with complex structures, which are often found among destinations, can gain time-related, monetary and qualitative advantages along with increased flexibility through virtual networking (Ndou & Petti, 2004). Consequently, it is not surprising that most of the established Virtual Tourism Networks (VTN) can be found at the destination level. Contemporary literature continuously refers to Destination Management Systems (DMS) in this context. Simply, they offer a collection of digital information on a destination which can be accessed interactively with the objective of presenting, advertising and marketing the destination as a single unit (Buhalis, 2003). As such, a DMS is based on bundling comprehensive information and is therefore characterised by its central nature. A true network, on the other hand, is decentrally structured. It includes nodes which can be considered as information hubs, but it bases its reason for existing on the networking of individual participants. Even though bundling creates economies of scale and scope, the value created through true networking, deploying the full potential of the Internet, is significantly larger.

Therefore, it can be seen that the potential of many VTNs has not been fully exploited to date. One reason for this is that the integration and networking of the parties involved are insufficient. Another reason is that standardisation and compatibility problems often arise (Ndou & Petti, 2004; Buhalis, 2003).

3 TANDEM – Developing a VTN Prototype

In order to counteract the aforementioned information deficit and fulfill networking requirements at the destination level, the Centre for Futures Studies of the *Forschung Urstein GmbH* developed the "TANDEM" prototype. This is a Virtual Tourism Content Network that was promoted within the framework of the TEC Dynapro research project using monies from the "*Innovative Maßnahmen des EFRE – Salzburg*" programme.

The goal of the prototype is not the creation of a new central source of information, but the above mentioned information networking of individual parties in order to eliminate the deficits outlined in Table 1. The central idea is to leverage the participating partners' existing infrastructure and competence. The TANDEM system serves as a virtual interface between content providers (Attractions & Activities) and content users (accommodation facilities). Using the TANDEM web interface, content providers can make their information available to other partners. Content users, on the other hand, select the information packages that are to be presented on their web site in the future from the available data. The content user creates a type of subscription with destination information organised according to target groups, geographical or seasonal relevancy for his or her site. The hotelier is thus able to provide guests with an electronic recommendation function which previously was only available on-site, at the hotel reception desk.

As end users, tourists do not have any direct contact with the system. They only see the information selected by the content user on the web site. Using the TANDEM system, content users can adapt the information to be integrated into their web sites with just a few clicks. In addition to colour, font, etc., they may also select from a variety of presentation forms (list displays, containers, independent pages, etc.) for information packages. The integration of content by means of a container is demonstrated in Figure 1. By clicking on one of the offers, a page opens displaying detailed information.

Fig. 1. Example of the integration of TANDEM information in a web site

From a technical perspective, the technology can also be viewed as a Content Syndication System. For these systems there exist a number of established data formats, such as RSS and ATOM (Hammersley, 2003) which have been used in tourism (Michopoulou & Buhalis, 2006). On the other hand, a number of efforts are being made to develop custom data formats for information exchange in tourism, for example Harmonize (Fodor, 2004).

Harmonize offers a semantic description of tourist offerings, which is modularly scaled for use as an ordering and booking system. It solves the problem of interoperability and data exchange between different players in tourism. The complexity of the Harmonize data structure is correspondingly high. The problem area addressed by TANDEM neither requires nor justifies this level of complexity. Therefore, a decision has been made to select an internal data structure for the TANDEM prototype system that is as simple as possible, yet sufficient. This simple data structure is shown in Table 2. For future versions of TANDEM, the possibility to import Harmonize data may prove to be beneficial.

Table 2. TANDEM data structure for static information

Visible for the tourist as an end user	Visible for the content user	Visible only internally
Title Short description (teaser) Description (full-text) Price or free of charge Dynamic data (e.g. special offers) An image Imprint (of content provider)	Address Geographical coordinates (Lat/long) Category URL	Contact person E-mail, Telephone Billing address

The data made available by the provider can have two general characteristics. Either they are static (all data that never or rarely change, such as the service description or the geographical location) or dynamic (such as operating hours, pricing, special offers, maintenance and facility holidays). Static information is given in either the short teaser or longer description form. For dynamic information, freely configurable "dynamic lines" can be created. In order to provide the content user with an additional competitive advantage through the implementation of third-party content, static content can also be individually optimised for search engines for each content user, as long as the provider approves. If the provider makes changes to dynamic content (e.g. changes to operating hours), these changes will be synchronised automatically on the content user's site. Figure 2 shows the data flow of static and dynamic data from the content-provider to the content-user.

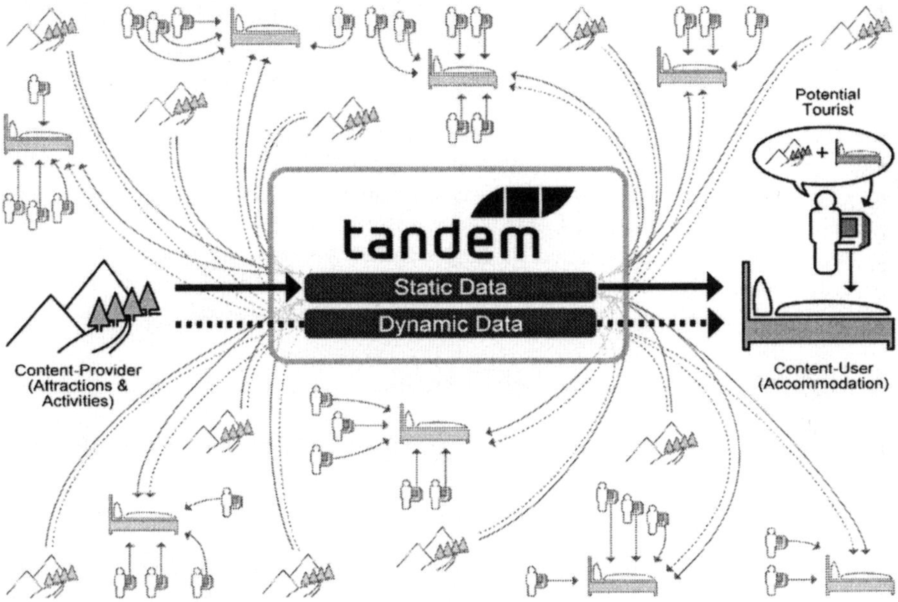

Fig. 2. Schematic representation of TANDEM

During the entire development process SMTEs were integrated into the project in the role of "friendly users". Through surveys, workshops and test accounts, data was gathered on the general conditions and requirements which provided the necessary information for a market-oriented conceptual design.

3.1 Technical Specifications

There are several alternative technical solutions available for content syndication. To choose the right solutions we used the following approach:

In order to keep interoperability problems at a minimum, the existing infrastructure and the competence of potential participants was ascertained. Since little information could be gained from interviewing the content users, due to a lack of understanding of technical details (XML, PHP, SSI), a probe was developed. This probe consisted of a set of files which the content users uploaded to their web space. These files were constructed in such a way as to test various features of the web space and provide information on them when accessed via the web server.

These studies showed that a prototype solution using XML or PHP on the content users webserver would have to be discarded. A decision was made to implement a solution using iframes and a solution using push from the TANDEM server to the content users webserver. Tourists, as end users, are unable to detect any difference between the iframe and push alternatives. The push alternative does present the content user with higher configuration expenditure, but at the same time, it is the only method that allows content to be optimised for search engines. For the iframe alternative the content of the iframe is loaded from the TANDEM server. From the perspective of a search engine the content of the iframe is not part of the content users website, but part of the TANDEM website.

The TANDEM prototype was completed at the end of August 2006. Information from 20 content providers was entered within the scope of the workshops carried out in the development phase. This information was subsequently selected by 20 content users via TANDEM and integrated into the respective web site. Consequently, the prototype has aptly demonstrated its functionality. All users of TANDEM showed great interest in the project and were highly cooperative. A detailed user evaluation was not made since TANDEM is still in an early prototype stage.

3.2 Value Creation through TANDEM

The following paragraphs provide an overview of how the system's main stakeholders (as presented in Table 1) can overcome the existing deficits caused by a lack of networking.

Attractions and Activities providers enter their data directly into TANDEM. In doing so, they are not only able to present their services on tourist organisation web sites as in the past, but they also appear automatically on numerous web sites of accommodation facilities which also provide access to the target guest groups. Changes to the hours of operation or prices are entered only once, centrally in the TANDEM system, and are then immediately updated on all other web sites. Content providers therefore profit from a multiplier effect and can also be found indirectly through the search engine results of the hotel web sites.

Accommodation: The hotelier selects the leisure offerings for his or her guests from TANDEM and presents them online. All of the necessary information is integrated dynamically and is automatically updated. The one-time expenditure incurred for creation is minimal and future maintenance expenditure is not required at all. Offerings can be exchanged with the click of a button, a feature which is especially valuable for seasonal facilities. The hotelier can convey the message that he or she is not only capable of providing attractive offers for room and board but also that the guest will be able to find an appealing selection of leisure time activities in the immediate area. At the same time, TANDEM makes it possible for search engines to find the integrated text elements. This increases the competitiveness of the hotel and is enhanced by higher levels of transparency for the destination offerings.

Potential *tourists* receive a single, pre-selected and relevant selection of cultural and leisure activities that is in tune with their specific interests. The quality of the information is high due to the freshness of the content. On-site activities can be planned online with minimal effort. In the end, an optimised information process is seen in an increased level of customer satisfaction, which has a sustained effect on buying and repeat buying behaviour.

Destination Management Organisations can integrate the TANDEM system information into their web site as well, gaining access to an optimised database in order to offer their on-site guests maximum levels of information and consultation quality. Non-commercial offerings, such as hiking trails or natural monuments which until now were only displayed on destination web sites, are available via TANDEM on the hoteliers' web sites, blurring the line between currently existing destination borders.

4 Discussion and Conclusion

In contrast to previous efforts to connect service providers from a single destination with each other, TANDEM does not attempt to make information available to end users via a central system. It appears to be significantly more effective and efficient to offer a platform which allows the individual providers to connect with each other in a self-regulating process. The approaches presented in this paper present only a few selected possibilities that a system like TANDEM can offer. Naturally, it is possible to consider expanding information networks at the transaction level. This could allow customers to reserve admission tickets to a museum via the hotel web site, for example. The implementation of dynamic packaging solutions would no longer be restricted to destination web sites as a result. Of course, the system can also be utilised in the opposite direction. Attractions and activities could recommend hotels in their area and offer reservation possibilities or even implement TANDEM as a Content Management System for their own web site.

The future challenges for a successful implementation of TANDEM on the market are also multifaceted. For a system such as TANDEM, which is characterised by a strong networking effect, a critical mass of users and/or partners must first be established. In this respect, a business model must be developed which can be presented simply and comprehensibly and keeps the entrance barriers low. The high value of such a system is justified in the superordinate goal of creating a win-win situation for each and every participant. The objective of securing competitive advantages for all those involved, paired with an exceptionally customer-oriented focus, requires a neutral system operator. In this respect, it will be necessary to view and operate a system such as TANDEM as a tourist infrastructure.

References

Buhalis, D. (2002). *e-Tourism: Information Technology for Strategic Tourism Management.* London: Pearson (Financial Times/Prentice Hall).

Buhalis, D. & Molinaroli, E. (2003). Entrepreneurial Networks and Supply Communities in the Italian eTourism. *Information Technology & Tourism*, 5, 175-184.

Egger, R. & Filipp, G., Hörl, J. & Jooss, M. (2006). *Österreichische Online-Gästebefragung 2005. Akzeptanz und Nutzung des Internet und mobiler Endgeräte durch potenzielle Österreich-Urlauber*. Salzburg: Eigenverlag

European Commission (2003). Adapting e-business policies in a changing environment: The lessons of the Go Digital initiative and the challenges ahead. *COM(2003)148* final. Brussels.

Favier, J. (2006). European Net Travel Has Only Just Taken Off. Retrieved June 17, 2006 from http://www.forrester.com/Research/Document/Excerpt/0,7211,38994,00.html

Fodor, O. & Werthner, H. (2004). Harmonise: A Step Toward an Interoperable E-Tourism Marketplace. *International Journal of Electronic Commerce*, 9 (2), 11-40.

Hammersley, B. (2003). *Content Syndication with RSS*. Sebastopol: O'Reilly.

Hakolahti, T. & Kokkonen, P. (2006). Business Webs in the Tourism Industry. In M. Hitz, , M. Sigala, & J. Murphy (Eds.) *Information and Communication Technologies in Tourism* (pp. 453-462). Vienna, New York: Springer Verlag.

Michl, P. (2006). *Erhebung des Online-Buchungsvolumens / Online-Anfragevolumens der österreichischen Beherbergungsbranche*. Wien: ÖW-Eigenverlag.

Michopoulou, E. & Buhalis, D. (2006). Developing an eTourism Platform for Accessible Tourism in Europe: Technical Challenges. In M. Hitz, M. Sigala, & J. Murphy (Eds.) *Information and Communication Technologies in Tourism* (p. 170) Vienna, New York: Springer Verlag.

Mitsche, N. (2005). Understanding the information search process within a tourism domain-specific search engine. In A. Frew (Ed.) *Information and Communication Technologies in Tourism* (pp. 440-451). Vienna, New York: Springer Verlag.

Morris, L. J. & Morris J. S. (2002). The changing role of the middlemen in the distribution of personal computers. *Retailing and Consumer Services*, 9, 97-105.

Ndou, V. & Petti, C. (2006). Tailoring DMS Business Models to Destination Configurations. In M. Hitz, M. Sigala, & J, Murphy (Eds.) *Information and Communication Technologies in Tourism* (pp. 441-452) Vienna, New York: Springer Verlag.

Ndou, V. & Passiante, G. (2005). Value creation in tourism network systems. In A. Frew (Ed.), *Information and Communication Technologies in Tourism* (pp. 440-451). Vienna, New York: Springer Verlag.

Ndou, V. & Petti, C. (2004). Virtual Networks in the Tourism Industry. In A. Frew (Ed.) *Information and Communication Technologies in Tourism* (pp. 446-457). Vienna, New York: Springer Verlag.

Sheldon, P. (1997). *Tourism Information Technology*. Oxford: CABI.

Statistik Austria (2006). *Tourismus in Österreich*. Wien: Eigenverlag.

Starkov, M. & Price, J. (2005). Search Engine Marketing in Hospitality. Retrieved June 17, 2006 from http://www.hospitalitynet.org/news.4024607.print

Tapscott,D., Ticoll, A., & Lowy, D. (2000). *Digital Capital: Harnessing the Power of Business Webs*. McGraw-Hill.

UNWTO (2006) World Tourism Barometer. 4 (2).

Assessing eBusiness Models of U.S. Destination Marketing Organizations

Tanvi Kothari [a]
Daniel R Fesenmaier [b]

[a] Fox School of Business and Management, Temple University, USA
[b] National Laboratory of Tourism & eCommerce
School of Tourism & Hospitality Management, Temple University, USA
{tanvi, drfez}@temple.edu

Abstract

Information technology has made it imperative for destination marketing organizations to adapt their traditional business models in order to keep pace with emerging advertising strategies, changes in the consumer market, and growing competition. This paper reports on a study of the eBusiness models used by 555 American convention and visitors' bureaus. The results of the study indicate that despite the high rate of adoption of web marketing in the tourism industry most bureaus are still using the most basic business model for their bureaus web marketing strategies. The paper discusses the implications of these findings and offers ideas for future research.

Keywords: eBusiness models, destination marketing organizations, web marketing strategy.

1 Introduction

Convention and visitors bureaus (CVBs) are charged with the responsibility of marketing and branding destinations. Being information brokers of the tourism network, they collect and provide information from and to both ends of the value chain and often function as a catalyst for urban and regional development (McIntosh, Goeldner, & Ritchie, 1995). The proliferation of Internet technologies opens up completely new perspectives and opportunities for the CVBs. As a result, destination marketing organizations (DMOs) are trying to adjust existing marketing strategies (Werthner, 1996). However, researchers (Godin, 1999; Hoffman & Novak, 1996; Zeff & Aronson, 1999) suggest that successful online advertising is not just about technology and new communication channels, it is about deconstructing traditional business models and reinventing the organization. Recent research indicates that CVBs are trying to adjust their marketing strategies using the Internet for destination marketing (Fesenmaier, Gretzel, Hwang, & Wang, 2004; Yuan, Gretzel, & Fesenmaier, 2005). However, these studies indicate that CVBs face tremendous challenges which limit their capability to adapt to this new environment (Fesenmaier & O'Leary, 1998; Gretzel, 2004; Hoffman & Novak, 1996; Yuan, Gretzel, & Fesenmaier, 2003). The purpose of this paper is twofold. Firstly, it outlines a framework for defining consumer oriented eBusiness models for CVBs. The second objective corresponds to a field study conducted for observing, analyzing, and cataloguing the eBusiness models being adopted by the American CVBs.

This paper is organized in the following sections. The first section overviews the literature on business models with reference to defining the purpose of ebusiness models, identifying the components of various business models and listing measures used to evaluate these business models. The next section provides a description of the research methods used to collect the data followed by the results and discussion section wherein the authors discuss the web-based marketing practices of the tourism marketing organizations in the United States. Based on these analyses, the bureaus were classified into four types of eBusiness models and their web marketing strategies are assessed. Finally, the implications of these findings are discussed and new ideas for future research are proposed.

2 eBusiness Models

Several definitions exist that describe the nature and purpose of a business model. Pateli and Giaglis (2002) argue that the business model explains the logic of making business for a firm (Linder & Cantrell, 2001; Petrovic, Kittl, & Teksten, 2001; Rappa, 2001; Timmers, 1998) while others argue that it is the essential link between strategy, business processes and information systems (Nilsson, Tolis, & Nellborn, 1999; Osterwalder & Pigneur, 2002). Petrovic, Kittl, & Teksten (2001, p. 2), on the other hand, adopted a systems approach to define a business model as "the logic of a business system for creating value that lies behind the actual processes". Similarly, Linder & Cantrell (2001, p. 1) define a business model as "the organization's core logic for creating value". According to Applegate (2001, p. 53), "a business model is a description of a complex business that enables study of its structure, the relationships among structural elements, and how it will respond to the real world." Finally, Rappa (2001) and Hawkins (2002) define the business model from a financial perspective by emphasizing cost and revenue streams.

One of the earliest attempts to construct a taxonomy of eBusiness models was by Timmers (1998) whereby he identified architectures for business models via value chain deconstruction and reconstruction – that is identifying value-chain elements – and identifying possible ways of integrating information along the value chain. By combining interaction patterns with value chain integration, Timmers (1998) provides a qualitative mapping of eleven business models along two dimensions. Following Timmers (1998) and other authors (Linder & Cantrell, 2001; Petrovic, Kittl, & Teksten, 2001), it is posited in this study that the eBusiness models should describe in a structured way how CVBs receive and provide value to their customers. Based on this literature, the proposed framework considers two dimensions of the value exchange (monetary value and the non-monetary value) by the destination marketing organization with its customers. The first dimension focuses on the 'the level of eCommerce' capabilities of the CVB websites and the second dimension focuses on 'the level of interaction' of the CVB with its customers on its websites. This framework evaluates the success of the destination marketing organization based on one of the major business model elements; that is, value exchanged.

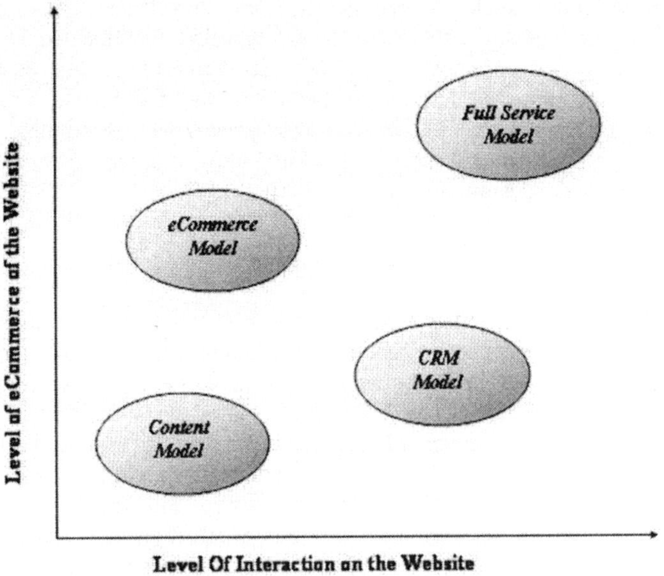

Fig. 1. Taxonomy of CVB eBusiness Models

As shown in Figure 1, the models used by CVBs can be classified into four core types. First is the 'Content Model' wherein the website plays the role of information provider. The CVBs adopting this model provide the most basic information to the visitors on its website; that is, persons visiting this website can only get information from the webpage and there are no functions that enable the user to provide information to, or interact with the CVB or its partners. The second model can be described as the 'Customer Relationship Model'. It is argued that the bureaus adopting this model provide value added services to their customers such as free news, email newsletters and at a more advanced level, they even personalize and customize the message content provided to their visitors. The websites also provide functions or features wherein the customer provides information to the CVB and there are opportunities for the customer to interact with the bureau and other customers. Thus, this model focuses on enhancing the customer relationship abilities of the bureau through its website.

The third eBusiness model can be described as an 'eCommerce Model'. Bureaus adopting this business model provide basic destination information but focus mainly on interacting with the customers in order to sell products/services to the visitors. As such, these models focus on generating revenue through the website rather than concentrating on maintaining or enhancing relationship with customers. Finally, the 'Full Service Model' is the most comprehensive model. Bureaus that adopt this model have a balanced web-strategy in terms of providing information to customers, enhancing relationship with customers and generating revenue through their website. The websites of these DMOs provide a range of functions which include value-adding offerings to customers such as free news, email newsletters, personalization - customization, and special offers/best buys; security function such as secure transaction through SSL, privacy policy, web seal certificate so that customers are assured that any eCommerce activity on the site is safe and secure; site stickiness programs such as community functions and customer loyalty programs, etc. These functions have been shown to create website stickiness, a crucial feature facilitating repeat transactions (Zott, Amit, & Donlevy, 2000).

3 Research Methods

A dataset of American convention and visitor bureaus was used as the sampling frame of this study. The complete dataset contains information about 1,676 American CVBs including the names of the bureaus, contact information (e.g., phone number, email address, and mailing address), and url addresses of the CVB websites. A survey questionnaire was designed and sent to the CEOs/Directors of 555 randomly selected tourism offices (approximately 1/3 of the population). A cover letter was included in the survey packet explaining the purpose of the survey and seeking assistance and support from the tourism organizations. The survey effort (which started in summer 2005 and ended in fall 2005) followed standard procedures and included an initial mail out, postcard reminder, and two additional mailings. Following Wang & Fesenmaier (2003; 2006) and Yuan et. al. (2003), the survey instrument included a number of questions related to the bureaus' web marketing strategies including: 1) Web marketing applications and eCommerce activities used; 2) Website promotion strategies; 3) Website objective and evaluation metrics; 4) Organizational characteristics such as size, innovativeness; and, 5) Organization IT climate such as management support to Internet operations and Internet literacy of the organization. The questionnaire took about 10 minutes to complete. A total of 70 surveys (12.61%) were returned due to invalid addresses for an adjusted sample of 485 bureaus. From this pool, a total of 181 organizations returned the survey, representing a 37.3% response rate.

4 Results and Discussion

4.1 eBusiness Models of American CVBs

Respondents were asked to identify the objective(s) that describe their website strategy. The three listed objectives were: a) The bureau's website is used primarily to broadcast information with the goal of providing information about the attractions, events, and accommodation in our area; b) The bureau's website includes advanced capabilities like personalization, recommendation, virtual community with the goal of encouraging interaction of visitors with our organization and destination businesses; and, c) The bureau's website facilitates/offers various trip planning activities with the goal of encouraging online booking, merchandise sales and payment capabilities. A fourth eBusiness model was constructed to reflect those bureaus indicating that their goal was to support visitors using all of the capabilities listed above.

The results of the survey indicate that almost 77% of the American CVBs have adopted the 'Content Model;' that is, they focus primarily on providing information about the attractions, events, and accommodations on their website. About 7% of the bureaus have adopted the 'CRM Model' whereby CVBs encourage a higher level of interaction with the customers. Interestingly, approximately 15% of the bureaus have adopted the 'eCommerce Model' which indicates that their websites are primarily used to broadcast information in order to encourage/support online booking, merchandise sales and payment capabilities. Finally, only 1.2% of the CVBs have adopted the 'Full Service Model' whereby the websites provide information about the attractions, events, accommodation, membership, encourage interaction of visitors with the CVB and destination businesses and provide advanced capabilities like personalization, recommendation etc. It is important to note that due to small sample size (n=2), those bureaus included in the Full Service Model were removed from further analysis.

The survey also asked CVB directors to indicate which information, functions, as well as CRM tools were offered on their website. This question provides a validity check of the bureaus and enables us to better understand the eBusiness focus of the respective bureaus. Analyses were conducted to assess the differences between the respective bureaus. As seen in Table 1, all bureaus provide basic information content on their website. However, bureaus adopting the CRM and the eCommerce eBusiness models provide significantly different functions on their websites. For example, bureaus adopting the CRM model are significantly more likely to use direct email campaigns, offer loyalty programs, and have personalization features on their websites. Bureaus adopting the eCommerce model, on the other hand, are much more likely to facilitate hotel reservations, sale of event tickets and merchandise/theme products on their websites. Further, in order to gain customer trust these bureaus also provide privacy policy, online chat rooms and secure transactions through SSL on their websites. Thus, it was concluded that the three eBusiness models reflect the range of strategies used by American convention and visitor bureaus.

4.2 Differences in Website Promotion Strategies

A series of analyses were then conducted to assess differences between the three CVB eBusiness models with respect to promotion strategies. The results indicate that there are few significant differences among bureaus; only the extent to which the bureaus use direct marketing strategies (done through the email list) was found to be significant (Scheffe=0.51,p=0.01). Analyses were also conducted to assess differences in the extent to which the American CVBs use different approaches to manage web site design, content, and maintenance. These analyses also indicate that there are no differences in the website maintenance strategies. Last, comparison of the bureaus with respect to website management practices indicates that there are no significant group differences in website design and search engine registration strategies. However, these analyses indicate that there is a significant group difference in website content management strategies (F=5.528, p=0.01); interestingly, the bureaus that adopt the eCommerce model are more likely to update the information content on their website as compared to the bureaus adopting the Content model (Scheffe = 0.998, p=0.05).

Table 1. Website Features by eBusiness Model (%)

Website Feature	Content (N=127)	CRM (N=11)	eCommerce (N=24)
Activities/Attractions Information	100	100	100
Accommodation information	98.4	100	100
Events Calendar	96.9	100	100
Brochure request capabilities	93.7	100	100
Links to Regional/City/Area pages	89.0	100	87.5
Restaurant information	87.4	81.8	100
Shopping information	86.6	81.8	100
Maps/Driving directions	81.1	81.8	91.7
Tour operator information	48.8	36.4	70.8
Search functions	47.2	45.5	62.5
Email Newsletter	44.9	72.7	62.5
Direct email campaign*	34.6	54.5	91.7
Trip/Vacation planner *	33.9	27.3	66.7
Incentive programs to attract new customers *	12.6	18.2	45.8
Personalization capability *	8.7	45.5	12.5
Interactive tools	18.9	36.4	25
Visitor comments - stories	9.4	18.2	20.8
Customer loyalty programs*	0	9.1	8.3
Virtual tours	7.1	27.3	8.3
Real time customer help capability	7.1	18.2	12.5
Recommendation System	6.3	18.2	16.7
Games and entertainment	7.1	18.2	8.3
Meeting planner support materials *	38.6	27.3	62.5
Privacy policy *	32.3	45.5	62.5
Highlight special offers/best buys *	26.8	54.5	83.3
Publications/Reports *	22.8	54.5	50
Hotel Reservations *	21.3	18.2	91.7
Secure transactions through SSL *	15	9.1	37.5
Classified/Banner advertisements *	12.6	27.3	33.3
Cross-selling/up-selling opportunities	12.6	18.2	25
Merchandise/Themed products *	9.4	9.1	33.3
Event tickets *	5.5	18.2	20.8
Community functions/chat rooms *	0.8	0	12.5
Attraction tickets	8.7	18.2	12.5

Note: * indicates significant differences at p= 0.05 using Pearson Chi Square.

4.3 Differences in Organizational Characteristics

At the organizational level, factors promoting or hampering the adoption and utilization of IT applications have been found to influence the innovation-adoption decision (Frambach, 1993; Rogers, 1995; Zaltman, Duncan, & Holbek, 1973). Further, a firm's financial resources can also be a major stumbling block to the adoption of sophisticated technologies. Following from this literature, a series of analyses were conducted in order to assess the nature of the various tourism organizations adopting the different eBusiness Models.

Table 2. Organization Profile and Internet Capabilities (in %)

Characteristics	Content (N=127)	CRM (N=11)	eCommerce (N=24)
Major markets served (multiple responses)			
Leisure travel	88.2%	72.7%	95.8%
Sports *	33.1%	36.4%	70.8%
Business travel *	25.2%	45.5%	50.0%
Festival/Special events	49.6%	54.5%	62.5%
Meetings/Convention *	52.0%	54.5%	91.7%
# of computers in use			
1 to 5	56.0%	45.5%	8.3%
6 to 10	27.2%	27.3%	37.5%
11 to 20	8.0%	27.3%	29.2%
21 to 50	6.4%	.0%	25.0%
51 to 100	1.6%	.0%	.0%
100 and more	.8%	.0%	.0%

Note: * indicates significant differences at p= 0.05 using Pearson Chi Square.

Specifically, the respondents were asked to identify from a list of different categories that represent the most important markets for their organization (see Table 2). The results indicate that the leisure travel market is the most important market to those bureaus that take a "Content" approach. This contrasts sharply with the "CRM" and "eCommerce" oriented bureaus that appear to be more balanced in travel markets. Indeed, the "eCommerce" bureaus appear to focus on all of the travel markets. Additional analyses of organizational characteristics indicate that while the eBusiness groups generally have the same size, those bureaus with more advanced eBusiness models tended to have more computers connected through the Internet ($F=33.829$, $p=0.005$), suggesting that they invest more of their resources in technology related systems.

4.4 Resource Allocation

An important characteristic of CVBs is that they are usually limited in their resources which include the financial resources dedicated to technology adoption and innovation. Almost 14% of the organizations have an annual budget less than $100,000 and almost 54% of the organizations have a budget higher than $100,001 but lower than $1,000,000. More than 26% of the organizations reported to have an annual budget higher than $1,000,001 but lower than $5,000,000. However, only 5% of the bureaus indicated to have a budget above $5,000,001. Analyses indicated that there is a significant difference (F=6.091, p=0.001) in the budgets of the CVBs based upon eBusiness model. This analysis indicates that, consistent with previous results, the "eCommerce" oriented bureaus have the largest budgets; however, a number of well funded bureaus have adopted the "Content" eBusiness model. Also, the "CRM" focused bureaus appear to have very similar budgets to those bureaus adopting the "Content" strategy.

Table 3. Organization Budget in Percent (in %)

Annual budget of the Bureau	Content (N=127)	CRM (N=11)	eCommerce (N=24)
Under $100,000	13.9%	9.1%	.0%
$100,001 - $250,000	23.0%	27.3%	.0%
$250,001 - $500,000	18.9%	18.2%	4.3%
$500,001 - $750,000	5.7%	9.1%	21.7%
$750,001 - $1,000,000	12.3%	9.1%	8.7%
$1,000,001- 2,000,000	16.4%	27.3%	30.4%
$2,000,001 - 3,000,000	3.3%	.0%	17.5%
$3,000,001 - 5,000,000	2.4%	.0%	8.7%
$5,000,001 and above	4.1%	.0%	8.7%

Note: Pearson Chi Square = 38.314, p = 0.01

Last, we examined the differences among the bureaus with respect to website specific budgets. The average annual website expenditure as reported by the bureaus (N=145) was approximately $32,000, with a range of values from $100 to $50,000, and represents approximately 6% of the total bureau budget. Bureau directors reported that, on average, their organizations spent 31% of the website budget for web site design, 27% for system maintenance, 24% for website personnel, 21% of the web budget for website content development, 17% for technology additions and upgrades, and 10% for website research. Statistical comparisons indicate that the total amount of expenditure on the website is significantly different (F=3.963, p=0.01) for the bureaus adopting different eBusiness Models. Specifically, the mean difference in the budget spent by bureaus adopting the "Content" model is significantly less as compared to the bureaus adopting the "eCommerce" model (Mean difference=$47,292.31, p=0.05).

5 Conclusions and Implications

IT plays a central role in destination marketing. The Web enables tourist principals to react to the current strategic challenges: globalization of tourism, the stagnation in developed destinations, changes in tourist behaviour and a demand for more and better information (Copeland & McKenney, 1988; Poon, 1993). The results of this study is consistent with the findings of recent studies (Gretzel & Fesenmaier, 2001; Yuan et al., 2003) which indicated that the potential of internet technologies has been largely unrealized by most DMOs. Also, the results indicate that most of the American CVBs use the Web as an online brochure for basic information dissemination, and do not take advantage of the interactive nature of the media. They focus mainly on core information oriented applications such as activities/attraction information, accommodation information, and clearly avoid the more advanced functions like personalization, customer interactive tools, etc. Post hoc analyses seem to indicate that this perspective is pervasive across all types/sizes of CVBs; however, it appears that bureau finances (or, lack thereof) may account for some of the lack of development of website functions/features.

By identifying the various eBusiness models that integrate the value flow both in monetary and non-monetary terms this study recognizes the necessity of changing the way in which DMOs conduct their business online and provide value. As the world moves to electronic business, some of the most important changes are occurring in what businesses do and how they derive value from doing these things; in other words, in what business models they use. In this digital era DMOs not only compete with each other but also have to combat the innovative strategies of other businesses like Expedia, Orbitz and Trip planner. Thus, it is essential for DMOs such as American CVBs to understand that in order to survive they need to change their fundamental role from being an 'information provider' to becoming a 'value enhancer'. DMOs can gain a competitive advantage by careful planning and by choosing an integrated model that expands the value chain for its customers.

References

Applegate, L. M. (2001). E-Business Models: Making Sense of the Internet Business Landscape. In G. W. Dickson & G. DeSanctis (Eds.), *Information Technology and the Future Enterprise: New Models for Managers*: Prentice-Hall.

Copeland, D. G., & McKenney, J. L. (1988). Airline Reservation Systems: Lessons From History. *MIS Quarterly, September,* 353-370.

Fesenmaier, D. R., Gretzel, U., Hwang, Y. H., & Wang, Y. (2004). Applications of Internet Technology In Travel And Tourism. In H. Bidgoli (Ed.), *The internet encyclopaedia* (Vol. 3, pp. 459-476). Bakersfield, CA: John Wiley & Sons.

Fesenmaier, D. R., & O'Leary, J. (1998). *The Challenges of Using Information Technology in Tourism.* Paper presented at the Workshop on Information Technology and Learning Environments in Tourism [Online].

Frambach, R. (1993). An Integrated Model Of Organizational Adoption And Diffusion Of Innovations. *European Journal of Marketing, 27*(5), 22-41.

Godin, S. (1999). *Permission Marketing: Turning Strangers Into Friends And Friends Into Customers*. New York: Simon & Schuster.

Gretzel, U. (2004). The Destination Website Dilemma: Where Has All The Marketing Knowledge Gone? *eReview of Tourism Research, 2*(6).

Gretzel, U., & Fesenmaier, D. R. (2001). Defining Internet Readiness for the Tourism Industry: Concepts and Case Study. In H. Werthner & M. Bichler (Eds.), *Lectures in e-commerce* (pp. 77-102). Wien; New York: Springer.

Hawkins, R. (2002, March 24-26). *The Phantom of the Marketplace: Searching for New E-Commerce Business Models.* Paper presented at the Euro CPR, Barcelona.

Hoffman, D. L., & Novak, T. P. (1996). Marketing in Hypermedia Computer-Mediated Environments: Conceptual Foundations. *Journal of Marketing, 60*(3), 50-68.

Linder, J. C., & Cantrell, S. (2001). *Changing Business Models: Surveying the Landscape*: Institute for Strategic Change, Accenture.

McIntosh, R. N., Goeldner, C. R., & Ritchie, J. R. (1995). *Tourism, Principles, Practices, Philosophies.* Toronto: John Wiley and Sons, Inc.

Nilsson, A. G., Tolis, C., & Nellborn, C. (1999). *Perspectives on Business Modelling - Understanding and Changing Organizations.* Berlin: Springer.

Osterwalder, A., & Pigneur, Y. (2002, June). *An E-Business Model Ontology For Modelling E-Business.* Paper presented at the 15th Bled Electronic Commerce Conference, Bled.

Pateli, A., & Giaglis, G. (2002). *A Domain Area Report on Business Model* (White Paper). Athens: ELTRUN: The eBusiness Center.

Petrovic, O., Kittl, C., & Teksten, R. D. (2001, October 31 – November 4). *Developing Business Models for eBusiness.* Paper presented at the International Conference on Electronic Commerce 2001, Vienna, Austria.

Poon, A. (1993). *Tourism, Technology and Competitive Strategies.* UK: Cab International.

Rappa, M. (2001). Managing the Digital Enterprise – Business Models On The Web. 2006, from http://ecommerce.ncsu.edu/business_models.html

Rogers, E. (1995). *Diffusion of Innovation.* (4 ed.). New York: The Free Press.

Timmers, P. (1998). Business Models for Electronic Markets. *Electronic Markets, 8*(2).

Wang, Y., & Fesenmaier, D. R. (2003). Web-Based Marketing Strategies Of U.S. Destination Marketing Organizations: Approaches, Issues, Trends And Implications: University of Illinois, Champaign.

Wang, Y., & Fesenmaier, D. R. (2006). Identifying the Success Factors of Web-based Marketing Strategy: An Investigation of Convention and Visitors Bureaus in the United States. *Journal of Travel Research, 44*, 239-249.

Werthner, H. (1996). Design Principles of Tourist Information Systems. In S. Klein (Ed.), *ICT in Tourism* (pp. 70-78). New York, NY: Springer.

Yuan, Y., Gretzel, U., & Fesenmaier, D. R. (2005). The Role Of Information Technology Use In American Convention And Visitors Bureaus. *Tourism Management, Forth Coming.*

Yuan, Y. L., Gretzel, U., & Fesenmaier, D. R. (2003). Internet Technology Use by American Convention and Visitors Bureaus. *Journal of Travel Research, 41*(3), 240-255.

Zaltman, G., Duncan, R., & Holbek, J. M. A. (1973). *Innovation and Organizations.* New York, NY: Wiley.

Zeff, R., & Aronson, B. (1999). *Advertising on the Internet* (2nd ed.). New York: John Wiley.

Zott, C., Amit, R., & Donlevy, J. (2000). Strategies For Value Creation In E-Commerce: Best Practice In Europe. *European Management Journal, 18*, 463-475.

Architectural Scenarios Supporting e-Business Models for a DMS

Claudio Petti[a]
Gianluca Solazzo[a]

[a] eBusiness Management Sector-ISUFI
University of Lecce, Italy
{claudio.petti, gianluca.solazzo}@ebms.unile.it

Abstract

Following recent studies and analysis conducted about Business Models for DMSs, this paper aims at discussing the interrelationships between destinations' configurations, business models, and architectural strategy for DMS platforms. In particular this work draws on recent attempts aimed at matching DMS business models design with specific characteristics of target destinations, to extend the same considerations towards the identification of the appropriate technological architectures and enabling software applications. In this aim a framework for selecting the appropriate DMS architecture is presented. The result of this analysis will thus lead to the identification of a set of technological architectures according to the different configurations that a destination might present.

Keywords: DMS, business models, DMS architecture, DMS technologies

1 Introduction

In the past ten years, the widespread diffusion of e-Business and the raising global competition have pushed a dramatic rethinking on the ways in which tourism business is organized. Destinations have emerged as the key competitive units and local cooperation and internetworking are becoming more and more relevant for attracting new tourism flows and retaining the profits of such activity. In this context Destination Management Systems, with their potential to enable local tourism authorities (DMOs) and private tourism enterprises (mainly SMEs) to better coordinate their own operations, manage their relationships and to develop customer-centered *online* and *offline* networks, are seeing their mission expanding from a mere marketing job towards a more incisive management role. However recent surveys (Salzburg/Brussels, 2005, WTO 2004) as well as the authors' department researches in the field, showed as there is still much progress to do towards the full and productive implementation of DMSs, in management practices as well as in academic studies. Among all the possible explanations about the difficulties that destinations are experiencing in implementing Destination Management Systems, from the ever-cited cost and know-how concerns to the somewhat overlooked awareness and methodological reasons, there is also some kind of a 'mismatch' between the DMS Business model and destination specific features. Basically the argument is that the choice and design of the DMS Business model may fail to take into account some destination's peculiar characteristics that have definitely an influence on the DMS implementation phase, such as the number of players involved in key decisions, the intensity of collaboration, or the managerial and technological capabilities of local DMOs (Petti & Ndou, 2006). Moreover, according to the same authors, there is also a co-evolutionary relationship between the implementation of DMSs and the related localized managerial and technological skill sets, which evolves and develops as a result of DMSs diffusion and adoption within the local community. Starting from these premises the aim of this work is to identify, building on this DMS-Destination features matching line of thought, the most suitable architectural strategy for each step within the framework proposed in Petti and Ndou (2006). More specifically actors, interrelationships between them will be depicted and major issues from a technological perspective will be raised. According to this purpose the paper is structured as follows: in section 2, a review of the main technologies used within the main European research projects on ICTs (Information and Communication technologies) and Tourism issues will be presented. In section 3, after a brief reference to the Petti and Ndou (2006) framework, an architectural and technological classification based on the four main scenarios previously identified is presented. Conclusions will highlight some of the main issues related to the choice of the appropriate DMS architectural and technological features.

2 Related Works

2.1 Relevance and Attractiveness: a proposed Classification for e-Tourism Technologies

This paper develops its arguments on the basis of a study undertaken in the framework of the authors' department research on new ICT-enabled organizational models for the development and management of tourism destinations. The aim of the study was to trace a state-of-the-art of European ICT Research for Tourism. At the end of 2005, 71 European Research Projects were surveyed. Projects have been analyzed according to three different dimensions: project overall objectives, project technical features and target users. Each dimension was further specialized in different categories to reflect the main functionalities researched (in rows in Table 1) and the technology-focus (in columns of Table 1) according to the different target actors of the project. As for any general classification most of the surveyed projects presented different and unambiguous characteristics, especially, for what concerns the topic of this work as related to the technology dimensions. For this reason having forced a project in a single cluster might seems, and is, reductive. Anyway, while doing such kind of studies, it is often possible to identify a "preferred" technology focus or a more characterising functionality. This 'prevalence' criteria are the ones that have determined the project classifications. The main result of the study are here reported. Table 1 below considers projects overall objectives versus technologies used.

Table 1. Overall Objectives Classification Vs Technology exploited

	Technology							
Type	**WS**	**LBS**	**DS**	**RM**	**NI**	**SW**	**AI**	**Total**
browsing, search & access	13	13		5	3	2	1	37
communication and promotion	4							4
e -distribution & commerce	3							3
integration & interoperability	1	4	2		3	1		11
management support	4	1		1			2	8
reservation / bookings / payment	7						1	8
Total	32	18	2	6	6	3	4	71

WS = Web Services; LBS = Location Based Services; DS = Distributed Systems; RM = Rich Media & Virtual Reality; NI = Network Integration (mobile networks-tcp/ip); SW = Semantic Web; AI = Artificial Intelligence

At a first glance, Web Services emerged as the most used technology. Web services, classified within this survey, are those services made available from a business's Web server for Web users or other Web-connected programs. This is a quite large definition that covers many different application based on the tcp/ip protocol. Sharing web services is the more and more common service oriented architecture strategy that researcher and companies are following to develop more efficient and manageable ICT systems. Location based services attracted interest too, probably because info-mobility may become the new frontier to ensure a more flexible tourism planning, as well as a more autonomous tourism experience. Anyway the main interest of the analysis was more on classifying rather than enumerating technologies surveyed. This has been done according to their level of *attractiveness* for innovation and research measured as the grade of feasibility in business processes and organisations (this matter strongly affects the final results of a project) and to their *relevance* within the overall project objective measured as the percentage of total project allocate in one of the technology variable. According to these criteria Web Services resulted both as the most attractive (45,07%) and as the more relevant (40%) technology to support tourism innovation, followed by Location Based Services (25,35% of attractiveness and 32% of relevance) and Rich Media & Virtual Reality technologies (8,45% of attractiveness and 12% of relevance). But if web services are mainly dedicated both to business to business and to business to consumer segment using devices and interfaces such as personal computers, and websites and portals that are common to average users, Location Based Services, Rich Media and Virtual Reality whereas promise to be an interesting path for the future still show some hurdles for their diffusion as they are more expensive, and use less common devices and more complex operating models. This increase costs, affects the usability of applications and the viability of the business model, which needs to be based on effective revenue sharing policies. The consideration above will be used in the next section for the definition architectural scenarios that take into account simultaneously the maturity of the technologies, their *evolution potential* (assured by interest in the European research context), and their *diffusion potential* on the technology market.

2.2. Matching DMS Business Models and destination configurations

Before getting to the definition of architectural scenarios, this section describes the framework within which those architectural scenarios will be framed (Table 2). The framework have been purposefully designed by Petti and Ndou (2006) adapting and integrating previous literature (Rispoli & Tamma, 1995; Tapscott, Ticoll, & Lowy, 2000; Tamma, 2002) with authors' project experience, to uncover the relationships between destinations' peculiar characteristics and DMS business model features. So it is particularly adapted for the purposes of the present paper.

More specifically, *Fragmentation* is characterized by a spontaneous entrepreneurship and scarce planning, a highly unstructured supply, no decisional centers or integration poles, weak relations and interactions among actors, scarcity of resources and capabilities (relational, managerial, and technical). In this context, the configuration of tourism experience is managed totally by the user through a series of point-to-point relations with each single operator. Single operators do not have any control on product configuration. So, the *aggregation* business model proposed in the table, needs to be seen in perspective as both the context and the result of an overarching destination management project aimed at creating the necessary 'platform' of human, structural and social capital for transforming fragmented models into more structured and competitive configurations on which to develop more incisive actions. So in this context the mission of the DMS is to support the creation of the necessary conditions to undertake wider destination management initiatives.

Table 2. DMS e-Business Models and Destination Models

	Form of Coordination			
Level of Integration	Autonomous	Cooperative	Centralized	Distributed
Variable				**Distributed Lead** *Alliance/Agora*
High			**Leadership** *Value Chain*	
Medium		**Cooperation** *Aggregation*		
Scarce/Low	**Fragmentation** *Aggregation*			
Resources & Capabilities	Scarce	Low	Medium/ High	High
Degree of Innovation	Low	Low	Medium/ High	High
Managing Actor	Internet Service Provider	Tourism Operators/ DMO	DMO	DMO/ Infrastructure Provider

Cooperation is characterized by a composed and relatively structured supply, a limited number of decisional centers. Moreover the relational dynamics of actors present diverse levels of intensity, can be short, medium or long term (consortiums, associations), characterized by operational or strategic content and a differentiated base of resources and capabilities. In this context the configuration of tourism experience is managed by some operators of the supply which assemble diverse alternatives on which they posses some extent of control, and among which the final user can effectuate a guided and qualified choice (i.e. the local tourism supply system has a network configuration). In this case, the appropriate business model for a DMS would be the *aggregation* as the integration level, required resources and capabilities are still low, as well as the innovation level. In these contexts the mission of the DMS will be to aggregate suppliers, tourism information and resources in a one single point-of-sale for its promotion and commercialization in the global tourism market. *Leadership* is characterized by a very structured supply, the presence of a unique decisional center and there exist some subjects that are capable to aggregate and control the supply. In this context the configuration of tourism supply is completely managed by the leader operator that resolves ex-ante the problems of uniqueness and coherence of supply (i.e. package). The appropriate business model for a DMS initiative is thus a *value chain.* In these contexts there is no need to start from aggregating and integrating information and resources, as aggregation and some level of integration are already realized by the decisional centers, i.e. the destination management organizations that are (now) present in the context. So, the DMS initiative is aimed at supporting destination organizations in its role of 'orchestrating' local tourism supply for the provisioning of integrated experiences and comprehensive solutions to prospect tourist segments.

Finally, *Distributed Leadership* is characterized by a strong maturity of the tourism destination context where the strong accumulation of human capital (in terms of management and technological capabilities), structural capital (in terms of technological infrastructures and applications), and social capital (in terms of culture and experience of collaboration), lowers the trade-off between coordination and integration. This reduces the need for a strong coordination between the different components of the local tourist supply, which rather tends to self-organize and converge around multiple offerings conceived to satisfy comprehensively the needs of different tourist segments. In a *distributed leadership* settings, where internetworking technologies allows for the distributed management of tourism in the destination, the level of integration can be high or low according to the kind of solution put in place, an *alliance* rather than an *agora*. A DMS initiative in these contexts needs to leverage on the integrated and collaborative culture of the context (so a value chain model seem a prerequisite for such a kind of models) to create distributed knowledge networks, composed by a set of dynamic linkages among diverse members who are engaged in deliberate strategic and operational exchanges of information, knowledge and services for design and produce both integrated and/or modular and personalized products. As pointed out, the choice of the business model in this case depends mainly on the strengths of ties and cooperation among actors, the capabilities related to the usage of advanced e-Business solutions and the extent of control of the context provider over the offerings.

3 Technological Scenarios for a DMS

Starting from characteristic of destinations and business models in each of the stages described in previous section, this section will identify different DMS architectural scenarios. Those scenarios will be described using the results of the classification of e-Tourism technologies presented in section 2.1. In particular, technologies enabling the adoption of Web Service as well as architectures compliant to these technologies will be preferred when depicting scenarios in which the destination is mature for such an implementation. Following scenarios have four categories of players:

- *Tourist actors* (TAs), who are the actors of the tourist chain, who might have an own Information System (IS) and want to join the network of enterprises that will enable the DMS settlement.
- An *Application Service Provider* (ASP), which is configured as an organization that provides base-infrastructural services and, eventually, value-added services (e.g. eBusiness, Knowledge Management and eLearning services). In addition, it should offer an environment of publication and execution of the DMS services. This actor represent the DMS's back-office.
- A *DMS*, that is the point of access to different services offered by TAs to final users. This actor should represent the DMS's front-office.
- Tourists, who are the *Consumers* of services offered by the DMS.

For all the following scenarios it has been assumed that a consumer access the DMS by internet and, after having chosen the preferred service category (e.g. hotel reservation) and having identified the service supplier, he closes the transaction. The first scenario depicted takes place in a *Fragmented* setting. Thus, it can be supposed that none of the TAs have an own IS, and that they are provided with very simple communication systems such as a fax or a GSM network, but they want to join the DMS in order to distribute their services through another delivery channel. It is possible to imagine that while the tourist asks for some products/services, the DMS publishes those electronic services and let the ASP manage the run-time environment (where the business logic of the services of each TA is held), and the TAs to notify the availability of the requested product/service. The DMS uses a component, previously published on the ASP, that implements the service chosen by the tourist. Through a gateway for communicating by fax or by the GSM network, a message is sent to the TA which has to communicate the availability of the product/service requested by the tourist. The architecture is shown in Figure1.

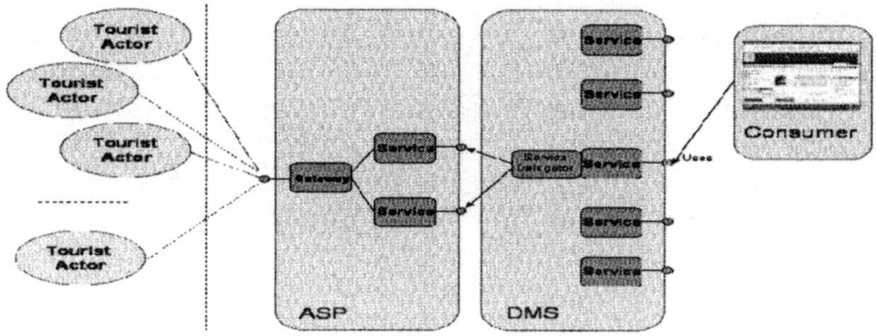

Fig. 1. Scenario 1 for Autonomous settings

A most suitable architecture for implementing a DMS in such a settings should take into account that a less pervasive integration with the pre-existing hardware/software infrastructures or systems, could be more successfully. In addition, such a scenario presents two valuable advantages: minimum effort required for the DMS implementation and low impact on the efficiency of both the TA and the DMO. A strong disadvantage is that the ASP acts as a single-point of failure for the whole architecture.

Moving towards a *cooperative* setting, it is possible to suppose that each TA has its own Information System, accessible by the internet, and that they want to join the DMS in order to have a new delivery channel for their services. The DMS, through a Service Delegator component, can activate the ASP's Adapter connected with the TA selected by the user, in charge of communicate and register the transaction on the TA's Information System. It is then necessary that each TA publishes on the DMS some ad-hoc components, that we called Adapters, which represent a specific view of other software components and perform a dynamic re-configuration without changing the client component's implementation. Adapters, whose formats, standards and runtime environment are decided by the ASP, allow the correct communication between the DMS and many Information Systems. An architecture for this scenario is represented in the Figure 2. This architecture is based on a tight coupling between the DMS and TAs, taking into account a low impact on the TA's information infrastructure as it does not require any kind of HW/SW upgrading, and leaving to the adapters the task of getting connected to systems that are in the TAs' information infrastructure. One of the major disadvantages in pursuing this strategy resides in the fact that the ASP acts as a single-point of failure for the whole architecture.

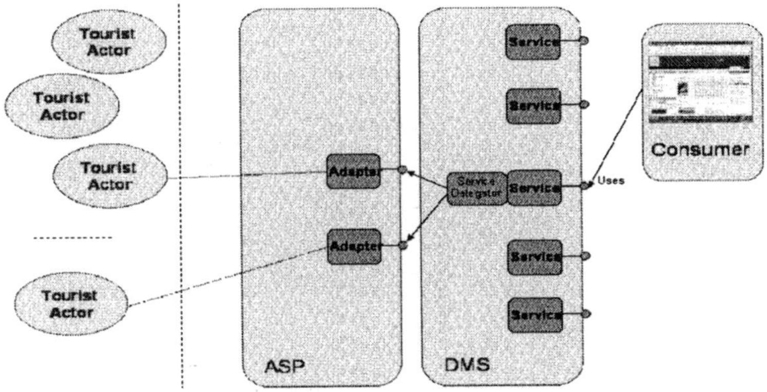

Fig. 2. Scenario 2 for Cooperative settings

Taking in consideration a *leadership* setting with a value chain business model it is possible to imagine, that the DMS plays a central role (for example by coordinating a background peer-to-peer architecture to which the DMS itself is connected) in the architectural configuration. Starting from the same business scenario in which a tourist has closed his transaction, after having chosen the service provider belonging to a certain service category, the DMS makes a lookup on a node of the peer-to-peer architecture, downloading a predefined proxy (a software generated to be used by other components and whose code is specific to the component implementation technology) (Herzum & Sims, 2000) for that service and establishing a connection with the TA's Information System selected by the tourist. The proxy will be in charge of communicating and registering the transaction on the TA's IS. The role of the ASP is now to provide just value-added services to the DMS, while the DMS will publish services and provide the technological infrastructure enabling the aggregation of heterogeneous services. Finally, the TA has to publish on a node of the peer architecture its services with the appropriate proxies. A possible implementation architecture is showed in Figure 3. In such a scenario, the DMS and TAs are more loosely coupled, because of a service registry. With a centralized service registry, its availability is not guaranteed but there is a continuous control on the TA's services availability.

Finally in a *Distributed Leadership* settings, internetworking technologies allows for the distributed management of tourism in the destination. It is possible thus, to extend the previous architecture, by allowing TAs to have its own services and publish them as Web Services on a UDDI (Universal Description, Discovery and Integration) registry, that is a platform-independent, XML-based registry for businesses worldwide to list themselves on the internet. An UDDI registry grants TAs and DMS to be loosely coupled, TAs to save transactions on its information system, DMS to be the aggregator of TA's product/services and make them available to consumers.

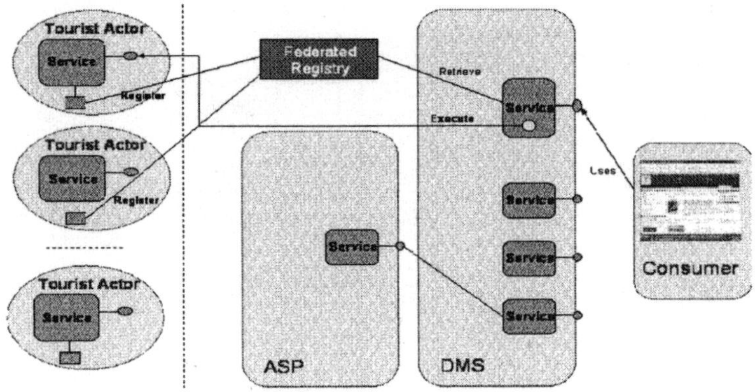

Fig. 3. Scenario 3 for Centralized settings

The DMS uses the software component corresponding to the service selected by the tourist. It can be published on the DMS itself or on the TA's Information System. Taking in consideration the case in which each TA has its software application on its information system, the TA has to develop a proxy component following technological standards for Web Service (xml-based protocols such as SOAP, interfaces that respects interoperability standards). So, the DMS can look up the UDDI registry and build an ad-hoc proxy component in order to use the TA's service.

This scenario is represented in Figure 4. It is clear that now the ASP has a marginal role though this do not imply that TA and DMS has to be tight coupled. In this hypothesis, TAs who want to join the network created by the DMS, must necessarily have an infrastructure HW/SW supporting web service standard, that means for TAs to face additional costs.

To sum up the four scenarios are represented in a schema which maps upon the Petti and Ndou (2006) framework stages and business models and takes in account further classification criteria. Classification criteria (represented in a set of three values) chosen are the *technological effort required* to the TA (in terms of development of new systems or customizations of the existing ones) and the *availability/impact* of the TA's Information System (where low means that the information system is made by a pc connected to the internet and an email address). The result of the mapping is represented in Figure 5. Described scenarios could imply complementary architectures but usually should be considered as subsequent steps that needs a not straight upgrading in terms of both technological (for instance SW/HW infrastructure) and organizational asset. In the case the DMS has to be implemented in a fragmented or cooperative settings, there is the necessity to design an "agile" solution that minimizes the coordination as well as the technological effort of the tourism actor (being a private tourism operator or the DMO).

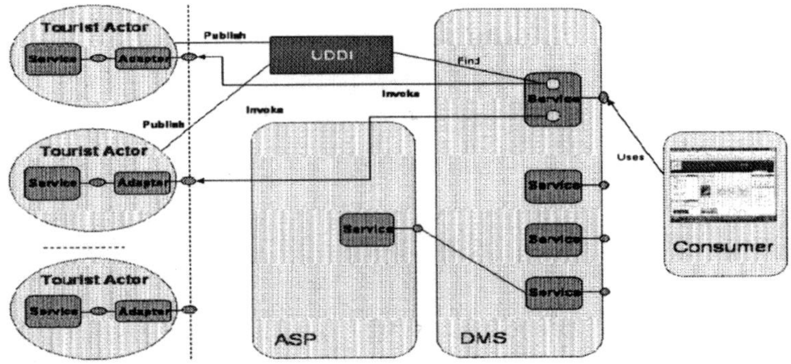

Fig. 4. Scenario 4 for Distributed Leadership settings

The first scenario is the one that most suits to a fragmented settings as it requires an internet connection for the services to work and no technological/organizational effort from TAs but the information management of the products/services offered. Whereas in fragmented towards cooperative settings, collecting/gathering and organising information, technology and data/content management are mechanisms that can be enabled in scenario 2 when adopting an architecture with low/medium technological impact on existing SW/HW infrastructures (TA's information systems) and a low/medium effort required to be realized. As it can be noticed, it is possible to realize a more loosely coupling between DMS and TA as much as the technological effort required and the availability of the TA's Information systems grow. The tradeoff stands on the need of a growing maturity and rich conditions to be set up.

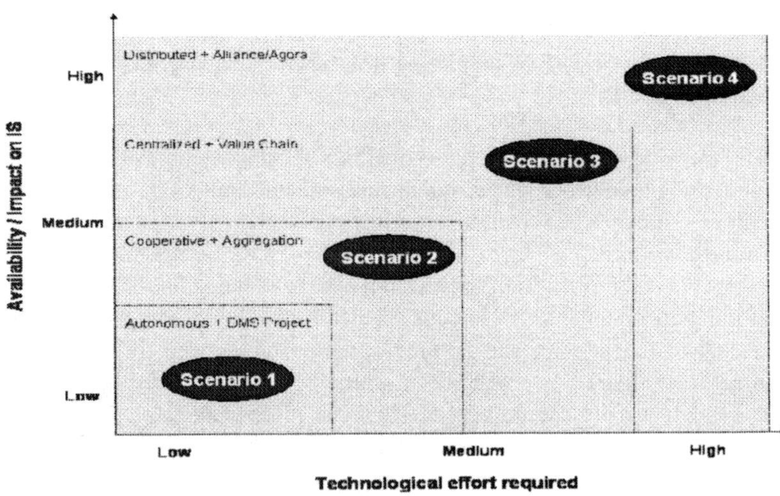

Fig. 5. Evaluation of scenarios within the DMS innovation framework

4 Conclusions and Future Work

The aim of this work was to integrate the discussions on the need to match business model design with destinations' specific characteristics along with DMS technological and architectural issues. So the thesis underpinning this paper is that as destination specific features shape the type of business model this has a consequence also architectural and technological choices that should be as appropriate as the business model and crafted to maximize its effectiveness.In this path web services have been identified as the most prevalent and relevant technologies with the potential to enable ICT-driven innovation in tourism. Moreover looking at the same analysis it emerges a strong marketing rationale behind the very recent developments of ICT solutions for tourism. In fact more than 50% of the projects surveyed focused on browsing, search, and access functionalities, and other data not shown in this study confirmed as most of the projects surveyed were targeted on final users. These results may be the case for ICT and tourism-related research to shift its focus from marketing to increase the focus on management issues.

Background analyses undertaken on most relevant technologies, destinations configuration characteristics and appropriate e-Business models typologies for each of them, have led to the elaboration of four different architectural scenarios that tried to give some hints on the issues of choosing the most appropriate technological architecture for a sustainable DMS initiative and the appropriate sequence of choices to be made. However, further detailed empirical analysis are needed to ascertain the different architectures used for DMS in different context, the extent to which those architecture match with the ones described in this paper and to measure the effectiveness of proposed choices through case studies. Future research is needed also to address the issues related to specific implementation of technological applications, human skills and managerial capabilities that are required in each evolutionary stage. Finally, a case study could also be needed to address issues related to the effectiveness in the development and deployment of scenarios.

References

Herzum, P., & Sims, O. (2000). *Business Component Factory*. Wiley Computer Publishing.

Petti C., & Ndou V. (2006). Tailoring DMS Business Models to Destination Configurations Networks in the Tourism Industry. In M. Hitz, M. Sigala and J. Murhpy (Eds.) *Information and Communication Technologies in Tourism 2006.* Vienna: Springer-Verlag.

Rispoli, M. & Tamma, M. (1995). *Risposte strategiche alla complessità: le forme di offerta dei prodotti alberghieri*. Giappichelli Editore. Torino.

Tamma, M. (2002) Destination Management: Gestire prodotti e sistemi locali di offerta. In Franch M. *Destination Management, Governare il turismo tra locale e globale.* Giapplichelli Editore.

Tapscott, D., Lowi, & Ticoll, D. (2000). *Digital Capital – Harnessing the Power of Business Webs.* Harvard Business School Press, Boston.

Salzburg /Brussel, (2005) *The European e-Business Market Watch. ICT and Electronic Business in the Tourism Industry. ICT Adoption and e-Business Activity in 2005.* European Commission, Brussels.

WTO (2004). *Survey of Destination Management Organization Report.* World Tourism Organization, Madrid.

Acknowledgements
Authors want to thank Valentina Ndou, for her precious contribution to the definition of the destination development framework to which this work refers, and Gianluca Lorenzo, for having inspired the features of architectural scenarios described in this paper.

Tour Operators in an eBusiness World
The Challenge of Change

Roberto Daniele
Andrew J Frew
Rune Todnem By

SITI research centre
Queen Margaret University College, UK
{rdaniele, afrew, rby}@qmuc.ac.uk

Abstract

Whilst much attention has been paid to the development of new tourism eMediaries, the growth of the Internet has also affected established tour operators. The aims of this paper are to examine the adoption of eBusiness by these players and explore issues linked to eBusiness driven change. The paper used a case study approach based on interviews with eBusiness executive from 3 of the 4 largest tour operators in UK and Europe and the analysis of supporting documentation such as company reports, journal and trade press articles. Findings highlight the fact that such companies have had to rethink fundamental aspects of their strategy and business models in order not only to survive but prosper. As a consequence considerable changes have also taken place in terms of organisational structures, organizational culture, business processes, skills-set requirements and technology infrastructure.

Keywords: Change Management, Organisational Strategy, Business Models, Organisational Structure, Organisational Culture; Business Processes, Tour Operator.

1 Background

The impact of eBusiness on organisations is well documented: Jackson and Harris (2003) suggest that the Internet is affecting the way in which companies operate and do business and therefore companies must be prepared to continually re-organise and restructure themselves. Kalakota and Robinson (2001:300) sum up the challenge by stating: "in the eBusiness world, companies must anticipate the need for transformation and be ready to re-examine their organisation to the core". Within the tourism industry, the last decade has witnessed the emergence of the web as an increasingly important distribution channel for the tourism industry and the emergence of new travel eMediaries such as Orbitz, Expedia and Lastminute to name a few. The rate and type of growth exhibited by eMediaries suggest that these organisations are assuming an increasingly central role in the travel and tourism value chain which is potentially more powerful and influential than the role played by any individual supplier and in certain cases, of entire industry sub-sectors (Daniele & Frew, 2004). The new business models being adopted by these players, essentially combinations or variants of agency, merchant model with dynamic packaging, have effectively seen them transforming from online travel agents to online tour operators thus bringing travel eMediaries in direct competition with the longer established tour operators such as TUI, MyTravel, Thomas Cook and First Choice, the main players in the creation and distribution of leisure package holidays in Europe. Far from standing still these tour operators have embarked on a journey of radical change involving substantial rethinking of their business models and strategies, organisational processes, culture and underlying IT infrastructure.

2 Aims and Methodology

The aims of this paper are to examine the adoption of eBusiness by "traditional" tour operators and explore issues linked to eBusiness driven change. The research builds on previous work (Daniele & Frew, 2006; By, 2005) and uses a case study method based on a mix of face-to-face and phone semi-structured interviews with eBusiness executives from three of the four largest tour operators in the UK and Europe. In addition, company annual reports, investor presentations and conference calls, press releases, academic and trade journals, conference proceedings, newspaper and magazine clippings, abstracting services, online sources and electronic databases provided further documentation for the case studies. Analysis of this additional documentation allowed the researchers to increase the research findings' reliability and validity through data triangulation. nVivo 7.0 was used to collect, organise and analyse this data. Such Computer Assisted Qualitative Data Analysis Software (CAQDAS) is well suited to the facilitation of a qualitative approach to research (Lewins & Silver, 2005). Data was imported and explored to identify and generate initial key concepts, ideas or categories which were stored in nVivo "free nodes". This then allowed the researchers to further explore themes contained at each node to establish relationships between issues and common themes/actions/strategies amongst the tour operators examined.

3 Tour Operator Challenges

Since the 1980s, the strategies of all large tour operators have placed an emphasis on increasing profitability through vertical integration. This in turn has produced substantial market concentration. For example in the UK, 53% of capacity is held by the top four players TUI/Thomson, My Travel, Thomas Cook and First Choice (Gountas, 2005). In recent years, the growth of web-based distribution and the arrival online intermediaries (eMediaries) combined with long term structural changes in consumer behaviour patterns towards more independent and flexible travel have created substantial challenges for traditional tour operators on many fronts.

The vertical integration strategies of the large European Tour Operators have not always produced the expected results with Dombey (2005) suggesting that the anticipated economies of scales did not materialise leaving these companies with the legacy costs of aggregation and limited benefits from their strategies. "No frills" airlines are providing tough competition for tour operators' charter airlines often offering a wider range of destinations and flight frequencies and dangerously competitive pricing levels (Buck & Lei, 2004). The rapid growth of travel eMediaries, increased B2C offers plus ongoing commission erosion has had a negative impact on travel agency profitability – including those of the large tour operators. Ownership of hotels has constrained some tour operators to specific short to medium haul destinations at a time when consumer preferences are shifting towards long destinations Dombey (2005).

Large, vertically integrated tour operators have been slow (or at least slower than travel eMediaries) in reacting to market changes and shifting consumer patters for four key reasons. Firstly, long product lifecycle: the traditional tour operating product lifecycle can be in the order of 6 to 24 months (Cooper, Fletcher, Fyall, & Gilbert, 2005). Secondly, limitations imposed by vertical integration: the operation of large tour operators becomes more cumbersome and less prone to change: as Gountas (2005:52) suggests, these companies resemble large machines: "with each part contributing to the optimum working of the other parts, often resulting in a degree of regimentation that reduces the organisation's responsiveness". Thirdly, limitations imposed by legacy ICT systems: many tour operators still run legacy systems developed in the 1970s and 1980s which, whilst adequate for the distribution through "bricks and mortar" travel agencies, have proven limiting in an online environment (Dombey, 2005). Finally, lack of clear online distribution strategy: until recently whilst many of the large tour operators enjoyed a high level of sales and brand awareness offline they seemed to have been less successful in developing a substantial online presence.

4 Response

After an apparently slow start, there is now substantial evidence to show that tour operators have been seriously re-examining their strategies and business models in light of the opportunities offered by the Internet. An analysis of their annual reports for example, shows that in the last two years, most players have started to address the issue by developing company-wide eBusiness strategies (as opposed to isolated and tentative eCommerce projects) and have set clear targets for their online distribution activities. As a result all the "big four" tour operators now appear in the top 10 agency sites visited in the UK (Hitwise, 2006). An analysis of the literature and interviews with key company executives responsible for the online activities at TUI/Thomson UK, MyTravel and Thomas Cook suggests that eBusiness induced changes can be summarised in the following categories:

4.1 Change in strategy and business models

One of the first challenges that companies face when attempting to embrace eBusiness and its technologies is how to move from being a "bricks and mortar" organisation to a "clicks and mortar" one, thus creating a more "virtual form" of organisation (Jackson & Harris, 2003). Krell and Gale (2005) suggest that eBusiness migration is a complex organisational change involving the adoption of "e-enabled" business processes, reassessment of strategies by virtue of technology changing both the nature of competition and the internal capabilities of the organisation.

Like in many other sectors, the Internet and eBusiness are having a fundamental impact on the very structure of the business models under which large tour operator groups have operated for the last two decades: in March 2006, for example, Thomas Cook announced a major rethink of its business model, including "a gradual departure from the ideal of an integrated leisure travel group, not because the model itself was bad but because it has outlived its usefulness". CEO Thomas Holtrop also said "we will create and implement a business model that ties up as little capital as possible while offering optimum flexibility (KarstadtQuell, 2006).

Most of the tour operators examined have been actively reducing their airline seats and hotel beds capacity as well as reducing the amount of risk exposure in the form of hotel/airline guarantees: Thomas Cook, for example, reduced its guaranteed contracts with hotels by 50% in 2004 as well as reducing its Condor fleet in Germany by 10 aircraft with re-orientation of activities with stronger focus on individual seat sales (Thomas Cook, 2005).

Finally, the advent of the Internet has provided the catalyst for these operators to pursue substantial online revenue contribution growth: preliminary 2006 figures quoted in the interviews are showing double, and in certain cases triple digit growth in the online activities of these operators. Tour operators are also trialling the development of separate seat/accommodation-only websites (often with different branding) partly to attract new customer segments and partly, in the words of one interviewee to "test the waters without cannibalising things" (i.e. without impacting on the packaged products sold on the main website). Finally all the tour operators considered were actively pursuing both white-label and affiliate agreements to expand their online reach and considered this as a key distribution strategy.

Whilst it would be premature to declare that the vertically integrated business model is obsolete, there is certainly enough evidence to suggest that all the tour operators examined have embarked on a journey towards what Chaffey (2004) refers to as "Vertical Disintegration", a model characterised by a substantial reduction in ownership of input; move away from mass production towards mass personalisation (through either increasingly more flexible traditional packages or dynamic packaging) and a closer and more interactive interaction with customers via sophisticated web channels and eCRM. One of the interviewees referred to this model, perhaps more appropriately as an "hybrid model" where the company in question is aiming to combine some of the advantages offered by the traditional vertically integrated model (stronger control and access to input and/or distribution; increased opportunities for branding at various customer contact points etc) with the advantages enjoyed by the new travel eMediaries who, to a certain extent are operating free from the traditional limitations inherent, to legacy non web-based ICT systems. Figure 1 illustrates in more detail the shift from vertical to virtual integration highlighting the current position of tour operators in relation to travel eMediaries.

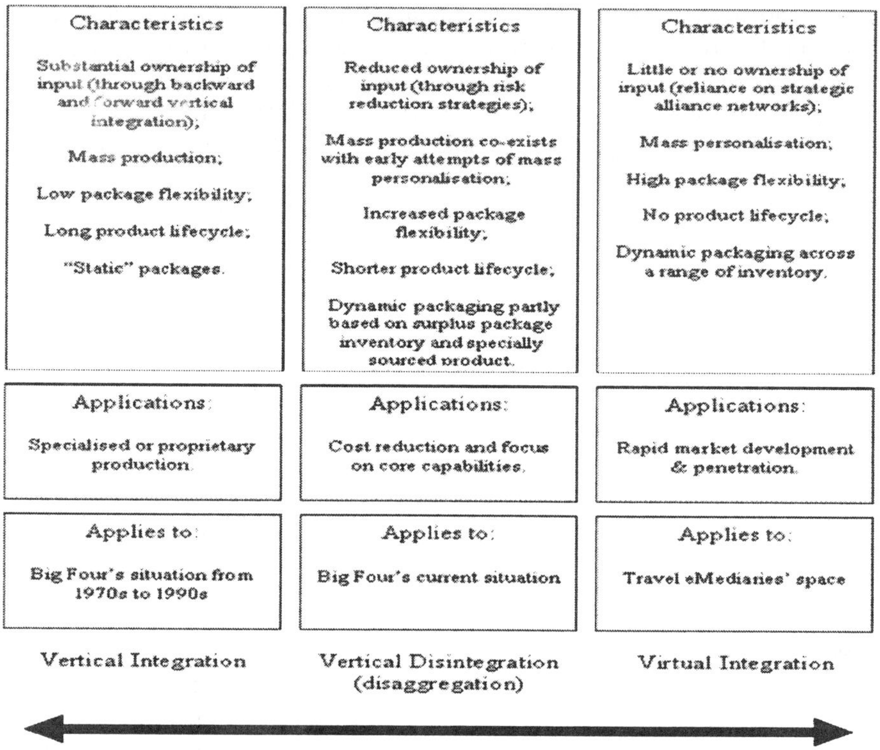

Fig. 1. From Vertical to Virtual Integration (adapted from Chaffey:2004)

4.2 Changes in organisational structure and culture

Changes of such magnitude are difficult to implement without a thorough re-think of the organisation structure and indeed, corporate culture.

With regards to organisational structure, Brett, Mahesh and Hartman (2005) argue that future organisations in the knowledge economy will look more like networks rather then current hierarchical structures, with lesser emphasis on strict departmentalisation (i.e. marketing, finance or sales) and more emphasis on informal networks. In other words: "power based structural hierarchies are seen as road blocks to getting work done and are crumbling in response to the impact of new eBusiness-based approaches" (Shand, 2000:1).

All of the managers interviewed suggested that eBusiness developments had been largely responsible for some changes in organisational structure: in one instance the Board of Directors had been recently reduced from 40 to 8 members to ensure that "fewer people take the important decisions quicker". At the same time most of the eBusiness divisions considered have grown to considerable prominence, moving from peripheral and experimental status to central key components of the organisation often seen as the drivers of new business development. In most cases the heads of these units now report directly to the company CEO.

The Internet not only challenges an organisation structure or technology: it will also challenge the organisation's mindsets, which are rooted in the organisational culture. Scherpereel and Lefebvre (2006) suggest that companies wishing to adapt to the changes created by eBusiness and the Internet should focus on their organisational culture first and technical expertise second.

In the case of the tour operators in question, it became apparent that a cultural shift was under way: themes which emerged strongly included the need to change the management attitudes and mindsets regarding the adoption of eBusiness, issues surrounding eBusiness induced conflict and conflict resolution and the need to enhance the consumer centeredness of the organisation.

With regards to change in top management's mindset it became rapidly clear that top level buy-in to radical eBusiness enabled change was a somewhat slow process to come by: an analysis of the companies' annual reports shows that none of the tour operators had significant organisation wide eBusiness migration plans until at least 2004/2005. Several of the eBusiness managers interviewed shared their frustrations with regards to: a) slow process of eBusiness implementation: *"We are a legacy business, we are oil tankers, it takes a lot time to turn around"*; b) management's difficulty in grasping new eBusiness models *"I know organisation like ours were sitting discussing low cost airlines saying it will never work when we had the opportunity to make it work"*; c) lack of awareness and understanding of technological developments: *"...and how do you have a sensible conversation with your Board about web 2.0, trying to explain the differences between you using one technology over another technology ... it is a huge challenge"*

As it is often the case, change can bring about both internal and external conflict. In the case of the tour operators in question, issues relating to conflict between divisions were identified, particularly in those units of the organisation where the adoption of eBusiness was perceived as potentially detrimental: commenting on the closure of several company owned retail outlets, one eBusiness manager suggested that: *"I think it is fair to say that people who work in the retail network see the Internet as a threat but the message has not yet put across to them that the Internet is a great way to attract customers to their shops"*. Interestingly, cultural conflict was also identified between the traditional IT departments and the newer eBusiness units: *"we are doing more and more in our division as opposed to the IT division because of the type of people and their ability to react a lot quicker, our IT division is quite a legacy division and still embroiled in the old ways of doing things, what I would say are not the most efficient processes"*.

The different pace of cultural shift within these organisations was seen as potentially problematic: *"we are almost creating a digital divide in our own organisation where you have a team of people who are almost running ahead at one level and the rest of the business is struggling to keep up with you"*.

The importance of companies becoming more customer centred as a result of being able to engage in rich customer conversations in an eBusiness environment is well highlighted by several authors: Siegel (2000) suggests that a genuine eBusiness strategy seeks to "foster conversations" with customers throughout the organisation by listening to customers in a strategic way, deepening relationships and loyalty.

Most of the eBusiness managers interviewed were acutely aware of the need to increase their organisation's focus on consumers: *"we need to ensure that everything we do is consumer led and fight that view through the entire business where you have commercial people and directors who are paid bonuses on profit and things like that"*. Likewise all interviewees agreed that the adoption of eBusiness practices increased the company's understanding of their customers in a way that was not possible before:

"eBusiness it is helping us even more because we are getting to realise through data, actually who are the customer that we really want to foster in terms of loyalty and relationships and obviously web data is allowing us to mine that and get a much more personalised and customised service to them".

Most managers also were aware that, as part of being a successful player in the online environment, they would have to face the challenges of developing the systems, processes and control mechanisms to empower the consumer to become more closely involved with package/service production and being prepared to loose some degree of control over the process:

"I think one of the challenges we are going to have as a business is that we are going to loose more control because it's going to the consumer. That is not a bad thing at all but a challenge because it ads a whole new level of complexity into your business that you need to manage for, particularly when you are talking about yield and margins. That is a tricky thing"

4.3 Changes in business processes

Adequately managing the eBusiness processes that facilitate the order fulfilment and delivery of services is a key operations management aspect for any company. Barnes, Hinton and Mieczkowska (2002) identify three key issues to be considered: business process integration (to what extent business processes for clicks & mortar organisations are aligned with those for bricks & mortar) information systems integration (to what extent intra and inter-organisational information systems are able to communicate and share information with each other) and the operating context (types of customers, business model and organisational factors). Focusing on the issue of business process integration, key drivers of change for the tour operators examined could be summarised in two major processes: the gradual deconstruction of the package tour and the adoption of dynamic packaging technologies.

Over the last two years the tour operators examined have effectively started to 'deconstruct' their package tours in order to be able to offer individual components of the trip which can then be either sold separately (e.g. flight only on a charter airline) or re-packaged in different combinations by the customer via dynamic packaging. All the tour operators analysed are now selling individual components of travel via their websites or specially created portals. This change has brought about considerable alterations to the business processes used to both contract and sell their inventory particularly through the adoption of company extranets (allowing suppliers to automatically load and manage inventory on the tour operator's reservation systems) on the buy side and the adoption of dynamic packaging technologies and business processed on the sell side.

Traditional tour operators are also implementing and constantly improving dynamic packaging technologies to meet emerging customer expectations and more effectively manage inventory and yields. All of the operators analysed either already had a dynamic packaging solution or were expecting to have one in place by the end of 2006. This was viewed as a key growth area by all tour operators as dynamic packaging commands an increasingly dominant share of the online packaging market. As well as being an important opportunity all tour operators interviewed agreed that dynamic packaging posed considerable implementation challenges both in terms of technology interfaces to the proprietary systems described earlier and in terms of re-designing business processes and business rules.

4.4 Changes in workforce's skills set requirements

The adoption of eBusiness is also changing the skills sets required both at the management and operational levels. With regards to the management level Brett, Mahesh and Hartman (2005:135) suggest that "owing to the fact that more jobs will be knowledge jobs, and the ability to interact with and even modify some aspects of a complex information system will be required, most managers will be less competent in their jobs than their employees". Mintzberg (1988) suggest that this shift of expertise will translate in a new role for managers, more aligned to the profile of an orchestra conductor rather than a shift supervisor. Either way, Druker (1999) suggests that most or even all management jobs, particularly at middle-management level, will be either greatly reduced or disappear altogether, and those management jobs left will have greater span of control.

Whilst it was difficult to identify such patterns across the organisations interviewed, they did mirror the experiences of at least one of the cases in terms of reduction of management numbers, and corresponding extension of span of control:

"if you take our board for example it is now made up of 8 people whilst it used to be made up by 40, we now operate as one business and we operate within a matrix structure within that business to get the maximum of the benefit we have very, very aggressively flattened the organisation so that we have less chiefs ... with fewer people making bigger decisions"

and in terms of more junior managers (senior managers in the eBusiness division) "educating" their superiors (company directors):

"what we did was to take the senior managers of that department and involve them at a very senior level at strategy meetings so they were involved in working with the directors in terms of how we drove the business forwards and we created a lot of business forums or steering committees that allowed us to call into there and articulate what we wanted to do and get approval and bring them along the journey".

At the employee level, Brett, Mahesh and Hartman, (2005) suggest that a different set of skills may be necessary to utilise new technologies effectively. They describe the emergence of the "information-empowered" employee, an individual who has "always on" access to both corporate and relevant external information via the network and is involved in supporting business processes permeated by IT: as a result, Brett, Mahesh and Hartman (2005:133) suggest that "much of the old workforce is no longer required to support productivity gains, and a different set of skills are necessary to utilize the new technology effectively".

In the case of one of the operators interviewed, out of the 80 staff that makes up their eBusiness division, *"all but a handful had to be recruited externally; we simply did not have the right skills set within the organisation*". Interestingly, the average age of this division is 26.

Even in more traditional areas of sales/retailing, clerical aspects of a travel agency or call centre staff are diminishing in importance since the data necessary to perform these tasks is available on the network and the business processes to construct a package are built into the information system (i.e. dynamic packaging). In the words of one of the interviewees:

"the biggest issue we have today quite frankly is that the website functionality is much better than anything we've got on our retail estate and that is an issue because our customers can go on our website and find a lot more information and be a lot more inspired they can by going into our retail estate".

Finding and recruiting this new set of skills was also considered a major challenge: *"it is difficult to get people who understand eMarketing, it is becoming a real, real challenge because there is not really a lot of really good people out there"*

4.5 Changes in technology infrastructure

Jackson and Harris (2003) suggest that one of the biggest problems for companies migrating from a traditional "bricks & mortar" environment to a "clicks and mortar" one is the need to migrate from legacy IT systems to an eBusiness infrastructure: whilst pure dot.com start ups have the advantage of a "clean sheet" to start with, "clicks and mortar" companies are often faced with complex migration and/or integration challenges as effective eBusiness solutions need strong integration of both front end systems (which are increasingly web-enabled), and back end systems (which are still relying on legacy applications that are nevertheless critical for the company's operations).

Whilst all the operators are still relying on fairly old proprietary reservation systems (i.e. TRACS for TUI/Thomson; TOS for Thomas Cook and ATOP for MyTravel) much work has been done to ensure that some of the problems that these systems have interfacing with a web environment are either eliminated or minimised. Whilst maintaining old proprietary systems in some areas of the business, some of the tour operators are also showing a gradual move to Internet based platforms: in the case of TUI/Thomson's airline, ThomsonFly, TRACS has been entirely replaced by Open Skies, an integrated web-enabled reservation and inventory system suite considered the de-facto standard for low cost carriers. More recently Thomas Cook has announced that it is embarking on a £67m, multi-year ICT project to replace all their legacy reservation systems (including TOS) with a single, multi-channel reservation platform covering its 34 tour operator brands and travel agency networks across Europe.

5 Conclusions

Challenged by a combination of shift in consumer behaviour and the emergence of travel eMediaries as significant new entrants in the travel and package holiday business, traditional tour operators are fighting back by re-examining their business models and their product/distribution channels mix. The processes of deconstruction of the package tour coupled with the strong growth of dynamic packaging is bringing both traditional tour operators and travel eMediaries in direct competition thus foreshadowing possible consolidation in the marketplace in the not too distant future.

Key to their survival and future prosperity will be their ability to positively manage the change involved in the transition from vertical to virtual integration (or hybrid model) driven by the adoption of eBusiness practices throughout the organisation without alienating key stakeholders in their networks, namely traditional and new customers, suppliers and intermediaries. Organisations adopting this path face several challenges in most cases likely to involve radical re-thinking of fundamental aspects of the company's business strategies with company structure, culture and organisational processes becoming much more customer centred. As Jackson and Harris (2003) suggest, in this process new skills, cultures and mindsets will need to be adopted and developed and resistance at all company levels may need to be overcome. To facilitate this, skilled change agents and leaders capable of championing eBusiness will be needed. Equally it is also important to refrain from "throwing the baby out with the bath water" and recognise that important aspects of the old business configurations and processes may still have currency in an eBusiness environment.

Despite the challenges highlighted in this paper, most of the tour operators analysed seemed well placed and prepared to operate in this eBusiness environment thanks to their ability to leverage their traditional strengths of strong brand names, close or, in some cases exclusive links with suppliers, substantially larger customers base and stronger CRM opportunities due to their higher number of touch points with customers. Future research aims to examine more closely the variety of business models that are emerging from these developments with particular regards to determinants of competitive advantage. In addition the paper highlights the need for further research in the management of change in traditional bricks and mortar organisations moving into an eBusiness driven "clicks and mortar" environment:

References

Barnes, D., Hinton, M., Mieczkowska, S. (2002). Developing a Framework to Investigate the Impact of E-commerce on the Management of Internal Business Processes, *Knowledge and Process Management*, 9(3), 133-142.

Brett, J.L., Mahesh, S. & Hartman, S. (2005). The changing nature of work in the age of eBusiness, *Journal of Organizational Change Management*, 18(2), 132-144.

Buhalis, D. (2003). *eTourism - Information technology for strategic tourism management.* Harlow: Prentice Hall.

Buck, S. & Lei, Z. (2004). Charter Airlines: Have they a future. *Tourism and Hospitality Research.* 5(1), 72-78.

By, R. T. (2005). Organisational Change Management: A Critical Review. *Journal of Change Management*, 5(4), 369-380.

Chaffey, D (2004). *eBusiness and e-Commerce Management*, 2nd Edition. London: Prentice Hall Financial Times.

Cooper, C, Fletcher, J., Fyall, A. & Gilbert, D. (2005). *Tourism Principles and Practice.* 3rd Edition. Harlow: FT Prentice Hall.

Daniele, R. & Frew, A. J. (2006). The Giants Fight Back - Tour Operators' Strategies. In A. J. Frew (E d.) The Face Of Competition from Travel eMediaries, *Proceedings of the Travel Distribution Summit, Europe – Research Conference,* (pp. 11 – 22) London: Axon Imprint.

Daniele, R. & Frew, A. J. (2004). From Intermediaries to Market-Makers: an Analysis of the Evolution of E-Mediaries. In A. J Frew. (Ed.) *ENTER 2004 – Information and Communication Technologies in Tourism*, (pp. 546 – 557). Wien: Springer - Verlag.

Dombey, A. (2005). *Navigating a Route to Profitability: The Future of Tour Operator Distribution,* a Towards Europe report, London: Towards Europe Limited.

Drucker, P. (1999). *Beyond the Information Revolution.* Charleston: Atlantic.

Gountas, S. (2005). Tour Operations Management. In Pender, L. and Sharpley, R. (Eds.), *The Management of Tourism*, (pp. 47-67). London: Sage.

Hitwise (2006). *Top 10 Travel Agency sites in the UK.* June 2006. Retrieved August 7, 2006 from http://www.hitwise.com.

Jackson, P. & Harris, L. (2003). EBusiness and Organisational Change: Reconciling traditional values with business transformation. *Journal of Organizational Change Management*, 16(5), 497-511.

Karcher, K. (1996). Re-engineering the Package Holiday Business. In Klein, S. Schmid, B.Tjoa, A.M. (Eds.), *ENTER 1996 – Information and Communication Technologies in Tourism* Conference Proceedings (pp. 221- 234). Wien: Springer - Verlag.

KarstadtQuelle (2006). *Thomas Cook AG to realign its business*. Retrieved August 17, 2006 from www.karstadtquelle/englisch/presse/1072_8378.asp

Krell, T. and Gale, J. (2005) EBusiness migration: a process model. *Journal of Organizational Change Management*, 18(2), 117-131.

Lewins, A. and Silver, C. (2005). *Choosing a CAQDAS Package*, a working paper, 3rd edition Nov 2005. Retrieved August 14, 2006 from http://caqdas.soc.surrey.ac.uk/ChoosingLewins&SilverV3Nov05.pdf accessed on 7/09/2005

Mintzberg, H. (1998). Covert leadership: notes on managing professionals. *Harvard Business Review*, 76(6), 140-147.

Pender, L. & Sharpley, R. (2005). *The Management of Tourism,* London: SAGE Publications.

Rieley, J. B & Clarkson, I. (2001). The Impact of Change on Performance. *Journal of Change Management*, 2(2), 160-172.

Scherpereel, C. & Lefebvre, J. (2006). Shocking the legacy mindset: management development and the internet. *Journal of Management Development*, 25(3), 232-248.

Shand, D. (2000). Dynamic Organization. Retrieved August 21, 2006 from http://www.destinationkm.com/print/default.asp?ArticleID=44

Siegel (2000). *Futurize Your Enterprise: Business Strategy in the Age of the E-customer,* New York: Wiley.

Thomas Cook (2005). *Annual report 200. Retrieved August 18, 2006 from,* http://www8.thomascook.de/tck/6168.jsp

A Review of Hospitality Website Design Frameworks

Noor Hazarina Hashim[a]
Jamie Murphy[a]
Rob Law[b]

[a] University of Western Australia Business School
{hashin01}@student.uwa.edu.au
{jmurphy}@biz.uwa.edu.au

[b] School of Hotel and Tourism Management,
The Hong Kong Polytechnic University
{hmroblaw}@polyu.edu.hk

Abstract

An effective website is vital for a hotel to strengthen its customer relationships and harvest online sales. Yet despite the proliferation of hotel website studies, research seems to have under-emphasised a fundamental first step, the development of valid and reliable constructs and features for evaluating websites. Based on a literature review, expert judgement and in-depth interviews, this study proposes a framework for evaluating hotel websites. The results are five dimensions of website quality – information and process, value added, relationships, trust, and design and usability – reflected by 74 websites features. The paper closes with a proposed process for developing a website evaluation framework and future research opportunities.

Keywords: hospitality, website design, meta-analysis

1 Introduction

Research suggests that website content can augment advertising and marketing activities (Barwise, Elberse, & Hammond, 2002; Wan, 2002). For example, customers satisfied with a website return to that same website (Kim & Stoel, 2004). Given the Internet's growing importance as a hospitality distribution and marketing channel (O'Connor & Frew, 2002), hoteliers must routinely evaluate their websites to ensure that the site is efficient, appropriate and useful to customers (Baloglu & Pekcan, 2006). Yet despite the Internet's increasing role in tourism and hospitality, research related to website evaluations seems lagging and requires further effort (Morrison, Taylor, & Douglas, 2004).

In the first instance, there is lack of consensus on the important features and dimensions of a hotel websites (Morrison et al., 2004). Website evaluation studies differ on dimensions of website quality (Aladwani & Palvia, 2002; Barnes & Vidgen, 2001). For example, Chen, Clifford and Wells (2002) identify three dimensions, while Liu and Arnett (2000) mention five dimensions. As the number of studies grows, dimensions of website quality begin to converge (Heinze & Hu, 2006) and suggest that website quality has multidimensional constructs such as information, interactivity, ease of use and trust (Kim & Stoel, 2004).

Despite this seeming convergence, most studies fail to explain how website dimensions form or the domain of the measured construct, and even fewer studies establish the validity and reliability of their measures (Susser & Ariga, 2006; Wolfinbarger & Gilly, 2003). For example, Liu and Arnett's (2000) factors related to website success included features about information to support business objectives, empathy to customer problems, and follow-up services to customers. These three features loaded on the same factor, information quality, yet there was no discussion of forming or classifying that factor (Kim & Stoel, 2004).

Finally, there seem to be two major research streams that analyse website features. One stream measures user perceptions of website quality (Law & Cheung, 2006; Law & Hsu, 2006) such as the E-S-Qual scale (Parasuraman, Zeithaml, & Malhotra, 2005). This stream examines perceived characteristics of effective and successful website and a complementary stream verify these variables in actual practice. These studies content analyse features on a website, using either humans (Murphy, Olaru, Schegg, & Frey, 2003) or computers (Scharl, Wöber, & Bauer, 2004; Schegg, Steiner, Frey, & Murphy, 2002) to count the presence of each feature.

In essence, websites are important to the hotel industry but there is little consensus on a valid and reliable website evaluation framework. Thus, this paper reviews key website evaluation studies across multiple disciplines from information management, e-commerce, electronic marketing, hospitality and tourism in order to propose and help validate an evaluation framework that will assist (a) hoteliers improve their website presence and (b) academics evaluate hospitality websites. The next section explains the methodology, an analysis of almost 50 website studies. After discussing the findings, the paper closes with academic and managerial implications of the study.

2 Methods

2.1 Defining websites dimensions and features

This study employed a two-step process to build content validity, a literature review of website evaluation studies and expert judgement to confirm and validate the dimensions. The literature review helps achieve content validity ensure the theoretical meaningfulness of a construct (Hinkin, 1995, p.969). A sound conceptual and theoretical basis of the construct must precede the development of website dimensions (Tsai & Chai, 2005).

The study started with a broad review of management information system, internet marketing and electronic commerce literature, as website evaluation studies often progressed from these disciplines. A July 2006 search of online databases – *Google Scholar* (Jacsó, 2005), *JSTOR*, *ProQuest International*, *PsycINFO*, *Business Source*

Premier, *Wiley Interscience* and *ScienceDirect* – with keywords *website evaluation*, *website study* or *web site study* – yielded 17 articles from nine journals from 1997-2005 that explained developing or constructing website dimensions (see Table 1).

Table 1. Website quality dimensions and features across studies

Authors	Dimensions and features
Liu, Arnett, Capella & Beatty (1997)	Products/services, overview, feedback, what's new, financial, customer service, search, employment, guest book, index/directory, online business, other sites, CEO messages and FAQs
Ho (1997)	Matrix of purpose (promotion, provision and processing) by value (timely, custom, logistic and sensational)
Chen & Wells (2002); Chen et al.,(1999)	Entertainment, informativeness, and easy to use and understand
Johnson & Misic (1999)	Functional/navigational issues, content and style and contact information
Lin & Lu (2000)	Information quality, response time, and system accessibility
Liu & Arnett (2000)	Quality of information and service, system use, playfulness, and system design quality
Zhang & von Drand (2001)	Information content, cognitive outcomes, enjoyment, privacy, user empowerment, visual appearance, technical support, navigation, organisation of information, credibility, and impartiality
Barnes & Vidgen (2001)	Usability, design, information, trust and empathy.
Cox & Dale (2002)	Ease of use, customer confidence, on-line resources, and relationship services.
Palmer (2002)	Download delay, navigability, site content, interactivity and responsiveness
Ranganathan & Ganapathy (2002)	Information content, design, security and privacy.
Aladwani & Palvia (2002)	Technical adequacy, content quality, specific content, and appearance
Wolfinbarger & Gilly (2003)	Fulfilment and reliability, website design, privacy and security and customer relationship
Kim & Stoel (2004)	Information, transaction, ease of use, entertainment, trust, consistent image
Hong & Kim (2004)	Structural robustness (Internal reliability and external security), functional utility (useful content and usable navigation) and aesthetic appeal (system interface and communication interface)
Tsai & Chai (2005)	Impression, download and switch speed, accessibility and convenience, web page content, service function and compatibility with common browsers

The first study introduced 12 features to evaluate Fortune 500 company homepages (Liu et al., 1997). Exploratory and descriptive, it failed to discuss reliability and validity. Later studies however, addressed this shortcoming. For instance, Tsai and Chai (2005) developed and validated a questionnaire for nursing websites. Their 32-item questionnaire covered six website quality criteria of impression, download and switch speed, accessibility and convenience, web page content, service function and compatibility with common browsers.

An analysis of the 17 articles also identified the 79 website dimensions and features in Table 1. While these studies contribute to website evaluation and design, a main limitation is research inconsistencies in addressing different aspects of website design factors, purposes, and user categories (Zhang & von Drand, 2001, p.11). Wolfinbarger and Gilly (2003) noted that lists of quality website dimensions were long, varied and oftentimes, different terms denoted the same construct. For instance to reflect ease of use, two studies use 'organisation of the site' (Chen et al., 2002; Chen & Wells, 1999) and another uses 'system design quality' (Liu & Arnett, 2000).

This study uses structured conceptualisation, a technique to organise thoughts, ideas, theories, and problem statements into conceptual representations (Trochim & Linton, 1986). The researcher starts with a brainstorming session, in this case based on the 17 articles, to generate a large set of topical information. Then, the researcher sorts the information into similar groups and a pictorial representation called a concept map (Trochim & Linton, 1986, p.293).

Lastly, the researcher interprets and defines the meaning of each group in the concept map. For example, Wolfinbarger and Gilly (2003) used structured conceptualisation to identify five dimensions of retail website quality: information, interactivity, relationships, trust, and design and usability. Structured conceptualisation of the results in Table 1 yielded the five dimensions of website quality in Figure 1: information and process, value added, relationships, trust, and design and usability.

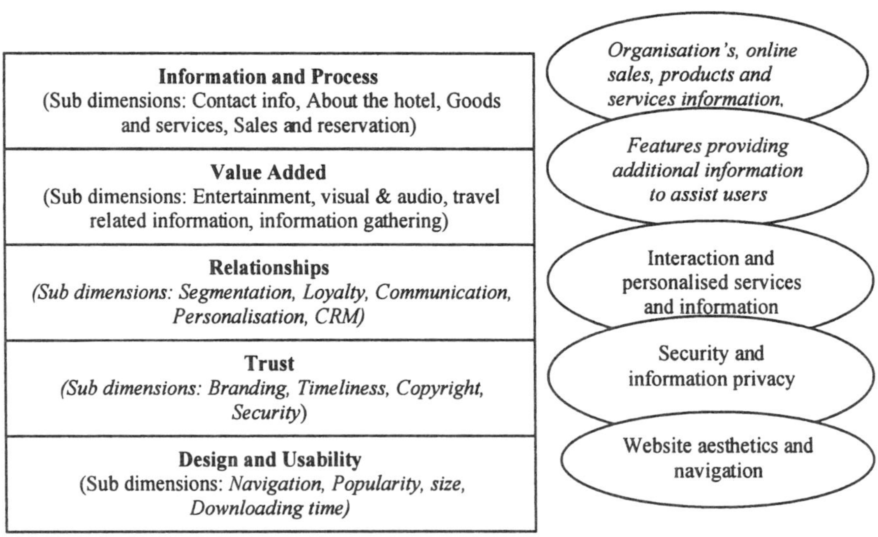

Fig.1. Dimensions of Hotel Website Quality

To help validate and generalise these dimensions to the hospitality industry, the researchers conducted 17 in-depth interviews in Kuala Lumpur and Johor Bahru, Malaysia in January 2006. The interviewees were 13 managers from one-five star hotels, two website designers specialising in hotel and destination marketing, and two university academics in e-commerce. The face-to-face, tape-recorded interviews relied upon semi-structured questions, whereby respondents described criteria for high quality websites. Transcribing and reviewing the interviews supported the framework in Figure 1 as well as identifying hotel-specific features. The following section complements these qualitative results by reviewing website evaluation studies in tourism and hospitality.

2.2 Classifying website features into dimensions

Wolfinbarger and Gilly (2003) argue that a website conceptual framework should capture online activities from the beginning to the end of transactions, including information search, website navigation, ordering, customer service interactions, delivery and satisfaction with the ordered product (p.183). Morrison et al. (2004) add that holistic website evaluations should assess technical details as poor technical performance could undermine good website content and sound marketing.

A literature review using the sources described in section 2.1 identified 25 tourism and hospitality website studies from 1996-2006 (see Appendix A). Research in website evaluation in tourism and hospitality took off only in mid 1990s (Morrison et al., 2004), as these 25 studies illustrate. There was one study from 1996-2001, three in 2002, five in 2003, three in 2004, two in 2005 and seven in 2006. Of the 25 studies, 12 are descriptive and explaining the frequency of each feature, ten studies measure the association of website features with dependent variables such as website marketing performance (Wang & Fesenmaier, 2005) and website effectiveness (Scharl et al., 2004) and three articles are case studies.

Reviewing the 25 articles generated 235 website features. Data consolidation of these features focused on similar names for the same website feature. For instance, three studies used the term 'electronic postcard' (Doolin, Burgess, & Cooper, 2002; So & Morrison, 2004; Yuan, Gretzel, & Fesenmaier, 2006), while a fourth noted 'send friend a postcard' (Schegg et al., 2002). Combining similar terms strengthens discriminant validity, that features differ, and construct validity or that a feature measures what it claims measure (Malhotra, Hall, Shaw, & Oppenheim, 2002).

Consolidation and structured conceptualisation of the 235 features yielded 74 features in 15 sub dimensions and five dimensions. Table 2 shows the final results and the frequency count of how often each feature appeared in the 25 studies. The top three dimensions and features based on frequency counts resemble literature discussing the evolution of websites, from providing information to providing personalisation and adding value (Piccoli, Brohman, Watson, & Parasuraman, 2004). Yet combined, the personalisation and added value dimensions did not garner as much research interest as the top dimension, information and processes.

Table 2. Dimension, Sub Dimension and Feature Frequency Counts

Information and Process (125)	**Value Added (55)**	**Design and Usability (49)**
• ***Sales or reservation (35)*** Search capability (14) Online reservation (9) Secure payment (8) Online cancellation (3) Booking confirmation (1) • ***Contact info (35)*** Email (14) Physical address (7) Phone (7) Map (4) Fax (3) • ***Sales promotions (23)*** Special promotions (8) Groups (5) Family/kids (5) Business travel (2) Honeymooners (1) Gift certificate (1) Bonus/coupons (1) • ***Goods and services (23)*** Download and printables (8) Room classifications (5) Facilities information (4) In-room photo (3) Technical information (1) Room infrastructure (1) View out of the room (1) • ***About the hotel (9)*** Short hotel description (3) Mission or purpose (2) Opening period (1) Organisation (1) People (1) Shareholder info (1)	• ***Travel information (34)*** External links (11) Events calendar (5) Transportation (5) Local sites (5) News (3) Climate/weather (2) Exchange rate (2) Interactive map (1) • ***Entertainment (21)*** Video or animation (11) Contest (4) Send an e-card (4) Viral Marketing (2) **Relationships (55)** • ***Loyalty/CRM (27)*** Guestbook (8) Newsletter subscription (6) Permission marketing (3) Membership/Club (2) Restricted area for loyal guest/personal login (2) Frequent visitor program (2) Data collection for profiling (2) Cookies (2) • ***Personal interest (28)*** Comments/Feedback (11) Online chat (6) Brochure request (5) Customised packages (3) Survey (3)	• ***Navigation (31)*** Multilingual site (11) Sitemap (9) FAQs (9) Consistent theme (2) • ***Technical (13)*** Website or Web page size (9) Browser compatibility (3) Option of browser versions (1) • ***Success metrics (5)*** Popularity ranking (4) Number of incoming links (1) **Trust (27)** • ***Copyright and security (10)*** Privacy statement (5) Copyright (2) Corporate identity (2) Site usage term (1) • ***Timeliness (9)*** Date last update (6) Current and timely info (3) • ***Branding (8)*** Branded URL (4) Branded email (3) Trademark (1)

The most researched features, over one-third of the total frequency count of 311, fell into the Information and Process dimension. Within this dimension and in decreasing order, the five sub dimensions related to sales, contact information, promotions, product descriptions and about the hotel. The top two sub dimensions were the most popular of all 15 sub dimensions. With a frequency count of 14, the ability to search a website and the presence of an email address, tied as the most popular feature in this dimension and all other dimensions.

The value added and relationship dimensions had the same frequencies. Value added features fell into two sub dimensions, travel information and entertainment. The top two value added features, 11 times each in the 25 studies, seemed at opposite ends of implementation costs. External links are free and easy to add while animated features are much more complicated and expensive. The two sub dimensions of relationships related to either loyalty or personal care. The most popular studied relationship feature was inviting customers to comment.

The design and usability dimension contained three sub dimensions: navigation, technical and success metrics. A multilingual site with 11 mentions, led this dimension, closely followed by Sitemap, FAQs and webpage size with nine mentions each. Despite growing calls for measuring website success (Morrison et al., 2004; Murphy, Ho, & Chan, 2005), success metrics was the least popular feature.

Studies highlight trust an essential element to create positive costumer relationship and pleasant online experience (Corbitt, Taylor, & Han, 2003). Yet this was the least studied dimension; less than one in ten frequency counts related to trust. Features such as timeliness information, branded URLs and email addresses, and privacy statements help increase customer with the hotel website and thus support and encourage customer relationships and loyalty.

A few studies showed relationship between some features and website performance. For instance, the search capability, download and printables, external link, video and animation, comments/feedback and multilingual site features had a significant relationship with dependent variables such as email reply quality (Murphy et al., 2003) and hotel's internet marketing activities (Wang & Fesenmaier, 2005). For instance, hotel websites with animation had low quality email replies, while websites that provided external links or brochure requests had high quality email replies (Murphy et al., 2003).

3 Conclusion and Future Research Directions

The list of reviewed articles is by no means exhaustive, yet peer-reviewed articles provide useful and dependable information. Furthermore, the qualitative interviews took place in Malaysia, which could bias the framework. Future research should use a more heterogeneous set of experts and a larger set of articles. This study reviewed the presence of website features. Future research could extend and complement this study by including more quantitative studies and investigating the presence of other variables in those studies. For example a few studies examined relationships between these features and either organisational characteristics such as size and star category (Murphy et al., 2003), or consumer preferences (Law & Hsu, 2006).

This developed framework helps hoteliers reflect on their current and future website design. The five dimensions help management understand important areas for their site. Offering the right information is critical, as customers with purchase intention seek specific product information and spend minimal browsing time on the web (Moe, 2003). It also gives hotels a list of features to gauge their website versus their competitors' sites. For example, the website ranking features demonstrates the visibility of the website on the Internet.

Academically, this framework helps consolidate existing studies on website evaluation and lays a foundation for future research. Research requires valid and reliable instruments, yet website evaluation studies often fail to verify or discuss dimension identification and measurement (Aladwani & Palvia, 2002). This study takes a small step forward, beyond the descriptive and narrative evidence to propose a website evaluation framework and corresponding features. A review of dozens of website evaluation studies helps ensure comprehensiveness and avoid missing important aspects of effective websites.

This paper comprises the first two of four proposed steps of a systematic and comprehensive study of website dimensions and features (see Figure 2). These phases cover six key validity types: content, construct (convergent and discriminant), criterion (predictive and concurrent), internal, statistical and nomological (Bagozzi, 1981; Hinkin, 1995; Straub, 1989).

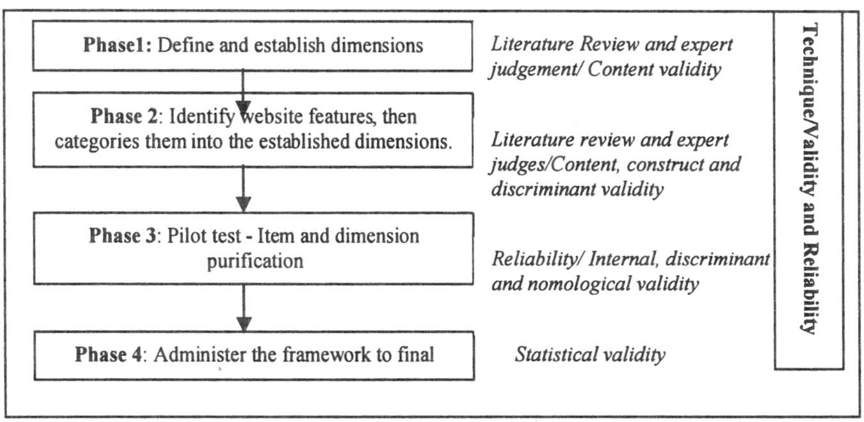

Fig.2. Proposed Website Evaluation Framework Development and Validation Process

This study defined dimensions for, and features of, a website evaluation framework. Both theory and understanding build a foundation for deciding website dimensions and features. The third phase deals with reliability, pre-tests coding the features on a few websites before the final step of coding the features present on the final sample.

Lastly, future research should pre-test the framework and most features on a sample of hotel websites. A pre-test allows the researcher to refine and purify the framework before administering to the final sample. For example, a feature can be ambiguous and misunderstood by coders, which leads to unreliable coding of the feature (Krippendorff, 1980; McMillan, 2000).

Appendix A: Tourism and Hospitality studies in this study

Baloglu, S., & Pekcan, Y. A. (2006). The Website Design and Internet Site Marketing Practices of Upscale and Luxury Hotels in Turkey. *Tourism Management, 27*(1), 171-176.

Benckendorff, P. J., & Black, N. L. (2000). Destination Marketing on the Internet: A Case Study of Australian Regional Tourism Authorities. *Journal of Tourism Studies, 11*(1), 11-21.

Blum, V., & Fallon, J. (2001). Welsh Visitor Attraction Websites: Multipurpose Tools or Technological Tokenism. *Information Technology & Tourism, 4(3-4)*, 191-201.

Cano, V., & Prentice, R. (1998). Opportunities for Endearment to Place through Electronic Visiting: WWW Homepages and Tourism Promotion of Scotland. *Tourism Management, 19*(1), 67-71.

Chung, T., & Law, R. (2003). Developing a performance indicator for hotel websites. *International Journal of Hospitality Management, 22*(1), 119-125.

Doolin, B., Burgess, L., & Cooper, J. (2002). Evaluating the Use of the Web for Tourism Marketing: A Case Study from New Zealand. *Tourism Management, 23*(5), 557-561.

Essawy, M. (2006). Testing the Usability of Hotel Websites: The Springboard for Customer Relationship Building. *Information Technology and Tourism, 8*, 47-70.

Feng, R., Morrison, A. M., & Ismail, J. A. (2003). East vs. West: A Comparison of Online Destination Marketing in China and the USA. *Journal of Vacation Marketing, 10*(1), 43-56.

Jeong, M., Oh, H., & Gregoire, M. (2003). Conceptualizing Web Site Quality and its Consequences in the Lodging Industry. *International Journal of Hospitality Management, 22*(2), 161-175.

Küster, I. (2006). Relational Content of Travel and Tourism Websites. *Asia Pacific Journal of Tourism Research, 11*(2), 119-133.

Law, R., & Cheung, C. (2006). A Study of the Perceived Importance of the Overall Website Quality of Different Classes of Hotels. *International Journal of Hospitality Management,* 25(3), 525-531.

Law, R., & Hsu, C. (2006). Importance of Hotel Website Dimensions and Attributes: Perceptions of Online Browsers and Online Purchasers. *Journal of Hospitality & Tourism Research, 30*(3), 295-312.

Law, R., & Wong, J. (2003). Successful Factors for a Travel Web Site: Perceptions of Online Purchasers in Hong Kong. *Journal of Hospitality & Tourism Research, 27*(1), 118-124.

Morrison, A. M., Taylor, J. S., & Douglas, A. (2004). Website Evaluation in Tourism and Hospitality: The Art Is Not Yet Stated. *Journal of Travel and Tourism Marketing, 17*(2/3), 233-251.

Morrison, A. M., Taylor, J. S., Morrison, A. J., & Morrison, A. D. (1999). Marketing Small Hotels on the World Wide Web. *Information Technology & Tourism, 2*(2), 97-113.

Murphy, J., Forrest, E. J., Wotring, C. E., & Brymer, R. A. (1996). Hotel Management and Marketing on the Internet. *Cornell Hotel and Restaurant Administration Quarterly, 37*(3), 70-82.

Murphy, J., Ho, P., & Chan, C. (2005). Competitive Analyses for Marketing Electronic Wine Tourism. *International Journal of Wine Marketing, 17*(3), 39-54.

Murphy, J., Olaru, D., & Schegg, R. (2006). Investigating the Evolution of Hotel Internet Adoption. *Information Technology & Tourism.*, forthcoming.

Murphy, J., Olaru, D., Schegg, R., & Frey, S. (2003). The Bandwagon Effect: Swiss Hotels' Website and E-mail Management. *Cornell Hotel and Restaurant Administration Quarterly, 44*(1), 71-87.

Scharl, A., Wöber, K. W., & Bauer, C. (2004). An Integrated Approach to Measure Web Site Effectiveness in the European Hotel Industry. *Information Technology & Tourism, 6*(4), 257-271.

Schegg, R., Steiner, T., Frey, S., & Murphy, J. (2002). Benchmarks of Web Site Design and Marketing by Swiss Hotels. *Information Technology & Tourism, 5*(2), 73-89.

So, S. I., & Morrison, A. M. (2004). Internet Marketing in Tourism in Asia: An Evaluation of the Performance of East Asian National Tourism Organization Websites. *Journal of Hospitality and Leisure Marketing, 11*(4), 93-117.

Wan, C. S. (2002). The Websites of International Tourist Hotels and Tour Wholesalers in Taiwan. *Tourism Management, 23*(2), 155-160.

Wang, Y., & Fesenmaier, D. R. (2005). Identifying the Success Factors of Web-based Marketing Strategy: An Investigation of Convention and Visitors Bureaus in the United States. *Journal of Travel Research, 43*(3), 1-11.

Yuan, Y. L., Gretzel, U., & Fesenmaier, D. R. (2006). The Role of Information Technology Use in American Convention and Visitors Bureaus. *Tourism Management, 27*(2), 326-341.

References

Aladwani, A. M., & Palvia, P. C. (2002). Developing and Validating an Instrument for Measuring User-Perceived Web Quality. *Information & Management, 39*(6), 467-476.

Bagozzi, R. P. (1981). An Examination of the Validity of Two Models of Attitude. *Multivariate Behavioral Research, 16*(3), 323-359.

Baloglu, S., & Pekcan, Y. A. (2006). The Website Design and Internet Site Marketing Practices of Upscale and Luxury Hotels in Turkey. *Tourism Management, 27*(1), 171-176.

Barnes, S. J., & Vidgen, R. (2001). An Evaluation of Cyber-Bookshops: The WebQual Method. *International Journal of Electronic Commerce, 6*(1), 11-30.

Barwise, P., Elberse, A., & Hammond, K. (2002). Marketing and the Internet: A Research Review. In B. A. Weitz & R. Wensley (Eds.), *Handbook of Marketing* (pp. 527-558). London: Sage Publications.

Chen, Q., Clifford, S. J., & Wells, W. D. (2002). Attitude toward the Site II: New Information. *Journal of Advertising Research, 42*(2), 33-45.

Chen, Q., & Wells, W. D. (1999). Attitude toward the Site. *Journal of Advertising Research, 39*(5), 27-37.

Corbitt, B. J., Taylor, J. S., & Han, Y. (2003). Trust and Hospitality: The Art Is Not Yet Stated. *Journal of Travel & Tourism Marketing, 2*(3), 203-215.

Cox, J. L., & Dale, B. G. (2002). Key Quality Factors in Web Site Design and Use: An Examination. *International Journal of Quality and Reliability Management, 19*(7), 862-888.

Doolin, B., Burgess, L., & Cooper, J. (2002). Evaluating the Use of the Web for Tourism Marketing: A Case Study from New Zealand. *Tourism Management, 23*(5), 557-561.

Heinze, N., & Hu, Q. (2006). The Evolution of Corporate Website Presence: A Longitudinal Study of Large American Companies. *International Journal of Information Management, 26*(4), 313-325.

Hinkin, T. R. (1995). A Review of Scale Development Practices in the Study of Organization. *Journal of Management, 21*(5), 967-988.

Ho, J. (1997). Evaluating the World Wide Web: A Global Study of Commercial Sites. *Journal of Computer Mediated Communication (Online), 3*(1), http://jcmc.indiana.edu/vol3/issue1/ho.html.

Hoffman, D. L., & Novak, T. P. (1996). Marketing in Hypermedia Computer Mediated Environments: Conceptual Foundations. *Journal of Marketing, 60*(3), 50-68.

Hong, S., & Kim, J. (2004). Architectural Criteria for Website Evaluation - Conceptual Framework and Empirical Validation. *Behaviour and Information Technology, 23*(5), 337-357.

Jacsó, P. (2005). Google Scholar: The Pros and the Cons. *Online Information Review, 29*(2), 208-214.

Johnson, K. L., & Misic, M. M. (1999). Benchmarking: A Tool for Website Evaluation and Improvement. *Internet Research, 9*(5), 383-392.

Kim, S., & Stoel, L. (2004). Dimensional Hierarchy of Retail Website Quality. *Information and Management, 41*(5), 619-633.

Krippendorff, K. (1980). *Content Analysis: An Introduction to Its Methodology*. California: SAGE Publications Inc.

Law, R., & Cheung, C. (2006). A Study of the Perceived Importance of the Overall Website Quality of Different Classes of Hotels. *International Journal of Hospitality Management, 25*(3), 525-531.

Law, R., & Hsu, C. (2006). Importance of Hotel Website Dimensions and Attributes: Perceptions of Online Browsers and Online Purchasers. *Journal of Hospitality & Tourism Research, 30*(3), 295-312.

Lin, J. C. C., & Lu, H. (2000). Towards an Understanding of the Behavioural Intention to Use a Website. *International Journal of Information Management, 20*(3), 197-208.

Liu, C., & Arnett, K. P. (2000). Exploring the Factors Associated with Web site Success in the Context of Electronic Commerce. *Information & Management, 38*(1), 23-33.

Liu, C., Arnett, K. P., Capella, L. M., & Beatty, R. C. (1997). Websites for the Fortune 500 Companies: Facing Customers through Homepages. *Information & Management, 31*(6), 335-345.

Malhotra, N., Hall, J., Shaw, M., & Oppenheim, P. (2002). *Marketing Research: An Applied Orientation*. New South Wales, Australia: Pearson Education Australia Pty Ltd.

McMillan, S. J. (2000). The Microscope and the Moving Target: The Challenge of Applying Content Analysis to the World Wide Web. *Journalism and Mass Communication Quarterly, 77*(1), 80-98.

Moe, W. W. (2003). Buying, Searching, or Browsing: Differentiating Between Online Shoppers Using In-Store Navigational Clickstream. *Journal of Consumer Psychology, 13*(1&2), 29-39.

Morrison, A. M., Taylor, J. S., & Douglas, A. (2004). Website Evaluation in Tourism and Hospitality: The Art Is Not Yet Stated. *Journal of Travel & Tourism Marketing, 17*(2/3), 233-251.

Murphy, J., Ho, P., & Chan, C. (2005). Competitive Analyses for Marketing Electronic Wine Tourism. *International Journal of Wine Marketing, 17*(3), 39-54.

Murphy, J., Olaru, D., Schegg, R., & Frey, S. (2003). The Bandwagon Effect: Swiss Hotels' Website and E-mail Management. *Cornell Hotel and Restaurant Administration Quarterly, 44*(1), 71-87.

O'Connor, P., & Frew, A. J. (2002). The Future of Hotel Electronic Distribution. *Cornell Hotel and Restaurant Administration Quarterly, 43*(3), 33-45.

Palmer, J. W. (2002). Web Site Usability, Design, and Performance Metrics. *Information Systems Research, 13*(2), 151-167.

Parasuraman, A., Zeithaml, V. A., & Malhotra, A. (2005). E-S-QUAL: A Multiple-Item Scale for Assessing Electronic Service Quality. *Journal of Service Research, 7*(3), 213-233.

Piccoli, G., Brohman, M. K., Watson, R. T., & Parasuraman, A. (2004). Net-Based Customer Service Systems: Evolution and Revolution in Website Functionalities. *Decision Sciences, 35*(3), 423-453.

Ping, Z., & von Drand, G. M. (2001). User Expectations and Rankings of Quality Factors in Different Web Site Domains. *International Journal of Electronic Commerce, 6*(2), 9-33.

Ranganathan, C., & Ganapathy, S. (2002). Key Dimensions of Business-to-Consumer Websites. *Information and Management, 39*(6), 457-465.

Scharl, A., Wöber, K. W., & Bauer, C. (2004). An Integrated Approach to Measure Web Site Effectiveness in the European Hotel Industry. *Information Technology & Tourism, 6*(4), 257-271.

Schegg, R., Steiner, T., Frey, S., & Murphy, J. (2002). Benchmarks of Web Site Design and Marketing by Swiss Hotels. *Information Technology & Tourism, 5*(2), 73-89.

So, S. I., & Morrison, A. M. (2004). Internet Marketing in Tourism in Asia: An Evaluation of the Performance of East Asian National Tourism Organization Websites. *Journal of Hospitality and Leisure Marketing, 11*(4), 93-117.

Straub, D. W. (1989). Validating Instruments in MIS Research. *MIS Quarterly, 13*(2), 147-169.

Susser, B., & Ariga, T. (2006). Teaching E-Commerce Webpage Evaluation and Design: A Pilot Study using Tourism Destination Sites. *Computers and Education, 47*(4), 399-413.

Trochim, W. M. K., & Linton, R. (1986). Conceptualization for Evaluation and Planning. *Evaluation and Program Planning, 9*(4), 289-308.

Tsai, S. L., & Chai, S.-K. (2005). Developing and Validating a Nursing Website Evaluation Questionnaire. *Journal of Advanced Nursing, 49*(4), 406-413.

Wan, C. S. (2002). The Websites of International Tourist Hotels and Tour Wholesalers in Taiwan. *Tourism Management, 23*(2), 155-160.

Wang, Y., & Fesenmaier, D. R. (2005). Identifying the Success Factors of Web-based Marketing Strategy: An Investigation of Convention and Visitors Bureaus in the United States. *Journal of Travel Research, 43*(3), 1-11.

Wolfinbarger, M., & Gilly, M. C. (2003). eTailQ: Dimensionalizing, Measuring and Predicting eTail Quality. *Journal of Retailing, 79*(3), 183-198.

Yuan, Y. L., Gretzel, U., & Fesenmaier, D. R. (2006). The Role of Information Technology Use in American Convention and Visitors Bureaus. *Tourism Management, 27*(2), 326-341.

Zhang, P., & von Drand, G. M. (2001). User Expectations and Rankings of Quality Factors in Different Website Domains. *International Journal of Electronic Commerce, 6*(2), 9-33.

An Experimental Usability Study for Augmented Reality Technologies in the Tourist Sector

Aurkene Alzua-Sorzabal[a]
María Teresa Linaza[b]
Marina Abad[a]

[a] Faculty of Humanities, San Sebastian Campus
Deusto University, Spain
{aurkenea}@ud-ss.deusto.es
[b] Department of Tourism, Heritage and Creativity,
Visual Communication Technologies (VICOMTech), Spain
mtlinaza@vicomtech.es

Abstract

This paper presents the usability study of a new prototype based on Augmented Reality technologies, which has been tested on a tourist site in the North of Spain. The overall aim of the usability study of the prototype has been the development of typologies of users and standards, so that new interactive tourist experiences could be personalized in the future taking into account concepts such as usefulness and ease of use. Observation has been a key issue within the usability study so that the possibilities and limitations of the design of the prototype have been analysed on the basis of the behaviour of users. Most of the participants agreed that the approach of using Augmented Reality technologies enhances the interactive experience with tourist content. Moreover, they have positively assessed the usefulness of the prototype as a tourist information point due to its capability of providing Location-Based contents.

Keywords: usability studies, augmented reality, tourism, interactive experience.

1 Introduction

Added-value services based on innovative Information and Communication Technologies (ICT) have launched new research challenges related to content personalization. These services should enhance the experience of users and skip what they consider irrelevant content for them. Thus, behavioural models which relate acceptance and usability of ICT with user profiles are crucial, as they provide further information for demand identification. From the point of view of the theoretical analysis, innovative methodological approaches should include two main aspects in order to take into account all aspects related to the usability of ICT-based products and services: a quantitative analysis of the numerically measurable aspects influencing the acceptance of the technology and a qualitative analysis of the soft factors that determine its usability.

Several disciplines within the domain of Social Sciences have traditionally distinguished between quantitative and qualitative techniques. However, new trends have shown the convenience of combining both methodologies in a triangulation method, where both qualitative and quantitative methods are used in varying ways and degrees. The aim of quantitative analysis is the generation of standardized data in a statistically representative way so that methodologies can be replicated and results can be compared in further research. The qualitative approach includes new factors such as the "level of interest" and "suggestion". It is not enough to know whether technology is usable but to analyse whether users are willing to use it and under which conditions. It must be mentioned that the degree up to which these factors influence the attitudes of the users with regard to technology usage in tourism settings is difficult to measure. User acceptance of technology is typically measured by looking at the intentions. The stronger the intention to use a technology, the more that user is supposed to accept the technology.

This paper presents the usability study of a new prototype, combines the commonly known concept of tourist binoculars and Augmented Reality technologies. The usability study and evaluation of the prototype have been based on both qualitative and quantitative analysis. Section 2 presents a brief state of the art regarding concepts related to methodological approaches for usability analysis. The new prototype based on Augmented Reality Technologies called PRISMA is described in Section 3 from a technical point of view, including its main features and the usage of the prototype. Section 4 focuses on the developed methodology, which has been separated in qualitative and quantitative methods. Finally, some general conclusions are provided in Section 5.

2 Literature review

Several theoretical models have been developed to study user acceptance and usage of emerging Information Technologies. The Technology Acceptance Model (TAM) has become a well-established robust model for predicting user acceptance (Davis, 1989; Davis *et al*, 1989). The goal of TAM is "to provide an explanation of the determinants of computer acceptance that is general, capable of explaining user behaviour across a broad range of end-user computing technologies and user populations, while at the same time being both parsimonious and theoretically justified". Specifically tailored for modelling user acceptance of Information Technology, TAM is a valuable tool for predicting attitudes, satisfaction and usage from beliefs and external variables.

There are some examples regarding the application of the TAM to the tourism sector. Noor *et al* (2005) present a survey conducted to determine whether the perception of trust, risk and sharing has an effect on the sharing of information at a tourism website. The study was conducted using the tourism website www.virtualtour.com which has 400000 members. Rasinger (2006) describes the research results comprising measures for discovering accepted mobile information services in tourism and defining the process for customer-based mobile information services development. Dilworth & Shafer (2004) examine visitor attitudes towards and intent to use Intelligent Transportation Systems (ITS) in two of the National Park units in California.

Another approach different from the TAM is the Concept of Flow (Novak, Hoffman & Yung, 2000), including factors such as skill and control, challenge and arousal, or focused attention. These factors contribute to flow, a state of mind where the user is completely devoted to the user of a system and forgets everything else around him/her.

Another theoretical area relevant for this contribution is usability testing and system evaluation. Usability study has proven to be an invaluable tool for ensuring the quality of computerised systems. The studies of stationary computer systems are an established discipline within Human-Computer interaction with widely acknowledge techniques and methods. Most research investigating the design of tourism technologies has focused on the concept of guides. These devices help travellers and others unfamiliar with an environment to navigate, learn and perform situated actions.

Research into developing technologies to support tourism has been popular with those exploring contextual awareness issues, and virtual or augmented reality (VR/AR). Some examples could include the GUIDE system developed at Lancaster University (Cheverst, Davies, Mitchell, & Friday, 2000) or a study of tourist requirements for the design of a city guide conducted by Brown and Chalmers (2003).

3 Description of the Prototype

The key objective of the PRISMA prototype is the integration of Augmented Reality technologies into the widely known concept of tourist binoculars. By means of these technologies, the real scene can be enhanced by virtual information to increase users' experience. PRISMA is basically a video see through visualization system composed of a camera to record the real time video stream, binoculars as the visualization device and an inertial sensor mounted on the structure to track the point of view and rotation of the binoculars (Fritz, Susperregui, & Linaza, 2005; Alzua-Sorzabal, Linaza & Susperregui., 2006).

The field of view of the spectator is captured by the camera mounted on the binoculars and sent to the processing unit, where the graphical data is added and the augmented stream is sent back to the binoculars. The tracking of the system captures and records the current location and orientation of the binoculars. The central processing unit converts these data into an orientation vector and the system displays the correct information on the binoculars. The graphical objects, which represent highlighted tourist assets or other abstract information, are drawn to enhance and complement the perception of the user of the natural environment.

PRISMA provides different added-value multimedia content As soon as users begin the interaction, the system personalises the content regarding the language (Basque, Spanish, English and French). Each language has an associated target group of users. Then, users choose what kind of information they are interested in among previously personalized contents.

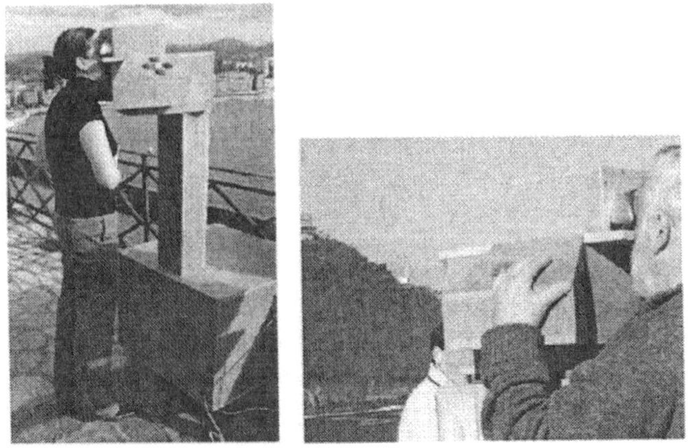

Fig. 1. PRISMA prototype in the real environment.

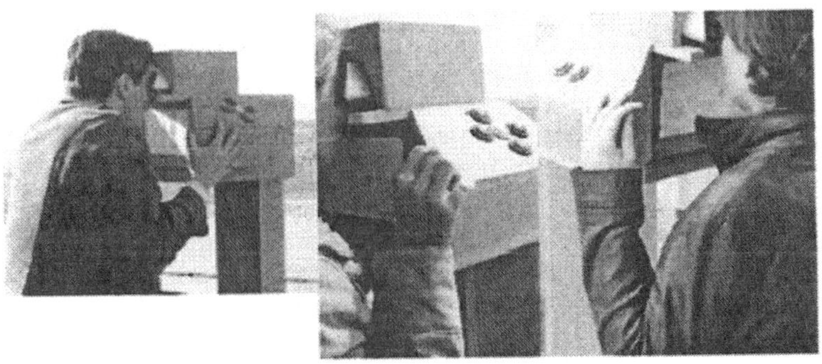

Fig. 2. Interaction interfaces for audiovisual contents.

An overview from one of the hills of Donostia-San Sebastian city in the North of Spain has been chosen as the real validation environment. The binoculars have been placed at the middle height of the hill to allow tourists and also local citizens to "visit" some of the interesting cultural and tourist attractions of the city, such as the Cathedral and Santa Clara Island in the middle of the bay.

When users discover a tourist asset about which they are interested in getting additional information, it is enough to click on the marker of the object and a menu with the available choices for the content. PRISMA allows tourists to gain multimedia personalized information about these tourist assets, including textual information (timetables, directions, telephone numbers), 2D photographs and maps, or even videos and 3D reconstructions.

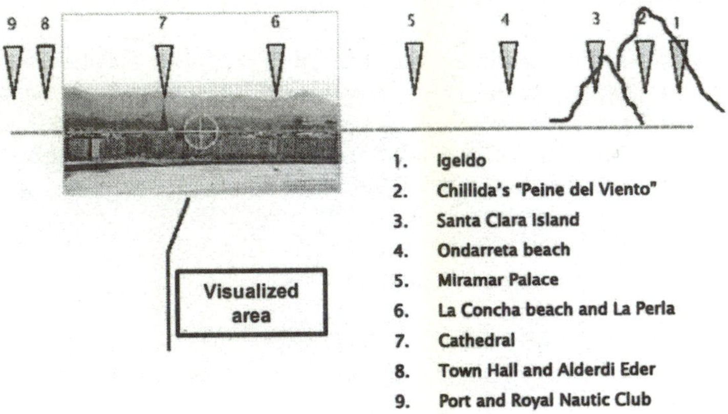

Fig. 3. Graphical augmentation of the point of view.

4 Evaluation Methodology for the Usability Study

The proposed evaluation methodology fits into the definition provided by Steele and Moss (1970), who defined the evaluation as "the systematic process of analysing what is better, more desirable, effective or suitable regarding some pre-defined criteria and objectives based on precise comparisons among several observation data with standardised criteria". Thus, objectivity is a must.

The overall aim of the usability study of PRISMA has been the development of typologies of users and standards, so that new interactive tourist experiences could be personalized in the future taking into account concepts such as usefulness and ease of use.

Therefore, the behaviour of the user when dealing with new technologies as a means of communication of tourist contents has been assessed. In order to achieve this aim, the quality of the communication between the prototype and the user has also been measured. Additionally, the usability study has identified the typology of users that may accept, use and even enjoy Augmented Reality technologies in tourism, leisure and cultural environments. Therefore, it is crucial to assess the impact of PRISMA within the added-value experience with the innovative 3D visualization prototype.

Concerning the sample, about 100 people took part in the usability study, from which 47 answered in-depth questionnaires, at the real scenario at the Monte Urgull in San Sebastian (Spain) in March 2006. The average profile of the participant is a man between 20 and 35 years old (61% of the sample) and quite familiar with the use of new technologies (mobile devices, laptops, digital cameras, Internet). Some of the participants worked in the tourism sector, including destination managers and content providers, because the usability study was also devoted to have feedback for the business exploitation plan of the prototype.

4.1 Quantitative analysis

The main objectives of the quantitative analysis of PRISMA are the assessment of the behaviour of the sample regarding the integration of ICT in tourist environments and the validation of the added value of Augmented Reality technologies to tourist attractions. Data has been collected on the basis of one specific questionnaire developed for the usability study of PRISMA, including aspects related to different constructors such as the perceived usefulness (PU) of the device, its perceived ease of use (PEOU) or the perceived added-value. The main difficulty has been related to the design of the questions which could bias the answers.

This questionnaire included 30 questions and has been filled by the participants of the survey just after experiencing the device. The answers were coded and processed using statistical software. The parameters that have been analysed included the profile of the user (socio-demographic data of the sample and familiarity with new technologies), parameters of the usability study (basically usefulness and ease of use), assessment of the contents (data about usefulness, scientific and technical quality of multimedia contents) and assessment of the prototype (perceived added-value of the prototype and willingness to pay).

Before experiencing the prototype, the evaluation team presented the project briefly an gave some basic instructions about the use of the prototype. Most of the participants (55%) agreed on the suitability of the explanations provided and found themselves confident when experiencing the prototype afterwards.

Table 1. Some of the statements for the quantitative analysis.

H1: I know the basic technological issues in order to experience the prototype.
H2: The provided explanations were enough to use the device correctly.
H3: The use of new technologies enhances the experience with cultural and natural resources.
H4: PRISMA provides new, interesting and useful information about the city.
H5: PRISMA is a new tourist information point.
H6: The experience of interacting with the prototype has been amazing and enriching.
H7: Interacting with PRISMA is quite simple.
H8: I have been able to navigate through and access easily the provided contents.
H9: I have learnt new subjects about the city.

Firstly, the usefulness of advanced technologies such as PRISMA within tourist environments was assessed. Two thirds of the sample agreed with the statement that PRISMA enhances the access to cultural goods and tourist assets. The same percentage affirmed that PRISMA is a useful tourist information point. They also described the overall interactive experience with the prototype as amazing and enriching. The values of the survey also showed a positive trend (more than half of the sample) when studying the usefulness of the prototype in order to communicate contents and develop affective relations.

The following statements dealt with the ease of use of the prototype and with the searching for additional contents. The usage of the prototype was quite simple for half of the sample, although it must be mentioned that 25% of the sample found it very difficult. However, this pattern was not extensible to the perception of users regarding the intuitiveness of the prototype. Therefore, it can be concluded that users found it easier to learn the usage of the prototype rather than to practically use it. Regarding the navigation and the ease of access to the desired contents, more than half of the participants found the desired contents easily. None of the participants was intimated by the prototype or worried about damaging the prototype due to their interaction.

The usefulness and the quality of the contents, and the technical quality of the multimedia material have also been evaluated. As an overall conclusion, it can be said that contents have been positively assessed. Most of the participants agreed that they have learned something new from their experience, although they found that historical information about the city was too hard for a general profile of a user. Two thirds of participants were surprised by the displayed audiovisual material about the city.

Finally, the questionnaire focused on issues related to the perceived added-value of the prototype and the willingness to pay for the experience. Regarding the former, more than 85% of the sample agreed on the added-value of PRISMA compared to more traditional tourist experiences. Moreover, 75% of the users would recommend the system to other users. The same trend appeared when asking about the willingness to pay, with more than 80% of positive answers. The average expected price would be between one and three euros.

4.2 Qualitative analysis

The evaluation of tourist information services based on ICT such as PRISMA should take into account not only the added-value of the displayed contents, but also the fulfil of the requirements and desires of users when interacting with such services. Studying the reactions of users is the preferred way of getting this information within qualitative analysis. Generally speaking, qualitative analysis collects data using three main approaches: direct observation, interviews and analysis of written documents.

Within Social Sciences, observation can be defined both as the recognition process and the behaviour registration of people, objects and events. Although there are several observation techniques, all of them are based on the same principle: behaviours are a measurable image of thoughts, expectations and emotions concerning social interactions. Systematic register and its analysis try to explain human behaviour, defining relationships to standardise behavioural patterns and to extend those models to other contexts on the basis of the quality and representation of the sample.

Observation has been a key issue within the usability study of PRISMA. Therefore, it was crucial to analyse the behaviour of users in order to assess the possibilities and limitations of the design of the prototype. Observation has focused on three main aspects regarding Human-Device Interaction: body position (ergonomics, comfort);

dynamic interaction user-device-environment; and interaction choices during the navigation. Body position was the first factor for the assessment of adaptability and usability of the prototype. The height and the position of legs, arms and back have been considered as indicators of the comfort of the users during the experience.

The height of the prototype was a big limitation for people smaller than the position of the visualization device (1.6 meter from the ground). In some cases as shown in Fig. 4, the user stood on a step in order to reach the binoculars. People much taller had to adjust their body position as well.

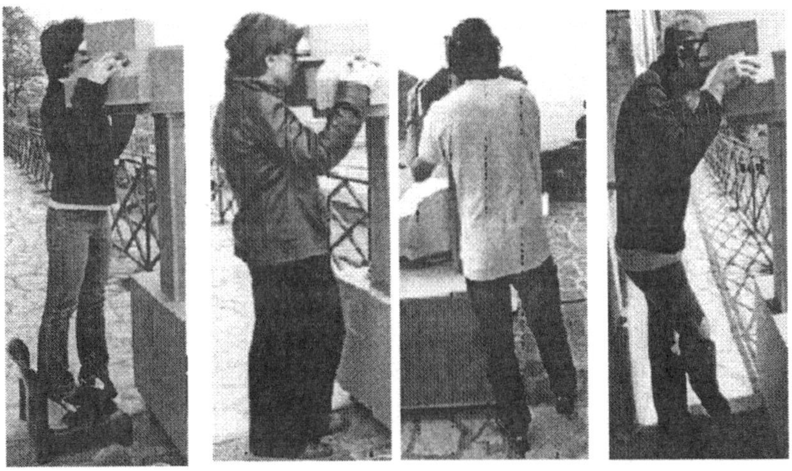

Fig. 4. Body position for some of the participants.

The position of the hands during the interaction with the buttons was quite diverse due to the different number of buttons on each side of the prototype. Although zoom buttons on the left side of the prototype were easily used, several difficulties arose when interacting with the navigation buttons on the right side. Only few participants have maintained the hands on these buttons during the whole experience, but most of them took them away and only placed them again during the interaction. Thus, the diversity of behaviours made it very difficult to find profiles and patterns of usability.

Fig. 5. Position of the fingers regarding the interaction buttons.

Although observation of the reactions of participants when interacting with contents was quite limited, it provided very interesting material for the usability study. As expected, tourist assets placed on the borders of the scenario were less visited than the central ones (Fig. 6). Moreover, no pattern could be defined regarding the selection between historical and practical contents.

Apart from direct observation, qualitative analysis has also included in-depth interviews. Due to field limitations, the designed sample was selected on the basis of its professional profile: a representative group of technicians, professionals from the tourist and cultural sector, and a group of pre- and post-graduated students.

Most of the participants live in San Sebastian, so they have a deep knowledge of the validation scenario.

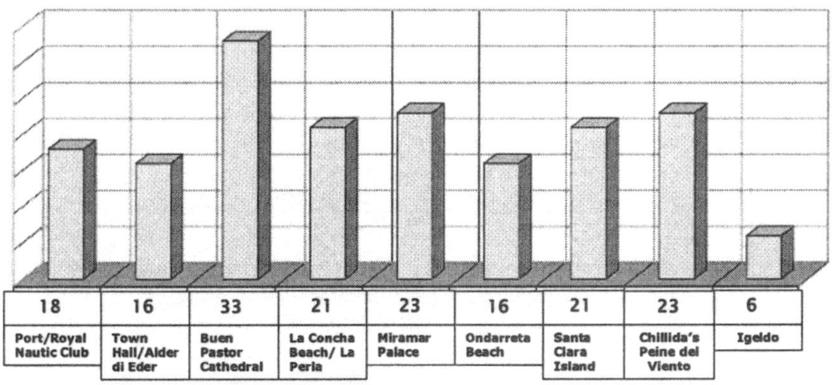

Fig. 6. Frequency of visits to the different contents.

In order to fulfil the requirements of a semi-structure interview, the four conceptual areas of the TAM were included in the evaluation, namely performance expectancy (perceived usefulness, extrinsic motivations and added-value), effort expectancy (complexity of the system and ease of use), social influence and facilitating conditions (perceived performance, facilitating conditions). All the interviews have been recorded for further assessment.

Regarding the physical usefulness and ergonomics, the interviews reinforced the results of the observation. Many participants mentioned the associated problems related to the physical design of the prototype. The visualization device is about 1.60 meter high, which may be too high for general public and even inaccessible for children. Another aspect mentioned was the uncomfortable position of the arms during the experience, most of the time lying over the speakers. The navigation buttons were identified as one of the main difficulties concerning the comfort and ergonomics due to the big number of buttons and the lack of correspondence between the navigation direction and the physical location of the buttons on the right side.

Concerning the perceived added-value, PRISMA has been catalogued as an added-value tourist tool. Compared to books and brochures, there is a reduction on the effort that should be done by tourists: information is already there. Many of the participants agreed that the prototype is a very useful way of getting in contact with the city: it offers a panoramic view of the city, provides the user with in situ information and no tourist guide is needed.

Regarding the business model, most of the sample agreed on a pay-per-view model, although the prototype could be free of charge as part of the promotion strategy of the city.

5 Conclusions

In order to measure the scope of the results and conclusions, it must be mentioned that the profile of the sample has been a little bit biased, with some of the participants working in the tourism sector. It must be clarified their double role within the study: a common tourist role for the quantitative analysis and a professional of the tourist sector role for the qualitative one. The participants provided a critical vision taking into account not only their personal point of view, but also an extended discussion about further developments of the prototype. The conclusions have been grouped on the basis of the issues that have been highlighted within the evaluation process.

Most of the participants agreed that the approach of using advanced visualization technologies such as Augmented Reality enhances the interactive experience with tourist content. The interviews concluded that PRISMA provides added-value multimedia contents in an interactive way. This way, information is more accessible with new visualization means and innovative interaction metaphors. Moreover, more than 80% of the participants were willing to pay up to three euros for the experience. As a conclusion, the participants have positively assessed the usefulness of the prototype as a tourist information point for urban environments due to its capability of providing Location-Based contents to allow better route planning.

Concerning the ease of use, the results of the quantitative analysis were mostly positive, although issues related to interaction, comfort and simplicity in the access to contents have to be improved. Many limitations or usability problems were related to the fixed height and the restricted physical adaptability of the prototype to the physical conditions of the user. Position of legs, arms and hands of the user was influenced by the binoculars, the interaction devices, the mechanical rotation of the visualization device and the design of the device as a whole. Further improvements in the physical design of the device will have a great impact not only on a more comfortable experience for the user, but also on a smaller damage when using the device. A final recommendation was the need of the contextualization of the prototype in order to facilitate its usage.

Regarding the contents, more than half of the sample found them usable, interesting and innovative. Moreover, two thirds of the users were impressed by the historical images that were displayed. Interactive contents based on QuickTime panoramas had the greatest impact, specially the navigation and zooming inside the Cathedral of the city. However, the potential of the prototype could be extended by panoramic approaches, holograms or non-linear story-telling techniques. As a final conclusion, it can be said that PRISMA can be considered as a prototype with a great potential impact over the tourist sector. Further application scenarios such as environmental impact of architecture planning projects have been suggested.

References

Ajzen, I. & Fishbein, M. (1980). *Understanding Attitudes and Predicting Social Behavior.* Prentice-Hall, Inc.

Alzua-Sorzabal, A., Linaza, M. T. & Susperregui, A. (2006). Providing On-Site Augmented Information to Tourists. M. Hitz, M. Sigala and J. Murphy (Eds.) *Information and Communication Technologies in Tourism 2006.* Wien New-York: Springer.

Brown, B., & Chalmers, M. (2003). Tourism and mobile technology. In: Kari Kuutti and Eija Helena Karsten (Eds.). *ECSCW 2003: Proceedings of the Eighth European Conference on Computer Supported Cooperative Work, Helsinki, Finland, 14–18 September 2003.* Dordrecht: Kluwer Academic Press.

Cheverst, K., Davies, N., Mitchell, K., & Friday, A. (2000). Experiences of developing and deploying a context–aware tourist guide: The GUIDE project. *MobiCom 2000: Proceedings of the Sixth Annual International Conference on Mobile Computing and Networking.* August 6–11, 2000, Boston, Massachusetts.

Davis, F. D. (1989). Perceived usefulness, perceived ease of use, and user acceptance of information technology. *MIS Quarerly* (September): 319-340.

Davis, F. D., Bagozzi, R. P. & Warshaw, P. R. (1989). User Acceptance of Computer Technology: A Comparison of Two Theoretical Models. *Management Science* 35: 982-1003.

Dilworth, G. & Shafer, S. (2004). Visitor Preceptions of Intelligent Transportation Systems in a National Park. *In Proc. of the 2004 Northeastern Recreation Research Symposium.*

Fishbein, M. & Ajzen, I. (1975). *Belief, Attitude, Intention and Behavior: An Introduction to Theory and Research.* Reading, Addison-Wesley.

Fritz, F., Susperregui, A. &. Linaza, M. T (2005), Enhancing Cultural Tourism Experiences with Augmented Reality Technologies. In *Proc. of the 6th International Symposium on Virtual Reality, Archaeology and Intelligent Cultural Heritage VAST2006.*

Noor, N. L., Hashim, M., Haron, H. & Ariffin, S. (2005). Community Acceptance of Knowledge Sharing System in Travel and Tourism Websites: an Application of an Extension of TAM. *In: Proc. of the European Conference on Information Systems.*

Novak, T. P., Hoffman, D. L. & Yung, Y.-F.- (2000). Measuring the Customer Experience in Online Environments: A Structural Modeling Approach. *Marketing Science,* 19(1), 22-42.

Rasinger, J., Fuchs, M., Höpken, W. & Tuta, M. (2006). A Customer Based Approach to discover Accepted Mobile Information Services in Tourism. In: Research@EyeforTravel, London, 5-6 June, pp. 31-46.

Acknowledgements

This paper is part of the project "PRISMA- Augmented vision for Cultural Tourism Applications", financed by The Movie Virtual and Ereiten Kultur Zerbitzuak within the INTEK program of the Department of Industry of the Basque Government.

A Conceptual Framework of Persuasive Architecture of Tourism Websites: Propositions and Implications

Cristian Morosan[a]
Daniel R. Fesenmaier[b]

[a] Department of Hotel, Restaurant, Institution Management and Dietetics
Kansas State University, Manhattan, KS, U.S.A.
cmorosan@ksu.edu
[b] National Laboratory for Tourism & *e*Commerce
School of Tourism and Hospitality Management
Temple University, Philadelphia, PA, U.S.A.
drfez@temple.edu

Abstract

This paper proposes a conceptual framework describing the persuasive architecture of tourism websites. The components included in this framework are organization, consumers, and industry that are in continuous communication with each-other. The organization uses a set of persuasive features to persuade consumers to purchase or remain on the site. Acting as catalysts in the persuasion process, the consumers and the industry contribute to the effectiveness of the website features. This study outlines four propositions for website design that destination marketing organizations can use to increase the persuasiveness of their websites.

Keywords: Persuasion, consumer behavior, online information search, website design.

1 Introduction

Today's Web environment is characterized by the over-saturation of information. This is a result of the enthusiastic adoption of the online environment by tourism organizations. This Web orientation enables consumers to access a wide assortment of information and transaction environments. However, the relatively large number of information sources makes it difficult for consumers to locate the right piece of information. For example, a simple search for the sequence "travel information" on a popular search engine returned more than 1.6 billion pages, while a search for "airline tickets" returned more than 52.3 million pages (using Google August 5, 2006). Paradoxically, despite the popularity of a few branded websites, most tourism-related websites provide information that is not always relevant to the travelers (Jeong et al., 2006). In the context of the dilution of informational value of the vast amount of information available online, both researchers and practitioners have been preoccupied with enhancing the websites' ability to influence visitors' purchase or visitation decisions. One of the most recent endeavors in this direction is the persuasive technology paradigm outlined by Fogg (2003). This study builds on this work and that of Kim and Fesenmaier (2005, 2006) to elaborate further the notion of persuasive architecture, which is based on the three dimensions of online communication (the organization, the consumers, and the industry). Thus, the purpose of this study is to discuss the relationships among the three dimensions in order to explain how tourism organizations can increase the influence of their websites by integrating persuasive features. The study formulates four propositions for guiding destination website design, arguing that more persuasive communications will impact tourism visitation.

2 The Concept of Persuasion

The concept of persuasion can be dated back to Socrates, as he linked persuasion with rhetoric. Rhetoric can be used as to give effectiveness to the truth, which is sometimes hard to uncover. Persuasion was later defined as "human communication designed to influence others by modifying their beliefs, values, or attitudes" (Simons, 1976, p. 21). Simons viewed persuasion as a form of attempted influence that seeks to alter the way others think, feel, or act. However, in Simons' view, persuasion differs from other forms of influence in that it is not coercive. Rather, persuasion involves guiding people towards the adoption of attitudes, beliefs, or behaviors preferred by the persuader through reasoning and emotional appeals (Reardon, 1991).

3 The Communication Triad

In this study, we propose a framework which posits that the primary purpose of a destination marketing website is to persuade its visitors to change their attitudes about the destination. The proposed framework is adapted from the communication literature where persuasion has been investigated extensively and proven to enhance an organization's communication efforts. This literature has advanced the idea that an organization's communication environment is based on three axiomatic components: (1) the destination marketing organization, (2) consumers, and (3) the industry. A representation of this environment is illustrated in Fig. 1.

Fig. 1. The communication triad

Within this framework, communication is carried out as a consequence of the various goals of the three components. For example, consumers might have the goal of searching for tourist information on a destination's website. In this case, they will communicate with the organization, but also indirectly with the industry. Thus, the more persuasive the communication, the greater the likelihood that the consumers will complete the process with a purchase decision or extend their visits on the website.

The destination marketing organization

The destination marketing organization (DMO) is the first component of the framework. To increase persuasion, DMOs can integrate into their websites two major types of features: hygiene and motivational features. The hygiene features (i.e., information quality, usability, and credibility) are the foundation for motivational features and absence of the prior makes the latter invalid. The motivational features (i.e., branding, reinforcement, involvement, inspiration, and e-commerce) attempt to persuade the consumer to either travel to the destination or, simply, consider visiting the website (Fig. 2).

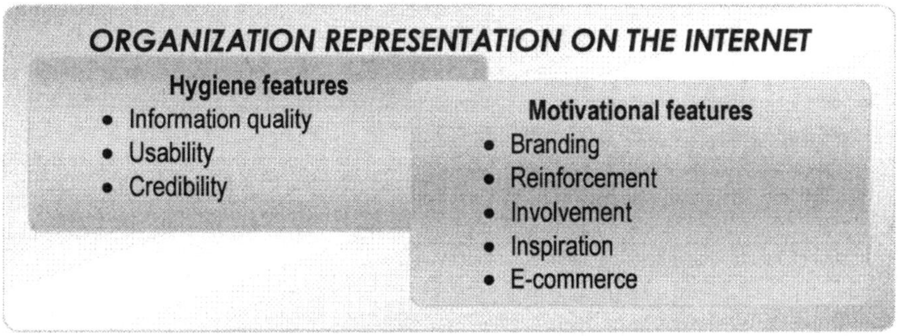

Fig. 2. The organization and its persuasive features

As information quality is essential to consumers, and the way information is delivered online, in content and organization, can facilitate or impede its utilization (Rosen & Purinton, 2004). An important goal of websites' information quality is providing accurate information to consumers. There are two important aspects of information quality: (1) complexity, referring to the amount of information that a website is perceived to offer and (2) novelty, which can take the form of new experiences and information or a combination of the two (Huang, 2003).

Credibility is another aspect of the website that affects its persuasiveness. For example, price incentives backed by source credibility is an efficient method of motivation that could lead to persuasion (Sternthal, Dholakia, & Leavitt, 1978). Moderately credible sources are more persuasive than the high credible ones when credibility cues are presented before the message, while highly credible sources induce a more positive attitude when the credibility cue follows the communication (Sternthal et al., 1978). Extensive research has been dedicated to understanding the dimensions of credibility. Two major dimensions have been found: (1) expertise (i.e., qualifications, skills, and training of the communicator, and his/her ability to know the truth) (Baudhuin & Davis, 1972), and (2) trustworthiness (i.e., the communicator is likely to tell the truth as he/she perceives it) (Tuppen, 1974). Examining communicator credibility, O'Keefe (2002) identified two main characteristics: (1) credibility and (2) likeability. O'Keefe regarded credibility as perceived credibility, as consumers often judge the communicator's believability. Thus, credibility has not been merely viewed as an intrinsic characteristic of a communicator (O'Keefe, 2002). A series of concepts have been examined as potential antecedents of credibility: education, occupation, and experience (Hurwitz, Miron, & Johnson, 1992), fluency in delivery (Pearce & Brommel, 1972), citation of evidence sources (Ostermeier, 1967), liking of the communicator (Bowers & Phillips, 1967), and humor (Chang & Gruner, 1981). Based on these findings, the following proposition was formulated:

Proposition 1. The persuasiveness of a destination marketing website can be enhanced by increasing the quality, usability, and credibility of information presented.

Motivational features of the destination marketing website include: (1) branding, (2) reinforcement, (3) involvement, (4) inspiration, and (5) e-commerce. As major components of tourism packages sold in the U.S. are branded (i.e., hotels and restaurants), building brand equity is a significant challenge. Despite brand incorporation in products and services sold in tourism, the use of brands by destination marketing organizations is not substantial (Cai, 2002). Thus, an important way in which tourism organizations can benefit from branding in an e-commerce context is to select a mix of brand elements to identify and build a destination image (Cai, 2002). According to Lee, Cai, and O'Leary (2006), tourism branding on the Internet can serve the organization better than on traditional media as the Internet incurs low cost and provides deep market penetration.

Reinforcement refers to the ability of the website to communicate effectively one or more components of the brand and actually move the consumer along with the brand. As a multidimensional construct, reinforcement can be achieved via interactivity (involving consumers in the website experience), website feedback, and customer relationship management. The purpose of reinforcement is threefold: (1) to expand the consumers' experience with the brand, by increasing brand awareness and improving their attitudes toward the brand; (2) to facilitate the communication of the different components of the brand (i.e., symbols, messages, or logos) in an attempt to make the consumer familiar with as many aspects of the brand as possible; and, (3) to make the experience more memorable for the consumers by exposing them to a variety of images that convey the same things: the brand attributes. Regardless of how reinforcement is carried out, its ultimate role is to change consumers' attitudes toward a product or service, in this case, toward a tourist destination. Therefore, from an organizational perspective reinforcement has a critical role in persuasion (Fog, 2003).

Development of involvement features is viewed as a very important aspect of website design (Huang, 2003). So far, the majority of the websites have used mostly functional features, in which the information has been provided to tourists in attractive ways, without involving them extensively. From a functional perspective, the simple visit to a destination marketing organization website can perceived as a boring task, and most tourists abandon it once a sufficient amount of information has been acquired or there are too frustrated to continue. However, realizing the importance of involving the tourists in their web surf experiences and based on the flow theory (Csikszentimihalyi & Csikszentimihalyi, 1988), tourism organizations have started to integrate website features that not only provide the content that is desired by the tourists, but they do it in an interactive, captivating way. Since involvement on tourist websites can induce changes in travelers' attitudes toward the destination, it is argued that a positive relationship exists between involvement and persuasion on state tourism websites.

Inspiration refers mostly to mental simulation, which has been viewed as the cognitive construction of hypothetical scenarios (i.e., stories or narratives) (Green & Brock, 2000). Consumers typically engage in narrative processing as a result of mental simulation. This has the role of diverting the attention away from critical thoughts. It will ultimately generate positive affect, with an impact on attitudes and evaluation of brands (Green & Brock 2000). Conversely, non-simulating consumers will eventually engage in analytical thought processing, which results in fewer critical thoughts and fewer positive emotions. The impact on attitudes and brand evaluation is typically lower (Escalas, 2004). However, it is believed that mental simulation evokes narrative transportation, which persuades the consumers via positive feelings and reduced critical thinking (Green & Brock, 2000).

Electronic commerce refers to the transactional capability of the website. The majority of the tourism websites has a strong information provision character, providing information to potential consumers. Recently, however, destination marketing websites have adopted a few new electronic commerce applications, targeted to selling of souvenirs, memorabilia, and most recently, hotel or airline booking engines. The electronic commerce features of a website affect persuasion in a number of ways. First, electronic commerce exposes consumers to additional products and services carrying the brand of the destination, which will impact consumers' attitudes toward the destination. Second, by engaging in transactional activities on the website, consumers would automatically navigate through more Web pages, increasing their exposure to the informational content, and increasing their familiarity with it. Third, engaging in online transactions poses a risk for some consumers. This is why they would eventually look for additional security features (i.e., third party endorsements) on the website, increasing their exposure to the website.

The five motivational features can have a considerable impact the persuasiveness of destination marketing websites. As a guarantee of quality, the brand can be a very powerful persuader. Reinforcement ensures that the appropriate messages about to the brand are interactively communicated with the consumers. Involvement confirms that the consumers' experiences on the website are deeper than just seeking the appropriate travel information. Inspiration can then change consumers' attitudes by helping them simulate the website environment. Finally, the electronic commerce capabilities not only provide the travelers with products and services that expose the consumers to the destination's brand elements, but also help users stay longer on the website while emerging in deeper experiences. Therefore, the following proposition has been formulated:

Proposition 2. The persuasiveness of a destination marketing websites can be enhanced by improving visitor experiences with branding, reinforcement, involvement, inspiration, and electronic commerce.

The consumers

Consumers represent the second component of the communication triad. In tourism, based on their goals, consumers may have two different types of Website involvement, which leads to two different behaviors: (1) goal-directed search (i.e., airline ticket purchase) and (2) browsing (i.e., finding general information about a destination) (Vogt & Fesenmaier, 1998; Pan & Fesenmaier, 2006). A popular model often used to explain these two types of behaviors is the Elaboration Likelihood Model (ELM) (Petty, Cacioppo, & Schumann, 1983; Petty & Cacioppo 1986). In ELM, when the likelihood of the message elaboration is low, an increase in the number of arguments leads to an enhancement in the persuasiveness of the message, and vice versa. The level of involvement is high and the consumers know exactly what kind of information they are looking for they follow the central route and are goal-directed. Thus, they are likely to follow a path described by the classical decision-making theory, passing through the five stages of decision making: need recognition, information search, evaluation of alternatives, purchase decision, and post-purchase evaluation. However, recent studies have found that there is a mixed route which combines the elements from the both original ELM routes (Fig. 3).

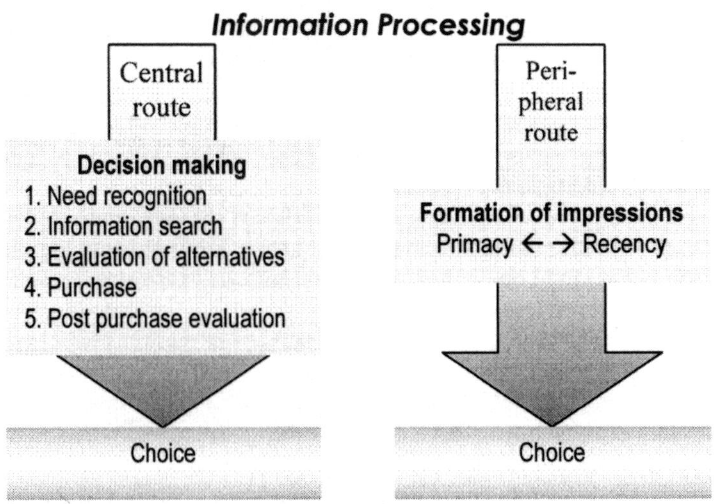

Fig. 3. Consumer processing of travel websites

Consumers following the peripheral route are generally led by hedonic needs and therefore, their level of involvement is low. In this case, the website should focus on exposing consumers to emotional cues that can facilitate the creation of impressions. Impressions are powerful motivators for consumers to continue visiting websites, as generally, impressions are viewed as sub-attributes of satisfaction, which can influence consumers' images of products and companies (Hu, Shima, Zhao, Takemura, & Matsumoto, 2004). In brick-and-mortar commerce, impressions are generally formed as a result of the efforts on sales personnel whereas in electronic commerce, impressions elicited by web pages will influence the consumers' visitation of the website.

Exploring usability and persuasion in human-computer interaction, Mak, Schmitt, and Lyytinen (1997) argued that based on the ELM theory two mechanisms may exist when consumers seek advice from a computer system. First, they argued that consumers who participate in updating the system knowledge will reduce the ambiguity of the decision setting and will accept the system's recommendation. Second, they found that users with a low level of participation will tend to accept the system's advice is determined if the system is perceived as credible.

A number of functionality design features can be employed to persuade consumers to consider the purchase. These features including search engines and reservation systems have a substantial role in helping consumers focus on the products and services they specifically look for. However, the role of the functionality cues is the most effective in the information search and evaluation of alternatives phases. Thus, as the consumers are goal-directed, the website should provide precise and up-to-date information about the details of the products and services that are necessary to make a decision (i.e., price, availability, and choices of accommodation, transportation, or events). Functionality cues can also be effective during the evaluation of alternatives. These cues can persuade the consumers by summarizing the characteristics of products and services, with an emphasis on their most salient features. During this phase, product comparisons could have a direct impact on the consumers as they often attempt to rank their choices based on critical attributes.

Although impressions have been examined extensively (Nielsen, 1994, 1999) their role has not been completely understood (Hu et al., 2004). It has been initially agreed that consumers behave as intuitive statisticians who transform information into abstract traits. However, despite extensive research, most of the models attempting to explain formation of impressions, including the popular model of information integration framework (Anderson, 1971), have been criticized for lacking psychological plausibility (Van Overwalle & Labiouse, 2004). That is, the claim that consumers perform all the weighing described in these models was deemed implausible, and alternative models have been proposed (Weinberg., Berger, & Hanna, 2004).

Formation of impressions relies on two critical components: (1) primacy and (2) recency (Richter & Kruglanski, 1998). Primacy refers to the consumers' tendency to rely mostly on information received early, remaining relatively unpersuaded by later information. Primacy has been attributed to the fact that consumers believe that the most important information is likely to be delivered first or they simply get bored (Kashima & Kerekes, 1994), or because they tend to be consistent in their judgments and could alter later information so that they become consistent with information received earlier (Steiner & Rain, 1989).

Primacy refers to the creation of first impressions. For the Internet, the home page carries considerable importance, as most consumers will eventually anchor their judgments on the information found on this page, guiding their perceptions of the rest of the website based on primacy. Primacy can be accomplished through the use of emotional cues and be instrumented through aesthetic, interactive, fun, playful features. Ultimately, the impressions can contribute to developing attitudes toward both the Website and the destination. Once the website has captured the attention of the prospective consumer, the next stage is to stimulate a high level of involvement.

The second aspect of impression formation is recency which refers to consumers' tendency to form impressions based on information received later (Richter & Kruglanski, 1998). According to Hogarth and Einhorn (1992), the mode of information processing impacts the order effect. Thus, when an objective is set from the start, end-of-sequence processing takes place, in which consumers make a judgment after being exposed to all the information. Step-by-step processing, on the other hand, involves updating judgments after being exposed to each of the informational segment and thus, is likely to yield recency (Kashima & Kerekes, 1994).

Consumers are exposed to a series of emotional cues, which are expected to determine an attitude toward the system. Emotional cues are signals derived from media properties (Obrenovic, Garay, López, Fajardo, & Cearreta, 2005) and are very important in stimulating visitors' emotions toward the tourist Website or destination. Emotions have been studied extensively in human-human interaction, but more research needs to be done to understand the role of emotions in human-computer interactions (Holzapfel, Fuegen, Denecke, & Waibel, 2002). Perhaps the most important category of emotional cues on Websites is represented by aesthetics, or those features that stimulate liking of the Website. These features include color, font type, pictures, and videos, meant to stimulate affect. Consumers do more than merely process information to make purchasing decisions (Olshavsky & Granbois, 1979), and, furthermore they might engage in imaginative, emotional, and appreciative consumption experiences. For this, they need a second category of emotional cues, which consists of interactive and playfulness features. Playfulness items that can stimulate emotions of travelers on a Website could include interactive planning tools for trips, interactive maps and driving directions, online games, and also interactive navigational tools allowing them to navigate through the attractions offered by the state. These tools have the role of engaging the traveler in a memorable experience online, eventually leading to flow.

Generally, any tourism website has to recognize different types and levels of consumer involvement. To fully take advantage of consumer involvement, website designers have to understand how various features fit into the two types of consumer involvement. From this perspective, the following proposition has been formulated:

Proposition 3. The persuasiveness of destination marketing websites can be enhanced by including functional cues oriented toward consumers involved in goal-directed behavior, and emotional cues oriented toward consumers involved in browsing.

The industry

The industry as a whole can impact communication by substantive means: (1) integration of experiences (bundling), and (2) providing third party information/endorsement. The integration of experiences is not at all new to the tourism industry. From the earliest stages of tourism development, various vendors and even destinations have come together to bundle products and services. Bundling is a very common practice used to reduce the cost of producing, marketing, and selling the products (Baumol, Willig, & Panzar, 1987). But, perhaps the greatest advantage of bundling is stimulating the demand for other products (Bakos & Brinjolfsson, 1999).

In the digital age, bundling becomes more challenging, yet more beneficial. Bundling in tourism has important reverberations throughout the entire value chain. For example, one of the benefits of bundling is cost reduction. In most cases, cost reduction will result in a reduction of the retail price. That is, the same products and services will be available to consumer at lower prices. Given that in today's market the consumer seek to replace a memorable (but more expensive) with a low-cost experience, bundling can enhance the attractiveness of many of the packages offered on tourism websites.

From an information provision standpoint, the industry plays a major role in providing the information from multiple destinations. In most cases, consumers are in search for information for multiple destinations as they generally don't visit a single destination (Hwang & Fesenmaier, 2003). Thus, websites integrating information from multiple destinations can be relatively persuasive for consumers seeking tourist information. One such pioneering website is vacationfun.com, which, by combining information about a multitude of destinations, managed to increase its influence on consumers' decisions to travel more so than single-destination state-sponsored tourism websites (Vacationfun.com, 2006). Considering the role of the industry in increasing the persuasiveness of tourism websites, the following proposition has been formulated as follows:

Proposition 4. The persuasiveness of destination marketing websites can be enhanced by increasing industry's involvement in presenting useful and credible tourist information online.

4 Conclusions and Implications

This paper describes a persuasive architecture of the B2C tourism environment. It is argued that the understanding of persuasive architecture design can help destination marketing organizations and other tourism-based organizations to develop websites that communicate more effectively with their visitors. This study identified a variety of persuasive tools that can be integrated into website design, enabling designers to open the door to new creative meanings. Thus, they can provide the future generation of tourist Websites with an edge in influencing consumers' decisions to purchase tourism packages.

The implications for the industry are substantial. First and foremost, this study and its propositions outline a new vision for website design whereby a number of features can be incorporated in website design to increase persuasiveness. For example, one way to increase the quality, usability, and credibility of information presented online, is provide only the information that is relevant to the travelers. In addition, to improve usability, the navigation capabilities of the website can be emphasized. Thus, adding suggestive links, pictures, and other navigational cues can help travelers perceive the websites as more useful. As credibility of information plays a critical role in persuasion, designers should incorporate features such as third-party endorsements, testimonials from actual travelers, and online communities to encourage travelers to view the website as a credible source of information. As brands are still powerful tools in today's marketing communications, the persuasiveness of website content can be enhanced by adding branded content. To accomplish this, the DMOs can work with trusted brands or include bundled packages containing branded components. Another increasingly important design feature is involvement. From this perspective, websites should incorporate interactive features such as trivia, maps, driving directions, chat rooms or even more challenging applications such as online games, question-and-answer, forums, or peer-reviewed sections.

One final implication is to emphasize the complementarities among various travel service providers at the destination level. From this perspective, the DMOs' websites could act as destination portals in that they will not only provide travelers with pertinent information about the destination, but will also provide links for the consumers to visit the various destination-related organizations. By adopting this new business model, DMOs can assume a leadership role within the destination and will enhance the credibility of the destination as a whole.

5 Directions for Further Research

This study serves as a theoretical foundation for a number of future studies that will continue to investigate the persuasiveness of travel websites. Despite the large number of studies providing empirical evidence for separate parts of this framework, an integrative empirical study must be conducted to confirm the structure of the proposed framework. Another direction for further research is to investigate the role of the DMO that is assuming a more intense leadership role in the management of the online marketing strategy for the whole destination. From this perspective, more studies will be necessary to investigate the complementary roles of various destination actors in providing persuasive information about their organizations, and their integration into a persuasive package at the level of the DMO. Overall, this study will open a new direction for research that will attempt to understand how to persuade the travelers to stay longer on a DMO website and how to encourage optimize the industry's efforts to encourage visitation of the advertised destinations.

References

Bakos, Y., & Brynjolfsson, E. (1999). Bundling information goods: Pricing, profits, and efficiency. *Management Science, 45*(2).

Baudhuin, E. S., & Davis, M. K. (1972). Scales for the measurement of ethos: another attempt. *Speech Monographs, 39*, 296-301.

Baumol, W., Willig, R., & Panzar, J. (1987). *Contestable Markets and the Theory of Industry Structure*: Dryden Press.

Bowers, J. W., & Phillips, W. A. (1967). A note on the generality of source-credibility scales. *Speech Monographs, 32*, 154-158.

Cai, L. A. (2002). Cooperative branding for rural destinations. *Annals of Tourism Research, 29*(3), 720-742.

Chang, M. J., & Gruner, C. R. (1981). Audience reaction to self-disparaging humor. *Southern Speech Communication Journal, 46*(419-426).

Csikszentimihalyi, M., & Csikszentimihalyi, I. S. (1988). *Optimal experience: Psychological studies of flow in consciousness*. Cambridge: Cambridge University.

Escalas, J. E. (1998). Advertising Narratives: What Are They and How Do They Work? In *Representing Consumers: Voices, Views, and Visions*. London: Routledge.

Fogg, B. J. (2003). *Persuasive Technology: Using Computers to Change What We Think and Do*. San Francisco, CA: Morgan Kaufmann Publishers.

Green, M. C., & Brock, T. C. (2000). The Role of Transportation in the Persuasiveness of Public Narratives. *Journal of Personality and Social Psychology, 79*(5), 701-721.

Hoffman, D. L., & Novak, T. P. (1996). Marketing in hypermedia computer-mediated environments: Conceptual foundations. *Journal of Marketing, 60*, 50-68.

Hogarth, R. M., & Einhorn, H. (1992). Order effects in belief updating: The belief-adjustment model. *Cognitive Psychology, 24*, 1-55.

Holzapfel, H., Fuegen, C., Denecke, M., & Waibel, A. (2002). *Integrating emotional cues into a framework for dialogue management.* Paper presented at the Fourth IEEE International Conference on Multimodal Interfaces ICMI'02.

Hu, J., Shima, K. R. O., Zhao, J., Takemura, Y., & Matsumoto, K. (2004). An empirical study of audience impressions of B2C Web pages in Japan, China, and the UK. *Electronic Commerce Research and Applications, 3*, 176-189.

Huang, M. H. (2003). Designing website attributes to induce experiential encounters. *Computers in Human Behavior, 19*(2), 425-442.

Hurwitz, S. D., Miron, M. S., & Johnson, B. T. (1992). Source credibility and the language of expert testimony. *Journal of Applied Social Psychology, 24*, 1909-1939.

Hwang, Y. H., & Fesenmaier, D. R. (2003). Multidestination pleasure travel patterns: Empirical evudence from the American Travel Survey. *Journal of Travel Research, 42*(2), 166-171.

Jeong, M., Morosan, C., & Park, M. (2006). Understanding visitors' perception of a state tourism website by their socio-demographic profiles. *Proceedings of the Hospitality Information Technology Association (HITA) Conference 2006*, Minneapolis, MN.

Kashima, Y., & , & Kerekes, A. R. Z. (1994). A distributed memory model of averaging phenomena in person impression formation. *Journal of Experimental Social Psychology, 30*, 407-455.

Kim, H., & Fesenmaier, D. R. (2005). *Persuasive designs of tourism websites in the United States*, Presented at the Annual Conference of the Travel and Tourism Research Association, New Orleans, June.

Kim, H., & Fesenmaier, D. R. (2006). *Persuasion and first impression of state tourism websites*. Presented at the Annual Conference of the Travel and Tourism Research Association, Dublin, June.

Lee, G., Cai, L. A., & O'Leary, J. T. (2006). WWW.Branding.States.US:An analysis of brand-building the US state tourism websites. *Tourism Management, 27*(5), 815-828.

Logan, R., Augaitis, S., & Renk, T. (1994). Design of simplified television remote controls: a case for behavioral and emotional usability. In *Proc.CHI 91,Human Factors in Computing Systems* (pp. 365–369). Boston, MA: ACMPress.
Mak, B., Schmitt, B., & Lyytinen, K. (1997). User participation in knowledge update of expert systems. *Information & Management, 32*, 55-63.
Nielsen, J. (1994). Report from a 1994 web usability study [Electronic Version] from http://www.useit.com/paper/1994_web_usability_report.html.
Nielsen, J. (1999). User interface directions for the web. *Communications of the ACM, 42*(1), 65-72.
O'Keefe, D. (2002). *Persuasion: Theory and Research* (2nd Ed.). Thousand Oaks, London: Sage Publications.
Obrenovic, Z., Garay, N., López, J. M., Fajardo, I., & Cearreta, I. (2005). An Ontology for Description of Emotional Cues. In Tao J., Tan T. & Picard R. W. (Eds.), *1st International Conference on Affective Computing and Intelligent Interaction (ACII2005) Proceedings. LNCS 3784* (pp. 505-512): Springer.
Olshavsky, R. W., & Granbois, D. H. (1979). Consumer decision making-Fact or fiction? *Journal of Consumer Research, 6*, 93-100.
Ostermeier, T. H. (1967). Effects of type and frequency of reference upon perceived source credibility and attitude change. *Speech Monographs, 34*, 137-144.
Pan, B., & Fesenmaier D. R. (2006). Exploring the structure of travel planning on the Internet, *Annals of Tourism Research, 33*(3), pp. 809 – 832.
Pearce, W. B., & Brommel, B. J. (1972). Vocalic communication in persuasion. *Quarterly Journal of Speech, 58*, 298-306.
Petty, R. E., & Cacioppo, J. T. (1986). *Communication and Persuasion: Central and peripheral routes to attitude change*. New York, NY: Springer-Verlag.
Petty, R. E., & Cacioppo, J. T. (1986). The elaboration likelihood model of persuasion. In L. Berkowitz (Ed.), *Advances in experimental social psychology* (pp. 123-205). San Diego, CA: Academic Press.
Petty, R. E., Cacioppo, J. T., & Schumann, D. (1983). Central and Peripheral Routes to Advertising Effectiveness: The Moderating Role of Involvement. *Journal of Consumer Research, 10*(3), 135-146.
Reardon, K. K. (1991). *Persuasion in Practice*. Newbury Park, CA: Sage Publications.
Richter, L., & Kruglanski, A. W. (1998). Seizing on the latest: motivationally driven recency effects in impression formation. *Journal of Experimental Social Psychology, 34*, 313-329.
Rosen, D. E., & Purington, E. (2004). Website design. Viewing the web as a cognitive landscape. *Journal of Business Research, 57*(7), 787-794.
Simons, H. W. (1976). *Persuasion: Understanding, practice and analysis*. Reading, MA: Addison-Wesley.
Steiner, D. D., & Rain, J. S. (1989). Immediate and delayed primacy and recency effects in performance evaluation. *Journal of Applied Psychology, 74*, 136-142.
Sternthal, B., Dholakia, R., & Leavitt, C. (1978). The Persuasive Effect of Source Credibility: Tests of Cognitive Response. *Journal of Consumer Research, 4*, 252-260.
Sternthal, B., Philips, L., & Dholakia, R. (1978). The Persuasive Effect of Source Credibility: A Situational Analysis. *Public Opinion Quarterly, 42*(3), 285-314.
Tuppen, C. J. S. (1974). Dimensions of communicator credibility: an oblique solution. *Speech Monographs, 41*, 253-260.
Vacationfun.com. (2006). Travel directory. Retrieved July 22, 2006, from http://www.vacationfun.com/travel.htm
Vogt, C. A., & Fesenmaier, D. R. (1998). Expanding the functional information search model. *Annals of Tourism Research, 25*(3), 551-578.
Weinberg, B., D., Berger, P. D., & Hanna, R. C. (2004). A Diagnostic Tool for Assessing the Relative Importance of Information in Impression Formation: Application in Order Effects. *Marketing Letters, 15*(2-3), 113-128.

The Persuasive Architecture of Destination Websites: The Effect on First Impressions

Heejun Kim[a]
Daniel R. Fesenmaier[b]

[a] Department of Recreation, Sport and Tourism
University of Illinois at Urbana-Champaign, U.S.A.
hkim12@uiuc.edu
[b] National Laboratory for Tourism & eCommerce
School of Tourism and Hospitality Management
Temple University, U.S.A.
drfez@temple.edu

Abstract

The design of websites can be a powerful tool to influence information seeking and choice. Recent studies have indicated that designing websites which evoke a favourable first impression is extremely important. The goal of this study was to investigate the key design factors in the formation of impressions towards web interfaces. An empirical study based on a self-report questionnaire was conducted and found that design elements related to inspiration, usability and credibility were significant drivers in the formation of first impression towards web interfaces. The paper concludes by discussing the implications of the empirical results and directions for future study.

Keywords: destination website design, persuasion, first impression.

1 Introduction

The design of tourism destination websites can be a powerful tool to influencing destination choices. The first few moments of interacting with websites are extremely important, and as a result, web designers now face increasing pressure to convey good impressions and enhance the perceived qualities of their web pages within that short period of time. Therefore, this study aims to: 1) examine drivers in website design that form a positive first impression towards tourism destination sites; and, 2) provide implications for further development of the persuasive design of destination websites.

2 Process of Information Search Using the Internet for Trip Planning

The process of information search using the Internet can be understood as comprising three distinct stages (see Fig. 1). Information searchers often begin their trip planning by using search engines to find and choose useful information sources (Marchionini, 1995; Wöber, 2006; Xiang & Fesenmaier, 2006). In the absence of favourite websites or the lack of information, information searchers choose a search system (i.e., Yahoo,

Google, etc.), formulate a query and execute the search; they are then presented results of their query (Marchionini, 1995; Xiang & Fesenmaier, 2006).

The second stage of the search process focuses on the impression formation and selection of a particular webpage. When information seekers use search engines their choice of information source is often made based upon the intensity of persuasiveness of metadata presented in the search results (Xiang & Fesenmaier, 2006). The use of metadata is crucial at this stage in that it functions as a cue that helps information seekers evaluate the search results and build expectancies towards information sources (i.e., websites). That is, metadata contributes to the information search process by creating first impressions about respective webpages. If a website fails to present a strong persuasive message at this stage, it is difficult to expect that the website will achieve its goal as an advertising channel.

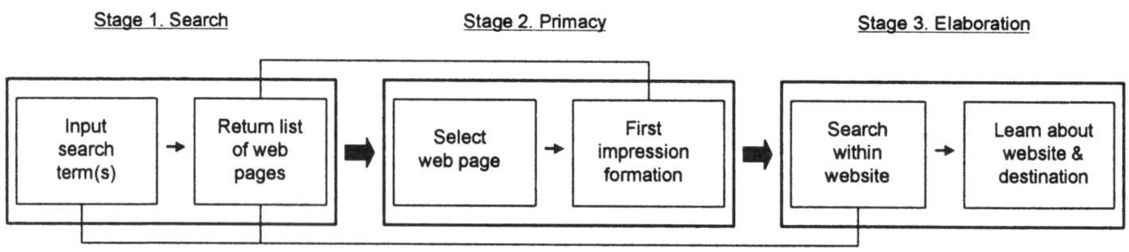

Fig. 1. Process of information search using the Internet for trip planning

When an information seeker first evaluates the relevance/usefulness of a website, he/she evaluates the website within a short period of time in an attempt to form an overall impression of the website. Studies indicate that when information searchers access a website, a rapid and almost unconscious but complex thought process is activated. Such a reaction is instantaneous but rational whereby the brain instantly tries to categorize and filter a website into a certain type (e.g., maybe approve, maybe disapprove or uncertain) (Fiske & Neuberg, 1990; Fiske, Lin, & Neuberg, 1999; Gladwell, 2005). Thus, this research indicates that first impressions aroused through an immediate interaction with webpage enables information searchers to make a quick choice about the particular website and even subsequent decisions. Importantly, these reactions are potentially long-lasting effect. For instance, website visitors with favourable first impressions toward the site may disregard or downplay possible negative aspects (e.g., dead links, slow downloads, outdated information, etc.). As such, information searchers tend to be consistent with their initial judgment in the following decision-making or behaviours in websites unless the site strongly disappoints them. However, it is also presumable that repeat visitors to website may take a different route in terms of process/interpretation of web interfaces as compared with web visitors with no or moderate experience with the sites. Thus, the primacy effect will be substantially enhanced for new visitors in the process of choosing an information source for trip planning. The final step of the information search process is a choice of whether or not to use (i.e., navigate within) the website. Information searchers with favourable first impressions towards a webpage are more likely to stay on the website and elaborate on their trip planning. If a website fails to appeal to and evoke good impressions to website visitors, they are more likely to stop browsing the site, go back to the search results and repeat the same procedure until they find a satisfactory information source.

3 Persuasive Architecture and Website Design

Recently, Kim and Fesenmaier (2005) proposed a dual-factor model based upon Zhang and von Dran (2000); specifically, it was posited that six web design factors can be used to define the persuasive architecture of destination websites; they can be divided into two sets of factors: (1) basic factors that trip planners perceive essential in tourism websites and (2) persuasive factors that increase the power of changing/reinforcing attitudes toward the site. Information and usability were found to be basic factors whereby credibility, inspiration, involvement and reciprocity to be persuasive factors. In this research the six design factors of Kim and Fesenmaier's study (2005) was adopted for further analysis in the context of the formation of impression towards tourism web interface. The conceptual framework for this study is briefly described below.

3.1 Informativeness-related design factors of destination websites

Functional information needs are the primary motivation for Internet users (Cole, 2000). Bauer and Greyser (1968) suggest that media users consider advertising's ability to provide audience information the fundamental reason for accepting the advertising. As the number of webpages continue to be developed and the amount of information available online increases; accordingly, information searchers tend to infer the overall quality (e.g., variety, currency, usefulness, helpfulness, and complexity) of a destination website in terms of information contents by browsing the webpage. For example, Ducoffe (1995; 1996) found a significant correlation between informativeness and advertising value, and attitude to advertising. Luo (2002) also found that informativeness of the website is positively associated with attitude toward the website. Based upon these results, it is hypothesized:

Hypothesis 1: The more informative a destination webpage is perceived to be, the more likely information searchers are to form a favourable first impression towards the webpage.

3.2 Usability-related design factors of destination websites

Researchers have proposed several different approaches to measuring website usability of which one element is functional convenience. Following from this research, it is argued that ease of use a system is a central concept in persuasion. Ease of use is composed of two distinct aspects: 1) ease of understanding, and 2) ease of navigation (Loiacono, Watson, & Goodhue, 2002). Websites should be designed clearly so that visitors easily understand who sponsors the site, what the goals of the sites are, and what they can achieve on the websites. Navigation is another important issue. Ease of navigation allows users to acquire more information they are seeking and make the information easier to find (Machlis, 1998). The perceived ease of use, in turn, influences an overall satisfaction with the use of system and behavioural intentions. Thus, the following hypothesis was made.

Hypothesis 2: The more usable a destination webpage is perceived to be, the more likely information searchers are to form a favourable first impression towards the webpage.

3.3 Credibility-related design factors of destination websites

Credibility has long been considered an important aspect of persuasion (Fogg, 1999). Wang, Beatty and Foxx (2004) proposed that trust is both cue-based and experience-based. Cue-based trust is consistent with the surface credibility proposed by Fogg and Tseng (1999), which describes how much a website visitor believes the website based on simple inspection of credibility cues the website contains. This study borrows the concept of cue-based trust and posits that website visitors can judge the quality of website in terms of credibility with a less mental effort whether or not the site is credible to allow for the possibility of subsequent communication. It suggests that information seekers can infer the level of trustworthiness of the website during an initial visit based only on available cues. In addition, Fogg (2003) argues that if a website is perceived to be credible, visitors tend to form positive attitudes toward the website. Thus, the following hypothesis was developed.

Hypothesis 3: The more credible a destination webpage is perceived to be, the more likely information searchers are to form a favourable first impression towards the webpage.

3.4 Inspiration-related design factors of destination websites

Inspiration is defined an infusion of some idea, purpose, etc. into the mind which includes a suggestion, awakening, or creating of a feeling or impulse. Thrash and Elliot (2003) argued that inspiration can be understood as an indicator of motivation involving the energy and direction of behaviour. Inspiration is evoked by trigger stimuli rather than initiated directly through an act of will. Importantly, inspiration is referred to as a temporal state of being motivated to creating positive affect towards web interface in this study. It is presumable that inspiration plays a role as a precursor of motivation, which exerts substantial influence in a positive way to enhancing favourableness and/or behavioural intentions. Thus, it was hypothesized that:

Hypothesis 4: The more inspiring a destination webpage is perceived to be, the more likely information searchers are to form a favourable first impression towards the webpage.

3.5 Involvement-related design factors of destination websites

Involvement is generally referred to as one's motivational state toward an object where that motivational state is activated by the relevance or importance of the object (Bloch & Richins, 1983; Rothschild, 1984; Zaichkowsky, 1985). Involvement is perceived as a motivational force which is related directly to various behavioural outcomes including the number and types of choice criteria, extensiveness of information search (Beatty & Smith, 1987), length of decision-making process, variety seeking, and brand attitude (Mitchell, 1980; Bloch & Richins, 1983). Within the online environment, interactivity is perceived as one of the most significant determinants influencing the level of involvement with the use of computer system along with personal characteristics and situational factors. Recent research indicates that an increase in the interactivity of website contributes to a corresponding increase in the level of liking (Stromer-Galley, 2004). Also, playful and enjoyable websites invite browsers to visit, keep them entertained and increase their depth of exploration. Thus, it was hypothesized that:

Hypothesis 5: The more information seekers perceive to be involved with a webpage, the more likely they are to form a favourable first impression towards the webpage.

3.6 Reciprocity-related design factors of destination websites

It is posited that communication is more persuasive when reciprocity is perceived and when the rewards for the communication are perceived to be more or less equal (LaGaipa, 1977). Reciprocity connotes that each party has rights and duties (Gouldner, 1960). One party should give benefits to those who give the other party benefits, implying that reciprocity entails mutual dependence. Therefore, reciprocal transaction exhibits mutually gratifying patterns of exchanging goods and services. Reciprocity is a powerful motivator of human conduct (Johnson & Eagly, 1989; Cialdini, Green, & Rusch, 1992) and it gives an explanation for a number of human behaviours. Thus, this concept is widely applied to the marketing settings. Kane, Johnson, Town and Butler (2004) investigated the impact of economic incentives on consumers' attitudes and behaviours and found that they were effective in increasing consumer's willingness to provide what the counterpart requested. Applied to the online environment, reciprocity is referred to as the extent to which a website is perceived to provide or support two-way information exchange between the destination and users (Huang, 2003). Within destination marketing websites, travel brochures/guidebooks and special offers/deals, and sweepstakes/contests are examples of benefits offered to visitors in hopes of building the reciprocal loop. Based upon this research, the following hypothesis was developed.

Hypothesis 6: The more reciprocal a destination webpage is perceived to be, the more likely information searchers are to form a favourable first impression towards the webpage.

4 Methods

4.1 Scale development

Dependent variable. First impression was defined as one's attitude towards the destination website and measured using a single favourableness question on the 5-point Likert scales (1: very unfavourable; 5: very favourable) created within a short period of time. Researchers have found that individuals form an initial impression of an object within seven to eight seconds (WNetwork, 2006); however, recent researchers suggest that the time frame is maybe shorter (e.g., 50 milliseconds (Hotchkiss, 2006; Lindgaard, Fernandes, Dudek, & Brown, 2006); 3 seconds; 4 seconds (Brainstorm & Raves, 2001; Kaiser, 2001); 5 seconds (Perfetti, 2005). In this study, a viewing time of each webpage was limited to seven seconds because it was perceived sufficient for an individual to review the entire webpage for the various cues needed to evaluate the "value" of the site.

Independent variables. The independent variables included in this study were the perceived qualities of destination webpages in terms of six web design factors. Following Straub (1989), prespecified constructs were utilized for the scale development where possible. Three items used to measure the information construct were adapted from Rieh (2002). For usability, Loiacono, Watson, and Goodhue's (2002) scales were integrated. For credibility, the concept of cue-based trust proposed by Wang, Beatty and Foxx (2004) was borrowed and three items were selected from several sources (Doney, 1997; Finberg, et al., 2001) to measure the perceived credibility of destination website. Because we did not find appropriate scales for inspiration, we operationalized this concept based upon Scioli and Averill (1998)'s definition and generated three items by decomposing the tourism destination homepages into individual design elements. Involvement with the web page was opertationalized following McQuarrie and Munson (1991). Last, reliable scales were not available to measure reciprocity; we developed four new items. All items were measured using a 5-point Likert scale, with 1 indicating that the respondent strongly agree with the statement and 5 indicating strong disagreement. A 'don't know' option was also provided in respective statements. The initial item pool was initially reviewed by ten experts to asses face validity and construct validity. The scales were subsequently reworded and refined based upon the results of the sorting task. The reduced item pool consisted of eighteen statements and is presented in Table 1. A pre-test of the scales was then performed using thirty students; based upon these responses Coefficient Alpha and confirmatory factor analyses were conducted. The results showed a high degree of internal consistency of the six design factor scales.

4.2 Treatment

Screenshots of homepages of the fifty official state tourism websites in the United States were used as treatments to measure participants' overall impressions toward destination homepages. The screenshots of the homepages were taken within an Internet Explore 6 browser at 1024 × 768 pixel resolution in 32-bit true colour. The fifty screenshots were then blocked into three sets according to the names of state in an alphabetical order, and as a result, each set included sixteen or seventeen treatments plus two additional webpages that were included as a "warm-up" exercise. A hypertext system was developed using Microsoft PowerPoint that displayed a webpage for exactly seven seconds and then prompted the respondent to complete the questions included in the survey. Importantly, the survey system did not allow study participants to go back and forth between destination webpages. It must be noted that applying snap shots might include a considerable weakness in that it did not promise an identical environment to the web in terms of the level of interactivity. However, considering that this study had an aim of understanding the blink effect towards web interface at the moment website visitors were exposed to and new visitors were more likely to demand a certain amount of time to learn about the new webpage, it is reasonably arguable that the lack of interactivity might not distort to great extent web visitors' perceptions.

4.3 Survey procedure and data collection

Participants in this study were randomly assigned by a computer to one out of three sets of treatments. They were first given a general description of the study. A paper-based questionnaire was then provided to subjects for each website to report their answers. A total of one hundred five students taking a tourism marketing class at a major university located in the north east United States were invited to participate in this study. Extra credit was provided as a means of motivating subjects' participation. In total, sixty five students completed a survey, resulting in a response rate of 79%. One must note that appropriateness of student subjects is still under debate whereby researchers question the external validity of such studies. It argued that students can be perceived to be representative of Internet user population due to their skills with the Internet; in addition, it is argued that the basic processes of information search are same as other individuals. Thus, it was concluded that this segment was appropriate to study the characteristics/attitudes/behaviours of information searchers in the web-mediated environment.

Table 1. Items of homepage design factors in DMO websites

	Items
	The destination homepage
Basic Factors	1. Informativeness : provides a variety of information. (INFO1) : provides up-to-date information.(INFO2) : provides useful information. (INFO3)
	2. Usability : is easy to understand. (USE1) : is easy to use. (USE2) : helps me to easily find the information I need. (USE3)
Persuasive Factors	1. Credibility : is trustworthy. (CRED1) : represents a tourism information provider I can trust. (CRED2) : represents a tourism office that will keep its promises. (CRED3)
	2. Inspiration : represent the destination in an appealing way. (INSP1) : helps me to be imaginative about the destination. (INSP2) : inspires me to visit the destination. (INSP3)
	3. Involvement : is highly interactive. (INV1) : helps me become involved in planning my trip. (INV2) : is enjoyable/fun to plan my trip. (INV3)
	4. Reciprocity : offers travel brochures I like to request. (RECP1) : enables me to directly contact the tourism office. (RECP2) : provides helpful customer service. (RECP3) : enables me to register for special offers, newsletter, personalization, etc. (RECP4)

5 Data Analysis and Results

Data analysis was conducted in three steps. First, Coefficient Alpha was computed and confirmatory factor analysis was conducted to test the reliability and unidimensionality of each construct. Second, a descriptive analysis was performed using six website design factors. Last, multiple regression analysis was conducted in order to identify the importance of these drivers in determining the subjects' first impression of the respective destination webpages. Responses to the warm-up exercises were excluded from the data analysis and 'don't know' were treated as missing data.

5.1 Completion of survey items

In total, 1,080 homepages of U.S. state tourism websites were evaluated. On average, respondents completed 14 items out of 19 for each webpage. More than two thirds of participants completed survey questions regarding an overall impression and the website qualities. However, a response rate was shown much lower in credibility and reciprocity-related questions (see Table 2). In addition, only approximately 50% of participants reported their opinion for questions concerning the currency of information.

Table 2. Completion of survey questions

Construct	The destination webpage	Percentage of completion
First impression	Overall impressions of homepages	82.7%
Informativeness	INFO1	95.1%
	INFO2	88.3%
	INFO3	54.2%
Usability	USE1	88.2%
	USE2	85.6%
	USE3	91.2%
Credibility	CRED1	70.9%
	CRED2	51.1%
	CRED3	50.0%
Inspiration	INSP1	93.5%
	INSP2	92.9%
	INSP3	94.6%
Involvement	INV1	82.8%
	INV2	76.9%
	INV3	77.1%
Reciprocity	RECP1	59.5%
	RECP2	48.4%
	RECP3	39.9%
	RECP4	43.4%

5.2 Instru ment validation

Analyses were first conducted to test the reliability and validity of the respective constructs. Reliability was assessed using Cronbach's α and validity was assessed using factor analysis. Table 3 provides an overview of the items included in respondents' perceptions of homepage design regarding internal consistency and unidimensionality. The scales used in this study show acceptable levels of internal consistency and reliability (i.e., α = .79 for information; α = .86 for usability; α = .85 for credibility; α = .91 for inspiration; α = .81 for involvement; and, α = .85 for reciprocity). Unidimensionality of the scales was evaluated using factor analysis with an orthogonal rotation (varimax solution); as can be seen, the results also confirmed the unidimentionality of each design factor (see Table 3).

5.3 Basic vs. persuasive factors of destination homepages

Descriptive analyses were conducted to assess respondents' evaluation of the design features of the destination webpages; the results appear to be consistent with the results of two-factor model proposed by Huang (2001). Specifically, respondents reported high ratings for basic factors (i.e., informativeness: mean = 3.7; *SD* = .79, usability: mean = 3.7; *SD* = .87). In contrast, the persuasive factors were rated somewhat lower (i.e., credibility: mean: 3.5; *SD* = .77, inspiration: mean = 3.3; *SD* = 1.10, involvement: mean = 3.5; *SD* = .89, reciprocity: mean = 3.5; *SD* = .86).

Table 3. Reliability and validity results

Items in Scale	**Internal Consistency**	**Unidimensionality**	
Homepage Design Factors	Cronbach's Alpha	Factor Loading	Variance Explained
Informativeness	.79		70.4%
INFO1		.85	
INFO2		.87	
INFO3		.80	
Usability	.86		77.4%
USE1		.89	
USE2		.87	
USE3		.88	
Credibility	.85		76.8%
CRED1		.85	
CRED2		.89	
CRED3		.89	
Inspiration	.91		84.6%
INSP1		.92	
INSP2		.93	
INSP3		.91	
Involvement	.82		74.1%
INV1		.88	
INV2		.85	
INV3		.85	
Reciprocity	.85		68.5%
RECP1		.80	
RECP2		.84	
RECP3		.85	
RECP4		.82	

5.4 Drivers to forming first impression towards destination homepages

Multiple regression analysis was used to assess the impact of website design factors on the formation of first impression towards the destination homepages. The independent variables were the overall mean values of the items used to construct the six design factors. As shown in Table 4, the beta coefficients for inspiration, usability and credibility were significant ($p < .001$ for inspiration and usability; $p < .005$ for credibility) and positive. Specifically, inspiration (ß = .30) was the most significant driver in forming favourable first impression, followed closely by usability (ß = .26). Credibility was also significant at the level of .05; however, it was notably lower in importance (ß = .16) as compared with the other two drivers. The multivariate regression showed a high R^2 (.757) indicating that the model fits extremely well (see Table 4).

Table 4. Multiple regression results

Dependent Variable: Overall impression towards a destination homepage

Goodness of fit

Multiple $R = .870$, $R^2 = .757$, Adjusted $R^2 = .750$, $SE = .439$

Independent variable	B	*SE* B	Beta	*T*	Sig.	Tolerance Value
Constant	-.11	.14		-7.33	.46	
Information	.15	.09	.14	1.72	.09	.165
Usability	**.26**	**.09**	**.24**	**3.00**	**.00****	**.182**
Credibility	**.16**	**.08**	**.14**	**2.08**	**.04***	**.244**
Inspiration	**.30**	**.05**	**.30**	**6.04**	**.00****	**.465**
Involvement	.13	.08	.12	1.55	.12	.193
Reciprocity	.03	.08	.03	.35	.70	.209

Note: * significant at p < .05, ** significant at p < .01

6 Conclusions

The primary goal of this research was to investigate key elements in the formation of first impression of destination webpages. This study confirmed that the perceived usability of destination webpages is a very important feature in persuading trip planners using the Internet. Two design factors (i.e., credibility and inspiration) were also perceived as one with substantial impact in the process of persuasion. Among the design factors, inspiration-related design elements had the greatest impact. That is, the homepages of DMO websites inspiring information searchers to visit their destinations are more likely to elicit a favourable response towards their websites. Thus, considering travel products and services are experiential products, destination web designers can take advantage of innovations in website design to by creating sensory associations by integrating persuasive web tools. Credibility was also a significant driver of first impression. This finding implies the need to recognize the trustworthiness or expertise of the websites is an important concern of potential visitors. Recently, cues such as "official" have been incorporated into many websites so as to convey some sort of credibility (Xiang & Fesenmaier, 2006).

A few limitations of this study must be identified along with the directions for future study. First, the survey system developed for this study did not provide an environment whereby respondents could interact directly with the destination webpages. Thus, future studies should fine-tune the study design whereby the survey system enables direct access to the respective websites. Secondly, this study did not examine where the differences in respondents' perceptions towards destination webpages were derived from (i.e., the use of particular design components or the effective use of message cues). Third, respondents' images/prior experiences with states as tourism destinations were not controlled in this study. It is expected that destination images may exert some influence on the evaluation of destination websites. Fourthly, this study did not examine the effect of personal and situational factors. It is presumable that personal traits (e.g., computer skills, experiences of using the Internet, information processing style, the level of involvement, travel interests, disposition of being persuaded, etc.) and situation factors (e.g., stage of trip planning, time constraint, etc.) play a certain role on information seeking behaviour and choice. In addition to the limitations and proposed directions for future studies described above, it is highly recommended that following studies use non-student subjects to generalize the findings of this study to a larger portion of consumers. Despite of the limitations this study contained, however, it is argued that the present study provides the foundation for future research that wishes to design more effective destination websites that achieve a goal of actually affecting visitor behaviour.

References

Bauer, R. A., & Greyser, S. A. (1968). *Advertising in American, The consumer view.* Boston, MA: Harvard University.

Bloch, P. H., & Richins, M. L. (1983). A theoretical model for the study of product importance perceptions. *Journal of Marketing*, 47 (Summer), 69-81.

Brainstrom & Raves (2001). *4 seconds to grab visitor's attention?* Retrieved from http://brainstormsandaves.com/achives/2001/03/10 4_seconds_to_grab_visitors_attention/.

Scioli, A., & Averill, J.R. (1998). Emotion and Cognition. In H.S. Friedman (Ed.), *Encyclopedia of Mental Health*. NY, Academic Press.

Cialdini, R. B., Green, B. L., & Rusch, A. J. (1992). When tactical pronouncements of chance become real change: The case of reciprocal persuasion. *Journal of personality & Social Psychology*, 63, 30-40.

Cole, J. I. (2000). *Surveying the digital future*, Los Angeles, CA: UCLA Center for Communication Policy.

Dijksterhuis, A., Bos, M. B., Nordgren, L. F., & van Barren, R. B. (2006). On making the right choice: the deliberation-without-attention effect. *Science*, 311(17), 1005-1007.

Doney, P., & Cannon, J. P. (1997). An examination of the nature of trust in buyer-seller relationships. *Journal of Marketing*, 61(April), 35-51.

Ducoffe, R. H. (1996). Advertising value and advertising on the web. *Journal of Advertising Research*, (Sep/Oct), 21-35.

Ducoffe, R. H. (1995). How consumers assess the value of advertising, *Journal of Current Issues & Research in Advertising*, 17(1), 1-18.

Finberg, H., Stone, H., & Lynch, D. (2001). *Digital Journalism Credibility Study*. Retrieved from www.journalists.org/Programs/credibility_study.pdf.

Fiske, S. T., Lin, M., & Neuberg, S. L. (1999). The continuum model: Ten years later. In S. Chaiken & Y. Trope (Eds). *Dual process theories in social psychology* (pp. 231-254). New York: Guilford.

Fiske, S. T., & Neuberg, S. L. (1990). A continuum model of impression formation, from category-based to individualing processes: Influences of information and motivation on attention and interpretation. In M. P. Zanna (Ed.), *Advances in experimental social psychology* (Vol. 23, pp. 1-74). New York: Academic Press.

Fogg, B. J. (1999). Credibility and computing technology. *Communications of the ACM*, 42(5), 39-44.

Fogg, B. J. (2003). *Persuasive technology: Using computers to change what we think and do.* San Francisco: CA: Morgan Kaufmann Publishers.

Fogg, B. J., & Tseng, H. (1999). *The elements of computer credibility.* Proceedings of CHI 99, pp. 80-87. New York, NY: ACM.

Gladwell, M. (2005). *Blink: the power of thinking without thinking.* Little, Brown & Company.

Gouldner, A. W. (1960). The norm of reciprocity: A preliminary statement. *American Sociological Review*, 25 (2), 161-178.

Hotchkiss, G. (2006). *The 50 milliseconds judgment.* Retrieved from http://www.searchengineguide.com/hotchkiss/2006/0206_gh1.html.

Huang, M. (2003). Designing website attribute in induce experiential encounters. *Computers in Human Behavior,* 19, 425-442.

Johnson, B. T., & Eagly, A. H. (1989). Effects of involvement on persuasion: A meta-analysis. *Psychology Bulletin*, 104, 290-314.

Kaiser, S. (2001). *Your web site's first impression happens only once.* Retrieved from http://skdesigns.com/newsletter/v2n2.shtml.

Kane, R. L., Johnson, P. E., Town, R. J., & Butler, M. (2004). A structured review of the effect of economic incentives on consumers' preventive behavior. *American Journal of Preventive Medicine* 27(4), 327-352.

Kim, H. J., & Fesenmaier, D. R. (2005). *Persuasive Design of Tourism Websites in the United States, Proceedings*, The Annual Conference of the Travel and Tourism Research Association, New Orleans, pp. 17-21.

LaGaipa, J. J. (1977). Interpersonal attraction and social exchange. In S. D. Duck (Ed.), *Theory and practice in interpersonal attraction* (pp. 129-164). London: Academic Press.

Lindgaard, G., Fernandes, G., Dudek, C., & J. Brown (2006). Attention to designers: You have 50 milliseconds to make a good first impression! *Behavior & Information Technology,* 25 (2), 115-126.

Loiacono, E., Watson, R., & Goodhue, D. (2002). *WebQual™: A web site quality instrument.* Paper presented at the American Marketing Association: Winter Marketing Educators, Austin, TX.

Luo, X. (2002). Uses and gratification theory and e-consumer behaviors: a structural equation modelling study. *Journal of Interactive Advertising*, 2(2).

Marchionini, G. M. (1995). *Information seeking in electronic environments.* Cambridge, Eng.: Cambridge Univ. Press.

Machlis, S. (1988). Believe it or not, Web stores can make money. *Computerworld*, 32 (20), 4.

McCquarrie, E., & Munson, J. (1991). *A revised product involvement inventory: improved usability and validity* (Vol. 19). Provo: UT: The Association for Consumer Research.

Mitchell, A. A. (1980). Involvement: A potentially important mediator of consumer behaviour. In W. L. Willkie (Ed.), *Advances in Consumer Research* (Vol. 14). Ann Arbor, MI: Association for Consumer Research.

Perfetti, C. (2005). *5-seconds tests: Measuring your site's content pages.* Retrieved from http://www.uie.com/articles/five_second_test/.

Rieh, S. Y. (2002). Judgment of information quality and cognitive authority in the web. *Journal of American Society for Information Science & Technology*, 53(2), 145-161.

Rothschild, M. L. (1984). Perspectives on involvement: current problems and future directions. *Advances in Consumer Research*, 11, 216-217.

Straub, D. (1989). Validating instruments in MIS research. *MIS Quarterly*, 13(2), 147-169.

Stromer-Galley, J. (2004). Interactivity as process and interactivity as product. *The Information Society*, 20(5), 391-394.

Thrash, T. M., & Elliot, A. J. (2003). Inspiration as a psychological construct. *Journal of Personality and Social Psychology*, 84, 871-889.

Wang, S., Beatty, S. E., & Foxx, W. (2004). Signaling the trustworthiness of small online retailers. *Journal of Interactive Marketing*, 18(1), 53-69.

WNetwork (2006). *Style by Jury's first impression tips.* Retrieved from http://www.wnetwork.com/articles/styleT1.asp?id=625.

Wöber, K. (2006). Domain specific search engines. In D. R. Fesenmaier, H. Werthner & K. Wober (Eds.), *Travel destination recommendation systems: Behavioral foundations and applications:* CAB International.

Xiang, Z., & Fesenmaier, D. R. (2006). Assessing the initial step of online persuasion process: Meta tags on tourism websites. *Journal of Information Technology & Tourism,* 8 (2), 91-104.

Zaichkowsky, J. L. (1985). Measuring the Involvement Construct. *Journal of Consumer Research*, 12(Dec), 341-352.

Zhang, P., & von Dran, G. M. (2000). Satisfiers and dissatisfiers: A two-factor model for website design and evaluation. *Journal of the American Society for Information Science*, 51(14), 1253-1268.

Evaluation of the Usability of Chinese Destination Management Organisation Websites

QI Shanshan[a]
Dimitrios Buhalis[a]
Rob Law[b]

[a] School of Management, University of Surrey, UK
ss79802004@yahoo.com.cn and D.Buhalis@surrey.ac.uk
[b] School of Hotel & Tourism Management,
Hong Kong Polytechnic University
hmroblaw@polyu.edu.hk

Abstract

Website usability reflects the quality of a website. Presently, there are only few prior studies that focused on Destination Management Organisation (DMO) website usability. There is also limited, if ever any, research on Chinese DMO websites. Since China is predicted to be the top destination in the world by 2020, it is important to examine the readiness of its web destination websites. By using a modified heuristic evaluation methodology, this research identified the current situation of Chinese DMO websites and evaluated the usability of Chinese provincial DMO websites. The research findings indicate that many DMOs in China have gradually introduced websites to promote their destinations and that overall the Chinese provincial DMO websites have medium usability problems. This study demonstrated that there is no relation between the tourism income of a destination and the performance of its website.

Keywords: DMO, DMS, China, usability, heuristic evaluation method, website.

1 Introduction

Information & Communication Technologies (ICTs) have revolutionised DMOs' operation. Most DMOs in the world have established their own websites to promote their service/products globally (Hanna & Millar 1997; Tunnard, & Haines, 1999; Buhalis, 2003, 2005; WTOBC, 2001, 2005). The main purpose of a DMO website is to attract more consumers and to increase visitation to the destination. Usability of DMO websites, therefore, plays a great role in achieving this objective. If a website has poor usability, the users tend to leave the website easily (Nielson, 2000). Souze, Manning, Goldman, and Tong (2000, in Au Yeung & Law, 2003) reported that 65% of users left retail websites because of usability barriers. A good performance in website usability saves customers' time and money; and improves a website's effectiveness. Therefore, usability performance is an important factor for a successful website (Douglas & Mills, 2004; Elges, 2004; Nielsen, 2003; Nielsen & Norman, 2000; Olive, 2002; Au Yeung & Law, 2003).

China has become the largest tourist destination in Asia and the UNWTO predicts that China will become the most popular destination by 2020 (Wang, Yu, & Avgoustis, 2005;

China Daily News, 2004). According to CINIC's (China Internet Network Information Centre) 2006 statistical report on the Internet development in China, the total number of Internet users has reached 111 million by Year 2005. Hence, there is a huge and emerging eTourism market in China and plenty of potential travel service users.

There are many prior studies on tourism website research and website evaluations (Buhalis & Molinaroli, 2003; Morrison, Taylor, Morrison, & Morrison,, 1999) but few are focused on DMO websites. Although a number of destination research projects have been published (Douglas & Mills, 2004; Ismail, Labropoulos, Mills, & Morrison, 2002; Benckendorff & Black, 2000; Buhalis, 1999; So & Morrison, 2004; Kaplanidou & Vogt, 2004), few of them are focused on the evaluation of DMO website usability. There are even less, if any, published research papers on DMO website developments and their usability in China. This research therefore aims to achieve a better understanding of the DMO websites in China and to evaluate their usability.

2 The Theoretical Background

DMO websites can promote destination products, develop partnership between public and private sectors, and bring benefit to both the supply and demand sides (WTOBC, 2001). On the demand side, DMO websites provide convenience to tourists, help them build destination images, cater for different personalities and needs, develop individualised itineraries and assist them purchase tourism products. On the supply side, DMO websites enable local businesses and travel intermediates to promote their service/products and communicate with their markets (Buhalis, 1999; 2003; Pike 2005; Tunnard, 1999).

Among other success criteria, effective DMO websites should have a high degree of usability. Nielsen (2000; 2003) proposed a definition of usability, which examines whether the design of a website's interface can satisfy certain criteria, including: "ease to use", "ease to learn", "memorability", "consumer's satisfaction", and "low user error rate". The usability of a website can reflect its effectiveness in providing convenience to users and in saving their time. In order to better serve customers, DMO websites should have excellent usability.

3 Methodology

This research endeavours to achieve a better understanding of DMO website usability and to produce useful evaluation results for analysing the usability of Chinese DMO websites. The objective of this research is therefore to evaluate the usability of Chinese provincial DMO websites. The heuristic evaluation is one of the most popular methods in usability examination (Nielsen,1993). Au Yeung and Law (2003) modified this method in their research and successfully evaluated the usability of Hong Kong hotel websites. This research uses a modified heuristic usability evaluation method adopted from Au Yeung and Law (2003).

Normally, the heuristic method requires a small group of evaluators. Every evaluator works individually and the researcher is in charge of collecting and analysing data. Evaluators are requested to be familiar with the products and to agree with a set of usability principles before the evaluation begins (Nielsen & Molich, 1990; Nielsen, 1992; Landauer & Nielsen, 1993). In this paper, a new usability criterion was developed to evaluate Chinese provincial DMO website usability, by combining DMO website success factors with website usability criteria as stipulated by Nielsen (2000, 2003) and Abeleto (2004).

The research process is shown in Figure 1. The process can be divided into three stages. The first stage developed new usability criteria for DMO websites, by combining website usability hazard criteria with critical success factors for DMO websites. In the second stage, two questionnaires were designed. The first one is about developing a new checklist to evaluate DMO websites. The second one is to evaluate 31 Chinese DMO websites. The third stage is to calculate Usability Hazards of DMO websites.

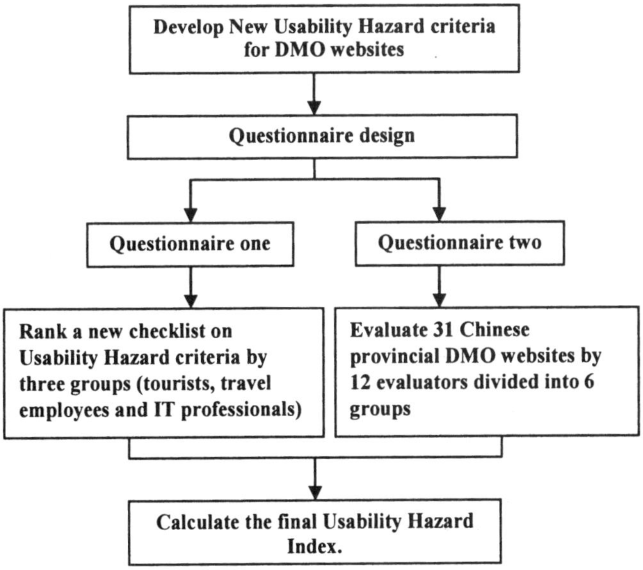

Fig. 1. Research procedure

3.1 New Usability Hazard criteria for DMO websites

To develop a comprehensive instrument, the usability hazard criteria are combined by critical success factors for DMO websites as reported in several studies (Morrison, 2002; Ismail et al., 2002; WTOBC 2001, 2005; So & Morrison, 2004; Kaplanidou & Vogt, 2004; Douglas & Mills, 2004). Website Usability Hazard Criteria are adopted from Nielsen (2000, 2003) and Abeleto (2004). These include 30 criteria that present problems which can damage the DMO websites performance. These criteria were divided into 5 dimensions as proposed by Abeleto (2004), namely: *Language,* that refers to the choice of words used to present information on the Web; *Layout and Graphics,* that pertain to how elements are visually rendered on the Web page; *Information Architecture,* that relates to how the content and features of a website can be arranged; *User Interface,* that determines the ease of navigating through content; and *general* that refers to the download speed, general practice of design and maintenance.

3.2 Questionnaires and Respondents

The aim of questionnaire one was to "range the DMO website usability criteria" and to establish a new checklist for DMO website usability in order to calculate the parameter of "Ir" (Importance Index of criterion). The questionnaire was administrated on 90 Chinese respondents who were divided into three groups, namely: tourists, travel industry employees, and IT professionals, who have visited DMO websites before. Each group had 30 respondents. All of the questions were closed-end questions, and respondents were required to rank the 30 DMO criteria within the five main dimensions. The final rating in section three was calculated based on the relative importance of responses from each group. In order to ensure research reality and validity, the first question used a qualifying question: "Have you ever visited any destination website before? If "yes" please go to section two, otherwise please go to section four" to distinguish the respondents.

The purpose of questionnaire two was to evaluate the 31 Chinese key provincial DMO websites. A five-point Likert scale was used to evaluate the websites, which ranged from point one "no problem on this criteria", to point two "minor problem", point three "medium problem", point four "major problem" and point five "destructive problem". The 12 evaluators were divided into six groups with two people in one group. The evaluators then rated the websites according to their performance.

3.3 Data analysis process

The model used in this research is adopted from Au Yeung and Law (2003). The modelling process was divided into two steps: (A), ranking a new checklist for DMO website usability criteria, and calculating "Ir" (Importance Index of Usability criterion) according to the respondent's perceptions of damage to the DMO website. (B), calculating "D" the Usability Hazard Index of the whole DMO website based on a questionnaire that used a five-point Likert scale to evaluate the DMO website. The advantage of the Likert scale technique is that the responses can be quantified and the attitude of respondents is easy to identify. For each DMO website and in each criterion, a mean rating score was calculated based on the result of group evaluation.

4 Research Findings

4.1 Different attitudes from different groups

All of the groups paid attention to website services and pertinent standard on website operation. However, different perspectives also emerged in the three groups. People in the tourist group seemed to care more about the website's ease of use and service functions. The IT professional people paid more attention to the website technology functions, and the group of travel employees cared more about the website's general performance, website target market and the relation between business partners.

4.2 Importance Index of Usability Criteria

The results of the 90 completed questionnaires on Importance Index of Usability Criteria are presented in Table 1. The results are arranged according to the respondents' general perception about the degree of damage to a DMO website. Therefore, higher scores mean that this criterion is more dangerous to the website.

Table 1 demonstrates that "Text is not readable and understandable", "disordered website structure", "improper use of systematic navigation labelling", "Dead links" and "Long sever responding time" are the major hazard criteria in website usability. In contrast, "Internet jargon using", "No print-out options" "No separate information for business co-operators" , "outstanding colour of hyperlinks" and "No accessible pages" are perceived to be minor hazards in website usability.

4.3 Chinese DMO Websites' Usability Hazards Indices in Five Dimensions

Table 2 shows mean scores of all Chinese provincial DMO websites' usability hazard indices of five dimensions and 30 criteria. The score of each dimension is the sum of this dimension's criteria. The maximum score of each dimension is 20 (from 0 "no problem" to 20 "destructive problem") (Au Yeung & Law, 2003).

Table 2 shows that the dimension with the best performance on Chinese provincial DMO websites is dimension one "language" scored 3.681. The dimension that has the worst performance is dimension four: "Information Architecture" which scored 7.192. These results implied that Chinese DMO websites have good language allocation in presenting website information and medium problems in dimension four. Moreover, "Using lots of internet jargon buzzwords", "Using Graphical bullet / divider bars in a wrong way", "No separate information for Business partners" and "Imperfect basic webpage elements" obtained the lowest score within their relative dimensions, which means these criteria have good performance. Otherwise, the criteria of "Texts are not readable and understandable", "Disordered website structure", "Doesn't mark changed URLs in the old web", "Without an internal search engine" and "No accessible pages for disabled people" obtained the highest scores within their dimensions, which implies Chinese provincial DMO websites have inadequate performance on these criteria.

Table 1. Importance Index of Usability criteria

Dimension 1. Language	**Importance Index**
1. Spelling and grammar mistakes	0.339
2. Use lots of Internet jargon buzzwords	0.245
3. Texts are not readable and understandable (include the headlines)	0.416
Dimension 2. Website Layout	
1. Using graphical bullet / divider bars in a wrong way	0.175
2. Web page is too long	0.139
3. Horizontal scrolling under the common screen's resolution	0.149
4. No print-out options	0.089
5. Non-standard text colours	0.135
6. Disordered website structure	0.196
7. Not using multimedia images	0.117
Dimension 3. Information Architecture	
1. Doesn't mark changed URLs in the old web	0.134
2. Poor data references	0.133
3. Improper use of Systematic navigation labelling	0.169
4. Poor Destination information	0.225
5. No relevant links (airports, travel agencies)	0.136
6. No separate information for Business partners	0.073
7. Without comment mechanism and tourism destination forum	0.130
Dimension 4. User interface and Navigation	
1. Links opening a new browser window	0.111
2. Imperfect basic web page elements	0.118
3. Dead links	0.191
4. Lack of Navigation support	0.148
5. The colour of visited hyperlinks is not significant	0.076
6. Lack of international service	0.087
7. Doesn't have a "Go Back" button	0.124
8. Without an internal search engine	0.145
Dimension 5. General	
1. Long sever responding time	0.255
2. Download time is too long	0.185
3. Bad browser compatibility	0.219
4. Program not accurate	0.220
5. No accessible pages for disabled people	0.121

4.4 The Performance of General Usability Hazard Indices on Chinese Provincial DMO Websites

The general usability hazard index of Chinese DMO websites is shown in Table 3. Because the total score is 100, all of the usability hazard indices could be sorted into four levels: 0-25.00 as level one [perform well on website usability with only minor problems appear on the website]; 25.01-50.00 as level two [their website usability performed normally, and only some medium problems need to be fixed in a short time]; 50.01-75.00 as level three [major problems were found on this website]; 75.01-100 as level four [destructive problems were found on this website].

Table 2. Usability Hazard Indices of Chinese DMO websites (mean score)

Dimension 1. Language	**Usability Hazards Index**
1.Spelling and grammar mistakes	1.695
2. Use lots of Internet jargon buzzwords	0.040
3. Texts are not readable and understandable (include the headlines)	1.946
Dimension total	3.681
Dimension 2. Website Layout	
1. Using Graphical bullet / divider bars in a wrong way	0.395
2. Web Page is too long	1.076
3. Horizontal Scrolling under the common screen's resolution	0.096
4. No print-out options	1.120
5. Non-standard text colours	0.697
6. Disordered website structure	1.201
7. Not using multimedia images	0.642
Dimension total	5.227
Dimension 3. Information Architecture	
1. Doesn't mark changed URLs in the old web	1.340
2 Poor data references	1.030
3. Improper use of systematic navigation labelling	0.273
4. Poor Destination information	0.980
5. No relevant links (airports, travel agencies)	0.680
6. No separate information for Business partners	0.365
7. Without comment mechanism and tourism destination forum	0.671
Dimension total	5.339
Dimension 4. User interface and Navigation	
1. Links Opening a new browser window	0.895
2. Imperfect basic webpage elements	0.571
3. Dead links	1.140
4. Lack of Navigation support	0.477
5. The colour of visited hyperlinks are not significant	0.785
6. Lack of international service	1.235
7. Doesn't have a "Go Back" button	0.920
8. Without an internal search engine	1.169
Dimension total	7.192
Dimension 5. General	
1. Long sever responding time	1.357
2. Download time is too long	1.208
3. Bad Browser Compatibility	0.071
4. Program not Accurate	0.958
5. No accessible pages for disabled people	2.098
Dimension total	5.692

Table 3 shows that the Usability Hazard Index of industrial performance is 27.131, which is between 25.00 to 50.00, belonging to level 2, and means there are medium problems on Chinese provincial DMO websites. Abeleto (2004) stated that medium hazards can cause visitor loss if these aspects cannot get improvements. They should obtain a high priority during site maintenance. Among the five dimensions, User interface and Navigation are the most problematic, followed by General, Information Architecture and Website Layout, whose scores are rather close to each other. Language is the least of the problems among all dimensions.

Table 3. Usability Hazard Indices of Chinese DMO Websites

Dimensions	Usability Hazards Index
Dimension 1. Language	3.681
Dimension 2. Website Layout	5.227
Dimension 3. Information Architecture	5.339
Dimension 4. User interface and Navigation	7.192
Dimension 5. General	5.692
Industrial performance	27.131

4.5 Chinese DMO Websites Usability Hazard Index and Tourism Receipts

In order to explore the relationship between the development of tourism destinations and the performance of tourism websites, this study classified destinations into three categories according to their total tourism receipts in 2004 (CNTA 2005). The categories were classified with total tourism receipts between US$10,000 to 21,000; US$4,000 to 7,500; or less than US$4,000 Million. Tables 4 and 5 list the dimensions and overall website usability hazard indices for different destinations according to 2004.

Table 4 shows that the performance of the six destinations with the highest tourism receipts income in Year 2004 between 10,000-21,000 million dollars. The total DMO website hazard index of these six websites reflects a good usability performance. The average score was 23.346, which implied minor problems. Amongst these websites the Guangdong Province seems to have medium problems in usability hazards as it is scored 32.46.

Table 4. Usability Hazards Index of Destinations with Total Tourism Receipts between 10000-21000 Million dollars (2004)

Dimension / Province	1. Language	2. Website Layout	3. Information Architecture	4. User Interface and Navigation	5. General	Usability Hazards Index of DMOs	Total tourism receipts Million dollars
Guangdong	3.775	9.885	3.400	7.480	7.920	32.460	20599.450
Jiangsu	3.775	6.235	4.715	3.080	3.713	21.518	17728.01
Zhejiang	3.775	3.685	4.050	4.505	2.438	18.453	12505.262
Shandong	3.775	5.545	3.690	7.545	3.520	24.075	10086.166
Shanghai	3.775	4.575	4.915	7.425	7.140	27.830	18147.558
Beijing	3.775	3.290	2.685	3.075	2.915	15.740	17345.353
Average	3.775	5.536	3.909	5.518	4.608	23.346	

In Table 5 for destinations with tourism income in 2004 between 4,000 and 7,500 million dollars, the average website usability performance was 29.863, which means these websites have medium problems. Among the performance of these tourism websites the worst one is Hebei's DMO website which scored 33.160 and has medium usability problem.

Table 6 includes sixteen Usability Hazard results for the low tourism income destinations (less than 4,000 million dollars). The average usability performance of their websites was 26.97, which means they has medium usability problems. The best destination website was Guizhou which scored 18.390. The worst DMO website usability performance was in Ningxia, whose usability hazards index was 39.030 and has medium usability problems.

Table 5. Usability Hazards Index of Destinations with Total Tourism Receipts between 4000-7500 Million dollars (2004)

Dimension / Province	1. Language	2. Website Layout	3. Information Architecture	4. User Interface and	5. General	Usability Hazards Index of DMOs	Total tourism receipts Million dollars
Hebei	3.775	5.930	7.680	7.855	7.920	33.160	4338030
Sichuan	3.775	3.580	3.955	7.495	9.958	28.763	7009681
Liaoning	3.775	6.730	2.640	5.350	9.020	27.515	7056726
Yunnan	5.000	5.925	7.575	4.730	4.620	27.850	4571644
Fujian	3.775	6.375	8.675	6.755	7.013	32.593	6818283
Henan	3.775	7.425	6.415	7.990	6.813	32.018	7092923
Hubei	3.775	4.660	4.460	7.830	7.013	27.738	5072531
Tianjing	3.775	4.035	4.640	7.225	6.040	25.715	6418141
Hunan	3.775	6.738	5.125	6.160	11.220	33.018	4600366
Average	3.911	5.711	5.685	6.821	7.735	29.863	

5 Summary of Research Findings and Conclusions

The overall Usability Hazard score of Chinese DMO websites is 27.131, which reflects moderate problems. T he most dangerous dimension is user interface and navigation. Table 7 refers to the usability criteria that scored the worst marks. "Texts are not readable and understandable", "Disordered website structure" and "Dead links" are major hazards to usability on Chinese DMO websites. Therefore, Chinese local DMOs should consider improving these functions. Besides, the two criteria "Doesn't notify users URLs have been changed" and "Without an internal search engine" are medium hazards to usability on Chinese DMO websites. The problems that are popular and persistent on the website can lead to visitor dissatisfaction and need to be addressed. Finally, the criterion of "No accessible pages for disabled people" is a minor hazard to DMO usability. This problem only affects the online experience of disabled users and hence it is usually ignored by designers.

Table 6. Usability Hazards Index of Destinations with Total Tourism Receipts Less than 4,000 Million dollars (2004)

Dimension / Province	1. Language	2. Website Layout	3. Information Architecture	4. User Interface and Navigation	5. General	Usability Hazards Index of DMOs	Total tourism receipts Million
Mongolia	1.695	2.290	9.450	8.415	2.420	24.270	1789.262
Guangxi	3.775	5.390	2.670	5.435	6.280	23.550	3148.98
Jilin	1.695	4.325	8.505	9.935	2.420	26.880	2277.961
Guizhou	3.775	2.510	0.670	3.965	7.470	18.390	2074.925
Shanxi	3.775	3.200	9.455	9.145	3.695	29.270	1987.787
Heilongjiang	3.775	3.310	3.595	7.290	5.720	23.690	3098.769
Shaanxi	3.775	3.665	4.430	9.535	10.120	31.525	2650.341
Tibet	3.775	4.950	4.425	3.865	4.620	21.635	189.665
Qinghai	3.775	5.550	6.915	8.300	3.345	27.885	250.411
Anhui	3.775	5.360	3.795	5.945	2.613	21.488	3298.769
Gansu	3.775	7.115	8.785	6.420	4.620	30.715	683.067
Xinjiang	3.775	7.878	6.455	10.515	4.445	33.068	1439.949
Jiangxi	3.775	5.925	8.015	11.445	5.720	34.880	2981.281
Chongqing	3.775	3.985	4.000	5.915	5.720	23.395	3210.403
Hainan	3.775	5.540	2.670	6.540	3.713	22.238	1374.328
Ningxia	3.775	6.425	7.295	13.615	7.920	39.030	186.941
Average	3.515	4.839	5.670	7.893	5.053	26.97	

Finally, the Chinese DMO websites' usability hazard index is listed in Table 8 for destinations with different income. The average Usability Hazard Index for tourism income between 10,000-21,000 Million dollars (2004) indicates that these DMO websites have minor problems whilst destinations with tourism income between 4,000-7,500 Million dollars and less than 4,000 Million dollars (2004) score 29.863 and 26.97, respectively indicating that they have medium problems. These findings show that for DMO websites with high tourism income perform slightly better than those destinations provided by DMOs websites with medium or low tourism income. However, DMO websites of destinations having low tourism income also have better performance than DMO websites of destinations having medium tourism income.

Table 7. Usability Criteria having the Worst Performance

Usability Criteria	Dimensions	Usability Hazards
Texts are not readable and understandable	1	Major
Destroyed website structure	2	Major
Doesn't mark changed URLs in the old web	3	Medium
Without an internal search engine	4	Medium
Dead links	4	Major
No accessible pages for disabled people	5	Minor

Table 8. Average Usability Hazard Index of Chinese DMO websites for destinations with different income in 2004

	Tourism income was between *10000-21000 Million dollars (2004) (n=9)*	**Tourism income was between *4000-7500 Million dollars (2004) (n=6)***	**Tourism income was *Less than 4000 Million dollars (2004) (n=16)***	**All websites**
Average Usability Hazard Index	23.346	29.863	26.97	27.131

Therefore, there is no relation between destination development/income and DMO websites performance, indicating that the usability performance is a matter of design and availability of expertise rather than economic development. In conclusion, overall the Chinese provincial DMO websites have medium usability problems and there is a need for addressing those issues through redesign or maintenance. Although most regions have developed websites, these websites need to be developed further and expanded to address the emerging needs of both domestic and international visitors.

References

Abeleto (2004). Objective evaluation of likely usability hazards – preliminaries for user testing. Retrieved July 15, 2006 from http://www.abeleto.nl/resources/articles/objective1.html.

Au Yeung, T. and Law, R. (2003). Usability Evaluation of Hong Kong Hotel Websites. In A. J. Frew, M. Hitz & P. O'Connor. (Eds), *Information and Communication Technologies in Tourism 2003*. pp. 261-269.

Benckendorff, P. J., & Black, N. L. (2000). Destination marketing on the Internet: a case study of Australian regional tourism authorities. *Journal of Tourism Studies*, 10(1), 11-21.

Buhalis, D. (1999). Marketing the competitive destination of the future. *Tourism Management,* 21 97-116.

Buhalis, D. (2003). *E-tourism information technology for strategic tourism management*, Prentice Hall.

Buhalis, D., (2005). Information Technology in Tourism. In Cooper, C., Fletcher, J., Fyall, A., Gilbert, D., & Wanhill, S., *Tourism Principles and Practice*, 702-730.

Buhalis, D., & Molinaroli, E., (2003). Entrepreneurial Networks in Italian eTourism. In A. J. Frew, M. Hitz,& P. O'Connor, (Eds.) *Proceedings Information and Communication*

Technologies in Tourism, ENTER'03, Helsinki, Springer-Verlag, Wien, .86-95.

China daily 13/05/2004. Retrieved July 15, 2006 from http://www.chinadaily.com.cn/english/doc/2004-05/13/content_330514.htm.

CINIC (China Internet Network Information Centre), (2006). Statistical report on the Internet development in China, China.

CNTA, (2005). *The Year book of China Tourism Statistics*, Beijing: China Tourism Press.

Douglas, A., & Mills, J. E. (2004). Staying Afloat in the Tropics: Allying a Structural Equation Model Approach to Evaluating National Tourism Organization Website in the Caribbean. In Law, R.,& Mills, J., *Handbook of Consumer Behaviour, Tourism, and the Internet*, 269-293.

Elges, M. (2004). Why Worry About Web Site Usability? *Credit Union Executive Newsletter,* 30 (19), 8.

Hanna, J. R. P. & Millar, R. J. (1997). Promoting tourism on the Internet. *Tourism Management*, 18 (7), 469-470.

Ismail, J. A., T. Labropoulos, J. E. Mills, & Morrison, A. (2002). A Snapshot in Time: The Marketing of Culture in European Union NTO Web Sites. *Tourism Culture & Communication,* 3 (3) 165-179.

Kaplanidou, K. & Vogt, C. (2004), *Destination Marketing Organization Websites (DMOs) Evaluation and Design What you need to know*. Michigan State University. http://www.travelmichigannews.org/Research.htm

Landauer, T. K & Nielsen, J. (1993). A mathematical model of the finding of usability problems. *Proceedings of ACM INTERCHI'93 Conference*, (pp. 206-213) Amsterdam, The Netherlands, 24-29 April 1993.

Morrison, A. M., Taylor, S., Morrison, A. J., & Morrison, A. D. (1999). Marketing small hotels on the World Wide Web. *Information Technology & Tourism*, *2*(2), .97-113.

Morrison, A. M. (2002). *Hospitality and travel system* (4th ed.). Dubuque. IA: Kendall/Hunt Publishing.

Nielsen, J. (1992). Finding usability problems through heuristic evaluation. *Proceedings ACM CHI'92 Conference* (pp. .373-380), Monterey, CA, May 3-7.

Nielsen, J. (1993). *Usability Engineering.* London, Academic Press Limited.

Nielsen, J. (2000). *Designing Web Usability: The Practice of Simplicity.* New York, New Riders.

Nielsen, J. (2003). *Usability 101: Introduction to Usability.* Retrieved July 11, 2006 from http://www.useit.com/alertbox/20030825.html.

Nielsen, J., & Molich, R. (1990). Heuristic evaluation of user interfaces. *Proc. ACM CHI'90 Conf.* (pp. 249-256), Seattle, WA, 1-5 April.

Nielsen, J.& Norman, D. A. (2000). Usability on the Web Isn't A Luxury. *Information Week,* (773): 65-69.

Olive, E. G (2002). Usability: Marking the Web Work. *Intercom.* 49, 8-10.

Pike, S. (2005). *Destination Marketing Organisations*, Elsevier, Oxford.

So, S. I. & Morrison A. M. (2004). Internet Marketing in Tourism in Asia: An evaluation of the Performance of East Asian National Tourism Organization Web Sites. *Journal of Hospitality & Leisure Marketing,* 11(4), 93-118.

Tunnard, C. R. & P. Haines (1999). Destination Marketing Systems – a new role for tourist board marketing in the information age. *Journal of Vacation Marketing*, 1(4), 43-56. http://www.infocentre.com/news/DMS.htm

Wang, S., Yu, T., & Avgoustis, S., (2005). The "The Top City" Rating System: A Case Study of China's NTO Functions. In China Tourism Research (374-384). The Hong Kong Polytechnic University.

WTOBC, (2001). *E-business for Tourism, Practical guidelines for destinations and businesses.* Published by the World Tourism Organization.

WTOBC, (2005). *Evaluating and Improving Websites, The Destination Web Watch.* Published by the World Tourism Organization.

The Websites of a Tourism Destination: a Network Analysis

Rodolfo Baggio[a,b]
Magda Antonioli Corigliano[a]
Valeria Tallinucci[c,d]

[a] Master in Economics and Tourism, Bocconi University, Italy
{rodolfo.baggio, magda.antonioli}@unibocconi.it
[b] School of Tourism, The University of Queensland, Australia
[c] EURAC research, European Academy of Bolzano, Italy
valeria.tallinucci@eurac.edu
[d] Centro Studi della Banca dell'Elba, Italy

Abstract

How to reveal throughout a quantitative survey of the websites the cooperation development of a tourism destination? The analysis of the links among the tourist websites of a destination allows it. The website network of a tourism destination is examined and the main statistical characteristics of the underlying graph are calculated. The general topology of the network is similar to the one characterizing such systems. However, differences are found, mainly due to the relatively poor connectivity among the vertices of the network. These results are discussed and interpreted. Moreover, the usage of quantitative network parameters is shown to be able to measure the degree of collaboration and cooperation among the destination stakeholders and their tendency to act in such a way.

Keywords: tourism destination, Internet, web, cooperation, economic and social integration, complex networks.

1 Introduction

The destination management approach has emerged, in the last years, as an important strategic and operational approach to foster the development of areas where tourism is a relatively important activity and where the economy may be significantly influenced by tourism revenues (Ritchie & Crouch, 2003). The spectrum of definitions describing Tourism Destination (TD) is quite extensive and there are many difficulties in setting clear borders to it (Jafari, 2000). Beside the definition issues, a TD is the archetype of a complex adaptive system (CAS). It shares many (if not all) of the characteristics usually associated with a CAS: non-linear relationships among the system components, self-organization of the structures, resilience to external shocks (Holland, 1995). As for many such systems, it can be represented by a network graph whose vertices are the organisations (public or private) belonging to the local tourism system.

Information technologies, and the Internet in particular, have shown to be a crucial tool for the operations and the development of this "information intensive" sector (Poon, 1993). A website looks to be a major (and, probably, it will be the only one in the future) tool to conduct business in the tourism field (Law, Leung, & Wong,, 2004). Furthermore, the network system based on the Internet may represent, for a destination, the tool to bind together the local tourism supply operators allowing them to integrate the destination product/service chain and to develop common competences and know-how (Laesser, 2003; Pollock, 1995) Integrating the offer of a TD requires an adaptation of the operators in overcoming the internal competitive reality. They are required to acknowledge the need to cooperate in order to recommend the destination to the international tourism market and to promote a unique selling proposition.

The network is a virtual space where the operators can meet, exchange information and experiences, develop common projects and build partnerships with the objective of reducing risk, distribution efforts, and financial costs. Moreover, promoting a common project through interlinked websites provides increased visibility. Even a single organisation can thus have a higher probability to be seen and selected among the huge offering of the World Wide Web. This is also due to the score system set up by the main search engines, which recognises and values the importance of the interlinking among websites (Brin & Page, 1998).

The Web, by its very nature, is a complex dynamically growing network and, in this respect, its global properties are closely related to its topological structure. In the last years, a vast catalogue of studies on complex networks has been compiled (Boccaletti, Latora, Moreno, Chavez, & Hwang, 2006; Pastor-Satorras & Vespignani, 2004). The tourism sector, however, has not yet been included in this collection. This paper aims at filling this gap by presenting an investigation on the websites network of a tourism destination. Moreover, it will be shown that some of the network topological metrics can be profitably used to characterise important properties of the network and of the underlying social and economic system.

2 Network Models

Although almost 200 years old, the origins are ascribed to a famous paper by Leonhard Euler dated 1736, the so called "science of networks" has had an incredible thrust only in the last few years. The topology of complex systems, portrayed as networks, has been shown to be a fundamental feature of such systems (Boccaletti et al., 2006) Behaviours and processes can be described and explained by taking into account the system's general connectivity properties. The spread of viruses over a computer network or of diseases in a population, the formation of opinions, the diffusion of information or knowledge, the resilience after external shocks, all exhibit a strong dependence on some basic topological features of the network representing a system.

Many metrics have been used to describe complex networks (da F. Costa, Rodrigues, Travieso, & Villas Boas, 2005). Most of them come from the long tradition of social network analysis and have been increased by the recent work of the community of statistical physicists. A handful of these, are the ones commonly employed to fully characterise topology and behaviours of a complex network:

- *degree distribution P(k)*: the statistical distribution of the number (and sometimes the type) of the linkages among the network elements;
- *average path length L*: the mean distance between any two nodes;
- *diameter D*: the maximal shortest path connecting any two nodes;
- *clustering coefficient C*: representing how concentrated is the connection of the node's neighbours in a graph and giving a measure of the inhomogeneity of local density of links;
- *efficiency* (at a local E_{loc} or global E_{glob} level): which can be interpreted as a measure of the capability of the system to exchange information over the network;
- *assortativity*: which gauges the correlation between the degrees of neighbour nodes. If positive, the networks is said assortative; in it well-connected elements tend to be linked to each other. This quantity, connected to the clustering coefficient, has been recently shown to influence directly the formation of strongly connected subnetworks or communities and to give an indication of their strength (Quayle et al., 2006).

The mathematical expressions for these quantities can be found in one of the recently published reviews of the research in this area (Albert & Barabási, 2002; Boccaletti et al., 2006). These parameters can be used to classify the networks into three broad classes (Amaral, Scala, Barthélémy, & Stanley, 2000):

- *single-scale networks*: in which P(k) exhibits exponential (Poissonian or Gaussian tails). This class contains the random graphs (ER) and the small world (SW) networks described by Watts and Strogatz (1998) which are characterised by large clustering coefficients and short average path lengths;
- *scale-free networks*: P(k) has a power-law distribution: $P(k) \sim k^{-\gamma}$. The distribution is largely uneven, there is no characteristic mean nodal degree (the mean of a Poissonian ER distribution), but some (few) nodes act as very connected hubs, with very large number of ties, while the majority of nodes have a small number of links (Barabási & Albert, 1999);
- *broad-scale networks*: for which the degree distribution has a mixed behaviour, a power law regime followed by some sharp cut-off (exponential or Gaussian decay) of the tail.

The general topological properties of the World Wide Web have been studied by a number of authors. In particular, it has been possible to highlight a complex structure of its components (web pages or websites). According to Broder, Kumar, Maghoul, Raghavan, Rajagopalan, Stata, Tomkins, and Wiener, (2000) the structure has a "bow-tie" shape (see Fig. 1), in which it is possible to recognise a number of components according to their connectivity characteristics. The model, widely accepted, calls for a strongly connected component (SCC), formed by all pages mutually connected by a directed link, an in-component (IN) and an out-component (OUT), formed by nodes connected to the SCC in a monodirectional way. In addition to these, there is a series of secondary structures called TENDRILS, containing pages that do not link the SCC and cannot be reached from it; TUBES, directly linking the IN and OUT parts without crossing the SCC and some disconnected elements (DCC), similar to isolated islands, with no connection at all to the other components. This structure has also been identified in several subnetworks of the whole Web, strengthening the hypothesis of a self-similar arrangement, i.e. the fact that subnetworks of the Web show similar structures (Dill, Kumar, McCurley, Rajagopalan, Sivakumar, & Tomkins, 2002).

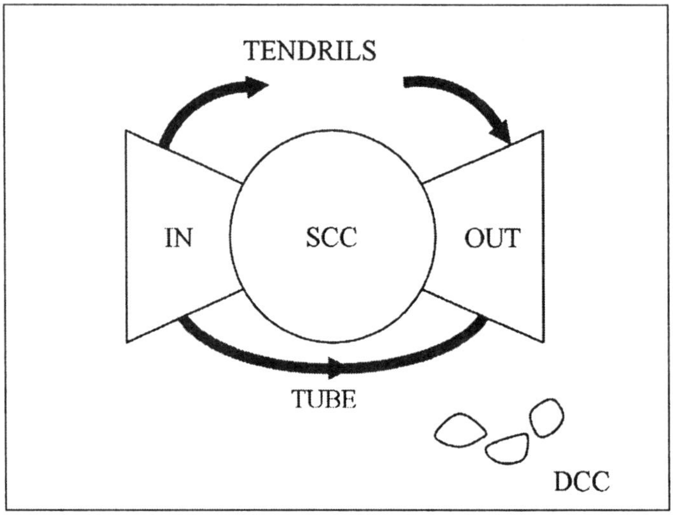

Fig. 1. A bow-tie model for the Web (after Baggio, 2006)

3 Methods

The websites of a tourism destination have been analyzed. The destination is the island of Elba, the main of the Tuscany Archipelago National Park and the third Italian island. It is an important environmental resource. Its geographic position, temperate climate, and the variety and beauty of its landscapes, coast and sea, make it a sea, sport and culture destination famous all over the world with almost 500 000 arrivals and 3 million overnights per year and several hundreds accommodation establishments (Tallinucci & Testa, 2006: 15-45). As for many other destinations, the Web has become, in the last years, an important means of promotion and commercialization for the whole community of local tourism operators. A previous study (Pechlaner, Tallinucci, Abfalter, & Rienzner, 2003) had been conducted in order to reveal the interest to develop a business model based on the Internet as a local network platform able to manage a small island tourism destination. The empirical enquiry on the accommodation entrepreneurs showed a good *Internet attitude* (88.8% of the responders had their own homepage and 68,5% a site within a local tourism portal). The main motivations for a presence on the network were identified in the possibility to achieve visibility on a wider market and to acquire new customers, the speed of communication with their customers, but also the passive need to be present on the web. The independence of the operators emerged from the surprisingly high proportion of self-made websites (more than 30%). The websites were linked from some general destination portal (often an internet service provider), but the local suppliers tried to maintain independent and personal styles and direct connections with their guests.

The study presented here refocuses on the Elban network formed by websites belonging to "classical" tourism operators: accommodation (hotels, residences, camping sites etc.), intermediaries (travel agencies and tour operators), transport, regulation bodies, services etc in order to reveal their connectivity. The whole size of the network is of 468 elements (websites). It is not huge, but of a size which can be considered sufficient to show meaningfully the graph's statistical properties (Angeloudis & Fisk, 2006; Dunne, Williams, & Martinez, 2002).

The websites have been analyzed considering them as the nodes of a complex network. Links among the websites have been listed by using a simple crawler and complementing the data obtained with a "manual" count of the hyperlinks to overcome the limitations of the program used (such as, for example, the impossibility to find hyperlinks embedded in Flash applications or Java applets). All links are considered of directed nature. The statistical analysis of the network thus obtained has been carried on by using standard software packages such as Pajek (Batagelj & Mrvar, 2004) and programs written by the one of the authors using the Matlab (MATLAB, 2004) development environment.

4 Results: The Elba Tourism Web Graph

The graphical representation of the Elba websites' network obtained is given in Fig. 2.

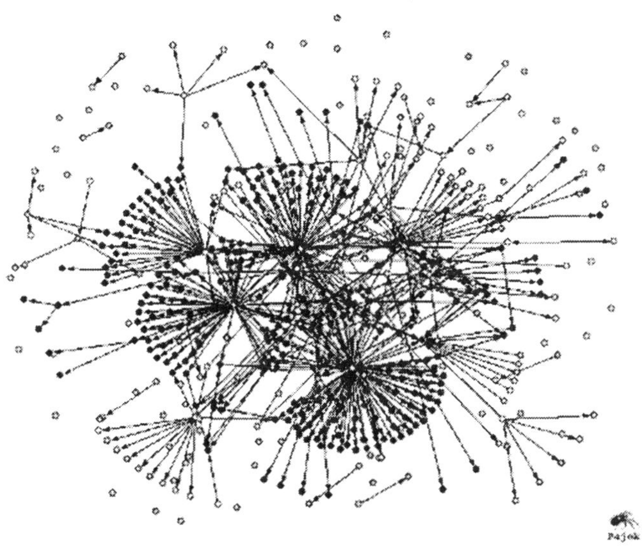

Fig. 2. The network of the Elban tourism websites

As it can be seen, the network exhibits a well identifiable structure. The network is rather sparse, its link density is d = 0.002 and almost 21% of the websites have no connection whatsoever to other sites. The diameter is D = 11, the average distance L = 4.5. These values are almost in line with those exhibited by similar networks (Albert & Barabási, 2002; Boccaletti et al., 2006; Pastor-Satorras & Vespignani, 2004).

The global clustering coefficient is: C = 0.003. Local and global efficiency (Latora & Marchiori, 2001) are: E_{loc} = 0.0145 and E_{glob} = 0.16981. These values are sensibly lower than those found for similar systems. The local efficiency value confirms the poor clusterisation of the network.

Key parameters characterising the structure of a directed network are the in-degree (k_{in}) and out-degree (k_{out}) distributions (the distributions of the number of links incoming to a node or outgoing from it). The cumulative degree distributions are shown in Fig. 3. Both display an almost perfect power law decay $P(k) \sim k^{-\gamma}$. The exponents calculated are: out-degree: $\gamma_{out} = 1.89$ and in-degree: $\gamma_{in} = 2.96$.

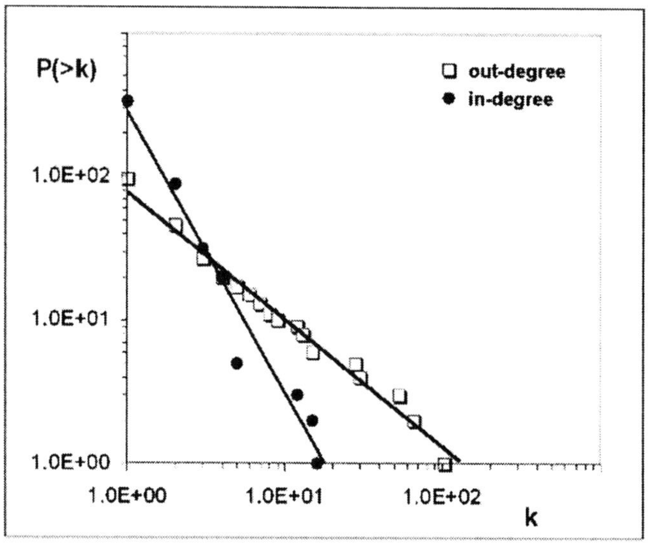

Fig. 3. In-degree and out-degree cumulative distributions for the Elba tourism websites' network

The in-degree exponent is higher and the out-degree exponent is lower than those typically measured for the Web: $\gamma_{in} \sim 2.1$ and $\gamma_{out} \sim 2.7$ (Broder et al., 2000). A spectral analysis confirms the main topological characteristics of the network, also acknowledging the scarce connectedness of the network.. Similar results were previously obtained, by using different techniques, in an assessment of the institutional websites of the island (Tallinucci & Testa, 2006: 126-135). The assortativity coefficient, calculated as the Pearson correlation coefficient between the degrees of adjacent vertices in the network (Newman, 2002) is: -0.101 ± 0.094. The Elban network, besides the general low connectivity among its websites, still shows evidence of a bow-tie structure. Table 2 displays the estimated proportions for the components along with the values accepted for the whole Web (Broder et al., 2000). To be noted is the very low size of a central strongly connected component.

Table 1. Relative size of the components for the Elba network and the Web in the hypothesis of a bow-tie structure

<table>
<tr><th></th><th>Elba Network (%)</th><th>Web (%)</th></tr>
<tr><td>SCC</td><td>3.4</td><td>28.0</td></tr>
<tr><td>IN</td><td>2.1</td><td>21.0</td></tr>
<tr><td>OUT</td><td>52.4</td><td>21.0</td></tr>
<tr><td>TENDRILS</td><td>15.6</td><td>21.0</td></tr>
<tr><td>TUBE</td><td>1.3</td><td rowspan="2">9.0</td></tr>
<tr><td>DCC</td><td>25.2</td></tr>
</table>

Summarising the results of the statistical analysis of the Elba tourism websites' network, it is possible to say that:

the results show a general agreement with similar results obtained by studying the Web and websites configurations (Broder et al., 2000; Dill et al., 2002). This may reinforce the idea of a substantial self-similarity in the structure of the Web space;
some of the values, though, show quite different characteristics: basically, a much lower connectivity and a higher sparseness of the network (Pastor-Satorras & Vespignani, 2004); moreover, a very small and negative correlation among the degrees of the nodes has been found (assortativity coefficient), i.e.: nodes with high degree tend to connect with nodes with low degrees. This behaviour is opposite to what is typically found for social networks (Newman, 2002, 2003).

5 Discussion

The main consideration, which can be drawn from the results shown in the previous section, concerns the network in itself and the usage of the technological connections among the organisations acting at the destination. The web network of Elba tourism stakeholders shows a very low connectivity and very low modularity (i.e.: low and sparse number of connected communities). This represents, essentially, a waste of resources both from a technical and an organisational point of view. It can be seen as a lost occasion in capturing the benefits and the advantages of cooperation mechanisms on the Internet. Mechanisms that could greatly ease the management of the destination and the efficiency in dealing with a globalised and highly competitive market (Barua, Whinston, & Yin, 2000; McLaren, Head, & Yuan, 2002). Moreover, on a strategic perspective, it should be taken into account that the future search engines and recommendation systems will be based on dynamic agents whose task will consist in identifying connected communities on the web. Not forming a "community" will inevitably result in very poor reachability for a casual user, with detrimental consequences for the effectiveness of the marketing and communication activities and their economic outcomes (Baggio, 2006; Lawrence, 2000).

In this scenario, the quantities measured above assume also one more important meaning. First of all, the low connectivity of the Elba tourism network gives us an indication of a poor degree of "technological" collaboration or cooperation among the stakeholders. More importantly, two measurements, the clustering coefficient and the assortativity index, can be used as quantitative assessments of this specific characteristics. For their nature, the first one (clustering coefficient) can be thought as a "static" measurement of cooperation, i.e.: formation of cohesive communities inside the destination, while the second one (assortativity) can be interpreted as representing the tendency to form such communities.

In the case of Elba, these conclusions have been already shown elsewhere by performing more "traditional" qualitative analyses (Pechlaner et al., 2003; Tallinucci & Testa, 2006). It has been argued that the low propensity to reference the external world could find a foundation on the strong independent way to conduct the family-run enterprises and on the high rate of loyalty guests which produce a good *word-of-mouth* promotion.

6 Conclusive remarks

The network formed by the websites of a tourism destination has been analysed. The statistical mechanics tools developed in the last years for this purpose have been used to derive the main topological characteristics of this network. The results show a general agreement with similar results, obtained by studying the Web and websites configurations. This reinforces the idea of a substantial self-similarity in the structure of the Web space. Some of the values, though, show different characteristics: basically a lower connectivity and a higher sparseness.

Four years after the first survey (Pechlaner et al., 2003), the *Internet attitude* of Elba's tourism operators has evolved, but less than their international competitors. In 2002, the web was seen as an opportunity to reach new guests and to open a window over the world, which potentially allowed to promote the destination on a global scale. Today, the advanced international destinations are able to sell integrated products and the individual tourist can satisfy their informational needs navigating through a well interconnected subnetwork. Elba, instead, still shows a very a scarce connectivity and a high rate of disconnected elements. This means, for example, that a guest has to identify a single supplier's website address in order to compose a holiday package. More importantly, this also means that the entrepreneurs are not cooperating to offer integrated products and services. The analysis of the Elba's website network allows to complement, with a quantitative assessment, analyses conducted with indirect or with qualitative methods, thus reinforcing the validity of those conclusions and allowing to overcome some of the limitations of those, such as the representativity of the samples chosen.

The authors believe also that by using structural network analysis methods, future work, already under way, may be able to better investigate the relationships between the technological network of websites and the real network of linkages among the stakeholders of a tourism destination. In this case some more tools may become available to address collaboration and cooperation issues, considered, by many, to be an important element for the success of a destination (Bramwell & Lane, 2000).

References

Albert, R., & Barabási, A.-L. (2002). Statistical mechanics of complex networks. *Review of Modern Physics, 74*, 47-91.

Amaral, L. A. N., Scala, A., Barthélémy, M., & Stanley, H. E. (2000). Classes of small world networks. *Proceedings of the National Academy of the Sciences of the USA, 97*, 11149-11152.

Angeloudis, P., & Fisk, D. (2006). Large subway systems as complex networks. *Physica A, 367*, 553-558.

Baggio, R. (2006). Complex systems, information technologies and tourism: a network point of view. *Information Technology and Tourism, 8* (1), 15-29.

Barabási, A.-L., & Albert, R. (1999). Emergence of scaling in random networks. *Science, 286*, 509-512.

Barua, A., Whinston, A. B., & Yin, F. (2000). Value and Productivity in the Internet Economy. *Computer, 33* (5), 102-105.

Batagelj, V., & Mrvar, A. (2004). *Pajek - Program for Large Network Analysis*. Retrieved December, 2005, from http://vlado.fmf.uni-lj.si/pub/networks/pajek/.

Boccaletti, S., Latora, V., Moreno, Y., Chavez, M., & Hwang, D.-U. (2006). Complex networks: Structure and dynamics. *Physics Reports, 424* (4-5), 175-308.

Bramwell, B., & Lane, B. (2000). *Tourism Collaboration and Partnerships: Politics Practice and Sustainability*. Clevedon, UK: Channel View Publications.

Brin, S., & Page, L. (1998). The Anatomy of a Large-Scale Hypertextual (Web) Search Engine. *Computer Networks and ISDN Systems, 30* (1-7), 107-117.

Broder, A. Z., Kumar, S. R., Maghoul, F., Raghavan, P., Rajagopalan, S., Stata, R., Tomkins, A., & Wiener, J. L. (2000). Graph structure in the web. *Computer Networks, 33* (1-6), 309-320.

da F. Costa, L., Rodrigues, A., Travieso, G., & Villas Boas, P. R. (2005). *Characterization of complex networks: A survey of measurements* (Preprint arxiv/cond-mat/0505185): ArXiv e-prints archive. Retrieved June, 2006, from http://arxiv.org/abs/cond-mat/0505185.

Dill, S., Kumar, S. R., McCurley, K., Rajagopalan, S., Sivakumar, D., & Tomkins, A. (2002). Self similarity in the web. *ACM Transactions on Internet Technology (TOIT), 2* (3 - August), 205-223.

Dunne, J. A., Williams, R. J., & Martinez, N. D. (2002). Food-web structure and network theory: The role of connectance and size. *Proceedings of the National Academy of the Sciences of the USA, 99* (20), 12917-12922.

Holland, J. H. (1995). *Hidden Order: How Adaptation Builds Complexity*. Reading, MA: Helix Books.

Jafari, J. (Ed.). (2000). *Encyclopedia of Tourism*. London: Routledge.

Laesser, C. (2003). Destination management: sfide per la politica turistica del futuro. In H. Pechlaner, K. Weiermair & C. Laesser (Eds.), *Politica del turismo e destination management* (pp. 43-71). Milano: TCI.

Latora, V., & Marchiori, M. (2001). Efficient behavior of small-world networks. *Physical Review Letters, 87*, 198701.

Law, R., Leung, K., & Wong, J. (2004). The impact of the Internet on travel agencies. *International Journal of Contemporary Hospitality Management, 16* (2), 100-107.
Lawrence, S. (2000). Context in Web Search. *IEEE Data Engineering Bulletin, 23* (3), 25-32.
MATLAB. (2004). MATLAB (Version 7, R14 - 2004). Natick, MA: The Matworks Inc.
McLaren, T., Head, M., & Yuan, Y. (2002). Supply chain collaboration alternatives: understanding the expected costs and benefits. *Internet Research: Electronic Networking Applications and Policy, 12* (4), 348-364.
Newman, M. E. J. (2002). Mixing patterns in networks. *Physical Review E, 67*, 026126.
Newman, M. E. J. (2003). The structure and function of complex networks. *SIAM Review, 45*, 167-256.
Pastor-Satorras, R., & Vespignani, A. (2004). *Evolution and structure of the Internet - A Statistical Physics Approach.* Cambridge, UK: Cambridge University Press.
Pechlaner, H., Tallinucci, V., Abfalter, D., & Rienzner, H. (2003). Networking for Small Island Destinations – The Case of Elba. In A. J. Frew, M. Hitz & P. O'Connor (Eds.), *Information and Communication Technologies in Tourism* (pp. 105-114). Wien: Springer.
Pollock, A. (1995). Occasional Studies: the impact of information technology on destination marketing. *EIU Travel and Tourism Analyst, 3: 66-83.*
Poon, A. (1993). *Tourism, technology and competitive strategies.* Oxon, UK: CAB International.
Quayle, A. P., Siddiqui, A. S., & Jones, S. J. M. (2006). Modeling network growth with assortative mixing. *The European Physical Journal B, 50*, 617-630.
Ritchie, J. R. B., & Crouch, G. I. (2003). *The Competitive Destination: A Sustainable Tourism Perspective.* Oxon, UK: CABI Publishing.
Tallinucci, V., & Testa, M. (2006). *Marketing per le isole.* Milano: Franco Angeli.
Watts, D. J., & Strogatz, S. H. (1998). Collective dynamics of 'small world' networks. *Nature, 393*, 440-442.

Collaboration Agents

Josef Withalm
Walter Woelfel
Ivan Smolak

Program and System Engineering, Siemens AG
{josef.withalm, walter.woelfel, ivan.smolak}@siemens.com

Abstract

One of the most essential tasks of Destination Management Organisations (DMOs) will be to encourage the building of networked organisations with their main tasks to align partners on business strategies (BS), business models (BM), and business processes (BP). These networks should encompass all organisations, whose activities affect in some way those of the realm of the DMO, and to get a high level of preparedness for building opportunity driven Collaborative Networked Organisations (CNOs). In this paper it will be outlined, how the building of CNOs will be facilitated using Semantic Web and Collaboration Agents. Semantic Web and Collaboration Agents will enable the implementation of the SMTE's offers concerning collaboration together with their tourism ones enhancing their web portals looking for appropriate partners, and evaluating their collaboration and tourism offers. Experiences with agent negotiations have shown big challenges. Substitution of these obstacles by Semantic Web seems feasible and would facilitate the work of DMOs.

Keywords: Agents, CNO - Collaborative Networked Organisations, DMO - Destination Management Organisation; OWL - Ontology Web Language, RDF - Resource Description Framework, semantic web.

1 Introduction

DMOs tasks are to bundle and provide all tourism services in a region/destination. Therefore many organisations should cooperate, and the DMO should build Virtual Breeding Environments (VBE).

In ENTER 2005 (Withalm & Wölfel, 2005) the importance of Virtual Organisations in tourism was introduced. The next step now explains how Semantic Web empowered by Agents will enable the building of Virtual Breeding Environments (VBE) and above all within such a VBE the setting up of a Virtual Organisation (VO).

In ECOLEAD (ECOLEAD, 2004) reference models were developed for companies, which are interested to join a collaborative network dependent of the respective phase (i.e. VBE, PVC, and VO), in which this organisation may reside actually. These reference models encompass checklists, templates, interfaces (to exist in software), tools, prototypes, specifications, architectures. These artefacts may be applied to facilitate the agreement concerning business strategies, business models and above all business processes for organisations which are due to join a collaborative network. If 'business strategies' are mentioned, then subtasks as legal issues, trust building, and so on must be covered, also. Each company is than empowered to configure / implement essential business processes to join a collaborative network in the respective phase.

But some questions arise:

1. Who will initiate a call for participation?
2. Is there some automatism for facilitating the bidding process?

First question will clearly be answered by the appropriate DMO. In answering the second question Agent technologies combined with Semantic Web could be an adequate approach, which will be explained in more detail in the following chapters.

Brief forecast of this explanation: with help of Semantic Web organisations may configure/implement concrete tools/interfaces, which are exposed in the ECOLEAD portals / reference models (dedicated to respective phases as VBE, VO, and PVC). These implemented/configured artefacts of the reference models are transformed into OWL and therefore visible for Agents. In that way Agents may find out, which organisations may best suitable for a collaborative network that is intended to be built. Concisely that means that Agents will clarify, if an organisation fits concerning business domain, business strategy, and business model. If that is true, you may tackle issues of business processes, which really executes the business.

Especially in the case of operation of a VO heavy business processes will be initialised by the Collaboration Agents. Concisely that means that Agents will synchronously/ asynchronously call processes, which are implemented by the organisation in following the specification of ECOLEAD. These processes will enable interoperation with existing systems on the one hand within the own organisation and on the other hand with existing systems of other organisations of this VO.

Prerequisites are that all issues of Enterprise Application Integration (EAI) are already tackled, so that ECOLEAD only enables the cooperation of applications between different organisations. In the scope of a VO such cooperation tasks could encompass procurement, delivering, developing, and manufacturing (well known business processes as is already known from supply chain). In that way organisations proceed step by step to reach the VO phase.

The previous phase is called Virtual Breeding Environment as all mentioned issues or prerequisites must already be tackled, i.e. trust building (see ECOLEAD, 2004), settling of legal issues, agreeing on common business strategies, business models, business processes but also issues concerning the ICT-I (Information and Communication Technology Infrastructure), for instance EAI tasks.

These results will be applied on three tourism projects. The first was already introduced in ENTER 2002 (Withalm, 2002), the second one in ENTER 2000

(Withalm, 2000), and the third one in ENTER 2001 (Withalm, 2001). Especially the later one will be applied in the fields of mega events and DMOs.

2 Theory/Issues

Meeting the requirements the following theories/issues must be discussed. On the one hand Semantic Web will be introduced, which could have a bright future in tourism. Already Tim Berners-Lee (2001, p.34), inventor of the World Wide Web, pointed out, which enormous potential is inherent in this approach. On the other hand Ontology must be taken into account. Before introducing the theory of Ontology the encountered challenges will be analyzed. Above all these technologies will be checked, how they can be approved in the area of Collaborative Networks.

Whenever Ontology has proved its usefulness in areas as tourism - see RMSIG on http://www.rmsig.de/ [Oct. 7, 2006], HARMONISE in (Werthner, 2001) - the transformation to collaborative networks raises some challenges. One of the most serious challenges is the application of Ontology to be applied on the sociological behaviour. Ontology has meshes of meaning, i.e. standardized expressions of meaning. So, usually hierarchical structures of terms are brought into relationship through predefined associations. Of course the definition of subclasses is the most common way of establishing a hierarchy, i.e. a specialization of the terms. Some examples for the area of tourism may clarify these explanations, i.e.

- Travel type (cruises, adventure trips, wellness, culture, etc)
- Tourism intermediaries (travel agent, tour operator, agent, etc)
- Type of traveller (seniors travellers, travellers with children, disabled travellers, etc)
- Geographical entities (countries, regions, cities, etc)
- Accommodation (reservations, camping, hostels, private rooms, pensions, hotels, etc)

After these very accurate and impressive examples for tourism the field of collaborative networks will be tackled. Issues like business strategies, business models, business processes must be followed.

Are trust issues specialisations of business strategies for instance, respectively what are specialization of trust issues (i.e. security, potential competitors)? Are these specializations of trust issues 'is of' or 'part of' relationships? Are there really clear distinctions between these subclasses or are some subclasses overlapping? All these issues must be solved, and especially large endeavours will be undertaken to find out, if RDF/OWL is the right formal language in this area of collaborative networks.

2.1 Semantic Web

The goal of the Semantic Web initiative is to create a universal medium for the exchange of data where data can be shared and processed by automated tools as well as by people. For the Web to scale, tomorrow's programs must be able to share and process data even when these programs have been designed totally independently. The Semantic Web will smoothly interconnect personal information management, enterprise application integration, and the global sharing of commercial, scientific and cultural data. Facilities to put machine-understandable data on the Web are quickly becoming a high priority for organisations, individuals and communities.

Most of the Web's content today is designed for humans to read, not for computer programs to manipulate meaningfully. Computers can adeptly parse Web pages for layout and routine processing but in general, computers have no reliable way to process the semantics.

The Semantic Web will bring structure to the meaningful content of Web pages, creating an environment where Software Agents roaming from page to page can readily carry out sophisticated tasks for users. The Semantic Web is not a separate Web but an extension of the current one, in which information is given well-defined meaning, better enabling computers and people to work in cooperation.

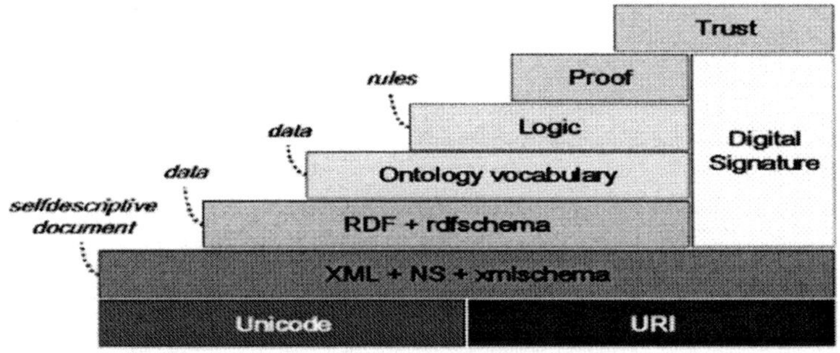

Fig. 1. Semantic Web Layers [Tim Berners-Lee]

Three important technologies for developing the Semantic Web are already in place: eXtensible Markup Language (XML), the Resource Description Framework (RDF) and Ontology Web Language (OWL) as Ontology vocabulary (see Fig. 1).

2.2 Ontology

Assume a user asks at a Web Search Engine for S*afari*, whereby he means in fact *safari adventure*. Today he would get minimum over twenty two thousand answers for this query. These answers would include not only safari adventures, but also announcements of an internet browser named Safari, a model of Land Rover called Safari, a subscription service for electronic access to books, and so on.

<u>Safari Example</u>: A photo safari is a Safari.
A hunting safari is a Safari.
A Safari is an adventure.
An adventure is a travel type.

This example shows that a Software Agent in the Web of todays could not find suitable matches for every query so easy. A solution to this problem is provided by the fourth basic component of the Semantic Web, collections of information called Ontology. This means that Ontology must be created to solve the problem. Therefore all relevant relationships in the travel domain have to be described by RDF/OWL.

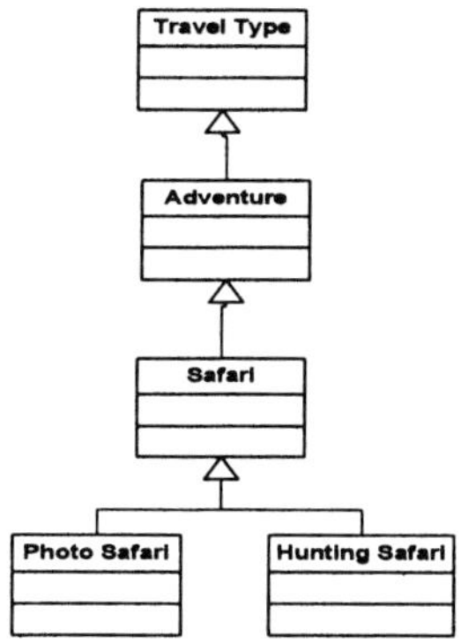

Fig. 2. Ontology Example

So the Semantic Web and Software Agent respectively can "understand" that the user means with safari not a browser, not a car, not a subscription service, but rather a travel type.

In philosophy, Ontology is a theory about the nature of existence, of what types of things exists; Ontology as a discipline studies such theories. Artificial Intelligence and Web researchers have co-opted the term for their own jargon, and for them Ontology is a document or file that formally defines the relations among terms. The most typical kind of Ontology for the Web has taxonomy and a set of inference rules. The taxonomy defines classes of objects and relations among them. For example, an *address* may be defined as a type of *location*, and *city codes* may be defined to apply only to *locations*, and so on.

Ontology can enhance the functioning of the Web in many ways. They can be used in a simple fashion to improve the accuracy of Web searches - the search program can look for only those pages that refer to a precise concept instead of all the ones using ambiguous keywords. More advanced applications will use Ontology to relate the information on a page to the associated knowledge structures and inference rules as in our example above. Another example of a page marked up for such use is online available on http://www.cs.umd.edu/~hendler/ [Oct. 8, 2006] from J.A. Hendler. In addition, Ontology makes it much easier to develop programs that can tackle complicated questions whose answers do not reside on a single Web page.

3 Methods/Procedures

To apply the required theories - namely Semantic Web and Ontology - some methods/procedures are in place and partially standardized. Ontology, as explained in chapter 2.2, is derived from AI and OO. The application in a sociological environment, as i.e. in Business Modelling, was not researched until yet. So these approaches, which were developed in ECOLEAD, will be introduced. Furthermore a very interesting approach of Business Model Ontology will be discussed, which was published by (Osterwalder, 2004). To make the web understandable to machines (i.e. Agents) also RDF and OWL must be taken into account (see Fig. 1).

Finally Collaboration Agents will be roughly introduced, which use Business Model Ontology. This Business Model Ontology will be implemented by enhancing the web portal (which is implemented usually in HTML) through RDF/OWL.

3.1 Business Models in ECOLEAD

ECOLEAD (ECOLEAD, 2004), which was already introduced in ENTER 2005 (Withalm & Wölfel, 2005), undertakes efforts to develop Business Models for each phase of a Collaborative Network (i.e. VBE, VO, and PVC). There a Business Model template (see Fig. 3) was implemented, which every SMTE may establish, when considering joining a Collaborative Network in finding out, if participation makes sense to them. Of course not only Business Models must be established, but also Business Strategies and Business Processes. And above all a SMTE must decide, if Business Strategies, Business Models, and Business Processes are aligned to their own ones and these of the DMO.

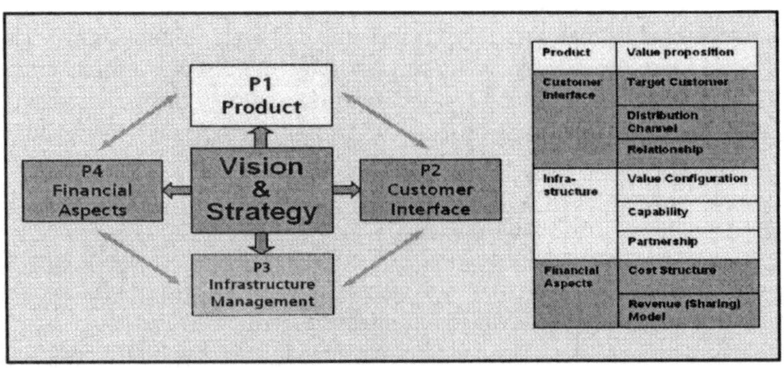

Fig. 3. Business Model

3.2 Business Model Ontology

At first collaborative networking organisations (led by the CNOs) need Ontology to find partners to join a Virtual Breeding Environment, in which they reach a preparedness to form a virtual organisation. In that sense Ontology has to be found, that facilitates opportunities to automatically evaluate, if partners are the right ones for a proposed network. How potential partners can be evaluated and how can the right ones be selected? Of course business strategies, business methods and processes must meet or at least converge.

Osterwalder has developed a business model Ontology (Osterwalder, 2004) which may be a very appropriate starting point for our discussion concerning Ontology. Osterwalder stated four pillars - according to the Ontology theory - four classes, for which he found subclasses. Relations exist between these classes and subclasses, and every subclass or term is structured further by attributes. A brief overview about Osterwalder's results is given below. The main goal of the Osterwalder's dissertation is to provide an Ontology that allows to accurately describing the business model of a firm. In a first step, there are four main areas identified that constitute the essential business model issues of a company: Product, Customer Interface, Infrastructure Management and Financial Aspects.

In a second step these areas have been broken down into a set of nine interrelated building blocks that allow to conceiving a business model. While the four areas are a rough categorization, these nine elements below is the core of the Osterwalder's business model Ontology: Value Proposition, Target Customer, Distribution Channel, Relationship, Value Configuration, Capability, Partnership, Cost Structure and Revenue Model.

The Business Model Ontology is a set of elements and their relationships that aim at describing the money earning logic of a firm. As outlined above the Ontology contains nine business model building blocks, so-called business model elements. Every business model element can be decomposed into a set of defined sub-elements. This decomposition allows studying business models on different levels of granularity in more or less detail and according to specific needs. Every business model element can be described precisely, textually and graphically. In the graphical descriptions the elements and sub-elements are related to each other through a "setOf" and "isA" relationship (see Fig. 4).

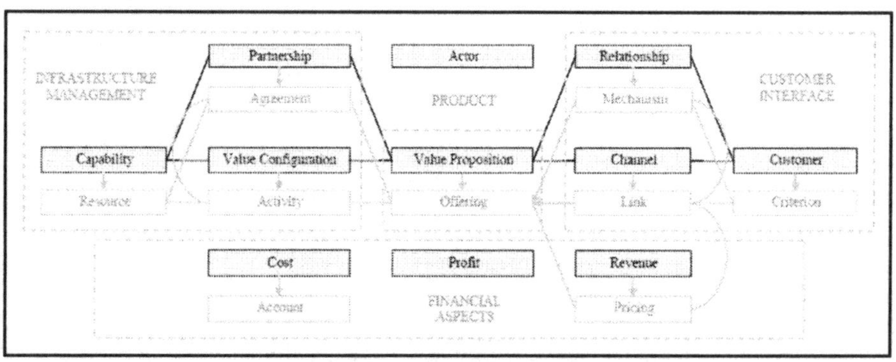

Fig. 4. Business Model Ontology (Osterwalder 0)

Similarly Ontology for business strategies and business processes will be established. When establishing Ontology for business strategies Balanced Score Cards (BSC) should be taken into account. BSC proceeds in finding disjoint classes of strategies which an organisation should follow. These strategy classes are strategies concerning customers, employees, internal processes - here you must be careful that overlapping to the Business Model Ontology could occur - and finally strategies concerning financial results. Each of these classes may be specialized (see business drivers) and so on. Each of these classes and subclasses has relationships and each subclass or term can be structured further by attributes. However, it could be an appropriate approach for establishing Ontology for business strategies.

Especially when deriving Ontology for business strategies, important terms - as trust building and legal issue - have to be taken into account, which unfortunately are very often neglected, and in doing so many business projects either failed or were very late. Useful approaches are found in (Kaplan & Norton, 1992; SBS, 1996).

Finally the business processes will be considered. Ontology is well established in this area. Horizontal and vertical business processes are differentiated. However horizontal processes are for instance procurement, delivering, maintaining, developing, and manufacturing. Vertical Business processes belong to domains as tourism, health care, chemistry, automotive. So as a rule, each of the mentioned horizontal business processes have a vertical specialization.

3.3 RDF/OWL

Meaning is expressed by RDF, which encodes it in sets of triples, each triple being rather like the subject, verb and object of an elementary sentence. These triples can be written using XML tags. In RDF, a document makes assertions that particular things (people, Web pages or whatever) have properties (such as "is a sister of," "is the author of") with certain values (another person, another Web page). This structure turns out to be a natural way to describe the vast majority of the data processed by machines.

OWL (Ontology Web Language, see details on http://www.w3.org/2004/OWL/ [Oct. 2, 2006]) is a Web Ontology language. Where earlier languages have been used to develop tools and Ontology for specific user communities (particularly in the sciences and in company-specific e-commerce applications), they were not defined to be compatible with the architecture of the World Wide Web in general, and the Semantic Web in particular.

OWL uses both URIs (http://www.w3.org/Addressing/ [Oct. 2, 2006]) for naming and the description framework for the Web provided by RDF (http://www.w3.org/RDF/ [Oct. 2, 2006]) to add the following capabilities to Ontology: ability to be distributed across many systems, scalability to Web needs, compatibility with Web standards for accessibility and internationalization, openness and extensibility.

OWL builds on RDF (Resource Description Framework, see details on http://www.w3.org/RDF/) and RDF Schema and adds more vocabulary for describing properties and classes: among others, relations between classes (e.g. disjointedness), cardinality (e.g. "exactly one"), equality, richer typing of properties, characteristics of properties (e.g. symmetry), and enumerated classes.

But what does OWL add that RDF-schema doesn't? The answer to this question is: OWL extends RDFS to allow for the expression of complex relationships between different RDFS classes and of more precise constraints on specific classes and properties.

Both OWL and RDF must prove to be appropriate in the collaborative network domain. RDF is the basis for expressing information about all things that can be addressed by a URI basis. In any case you are confronted with a lot of such things, which is in some sense not a reification of natural things. Often only real world things are considered (see RMSIG http://www.rmsig.de/ [Oct. 7, 2006], (Werthner, 2001)), but you have also to take into account domain specific processes (as for instance reservation, booking or cancelling are not really reifications of a real world thing). RDF has already proved its relevance.

An evaluation process is very important. Experiences coming from RMSIG and HARMONISE (Werthner, 2001) will be very useful. Nevertheless it seems that booking, reservation and cancelling are very well understood and defined. But what is the situation with value proposition for instance.

As before mentioned RDF was only applied in very similar/exact Ontology so far, in tourism for instance for reservation, cancelling ... Usually all this Ontology- when speaking of simple Ontology - has clear disjoint classes and subclasses. But Osterwalder introduces much more complex relationships between the four disjoint pillars. To describe these high complex relations with the range of RDF/OWL vocabulary seems a big challenge. The Business Model Ontology will be implemented, either basing on the standardized RDF/OWL vocabulary or in enhancing this vocabulary a bit according the requirements of the given Ontology.

Travel type Ontology

```
<owl: Class rdf: ID="Travel Type"/>
<owl: Class rdf: ID="Adventure">
    <rdfs:subClassOf  rdf: resource="#Travel Type"/>
</owl>
<owl: Class rdf: ID="Safari">
    <rdfs:subClassOf  rdf: resource="#Adventure"/>
</owl>
<owl: Class rdf: ID="Photo Safari">
    <rdfs:subClassOf  rdf: resource="#Safari"/>
</owl>

<owl: Class rdf: ID="Hunting Safari">
    <rdfs: subClassOf  rdf: resource="#Safari"/>
</owl>
```

Data of the Travel agency

```
<Travel Agency>
   <Agency Data>
            <Tel href="Tel: +431234567">Contact</Tel>
            <Office Hours>Mo-Fr 10:00-18:00
            </Office Hours>
   </Agency Data>
   <Travels>
   <Africa>
      <Hunting Safari>
         <Price>1900</Price>
         <Travel Duration>21 Days</Travel Duration>
         <Number of Persons>1 Person
         </Number of Persons>
      </Hunting Safari>
   </Africa>
   <Australia>
   ...
   </Australia>
   </Travels>
```

Fig. 5. RDF/OWL Example

3.4 Collaboration Agents

Agents were already introduced in (Withalm, 2000). Now the most essential behaviours of Agents will be described. Agents will roam through the portals of participating organisations and looking for ideal partners. Agents will be programmed by the DMO in that way that it may decide which partner may be best suitable according Business Strategies, Business Models and Business Processes. To do so it must look for Semantic Web portals - they are characterized, that their contents are presented in RDF/OWL. So partners, which are interested to co-operate in a breeding environment must implement their BS, BM, BP in RDF/OWL according to the established outcomes of the ECOLEAD project and using the proposed ICT-I of ECOLEAD. In applying this, ICT-I should contain RDF/OWL generators facilitating the preparation of this collaborative Semantic WEB. On the other hand the required RDF/OWL generators for implementing the Agents are also contained in the ECOLEAD ICT-I. Agents must also be modified according the concrete requirements of the respective domain (including BS, BM, and BP). These modifications should be done via attribute based programming. Agents are now in the position roughly to look for appropriate organisation.

As already outlined it seems feasible that the negation process of agents on the e-marketplace may be substituted by Semantic Web. In ENTER 2004 (Withalm, 2004) the crucial problems (see FIPA (Foundation for Intelligent Physical Agents organisation); on http://www.fipa.org/ [Oct. 2, 2006] of negotiation issues of agents were already discussed.

4 Results

This approach will be applied in DMOs of the specific region, which is involved in oncoming projects (as for instance Olympic Games, ski championships, EURO2008).

Within the proposed DMO the building of virtual organisations is intended, providing ticketing, entertainment, travelling, and transportation, together with all organisations, which could be involved in such a mega event.

But before creating VOs the project team together with the DMO will be involved in preparation endeavours, and in the first phase all results how to build a breeding environment will be realized. In that phase many of the already developed guidelines, checklists, tools will be applied in that sense that especially all questions concerning the business strategies – above all trust buildings and legal issues – and business models will accelerate the decision process, which organisations should/could participate.

Especially applying rules for trust building and business models (particularly those concerning pillar 2 ‘customer interface’, see Fig. 3) will clarify that some organisations are direct competitors and it does not make sense in continuing negotiations by collaboration agents with all of them. But on the other hand it will become clearer, which organisations are more appropriate to join the network then others. Especially pillar 1 and pillar 3 (see Fig. 3) - value proposition and infrastructure management - will be useful to select the right organisation.

Value proposition and infrastructure management will indicate, if organisations prepare a common value proposition and infrastructure management in a virtual organisation. For instance, if infrastructure management does not align, all efforts to automate these business processes are likely to fail.

Further questions will be answered:

- Are RDF/OWL ready for Sociological Ontology?
- Are SMTEs able to enhance their web portals with Collaboration and Tourism Ontology by applying RDF/OWL?
- Have Collaboration Agents the ability to select appropriate partners according their business oriented properties?
- Is the programming of Collaboration Agents feasible for DMOs?
- Has Semantic Web the potential to substitute the crucial negotiation issues of Agents on e-marketplaces (see FIPA on http://www.fipa.org/)?

5 Conclusions

Because of time/cost constrains, many aspects, which are introduced in previous chapters, will not be implemented in the first phases of the foreseen mega events. Nevertheless the concept should prove to be very efficient, and that's why a step by step implementation of all these aspects is foreseen, which were/will be developed during the project life time of ECOLEAD.

Whenever the application of all these checklists, templates and tools improves and accelerates the negotiation process, the full power will come, if all these concepts for finding appropriate partners for a breeding environment will be implemented by means of Semantic Web (i.e. Ontology, RDF/OWL, Agents).

Tourism applications will encompass the SMART-UP Initiative (Withalm, 2002), the SAPA-approach (Withalm, 2004) and the A-Net Initiative of the Austrian government. These concepts will also be demonstrated and verified in other domains than tourism, for instance in health applications.

However, Semantic Web will proceed step by step pragmatically. If organisations recognize the benefits of offering their business oriented properties to have the possibility in joining a Virtual Breeding Environment, they will implement all these RDF/OWL code and therefore are reachable and understandable for Collaboration Agents, which are looking for and evaluating potential partners.

Finally in that way e-business projects will transcend to Collaborative Networks, which minimize the possibility of failing enormously.

Collaboration Agents could have a bright future in tourism insofar as:

- First progresses are already accomplished with Ontology issues in tourism, i.e. RMSIG, HARMONISE (Werthner, 2001).
- ECOLEAD provides frameworks, reference models, guidelines ... for settling issues, how Collaborative Networks agree on common Business Strategies, Business Models, and Business Processes.
- SMTEs are enabled to implement Tourism and Collaborative Ontology with the help of RDF/OWL enhancing their web sites and therefore are accessible to Collaboration Agents.
- Collaboration Agents are implemented by DMOs, which intend to create a Collaborative Network organizing mega events.
- Negotiation vocabulary and behaviour of Collaboration Agents according to FIPA will not be taken into account by SMTEs. It's up to the DMO to implement the Collaboration Agent. Therefore knowledge and responsibility of implementation of Agents are withdrawn from the bulk of involved organisations to the DMO.

References

Berners-Lee, T., Hendler, J., & Lassila, O. (2001) The Semantic Web *Scientific American*, 284 (5), May 2001, 28-37.

ECOLEAD (2004). Contract for: Integrated Project – Annex 1: Description of Work. European Collaborative networked Organisations LEADership (IST-1-506958).

Kaplan, R. S., & Norton, D. P. (1992). The balanced scorecard: measures that drive performance. Harvard Business Review Jan – Feb pp. 71-80.

Osterwalder A. (2004). The Business Model Ontology. A Proposition in a Design Science Approach. THESE Présentée à l'Ecole des Hautes Etudes Commerciales de l'Université de Lausanne.

SBS Siemens Business Services GmbH & Co. OHG. (1996). Consulting: Chestra V3 – For companies on the move; Überblick über Chestra. Band 1, Aug 1996

Werthner H. (2001). Harmonise. Retrieved from: http://dbs.cordis.lu/fep-cgi/srchidadb?ACTION=D&CALLER=PROJ_IST&QM_EP_RCN_A=57155

Withalm, J. (2000). Agents Solving Strategic Problems In Tourism. In K. W. Wöber et al. (Eds.). *Information and Communication Technologies in Tourism 2000.* Wien: Springer-Verlag.

Withalm, J. (2001). ASA - Additional Services Architecture. In P. J. Sheldon, K. W. Wöber, & D. R. Fesenmaier (Eds.). *Information and Communication Technologies in Tourism 2001.* Wien: Springer-Verlag.

Withalm, J. (2002). Small and Medium Sized Enterprises Alliance through Research in Tourism. In K. W. Wöber, A. J. Frew, & M. Hitz (Eds.). *Information and Communication Technologies in Tourism 2002.* Wien: Springer-Verlag.

Withalm J. (2004). Travel Angel or how I learned to stop worrying and love the traveller agent. *ENTER 2004.*

Withalm J., Wölfel W. (2005). Introducing Virtual Organisations to Tourism. *ENTER 2005.*

Destination Management Systems: Technical Challenges in Developing an eTourism Platform for Accessible Tourism in Europe

Eleni Michopoulou1[a]
Dimitrios Buhalis1[a]
Spyros Michailidis[b]
Ivor Ambrose[b]
[a] School of Management, University of Surrey, UK
{E.Michopoulou, D.Buhalis}@surrey.ac.uk
[b] EWORX S.A., Greece
{sm, ia}@eworx.gr

Abstract

This paper demonstrates how destinations can utilise ICTs to strengthen their competitiveness and capture profitable market segments; in particular the accessibility requiring market. Sixteen focus groups conducted during three workshops and interviews, provided qualitative data on the disabled user requirements regarding tourism information. In order to accommodate these requirements and serve this market effectively, an e-Portal that provides accurate, relevant, reliable and accessible tourism information is required. Building and operating such a portal entails four critical technical challenges, namely: Interoperability, Content Integration, Accessible Design and Personalisation. Results indicate a number of trade-offs that system developers need to decide upon when incorporating user requirements in the design process. The paper concludes by demonstrating how destinations need to utilise ICTs in order to effectively address the disabled traveller requirements and capitalise on this market.

Keywords: User requirements, disability market, accessible tourism, destination marketing.

1 Introduction

While addressing different market segments is strategically significant for destinations, the accessibility tourism market is currently underserved (Burnett & Baker, 2001; McKercher, Packer, Yau, & Lam, 2003). People with accessibility requirements not only have equal rights to travel like every one else, but they also represent an increasingly important, yet neglected market niche. For the disabled traveller, determining accessibility is complex and often influences the very decision of engaging in travel or not (Tucker, 2005). However, their travel experiences are still highly restricted by physical accessibility barriers, such as: transportation constraints, inaccessible accommodation and tourism sites, as well as information barriers such as a general lack of information or poorly designed web sites. The tourism industry has on the one hand neglected to provide information about accessibility, and on the other hand to adopt inclusive design principles. This is because of lack of enforcement of statutory building regulations, lack of knowledge and misperception about disabled and elderly customers' actual requirements, and social segregation and stereotype challenges of catering for disabled and elderly customers.

For the tourism industry to develop suitable product offerings and capitalise on this market, user requirements need to be investigated. There are three interlinked user requirements, namely: *physical accessibility*, *information about accessibility* and accessible *information on-line*. While the architectural requests for barrier free environments as well as the web accessibility requirements have been well established (ADA, 1993; WAI & Initiative, 2005), the information required prior to travel has not been adequately elaborated.

Hence, this paper focuses on the informational needs of the disabled user group and proposes an informational system to address these needs. The OSSATE [One-Stop-Shop for Accessible Tourism in Europe, co-funded by the EC e-Content Programme] project aims to develop a prototype multi-platform, multi-lingual, digital information service that provides reliable, understandable, relevant and easy to find information that refers to the whole value chain of the accessible tourism destination. The result of this project is the "Europe for All" (EFA) web Portal. The development of such a Portal entails multiple technical challenges that can be narrowed down to four distinct categories, namely: Interoperability, Content Integration, Accessible Design and Personalisation.

2 Theoretical Issues

Globalisation has intensified competition amongst destinations, resulting in a continuous effort to maximise attractiveness and competitiveness. Destinations need to satisfy the needs and address the specific requirements of different target markets. Segmentation enables destinations to attract and retain profitable tourist segments by providing customised products and services; creating a distinct competitive advantage in the fiercely antagonistic travel marketplace (Buhalis, 2003). The disabled traveller market is neither homogeneous nor consistent. There are different types of disablement, including mobility, hearing, visual, and mental. There are also different extents of each disability. Mobility impaired for instance, can be an older person walking with a stick, a wheelchair user that can also use a stick to overcome a couple of steps, or a tetraplegic full-time wheelchair user with an assistant. Hence, there are many user sub-segments within the disability market, having different requirements according to type and extent of disability (Burnett & Baker, 2001).

The accessibility requiring market is significant in terms of size as well as spending power. It has been estimated that over 750 million people worldwide have some type of disability. In Europe, the number of people with accessibility requirements is almost 130 million, when including the elderly (Buhalis, Eichhorn, Michopoulou, & Miller, 2005), as there is a strong and positive correlation between ageing and disability (Bloch, 2000; Gerlin, 2005). This market will continue to grow due to the ageing of the baby-boom generation of 1945 to 1965 reaching 65+ in 2010, the decrease of fertility rates since 1965, and finally, the increase of life expectancy at older ages. This market is also important due to its spending power. The discretionary income of the disability market in 1998 was estimated around $200 billion in the US (Burnett & Baker, 2001), while according to the UK Government, the spending power of the disabled market in the UK alone, is estimated to be £80 billion pounds per annum (Spink, 2004).

To address the accessibility requiring market and benefit from the multiplier effects generated by friends and relatives travelling with them (Pühretmair, 2004), destinations should reassure accessibility in both physical/built and on-line environment. Dissemination of information regarding tourism accessibility is of utmost importance, to enable disabled people make informed decisions and engage in travel. Destination Management Organisations (DMOs) therefore need to gather and disseminate reliable and accurate information on accessibility. Information Communication Technologies (ICTs) and Destination Management Systems (DMSs) in particular provide a vehicle to addressing the specific requirements of this market segment.

3 Methodology

A comprehensive review of the disability tourism literature identified key themes, issues and challenges. It demonstrated that research on this area is at its infancy and that we should understand better the key needs and requirements of these markets.

Given the complexity of the issue examined, exploratory, qualitative research design was adopted. Primary research concentrated on qualitative research that included workshops, interviews and focus groups with a range of stakeholders, including: National Tourism Boards, Hotel distributors, Destination Management Systems and the disabled community. The respondents who were selected to participate in the workshops and focus groups consisted of top level disability experts, travel professionals and e-business managers. The sample design was purposive and judgmental, and enabled the research team to access considerable expertise.

A total of 16 focus groups investigated 4 different thematic areas, namely: destination marketing, disability market analysis, disabled traveller requirements and web personalisation / Customer Relationship Management. They took place in two international workshops. The first workshop took place in London UK, on the 12th - 13th May 2005 with a total of 68 participants, while the second workshop numbered 131 participants and occurred 8th -9th of September 2005 in Athens, Greece.

To analyse and overcome the various challenges raised in the focus groups and workshops, critical stakeholders were invited to provide further feedback on key issues. A number of semi-structured interviews were also conducted with stakeholders in order to acquire in-depth knowledge from their experience. Qualitative methods were adopted and content analysis was used for coding the discussion and comments made (Weber, 1990).

The results revealed the informational requirements of the disabled user group as well as key challenges of building and operating a system that addresses these requirements, namely: interoperability, content integration, accessible design and personalisation.

4 Findings: User Requirements and Challenges

4.1 User Requirements

After a thorough literature review and the results of the workshops, disabled traveller market requirements were grouped in three major categories, namely: Accessibility of the physical/built environment, information regarding accessibility and accessible information.

The first basic requirement of the disabled traveller market is accessibility of the physical/build environment. Making the built environment accessible will give tourists access to more facilities and services, and the right to choose according to personal preference. Legislation, corporate responsibility and architecture practice gradually address these requirements.

Secondly, information regarding accessibility is a fundamental requirement for the disabled traveller market in order to engage in travel. *Richness of information* is a key determinant, as information regarding tourism accessibility is highly fragmented and scattered amongst different industry players. The presentation of the linkages between accessible tourism and transport facilities is of paramount importance. The demonstration of *accessibility paths* within the destination, as well as between the origin, the transit area and the destination is critical for creating a *door-to-door* access map. *Reliability* and *accuracy* are also vital in order for disabled travellers to *trust* the information source. This is mainly due to the limited flexibility of this market to trade off between travel attributes. For instance, if information regarding the width of a door is false, a wheelchair user may simply not be able to enter the hotel and there is not always an option to go to another nearby hotel. The need for *objective measurements*, rather than prescriptive information or classifications, enables users to judge accessibility according to their individual abilities.

Finally, the third indispensable requirement is the accessibility of information on-line. Websites that are not designed with web accessibility in mind cannot support a variety of assistive technologies used by disabled users. Accessibility of information on-line can provide this market with access to more content. It seems that the more generic the tourism content, the more inaccessible the websites tend to be.

The EFA portal addresses these requirements by providing comprehensive information about the accessibility of tourism facilities within three destinations in the pilot phase, namely: Belgium, Greece and UK. Ensuring accessibility by a wide range of users, set web accessibility, as one of the key website design priorities. To develop a portal that is accessible and disseminates accurate and reliable information about accessible destinations, four key challenges have to be overcome.

4.2 Interoperability

Interoperability is a major issue throughout the tourism industry. All elements of the tourism industry operate different systems, as their scale and scope of service vary significantly. Research has shown that interoperability obstacles can be overcome at a semantic level, by specialised ontology development (Dongsong, 2004; Werthner & Fodor, 2005). Interoperability will be critical for creating an accessibility path, i.e. the interlinking of all accessible products and services required. Hence, interconnecting value chain elements of the tourism industry and creating an accessibility path amongst accessible components will be critical for providing accessible tourism experiences. Within the range of EFA interests, a comparative analysis of the database structure of three major European Accessibility Schemes, namely: Visit Britain, Toegankelijk Vlaanderen Bureau and Association Nationale pour le Logement des Personnes Handicapées that was carried out. This revealed that there is a total of over 1200 different fields describing accessible tourism supply. Additionally, not more that 10% of the fields where found in common. Hence, there is a need to develop the accessibility tourism ontology to support the major players interoperate their databases towards building a European portal.

EFA is tackling interoperability by providing interfacing modules to existing national and regional tourist information databases, as well as by making use of the XML language and the Harmonise project outcomes. Additionally, to support a multidisciplinary group of stakeholders, data gathering tools for new venues and recently established 'accessible tourism information schemes' are introduced, with a dedicated data entry service. By promoting interoperability and interconnectivity amongst the different players, the EFA platform will allow the comprehensive integration of a wide range of products and services. Furthermore, it will support accessible tourism companies to network and exchange information in a seamless manner.

4.3 Content Integration

Research has demonstrated that the provision of specialised and detailed information tends to be inadequate, as the level of accessibility requirements increases (Miller & Kirk, 2002). A survey on 43 Accessibility Schemes in 19 countries revealed that although these organisations provide accessibility specific information, the content tends to focus mostly on mobility impairments; neglecting other types of disabilities. Information is often available in different patterns and languages. It is often scattered amongst different industry players, including DMOs, national, regional or local Accessibility Schemes, and hotel aggregators. This content can be found in different formats, setting an extra burden to the integration process that will enable reliability and consistency (Werthner & Ricci, 2004). Consequently, the EFA platform aims to integrate content from the largest possible range of reliable sources, addressing the multi-faceted needs of a wide range of users; as the perceived information quality has a direct effect on system use (D'Ambra & Mistillis, 2005). This holistic approach will encapsulate accessibility-specific and tourism-generic content, in order to satisfy different sets of requirements, and covering all markets from severely disabled to able-bodied persons.

For this purpose, EFA has developed 3 scalable data sets that reflect three informational levels as illustrated in figure 1. The EFA system allows for three levels of assessment of venue accessibility, level 1 (self-assessment by venue owners), Level 2 (professional assessment by auditors) and level 3 (third-party regional or national accessibility schemes). The more detailed the information available, the more reliable the source. The developed database schema will cater for all three levels by identifying and analysing the imported data at different component levels. If a component (and all underlying checklists and questions) needs to be filled at more than one level, then two different component entities will be created in the database. This means that a venue owner may have entered their self assessment questionnaire and when the auditor fills in the level 2 assessment the previous data will not be deleted. Obviously precedence between the 3 levels is given to higher levels when querying the database (L3>L2>L1).

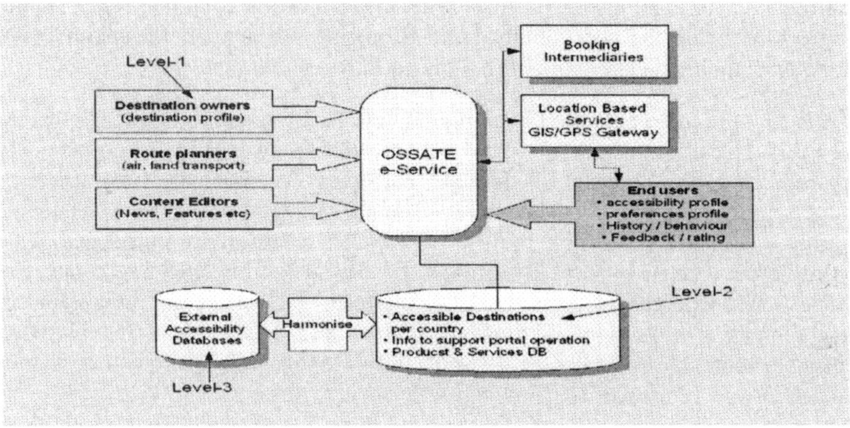

Fig.1. EFA System Information Flow

4.4 Accessible Design

Accessible design of websites is critical for both visually impaired as well as those using assistive technologies to navigate the site. The OSSATE project has examined the WAI standards thoroughly and has conducted an extensive web research of numerous websites of different groups, including: governmental websites, Destination Management Organisations (DMOs), Content Aggregators, Tourism Suppliers and Disability Organisations in order to identify best practise examples. The majority of these websites were found inaccessible with very few exceptions, mainly those targeting exclusively the disabled audience. A strong and positive correlation appeared between disability content and accessibility, as the more generic the content is the more inaccessible the website is. One of the most common trade-offs web developers are faced with is that of the web pages layout. Elements such as low colour contrast, rich graphics and animation components and pop-ups are not recommended or even prohibitive for creating accessible websites (Han & Mills, 2006). One of the challenges for EFA is that the three columns approach, as illustrated in figure 2, is most common amongst the mainstream travel websites. It looks professional and appealing to end users as they are familiar to this design. It also provides sufficient space for presentation on the landing page. However, from an accessibility point of view, this layout has some inherent drawbacks. In particular, when attempting to increase the font size, the columns either get out of proportion resulting in a damaged layout, or they retain their size and the larger font-sized content cannot fit within the same space.

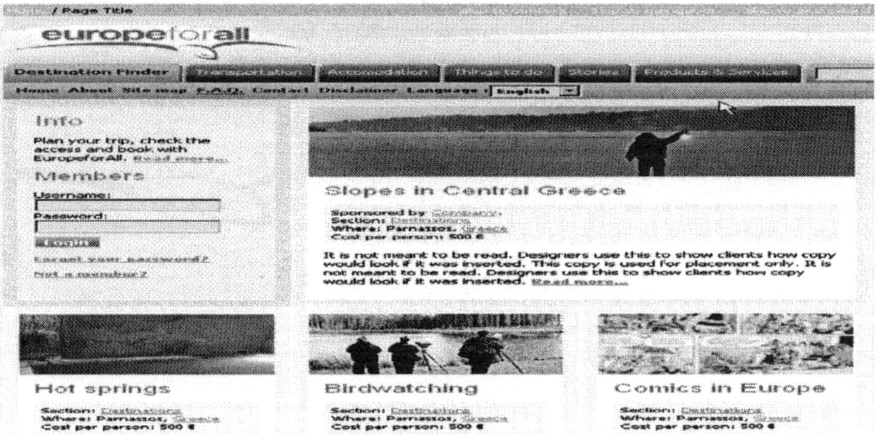

Fig.2. Three Column GUI Layout

To overcome these problems, a slightly modified approach was deployed, using two instead of three content columns, as illustrated in figure 3. This way, when increasing either the font size or even the window size, the layout remains consistent. Text and images take up any additional space and adapt to the initial layout.

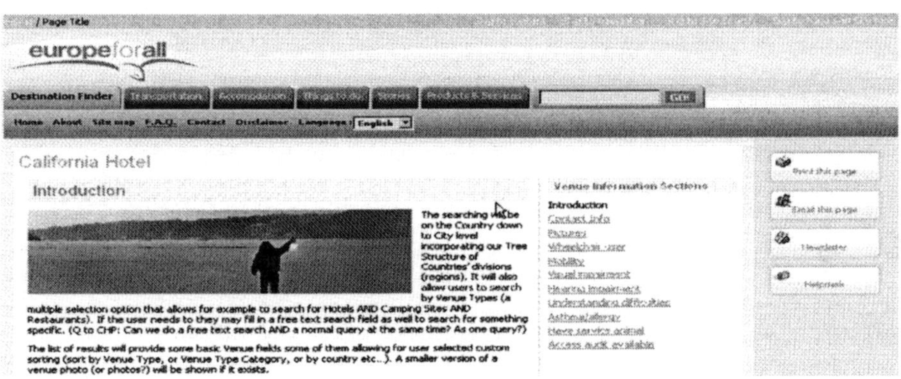

Fig.3. Two Column GUI Layout

4.5 Personalisation

Finding the right content on-line can be hard and time consuming, especially for people seeking specific information. Personalisation allows Internet users to specify their requirements and interests in order to access the required information at the desirable format. Travellers normally have a wide range of requirements and preferences and this has created the need for travel recommender systems (Ricci & Delgado, 2004). These may range from the preferred hotel chain to the language that the information should be presented (Pierrakos, Paliouras, Papatheodorou, & Spyropoulos, 2003). The disabled traveller market, in particular, places additional requirements that relate with the type and severity of disability. Interviewees expressed therefore the need to be able to personalise their travel information search according to their own needs. A blind person may choose to visit only places that have Braille displays and audible queues, whilst a full time wheelchair user may request to retrieve and consider information only for wheelchair accessible hotels. Users may also request the provision of information in a particular format that suits best their computer usage needs.

The EFA system enables individual users to build their profiles, thus enabling them to perform personalised searches and retrieve suitable specialised content (Greer & Murtaza, 2003). The configuration of individual user profiles is a continuous process where the system allows the user to build their profile in an initial stage and then to update it progressively according to the user's input and actions over time. User profiling is utilised in order for the system to filter the search results and to provide the relevant content to the target user. An example of an advanced venue search use case scenario is illustrated in figure 4.

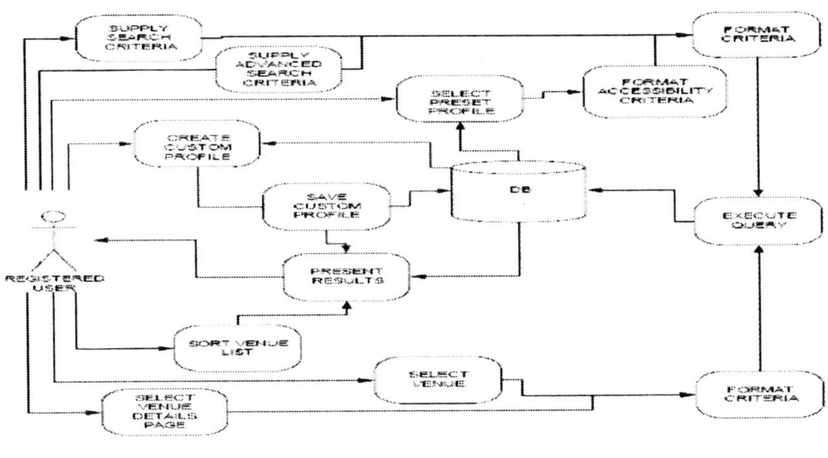

Fig. 4. Advanced Venue Search Use Case Scenario

The EFA portal, will also offer personalisation features to provide customised content aggregation or syndication to users. In order to achieve such functionalities Portlets (Portlet Specification and API 1.0) are deployed. EFA uses portlets as pluggable content components that are integrated in the presentation layer. The content retrieved by a Portlet can be aggregated with the content of other Portlets to form a portal page, thus allowing for further customisation of the user's personal space. Additionally, EFA, as a tourism content distributor, is exploiting the XML-based RSS feature to provide information to RSS-aware programs that can check the feed for changes and deliver the new content to end-users' personalised web pages.

Still, as the degree of disability varies, users should be able to choose the products and services that best serve their individual abilities and preferences by trading off with parameters such as available facilities, venue location or price This is possible for a wide range of facilities, products and services that are not restricted by the 'veto principles' (Israeli, 2002). According to the 'veto principle', when a certain condition cannot be met then the venue in question cannot be considered as accessible for a particular type of disability. For example, a hotel with no elevator cannot be considered accessible for a full time wheelchair user (veto principle applies) but can be suitable to a hearing impaired. Therefore, the provision of a flexible, personalised service should allow the end-user to make informed choices and compromises between different travel products according to their ability, preference and individualised criteria (De & Radha Krishna, 2002).

5 Conclusion

The competitiveness and prosperity of destinations depends on their effectiveness in the acquisition, conversion and retention of profitable market segments. The disabled traveller market is lucrative both in size and spending power. However, the travel industry has long neglected this market due to misperceptions regarding its requirements. This paper investigates these requirements and distinguishes three basic categories, namely: physical/built environment accessibility, information about accessibility, and accessible information on line. While there are well established guidelines addressing physical and on-line accessibility, there is a gap regarding information about accessibility. Hence, leading destinations should address this requirement by collecting and disseminating information about accessible tourism facilities and services available. The EuropeforAll (EFA) Portal aims to aggregate such accessibility information from multiple destinations and leverage it to a European level. However, the design and development of the platform entails multiple challenges that can be classified into four categories, namely: interoperability, content integration, accessible design and personalisation. To overcome these challenges, the system developers created specialised information collection tools; designed a scalable database to store and manage the data; decided upon the trade-offs of accessible GUI; and deployed technologies such as RSS and Portlets to deliver dynamic, specialised content to the end-users. Hence, the EFA platform will enable accessible travel suppliers to "plug and play", creating a pool of resources, and provides disabled consumers the ability to customise the way they retrieve and interact with information.

References

ADA. (1993). *Covering Public Accommodations and Commercial Facilities.* Retrieved April 4, 2006 from http://www.usdoj.gov/crt/ada/taman3.html.

Bloch, D. (2000). *OECD Tables and Figures on Ageing.* Retrieved August 30, 2006 from http://www.oecd.org/dataoecd/27/44/2345400.pdf.

Buhalis, D. (2003). *e-Tourism: information technology for strategic tourism management.* UK: Prentice Hall.

Buhalis, D., Eichhorn, V., Michopoulou, E., & Miller, G. (2005). *OSSATE Accessibility Market and Stakeholder Analysis* (No. Deliverable 6.1.): http://www.ossate.org/library_news_002.jsp.

Burnett, J. J., & Baker, H. B. (2001). Assessing the Travel–Related Behaviors of the Mobility–Disabled Consumer. *Journal of Travel Research, Vol. 40* (1), 4-11.

D'Ambra, J., & Mistillis, N. (2005). *Analysis of perceived quality of information resources and a priori web usage at the Sydney visitor information centre.* Paper presented at the ENTER 2005, Innsbruck, Austria.

De, S. K., & Radha Krishna, P. (2002). Mining Web Data Using Clustering Technique for Web Personalization. *International Journal of Computational Intelligence & Application, 2* (3), 255-265.

Dongsong, Z. (2004). Web services composition for process management in e-business. *Journal of Computer Information Systems, 45*(2), 83-91.

Gerlin, A. (2005). *Access Denied,* Retrieved August 30, 2005, from *http://www.time.com/time/europe/magazine/article/0,13005,901050411-1044655,00.html?promoid=rss_world.*

Greer, T. H., & Murtaza, M. B. (2003). Web personalization: The impact of perceived innovation characteristics on the intention to use personalization. *Journal of Computer Information Systems, 43* (3), 50-55.

Han, J., & Mills, J. (2006). *The mutual designing of travel websites: Perceptions of the visually impaired.* Paper presented at the ENTER 2006, Lausane, Switzerland.

Israeli, A. A. (2002). A Preliminary Investigation of the Importance of Site Accessibility Factors for Disabled Tourists. *Journal of Travel Research, 41* (1), 101-104.

McKercher, B., Packer, T., Yau, M. K., & Lam, P. (2003). Travel agents as facilitators or inhibitors of travel: perceptions of people with disabilities. *Tourism Management, 24* (4), 465-474.

Miller, G., & Kirk, E. (2002). The Disability Discrimination Act: Time for a stick? *Journal of Sustainable Tourism, 10* (1), 82-88.

Pierrakos, D., Paliouras, G., Papatheodorou, C., & Spyropoulos, C. D. (2003). Web Usage Mining as a Tool for Personalisation. *User Modeling and User-Adapted Interaction, 13* (4), 311-372.

Pühretmair, F. (2004). *It's time to make eTourism accessible.* Paper presented at the Computers helping people with special needs, 9th International Conference, ICCHP 2004, Paris, France.

Ricci, F., & Delgado, J.E. (Eds.). (2004). *Information Technology and Tourism (Special Issue on Travel Recommender Systems)* (Vol. 6): Cognizant Communication Corporation.

Spink, A. G. (2004). *Last of the big disabled spenders.* Retrieved August 28, 2005, from http://news.bbc.co.uk/1/hi/business/4105385.stm.

Tucker E., S. E., Hazel J. (2005). Tourism and Disability: Issues beyond Access Tourism. *Review International, 8*, 211-219.

WAI, & Initiative, W. A. (2005). *WAI Guidelines and techniques.* Retrieved March 7, 2006, from *http://www.w3.org/WAI/guid-tech.html.*

Weber, R. P. (1990). *Basic Content Analysis.* U.S.A.: Sage Publications, Inc.

Werthner, H., & Fodor, O. (2005). Harmonise: A step towards and interoperable tourism marketplace. *International Journal of Electronic Commerce, 9* (2), 11-39.

Werthner, H., & Ricci, F. (2004). E-commerce and tourism. *Communications of the ACM, 47* (12), 101-105.

Acknowledgements

This paper was developed as part of the OSSATE project no. EDC-11278 funded by the eContent programme of the European Commission. The authors would like to acknowledge contribution by the entire OSSATE team to this paper.

Electronic Customer Care in Tourist Destinations - Exploring the Effects of Offer Inquiry Systems

Michael Fux
Stefan Eggel
Barbara Scholl

Department of Business Administration, Institute of Information System
University of Bern, Switzerland
{michael.fux, stefan.eggel, barbara.scholl}@iwi.unibe.ch

Abstract

Customer care in an online and offline environment is crucial for success in tourism. In our days, actors in tourism are implementing web-based systems to facilitate online interaction with customers. This study explores the effects of inquiries sent via offer inquiry systems (OISs) and by e-mail. The offers were assessed in three service quality dimensions: response behaviour, content quality and level of individualization. The analysis revealed only minor differences between the two inquiry channels but an interesting comparison of the type of offer sender (destination management organisation (DMO) vs. hotel). Nevertheless, the latest reply sent by a DMO via OIS is revealing one considerable advantage of an OIS: The inquiry processing system is managed by the DMO as supervisor, so that if the customer does not receive a reply from at least one hotel, the DMO can step in and provide the customer with various offers.

Keywords: electronic customer inquiry, customer service, offer inquiry system

1 Introduction

With the rapid spread of Internet technology, new means of communication have become commonplace. Nowadays, many people frequently use the Internet as an alternative to the telephone or traditional 'snail' mail. Moreover, people expect their correspondents to be accessible at all times via this new medium. Clearly, this development poses a considerable challenge for organisations to offer an e-channel and to handle incoming communication effectively and efficiently via this channel. Tourism intermediaries such as destination management organisations, in particular, depend on reliable e-channel management as their guests increasingly go online for information and bookings. Nevertheless, they seem to face difficulties answering online inquiries, as the results of a preliminary research study have shown (Fux, Noti, & Myrach, 2005): A mystery guest received no reply from one third of the DMOs contacted. This result is in line with other findings of electronic customer research in the tourism industry (Frey, Schegg, & Murphy, 2003).

This study will present the opportunities provided by web-based systems to improve the service quality of responses to electronic offer requests. Service quality is measured in terms of response behaviour, content quality and level of individualization. The inquiries about ski-holidays were sent to DMOs by e-mail or via offer inquiry systems (OISs). Inquiries sent via OISs were typically answered by hotels and not by DMOs. This set-up was used to answer the two following questions:

1. What are the effects of an OIS in terms of response behaviour?
2. What are the effects of the different processors in terms of response behaviour, content quality and level of individualization?

The paper is organized as follows: it begins with a few conceptual foundations concerning offer inquiries from the customer and business perspective and goes on to present the research set-up. In the following section, the results are described and discussed. The paper concludes with several implications and an outlook to further research.

2 Processes of an Offer Inquiry and Offer Management

2.1 Customers` Perspective of an Offer Inquiry

There are three principal stages to differentiate in the purchase and consumption of tourism products: before the journey, during the journey and after the journey (Vandermerwe, 1996; Werthner & Klein, 1999). In terms of visiting a destination, Beritelli (1999) defines the following phases: awareness, decision making, booking, preparation, arrival, stay, return journey and processing of the journey. In this paper, the decision-making stage will be studied more closely; especially the interactions during a customer inquiry. In this stage - also known as the 'evaluation phase' in the customer buying cycle (Muther & Österle, 1998) - customers seek detailed information about different offers which can be considered and have the potential to satisfy the desire for a journey. The customer then evaluates the different offers in relation to his or her needs. During this stage, customers intend to develop a certain attitude towards a product and to form a purchase intention for one offer. This last step of the evaluation stage can be considered the actual buying decision (Gierke, 2005).

2.2 Business Perspective of Processing Offer Inquiries

Effective handling of electronic inquiries is considered an essential and critical means for customer service and customer relationship management (Yang & Jun, 2002; Zemke & Connellan, 2001). As the quality of customer service directly affects the customer's buying decision, companies should attach great importance to fulfilling customers' needs during the decision-making process. This study focuses on inquiries submitted by e-mail and via OISs. The process of handling an offer inquiry may be structured in three steps: accepting, processing and transmitting the inquiry (see Figure 1). The corresponding activities are described in the following paragraph and illustrated in Figure 1.

If customers contact the DMO for an offer, it is usually the DMO that handles the inquiry. Upon receiving an inquiry, the DMO will generally begin by running a check to identify repeat customers and entering any new customers in its customer database. After that, the inquiry has to be classified according to its content. If the inquiry is not processed immediately, the customer must be informed of further steps and the expected handling time. Crucial for the performance of this first step are the availability of different contact channels to take inquiries as well as an ingenious system for classifying inquiries. Once the inquiry has been accepted, further steps can be taken by the DMO itself or by the hotel. Both routes were observed in empirical research. When an inquiry is processed, information about room availability is highly important as is customized offer bundling to achieve a high level of individualized, unique treatment for each inquiry. This step can be increasingly supported by information systems as explained in the following paragraphs. When an offer is sent, the choice of channel should not be dictated exclusively by costs but should also reflect customer preferences in order to guarantee a high level of customer service. All interactions between customers and DMOs or hotels must be tracked in the customer database (Merzenich, 2005; Schumacher & Meyer, 2004).

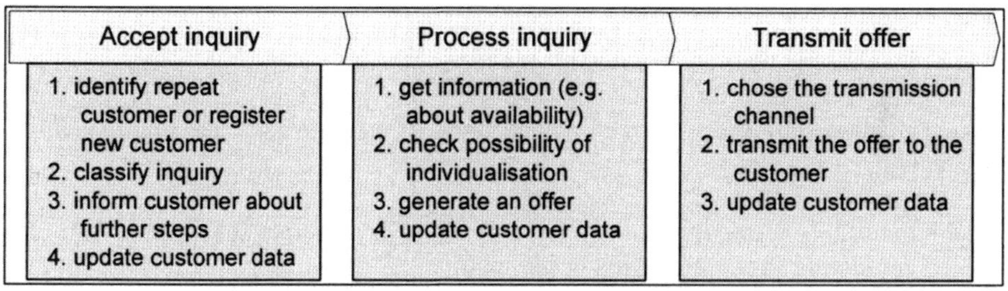

Fig. 1. Inquiry processing

2.3 Offer Inquiry System

The main purpose of an Offer Inquiry System (OIS) as part of a Destination Management System (DMS) is to relieve the DMO of its heavy daily flow of inquiries through efficient handling processes. Furthermore, the system should facilitate an excellent customer service level with more customised professional responses to inquiries. Therefore, potential customers seeking offers from a tourist destination are required to concretise their wishes online so that no further manual data input is necessary by the DMO. The customer has to go through a multi-level online form - which typically includes three steps - and specify his or her requirements to offers according to wishes (see Figure 2). The submitted data is stored in a database system called an 'inquiry pool', access to which is restricted to participating accommodation providers. Any provider which meets the criteria can read the inquiries and send a customised offer directly to the customer via the system. In order to be able to track interactions with customers, maintain an accurate customer history and analyse customer statistics, it is essential that hotels record their transmission of offers in the system.

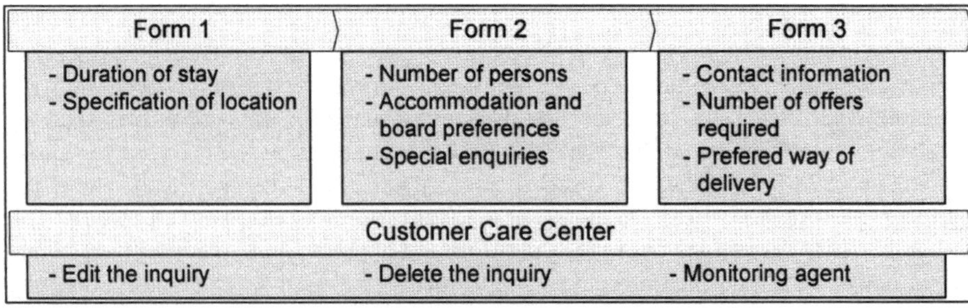

Fig. 2: Process of an inquiry sent via an OIS

Figure 2 shows the typical process of submitting an inquiry via a web-based system. The first step when going through the multi-level online form is to determine the duration of one's stay and specify the desired location within the destination. Number of persons, accommodation, board preferences and special requests are entered in the second form. In the final step, (potential) customers are required to validate their inquiry by entering their contact details, the required number of offers and the method of delivery. The last requirement highlights the importance of identifying the right contact medium in a multi-channel environment in order to generate high customer satisfaction.

After submitting the inquiry, the customer receives an automated response from the OIS recapitulating the details of his or her inquiry and confirming successful delivery. Once the inquiry is saved in the inquiry pool, the (potential) guest may access it at any time via the web-based customer care centre, which allows him or her to edit or even delete the inquiry and monitor the response process. Thus, if hotels send their offer via the system, customers are able to keep track of received and pending offers. Moreover, the customer care centre serves as an innovative online platform for lodging complaints or providing positive feedback. After exceeding the system's time limit, the (potential) guest receives a summary by e-mail listing all the hotels that have replied through the system. If no hotel has answered the inquiry, it is up to the DMO as the monitoring agent to step in and prompt matching hotels to respond.

3 Research Design

3.1 Sampling

In order to compare the effects of an OIS, two disjoint samples were required for this survey: one includes destinations using OISs for offer inquiries, the other offering e-mail as inquiry channel. The first sampling relied on reference customers from OIS providers and included 30 alpine destinations mainly in Austria. The 41 destinations of the second sample were randomly chosen among the remaining Swiss and Austrian destinations which have not implemented an OIS. All destinations considered attract leisure travellers for winter sports such as skiing as well as tourists seeking nature in all seasons (Buhalis, 2000).

3.2 Data Collection and Experimental Design

A mystery-guest approach was used to assess the responses of selected tourist destinations to electronic offer requests submitted via OIS or e-mail. This means that inquiries by a fictitious person - in this case a father of a family of four - were simulated and actual hotel and DMO responses were studied. Mystery guests are widely used as a method of assessing quality in service industries (Matzler, Pechlaner, Abfalter, & Wolf, 2000). OIS forms were filled in on Tuesday, 13 December 2005 between 2p.m. and 4p.m., and e-mails were sent one week later. To reduce further bias, the e-mail inquiry stemmed from a private e-mail address rather than a free commercial address, and the e-mails were sent individually to override filtering programs that protect tourism organisations from information overload and spamming (Matzler, Pechlaner, & Kohl, 2005).

As with traditional channels, service quality and customer satisfaction are key determining factors for successful Internet transactions. Therefore, the replies were analysed in relation to three dimensions - response behaviour, content quality and level of individualization - consisting of several variables. These three dimensions are now briefly explained.

3.3 Assessment Criteria

Strauss and Hill's (2001) study of customer complaints by e-mail revealed that responding quickly is a simple way to raise the perceived quality of customer service. Therefore, response behaviour was assessed according to four aspects: whether or not the mystery guest received a reply, and, if so, the response time. A response time of less than four hours was considered very well, and between four and 48 hours (approaching the OIS time limit) was still satisfactory. The analysis went on to examine the number of e-mails which the prospective guest received and whether or not he obtained follow-up e-mails inquiring after the status of the booking process.

The following five items indicate content quality (Frey et al., 2003; Leuenberger, Schegg, & Murphy, 2003; Murphy & Tan, 2003): The DMOs or hotels were supposed to address the mystery guest politely and personally, thank him for his interest and disclose the hotel's and the electronic receptionist's identity. In addition, the offer was expected to include the correct date and the total price of one week's accommodation for a family of four. In the case of a booking, the mystery guest expected to find information on how to confirm the offer, e.g. by telephone or via an online booking engine.

In order to analyse the level of caring and individualized attention which a business affords its customers (Parasuraman, Zeithaml, & Berry, 1988), the mystery guest explicitly asked for (1) a family friendly (2) 3/4-star hotel (3) located next to ski lifts with a (4) sauna, (5) indoor pool and (6) parking. The inquiry was completed by a question relating to the event programme for the period in question. In the assessment, each specification received one point if it was mentioned and no point if ignored. Only the hotel's star rating was effectively verified on the hotel's website: the other criteria were not tested. A simple mention in the offer regarding availability was adequate.

3.4 Research Model

The main focus of this study is on significant differences in three service quality dimensions caused by different inquiry modes (OISs vs. e-mail) and inquiry processors (DMOs vs. hotels). By treating service quality as a dependent variable and the inquiry channel and processors as independent variables, we are emphasizing the significant effects of an OIS. The study analysed relationships between the inquiry channels and the response behaviour as well as between the different inquiry processors and the three service quality constructs (see Figure 3).

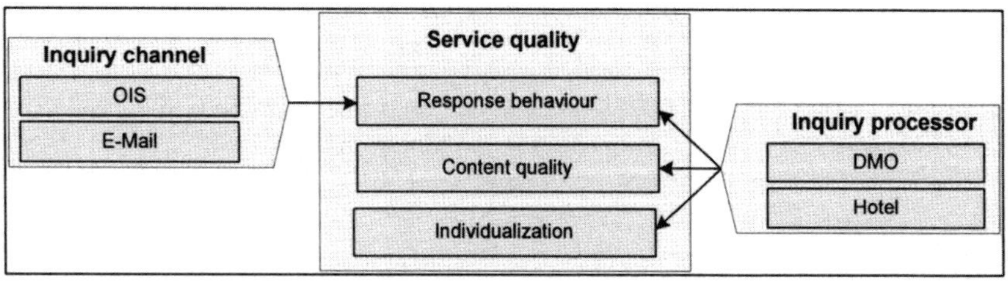

Fig. 2. Research model

Significant differences ($p<0.05$) based upon the independent variables 'inquiry channel' and 'inquiry processor' were evaluated with Pearson's chi-square. The phi coefficient is used as a measure of the degree of association between the binary variables. Values over 0.3 indicate an association between the analysed variables (Backhaus, Erichson, Plinke, & Weiber, 2006).

4 Results

4.1 Response Behaviour

The excellent response rate is spread fairly equally across the OIS and e-mail samples (96.7%; 94.9%). Indeed, only three inquiries out of a total of 71 remained unanswered. On the contrary, fewer than four in ten destinations answered with the required 3-5 offers. From the customer's point of view, five offers would be the desired response behaviour, but on average one inquiry generated fewer than three responses regardless of the releasing source.

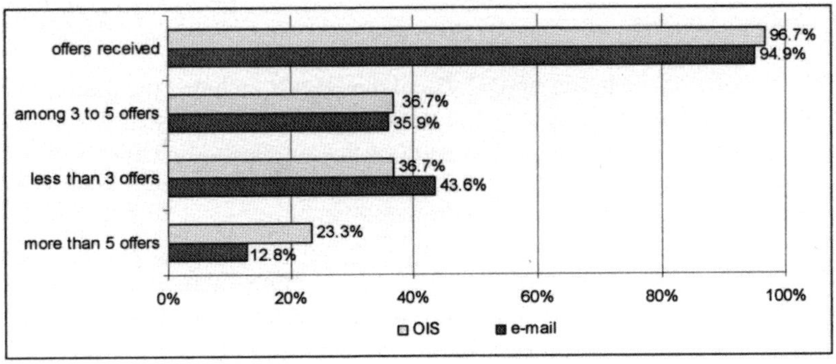

Fig. 3. Response behaviour by inquiry channel

Response time varies considerably between inquiry processors: 67% of the answering DMOs took less than four hours to respond whereas only 29.3% of hotel offers could keep up with this. The shortest response time was two minutes and stemmed from a DMO; the longest response time was 142 hours - although it must be said that the inquiry in question was handled by the DMO, which, after realising that the inquiry had remained unanswered via its OIS database, had stepped in and sent offers to the customer itself. However, over 90% of all destinations sent their offer within two days, which is an acceptable result.

Receiving follow-up e-mails from DMOs and hotels was hardly seen. In only ten out of 252 offers the sender asked the mystery guest about the status of his travel planning process and offer further advice.

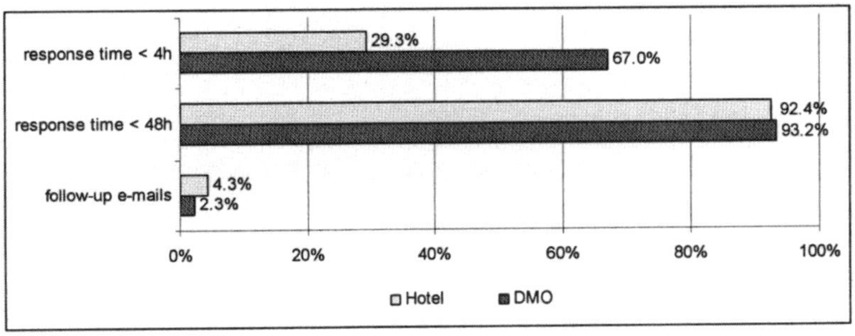

Fig. 4. Response behaviour by inquiry processor

An evaluation of these results reveals no differences in terms of the 'inquiry channel' variable. Hence, the medium by which inquiries are sent to the DMO (e-mail or OIS) does not affect the response behaviour. Instead, the processor of the inquiry (DMO or hotel) has a significant effect on the response time: DMOs respond within four hours much more often than do hotels.

4.2 Content Quality

While almost 90% of the hotels and 97.7% of the DMOs included the guest's name in their reply, only slightly more than six in ten senders thanked the guest for his inquiry. Expecting a correct and complete offer whittles the numbers down even further. Less than 18% of the hotels contacted were able to meet this criterion while 68.2% of the DMOs sent a complete offer with a total price. Many hotels and DMOs also failed to give information on how to proceed to book the offer. However, 48.9% of offers from the DMOs included further booking instructions, significantly more than those of the hotels (13%). The identity of the electronic receptionist was given by more than 90% of the DMOs, but only by 48% of the hotels.

As already mentioned, there are some significant effects on content quality: DMOs acting as intermediaries were more likely to send a correct, complete and signed offer and include further booking instructions.

Table 1. Significance test for response quality (* indicates significance at p=0.05)

	Hotel (N=184)	DMO (N=88)	$\chi 2$	φ
Personalized e-mail	89.67%	97.73%	na	
Thanked for the inquiry	60.87%	67.05%	0.97	
Complete and correct offer	17.39%	68.18%	68.61	0.50*
Information about booking	13.04%	48.86%	41.14	0.39*
Identity of the receptionist	47.83%	92.05%	49.47	0.43*

4.3 Individualization

The elements of individualization reveal substantially different results. Some offers do not contain any elements of individualization and refer to a website. Other propositions fulfilled every desire and even provided additional information. The level of individualization was assessed according to seven questions/requests to the supplier. If the variable 'inquiry processor' with the forms 'hotel' and 'DMO' is linked to the criteria of individualization, significant interdependencies can be calculated for the criteria 'family friendly' and indications of 'parking'. The hotels refer significantly more often to the 'family friendliness' of their offer, whereas the DMOs mention the availability of parking significantly more frequently.

Besides the significance analysis, the following descriptive results offer some insight into individualization. On average, 10% of all offers answered the question about events during the holiday period. The star rating is omitted in 18.5% of all offers sent by hotels but in only 9.1% of offers sent by DMOs. The criteria 'family friendly' (hotels: 80.4%, DMOs: 47.7%) and 'located next to ski lifts' (hotels: 54.3%, DMOs: 30.7%) are fulfilled better by hotels than by DMOs. The criterion 'indoor pool' is better fulfilled by the hotels, whereas the question regarding the sauna was better answered by the DMOs.

Table 2. Significance test for individualization (* indicates significance at p=0.05)

	Hotel (N=184)	DMO (N=88)	$\chi 2$	φ
3/4-star hotel	81.52%	90.91%	4.02	0.12
Family friendly	80.43%	47.73%	30.24	0.33*
Located next to ski lifts	54.35%	30.68%	13.40	0.22
Indoor pool	51.09%	62.50%	3.13	
Sauna	66.85%	70.45%	0.36	
Parking	20.65%	55.68%	33.58	0.35*

5 Discussion and Further Research

In conclusion, the results of this study do not indicate significant differences between the offers arising from e-mail inquiries and inquiries sent via an OIS. In some cases the potentials of OIS are not fully exploited. Because the hotels either take inquiry from the database and fail to send an offer or the hotels do not record their transmission of offers in the system. This leads to the situation where the potential guest does not receive the desired number of offers and the DMO as supervisor loses control of inquiry processing.Nevertheless the latest response, which was in connection with an inquiry sent via an OIS, shows one advantage of an OIS. The inquiry processing system is managed by the DMO, and if the customer does not receive a reply from at least one hotel, the DMO can step in and provide the customer with various offers. This form of supervision is highly useful if many hotels are fully booked, and the hotels show no interest in further inquiries.

The reason why significantly more offers sent by DMOs contained a complete offer with a total price might be explained by usage of an offer preparation application in the destination management systems. These applications generate offers containing all the details and a total price. The offers created by the system have a uniform layout, making it easier to compare prices and conditions. Similar functionalities like automatic processing of standard requests are provided by e-mail response solutions, but the existing systems are tailored for large enterprises and are therefore too expensive for an implementation in SMTE. For that reason small tourism operators are forced to handle all inquiries manually. The individual editing of each inquiry is labour-intensive and may lead to resource problems. As already mentioned, the quality of the replies sent by the DMOs is better on average. Therefore, further research might explore as well the perceived potentials and risks of outsourcing electronic customer interactions like e-mail inquiries or online bookings from hotels to DMOs instead of focussing on OIS that leaves these activities in hotel`s responsibility. In an outsourcing scenario hotels could concentrate on their core capabilities, and DMOs would take care of inquiries and bookings. Another area for further research is the adoption of DMS applications by service providers. Within the context of the research project, a possible research subject might be an application supporting offer creation provided by the DMO. This system would enable the hotel to create offers in a standardised manner. Because of its integration in a comprehensive DMS, integrated CRM processes from inquiry through to booking would be possible.

References

Backhaus, K., Erichson, B., Plinke, W. & Weiber, R. (2006). *Multivariate Analysemethoden. Eine anwendungsorientierte Einführung*. Berlin et al.: Springer.

Beritelli, P. (1999). Qualität im Destinationsmanagement. In Mussner, R., Pechlaner, H. (Eds.), *Destinationsmanagement* (pp. 31 - 43). Chur: Rüegger.

Buhalis, D. (2000). Marketing the competitive destination of the future. *Tourism Management*, 21 (1), 97-116.

Frey, S., Schegg, R. & Murphy, J. (2003). E-mail customer service in the Swiss hotel industry. *Tourism & Hospitality Research*, 4 (3), 197-212.

Fux, M., Noti, M. & Myrach, T. (2005). Quality of Feedback to E-Mail Request - An Explorative Study in Alpine Tourism Destinations. In M. Hitz, M. Sigala & J. Murphy (Eds.), *Information and Communication Technologies in Tourism 2006* (pp. 370). Wien, New York: Springer.

Gierke, F. (2005). *Kundenorientierung im E-Commerce-Prozess*. Hamburg: Verlag Dr. Kovac.

Leuenberger, R., Schegg, R. & Murphy, J. (2003). E-mail customer service by upscale international hotels. In A.J. Frew, M. Hitz, & P. O'Connor (Eds.), *Information and communication technologies in tourism* (pp. 20-28). Wien, New York: Springer.

Matzler, K., Pechlaner, H., Abfalter, D. & Wolf, M. (2005). Determinants of response to customer e-mail enquiries to hotels: evidence from Austria. *Tourism Management*, 26 (2), 249-259.

Matzler, K., Pechlaner, H. & Kohl, M. (2000). Formulierung von Servicestandards für touristische Dienstleistungen und Überprüfung durch den Einsatz von "Mystery Guest". *Tourismus Journal*, 4 (3), 157-176.

Merzenich, M. (2005). *Prozessmanagement im Customer Relationship Management - Gestaltung und Implementierung kundenorientierter Geschäftsprozesse*. Berlin: Logos Verlag.

Murphy, J. & Tan, I. (2003). Journey to nowhere? E-mail customer service by travel agents in Singapore. *Tourism Management*, 24 (5), 543-550.

Muther, A. & Österle, H. (1998). Electronic Customer Care - Neue Wege zum Kunden. *Wirtschaftsinformatik*, 40 (2), 105-113.

Parasuraman, A., Zeithaml, V. A. & Berry, L. L. (1988). SERVQUAL: A Multiple-Item Scale for Measuring Consumer Perceptions of Service Quality. *Journal of Retailing*, 64 (1), 12-40.

Schumacher, J. & Meyer, M. (2004). *Customer Relationship Management strukturiert dargestellt*. Berlin/Heidelberg: Springer Verlag.

Strauss, J. & Hill, D., J. (2001). Consumer Complaints by E-Mail: An exploratory investigation of corporate responses and customer reactions. *Journal of Interactive Marketing*, 15 (1), 63-73.

Vandermerwe, S. (1996). *The Eleventh Commandment: Transforming to "Own" Customers*. Chichester et al.: John Wiley & Sons.

Werthner, H. & Klein, S. (1999). *Information technology and tourism: a challenging relationship*. Wien: Springer.

Yang, Z. & Jun, M. (2002). Consumer perception of e-service quality: from Internet purchaser and non-purchaser perspectives. *Journal of Business Strategies*, 19 (1), 19-42.

Zemke, R. & Connellan, T. (2001). *e-service*. New York: Amacom.

Identification of Six Socio-types of Internet Users and their Impact on the Interactivity of Tourism Websites

Francine Charest[a]
François Bédard[b]

[a]Department of Communication
Université du Québec à Montréal, Canada
Charest.francine@uqam.ca

[b]Department of Urban and Tourism Studies
School of Business, Université du Québec à Montréal, Canada
Bedard.francois@uqam.ca

Abstract

Many studies have shown that Internet users do not form a homogenous group in regard to the way in which they appropriate websites. Socio-demographic profiling (age, sex, education, social status) is the usual method for explaining the different website usages of Internet users. This article proposes a new approach – that of socio-types – to understand and manage the different usages. Laboratory observation sessions were conducted about Internet users and their appropriation of the website of a destination management organization. These sessions allowed to identify six socio-types among Internet users of tourism sites: (i) the "Explorer", (ii) the "Agenda Setter", (iii) the "Demanding Type", (iv) the "Party Type", (v) the "What To Do Type" and (vi) the "Google Addict". A good knowledge of each of those socio-types will prove very useful for managers in charge of building or redesigning a website. Moreover, that knowledge will make the managers more aware of the need to invest in the interactivity of their websites so that each visitor, whatever his/her socio-type, can find their area of interest.

Keywords: Internet user socio-types, appropriation theory, website design.

1 Introduction

This article concerns a study that allowed to identify six socio-types of Internet users of tourism websites. The first section describes the theoretical framework of the study that was inspired mainly by works of de Certeau in the field of communications. The second section explains the procedure of the laboratory experiments conducted with Internet users. The third section describes each of the six socio-types which the analysis of the data gathered in the laboratory allowed to identify. The fourth and last section discusses some implications which the study has for management.

2 Background, Theory and Issues

The appropriation approach of Internet usage by users

The theoretical foundations of this research topic has its origin in works on mass communication and ICT and, more particularly, on the phenomenon of appropriation of the Internet by users. The topics investigated in the appropriation approach followed the same conceptual course as the studies carried out on mass communication. In reaction to the limits of the quantitative studies issued from the dissemination approaches, as well as to the growing number of ICT users, the interest of researchers moved toward the appropriation of ICT by means of sophisticated qualitative user studies. The force of that approach resides in, on the one hand, the analysis of *how* the different usages manifest according to social group. On the other hand, its force rests on the analysis of the *sense* or meanings which those usages assume for the users.

Academic literature recognizes de Certeau as the forerunner of the appropriation approach, considered to commence with the publication of his book "*L'Invention du quotidien*" (*Invention of the daily)* (1980). De Certeau is interested in the *ways and habits* of *ordinary people* in their daily lives when exposed to new objects. These habits of active and crafty users generate a creativity of *tactics* or *poaching* that has little in common with the prescribed *strategies*. The recognition accorded to de Certeau concerns essentially the paradigm of the active user.

De Certeau's theory is based on three propositions: (i) there is a discrepancy between the representation offered by the dominant production and the one which the user effectively appropriates; (ii) user's operations, ruses and poached actions are part of a power play in which users try to seize benefits where possible; (iii) there must be a logic to those practices.

De Certeau tries to understand what people *actually* do with the products they are *prescribed.* The great value of de Certeau's model resides in considering the *user* as a *point of departure* in the production of objects. The main advantage of de Certeau's model, according to Chambat (1994), is that it denounces the methodological limits of variables normally retained in other types of traditional analyses. He refers here to the variables income and socio-demographic generally retained in empirical studies (1994, p.260). According to researchers in the appropriation approach (Chambat, 1994; Jouet, 2000; Lafrance, Brouillard, 2002; Breton, Proulx 2002; Harvey, 2004; Fusaro, 2004; Marec, 2004), the analysis of those variables does not always explain the *real* usages of users. Moreover, it is precisely those limits that have led researchers to perform excessive traditional macro-social analyses rather than take on micro-social measures, such as in-depth interviewing techniques. The many types of appropriation then become cross contributions and converge toward intertwined universes that influence one another and that become less and less separable. As Jouet emphasized (2000): "The user is no longer a simple and passive consumer of products and services offered to him, [...] he becomes an actor (2000, p.502-503).

Interaction *man-machine*

Aside from the specific theoretical framework of the appropriation approach, this paper will also refer to studies conducted from the viewpoint of the interaction *man-machine*. Kim and Lee (2002) identify four elements necessary for the evaluation of websites. (i) Content: An important design factor for content is the decision regarding features to be shown for a product or service. A related question is how to decide which information is appropriation. There are various types of knowledge: facts, concepts, procedures, processes and principles. (ii) Structure: Once the products or services have been identified and the appropriate information collected, the knowledge must be organized to enable customers to understand the domain with minimum effort. Several different structures are possible, such as the hierarchic, network and grid structures. (iii) Interaction: The interaction element determines the types of navigation aids necessary to enable customers to interact effectively with the system, including various browsing and search facilities. (iv) Presentation: This element determines how the information is actually displayed on the screen (pixel size, background, logo, image, icons, color, polygons and page layout) (2004, p. 186-187).

Bastien and Scapin (1993), for their part, have carried out analyses of more than forty websites. This allowed them to identify numerous ergonomic evaluation criteria that proved to be indispensable tools for evaluating websites. These criteria are listed on their website at http://www.ergoweb.ca/criteres.html. This paper focuses on the four criteria that appear to relate most directly with the four elements developed by Kim and Lee. (i) Guidance, classification and distinction between items, feedback and readability: "the entirety of means implemented to consult, orient, inform and guide the user during his interactions with the computer (messages, alarms, labels) including terminological aspects". (ii) Work load, conciseness, information density: "the entirety of interface elements that reduce the visual or mnemonic load for users and that increase the effectiveness of the dialogue". (iii) Homogeneity and coherence: "refers to the way in which interface design options (e.g. codes, names, formats, procedures) are stored for identical contexts or are different for different contexts". (iv) Significance of codes and names; "the aligning of objects or the information displayed or entered, and their referent [...] Codes and names "signifiers" have a strong semantic relation with their referent".

Ergonomic evaluation criteria applied to the tourism sector

The application of ergonomic evaluation criteria to the tourism sector has inspired the works of Pan and Fesenmaier (2003). They analyze the users' search process on websites by the use of symbols. They show that users' processes are different from the process proposed by the websites: "*...travelers appear to have a different mind set compared with the information on the Internet and the discrepancy contributed to the usability problem of the Internet*" (2003, p.249). According to Xiang and Fesenmaier (2004), symbols or icons used by designers are generally relied on as a valuable and universal tool by those who search for pertinent and efficient information on precise destinations. However, many sites use symbols inappropriately, thereby causing more confusion than assistance: "*inappropriately used metaphors can potentially make a website confusing*" confirms Garret (cited by Xiang, Fesenmaier, 2004, p. 185). In that sense, the authors remind of the five key principles developed by Nielsen to which interface designers should adhere: "*easy to learn, efficient to use, easy to remember, few errors and pleasant to use*" (Nielsen cited by Xiang, Fesenmaier 2004, p. 191). Dearden and Lo (2004) show that there is a great inconsistency among the tools at the disposal for Internet users when searching tourism information. Those tools do not always correspond to the information needs of Internet users: "*Many existing web-based tools to support tourism decision-making are poorly matched to the needs of Internet users*" (2004, p. 172).

3 Methodology

Methodology used in this paper to gather data on the ways of users in their appropriation of tourism websites consisted of laboratory observation sessions using a method developed by Nantel (2005). The main objective of this type of laboratory testing is to analyze the user-friendliness and functional effectiveness of websites. It is based on a systematic approach to consumers' decision-making processes in a navigation situation. It is also based on concurrent verbalizations (protocol analysis), on analyses of consumers' navigation processes (log analysis) and on in-depth interviews. A second objective of the laboratory test is an in-depth analysis of consumers' evaluations of websites by reviewing: appearance; navigation and clarity of a site; format of data posted; page downloading time; confidence in the site and the company; confidence in the security of the site; online forms, special offers on the site; and search engine used. To evaluate the efficiency of a particular website, the following variables are measured: degree of difficulty of the task; degree of accessibility of information posted on the site; way in which the information is evaluated and understood by the consumer; moments of frustration and doubt during navigation; and 'dead ends' (moments of 'going nowhere'). By measuring these variables, an attempt is made to identify strengths and weaknesses of tourism website navigation.

In order to meet the objectives of this study, i.e. the identification of socio-types of Internet users, two modifications were made to the Nantel method: (i) the adding of an interview held before the navigation (pre-navigation), (ii) more in-depth, semi-directed interviews conducted after the navigation (post-navigation). The pre-navigation interviews allowed to identify the needs and expectations of Internet users before their appropriation of the site. The post-navigation interviews allowed to verify and validate whether the site studied during the laboratory observation sessions had effectively responded to the user's needs.

The Nantel method requires between twenty and thirty participants. For this study, candidates were recruited from ads placed in national newspapers in 2004 and 2006. Of those candidates, 24 final participants were then selected based on the following criteria: Internet users (i) with average or no experience who search for information or who wish to make bookings on websites; (ii) who have effected less than 25 information searches on tourism websites over the past 12 months; (iii) who have effected less than 10 bookings on tourism websites over the past 12 months. Even though Internet users were encouraged to verbalize what went on in their heads during the navigation, they expressed more during the post-navigation interview about their level of appreciation with the site. This allowed the researcher-interviewer to observe concrete examples of usages of the site. It was thus possible to ask Internet users about the scope of websites by Kim and Lee and about the ergonomic criteria of Bastien and Scapin by referring to concrete examples of their own interaction with the website. In this way it was possible to validate whether or not the site responded to their needs.

That way of employing the different techniques of the Nantel model and of intensifying the investigation by measuring, before and after, the scope and the ergonomic evaluation criteria of the website, allowed to identify the usage discrepancies between the following two types of dimensions: the "interactive" functions and the structure or the organization of ideas on the site.

The in-depth investigation, conducted to measure the cognitive needs of interactivity of Internet users, allowed to discern the gaps between *prescribed* and *effective* usages of the site. This concerns the perceived gap of data gathered between the beginning and the end of the navigation and also between the navigation and the interviews. Concerning the data gathered during the navigation, a gap evolved between the data collected in the first two thirds of the navigation and the last third. This should allow us to identify the *modus operandi* of Internet users by observing their reactions until they leave the site. That direct method of observation, together with the actions and comments verbalized by the Internet users, allowed to better comprehend the evolution of a web navigation or to anticipate the self-evaluation of an Internet user concerning the accomplishment of a task given to them. The data gathered in a qualitative manner contradicted the quantitative data. In fact, the data about the navigation was more positive than the data obtained during the interviews. The descriptive, qualitative and hypothetical-deductive approach allowed to establish that conclusion.

4 Results and Discussion

The analysis of the results of the laboratory observation sessions allowed to define six socio-types of Internet users of tourism websites: the "Explorer", the "Agenda Setter", the "Demanding Type", the "Party Type", the "What To Do Type", and the "Google Addict".

“ExplorerType”

Internet users who correspond to the "**Explorer**" profile generally navigate the research test site starting with the "Discover" section. "Explorers" enjoy navigating the site, which they appreciate for its classic, convincing and high quality make-up. They find the informational content inspiring. They make abundant use of the navigation tools and enjoy doing so. They appreciate the suggestions and navigate from link to link by taking the time to read the information, in particular about the accommodations and packages. They also visit the more specialized sites. "Explorers" notice and value the visual quality of the site. They appreciate the straightforwardness and effectiveness of the search engine. They thus navigate with ease and without much difficulty, even if this means investing time to familiarize themselves with the site before obtaining the sought for information. In all, "Explorers" feel confident using the site and experience it as user-friendly and compatible to their needs.

"Agenda Setters"

"Agenda Setters" are Internet users whose search is centered around the "Plan" section, as well by using the "Quick Search" function. They are more restless than the "Explorers". Their first goal is to plan the accommodation. In a second step they will then search for information about nearby activities. In the beginning, they enjoy navigating the site, the first pages of which they find appealing. They have a precise idea of what they are looking for from the start. "Agenda Setters" generally read the content of the web pages by skimming through them and navigate for less than ten minutes. They also type in keywords in "Quick Search" to accelerate their search rather than searching the site. The latter function often provides them with satisfying search results. On the other hand, they quickly question the content of the distributed information if they don't find information about the specific establishment, prices or services they are researching. They question not only the site but also their own capacities for finding the information on "this" site. They become very restless during their navigation. The work involved in the search seems extensive to them. They would appreciate the assistance of an agent to guide them. They quickly become impatient when faced with the inefficiency and the slow response time of the site, above all if they want to open photos or links. They also become impatient when the site does not remember checked off options from one page to the next. In short, "Agenda Setters" who do not succeed in "planning" their accommodation quickly or in finding the desired information generally experience the work involved as extensive. Internet users who correspond to this profile nevertheless succeed in navigating the site. At times they feel assured when they at last find familiar pointers. However, their difficulty to adapt to the organization of ideas, i.e. the sometimes "incoherent" functioning of the transmitted or non-memorized messages, prevent the "Agenda Setters" from feeling comfortable with the research test site. They generally leave the site with a slightly negative impression.

"Demanding Type"

The **"Demanding Type"** represents the most challenging users of the site. They generally enter the site via the "Book" section. Similar to the "Agenda Setters", these users know exactly what they are looking for. They want to get that information as fast as possible – at maximum with two or three clicks. On the one hand, they appreciate that a site poses them two or three questions to the end of establishing a quick profile. On the other hand, they usually also expect accommodation, package and deal offers that correspond first of all to their choices and preferences and secondly to the requested price and availabilities. The "Demanding Type" appreciates viewing packages, deals and suggestions in thematic modules or as "tailor-made vacations". They are surprised that the research test site does not function on a per profile basis, i.e. in a more individualized and interactive manner. They are moreover surprised of not finding spaces reserved for suggestions or discussion forums, as can be frequently found on many other sites. They don't appreciate that the site does not remember pre-checked information and much less that it does not respond in a precise, coherent and satisfying manner to their requests. They rapidly judge the site in a negative way when more work is involved, when they have to repeat the action of checking reservation elements, and even more so when they have to restart a request. In general, the "Demanding Type" generally feels that the site is neither adequate to their needs, nor adapted to their demands, choices, preferences and interactive way of using sites. In short, they feel that the site does not correspond to their profile. They generally leave with a negative impression, feeling that the site is incompatible with their needs and expectations.

“Party Type”

The **"Party Type"** generally navigates the research test site via the "Events and Festivals" section. They usually start out by searching the site on the basis of events that attract their attention. It is thus festivals, events and other entertainment offers that inspire them. They begin their search from that aspect and let themselves be guided through the site. They generally don't have a preconceived idea of what they are really looking for when they begin their search. However, once they find an activity or event that responds to their needs, they then search the accommodation pages. They are attracted by evocative names such as Beluga Hotel that match the type of excursion they are planning, in this case a whale watch. Even though they are able to quickly find information about festivals and excursions, they have difficulty carrying out the hotel reservation. When checking the boxes during the booking procedure, they repeatedly obtain the "no result" response. They don't understand the reason for that response as the site does not indicate that additional information. They then question the validity of the information and start the procedure over and over again. After changing the hotel selection, they then often obtain a positive result at last, which then satisfies them. Once the information is obtained and the transaction completed, the "Party Type" generally wants to book directly on the research test site. They are not worried about transmitting information to the site, the "security" symbol sufficing to reassure them. Other than the symbol, the logos of the Destination Management Organization (DMO) and of the company give them confidence. They usually leave with a positive and favourable image of the site, even if the task seems difficult up to a certain point. The final success of their transactions suffices to satisfy them.

“What To Do Type”

The **"What To Do"** profile resembles the "Agenda Setter" in the sense that "What To Do" users as well seek first and foremost to plan. However, they differ in regard to the information required for the planning. "What To Do" users are guided more by the activities they are planning than by the type of accommodation. "What To Do" users like navigating the site. They appreciate the suggestions and would even like to see more of them on the site. Nevertheless, their search is first and foremost guided by the suggested activities. They don't always have precise ideas when entering the site. Once they have decided on an activity, they begin looking for information about the accommodation. Their navigation then leads them to the "Book" section. They also search information about packages and deals. "What To Do" users are the only ones who put the various web pages in their favourites and who resort to those during the procedure. "What To Do" users search above all sports activities, which limits their search fairly quickly. If anything, they find wellness and relaxation offers. They nevertheless continue to navigate for a fairly long time before realizing that they keep getting the same responses no matter how they use the site. This leaves them frustrated. Thus, even though the "What To Do" users look for a sports activity, they fail to find anything beyond the initially bookmarked information. Their navigation begins on a positive note and then changes to negative during the last third of their search. Faced with the repetition of data, the return to the same places no matter what method chosen, and the lack of information corresponding to their needs, "What To Do" users leave with an impression that the site is not suited to their needs. During the interview, this impression remained negative, even if the results of the navigation showed a positive perception of the site.

“Google Addict”

Similar to the "Demanding Type", users of the profile called **"Google Addict"** distinguish themselves by their extreme impatience. As their name indicates, these users leave the site after having opened only three or four pages, upon which they turn directly to the Google search engine. "Google Addicts" comprise users of all navigation approaches, i.e. they enter the site using the "Discover", "Plan" or "Book" sections. "Google Addicts" are impatient and demanding. If the site does not respond to their request instantaneously, they leave it precipitately for Google. They react very emotionally and negatively when the site does not immediately give them the exact information they are looking for on the basis of their profile, tastes and demands. This type of usage is becoming increasingly common. It reflects a new generation of Internet users who are used to functioning, thinking, searching and navigating according to the usage established by Google. The search engine's user-friendliness, speed and accessibility to an inexhaustible and instantaneous network of information seems to have become the standard for today's web surfers. "Google Addicts" are surprised as soon as a system does not interact like Google. In their words and actions, "Google Addicts" reflect Google. They constantly refer to Google and wonder if Google would have provided more information, if Google would have been faster or if the information provided by Google would have been more relevant. In short, "Google Addicts" wonder whether the search engine Google could be integrated into the research test website.

5 Conclusion

A good knowledge of each of those socio-types will prove very useful for managers in charge of developing or redesigning a website. Moreover, that knowledge will make them more aware of the need to invest in the interactivity of their website so that each visitor, whatever their socio-type, can find his/her area of interest. As early as 1986, Rogers identified interactivity as a chief determinant of user acceptance. He defined interactivity as “the capacity of the new communication systems to respond to users almost like an individual who is taking part in a conversation" (Rogers, cited in Harvey, 2004, p. 76). An immediate feedback that also has quality content establishes user confidence and satisfaction (Bastien & Scapin, 1993). By contrast, the lack of feedback as well as lengthy response delays can frustrate users and impede current transactions. Adaptability (here the capacity to react according to the context and according to user needs and preferences) as well as flexibility (here the ability to personalize an interface and the methods for reaching a given objective) represent ergonomic criteria that are essential for all interactive communication on websites. Interactivity is a notion at the centre of the debate on user autonomy (Kim & Lee, 2002). The supporters of the appropriation approach recognize that interactivity is among the prerequisites for proceeding with the evaluation on websites. Researchers studying interactive communication acknowledge the potential of the Internet to promote exchanges and study new ways of communicating by means of this new tool. Many of these researchers find that the Internet is still regarded more as an extension of a mass dissemination tool rather than an occasion to explore new communication methods: To communicate in networks in an interactive and personalized way would represent new challenges for the actors-producers of information as well as the actors-users, as underlined by Castells (2001). This paper may serve as a basis for future research. An interesting topic may be to identify measurable attributes of each user, collect data and then run a clustering algorithm to see if the same prototypes emerge.

References

Bastien, J. M. C., & Scapin, D. (1993). Ergonomic Criteria for the Evaluation of Human-computer Interfaces. *Technical report of the French National Institute of Research in Computer Science and Control*, No.156, and online at http://www.ergoweb.ca/criteres.html.

Breton, P., & Proulx, S. (2002). L'explosion de la Communication à l'aube du XX1è siècle. Montréal: Boréal.

Castells, M. (2001). The Internet Galaxy, Oxford; New York: Oxford University Press.

Chambat, P. (1994). Usages des Technologies de l'information et de la Communication (TIC): Évolution des Problématiques, *TIS*, 6(3), 249-270.

Dearden, A., & Lo, C. M. (2004). Using Cooperative Evaluation to Explore Travel and Tourism Decision-Making. In A.J. Frew (Ed), *Information and Communication Technologies in Tourism 2004*, proceedings of ENTER 2004 (172-183). New York: Springer.

De Certeau, M. (1990). L'invention au Quotidien. 1. Arts de faire. Paris: Gallimard.

Fusaro, M. (2002). Commerce Électronique Comment Créer la Confiance, St-Hyacinthe: Somabec.

Jouet, J. (2000). Retour Critique sur la Sociologie des Usages, *Réseaux*, 100, 487-521.

Harvey, P. L. (2004). Cyberespace et Communautique; Appropriation, Réseaux, Groupes Virtuels, Saint-Nicholas (Québec): Presses de l'Université Laval, p. 239.

Kim J., & Lee, J, (2002). Critical Design Factors for Successful E-commerce Systems, *Behaviour and Information Technology*, 21(3), 185-199.

Lafrance, J-.P., & Brouillard, P. (2002). Le Commerce Électronique, y a-t-il un Modèle Québécois? Sainte-Foy: Presses de l'Université du Québec.

Marec, J. (2004). Usages: Pratiques de Recherche et Théorie des Pratiques, *Hermès*, 38, 141-147.

Nantel, J., Mekki B. A. & Bressolles, G. (2005). L'efficacité des sites Web: Quand les Consommateurs s'en Mêlent, *Gestion*, 30(1), 16-23, www.net-question.com/chairerbc/.

Nantel, J., Sénécal, S., Mekki, B., & Berrada, A. (2005). The Influence of "Dead-ends" on Perceived Website Usability, *Journal of E-Business*, June.

Pan, B., & Fesenmaier, D. R., (2003). Travel Information Search on the Internet: A Preliminary Analysis in A. J. Frew, M. Hitz, & P. O'Connor (Eds). *Information and*

Communication Technologies in Tourism 2003. proceedings of ENTER 2003 (pp. 242-251). New York: Springer.

Xiang, Z., & Fesenmaier, D. R. (2004). Interface Metaphors and Their Roles in Travel-Related Websites. In A.J. Frew (Ed), *Information and Communication Technologies in Tourism 2004*, proceedings of ENTER 2004 (184-194). New York: Springer.

Exploring the Use of Emotional Features at Romantic Destination Websites

Alecia C. Douglas
Juline E. Mills
Raphael Kavanaugh

Department of Hospitality and Tourism Management
Purdue University, United States of America
{acdougla, millsje, raphaelk}@ purdue.edu

Abstract

Emotional connections with products have been identified as an influential factor in consumer decision making and the formation of desirable behaviours toward a brand. Currently, there is insufficient research investigating the emotional appeal of Websites with the concept being rarely addressed in travel and tourism. The purpose of this research was to therefore determine the extent to which the top ten romantic destinations used emotional features at their Websites. In addition, the Website Emotional Features Assessment Model (WEFAM) was developed and tested using confirmatory factor analysis (CFA). The model results showed that four WEFAM emotional features site activation, affection, surgency, and confidence are important in the Website design for romantic destinations.

Keywords: Emotions, romantic destinations, Website features, confirmatory factor analysis.

1 Introduction

Emotions have a long tradition in marketing, advertising, and consumer behavior research and have been studied in shopping experience, loyalty behaviors, purchase behaviors, and satisfaction (see Holbrook & O'Shaughnessy, 1984; Cohen & Areni 1991; Erevelles, 1998; Richins, 1997; O'Shaughnessy & O'Shaugnessy, 2003). Marketers have succeeded at manipulating senses in the traditional marketplace by strategically placing verbal and non verbal cues in a stimulating environment to appeal to customers' emotions. In the current study, the authors bring to light the growing importance of emotional usability at tourism destination Websites. As e-tourists continue to spend much of their time browsing from site to site they are demanding more engaging and interactive experiences that appeal to their emotional psyche. The goal of the study is to determine whether or not e-tourism marketers are capitalizing on that marketing power of emotions by incorporating emotional features at their Website.

2 Emotions in Marketing and Information Technology Research

Traditional marketing research indicates that a customer's emotional connection with a product/service can stimulate buying interest, guide choices, arouse buying intentions, and influence future buying decisions (O'Shaughnessy & O'Shaugnessy,

2003). In the context of advertising research, the manipulation and study of emotions can help to explain incremental variance in the purchase behaviour of consumers (Holbrook & O'Shaughnessy, 1984). Hirschman and Holbrook (1982) in their seminal work on hedonic consumption argue that emotions may be critical to the success of a product. A customer's buying decision, among competing brands, could be affected by realistic and enticing promises entrenched in human emotions (Travis, 2000). In the marketing of services, emotional appeals could be seen as profoundly attractive message strategies building upon the challenges of effectively tangibilizing the tourism product (Mattila, 2001). Investigating those sensorial needs and desires of a target market (Jin & Sook, 2003) can bring e-marketers one step closer toward building a deeper and closer relationship between the brand and the consumer.

However, the marketing power of emotions was neglected in information technology (IT) research until recently when Huang (2003), Jin and Sook (2004), and Lam and Lim (2004) studied the concept. These authors examined how emotional and/or hedonic features in Website design can fill the needs of consumers, induce experiential online encounters, and be incorporated in e-branding strategies. Research in information systems promotes the use of IT-enabled functional features on Websites that facilitates task completion and rational decision making (see Liang & Lai, 2002). Nevertheless, there is evidence that emotions are a critical determinant of consumer behaviour in an online environment. In a study by Huang (2003), emotional experiences in an online shopping environment were found to be positively related to a customer's intention to explore or purchase from the Website. As emotions influences a customer's memories of products and the decision making processes (Kim & Moon, 1998; Lee, 1998), more Websites are being designed to evoke specific emotions from their users (Schenkman & Jonsson, 2000; Kim, Lee, & Choi, 2003).

Designing Websites that activate users' senses may potentially increase the level of emotional engagement referred to as flow (Csikszentmihalyi, 1975). Flow is an individual's subjective experience of enjoyment while playfully interacting when completing a given task (Webster & Martocchio, 1992). In the online environment, Hoffman and Novak (1996) defined flow as: "the state occurring during network navigation which is: (1) characterized by a seamless sequence of responses facilitated by machine interactivity, (2) intrinsically enjoyable, (3) accompanied by a loss of self-consciousness, and (4) self-reinforcing." When experiential flow is operationalized, it is often in the context of enjoyment or interest in human and computer interactions (Huang, 2003).

3 Website Emotional Features Assessment Model

Using Holbrook and Batra's (1987) concept of emotions, Lim and Lam (2004) classified online features that evoked various emotions in customers. Holbrook and Batra (1987) developed a modest number of multi-item indices for measuring emotional responses to non-verbal components of advertising. These items also correspond with Mehrabian and Russell's (1974) pleasure-arousal-dominance (PAD) paradigm. Lim and Lam (2004) adopted this emotional response scale to the online environment arguing that it is important for Website designers to include features that will cater to the emotional needs of users. Findings from their study supported the argument that emotional Website features are an influential factor to be considered in electronic commerce. Table 1 lists the emotional features used in the current study as they relate to destination Websites.

Table 1. Website Emotional Features Adopted from Lim & Lam (2004)

Definition of Emotional Features	Examples
Site Activation: Emotional features that make e-tourists feel aroused, stimulated, and excited.	• *Attractive colour use* • *Vivid animation*
Site Affection: Emotional features that make e-tourists feel that the Website is sympathetic, empathetic, and/or caring toward them	• *Special interest sites for tourists* • *Foreign language version of site*
Site Confidence: Emotional features that make e-tourists feel confident with the Website and convey the message that the Website is competent.	• *Visitor testimonials* • *Guest Books*
Site Serenity: Emotional features that give e-tourists feelings of harmony, peace and relaxation.	• *Soft colour combination* • *Peaceful background music*
Site Superiority: Emotional features that make e-tourists feel like special members of a privileged club.	• *Visitor submitted photo* • *Personalized Website*
Site Surgency: Emotional features that make e-tourists feel the Website is fun and enjoyable.	• *Virtual postcard* • *Interactive destination map*

To guide the study, several research questions were formulated: (1) to what extent do romantic destinations use emotional features at their Website? (2) What emotional features are being used at romantic destination Websites? (3) Which romantic destination Website is the most emotional appealing? To address these research questions, the authors propose the Website Emotional Features Assessment Model (WEFAM) shown in Figure 1.

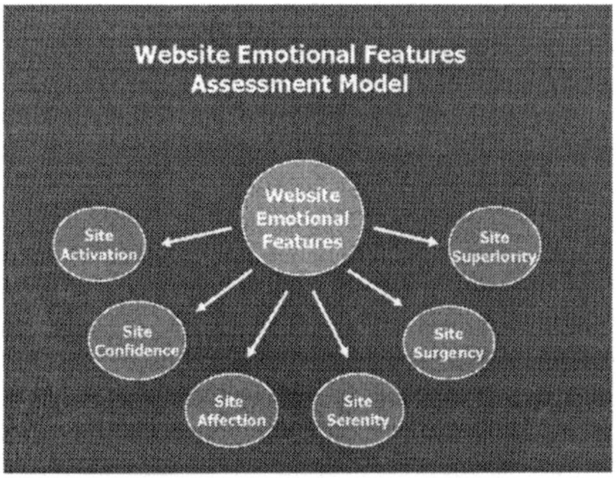

Fig. 1. Website Emotional Features Assessment Model (WEFAM)

4 Methods

To determine the extent to which tourism destinations incorporate emotional features in their Website design, the proposed WEFAM model was tested by evaluating the Websites of the top ten romantic destinations in 2005 according to Modern Bride Magazine (Wong, 2005). The official tourism destination Websites were selected to test the emotional features model as they are often times the starting point for collecting information and exploring the destination. Table 2 shows the list of the top ten romantic destinations, in random order, with their respective Website addresses. The questionnaire consisted of 25 items measuring site activation, confidence, affection, serenity, surgency, and superiority as the WEFAM model. All items were measured on a seven-point Likert-type scale ranging from strongly disagree (1) to strongly agree (7).

Table 2. Names and Website Addresses of the Destination Management Organizations Used in the Study

Romantic Destinations	Website Address
1. Hawaii	http://www.gohawaii.com
2. Italy	http://www.enit.it/default.asp?Lang=UK
3. Tahiti	http://www.tahiti-tourisme.com/
4. Anguilla	http://www.anguilla-vacation.com/
5. Fiji	http://www.bulafiji.com/
6. St. Lucia	http://www.stlucia.org/
7. Mexico	http://www.visitmexico.com
8. St. Barths	http://www.saint-barths.com/
9. France	http://us.franceguide.com/
10. Jamaica	http://www.visitjamaica.com

The survey was administered to undergraduate students at a U.S. Mid-Western University (n=36) in a controlled computer laboratory setting. The sample was selected because of their knowledge of tourism marketing on the Internet and prior training and experience in conducting Website evaluations. Student samples are useful for concept identification and construct analysis (Emory, 1980). Moreover, the homogeneous nature of student samples allow for more exact theoretical predictions than possible with a heterogeneous group (Calder, Phillips, & Tybout, 1981). Additionally, the likelihood of making false conclusions on covariations about the variables under examination is reduced (Calder et al., 1981).

Although the sample size limits the applicability of the findings, the research design considered Nevitt's (2000) approach/guidelines for using small samples in model development. Nevitt (2000) argues that maximum likelihood iteration performed in structural equation models (SEM) is capable of generating stable parameter estimates even when small samples are used. Further, Bentler and Yuan (1999) argue that sample size in SEM can be reduced to the point where the sample size is only slightly larger than the number of parameter estimates. In this case, a sample size as small as n=20 respondents would be sufficient for model building given that the proposed model is based on seven parameters and their corresponding error terms. Given the desirability for theoretical testing and the potential to yield stable parameter estimates, it was determined that data obtained from the sample was suitable for analysis. Nine romantic destination Websites were successfully evaluated with the exception of Jamaica due to inaccessibility of the site. Data were then analyzed using the Statistical Packages for the Social Sciences (SPSS 14.0) application to conduct normality, collinearity, and exploratory factor analysis (EFA). Using Analysis of Moment Structure (AMOS 4.0), a structural equation modeling (SEM) program, first and second-order confirmatory factor analysis (CFA) was performed to specify an appropriate WEFAM model. The mean scores of each construct from the second-order CFA were calculated to determine which romantic destination Website was the most emotionally appealing.

5 Results

Exploratory factor analysis (EFA) was conducted on all 25 items measuring site activation, confidence, affection, serenity, surgency, and superiority with the results appearing in Table 3.

Table 3. Emotional Features Factor Analysis Results

	Component					
	Site Activation	Site Confidence	Site Surgency	Site Affection	Site Information	6
Attractive Color	.918					
Aesthetics	.889					
Graphics	.884					
Soft Color	.841					
Animation	.619					
Testimonials		.816				
Message Board		.813				
Guestbook		.811				
Directory		.582				
Virtual postcard		.569				
Virtual Trip planner			.781			
Virtual map			.667			
Language				.803		
Foreigner				.639		
FAQs					.619	
Partners					.612	
Environment						.765

KMO = 0.831, Bartlett's X^2 2982.330; df = 276; p = 0.000; Total Variance Explained = 60%

6 Confirmatory Factory Analysis (CFA) Results

Model fit was not immediately achieved with the initial first-order CFA where X^2 = 240.5; df = 94; p = 0.001; GFI = 0.915; AGFI = 0.877; NFI = 0.896; CFI = 0.934; RMSEA = 0.069. As such, an iterative process was carried out to yield appropriate fit statistics. The final first-order CFA model produced X^2 = 68.245; df = 48; p = 0.029; GFI = 0.965; AGFI = 0.943; NFI = 0.963; CFI = 0.989; RMSEA = 0.036 (see Figure 2).

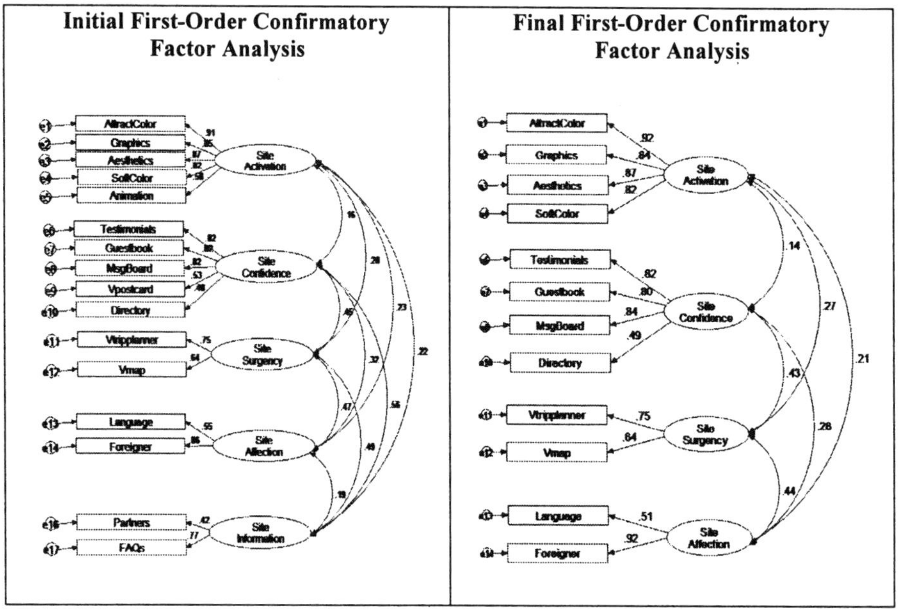

Fig. 2. Initial and Final First-Order Confirmatory Factor Analysis

The second-order CFA generated final model fit statistics of X^2 = 78.9; df = 53; p = 0.001; GFI = 0.960; AGFI = 0.941; NFI = 0.957, CFI = 0.985; RMSEA = 0.039. The final model shows that site activation, confidence, surgency, and affection are representative of the emotional features incorporated into the Website design of the romantic destinations evaluated. Although all items measuring site activation were strong (>0.80), respondents indicated that attractive use of colour to improve the visual appeal of the site (0.91) was more dominant over graphics (0.83), aesthetics (0.87), and soft colour (0.81). Message boards (0.85) were used more often than testimonials (0.82), guest book (0.81), and directory (0.57) when communicating the competence of the Website and making the viewer feel confident about the experience.

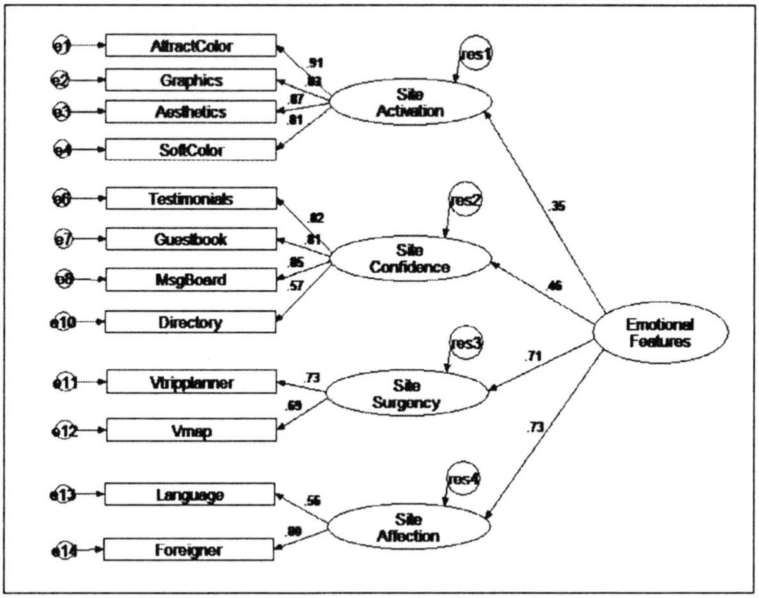

Fig. 3. Final Structural Equation for the Website Emotional Features Assessment Model (WEFAM)

Having a virtual trip planner (0.73) also increased the level of surgency of the Website. Specifically, features enhancing fun, entertainment, and interaction with the site while catering/tailoring the content based on the foreign visitor's interest (.80) was an influential factor of site affection. In general, site affection (0.73) was the most influential of all four emotional features followed by site surgency (0.71), site confidence (0.46), and site activation (0.35) respectively. This suggests emotional features that sympathize and/or empathize with the participant were more dominant in the sites evaluated. Not to be downplayed was the influence of site surgency in the emotional features mix which has the potential to increase or decrease Csikszentmihalyi's (1975) theory of 'flow' at the destination Website. Site activation (0.35) features that excite, stimulate, and/or arouse the senses were found to be the least important emotional features used in the current design of the top ten romantic destination Websites.

7 Romantic Destination Rankings

Using the final structural equation for the WEFAM model in Figure 3, a ranking of the top romantic destination Websites was conducted to determine which Website incorporated more emotional features in its design by computing the mean scores for each construct (see Table 4). From the descriptive results, St. Barths (mean score = 6.13) was ranked first under the site activation category suggesting that the use of colour, graphics, and aesthetic appeal in the design of the Website made it more stimulating and exciting to view than the others. Italy on the other hand was ranked the lowest for site activation with a mean score of 4.00 indicating that the site was not as arousing when compared to the others. For site confidence, St. Lucia (mean score

= 4.60) was ranked the highest by respondents at being competent in communicating the brand through a combination of testimonials, guest books, message boards that showcase the brand from the customers point of view. On the contrary, St. Barths, which was viewed as the most stimulating Website, was the least confident with a mean score of 1.51.

Table 4. Romantic Destination Website Emotional Features Ranking

Destinations	**Site Activation**		**Site Confidence**		**Site Surgency**		**Site Affection**	
	Mean	Rank	Mean	Rank	Mean	Rank	Mean	Rank
1. Hawaii	5.81	3	1.75	5	4.86	3	5.99	2
2. Italy	4.00	9	1.84	4	4.36	5	5.76	4
3. Tahiti	5.98	2	2.00	3	5.65	2	3.44	7
4. Anguilla	5.14	7	1.75	5	4.57	4	2.64	9
5. Fiji	5.15	6	1.55	8	3.22	9	2.77	8
6. St. Lucia	5.62	4	**4.60**	**1**	**6.30**	**1**	5.99	2
7. Mexico	5.34	5	2.24	2	3.75	8	**6.28**	**1**
8. St. Barths	**6.13**	**1**	1.51	9	4.36	5	4.59	6
9. France	4.99	8	1.74	7	4.06	7	4.61	5
Total	**5.35**	**1.36**	**2.11**	**1.50**	**4.57**	**1.90**	**4.67**	**2.04**

Overall Emotional Ranking:

1 – St. Lucia (5.63); 2 – Hawaii (4.60); 3 – Mexico (4.40); 4 – Tahiti (4.27); 5 – St. Barths (4.15) 6 – Italy (3.99); 7 - France (3.85); 8 – Anguilla (3.52); 9 – Fiji (3.17)

As it relates to emotional features that make browsing fun and enjoyable, St. Lucia's Website was once again ranked first for site surgency with a mean score of 6.30 ahead of Tahiti (5.65) and Hawaii (4.86). Fiji scored the lowest for site surgency with a mean score of 3.22 indicating that the Website was not enjoyable to browse. Lastly, Mexico was voted the most affectionate Website with a mean score of 6.28 closely followed by Hawaii and St. Lucia with scores of 5.99 each. This suggests that Mexico's Website appealed more on an empathetic level with Web users by providing emotional features on the site that cater to the varying interests of foreign visitors as well as tailoring the entire Web experience based on the visitor's country of origin. Anguilla was ranked the least affectionate romantic destination Website with a mean score of 2.64. A brief perusal of Anguilla's Website confirms that at the very least, there is no provision for tailoring the content to the potential visitor's language. A visitor from a non-English speaking country may have difficulty understanding the information presented by Anguilla.

Overall, St. Lucia (5.63) ranked as the most emotionally appealing destination Website followed by Hawaii (4.60) and Mexico (4.40) in third. An exploration of St. Lucia's Website revealed the simple elegance of the site complemented by panoramic views showcasing the life of the destination using a picture slideshow. Generally, there is a good balance of emotional and functional Website features incorporated in the Website design. Visitors to the site are reassured of the destination's competence as there is a prominent display of several industry awards. Verbal cues at the Website also exude emotional overtures. The choice of words used touches on a more personal and emotional level. For example, instead of the usual 'Contact Us' link common to most tourism Websites, St. Lucia enters into a conversation with the e-tourist by saying "Talk To Us." This is indicative of the extent with which St. Lucia is willing to be 'up close and personal' by creating an emotional gateway to heart of the e-tourist.

8 Discussion and Conclusion

This study sought to determine the extent to which romantic destinations use emotional features on their Websites. The value of the study is in its contribution to building a body of literature in the tourism discipline on the influential role emotions play specifically at destination Websites. Limited knowledge exists on the use of emotions in Website design in IT research and within the tourism literature. Although borrowing from mainstream IT, the study was exploratory in nature due to the unique characteristics of tourism destination Websites. As such, the emotional features identified were framed in the context tourism. Destination Websites evaluated were chosen for their romantic appeal to couples wishing to celebrate love and togetherness. Results of the study indicate that romantic destinations are capable of appealing on an emotional level with e-tourists because of their use of affect laden features in the design of the site.

To an extent, findings of the study suggest that emotional features particularly affection, surgency, confidence, and activation are being used in varying degrees at the destination Websites evaluated. From the data, the results of the factor analysis did not generate components representative of Website superiority and serenity. Therefore, we can conclude that site superiority and serenity are not well represented in the destination Websites evaluated. Items and constructs used in the study were developmental therefore limiting generalizations to larger populations. In assessing the sites of the top romantic destinations, it must be noted that the WEFAM model did not consider the "universe" of all elements representative of emotional Website features. For example, further development of the serenity construct may be extended to include items such as: 'use of verbal cues with subtle emotional tones,' 'harmonious use of pictures, text, and audio cues,' and 'inviting audio cues.' Nevertheless, this exploratory study provides direction for future research and model building with practical implications for destination Websites catering to travel markets that have more hedonic motives when planning their travel.

Building emotional features in the design of destination Website interfaces is likely to be an influential determinant in eliciting desirable behaviours in e-tourists. Literature suggests that evoking emotions in customers can stimulate interest in the destination or the tourism product, guide choices, arouse purchase intentions, and influence future buying decisions (O'Shaughnessy & O'Shaugnessy, 2003). Given these findings, a practical consequence of this research is attracting the attention of e-tourism marketers and researchers to the importance of emotional features at destination Website.

References

Bentler, P. & Yaun, K. (1999). Structural equation modeling with small samples: Test statistics. *Multivariate Behavioral Research*, 34, 181-197.

Calder, B. J., Phillips, L. W., & Tybout, A. (1981). Designing research for application. *Journal of Consumer Research*, *8*(1), 197-217.

Cohen, J. B. & Areni, C. S. (1991). Affect and consumer behavior. In A. Robertson and H. Kassarjian (Eds.). *Handbook of Consumer Behavior (pp.* 183-240).Prentice-Hall, Englewood Cliffs..

Csikszentmihalyi, M. (1975). *Beyond boredom and anxiety.* San Francisco: Jossey-Bass.

Emory, C. (1980). *Business research methods revised edition.* Homewood, Illinois: Irwin-Dorsey Limited.

Erevelles, S. (1998). The role of affect in marketing. *Journal of Business Research* (42), 199-215.

Hirschman, E. C. & Holbrook, M. B. (1982). Hedonic consumption: emerging concepts, methods and propositions. *Journal of Marketing*, 46(3), 92-101.

Hoffman, D. L. & Novak, T. P. (1996). Marketing in hypermedia computer-mediated environments: conceptual foundations. *Journal of Marketing, 60,* (July 1996), 50–68.

Holbrook, M. B., & Batra, R. (1998). Toward a Standardized Emotional Profile (SEP) useful in measuring responses to the nonverbal components of advertising. In S. Hecker and D. W. Stewart (Eds.). *Nonverbal Communication in Advertising.* Toronto: Lexington Books.

Huang, M. H. (2003). Designing website attributes to induce experiential encounters. *Computers in Human Behavior,* 19, 425–442.

Jin, K. Y., & Sook, K. E. (2003). E-brand design with 3C strategy: a case study of e-brand Website analysis. In proceedings of the *6th Asian Design Conference*, Tokyo, Japan.

Kim, J., & Moon, J. (1998). Designing towards emotional usability in customer interface. *Interacting With Computers, 10*(1), 1-29.

Kim, J., Lee, J., & Choi, D. (2003). Designing emotionally evocative homepages: an empirical study of the quantitative relations between design factors and emotional dimensions. *International Journal of Human Computer Studies, 59*(6), 899-940.

Lam, R. H. M. & Lim, K. H. (2004). Emotions in online shopping: fulfilling customer's needs through providing emotional features and customizing Website features. In proceedings of the *Twenty-Fifth Annual International Conference on Information Systems*, Washington D. C., United States: December 12-15.

Lee, K. (1998). Sensibility ergonomics: needs, concepts, methods and applications. *Journal of the Ergonomics Society of Korea, 17*(1), 91-102.

Liang, T. P., & Lai, H. J. (2002). Effect of store design on consumer purchases: an empirical study of on-line bookstores. *Information & Management, 39*(6), 431.

Mattila, A. S. (2001). Do emotional appeals work for hotels? An exploratory study. *Journal of Hospitality & Tourism Research,* 25(1), 31-45.

Mehrabian, A., & Russell, J. A. (1974). *An Approach to Environmental Psychology*, MIT Press, Cambridge, MA.

Nevitt, J. (2000) Evaluating Small Sample Approches for Model Test Statistics in Structural Equation Modeling. Paper presented at the Annual Meeting of the American Educational Research Association.

O'Shaughnessy, J. & O'Shaughnessy, N. J. (2003). *The marketing power of emotions*. Oxford, NY: Oxford University Press.

Richins, M. L. (1997). Measuring emotions in the consumption experience. *Journal of Consumer Research* (24), 127-146.

Schenkman, B., & Jonsson, F. (2000). Aesthetics and preferences of web page. *Behaviour and Information Technology, 19*(4), 367-377.

Travis, D. (2000). *Emotional branding: how successful brands gain the irrational edge*. Prima Publishing, California.

Webster, J. & Martocchio, J. J. (1992). Microcomputer playfulness: development of a measure with workplace implications. *MIS Quarterly,* 16(2), 201–226.

Wong, G. (2005). 10 Best honeymoon spots: travel agents pick their favorite destinations for newlyweds; luxury, spa resorts top trends. Retrieved from http://money.cnn.com/2005/06/08/pf/best_honeymoons/.

The Contribution of Technology-Based Heritage Interpretation to the Visitor Satisfaction in Museums

Sofía Reino[a]
Nicole Mitsche[b]
Andrew J. Frew[a]

[a]SITI Research Centre
School of Business and Enterprise
Queen Margaret University College
{sreinopardinas; afrew}@qmuc.ac.uk

[b]Tourism, School of Arts, Design, Media & Culture
University of Sunderland
nicole.mitsche@sunderland.ac.uk

Abstract

The tradition of heritage interpretation is moving away from purely conservational and educational goals to an entertainment- and experience-oriented interpretative provision. New technologies are gaining prominence in museums to enhance visitors' mindfulness, subsequent learning outcomes and satisfaction. Extant research literature reflects technology-based heritage interpretation; however, such studies implement predetermined outputs which have never been tested by the demand side. This paper seeks to assess technology-mediated heritage interpretation, merging both theory from the museums management and customer satisfaction literatures, and applying Importance-Performance Analysis. Results reveal that new technology does not represent a substitute for other interpretative applications. Its appropriate use in those museums with a traditional interpretative layout enhances displays′ multisensory provision and visitors′ perceived interactivity. The use of technology is more appreciated in traditional museums than in those with live interpretation.

Keywords Tourism, ICT, heritage interpretation, Importance-Performance Analysis, museums.

1 Introduction

Information and Communication Technologies (ICT) are affecting the *modus operandi* of entire industries (Crowston & Myers, 2004). As it has progressively taken place in other areas, museums are increasing their use of ICT, not only to support management operations, through data collection and analysis (Sheldon, 1997), but also to be directly used by visitors, in an attempt to enhance their experience of the exhibition. Publications which examine the use of technologies in heritage interpretation - both from the computer science and museum curatorship perspective - emphasise the benefits of technology implementation in heritage interpretation (Chalmers & Rushmeier, 2002; Beeho & Prentice, 1995). Museums have changed from the imposing sites designed to preserve relics and to exhibit collections, to places where a mix of enjoyment, learning and experience outcomes are also pursued (Moscardo, 1996). Furthermore, museums, as heritage attractions, are an important element of the tourism destination and must adjust to new consumers' needs (MacDonald & Alsford, 1991). On the other side, some authors consider that museums should maintain strict guidelines in their exhibits, making sure that no place has been given to the misinterpretation of the past (Uzzel, 1989) and react against a possible "over-interpretation", which might not leave place for the imagination (Meyer, 1993). According to some authors ICT increase museums' potential to compete with the entertainment industry (MacDonald & Alsford, 1991). However, little research has been carried out from the demand-side perspective and this study aims to address this gap in research using the Importance-Performance analysis to assess consumers' preferences in technology-based heritage interpretation.

2 Theoretical Background

ICT in museums is no longer confined to the support of data entry operations (MacDonald & Alsford, 1991). The increased demand for heritage-related activities, the continuous developments in technological appliances and museums' increased interest in attracting larger numbers of visitors have stimulated further developments in ICT usage to support heritage interpretation. Heritage interpretation - the process by which the history behind objects is packaged and offered to customers (Ashworth, 1990) - is considered an essential feature of the visitors' experience, due to the relevance that heritage has acquired as part of the tourism destination and the need to increase museums' competitiveness. The field of ICT and heritage interpretation has been extensively researched (Veltman, 2005). Some studies have approached the effectiveness of technological appliances in museums, such as Grinter, Aoki, Hurst, Szymanski, Thornton, and Woodruff (2002), whose research examined visitor use of mobile audio and visual devices. The work presented by these authors was carried out through interviews, bringing an insight in the understanding of how certain types of devices might enable social interactions when visiting a museum. Other works examine the introduction of specific technological devices, such as cinematic techniques in multimedia museum guide (Rocchi, Stock, Zancanaro, Kruppa, & Kruger, 2004), or three-dimensional audio devices (Hatala, Kalantari, Wakkary, & Newby, 2004). However, this line of research has been mainly carried out from the computer science perspective, in an attempt to augment the number of visits to museums by introducing 'high-tech' devices. Even though, theories of heritage interpretation have been considered to a certain extent in some of these projects – as for instance, the emotional significance of the exhibitions in Rocchi et al. (2004) – the validity of the adopted variables which measure the effectiveness of these applications has not been tested and arises from preconceived ideas of effectiveness outputs.

During the 17th century museums started to open their displays to the general public, as opposed to their previous exclusive dedication to scholars (Bennett, 1995). However, their interpretative provision was purely focused on educational outcomes (Moscardo, 1996). Nowadays, with the increased demand for heritage-related activities as part of the holidays, museums are becoming an important element of the tourism product, increasing the number of leisure-seekers visiting museums (Uzzel, 1989). On the other side, in social cognition research, entertainment and interactive displayes are now considered to enhance visitors' interest, and therefore, mindfulness and learning outcomes (Mellor, 1991; Moscardo, 1988). Technology-mediated heritage interpretation has been suggested to increase interactivity (Moscardo, 1996), similarly to that one achieved through live interpretation in museums (Beeho & Prentice, 1995), i.e. introducing costumed staff who explain the exhibitions (Alsford & Parry, 1991). However, some authors consider that there is a risk of spoiling some of the special character which distinguishes museums as formal institutions by breaking the boundary between fantasy and reality and eventually affecting the number of visitors (Uzzel, 1989). On the other side MacDonald and Alsford (1991) argue that the developments in technology and mass media communication do not jeopardise museums' special nature, but enhance their exclusivity as the leisure-related institutions where knowledge transfer is research-based, as opposed to the entertainment industry, where reality is commonly not firmly documented. In addition, with the emergence of a more diversified visitor profile, interpretation will have to address very different motivations and knowledge backgrounds, from the educated and experienced consumer who commonly seeks an "individualised, personalised, participative experience", to a more passive tourist who hardly acquires any pre-trip information (Hooper-Greenhill, 1992).

Heritage-related activities, such as visits to museums and centres of heritage interpretation, play a fundamental role in the overall tourism experience – forty per cent of tourism trips have a heritage-related activity (Timothy & Boyd, 2003). Due to the importance of the tourism satisfaction in determining the success of destinations (Kozak & Rimmington, 2000), visitors' preferences need to be recorded and implemented. In tourism, as in other business environments, the concepts "satisfaction" and "quality" have been imprecisely used (Bowen, 2001). According to Tribe and Snaith (1998) questionnaires tended to evaluate satisfaction from the "researcher's view of the world" rather than from the customers' perspective. The attributes which determine the potential achievement of customer satisfaction were stated by the researcher rather than by customers. According to these authors, customers should not only be asked to rate companies' performance in the suggested features, but also the importance that they give to the specific attributes in the purchasing decision. The outputs commonly used for the assessment of technology usage in heritage interpretation is mainly based on those traditional theoretical frameworks, which assume that learning is the only pursued outcome when visiting one of these institutions. Heritage interpretation is commonly acknowledged as an essential element for the understanding of museums' displays (Moscardo, 1996; Prentice, 1993). Aiming to enhance the benefits of heritage interpretation, ICT is currently being introduced as an interpretative instrument (MacDonald & Alsford, 1991). However, no research has been conducted to evaluate the demand side perspective as regards to technology-based interpretative provision. Therefore, this study is a first step in approaching the assessment of tourism satisfaction, as regards to the use of technology in heritage interpretation.

3 Methodology

This research aims to introduce the demand-side assessment method for technology implementation in heritage interpretation. Therefore, the Importance-Performance analysis (IPA) - commonly used in customer satisfaction studies (Ennew, Reed, & Binks, 1993) - has been here implemented to study visitors' predilection/dislike of technology implementation in museums, enabling visitors to assess the validity of each dependent variable of the study. In addition, relationships between the use of specific technology and the potential effectiveness outcomes are assessed enabling the satisfaction-dissatisfaction evaluation.

3.1 Importance-Performance Analysis

Importance-Performance Analysis (IPA) is the name given to the research instrument used in this investigation. This tool has been widely used in a variety of fields for the assessment of customer satisfaction (Tribe & Snaith, 1998). It stems from work developed by Fishbein (1967) where attitude is related to belief and evaluation and the method uses the confirmation/disconfirmation concept further developed by Oliver (1980) and Churchill and Surprenant (1982). In essence IPA brings together measures of both attributes "importance" and "performance" into a two-dimensional matrix (Fig. 1), in order to facilitate the data interpretation and analysis of results (Oh, 2001).

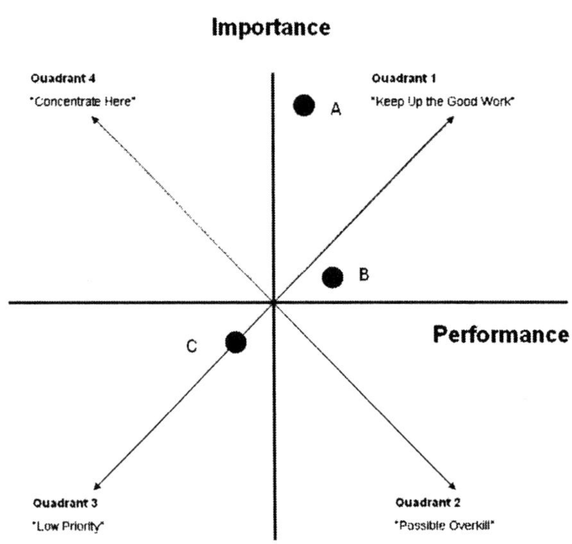

Fig 1. Traditional Importance-Performance Grid (Oh, 2001)

Quadrant 1, "keep up the good work", represents both those attributes which customers consider essential and in which clients have a positive perception of the company's performance. Similarly, "possible overkill" in Quadrant 2 shows those attributes of relatively little importance for customers, but where the company performs well. The third quadrant, so-called "low priority", represents attributes which customers rated of the lowest importance and performance and which are expected to receive a low priority in management decisions. Quadrant 4 represents those attributes in which the company needs to focus their efforts, as customers identify those as the most important to their purchase decisions. The Importance-Performance matrix has been adapted in this project to identify visitors' preferences in technology use for heritage interpretation purposes. The study consisted in a survey, which was carried out in two museums with different types of interpretative provision. One includes live interpretation and another one has no live interpretation, but incorporates the use of technology in its explanatory provision. Both of them also introduced some traditional interpretation, whose effect on customer satisfaction has also been surveyed.

3.2 The Survey

The survey evaluates the Importance-Performance of learning, entertainment and experience outcomes – commonly acknowledged as the main goals of heritage interpretation (Moscardo, 1996) - and the effectiveness of technology-based interpretative solutions in the enhancement of each of these outcomes. Furthermore, it compares the customer satisfaction achieved by technology-supported interpretation to those obtained through live interpretation and other more traditional forms of heritage interpretation. The questionnaire follows a paired structure, allowing customers to state the importance they give to each attribute and their perception of satisfactory performance as regards to each attribute. Tourism satisfaction occurs when companies' performances match customers' expectations. A simplified and adapted version of the methodology used by Tribe and Snaith (1998) has been applied in this study. Instead of the consumers being asked to rate their answers on a five-point scale, these surveys only establish two possible responses: yes and no.

A 120 questionnaire set was equally distributed in two museums with different interpretative provision, namely Beamish Museum (www.beamish.org.uk), a regional open air museum where live interpretation forms a central approach and enables a high level of interaction with the costumed staff without any type of technology as part of the interpretative provision; and The Bowes (www.thebowesmuseum.org.uk), a museum with a more traditional interpretative emphasis and layout, which has introduced some ICT tools, i.e. audio devices and some touch screens. The museums were selected according to the convenience of their location - north east England – and their different heritage interpretation provision – i.e. immersive and traditional. The questions included in the survey were derived from heritage interpretation literature and site visits to the location before. A pilot study was carried out with five participants, previous to the development of the final questionnaire, and their suggestions were considered for the design of the final survey. The data was analysed using SPSS. Sign tests were conducted to analyse the relationship between the expectation and performance and whether "the perception is different to the expectation" (dissatisfaction) or "the perception is equal to the expectation" (satisfaction). Furthermore, a crosstabulation (see Table 1) was also carried out aiming to describe the specific nature of the satisfaction-dissatisfaction results for each attribute and whether visitors considered that each of these attributes were "performed and expected", "not-performed but expected", "performed but not-expected" or "not-performed and not-expected. Finally, the results have been graphically represented in the Performance-Expectation Grid (Figure 2) which is an adaptation of the "Importance-Performance Grid" introduced by Oh (2001). Each attribute has been represented in the relevant/s quadrant/s, according to the results from the crosstabulation.

4 Results

The results are presented in two different sections; one is related to the analysis of the different interpretative elements which have been included in the research and the other one relates to the achievement of the studied outcomes "learning", "entertainment" and "experience" through technology-based interpretation as opposed to "live interpretation" and traditional interpretative devices. Both types of results will refer to the sign tests which have been carried out as part of the exploratory stage, the Crosstabulation which brings in a deeper understanding of the results (Table 1) and the Expectation-Performance Grid (Fig. 2 and Fig. 3) which graphically represents the results for the specific devices (Fig. 2) and for the specific outcomes (Fig. 3).

Table 1. Crosstabulation and Chi-square - Comparison between Museums

	Perf.-Exp. (%)		N. Perf.-Exp. (%)		Perf.-N.Exp. (%)		N.Perf.-N.Exp. (%)		
	Bea	TBw	Bea	TBw	Bea	TBw	Bea	TBw	Sig.
Entertainment Outcomes	96.7	93.3	1.7	5.0	0.0	1.7	1.7	0.0	0.386
Learning Outcomes	65.0	61.7	21.7	36.7	10.0	0.0	3.3	1.7	**0.034***
Experience Outcomes	88.3	81.7	1.7	18.3	5.0	0.0	5.0	0.0	**0.020**
Interpretation Provision	65.0	63.3	28.3	36.7	6.7	0.0	0.0	0.0	0.098
Staff Explanations	81.7	96.7	5.0	1.7	11.7	1.7	1.7	0.0	0.064
Written Information	20.0	93.3	58.3	0.0	0.0	6.7	21.7	0.0	**0.000***
Touch Screens.	0.0	5.0	28.3	33.3	0.0	0.0	71.7	61.7	0.158
Audio Devices.	6.7	76.7	25.0	5.0	0.0	15	68.3	3.3	**0.000***
Interaction with Objects	30.0	55.0	11.7	18.3	10.0	13.3	48.3	13.3	**0.001***
Poster	8.3	88.3	23.3	5.0	1.7	5.0	66.7	1.7	**0.000***
Combination of Elements	28.3	88.3	28.3	8.3	3.3	3.3	40.0	0.0	**0.000***

*** p<0.05**

This table represents the percentage of people who falls into each category, being the categories "People who found and have expected the attribute" (Perf.-Exp.), "People who did not found but have expected the attribute" (N.Perf.-Exp.), "People who found but did not expected the attribute" (Perf.-N.Exp.) and "People who did not found have not expected the attribute" (N.Perf-N.Exp.). Both museums are presented within this table, Beamish Museum (Bea) and The Bowes (TBw).

Demographic data was recorded but no significant differences in the results, related to the respondents' profile, were identified. So it was decided to skip this information in favour to other.

4.1 Interpretative Devices

Different results have been achieved within the technology-related devices. According to the results arisen on the sign test, high levels of customer satisfaction were achieved in both museums as regards to the attribute "touch screens" as 83 out of the 120 respondents were satisfied. Table 1 shows that 66.7% of the sample stated they did not expect and did not find touch screens in any of these museums. According to Moscardo (1996) touch screens are considered to enhance visitors' interactivity with objects, they increase the sense of control over their experience of the place and can provide a large amount of information about the collection in a reduced space. Even though the majority of the visitors stated they did not expect them, as reflected on Fig. 2 still a high percentage of visitors - 33.3% from The Bowes and 28.3% from Beamish – would have appreciated these interpretative devices being included in both museums. No significant differences have been identified when comparing the results from both museums in this attribute. As regards to the audio devices, the sign test reflected that 93 people out of the 120 who participated in the survey evaluated both museums' performance as satisfactory. Table 1 reveals that this satisfaction is due to two different results, 41.5 % of the people expected to find audio devices and did satisfy their expectations, while a still high percentage of people - 35.8% - stated their lack of expectation and performance as regards to this attribute. There are some significant differences between museums as regards to the feature "audio devices". As reflected on Table 1, people who visited Beamish did not expect these devices being introduced and did not find them (68.3%); while in The Bowes they did expect them and found them (76.7%). These results show high levels of satisfaction in both museums, although in opposite directions (see Fig. 2).

As opposed to the use of technology, the traditional types of heritage interpretation were also evaluated in this study. The sign test revealed that 99 visitors were satisfied as regards to the use (or otherwise) of posters for heritage interpretation. Table 1 reveals the different proportions of visitors who expected and achieved this attribute being performed by the visited museum (48.3%) and the people who didn't expect this interpretative provision and did not find it in the visited museum (34.2%). The reason for these contradictory figures is shown on Fig. 2. There are significant differences between museums. The majority of the people who visited The Bowes (93.3%) expected posters been displayed, and 88.3% of the people stated their satisfaction as regards to this attribute. However, only 31.6% of the people who visited Beamish Museum expected to find posters, and the majority, 58.3% did not expect to find them at all in Beamish. This indicates the higher importance of posters in traditional museums as opposed to those with live interpretation. As regards to staff explanations, the sign test has revealed a high level of equality in visitors' responses as 89.2% of them said to both have expected and obtained staff explanations during their visit to the museums and no significant differences have been identified between these museums, 96.7% in The Bowes and 81.7% in Beamish. Finally, Fig. 2 reflected that only 58.3% of the visitors expected and achieved to find a combination of elements within the interpretative provision of these museums and a still important percentage of the visitors, 20%, did not expect to find a combination of elements and did not find it in the museum they have visited. The vast majority of the visitors to The Bowes (88.3%) did expect and report a positive performance by the museum as regards to this attribute. However, Beamish does not show such a satisfactory result and only 40% of the visitors was satisfied by not finding combination of elements.

Generally, visitors reported a high level of perceived interactivity with the objects in both museums. The sign test stated that a total of 88 people out of the 120 participants have reported that they have fulfilled their expectations as regards to this attribute. The results from Table 1 and the Expectation-Performance Grid in Fig. 2 show important differences between museums as regards to this attribute. The majority of the people who visited The Bowes (55%) expected and found their expectations fulfilled, while in Beamish the highest percentage (48.3%) corresponds to those who did not expect and did not find interactivity during their visits. According to Koran, Morrison, Lehman, Koran, and Gandara (1984) visitors are more attracted by those objects that can be touched. Even though live interpretation - performed in Beamish Museum - is considered to improve visitors' interactivity with the exhibition (Timothy & Boyd, 2003), this traditional museum has shown to enhance interactivity with the objects at a greater extent than the museum which provides live interpretation.

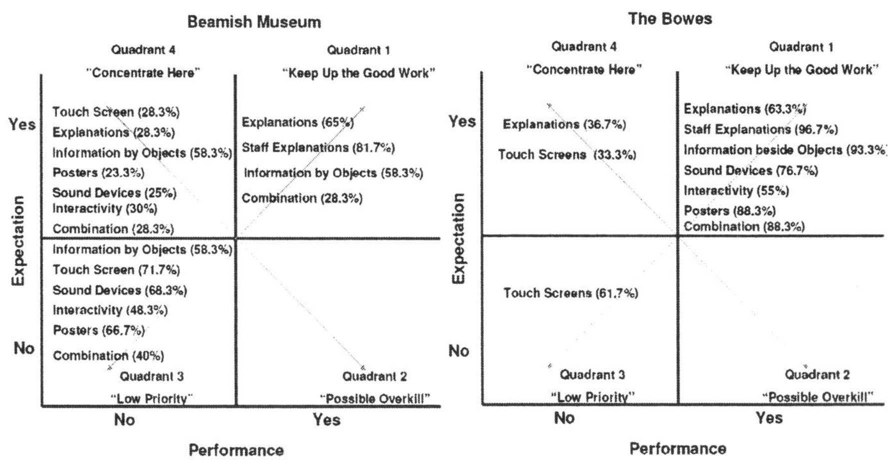

Fig. 2. Expectation-Performance Grid for Interpretative Devices in Beamish Museum and The Bowes.

4.1 Technology-Based Learning, Entertainment and Experience

The different outcomes considered in the heritage interpretation-related literature - learning, entertainment, and experience - have been examined within this study, as well as differences in expectation and performance related to the diverse types of interpretation techniques, namely live interpretation, technology-based and traditional interpretation. The results have been also obtained from the sign test and Table 1 and have been graphically presented in Fig. 3.

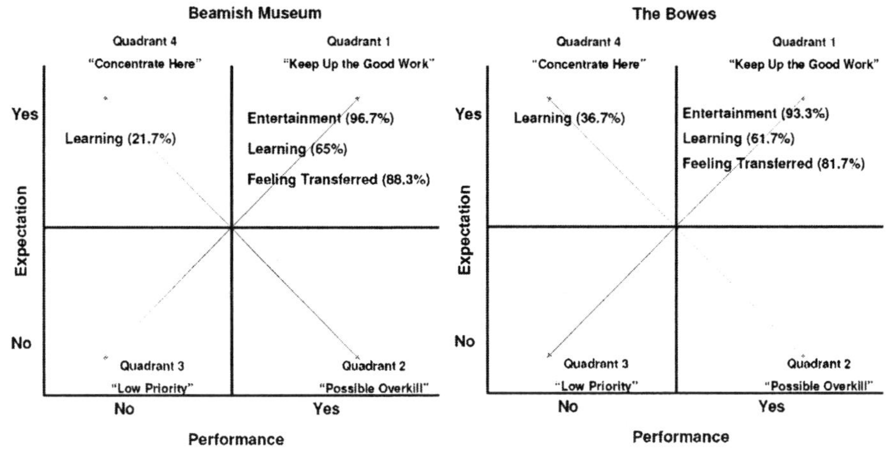

Fig. 3. Expectation-Performance Grid for Learning, Entertainment and Experience Achievement in Beamish Museum and The Bowes.

Learning, entertainment and the experience have been considered similarly important by the visitors to both museums. As shown on Fig. 3, visitors' satisfaction has been achieved as regards to all these three elements. The results show that both museums have similar outcomes regarding the learning attribute, even though still an important percentage (29.2%) of the visitors aim to learn more than they actually did. Nevertheless, the figures show an interesting variation from the percentage of visitors who expected to learn during their visit to Beamish Museum (86.7%), with live interpretation and the visit to The Bowes (98.4%), which could be related to the different types of motivation for visiting a traditional museum, with a higher level of educational purpose or one whose design is based on live interpretation, where visitors might have lower learning motivation.

There are no significant differences between museums as regards to the attribute entertainment, both museums show similar results, with the 96.7% of the visitors from Beamish expecting and achieving to be entertained, and the 93.3% of those who visited The Bowes also expecting and fulfilling this attribute. In Addition, more innovative formulas of interpretative provision, such as the one in Beamish Museum, which fully recreates the era to be displayed and could therefore enhance visitors' experience, do not seem to improve those learning outcomes. The results show that the examined museums have been generally satisfactory in terms of visitors' experiences. The majority of the visitors stated that they expected the feeling of being transferred before coming into the museums and their answers to the survey prove that they have achieved that prospect. Besides, there are no significance differences between both museums' results. The majority of the people who visited Beamish Museum and The Bowes confirmed they have learned, have been entertained and have had a fulfilling experience when visiting these museums.

5 Conclusions and Outlook

Previous research in technology implementation for heritage interpretation purposes has adopted learning as the only output to determine the devices' effectiveness. Several outputs have been identified during the examination of the heritage interpretation-related literature; these are not only learning but also entertainment outcomes as well as the experience itself. However, no consumer input has been considered for the establishment of these effectiveness indicators. Research in customer satisfaction states the need to identify the importance that customers assign to each attribute when assessing their overall satisfaction rate, in an attempt to understand the specific weight of each element in their purchasing decision. This research therefore combines both, tourism and customer satisfaction literature and major heritage interpretation theories, building a bridge between these two cognitive fields to analyse the use of technology implementation in museums. The Importance-Performance theory and the Expectation-Performance Grid have been proved to be of special usefulness in assessing visitor satisfaction as regards to the use of technology for heritage interpretation in museums.

The results show that different requirements apply to the diverse types of museums. The use of a combination of diverse interpretative tools such as posters, audio-visual devices described by Moscardo (1996) as facilitators of a multisensory provision seem not to play an essential role in immersive museums. The live interpretation provided in Beamish Museum seems to facilitate itself visitors' stimulation and as a result the combination of diverse interpretative tools such as posters and audio devices might not be needed for the enhancement of visitor satisfaction. The three elements considered in the literature as the main outcomes of heritage interpretation - learning, entertainment and experience - have been confirmed in the study as highly important for visitors to museums. Both visitors to Beamish and The Bowes have learnt in similar percentages, however, there are some differences between museums as regards to their learning expectations. A higher percentage of visitors to The Bowes than those who visited Beamish Museum have expected the achievement of learning outcomes. Visitor motivations vary should be addressed in further research from the consumer behaviour perspective.

As regards to the use of technology, people were in general terms satisfied without the availability of touch screens, nevertheless, a high percentage of visitors would have appreciated them in both museums. The use of audio devices was appreciated in the traditional museum, while those visiting the immersive museum didn't expect this type of device. Live interpretation seems to provide a state of mindfulness which allows museums' management to dispense with the combination of interpretative devices that would become essential in museums with traditional interpretative provisions. This suggests that technology seems not to represent a substitute for other interpretative applications, but when appropriated used does complement the interpretative provision in traditional museums, enhancing the interactivity and multisensory provision of the exhibition. Furthermore, interactive and multisensory devices, as well as the combination of different elements within the interpretative provision are more appreciated in the general understanding of the collection of traditional sorts of museums than in those with live interpretation. These differences between museums suggest that further research should then be directed to identify devices which enhance visitors' mindfulness in traditional museums, as a way to increase their competitiveness with museums that provide live interpretation.

Although there are some attempts in the literature to classify the different types of interpretation which might be offered by museums, these are too general and do not include the specific devices into specific categories. Therefore, further research aiming to define the different levels of heritage interpretation is required, developing categories from the most basic interpretation, which would be brought by the merely display of artefacts to the most sophisticated one which would be represented by the live interpretation/virtual reality, where the past is fully recreated and visitors' mindfulness and attention is at its highest. This study has practical implications for museums management, related to technology enhancement. Especially traditional museums are expected to engage in IT-related interpretation to enhance learning, experience and entertainment. The sector still needs more innovative ideas, and further research is needed to analyse the status quo of current IT use in museums.

There were some restrictions in the scope of this work, but these also point to opportunities for further research, e.g. the small museums' sample - only two - constrained the suitability to generalise the findings. This is thus a foundation study which aims to set the basics for further research, and should therefore be extended including examples from more museums. Furthermore, the application of this method to museums where a wider range of ICT applications were available would increase the validity of the results.

References

Alsford, S. & D. Parry (1991). Interpretive Theatre. A Role on Museums? *Museum Management and Curatorship* 10(1): 8-23.

Ashworth, G. (1990). The Historic Sites of Groningen; Which is Sold to Whom? *Marketing Tourism Places*. G. Ashworth & B. Goodall. Routledge, London.

Beeho, A. J. & R.C. Prentice (1995). Evaluating the Experiences and Benefits Gained by Tourists Visiting a Socio-Industrial Heritage Museum: And Application of ASEB Grid Analysis to Blists Hill Open-Air Museum, The Ironbridge Gorge Museum, United Kingdom. *Museum Management and Curatorship* 14(3): 229-251.

Bennett, T. (1995). *The Birth of the Museum: History, Theory, Politics*. Routledge, London.

Bowen, D. (2001). Antecedents of Consumer Satisfaction and Dis-satisfaction (CS/D) on Long-haul Inclusive Tours - A Reality Check on Theoretical Considerations. *Tourism Management* 22(49): 61.

Chalmers, A. & H. Rushmeier (2002). Computer Graphics in Art History and Archaeology. *IEEE Computer Graphics and Application*, September/October.

Churchill, G. & C. Surprenant (1982). An Investigation into Determinants of Customer Satisfaction. *Journal of Marketing Research* 19(491): 504.

Crowston, K. & M.D. Myers (2004). Information Technology and the Transformation of Industries: Three Research Perspectives. *Journal of Strategic Information Systems* 13: 5-28.

Ennew, C.T., G.V. Reed & M.R. Binks. (1993). Importance-Performance Analysis and the Measurement of Service. European Journal of Marketing, 27(2): 59-70.

Fishbein, M. (1967).*Readings in Attitude Theory and Measurement*. Wiley, New York.

Grinter, R.E., P.M. Aoki, A. Hurst, M.H. Szymanski, J.D. Thornton & A. Woodruff. (2002). Revisiting the Visit: Understanding How Technology Can Shape the Museum Visit. In proceedings of *ACM Conference on Computer Supported Cooperative Work*. New Orleans, Louisiana, USA: November 16-20, 2002.

Hatala, M.L., Kalantari, R. Wakkary & K. Newby (2004). Ontology and Rule Based Retrieval of Sound Objects in Augmented Audio Reality System for Museum Visitors. In proceedings of the *ACM symposium on Applied computing*, Nicosia, Cyprus, pp. 1045–1050.

Hooper-Greenhill, E. (1992). *Museums and the Shaping of Knowledge*. Routledge, London.

Koran, J., L. Morrison, J.R. Lehman, M.L. Koran & L. Gandara (1984). Attention and Curiosity in Museums. *Journal of Research in Science Teaching* 21: 357-363.

Kozak, M. & M. Rimmington (2000). Tourism Satisfaction with Mallorca, Spain, as an Off-season Holiday Destination. *Journal of Travel Research* 38(3): 260-270.

MacDonald, G.F. & S. Alsford (1991). The Museum as Information Utility. *Museum Management and Curatorship* 10: 305-311.

Mellor, A. (1991). Experiential Learning through Integrated Project Work: an Example from Soil Science. *Journal of Geography in Higher Education* 15: 135-149.

Meyer, S. (1993). Voyage to Discover or Road to Nowhere? *Museums Journal* 93(9): 24-25.

Moscardo, G. (1988). Towards a Cognitive Model of Visitor Responses in Interpretative Centres. *Journal of Environment Education* 20: 29-38.

Moscardo, G. (1996). Mindful Visitors - Heritage and Tourism. *Annals of Tourism Research* 23(2): 376-397.

Oh, H. (2001). Revisiting importance-performance analysis. *Tourism Management* 22(6): 617-627.

Oliver, R.L. (1980). A Cognitive Model of the Antecedents and Consequences of Satisfaction Decisions. *Journal of Marketing Research* 17(46): 49.

Prentice, R.C. (1996). Tourism as Experience. Tourists as Consumers. Insight and Enlightenment. Inaugural Lecture. Queen Margaret University College, Edinburgh p.55.

Prentice, R.C. (1993). *Tourism and Heritage Attractions*. Routledge, London.

Rocchi, C., O. Stock, M. Zancanaro, M. Kruppa & A. Kruger (2004). The Museum Visit: Generating Seamless Personalized Presentations on Multiple Devices. In proceedings of *Intelligent User Interfaces IUI 2004*. Madeira, PT: January 2004.

Sheldon, P. (1997). *Tourism Information Technology*. CAB, Oxford.

Timothy, D. J. & W. Boyd (2003). *Heritage Tourism*. Pearson Education Limited, Harlow.

Tribe, J. & T. Snaith (1998). From SERVQUAL to HOLSAT: Holiday Satisfaction in Varadero. *Tourism Management* 19(1): 25-34.

Uzzel, D. (1989) Introduction: The Visitor Experience. *The Visitor Experience*. D. Uzzel. Belhaven Press, London.

Veltman, K.H. (2005). Challenges for ICT/UCT Applications in Cultural Heritage. *e-Journal of the Humanities and Philology Studies of the UOC* 7 May.

Veverka, J. A. (1996). Interpretation as a Management Tool. *Trends* 34(4): 7-9.

Towards a Web-based Marketing Process Framework for City-based National Tourism Organizations

Mandy Lo[a]
Rob Law[b]

[a] Hong Kong Trade Development Council, Hong Kong
mandy.mk.lo@tdc.org.hk

[b] School of Hotel & Tourism Management,
The Hong Kong Polytechnic University, Hong Kong
hmroblaw@polyu.edu.hk

Abstract

The applications of Internet technology to tourism have led to the emergence of web marketing, which provides tourism organizations with a new opportunity to interact directly with stake holders. Although national tourism organizations [NTOs] have been using the Internet to promote their destinations and develop integral and consumer focused marketing programs, prior research on web marketing development in NTOs is limited. This paper reports on a study which formulated a marketing process framework for city-based NTOs. The framework was then applied to the NTO websites in Singapore and Hong Kong, two primary city-based travel destinations in Asia. Managerial implications for the success of web marketing are also provided.

Keywords: NTO, websites, Singapore, Hong Kong, web marketing

1 Introduction

Since the early 1990s, the growth of Internet technology has had a large impact on the tourism industry. Specifically, Internet technology has enabled the tourism industry, including tourism organizations, to directly reach worldwide customers in a cost effective way (Buhalis, 1998, 2003). In addition, the Internet can help tourism organizations implement different kinds of promotional activities and supplementing, if not replacing, offline promotion tools. This change is important as the Internet is generally considered as a multi-promotion tool and distribution channel (Gretzel, Yuan, & Fesenmaier, 2000). In the travel and tourism industry, customers search for travel related information, make online air ticket bookings, online room reservations, and other online purchases. Due to the increasing popularity of Internet applications, most tourism organizations such as hotels, airlines, and travel agencies have embraced Internet technology as part of their marketing strategy (Carson & Sharma, 2002). Since then, web marketing has become a core marketing development in travel and tourism.

In response to the increasing demand of Internet applications, the tourism industry has developed a high level of interest in using the technology as a global distribution channel to different parties in the world (Fesenmaier, Gretzel, Hwang, & Wang, 2003). In the context of destination promotion, the Internet provides new opportunities for tourism organizations to promote their destinations by developing integral and consumer focused marketing programs. Despite the existence of such opportunities, the existing tourism literature only has a limited number of prior studies on web marketing development of NTOs, and virtually no prior study has been attempted to analyze city-based NTOs. At present, the city-based NTOs are under unprecedented pressure of effectively promoting their destinations. In view of such an emerging challenge, this study is to analyze the marketing concept of city-based NTOs and the impact of web function on NTOs. More importantly, this study aims to develop a web marketing process framework for city-based NTO websites. The proposed framework is then applied to the websites of Singapore Tourism Board (STB) and Hong Kong Tourism Board (HKTB), two city-based NTOs in Asia that have used the Internet as one of their major marketing tools for promoting their travel destinations. The results should be able to offer valuable insights for tourism practitioners and policy-makers for NTOs in general, and for city-based NTOs in particular.

2 Literature Review

Web-based marketing began in the early 1990s when business attempted to use the Internet for commercial and financial purposes to promote various products and services. The development of the Internet and its growth as a business tool have created new opportunities for marketers to target consumers, achieving the marketing goals and objectives (Morrison, Mills, Chuvessiriporn, & Ismail,, 2002). The success of web-based marketing is evident as the percentage of online travel bookers who had used the Internet for their travel related purchase increased from 29 per cent in 2003 to 40 per cent in 2004 in the United States (TIA, 2004). The World Tourism Organization contends that the Internet is the ideal medium for promoting travel and tourism (WTO, 1999).

With the use of Internet based technologies, the travel and tourism industry has been able to promote services in a variety of ways ranging from mass marketing to mass customization (Morrison *et al.*, 2002). In addition, websites provide tourism organizations like NTOs a new opportunity to interact directly with individual tourists, and to attract them to visit specific travel destinations (Fesenmaier *et al.*, 2003). NTOs are non-profit, small and medium-sized, and information intensive organizations that provide a wide range of activities to co-ordinate the diverse components of the tourism industry (Gartrell, 1988). In this aspect, the role of NTOs is to liaise, collect and provide information to both consumers and the industry in order to facilitate tourism promotions and development of the specific travel destinations. Since the introduction of the Internet to non-official bodies, the management of NTOs has begun to realize that Internet marketing is an inseparable activity, which often determines parts of their overall marketing endeavor (Fesenmaier *et al.*, 2003). Specifically, using Internet technology enables NTOs to reach a large number of travellers at a relatively low cost and to provide more in-depth and quality information than traditional media. As a consequence, NTOs can better promote their tourist attractions and services, present associated organizations more equally, and collect customer information for effective customer relationship management.

Web marketing has become a new medium that offers the chance to increase richness and reach in a way that changes nearly all practices of the tourism marketplace (Dierich, Sy & Schertler, 2002). Likewise, the role of a NTO changes from simple distribution of information materials and administration of a destination towards global marketing and management of the specific destination (Dierich et al., 2002). Different from the past, NTOs no longer regard the Internet as peripheral and the territory of the IT Department (WTO, 1999). Web marketing now becomes an integral and important component of their marketing programs. In particular, innovative marketing and management strategies have evolved in the areas of web development, web advertising/promotion, e-commerce activities, customer relationship management, and the use of online destination management systems (Fesenmaier *et al.*, 2003).

According to Fesenmaier et al. (2003), there are three major stages in the development of NTO websites, including publishing, database retrieval and personalized interaction. The first stage makes available the same information to all users in a form of thousands of pages, pictures, sound and video. Later, when the website becomes mature, it then moves to the second stage which combines the publishing power of the first stage and responses to user requests. In other words, the interactivity and dialogue get started at this stage. The third stage requires the capabilities of the previous stages and customization of content and functions to the needs of specific users. In this way, the NTOs use web-based technologies in different approaches and with varying intensity to fit the needs of different cultural backgrounds, financial resources, and marketing objectives (Gzetzel et al., 2000).

The success of an NTO's web marketing strategy largely depends on the design of a website. Web designers have emphasized that an effective website design can be easily and rapidly developed by utilizing prototypes to identify its targeting users (Kentie, 2002; Niederst, 2006). Generally speaking, several stages are involved in web design. First, it defines the needs, which include the clients' needs and users' needs. Second, it defines ideas by collecting the concepts from participants. Third, the design is defined to build the website after the collection of ideas. The final step is delivery which enables the clients to construct their applications. This would determine the cost-benefit analysis for website development and support. Likewise, McCarthy and Aronson (2000) proposed an e-Commerce Web site Design Model to explain the concept of marketing integration in order to support consumer satisfaction. The framework was classified into four levels explaining customers' desire and response. In the model, the level of development of a website is classified as introductory, informative, interactive and intelligence. The model, however, only provided brief description of desired response and without any detailed discussions of what should be included in each stage. Still, this model forms the basis of this present study on city-based NTO websites.

3 Methodology and the Established Framework

This study uses a qualitative research approach. The qualitative research can be broadly defined as 'any kind of research that produces findings not arrived at by means of statistical procedures' (Strauss & Corbin, 1990, p.17). The qualitative methods can be used to better understand some lesser-known behaviors as well as to explore more in-depth information that may be difficult to convey quantitatively (Strauss & Corbin, 1990). In this study, in-depth interviews were firstly conducted with three senior executives and one web consultant of tourism organizations in Singapore and Hong Kong in a form of open-ended questions to form the initial framework, which was based on the e-Commerce Web site Design Model proposed by McCarthy and Aronson (2000). A jury of executive opinion group with ten stakeholders for STB and HKTB websites was then formed to refine and validate the proposed framework in a focus group discussion. A content analysis was then performed by three people to evaluate the HKTB and STB websites on the basis of the developed framework. Findings were finally verified by two leaders of tourism organizations. All participants were selected by convenience sampling and the research was conducted in the period June to December 2004.

3.1 Theoretical Studies The Two-Way Process

This study extends the marketing concept of two-way channel to city-based NTO websites. This approach attempts to represent the importance of the inter-relationship between city-based NTOs and web users by the impact of the Internet at a marketing-oriented level. NTO websites mainly serve as an information gateway for facilitating communications between NTOs and users. The two-way concept of the marketing role for city-based NTOs as indicated in Figure 1 clearly shows the flow and relationship between NTOs and their website users in an interactive and user-based environment. With the high level of interactivity of Internet technology, NTOs can expand their scope of data collection and user profile analysis on the basis of users' responses.

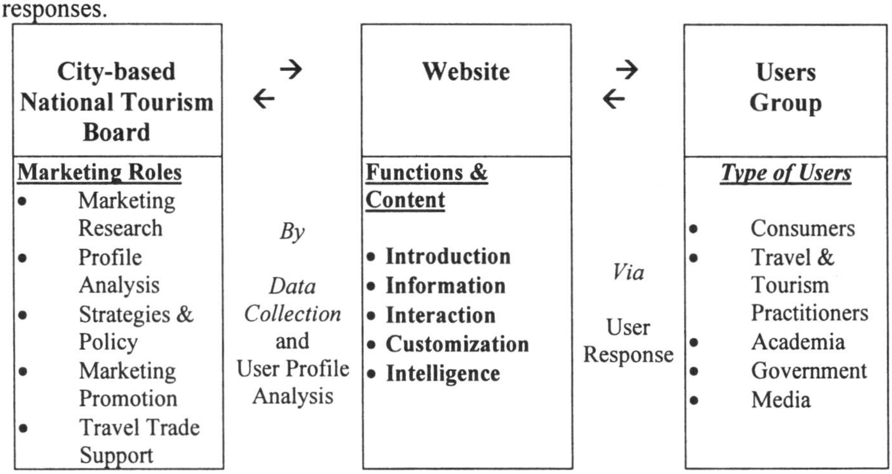

Fig 1. The "Two-way Channel" Concept of the Marketing Role in City-based NTOs by the Impact of Website Functions

3.2 Theoretical Studies The Proposed Framework

The proposed process framework for city-based NTO websites comprises five stages, each of which consists of different levels of functions. The levels in each stage move from simple to sophisticated applications. The framework is for city-based NTOs to adopt Internet technologies for their promotional and marketing purposes. Moreover, the five stages are equally important for a city-based NTO when using web marketing for promotion. The five stages can be grouped as "4I+1C" and are summarized in Table 1, and the remaining paragraphs in this section discuss these stages and their associated levels.

Table 1. A Web-based Marketing Process Framework for City-based NTO

Stage		Number of Levels
I	Introduction	1
II	Information	6
III	Interaction	2
IV	Customization	2
V	Intelligence	3

3.3 Introduction (Stage I)

This stage of the model consists of one level (Table 2). The level is developed on web page design and content presentation templates, together with brand building of a tourist destination. It also provides the name of the tourism destination together with a brief introduction on one single screen.

Table 2. Web-based Marketing Process Framework for NTO – Stage I (Introduction)

Stage	*Level*	Functions
Introduction	**1**	• Design web page layout and content presentation templates • Brand building of a tourist destination with market-specific/focus • Name of the tourist destination • A brief introduction about the tourist destination on one screen

3.4 Information (Stage II)

There are six levels of functions in this stage, which range from an initial phase to other phases of complexity (Table 3). The function in Level 1 includes brief information and description with photos of a tourist destination that show the geographic location and "how to get around" map. Level 2 is a basic level of interaction including the provision of a wide range of information, adding links to external providers of related services, flashing photos and graphics, and allowing online enquiries, a search function and a glossary. Level 3 provides in-depth and detailed information of the travel destination and lists events, activities and new tourism products of the destination. Online customer support in the form of FAQs is available to include tourist-related information like epidemics, war, government policy, passport/visa requirements, safety information and a currency converter. Level 4 contains the "themed" itineraries with special interest tours. Travelers can design and plan their own trips in a flexible and easy way. Level 5 consists of a more advanced technology that shows the visuals of the destination in a form of multi-media. Level 6 provides research statistics and annual reports of the travel destination. The NTO develops its own extranet on marketing plans and promotions, market intelligence, product updates and career development.

Table 3. Web-based Marketing Process Framework for NTO – Stage II (Information)

Stage	Level	Functions
Information	1	• Brief information (geographic location, how to get around and maps), with description and photos of the tourist attraction
	2	• Provide a wide-range of information (with sound effect), adding links to external providers of related services (hotels, airlines, travel agents, tourist attractions, government departments, airport) • Have flashing photos and graphics • Allow online enquiry, search function, glossary (language usage)
	3	• Provide in-depth and detailed information • List all the events/activities/new products of the tourist destination • Online customer support in the form of FAQs including all tourist-related information (epidemics, war, policy, safety)
	4	• Provide special interest tours and "themed" itineraries
	5	• Multi-media effects with animation, sound, video clips, virtual tours, web-cams and wallpaper
	6	• Provide research statistics, annual report • Develop extranet on market intelligence, product development, career opportunities

3.5 Interaction (Stage III)

Stage III has an interactive component that relates to "instant response" (Table 4). At Level 1, the products and services become a tool for exchange of information. This provides flexibility in planning itineraries for "Do-it-yourself" elements and online consumer promotion. At Level 2, an online forum and/or "members' corner" is created to show visitors' sharing of experiences and media coverage of the travel destination.

Table 4. Web-based Marketing Process Framework for NTO – Stage III (Interaction)

Stage	Level	Functions
Interaction	1	• Products and services as a tool for exchange of information • Itinerary planning for DIY elements • Online promotion e.g. online consumer contest
	2	• Visitors' sharing of experiences / media coverage of the tourist destination on an online forum and/or "members' corner"

3.6 Custo mization (Stage IV)

City-based NTO websites at Stage IV have reached a high level of sophistication (Table 5). At Level 1, they have market specific customization with the same content but local adaptation in the source markets. The local adaptation is due to the differences in languages, culture, and legal requirements. Level 2 of this stage provides segment specific information adapted to the market which includes entry visa requirements and cultural travel interests. Promotions in the source markets are identified by geographical locations, age groups, and target market segments along with the marketing strategy.

Table 5. Web-based Marketing Process Framework for NTO – Stage IV (Customization)

Stage	Level	Functions
Customization	1	• Market specific customization with local adaptation in the source markets, due to cultural differences, legal requirements, different languages (same content) • Same content in different languages
	2	• Segment specific information i.e. entry visas, cultural travel interests • Market promotions by geographical locations, languages, age groups and market segments e.g. tactical sales promotions, event promotions

3.7 Intelligence (Stage V)

Stage V is a more sophisticated stage. As revealed in Table 6, Level 1 utilizes intelligent agents to build and maintain user profiles, provides market research analysis based on the collected data, and offers advanced searching for a specified type of users' needs. It is based on users' desire and response, and to build a good reference by understanding individuals' needs for an effective integrated market planning and strategy at Level 2. At Level 3, travel trends are available in the form of tourism policies, travelers' behavior, as well as tourism products and development.

Table 6. Web-based Marketing Process Framework for NTO – Stage V (Intelligence)

Stage	Level	Functions
Intelligence	1	• Utilize intelligent agents to build and maintain user profiles • Market research analysis based on data collection i.e. personal details • Advanced search for a specified type of users' needs
	2	• Based on users' desire and response to understand individuals' needs for an effective integrated marketing planning and strategy i.e. integrated marketing programs
3.1	3	• Travel trend in the form of tourism polices, travelers' pattern and tourism products

4 Empirical Findings of HKTB and STB Websites

Different NTOs have recently invested in Internet technology in order to support a new way of marketing communication networks towards the Information Age in this decade (WTO, 1999). In this study, the city-based NTO websites in Singapore (www.visitsingapore.com) and Hong Kong (www.discoverhongKong.com), both are in Asia and have similar backgrounds in terms of economic and tourism development (Cheung & Law, 2002), were chosen for analysis in this study. In these two places, tourism is considered as one of the major economic pillars with strong government support. In addition, both destinations are competitors in general and in particular in tourism. These two NTOs thus have put a lot of efforts to promote their destinations in different marketing channels including web marketing. These NTOs are generally able to demonstrate a high level of integration of the Internet as one of the major marketing tools.

On the basis of the developed web-based marketing framework as presented in the previous section, a content analysis was performed on the extent of achievement of the NTO websites in Singapore and Hong Kong by checking the existence of the needed functions for each level in different stages using Yes/No. According to Cheung and Law (2002), such a method is direct and more accurate than complicated methods. While "Y" (Yes) showed that the NTO had the level of function indicated, "N" (No) indicated such a function is not available on the website. Counting the Y/S occurrences can imply the level of sophistication on a website. Table 7 presented next shows the findings of the content analysis of the two websites. As a whole, both websites are quite similar in terms of different levels of achievement. On the STB website, there were 29 "Yes" and 2 "No" among the 31 feature analyzed, whereas the corresponding numbers for the HKTB website were 30 and 1 respectively.

Table 7. Comparative Results of HKTB and STB Websites

		HKTB Website	**STB Website**
Stage	**Level**	**Y/N**	**Y/N**
Introduction	1	4Y	3Y/1N
Information	1-6	14Y/1N	15Y
Interaction	1-2	5Y	5Y
Customization	1-2	3Y	2Y/1N
Intelligence	1-3	4Y	4Y
Summary:		**30Y / 1N**	**29Y / 2N**

Generally speaking, both city-based NTO websites offered rich and attractive information for their destinations. This indicates both NTOs have made large investments to enable their websites to attain a high level of functions. The results of this study showed both city-based NTO websites were in an advanced stage of adopting web marketing. In terms of loading speed, both websites responded rapidly and were easy to access. At the "Introduction" stage, HKTB's website slightly outperformed STB's website. Brief information about the destination was not available on STB's website. At the "Information" stage, HKTB's website provided rich information and attractive photos and graphics in a multi-media form.

However, basic information like "glossary" was missing on the HKTB's website. The "glossary" information is useful for travelers, especially the first-time visitors. Also, both NTO websites have met a high level of functions at the "Interaction" stage. However, there was room for improvement in a couple of aspects. For instance, HKTB's websites could broaden the interaction level with other mirror sites, in addition to the sites in Japan and the U.S. At the stage of "Customization", the HKTB's website was at a more advanced level of development. Although STB's website offered language options, the content of the non-English web pages was not customized to the source market. At the stage of "Intelligence", both city-based NTO websites have reached a high level of functionality. However, it would be valuable to provide an advanced search engine for some sophisticated users and niche market segments. All together, the results of the content analysis indicated that both NTOs closely matched their targeted website development and were very competitive on web marketing promotions and development.

5 Conclusions

Summary

This study has made an initial attempt to address the web marketing issues that are important to travel and tourism in the context of city-based NTOs. Although the issues have rarely been examined in prior research, this study has analyzed the web-based marketing efforts of city-based NTOs. The results of this web-based marketing study of city-based NTOs have led to a few interesting findings. As the competition between the selected city-based NTOs is keen, Singapore and Hong Kong both shared many similarities, be it historical, financial, economic, social, or tourism related development.

Furthermore, the two-way channel concept of the marketing role in city-based NTOs is developed to represent the inter-relationship between NTOs and their stakeholders at a marketing-oriented level. The development of web-based marketing would be one of the key marketing foci for promoting a travel destination in a direct and cost-effective manner. Based on the developed web-based marketing framework for city-based NTOs, one would be able to review the level of functional achievements for individual websites, i.e. STB and HKTB websites in this study. The findings can provide insights and a good reference for the two city-based NTO websites, as well as other city-based NTO websites, to continuously improve and revamp their websites.

Implications to STB and HKTB

The STB website has demonstrated a high level of performance in web-marketing functions. The website, however, can be further enhanced in the "Introduction" stage. This could be done by including brief information with a write-up on the main page. This would offer its users a general idea of a variety of tourist attractions. Also, at the "Customization" stage, the STB website should have some attempts to develop and explore market promotions at a segmentation level. This could expand the marketing networks to different source markets, leading to the far reaching of their target audience in a focus-oriented approach. The necessity for ongoing improvement also goes to the HKTB website. For instance, at the "Information" stage, the website should make the "Contact Us" function using a large and eye-catching icon instead of using a small icon. In addition, it is recommended that the HKTB should create a glossary column on its website. This would provide more useful information to general consumers, especially the first-time visitors, to have a better understanding of the local culture and lifestyle. In order to have an interactive website, HKTB could consider creating a web page showing how the visitors can share their experiences as "sharing is earning" and "earning is sharing". Furthermore, the members' corners could be expanded into an online forum to the main website in order to increase the level of communications with users. At "Customization" stage, the HKTB website could expand the segment specific information to websites in other languages.

Lastly, additional efforts should be spent for the two city-based NTOs to explore their future market planning. This could be accomplished in a few ways. First, both NTO websites should have enhancement in terms of featuring different topics and providing the information that is required in the FAQ section. Second, with the increase of Frequent Independent Travelers (FITs) and its impact on traveling trends from long-haul and short-haul markets, both NTOs should consider enhancing their websites with more optional special interest tours and themed itineraries for tour planners on both English and non-English web pages. Third, with an increase in number of experienced travelers, the availability of advanced search functions for specific types of users would certainly help these sophisticated travelers.

Future Research

A natural extension of this study is to use the developed framework to evaluate the websites of other city-based NTOs. The established framework, albeit useful in its initial development, needs to be further modified from time to time. This ongoing modification is necessary because of rapid changes of computing and networking technologies, as well customer behavior. Also, it would be valuable to investigate if additional stages and/or levels that better reflect the latest development of marketing strategies are incorporated into the modified framework. The involvement of more people in the framework modification would certainly make it more comprehensive. In addition to city-based NTO websites, future endeavors can evaluate the applicability of the framework to NTO websites of other nature.

References

Buhalis, D. (1998). Tourism and information technologies: Past, present, and future. *Tourism Recreation Research.* 25(1), 41-45.

Buhalis, D. (2003). *eTourism – Information Technology for Strategic Tourism Management.* Harlow, Essex: Pearson Education.

Carson, D. & Sharma, P. (2002). A Model of Australian Tourism Information: Implications for Information Systems. In K. W. Wober, A. J. Frew,. & M. Hitz (Eds). *Information and Communication Technologies in Tourism 2002.* Proceedings of the International Conference in Innsbruck, Austria, pp. 49-58.

Cheung, C. & Law, R. (2002). Virtual MICE Promotion: A Comparison of the Official Websites in Hong Kong and Singapore. *Journal of Convention & Exhibition Management.* 4(2). 37-51.

Dierich, J., Sy, R. R. & Schertler, W. (2002). The Use of Internet-Marketing by National Tourism Organizations in Germany – An Empirical Approach. in Wober, K.W, Frew, A.J. and Hitz, M. (Eds). *Information and Communication Technologies in Tourism 2002.* Proceedings of the International Conference in Innsbruck, Austria, pp. 115-125.

Fesenmaier, D., Gretzel, U., Hwang, Y. H. & Wang, Y. (2003). The Future of Destination Marketing: e-Commerce in Travel and Tourism. *International Journal of Tourism Science.* 3(2), 191-200.

Gartrell, R. (1998). *Destination marketing for convention and visitor bureaus.* Dubuque, IA: Kendall/Hunt Publishing Company.

Gretzel, U., Yuan, Y. L., & Fesenmaier, D. R. (2000). Preparing for the New Economy: Advertising Strategies and Changes in Destination Marketing Organizations. *Journal of Travel Research* 39(Nov), 146-156.

Kentie, P. (2002). *Web design tools and techniques.* Berkeley, CA: Peachpit Press.

McCarthy, R. V. & Aronson, J. E. (2000-2001). Activating Consumer Response: A Model For Web Site Design Strategy. *Journal of Computer Information Systems* Winter. 41(2), 2-8.

Morrison, A. M., Mills, J. E., Chuvessiriporn, S., & Ismail, J. (2002). Where Are We Now? An Initial Analysis of Web-based Marketing Issues Affecting Travel and Tourism. In K. W. Wober, A. J. Frew, & M. Hitz (Eds). *Information and Communication Technologies in Tourism 2002.* Proceedings of the International Conference in Innsbruck, Austria, pp. 375-386.

Niederst, J. R. (2006). *Web design in a nutshell.* Sebastopol, CA: O'Reilly.

Strauss, A. & Corbin, J. (1990). *Basics of qualitative research: grounded theory procedures and techniques*. Newbury Park, California: Sage Publications.

TIA (2004). TIA Report Measures Continued Growth in Online Travel. *Press Release.* Travel Industry Association of America, September 9, 2004. Retrieved October 15, 2005 from http://www/tia.org/press.

WTO (1999). *Marketing tourism destinations online: Strategies for the information age*. World Tourism Organization Business Council. Spain: Madrid.

An Assessment of Innovation in Web Marketing: Investigating American Convention and Visitors Bureaus

Florian Zach
Zheng Xiang
Daniel R. Fesenmaier

National Laboratory for Tourism & eCommerce
School of Tourism and Hospitality Management
Temple University, USA
{fzach, philxz, drfez}@temple.edu

Abstract

Innovation has become an increasingly important issue for tourism businesses. The goal of this study was to evaluate innovation in Web marketing by American convention and visitors bureaus and the contribution of website features to the overall success of their Web marketing programs. The results indicate that innovation in Web marketing has been limited in that the majority of the American CVBs focus on basic content provision and website promotional activities. The findings also indicate that there is a perceived gap between the investment in innovative website features and their contribution to the overall Web marketing success.

Keywords: Innovation, web marketing; convention and visitors bureaus.

1 Introduction

The Internet has become the most important communication channel in tourism organizations' marketing activities (Buhalis, 1998, 2000; Wang & Fesenmaier, 2006). Within this context, tourism organizations have been forced to "re-invent" themselves in order to adapt to this new environment (Gretzel, Fesenmaier, Formica & O'Leary, 2006; Poon, 1993). However, the effective use of the Internet in Web marketing remains a substantial challenge for tourism organizations (Werthner & Klein, 1999). Recent research indicates that tourism organizations are faced with many barriers such as a limited budget, lack of leadership capabilities as well as a limited understanding of Internet technologies which constrain their ability to innovate (Buhalis, 2000; Yuan, Gretzel & Fesenmaier, 2003; Gretzel et al., 2006).

The capacity to innovate is becoming increasingly important for tourism organizations (Drucker, 1985; Hjalager, 2002; Prahalad & Hamel, 1990; Sundbo, 1997). Innovation is generally defined as a persistent and purposeful activity that requires long-term commitment and continuous effort (Drucker, 1985). While past studies have emphasized the importance of IT to the success of tourism organizations

(Poon, 1993; Werthner & Klein, 1999; Gretzel, Yuan & Fesenmaier, 2000), the role of innovation as a continuous process has not been well studied. As such, the goal of this study is to provide an understanding of innovation as a continuous effort in the Web marketing programs of American CVBs. Specifically, this study aims to: 1) assess the extent to which American CVBs innovate in their Web marketing efforts; and, 2) evaluate the contribution of these innovations to the overall success of their Web marketing programs.

2 Innovation as the Key to Competitive Advantage

Schumpeter (1947) and Rogers (2003) argue that innovation is the use of new ideas, practices and objects as well as doing things in a new way. Through innovative behaviour, organizations re-invent products, services, and processes to stay ahead of their competitors (Porter, 1985). As pointed out by Drucker (1985), organizations are constantly challenged by environmental change. By recognizing the threats and opportunities and integrating new knowledge, organizations can identify appropriate strategies to exploit the change for their own advantage. Thus, innovation is considered a central activity through which tourism organizations can create value in competition with other destinations (Hjalager, 2002; Ritchie & Crouch, 2000; Weiermair, Peters & Frehse, 2005).

Information technology (IT) has revolutionized the management and operation of businesses in that the effective use of IT allows businesses to increase their power in dealing with stakeholders (Porter & Millar, 1985) and to improve decision making in their marketing and promotion-related activities (Poon, 1993). However, innovations on the Internet, especially those related to marketing activities, are highly mobile as competitors can easily adapt certain website features and implement them into their own websites (Amit & Zott, 2001). As such, organizations are constantly forced to innovate in their Web marketing programs.

Innovations can be either incremental or radical (Nord & Tucker, 1987). Incremental innovation requires only minimal adaptations, while radical innovation, on the other hand, requires the modification of norms and values. Following this perspective, it is argued that the development of the Internet and the consequential rise of Web marketing can be considered as radical, whereas innovations in existing website features are incremental in nature because they focus on improving the current Web marketing strategies.

3 Web Marketing in American CVBs

Web marketing leverages new forms of direct and personalized interactions and transactions between marketers and consumers (Hoffman & Novak, 1996; Parsons, Zeisser & Waitman, 1998). The interactive and networking capabilities of the Internet allow tourism organizations to employ a variety of approaches to attract, engage, retain, and learn about visitors (Buhalis, 2000; Gretzel et al., 2000; Werthner & Klein, 1999; Wang & Fesenmaier, 2006). Recent research by Wang and Fesenmaier (2006) argues that CVBs' Web marketing activities consist of three functional areas: 1) Website content, including information provision related elements such as search functions and listing of attractions and services; 2) Website promotion, consisting of techniques used to attract visitors from other channels such as search engine optimization and advertisements in other websites; and, 3) Website eCommerce, represented by transaction related features that target behavioural outcomes from visitors. Other studies have found that American CVBs are at different stages of development with respect to their capacity to leverage IT (Yuan et al., 2003, 2006; Hanson, 2000; Wang & Fesenmaier, 2006). That is, the higher the stage they are in, the more sophisticated they have become in terms of taking advantage of the Internet as an interactive and networking communication channel. Thus, the use of Internet-based tools in a meaningful and innovative way is crucial to the overall success of the CVB.

4 Research Method

The goal of this study was to assess the extent to which American CVBs innovate in their Web marketing activities and to evaluate the contribution of implemented website features to the overall success of their Web marketing programs. The research methodology used to achieve this goal is outlined in the following sections.

4.1 Sampling and Data Collection

A sample of 554 out of a total of approximately 1,800 American CVBs was randomly selected for this study. A nine-page questionnaire, together with an explanatory cover letter, was sent to CVB directors/CEOs in spring 2006. A free copy of the executive summary of this study was offered as an incentive. Three weeks after the initial mailing a reminder was sent to all CVBs. Two additional mailings were conducted, three and seven weeks after the reminder, respectively, resulting in an overall response rate of 25.8%.

4.2 Measures and Data Analysis

Respondents were first asked to indicate whether their organization has a website and when it was established. Then, items for each type of website feature were identified through a comprehensive literature review (Wang & Fesenmaier, 2006; Kothari & Fesenmaier, 2006; Rita, 2000). Based upon this review respondents were asked to identify the features of their Website in terms of website content, website promotion, and website eCommerce. Specifically, 25 items were used to measure content, 15 items for promotion, and 11 items for eCommerce.

Measuring innovation is challenging as the "newness" of a feature is perceived differently by each CVB. In this study, the level of innovation in Web marketing efforts was measured in terms of the following: 1) whether a feature was implemented in the website; 2) whether it was implemented before or since January 1, 2005; and, 3) the extent to which it had been adjusted since January 1, 2005 (5-point Likert scale from 1="no adjustment" to 5="complete revamp"). The January 1, 2005 was selected as a "cut off date" as the survey took place in Spring, 2006. If the adjustment was rated either 4 or 5, the feature was considered to have experienced a major change. Respondents were also asked to identify up to three website features for each of the Web marketing areas that contribute most to the overall success of the Web marketing program. As suggested by Moorman & Rust (1999), it is argued that the perceptions of managers are considered valid and effective measures of success.

Based upon this information, a two-dimensional matrix was developed in order to assess the relationship between innovation and the success of the web marketing program. As described in figure 1, it is argued that adjustments/ changes in the website is appropriate when the feature is located in either Quadrants III or II where they can be characterized as Strategic Investments or Strategic Disinvestments. Website features located in Quadrant IV, however, represent Under Invested features whereas Quadrant I represents features which are perceived to cost too much effort relative to their perceived contribution to the overall Web marketing program (over-investment).

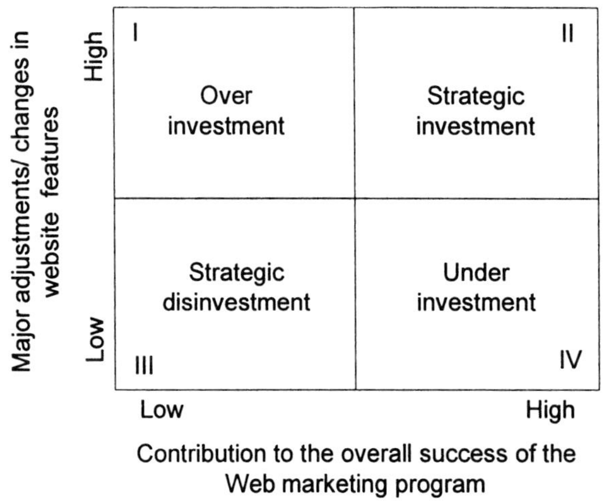

Fig. 1. Change – Contribution Matrix

5 Research Results

Research results first deliver descriptions about the organizational characteristics of CVBs; then, detailed results of the assessment of innovation by American CVBs are presented based on the three functional areas of Web marketing.

5.1 Characteristics of American CVBs

The characteristics of participating CVBs are presented in Table 1. About half of the CVBs are county level (45.1%); approximately one third (39.4%) are city level, and the remaining 15.5% are region level CVBs. Nearly half of the CVBs are independent organizations (46.1%) and 18.4% are a division of the chamber of commerce. The major markets of the CVBs are leisure travel, meetings/conventions, as well as festivals/special events. The majority of the CVBs (69.9%) are small organizations with fewer than 10 full-time employees. About one fifth of the CVBs (22.9%) have an annual budget between $250,001 and $500,000.

In terms of using the Internet as a marketing channel, all CVBs currently have an online presence. This suggests that Internet technologies have, indeed, been embraced by American CVBs as a tool to communicate with their visitor markets. However, it is interesting to note that, historically, nearly one quarter (23.1%) of the CVBs established their online presence the Internet before 1995, about one half (53.1%) by 1998 and about three-quarters (76.9%) by 2000.

Table 8. Characteristics of CVBs

Type of CVB	%	*Most important markets*	%
Independent organization	46.1	Leisure Travel	90.6
Part of county government	9.2	Business travel	51.3
Division of the Chamber of Commerce	18.4	Meetings/Conventions	67.4
Part of city government	13.5	Sports	57.0
Part of state government	2.1	Festivals/Special events	59.3
Division of Economic Development	2.8	Other	17.3
Other	7.9		
Annual budget	%	*Full-time employees*	%
<$100,000	11.4		
$ 100,001 – $ 250,000	17.9	No full-time employees	0.7
$ 250,001 – $ 500,000	22.9	1 to 9	69.2
$ 500,001 – $ 750.000	7.1	10 to 19	18.2
$ 750,001 – $ 1,000,000	7.9	20 to 49	9.1
$ 1,000,001 – $ 2,000,000	15.0	50 to 99	1.4
$ 2,000,001 – $ 3,000,000	3.6	100 to 199	0.7
$ 3,000,001 – $ 5,000,000	7.1	200 and above	0.7
$ 5,000,001 and above	7.1		

5.2 Innovation in Web Marketing Features

Website Content Features

Table 2 summarizes the results with respect to the implementation of website content features. As can be seen, the most implemented website content features are those related to information provision, which include: activities/attraction (97.2%), events (95.0%), accommodation (93.6%), links to area pages (92.2%), restaurants (86.5%), shopping (83.7%), maps/driving directions (75.2%), tour operators (60.3%), downloadable brochures (57.4%). There is a high degree of variability among interactive website features such as search tool (49.6%), trip planner (30.5%), virtual tours (20.6%), personalization capability (10.6%), and recommendation system (9.9%). It appears that the higher the technical requirements are, the fewer CVBs implemented such a feature. Features related to relationship management, including email newsletters (51.1%), e-cards (22.7%), online real time help (4.3%), virtual community (3.5%), and chat rooms (2.1%), exhibit the same pattern. The least implemented website features are those related to providing secure website access for trust building: privacy policy (42.6%), secure transaction with SSL (19.9%), and Web seal certificate (8.5%). Lastly, only 1.4% of the CVB websites have integrated mobile phone capabilities. Of the features implemented, the most popular website content features were chat rooms, virtual community, mobile phone capability, online real time help, and downloadable brochures. Interestingly, the majority of technically more sophisticated website features such as virtual tours, personalization capability, search tools, and Web seal certificates were implemented before January 1, 2005. Since January 1, 2005 at least half of the CVBs indicated that they had made major changes to personalization capabilities (60.0%), email newsletters (59.7%), event calendars (58.2%), downloadable brochures (55.6%), games and entertainment (50.0%), and mobile phone capability (50.0%). Features that experienced no or only limited major changes were Web seal certificate and chat rooms (both 0.0%), as well as virtual communities (20.0%), and online real time help (33.3%).

Table 2. Implementation of Website Content Features

Website Content Feature	Overall Rate	Implementation Before 01/01/05	Implementation Since 01/01/05	Major Changes Since 01/01/05
Activity/Attraction info	97.2%	95.6%	4.4%	48.9%
Event calendars	95.0%	90.8%	9.2%	58.2%
Accommodation info	93.6%	95.3%	4.7%	48.5%
Links to area pages	92.2%	91.7%	8.3%	36.2%
Restaurant information	86.5%	90.8%	9.2%	44.3%
Shopping information	83.7%	90.4%	9.6%	35.6%
Maps/Driving directions	75.2%	87.0%	13.0%	45.3%
Tour operator information	60.3%	87.7%	12.3%	41.2%
Downloadable brochures	57.4%	60.0%	40.0%	55.6%
Email newsletter	51.1%	79.4%	20.6%	59.7%
On site search tool	49.6%	87.1%	12.9%	44.3%
News	48.2%	90.2%	9.8%	39.7%
Privacy Policy	42.6%	89.3%	10.7%	26.7%
Trip planner	30.5%	76.9%	23.1%	44.2%
E-cards	22.7%	81.5%	18.5%	43.8%
Virtual tours	20.6%	76.0%	24.0%	34.5%
SSL for secure transaction	19.9%	69.2%	30.8%	42.9%
Personalization capabilities	10.6%	76.9%	23.1%	60.0%
Recommendation system	9.9%	71.4%	28.6%	42.9%
Games and entertainment	8.5%	77.8%	22.2%	50.0%
Web seal certificate	8.5%	83.3%	16.7%	0.0%
Online real time help	4.3%	57.1%	42.9%	33.3%
Virtual communities	3.5%	23.1%	76.9%	20.0%
Chat rooms	2.1%	20.0%	80.0%	0.0%
Mobile phone capability	1.4%	50.0%	50.0%	50.0%

Figure 2 shows a gap in CVBs' perception in their effort to change implemented features. The majority of website content features is located in Quadrant I (over investment). In Quadrant III features providing privacy policy and links to area pages are rather static, as changes might not occur on a regular basis. Accommodation info, events calendar, and activity/ attraction info are the three features that experienced the most strategic investment. Compared to these features, email newsletter, downloadable brochures, and maps/ driving directions are not perceived as major contributors to the overall Web marketing program.

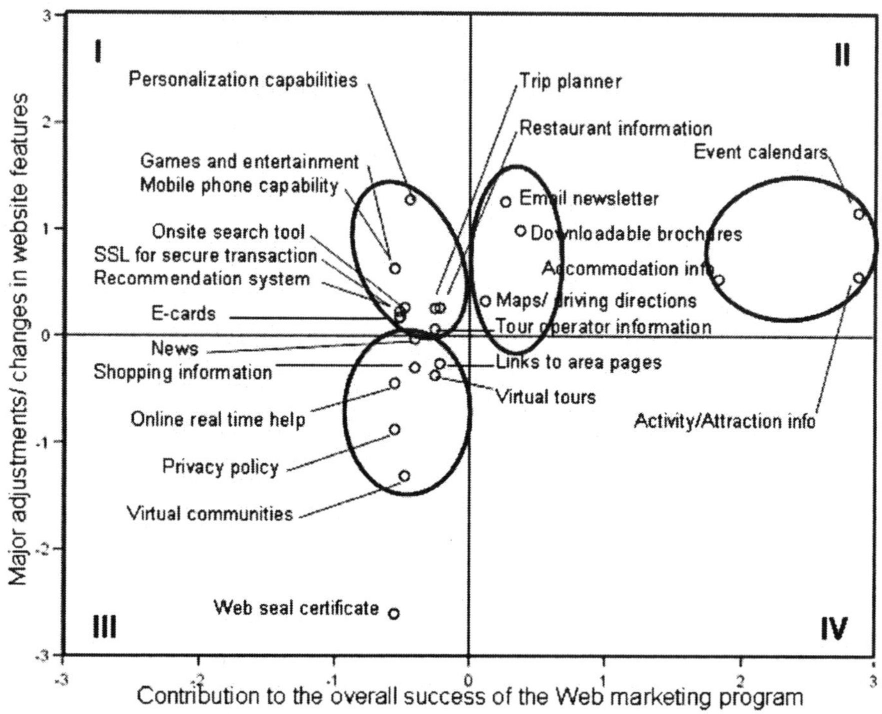

Fig. 2. Change - Contribution Matrix of Website Content Features

Website Promotion Features

The results for website promotion features are shown in table 3. Nearly every bureau includes its website address in print material (99.3%) and their emails (90.9%). Websites are also frequently promoted in traditional media such as magazines (88.1%), newspapers (86.7%), and radio (55.2%); however, TV (36.4%) and billboards (29.4%) are less frequently used. Listings in search engines are highly popular among CVBs; 76.2% of CVBs register with search engines. Additionally, keywords (75.5%) and meta-tags (55.2%) are used to optimize the website for search engines. However, only 17.5% of CVBs directly place ads in search engines. The use of "traditional" website promotion techniques varies from email campaigns (50.3%) to banner ads exchanges (23.8%). Lastly, guerrilla marketing through participation in virtual communities is the least used activity to promote websites (7.7%). However, this feature and ads in search engines are the most recently (since January 1, 2005) implemented promotional website features (22.2% and 31.8% respectively). The majority of promotional website features were implemented before January 1, 2005. Furthermore, participation in virtual communities and ads in search engines also have experienced major changes from the majority of the CVBs (72.7% and 60.0% respectively). Interestingly, nine out of the fifteen promotional website features were modified by at least 40.0% of the CVBs; even traditional, well established features like website address in print material (22.5%) experienced major changes.

Table 3. Implementation of Website Promotion Features

		Implementation		Major
Website Content Feature	Overall Rate	Before 01/01/05	Since 01/01/05	Changes since 01/01/05
Website address in print material	99.3%	94.8%	5.2%	22.5%
Promote website in magazine ads	90.9%	92.8%	7.2%	35.4%
Website address in email	88.1%	89.7%	10.3%	23.0%
Promote website in newspaper ads	86.7%	89.7%	10.3%	33.1%
Register with search engines	76.2%	83.5%	16.5%	42.2%
Keywords for search engines	75.5%	84.8%	15.2%	43.5%
Meta-tags for search engines	55.2%	84.2%	15.8%	49.4%
Promote website in radio ads	55.2%	83.3%	16.7%	35.4%
Direct marketing through email list	50.3%	82.5%	17.5%	44.4%
Incentive programs	36.4%	74.4%	25.6%	46.2%
Promote website in TV ads	36.4%	79.2%	20.8%	44.2%
Promote website on billboards	29.4%	81.1%	18.9%	35.7%
Banner ads exchange	23.8%	81.5%	18.5%	47.1%
Ads in search engines	17.5%	68.2%	31.8%	60.0%
Participate in virtual communities	7.7%	77.8%	22.2%	72.7%

Figure 3 clearly shows that only key words in search engines are perceived as strategic investments; thus, the majority of the features are considered either under or over investment (Quadrants IV and I). This finding clearly suggests that CVBs are not aware of how most promotional features support their website.

Website eCommerce Features

As shown in Table 4, eCommerce features are not widely implemented by American CVBs. The most widely implemented features (meeting planner material 52.1%, publications/reports 44.1%) focus on business-to-business relationships. Ecommerce features targeting consumers are used in a rather limited way. For example, special offers/deals and online hotel booking are implemented in 41.3% and 34.3% CVB websites, respectively. Similar to promotional website features, also here the least implemented features (attraction tickets, classifieds/banners, and event tickets) have been the recently most implemented features (38.5%, 35.7%, and 30.8% respectively). It also appears that CVBs are trying to catch up with hotel booking, as 29.5% of CVBs implemented this features since January 1, 2005. Interestingly, all implemented eCommerce features were subject to major changes since January 1, 2005, identifying the increased importance of eCommerce features for CVBs. Specifically, hotel booking (53.1%), as well as merchandising and attraction tickets (both 50.0%), and meeting planner material (49.4%) have been changed.

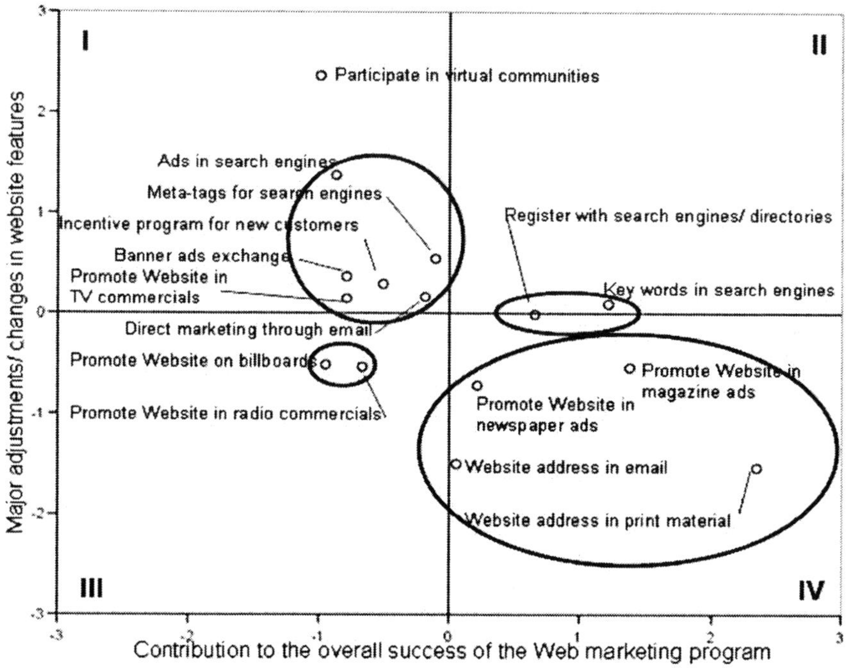

Fig. 3. Change – Contribution Matrix of Web Marketing Success

Table 4. Implementation of Website eCommerce Features

Website Content Feature	Overall Rate	Implementation Before 01/01/05	Implementation Since 01/01/05	Major Changes since 01/01/05
Meeting planner material	55.2%	78.6%	21.4%	49.4%
Publications/Reports	44.1%	84.9%	15.1%	42.9%
Special offers/Deals	41.3%	82.7%	17.3%	42.4%
Hotel booking	34.3%	70.5%	29.5%	53.1%
Coupons	23.8%	80.0%	20.0%	38.2%
Merchandising	18.2%	77.3%	22.7%	50.0%
Classifieds/Banners	14.0%	64.3%	35.7%	45.0%
Event tickets	11.2%	69.2%	30.8%	37.5%
Attraction tickets	9.8%	61.5%	38.5%	50.0%
Restaurant reservation	0.0%	0.0%	0.0%	0.0%
Parking tickets	0.0%	0.0%	0.0%	0.0%

Figure 4 clearly displays an alignment with the findings from table 4. Features that have been implemented recently and that experienced major change since January 1, 2005, are perceived as contributors to the overall web marketing success: hotel booking, meeting planner material, special offers/ deals. Interestingly none of the implemented feature was located in either Quadrant IV (under investment) or II (strategic disinvestment); identifying the importance of eCommerce for CVBs.

6 Conclusions and Implications

There is a fundamental need for tourism organizations to identify new ways of conducting business in order to establish competitive advantage (Poon, 1993). In particular, as the Internet becomes part of everyday life, tourism organizations must constantly engage in the search for, and development of, novel approaches in their Web marketing programs. This study examined the extent to which convention and visitors bureaus in the United States implement and improve their website features as a continuous effort.

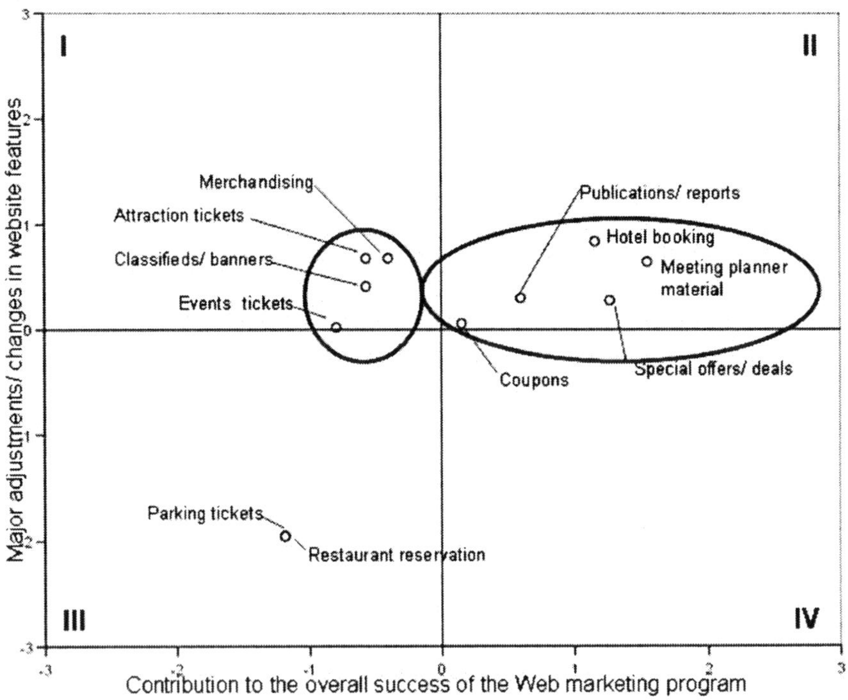

Figure 4. Change – Contribution Matrix of Website eCommerce Features

The results clearly indicate that recent innovation in website marketing by American CVBs focuses primarily on website features related to basic information provision and website promotion. Interactive website features, relationship management techniques, as well as transaction related features are used in a very limited way by CVBs. On one hand, this suggests that Web marketing based on information provision and promotion is still the dominant paradigm because they reflect the fundamental role of CVBs as the information service provider for destination visitors. On the other hand, it also implies that many CVBs are, indeed, in the early stages of IT use in that they fail to recognize and integrate the interactive and networking capabilities of the Internet into their marketing programs. As such, the findings of this study are consistent with a series of studies that focus on the adoption and use of Internet technologies in tourism organizations, especially in Web marketing (Buhalis, 2000; Werthner & Klein, 1999; Wang & Fesenmaier, 2006; Yuan et al., 2003, 2006).

Innovation is a continuous process (Drucker, 1985). It seems to be a promising sign that many CVBs are constantly making adjustments to website features. However, their efforts are fairly limited to the modifications of website features related to content and promotion. Other features, especially website eCommerce features, receive little attention regarding their implementation. This may lead to an unbalanced combination of website features in terms of the level of sophistication in supporting visitors' information use activities.

Generally speaking, it appears that CVB directors believe that basic website features such as providing information about the destination contribute the most to the overall success of their Web marketing programs. However, there seems to be a gap in CVB leaders' perception of the contributing factors in comparison with the investments towards adjustments. That is, for a significant number of website features, CVBs directors consider they have invested too much effort without realizing tangible outcomes. This suggests that CVB directors may not be convinced about the value of many website features.

This study offers useful insights into the nature of innovation in Web marketing by American CVBs with a focus on implementation of technological features. However, it is important to recognize that organizational capabilities need to be developed to be able to better respond to the constantly changing environment (Xiang & Fesenmaier, in press). Future research should further investigate the conditions and enablers for tourism organizations to improve their innovative activities.

References

Amit, R. & Zott, C. (2001). Value creation in E-business. *Strategic Management Journal*, 22 (6-7), 493-520.

Buhalis, D. (1998). Strategic use of information technologies in the tourism industry. *Tourism Management*, 19 (5), 409-421.

Buhalis, D. (2000). Marketing the competitive destination of the future. *Tourism Management*, 21 (1), 97-116.

Drucker, P. F. (1985). *Innovation and Entrepreneurship*. New York: HarperCollins Publishers.

Gretzel, U., Yuan, Y.-L. & Fesenmaier, D. R. (2000). Preparing for the new economy: advertising strategies and change in destination marketing organizations. *Journal of Travel Research*, 39(2), 146-156.

Gretzel, U., Fesenmaier, D. R., Formica, S. & O'Leary, J. T. (2006). Searching for the future: challenges faced by destination marketing organizations. *Journal of Travel Research*. 45(2), 116-126.

Hanson, W. (2000). *Principles of Internet Marketing*. Cincinnati, OH: South-Western College Publishing.

Hjalager, A.-M. (2002). Repairing innovation defectiveness in tourism. *Tourism Management*, 23(5), 465-474.

Hoffman, D. L. & Novak, T. P. (1996). Marketing in hypermedia computer-mediated environments: conceptual foundations. *Journal of Marketing*, 60(July), 50-68.

Kothari, T. & Fesenmaier, D.R. (2006). *The Web Marketing Strategies of Tourism Organizations in the United States*. White paper for the Directors of the American Convention and Visitors Bureaus based on a National Study conducted by the National Laboratory of Tourism & eCommerce, Temple University.

Moore, G..A. (2005). *Dealing with Darwin*. New York: Portfolio.

Moorman, C. & Rust, R. T. (1999). The Role of Marketing. *Journal of Marketing*, 63 (special issue), 180-97.

Nord, W. R. & Tucker, S. (1987). *Implementing Routine and Radical Innovation*. Lexington, MA: Lexington Books.

Parsons, A., Zeisser, M. & Waitman, R. (1998). Organizing today for the digital marketing of tomorrow. *Journal of Interactive Marketing*, 12 (1), 31-46.

Porter, M. E. (1985). *Competitive Advantage*. New York: The Free Press.

Porter, M. E. & Millar, V. E. (1985). How information gives you competitive advantage. *Harvard Business Review*, 64 (4), 149-160.

Poon, A. (1993). *Tourism, Technology and Competitive Strategies*. Wallingford, CT: CAB International.

Prahalad, C. K. & Hamel, G. (1990). The core competence of the corporation. *Harvard Business Review*, 68 (3), 80-91.

Rita, P. (2000). *Web Marketing Tourism Destinations*. In *proceedings of The 8th European Conference on Information Systems (ECIS)*, Vienna, Austria, July 3-5, 2000.

Ritchie, J. R. & Crouch, G. I. (2000). The competitive destination: a sustainability perspective. *Tourism Management*, 21 (1), 1-7.

Rogers, E. M. (2003). *Diffusion of Innovations (5th edition)*. New York: The Free Press

Schumpeter, J. A. (1947). The creative response in economic history. *The Journal of Economic History*, 7 (2), 149-159.

Sundbo, J. (1997). Management of innovation in services. *The Service Industries Journal*, 17 (3), 432-455.

Travel Industry Association of America (2005). *Travelers' Use of the Internet*. Washington, DC: Travel Industry Association of America.

Wang, Y. & Fesenmaier, D.R. (2006). Identifying the success factors of web-based marketing strategy: an investigation of convention and visitors bureaus in the United States. *Journal of Travel Research*, 44 (3), 239-249.

Weiermair, K., Peters, M. & Frehse, J. (2005). *Innovation in small businesses vs. MNEs*. In proceedings of the *AIEST (Association Internationale d'Experts Scientifiques du Tourisme) 55th Congress*. Brainerd, MN, USA: August, 28 – September, 1, 2005.

Werthner, H. & Klein, S. (1999). *Information Technology and Tourism - A Challenging Relationship*. Wien - New York: Springer-Verlag.

Xiang, Z. & Fesenmaier, D. R. (in press). Benchmarking as a strategic tool for destination marketing organizations: a proposed framework. *Journal of Travel and Tourism Marketing*.

Yuan, Y., Gretzel, U. & Fesenmaier, D. R (2003). Internet technology use by American convention and visitors bureaus. *Journal of Travel Research*, 41 (3), 240-255.

Yuan, Y., Gretzel, U. & Fesenmaier, D. R. (2006). The role of information technology use in American convention and visitors bureaus. *Tourism Management*, 27 (2), 326-341.

An Analysis of Hotel Trademark Abuse in Pay-Per-Click Search Advertising

Peter O'Connor
Institute de Management Hotelier International,
Essec Business School, France
oconnor@essec.fr

Abstract

Using Pay-per-Click (PPC) advertising helps overcome the limitations of search engine optimisation. Instead of attempting to manipulate web pages with little guarantee of success, advertisers can guarantee placement by bidding on the keywords which trigger sponsored listing on search engines and syndicated sites. However controversy has arisen over the use of trademarks as both keyword triggers, and in the text of sponsored listings? Legally the position is unclear. This paper s pecifically investigates trademark use in hotel searches. Using 90 properties in Europe, Asia and the USA, searches were performed to establish if third parties were using hotel trademarks in their paid placements. Findings indicate that abuse is rampant. While hotels perform well in organic search, they are usually preceded by paid listings using their trademarked terms. Customers are undoubtedly being diverted and urgent action is needed to reclaim hotel trademarks in the search environment.

Keywords: Search engine marketing, trademark abuse, hotel sector.

1 Introduction

Since its launch in 1994, the Web has continued to grow at a phenomenal rate, from an estimated one billion web documents in 2001 to over eleven billion in January 2005 (Gulli & Signorini, 2005). Navigating this ever expanding sea of data is a challenge. Search engines – sites that maintain indexes of web content - allow users to specify words / phrases and return a list of sites that potentially match these criteria – are a key way of finding information on the Web. Google, the world's largest search engine, is estimated to have indexed over 8 billion pages (Sullivan, 2004c) and to be used in nearly 50% of consumer searches (Nielsen NetRatings, 2006).

In the beginning, search engines were unbiased, displaying results that provided the most relevant answers to user queries (Sullivan, 2002). While many were supported by advertising, these were generally banners displayed across the top of the page and clearly differentiated from search results. Today, however, search engines need more workable business models to meet the substantial costs of maintaining their databases and improving their technology (Princeton Research Associates, 2002). For that reason, many now market their ability to route consumers towards specific websites. Like tour guides supplementing their income by bringing potential customers to restaurants or gift shops, many search engines now actively direct users to sites which have paid for placement on their results pages (Lastowka, 2002).

In most cases, these paid placements are based on advertisers bidding for the keywords under which they wish to be displayed. For example, an online sports retailer might wish to appear when users enter "running shoes" as a search criterion. Controversy has arisen, however, over the use of trademarked terms as keywords. For example, can the same online retailer bid on the keyword "Nike" and / or use the trademark "Nike" in the copy of their advert, thus potentially diverting shoppers who might otherwise have bought directly from Nike.com - the website of the trademark owner? While still a developing subject, this paper examines the ethical and legal position. In particular, the contrasting situation within and outside the USA is contrasted in the literature review section below. As an illustration the paper then surveys the use of trademarks in paid adverts displayed during searches for specific hotel properties to establish the extent to which hotel trademarks are being abused.

2 Background

Search engines have become an essential tool, with search volumes increasing at over twenty percent per year as users struggle to find information on the Web (Sen, 2005). Research has shown that users now also type URLs directly into search boxes, suggesting that they use search engines not just as data harvesting tools but for navigation (Smith, 2005). Furthermore, research by Jupiter shows that the vast majority of searchers don't look past the first two-pages of results (Thompson, 2004). Given such dependence, gaining a favourable position in results listings is important for anyone wishing to gain exposure to on-line customers. Search engine marketers use two main techniques to try to increase positioning. Search engine optimisation focuses on manipulating site structure and content in order to be naturally ranked highly under particular search terms, while paid placement instead pays for position, usually on a competitive cost per click basis, as will be discussed below.

2.1 Organic Search Engine Optimisation

Search engines use specialized software, known as *spiders*, to crawl the web, classifying each page they encounter and adding it to their databases so that it will subsequently appear in their search results. Marketers try to manipulate these spiders by modifying their HTML (for example the title tag, meta-tags, headings or links) and / or page content to convince the ranking algorithm to give that page a higher position than the others displayed on a search-results listing (Sen, 2005).

Organic optimisation suffers from several limitations. The search engine's algorithms are both secret and complex, making it difficult to establish what modifications are needed for better positioning. Algorithms also change frequently and thus any gain achieved may subsequently be lost. Each search engine stresses different issues, and thus optimising for one may negatively affect positioning on others. Lastly, pages must be re-evaluated for changes to be taken into account. Although spiders revisit periodically, it can take up to 120 days for the results of a campaign to become visible (Sen, 2005). SEO is thus time consuming and costly, with little guarantee of success in terms of consistently high rankings. Marketers have to adapt to ever changing classification strategies to both maintain position and improve rankings (Pasternack, 2006). Such limitations are driving many towards using paid placement.

2.2 Paid Placement

Instead of spending time manipulating sites with little guarantee of success, paid placement allows marketers to pay for positioning in search results (Sen, 2005). Such *sponsored links* are acquired by competitively bidding on specific keywords, usually on a Pay-per-Click (PPC) basis (Sullivan, 2004b). For example, if an advertiser wished to appear in top position for "running shoes", he might agree to pay 25 cents per click. If no one else offered to pay more, then he would appear in the number one spot. If someone else later decided to pay 26 cents, then he would fall to number two position, unless he increased his bid to regain the top position (Sullivan, 2004d).

Several paid search networks exist, with the biggest being Google AdWords and Yahoo! Search Marketing (formerly known as Overture) (Krol, 2006). These are networks in that in addition to displaying adverts within their own search results, both syndicate sponsored listings to third party sites (Sullivan, 2004b). For example, Google places sponsored listings on other search engines (such as Ask.com and AOLSearch) and on content sites (such as the NewYorkTimes.com, HowStuffWorks and MySpace), as well as a large number of smaller sites that allow Google to crawl their content and integrate relevant adverts in return for a revenue share (Sen, 2005). Some of the sites powered by Yahoo! Search Marketing include Altavista, CitySearch, CNN and NationalGeographic.com.

Sponsored listings are usually (but not always) segregated from organic results and labelled as adverts. Their position can vary. For example, on its own search results, Google normally displays AdWords down the right-hand side of the screen, separated from organic results by a vertical bar (Burden, 2005). Yahoo!, in contrast, displays its sponsored listings above and in the same format as its organic results, with the term ("sponsored") appearing beside each link. Google also sometimes positions sponsored matches above its organic listing, but shaded in a different colour to clearly distinguish them from normal results. However, particularly on syndicated sites, the line between 'results' and 'advertisements' has become extremely blurred (Lastowka, 2002). According to Sullivan (2004a), with old media like or television, consumers can identify adverts as they look different from normal content and over time they have established criteria to help them determine which is which. However, on the web, sponsored listings have only become commonplace relatively recently, which isn't much time to develop clues as to what's an advert (Sullivan, 2002).

Paid placement overcomes many of the limitations of SEO, as it effectively guarantees visibility under a desired set of keywords. Adverts appear instantly, can be changed at will, and the advertiser has total control over position, title, content and even where the user is taken if they click on the link. Changes in the ranking algorithm have no effect and adverts can be precisely targeted thus increasing the likelihood of delivering highly targeted traffic (Hansell, 2006). Payment is performance based and, with a budget per advert per day, costs are known in advance.

As a result, paid placement has become the search engine marketing strategy of choice for most on-line sellers. It accounted for approximately 83% of the estimated $5.75 billion spent on search engine marketing in 2005, compared to just 11% for organic search optimisation (Krol, 2006).

2.3 Trademarks and Paid Placement

Paid placement works by encouraging advertisers to bid on keywords which act as triggers to determine positioning when users enter search terms on the sites serviced by the network. Controversy has arisen over whether advertisers should be allowed to bid on another company's trademarks in such systems.

An estimated twenty percent of online searches are for trademark terms (Elixir Systems, 2006). Trademark owners argue that in such cases consumers are searching for information about, or to purchase, their company's products. When trademarks are used as keywords, bias in the result listings may mean that these products are sold indirectly (thus necessitating the payment of an unnecessary mark-up or commission) or even diverted to competitors and the sale lost entirely. Trademarks may also potentially be included in the text of these paid placements which, when combined with bidding on the trademark keyword, is a highly effective way to bait-and-switch consumers to alternative products. To combat this, trademark owners are often obliged to themselves participate in paid placement, engaging in costly bidding wars with competitors to protect their trademarks.

The search networks have in general taken a hands-off approach to dealing with this issue. Most placed the burden of responsible use on advertisers themselves, arguing that it is the latter who are abusing the system, and that trademark owners must resolve any infringement with the offender directly (Wehr, 2005). Quite recently, Yahoo! changed its position and announced that they will no longer allow advertisers to bid on trademarked terms (Pattison, 2006). As will be seen, however, Google still allows advertisers to bid on trademarks as keyword triggers as long as the term is not used in the advert title or advert copy (Miolina, 2004).

2.4 The Legal Perspective

A practice which raises similar concerns to paid placement is trademarks use in meta-tags – hidden lines of HTML code used to describe a page's contents to visiting spiders (Lastowka, 2002). While search engines maintain that they no longer give emphasis to meta-tags in ranking algorithms, it's still important to include appropriate phrases (including trademarks) in pages to help with organic positioning (Oliva, 2004). Competitors could also include these same trademarks in their meta-tags to try to appear alongside or above the company's site in search results and divert business (Howell, 2006). However such usage has in general been found to be unlawful.

While early rulings focused on trademark infringement under a likelihood-of-confusion analysis, *Brookfield Communications Inc v. West Coast Entertainment Corp* introduced a more useful initial-interest-confusion argument (Lastowka, 2002).

Even though "moviebuff" was a registered trademark of Brookfield, West Coast intended to set up a site at Moviebuff.com and use moviebuff in its meta-tags. Prohibiting the use of the domain name, the court also introduced a landmark judgment on meta-tags. While consumers viewing search results influenced by such meta-tags would be unlikely to be confused as to the real Brookfield site (thus negating the likelihood-of-confusion argument), the court ruled that there existed the real possibility of initial-interest-confusion – "the diversion of potential customers from the website they were seeking to another site, based on the belief that the second site is associated with the original one sought". If meta-tags placed West Coast's site among "moviebuff" results, this might divert consumers searching for Brookfield. The court compared this to a misleading billboard that directed consumers to exit a highway at the wrong place or to posting a sign with another's trademark in front of one's store, and ruled that such practices were not acceptable (Lastowka, 2002).

However the court did note that West Coast would be permitted to use the more generic term "movie buff", which it described as a "descriptive term ... routinely used in the English language to describe a movie devotee". The English Courts delivered a similar judgement in *Road Tech Computer Systems Limited v. Mandata* (CMS Cameron McKenna LLP, 2000). It's clear that the unauthorized use of trademarks (registered or not) is actionable in circumstances where they are being used to lure searchers away from the owner's website. However it's also worth noting that search engines have never been held liable in such cases (CMS Cameron McKenna LLP, 2000). Instead they have been characterized as passive conduits duped and outwitted by the infringing meta-tags (Lastowka, 2002).

Given such clear precedents, trademarks use in paid placement should follow similar logic. When third parties bid on trademarks or use trademarks in the text of their adverts, they are intentionally trying to appear in the results for search terms of the trademark owner. As the test for infringement looks to likelihood-of-confusion, it is difficult to see why the legal position should differ, and the courts have largely supported this argument. For example, in *Nissan Motor Co. Ltd v. Nissan Computer Corp.*, the court ruled that there was no good cause for not extending the protection offered in meta-tag cases to infringements in paid placement (Lastowka, 2002). The message is clear – when a trademark is being abused, the owner can take legal action against the advertiser to both prevent further infringement and recover damages for lost business (Thompson, 2004). However actually doing so can be problematic. Finding the offender can be difficult as domain name registrations can now legititamately hide the owner's contact details, and sites may be deliberately registered in foreign countries where enforcement is more difficult. An easier solution would be if the PPC networks actively policed trademark abuse.

As mentioned above, Google is the only major search network that currently allows advertisers to bid on trademarks as keywords (Coy, 2006). If a trademark owner objects, Google has one policy for the U.S. and another for the rest of the world. Outside the U.S., if a trademark owner objects to the use of their trademark in an advert's content or keyword triggers, Google will require the advertiser to remove the term. (Mirchin, 2005). In the U.S. however, Google will only act if the trademark is used within the advert copy. The purchase of trademarked terms as keyword triggers is not only allowed but actively promoted. This has been challenged in the US courts. In *GEICO v. Google Inc & Overture Services*, GEICO claimed that the search networks infringed upon its trademarks when it sold them as keywords to competitors, causing sponsored links to appear next to GEICO site in search results. GEICO claimed this was likely to confuse consumers, and that that the sponsored links were misleading as they implied an association between GEICO and the companies displayed (Mirchin, 2005). To prove infringement, GEICO needed to show that use of its trademark was "likely to confuse an ordinary consumer as to the source or sponsorship of the goods" (Mirchin, 2005). However the survey data presented failed to achieve this, with the court concluding that "initial interest confusion" is more difficult to prove in e-commerce than in the real world. While it might be time-consuming or expensive to retrace your steps if confused by a billboard using another's trademark, in the online world all the user needs to do is click the "Back" button (Mirchin, 2005). Ho wever the court did rule that consumers were indeed confused when trademarks were included in the heading or text of adverts. However this has less relevance as the search networks claim that they remove adverts which use trademarked terms without the owners' permission (Mirchin, 2005). The case was settled under terms of confidentiality, but is important for Google as it provides a meaningful legal argument to support their continued use of trademark terms as keyword triggers.

Similar rulings have been delivered in Germany. For example, *Nemetschek v. Google* ruled that it is advertisers, not the search networks, who are responsible for keywords chosen. However the latter need to be able to disqualify trademark terms as soon as they have been informed of violations. Similarly, in *Metaspinner media GmbH v. Google*, the court ruled that there is neither trademark infringement nor unfair competition as long as the trademark does not appear in the advert text, implying that use as keyword triggers is permissible. In France, however, the courts have ruled very differently. A number of high profile cases, including *Viaticum / Luteiciel v. Google, Louis Vuitton v. Google, Le Meridien v. Google* and *Accor v. Overture*, have all ruled that search networks are guilty of trademark infringement when they allow advertisers to bid on trademarked terms or suggest such terms as potential triggers in their keyword suggestion tools. In all cases, the networks have been ordered to discontinuing displaying the infringing adverts, delete the trademarks in question from their keyword generator and pay substantial damages.

The search network's claims that they remove adverts that use unauthorised trademarks are not in fact accurate. While Google will prevent advertisers from bidding solely on trademarks themselves, it does not disable keyword phrases composed of trademarks used in combination with generic terms – for example "Ford trucks" - the generic term "trucks" combined with the trademark "Ford" (Thompson, 2004). Yahoo! Search Marketing requires a trademark owners to provide evidence of confusion before disabling keywords (Thompson, 2004), and specifically allows bidding where the linked page primarily provides editorial or comparison data (Seda, 2004). The search networks are protected in such behaviour under arguments of comparative advertising and fair use. For example, in *Playboy Enterprises Inc. v.*

Netscape Communications Corp., the court ruled that the search engines could never be sure that a searcher was not looking for information on the generic word "playboy" rather than the trademark "Playboy". In the court's opinion, generic terms, even when sold to competitors for their trademark value, are incapable of possessing a trademark meaning (Lastowka, 2002).

3 Search and the Hotel Sector

Online travel continues to grow as consumers embrace internet sources to help plan and purchase travel (Future Foundation, 2005). Online travel revenues were estimated to have exceeded $60 billion in 2005 (ComScore, 2006b), with recent studies estimating that nearly one in three of the euros spent online by European consumers goes towards leisure trip bookings (Favier & Bouquet, 2006).

DoubleClick claim that search plays a role in approximately 75% of online travel purchases, considerably higher than the estimated 50% for e-commerce in general (DoubleClick, 2005). An estimated 50 million US Consumers research travel online each month (Saks, 2006), while Forrester Research claim that 56% of online European travellers use search to find websites (Forrester Research, 2005). ComScore (2005b) estimate that nearly one-third subsequently purchase within eight weeks - mostly, but not exclusively, through online channels. Search is regarded as highly relevant and useful; with 82% of users either satisfied or very satisfied with their use of web search for travel planning (ComScore, 2005b). Search is rated more highly than any other information source, including travel agents (63%) or family and friends (78%) (ComScore, 2005a). Travel search is also effective at attracting incremental customers. In a comparable UK study, ComScore (2006a) noted that 39% of respondents visited a travel site they had not planned to visit and 25% considered a new brand as a result of their placement at the top of search results. They also pointed out that the more fragmented nature of the travel sector (offline and online) in Europe, combined with the more varied travel options available to European travellers, results in a more intensive planning process and further drives consumers towards using search (ComScore, 2006a).

While most searches involve generic terms, for travel the use of brands becomes more prominent close to the actual purchase, peaking in the session in which the sale actually occurs (DoubleClick, 2005). DoubleClick conclude that buyers may start their searches with generic terms, but rely on branded searches to find sites in the period leading up to purchase. There is also evidence that branded searches may be more effective, with 16% of searchers who made a supplier related search making an instant purchase compared to only 5% of those who made a destination related search (DoubleClick, 2005). Hitwise also maintains that traffic from branded search terms has the highest conversion ratio, so brand hijacking can have a real impact on the bottom line (Hitwise, 2006). Given the importance of search, and branded search in particular for travel, the question must be asked as to whether trademarks are being abused in the online travel search environment? This paper focuses specifically on the hotel sector, a key component of travel and one which has become increasingly important in online travel sales (Carroll & O'Connor, 2005). Forrester claim that accommodation is the most researched item within travel (Favier & Bouquet, 2006). Are hotel's trademarks being abused? What is the estimated effect of such abuses? How should hotels react to protect their trademarks and insure that they get maximum benefit from trademarks in the online environment?

4 Research Methodology

The objectives, therefore, of this study were to establish if hotel trademarks were being abused in three separate but connected situations - in the meta-tags of third party sites; within the keywords of Pay-per-Click networks; or with the titles or content of the sponsored adverts displayed on these networks.

Ten hotels in nine major European, US and Asian cities were randomly selected from the ABC Hotel Guide 2005. Searches were carried out for each property on search sites serviced by either Google AdWords or Yahoo! Search Marketing. Three regional variations of each site (.com, .fr and .co.uk respectively) were searched to assess if differing regulations in each country affect the behaviour of either the networks themselves or advertisers. A total of 540 individual searches were performed during the first week of August 2006, with the hotel name used as the search criteria. If the latter did not contain the city name or the word "hotel", they were added for the sake of consistency. Thus, the criteria for the hypothetical "ABC Hotel" in Paris and "The Majestic" in Berlin would have been "ABC Hotel Paris" and "Majestic Hotel Berlin" respectively. Following each search, the results page was assessed, with the positioning of the trademark owner's website in the organic and sponsored results listings noted, along with any usage of trademarks in sponsored listings or within the meta-tags of first site to appear in the organic results. While the study suffers from a variety of limitations (such as for example, a possibility that the searches detailed above do not truly represent the real situation), the methodology used should help minimise these limitations and result in findings that are indicative of the current situation.

5 Selected Findings

In organic listings, hotels performed well, as can be seen from Table One. Direct websites appeared in first position in nearly two-thirds of cases, and in the top ten in approximately another one-fifth of cases. If result listings were based only on organic rankings, hotels would be positioned on the first page of search results the vast majority of the time (83%).

Table 1: Selected research findings

Topic	Overall	Altavista	Google	AdWords
Hotel in 1st position in organic listings	61%	54%	67%	n/a
Hotel in positions 2 to 10 in organic listings	22%	29%	16%	n/a
Sponsored links appear	74%	83%	64%	91%
with hotel in 1st position in organic listings	59%	54%	65%	58%
with hotel in position 2 - 10 in organic listings	23%	28%	18%	14%
Sponsored links include third party sites	89%	99%	76%	97%
Sponsored links include hotel site	24%	14%	38%	15%
Sponsored links feature only hotel site	11%	1%	24%	3%
Hotel appears first on sponsored links	11%	5%	20%	9%

However search engines display sponsored links above and around organic results. During this study, sponsored links appeared before organic search results in 74% of cases. When the hotel site appeared in first position, a sponsored link preceded it in nearly 60% of cases, while when the hotel site appeared elsewhere in the top ten; it was preceded by a sponsored link 78% of the time. The majority of these links (89%) were for third parties, primarily online intermediaries attempting to sell the hotel's product or divert customers to competing products. The hotel itself participated in sponsored links in only 25% of searches. In 11% of cases, it was the only link to appear, while it was in first position in the sponsored links section in another 11% of cases. Trademarks were also being abused within the text of the sponsored adverts. Where sponsored links were displayed, at least one of the third party adverts contained the trademark search term in 66% and 37% of cases on Altavista and Google respectively.

Google normally displays AdWords to the right of organic search listings in addition to its sponsored links across the top of the page. AdWords appeared in over 90% of the study's Google searches, including 58% of the time when the hotel site was listed in first position in organic results and 74% of cases when the hotel site was elsewhere in the top ten. As with sponsored links, the majority of AdWords were for third party companies, with only 15% including adverts for the hotel's direct site. The hotel site appeared first in only 9% of cases, and was the sole advert in only 3% of cases. Use of trademarked terms within the title and text of third party AdWords only occurred in 12% of cases. Lastly, trademarks were also being abused in the meta-tags of the third party sites that appeared in the search listings. Of the 211 searches that returned a third party site in first position, 86% included the hotel's trademark in their meta-description or meta-keywords html tags.

6 Conclusion

The use of trademarks as keywords in paid placement is clearly a controversial topic. While legally, in the US at least, the search networks are justified in allowing advertisers to bid on trademarked terms, most (with the exception of Google) have committed to helping trademark owners protect their brands by formally banning the use of trademarks as keywords or in advertising copy.

From the survey, it's clear that hotels are performing well in terms of search engine optimisation. In the majority of cases, the hotel's direct website appears either first (61%) or in the top ten (22%) of organic listings on searches for the hotel's name and location. However these favourable positions are being compromised by third party sites that have paid for placement on the hotel's trademarks and using these trademarks in their advertising copy. Sponsored links preceded the direct website's listing in 82% of cases during the study, while Google AdWords appeared to the right of search results in nearly 72% of cases. Hotel's trademarks are being used in the titles and copy of these sponsored listings in many cases. It's clear that despite the search networks claims that they help trademark owners to protect their brands, hotel's trademarks are being abused and customers being diverted.

Such findings demonstrate either a severe lack of knowledge or of attention on the part of hotel online marketers. All search networks (including Google) will disqualify the use of trademarked terms in the title and content of adverts. However findings indicate that in nearly nine out of ten searches, at least one of the sponsored links displayed included the hotel's trademark. The search network's defence is that they are not aware of which terms are trademarks. If informed of abuse on a case by case basis, they will then prevent advertisers from using trademarked terms. Such a policy places the burden of monitoring trademark use on paid search networks on the trademark owner – a task which is clearly not being done by hotel companies.

Managing the use of trademarks as keyword triggers is more difficult. While according to Lastowka (2002), some search engines respond well to informal complaints about the purchase of trademarks, Google actively promotes trademarks as potential keyword triggers in the U.S. market, and refuses to disqualify trademarks used in conjunction with generic terms worldwide. Trademark owners thus have to pursue the advertiser directly. Where the contact details of the offending site can be established, a cease-and-desist letter from the company's lawyer can be highly effective, with Seda (2004) estimating that 90% of infringements can be stopped in this way. Smaller sites in particular will usually remove trademarks to avoid a court battle, although in some cases legal action may be necessary. For this, evidence needs to be collected as by the time such a case gets to court, the illegal adverts in question will have disappeared. Thus it's important to capture a history of the activity (using screen captures) with as much detail as possible (Wehr, 2005).

It's also clear that hotel companies are failing to take advantage of the potential of paid placement to increase their visibility on search results. The study shows that only a small percentage is using PPC advertising, and an even smaller number using it effectively. Bidding on the hotel's own trademarks is essential as it overcomes the uncertainty of search engine optimisation, insuring that the hotel website is always presented in relevant consumer searches. When combined with effective monitoring and management of trademark use, it should also be extremely cost effective. Only the minimum bid should ever need to be paid as third parties should not be able to bid on trademarked terms without permission, and any clicks (and therefore any costs) should deliver highly qualified prospects.

Protection of a company's brand in the online environment has become an essential task, and one which hotels are failing to undertake. Failure to act may mean that the trademark may pass into "common use" and lose its trademark value. The best defence is a good offence, and thus trademark owners need to be proactive about finding and stopping those seek to profit from their brand (Wehr, 2005). Search audits need to be conducted frequently, examining both paid and organic search results for evidence of trademark infringement (Pattison, 2006). Where abuse is discovered, procedures by which both the search network in question and the advertiser are contacted to demand discontinuation should be established. Hotels should also be prepared to go to court to protect their online brand. While expensive and time consuming, not doing so will undoubtedly result in business being diverted to competing websites.

References

Burden, D. (2005). Marketing's haiku challenge. *Marketing (UK), 24 August 05,* 26.

CMS Cameron McKenna LLP. (2000). *Meta-tagging on search engines*. London.

ComScore. (2005a). *U.S. Travel Searchers*. Reston VA: ComScore Networks Inc.,.

ComScore. (2005b). *Web Search Plays a Key Role in the Travel research and Purchase Process*. Reston, VA: ComScore Networks Inc.

ComScore. (2006a). *Online Search Drove Nearly 10 Million UK Travel Purchases between December 2005 and February 2006*. Retrieved 3 August, 2006

ComScore. (2006b). *Understanding Consumer's Shopping and Buying Behaviour at Supplier and Agency Travel Sites*. Reston, VA: ComScore Networks Inc.

ComScore Inc. (2005). *U.S. Travel Searchers*. Reston VA.

Coy, P. (2006, 3/6/2006). The secret to Google's success. *Business Week,* 17.

Elixir Systems. (2006). *Online Reputation Management: Protect your brand*. Scottsdale, AZ.

Gulli, A., & Signorini, A. (2005). *The indexable Web is more than 11.5 billion pages*. Poster proceedings of the 14th international conference on World Wide Web, Chiba, Japan.

Hansell, S. (2006, 16/8/06). Seek (on the Web) and the advertisers shall find you. *International Herald Tribune,* p. 13.

Hitwise. (2006) *Best Practice for Search Engine Brand Management*. London.

Howell, B. (2006). Proving Web History. *Journal of Internet Law*(February), 3-9.

Krol, C. (2006, 16/1/06). Search engine marketing up 44% in 2005. *B to B, 91,* 3.

Lastowka, F. G. (2002). Search Engines Under Siege: Do Paid Placement Listings Infringe Trademarks. *Intellectual Property & Technology Law Journal, 14*(7), 1-7.

Miolina, H. (2004). The Google Trademark Controversy - Actionable Advice. *The Search Marketing Advisor Newsletter, 3*(1), (online).

Mirchin, D. (2005). Google wins U.S. keyword case. *Information Today, 22*(9), 1-5.

Nielsen NetRatings. (2006). *MegaView Search Engine Ratings*. NewYork: Nielsen NetRatings.

Oliva, R. (2004). Playing the Search: So little time, so many sites. *Marketing Management*(April), 48-51.

Pasternack, D. (2006). Good Organic Rankings Aren't Enough. In M. Alam Khan (Ed.), *Essential Guide to Search Engine Marketing*. New York, NY: Courtenay Communications Corporation.

Pattison, W. (2006, 9 March 2006). *Trademark Infringement Issues for Pay-per-Click (PPC) Advertisers*. Retrieved 25 August, 2006

Princeton Research Associates. (2002). *A Matter of Trust: What Users Want From Web Sites - A Report on Consumer Concerns About Credibility of Web Sites*. Yonkers, New York: Consumer Reports WebWatch.

Seda, C. (2004). *Search Engine Advertising*. Indianapolis, IN: New Riders.

Sen, R. (2005). Optimal Search Engine Marketing Strategy. *International Journal of Electronic Commerce, 10*(1), 9-25.

Smith, S. (2005). The Emerging Search Economy. *econtent*(Jan / Feb), 31.

Sullivan, D. (2002, 2 July). *FTC Recommends Disclosure to Search Engines*. Retrieved 3 September, 2006

Sullivan, D. (2004a, 22 November). *Buying your way in: Search Engine Advertising Chart*. Retrieved 2 September, 2006

Sullivan, D. (2004b, 13 Aug). *Pay Per Click Search Engine)*. Retrieved 2 September 2006

Sullivan, D. (2004c). *Search Engine Wars V Erupts*. Retrieved 27 August, 2005

Sullivan, D. (2004d, 5 July). *Submitting via Paid Listings: Overture & Google Adwords*. Retrieved 2 September

Thompson, C. (2004). Search Engines Invite New Problems. *Marketing Management*(April), 52-53.

Wehr, L. (2005, 10 May). *Thieves, Scallywags and Scoundrels: Combating Trademark Infringement in Search*. Retrieved 28 August, 2006.

Annotating Accommodation Advertisements Using CERNO

Nadzeya Kiyavitskaya[a]
Nicola Zeni[a]
Luisa Mich[b]
James R. Cordy[c]
John Mylopoulos[d]

[a] Dept. of Information and Communication Technology, University of Trento, Italy
{nadzeya, nzeni}@dit.unitn.it
[b] Dept. of Computer and Management Sciences, University of Trento, Italy
luisa.mich@unitn.it
[c] School of Computing, Queens University, Kingston, Canada
cordy@cs.queensu.ca
[d] Dept. of Computer Science, University of Toronto, Ontario, Canada
jm@cs.toronto.edu

Abstract

There has been great interest in applying Semantic Web technologies to the tourism sector ever since Tim Berners-Lee introduced his vision. Unfortunately, there is a major obstacle in realizing such applications: tourist (or other) information on the Web has to be semantically annotated, and this happens to be a very time- and resource-consuming process. In this work we present the application of a lightweight automated approach for the annotation of accommodation advertisements. The annotation tool, called Cerno, allows for annotation of text according to a predefined conceptual schema. Resulting annotations are stored in a database, allowing users to quickly find the best match to personal requirements. To evaluate our framework, we have conducted a series of experiments that support the efficacy of our proposal with respect to annotation quality and fulfilment of user information needs.

Keywords: semantic web, CERNO, semi-automatic annotation, accommodation ads

1 Introduction

The Semantic Web has been proposed as an extension of the World Wide Web where information is explicitly given well-defined meaning through semantic annotations. This vision has provoked great interest in the tourism sector since it was first proposed by Tim Berners-Lee in 1999 (Berners-Lee, Hendler, & Lassila, 2001). This interest is motivated largely by the importance of tourism in the world economy (for the U.S. see (Travel Industry Association of America, 2004), also (European Commission, n.d.) for Europe). Moreover, in the last years, the percentage of people using the Internet as a medium to find a destination for vacations and reserve related services has been increasing steadily (European Travel Commission, 2006).

Potential applications based on the availability of semantically annotated information in tourism are described in (Maedche & Staab, 2002), highlighting the feasibility of applying existing Semantic Web-based tools for next-generation tourism information systems. From a user viewpoint, the key idea is to allow the tourist to quickly retrieve all necessary information for organizing a vacation from the Web. This information relates to different phases of vacation planning - selection of a destination, finding the way to get there, choosing accommodation facilities, etc. - and must be provided in both efficient and effective ways. Thus far, users' experience in searching the data related to vacation planning shows that this process requires a long time and often gives unsatisfactory results. In this work we propose to demonstrate the merit of semantic web technologies as an instrument to improve the quality of service through a specific case study.

Many research projects work on implementing tools supporting the semantic annotation of documents, such as Kim (Kiryakov, Popov, Terziev, Manov, & Ognyanoff, 2005) and SemTag (Dill, Eiron, Gibson, Gruhl, Guha, Jhingran, Kanungo, McCurley, Rajagopalan, *Tomkins*, Tomlin, & Zien, 2003), to name just two of the most known. These projects are characterised by different levels of automation of the annotation process. Available tools range from user-friendly interfaces facilitating hand annotation, to semi-automatic annotation tools where the user intervenes in one or more phases, to systems automatically annotating documents. For the applications in the tourism area the first approach – "computer supported" manual annotation – cannot be applicable, because of the large number of documents to be annotated and the high cost of keeping up with the rapid changes in their content. On the other hand, given the state-of-the-art in the systems for completely automatic semantic annotation, existing tools do not provide satisfactory results for arbitrary content, but only for relatively limited domains. Thus, the challenge is to develop annotation environments for complex sectors such as tourism that produce good quality results within reasonable time and resource limits. To address this trade-off we have to identify the requirements that the annotation tool has to satisfy for each specific task. In some cases the priority is to find all possible answers even if the tool provides in addition a few incorrect answers. For other tasks it is more important to select only correct matches. Using terminology from information retrieval, this means that in the first case recall is given greater importance, whereas in the second case we are interested in higher precision results. For example, for a tourist looking for an accommodation close to the Coliseum in Rome, it is more important to have at least one suitable answer. While for an official tourist operator providing information about lodging possibilities in Rome, it is crucial to have many accommodation options, organised along one or more dimensions. Here, both high recall and precision are desired.

In this work we analyse the results related to the application of semantic annotation to accommodation ads in a city of art. We performed several experiments using a semi-automatic annotation tool (Kiyavitskaya, Zeni, Mich, Cordy, & Mylopoulos, 2006) (named *Cerno*) to annotate accommodation advertisements. Cerno is based on a lightweight text pattern-matching approach that takes advantage of a structural transformation system TXL (Cordy, 2006). The architecture and the performance of the tool are described in (Kiyavitskaya, Zeni, Cordy, & Mylopoulos, 2005). In this paper we assume the viewpoint of a web engineer that has to evaluate Cerno's ability to support the development of semantic annotation based applications.

From a linguistic viewpoint, online accommodation advertisements and similar documents pose a number of particular difficulties:

- partial and malformed sentences (for example, "30 square meters studio apt. in Rome center near FAO");
- abbreviations and short-forms ("Furn./equipp.");
- location-dependent vocabulary: names of geographical objects, both proper nouns ("Colosseum") and common nouns ("campo");
- presence of foreign language terms ("via", "Strasse", "Policlinico");
- monetary units ("Euro 73.00/83.00/93.00 p.n.", "€2000");
- date and time conventions ("from the 15/20th of july 2006").

From the functional viewpoint, such advertisements are present in various kinds of websites publishing classified ads. These websites can belong to B2C (business to consumer) applications, where owners of a website offer space for publishing announcements, or to C2C (consumer to consumer) applications, where the users interact directly, for instance, within a virtual community. Both cases involve *non-intermediate* tourism (i.e. the segment of tourists who do not defer to on an intermediary, in other words, "do-it-yourself" tourists) where the Web is used in order to make visible and promote individual offers.

Searching these kinds of ads is very often a real test of patience for the user who has to look for the information in long lists of accommodation ads. Analogous problems can emerge when finding a hotel on tourist portals: most of them offer a keyword-based search; an example of more sophisticated search tool can be seen in the European tourism portal (www.visiteurope.com [Sept. 7, 2006]), which enables "semantic queries" (for example, find all accommodation in the vicinity of the Coliseum). However, solutions of this type demand large investments and are affordable only for large organisations. Taking into account both linguistic and functional issues, it is important to explore lightweight tools for semantic annotation.

2 Semantic Annotation Using Cerno

Cerno is based on the parsing and structural transformation system TXL (Cordy, 2006), which allows by-example rapid prototyping of language descriptions, tools and applications. The architecture of Cerno (Fig. 1) is based on the LS/2000 software analysis architecture (Dean, Cordy, Schneider, & Malton, 2001), generalized to allow for easy parameterization by a range of semantic domains. To annotate input documents, Cerno uses context-free grammars, generates a parse tree, and applies transformation rules to generate output in a target format (Kiyavitskaya et al., 2005). The architecture of Cerno factors out reusable domain independent knowledge such as the structure of basic entities (email and web addresses, dates, and other word-equivalent objects) and language structures (document, paragraph, sentence), while allowing for easy change of semantic domain, characterized by vocabulary (category word and phrase lists) and semantic model (entity-relationship or UML class diagram and interpretation).

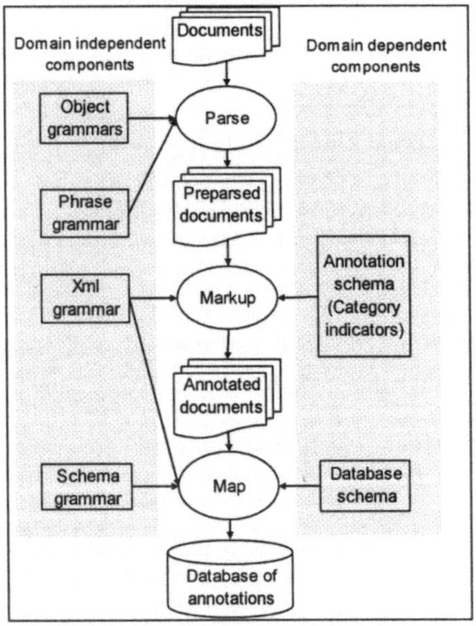

Fig. 1. Architecture of our semantic annotation process.

The annotation process consists of three main phases. In the first phase, a context-free grammar is used to efficiently obtain an approximate phrase structure parse of the source text. This stage results in a deterministic maximal parse. As part of this first stage, basic entities are recognized. The parse is linear in the length of the input and runs at compiler speeds (Kiyavitskaya et al., 2005). In the second phase, initial semantic annotation of the document is derived using a wordlist file specifying both positive and negative indicators for semantic categories. Indicators can be both literal words and phrases and names of parsed entities. Phrases are marked up once for each category they match – thus at this stage a sentence or phrase may end up with many different semantic annotations. Vocabulary lists are derived from the semantic model for the target domain. This stage uses the structural pattern matching and source transformation capabilities of the TXL engine similarly as for software markup to yield a preliminary marked-up text in XML form. The third stage uses the XML marked-up text to populate an XML database schema, derived from the semantic model for the target domain. Sentences and phrases with multiple annotations are copied, one for each different markup, before populating the database. In this way we do not prejudice one interpretation as being preferred. The final outputs are both the XML marked-up text and the populated database.

3 Semantic Annotation of Accommodation Ads

In our first experiment we used a set of several hundred advertisements for accommodation in Rome drawn from an online newspaper (Live In Rome & Italy, n.d.a), see an example in Fig. 2.

```
Very elegant apartment located in Piazza Dante, just a walk from
Fosse Ardeatine and 10 minutes to Colosseum by bus (Bus stop in the
square. 75 smq in a charming, and full furnished environment. 1.200
euro a month, utilities not included. Write to
pseudonym@somewhere.it or phone to 123.1234567
```

Fig. 2. Sample accommodation advertisement.

To annotate these ads, we designed a conceptual schema which represents the information needs of a tourist (Fig. 3). Then, as the first step to produce the annotation schema, we derived the most general concepts of the model: *Accommodation Type, Owner, Contact, Facility, Term* (of availability), *Location,* and *Price.*

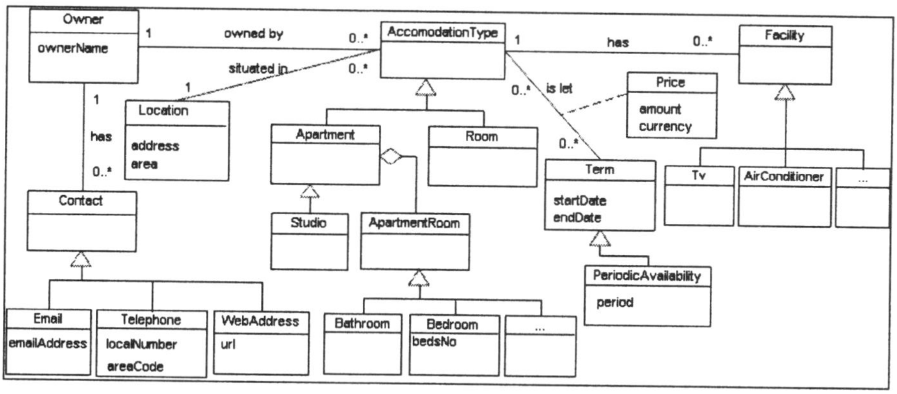

Fig. 3. Conceptual schema for accommodation ads represented in UML notation (http://www.uml.org/ [Sept. 7, 2006]).

First analysis of this list allows us to omit the concept of *Owner,* because this information is rarely provided in ads. Hence, the annotation schema derived consisted of the following concepts: *Type, Contact, Facility, Term*, *Location,* and *Price*. This schema is rather standard, given the nature of the documents. The goal of this experimental study was to identify and annotate the concepts in the advertisements according to the given conceptual schema, which was translated into XML (www.w3.org [Sept. 7, 2006]) for input to the Cerno tool. The tags, i.e. concepts, used for annotation are given in Fig. 4.

```
<ad>
      <location></location>
      <price></price>
      <contact></contact>
      <facility></facility>
      <term></term>
      <type></type>
</ad>
```

Fig. 4. Database template schema for accommodation advertisements.

To adapt our semantic annotation methodology to this experiment, the domain-related wordlists were constructed by hand from a set of examples. In order to make a realistic test of the "generality" of the method we restricted ourselves to some constraints. In particular, we avoided all proper names and locality-dependent words, and we did not pre-process the text of accommodation descriptions by formatting them or correcting errors. The output of the annotation was the annotated original advertisements (Fig. 5) and a database with one instance of the schema for each advertisement in the input.

```
<type><location>Very elegant apartment located in Piazza Dante, just
a walk from Fosse Ardeatine and 10 minutes to Colosseum by bus (Bus
stop in the square)</location></type>. <facility> 75 smq in a
charming, and full furnished environment </facility>.
<facility><price>1.200 euro a month, utilities not included
</price></facility>. <contact> Write to pseudonym@somewhere.it or
phone to 123.1234567 </contact>
```

Fig. 5. Example result of an annotated accommodation advertisement.

Next we performed a series of experiments in order to estimate the flexibility of the annotation tool to different geographic regions. In particular, we analysed accommodation ads in Venice (Live In Rome & Italy, n.d.b) and Paris (Rentcom.info Property Portal, n.d.). Both of these posed new problems compared to the ads in Rome, for example different document structure and vocabulary, and missing information, such as contact and price of accommodation.

4 Analysis of the Results

4.1 Evaluation Measures

The performance of semantic annotation tools is usually evaluated similarly to information extraction systems, i.e. by comparing with a reference annotation and calculating recall, precision and other quality measures. In order to evaluate our experimental results, we calculated a number of measures for the tool's automated annotation compared to manually-generated annotations:

Recall shows how well the tool performs in finding relevant items (i.e. the number of relevant items detected divided by the number of all relevant items in the collection):

$$recall = \frac{TP}{TP + FN} \quad (1)$$

Precision shows how well the tool performs in not returning irrelevant items (i.e. the number of relevant items detected divided by the number of all items detected):

$$precision = \frac{TP}{TP + FP} \quad (2)$$

Fallout measures how quickly precision drops as recall is increased:

$$fallout = \frac{FP}{FP + TN} \quad (3)$$

Accuracy measures how well the tool identifies relevant items and rejects irrelevant ones:

$$accuracy = \frac{TP + TN}{N} \quad (4)$$

Error rate demonstrates how much the tool is prone to accept irrelevant items and reject relevant ones:

$$error = \frac{FP + FN}{N} \quad (5)$$

In these formulas N is the total number of test items $N = TP + FP + FN + TN$, where:

TP (true positives) is the number of items correctly assigned to the category;
FP (false positives) is the number of items incorrectly assigned to the category;
FN (false negatives) is the number of items incorrectly rejected from the category;
TN (true negatives) is the number of items correctly rejected from the category.

All these measures were used during the analysis of the results.

4.2 Results of the Annotation

In order to estimate the quality of automatic annotations in our experiment, Cerno and a human marker were given one hundred advertisements to annotate. These documents were different from the training set used to tune the tool for the domain (a second human annotation was used to evaluate the confidence level of the reference annotation: differences were lower than 1% for all the measures). The tool was then compared against the human annotation to calculate the five measures described in this section (Table 1).

Table 9. Evaluating tool annotation (Rome, 100 ads)

Concept / **Measure**	Contact	Facility	Location	Price	Term	Type	*Average*
Recall	99.07	96.69	77.00	97.09	76.19	93.97	*90.00*
Precision	100.00	96.15	98.72	96.15	91.43	96.46	*96.49*
Fallout	0.00	2.62	0.29	1.16	0.74	1.20	*1.00*
Accuracy	99.78	97.10	94.64	98.44	97.10	97.54	*97.43*
Error	0.22	2.90	5.36	1.56	2.90	2.46	*2.57*

From the annotation tool viewpoint, these results are very promising. In fact, without local knowledge and using a very small vocabulary and only few TXL rules for non-trivial semantic concepts (most of which are not covered by traditional information extraction systems) we obtained results comparable to some of the best heavyweight annotation methods, albeit on a limited domain. The tool was also very fast, handling 100 advertisements in about 1 second on a 1 GHz PC.

Next we measured the effect of the initial automated annotation of the tool on human annotation productivity. The time taken by an unassisted human marker to semantically annotate a new sample of 100 advertisements was measured, and compared to the time taken by the same human marker when asked to correct the automated markup created by the tool. In this first evaluation the human annotator was observed to use 78% less time to mark up text with assistance than without, a significant saving. Because the system was shown in the first evaluation to be more aggressive than humans in markup, the majority of the correction work was removing markup inserted by the tool.

From an application viewpoint, the results in Table 1 represent a useful input to the designer of a semantic annotation based application. In fact, the annotation tool exhibited in average high level of recall, precision and accuracy; and a quite low level of fallout and error (the last column of Table 1). However, the results are not homogeneous for the different concepts. According to the table, the information on contact and price was more accurate than the information on the other concepts.

However, to interpret these results we should take into account that the relevance of these entities depends on tourist needs. To this end we adapted existing data to the information needs of a tourist looking for any kind of accommodation obtained from a large survey (Hepp et al., 2006). According to their list of the "relevant information categories" for the accommodation seeking problem, the subset of concepts used for our annotations, can be classified as follows, starting from the most important: *Location, Price, Type, Facilities. Contact* and *term* were not considered in the study, but we can assume that *contact* is more relevant than *term* (availability can be checked only if the contact is correctly given).

In this context, in respect to that classification, we could say that for a tourist looking for accommodation, the annotations of Cerno satisfy the requirements for the most relevant concepts, *contact* and *location* (with a high precision, even if the recall is not 100% we are sure that we would obtained only suitable accommodations, even if we will not find all of them). The results for the other concepts are also adequate (accuracy ranges from 94.64 to 99.78) for a single tourist search. However, for an exhaustive search, for example to classify all the accommodation in a given area of Rome for a tourist guide, we have to take into account that the system was not able to identify more than 23% of the location related information in the ads (given that ads could contain more than one location, this result represents an upper limit for the missing ads), so that the tool annotation would have to be revised by an human annotator. The (small) differences in the results are mainly due to the level of generality of the concepts: for example, for *facility,* on one hand there are a number of facilities that could be found in an accommodation; on the other hand, there are no linguistic forms (as for *contact*) or specific symbols (as for *price*); and for *term*, the results depend a lot on how this notion is defined (for example, phrases like "Studio available for holidays" and "Reductions for long term stay" implicitly contain information about the time for rent, but human markers may ignore it as not being relevant enough). Results obtained for the accommodation ads in Paris and Venice are given in table 2 and 3, respectively.

Table 2. Evaluating tool annotation (Paris, 10 ads)

Concept / Measure	Contact	Facility	Location	Price	Term	Type
Recall	-	78.79	69.57	50.00	100.00	81.25
Precision	-	100.00	88.89	50.00	66.67	100.00
Fallout	-	0.00	5.00	1.64	1.61	0.00
Accuracy	-	88.89	85.71	96.83	98.44	95.24
Error	-	11.11	14.29	3.17	1.56	4.76

The results show excellent quality rates for some concepts while there is a drop in performance for others. While some of the differences are due to the different styles of the ads (e.g., they were published on a different website for Paris), most of them are related to the geographical and cultural differences described in the introduction. Thus, these data give useful hints on how to tune the tool's domain-dependent components to obtain better quality results.

Table 3. Evaluating tool annotation (Venice, 10 ads)

Concept / Measure	Contact	Facility	Location	Price	Term	Type
Recall	-	92.86	58.33	100.00	100.00	100.00
Precision	-	92.86	100.00	90.91	50.00	100.00
Fallout	-	2.63	0.00	2.38	1.96	0.00
Accuracy	-	96.15	80.77	98.08	98.08	100.00
Error	-	3.85	19.23	1.92	1.92	0.00

5 Related Work

There are many other systems and projects related to semantic annotation; here we have room to name only two of the best known, to set our work in context. SemTag (Dill et al., 2003) annotates large numbers of web pages with concepts from TAP ontology, using corpus statistics to improve the quality of tags. The TAP knowledge base contains lexical and taxonomic information about such objects as musicians, movies, authors, athletes, states and cities, and other generic terms. SemTag detects the occurrence of these entities in web pages and disambiguates them. The KIM platform (Kiryakov et al., 2005) is an application for automatic ontology-based named entities annotation, indexing and retrieval. In KIM, as well as in SemTag, semantic annotation is considered as the process of assigning to the entities in the test links to their semantic descriptions, provided by ontology. The platform is based on GATE (General Architecture for Text Engineering). The main contribution of KIM is recognition of named entities with respect to the KIMO ontology, which covers such items as *Organisation, Person, Location, Event, TimeInterval* and others. Another tool that has been used on a large-scale is SCORE (Sheth et al., 2002), which integrates several information extraction methods, including probabilistic, learning, and knowledge-based techniques, then combines the results from the different classifiers. In contrast to all these tools our method uses a lightweight robust context-free parse in place of linguistic analysis. Moreover, in Cerno there is no learning phase, instead the tool has to be tuned manually when being ported to a particular application. Cerno does not rely on a knowledge base of known named entities, rather it detects them in the style of software analyzers – basing on the structural and vocabulary context of these entities (Kiyavitskaya et al., 2006). This advantage helps make our tool faster and less dependent on the additional knowledge sources.

Focusing on the tourism sector, in recent years, many large projects have been undertaken, especially in the area of ontology development. Among these is Harmonise (Dell'Erba et al., 2002), which aims at creating a comprehensive ontology for Tourism. Another group developing an ontology in this sector is DERI (http://e-tourism.deri.at). The DERI website gives also a long list of existing ontologies related to the tourism sector (E-Tourism Working Group, 2004). One of the more recent initiatives is the Open Travel Alliance (http://www.opentravel.org/ [Sept. 7, 2006]), which works on producing XML message specification schemas for trading partners. Our project does not use any specific ontology, but rather uses a small conceptual schema which could be derived from or integrated with any of these more general ontologies, translating to a standard ontology language such as OWL (http://www.w3.org/2004/OWL/ [Oct. 24, 2006]). Other projects have the goal to create an interactive environment which exploits semantically annotated documents to integrate the information available from different sources. For example, one of the few applications in tourism sector takes advantage of semantic annotations to enable dynamic packaging (Cardoso, 2006).

6 Conclusions

In this paper we have presented the application of Cerno, a lightweight tool for semantic annotation of web documents, to the annotation of accommodation ads. The results of the experiments, albeit preliminary, suggest that the quality of the output is adequate to develop web based applications supporting accommodation search. The main advantages using Cerno are the following:

- Cerno requires a limited use of external resources (no gazetteers, vocabularies, ontologies); if necessary, and for specific applications, the tool architecture allows the integration of such components with minimal effort.

- Cerno requires only limited computational resources, so that it could easily be adapted to "lightweight" interfaces to access tourist information or to online real-time applications.
- The effort to adapt Cerno to a new domain is minimal compared to what is required for other tools.

In addition, the comparison with data on the tourist information allows us to adopt a engineering approach that focuses on the feasibility of applications based on semantically annotated accommodation ads. For the designer of a semantic annotation based application the results of the experiments represent useful data suggesting how to adjust the tool to obtain adequate quality results for a particular task. Cerno has also been used to annotate tourist board websites with a very rich conceptual schema representing the knowledge of marketing experts with the goal of evaluating the communicative effectiveness of those websites.

Potential applications of the system presented in this paper are related to (a) the implementation of an interface to support accommodation search based on semantic annotation of documents (e.g., a web service usable both by human and artificial agents); (b) the integration of accommodations ads for a given city published on differently structured web sites. As regards further experimentation, the following topics need to be investigated: performance of the tool in case if external resources are used; identification of thresholds of the evaluation measures' values for a given application (for example, if the tool does not give "all" the accommodation ads that satisfy the tourist's needs, it is not a problem for the tourist, but it could be a problem for the owners of the missed accommodation).

References

Berners-Lee, T., Hendler, J., & Lassila, O. (2001). The semantic web: a new form of web content that is meaningful to computers will unleash a revolution of new possibilities. *Scientific American, 284* (5), 28-37.

Cardoso, J. (2006). E-tourism: creating dynamic packages using semantic web processes. *W3C Workshop on Frameworks for Semantics in Web Services.* Retrieved August 29, 2006, from http://www.w3.org/2005/04/FSWS/Submissions/16/paper.html.

Cordy, J. R. (2006). The TXL Source Transformation Language. *Science of Computer Programming, 61* (3), 190-210.

Dean, T., Cordy, J., Schneider, K., & Malton, A. (2001). Experience using design recovery techniques to transform legacy systems. *Proceedings of the 17 Int. Conf. on Software Maintenance (ICSM 2001)*, pp. 622-631.

Dell'Erba, M., Fodor, O., Ricci, F., & Werthner H. (2002). Harmonise: a solution for data interoperability. *Proceedings of the IFIP Conference on Towards The Knowledge Society: E-Commerce, E-Business, E-Government, 233,* 433-445.

Dill, S., Eiron, N., Gibson, D., Gruhl, D., Guha, R., Jhingran, A., Kanungo, T., McCurley, K. S., Rajagopalan, S., *Tomkins*, A., Tomlin, J. A., & Zien, J. Y. (2003). A case for automated large-scale semantic annotation. *Journal of Web Semantics, 1* (1), 115-132.

E-Tourism W*orking Group. (2004). Ontology collection in view of an e-tourism portal. Retrieved* September 13, 2006 from http://138.232.65.141/deri_at/research/projects/e-tourism/2004/d10/v0.2/20041005.

European Commission. (n.d.). *Tourism. Facts and figures about European tourism.* Retrieved September 7, 2006, from http://ec.europa.eu/enterprise/services/tourismeu.htm.

European Travel Commission. (2006). *World and regional overview*. Retrieved September 4, 2006 from http://www.etcnewmedia.com/review/default.asp?SectionID=10.

Hepp, M., Siorpaes, K., & Bachlechner, D. (2006). Towards the semantic web in e-tourism: can annotation do the trick? *Proceedings of the 14th European Conf. on Information System (ECIS 2006)*. Retrieved August 25, 2006 from http://www.heppnetz.de/files/hepp-siorpaes-bachlechner-annotation-ECIS2006.pdf.

Kiryakov, A., Popov, B., Terziev, I., Manov, D., & Ognyanoff, D. (2005). Semantic annotation, indexing, and retrieval. *Journal of Web Semantics, 2* (1), 49-79.

Kiyavitskaya, N., Zeni, N., Cordy, J. R., Mich, L., & Mylopoulos, J. (2005). Applying software analysis technology to lightweight semantic markup of document text. In S. Singh, M. Singh, C. Apte, & Perner P. (Eds.). *Proceedings of Int. Conf. on Advances in Pattern Recognition (ICAPR 2005)*, LNCS, *3686*, pp. 590-600. Springer Verlag.

Kiyavitskaya, N., Zeni, N., Mich, L., Cordy, J. R., & Mylopoulos, J. (2006). Text mining through semi automatic semantic annotation. In U. Reimer, & D. Karagiannis (Eds.), *Proceedings* of *Practical Aspects of Knowledge Management (PAKM'2006)*. LNCS, *4333*, pp. 143-154. Springer Verlag.

Live In Rome & Italy. (n.d.). *Apartments in Venice*. Retrieved March 4, 2005, from http://www.liveinrome.com/apartments/venice.htm.

Live In Rome & Italy. (n.d.). *Rome Ads - Classifieds for Rome, Italy*. Retrieved January 15, 2005 from http://www.liveinrome.com/classifieds.htm.

Maedche, A., & Staab, S. (2002). Applying semantic web technologies for tourism information systems. In K. Wöber, A. Frew, M. Hitz (Eds.). *Proceedings of the 9th Int. Conf. for Information and Communication Technologies in Tourism (ENTER 2002)*,. Springer Verlag.

Rentcom.info Property Portal. (n.d.). *Property in France-Paris apartments*. Retrieved March 4, 2005 from http://www.rentcom.info/paris-apartments/paris-apartments-2.html.

Sheth, A., Bertram, C., Avant, D., Hammond, B., Kochut, K., & Warke, Y. (2002). Managing semantic content for the Web. *IEEE Internet Computing, 6* (4), 80-87.

Travel Industry Association of America. (2004). *Economic research: economic impact of travel and tourism*. Retrieved September 7, 2006 from http://www.tia.org/Travel/econimpact.asp.

The Fototeddy Strategy – Web Site Attraction Through Physical Interaction

Peter Heinzmann[a]
Lothar Müller[b]
Stéphane Racine[b]
Ljiljana Vukelja[b]

[a] cnlab Information Technology Research AG
Rapperswil, Switzerland
peter.heinzmann@cnlab.ch

[b] HSR Hochschule für Technik Rapperswil,
University of Applied Science, Switzerland,
{lothar.mueller, stephane.racine, ljiljana.vukelja}@hsr.ch

Abstract

This paper introduces the "Fototeddy Strategy", which uses offline physical interaction to drive online virtual interaction at a designated website. A big Teddy sculpture, the Fototeddy, which functions as a photo booth demonstrates the strategy. The sculpture attracts through its size, colours, and most importantly, through a new and engaging way of interaction. People control the photo booth by gestures. This user engagement to take pictures with an interactive photo booth in the physical world extends to the virtual world by making the photos available online at www.fototeddy.ch. The experience with more than 20'000 people taking pictures with the Fototeddy at various events proves that it is possible to attract and engage people in the physical world, and then lead them to the virtual world. The paper outlines also how to implement the "Fototeddy Strategy" in tourism, based on a case study for a skiing resort.

Keywords: user experience, human computer interaction, gesture control, web site promotion

1 Introduction

Computing is moving beyond the desktop into new physical contexts asking also for new user interfaces like mobile phones or tangible interaction systems (Eran, 2001), (Rauterberg, Fjeld, Krueger, Bichsel, Leonhardt, & Meier,, 1998). Automatic point of sales systems like ticketing, teller (automatic teller machines, ATM) or beverage and food supply machines are examples of devices which look more and more like computer terminals than conventional machines. These devices are located in public and they increasingly get their own network connections which significantly extends the functionality of the machines. This is also true for photo booths, i.e. automated photography machines (Hines, 2005; Ratner & Evans, 2003). Photo booths were originally designed to quickly take and print portrait pictures to be used for documents like passports, transit passes, ski passes or to be exchanged with friends.

Many people like taking and exchanging pictures. This is not just true for the paper pictures of the physical space, it is also true for the electronic pictures taken and viewed in the virtual space. Web sites to share photos electronically are proliferating (Flickr, 2006), including geocoding images, i.e. tagging photos with geographic positions (Microsoft, 2006).

This paper presents an attractive type of photo booth which looks like a Teddy bear: the Fototeddy. It is designed to engage users to interact with an electronic camera system by gesture control. The experience with a physical object shall lead users to the virtual system, the Fototeddy web site. People who want to take pictures have to stand in front of the Fototeddy. In order to get photographed they must hold their hand horizontally and move it to four different positions. Fig. 1 shows two people standing in front of the Fototeddy and trying to take a picture by appropriate hand gestures.

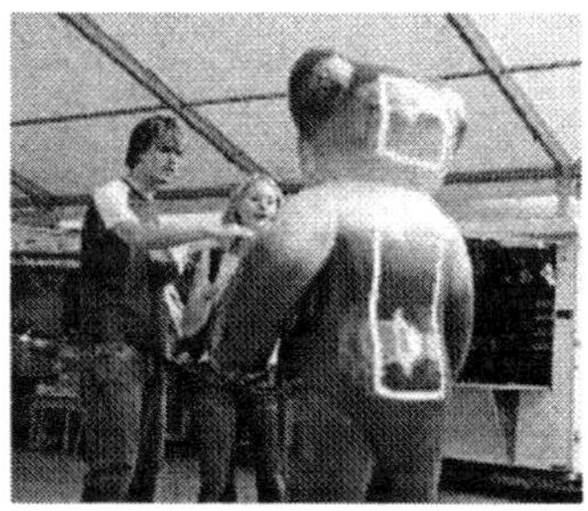

Fig. 1. Fototeddy in action

The Fototeddy is typically placed in public spaces where people have time for leisure, e.g. when visiting exhibitions, during shopping or while they are waiting for transportation.

The Fototeddy example is used to introduce a strategy to attract, engage and finally lead people to a web site by linking physical and virtual space. This strategy is therefore called “Fototeddy Strategy”. This paper reports on the experiences gained at exhibitions and events, discusses usage statistics and human computer interaction issues. Finally, it is outlined how to implement the “Fototeddy Strategy” for a skiing resort.

2 The Fototeddy Strategy

The Fototeddy system encompasses the Interactive Photo Booth, i.e. the Fototeddy machine, a web site and web browsers. People who want to take pictures have to stand in front of the physical object Fototeddy. In order to print and mail their pictures people have to visit a specific web site. Other people can also browse the pictures taken. Fig. 2 illustrates the Fototeddy system.

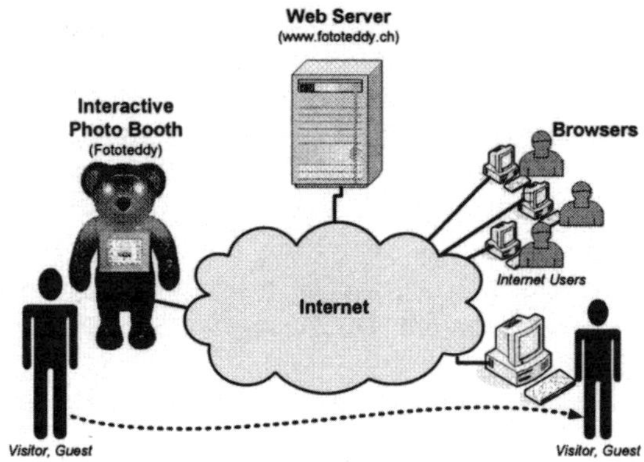

Fig. 2. Fototeddy system overview

With the example the authors introduce a new strategy called “Fototeddy Strategy” to attract, engage and finally lead guests to a web site by linking physical and virtual space. It consists of the following steps:

Attract people to a *physical object* through its appearance. In our case this is achieved by form and colour of the Fototeddy.
Engage people through an *uncommon usage experience.* In our case this is the activation of the camera by gestures. For many people this has some novelty touch.
Lead people to the accompanying web site *leveraging their engagement.* In our case people can review, mail or print the photos at a specific web site.

Many web sites try to attract attention of arbitrary surfers by increasing the page ranking position within the search engines (Brin & Page, 1998). The “Fototeddy Strategy” does not want to attract arbitrary visitors but visitors who already have been at specific physical locations. It has certain similarities with the Attract-Engage-Deliver pattern found in Jan Borchers *A Pattern Approach to Interaction Design*, 2001, in the context of visitors in exhibition halls (Borchers, 2001).

3 Fototeddy System

3.1 Background

In summer 2005 the Zurich City Association placed over 600 Teddy bears throughout Zurich. The organizers provided white fiberglass Teddy forms which were then imaginatively decorated by various artists. In a parallel action the Swiss Engineering Association asked Universities to build “Techno Teddies” for its 100 year celebration. At the University of Applied Sciences Rapperswil (HSR) it was decided to set up a Teddy which motivates people to physical interactions with the Teddy and leads people to the HSR web site. The plan was to provide a Teddy which takes pictures similar to a photo booth. However, unlike in the photo booth situation, the camera is not started by pushing a button, but by specific gestures. The resulting pictures are not printed, but displayed on a touch screen and sent to the web server www.fototeddy.ch. Hence, people need some gesture skills in order to have a picture taken, and people need to visit a web site in order to print or mail the picture. Guided by one of the authors, two students realized the system as a study project (Baumgartner & Höhener, 2005).

The idea of touch less computer interaction is not new. However, the special infrastructure used in other systems is rather expensive (Fraunhofer, 2006) whereas the Fototeddy works with cheap of the shelf components.

3.2 Fototeddy (Interactive Photo Booth) Functions and Software

Fig.3 illustrates the Fototeddy and its components. The appearance of the Fototeddy as chosen by the students reminds of Kodak colours. On the Teddy's belly there is a touch screen to display live images, gesture tasks and to locally inspect the pictures taken. The webcam to take the pictures sits in the nose of the Teddy. There are spotlights in the eyes which act as flashes when a picture is taken. Lights in the ears blink when the gesture movements successfully triggered a snapshot. At the same time, one can hear a "cheese" sound. The Fototeddy is connected to the Internet by twisted pair Ethernet or wireless LAN.

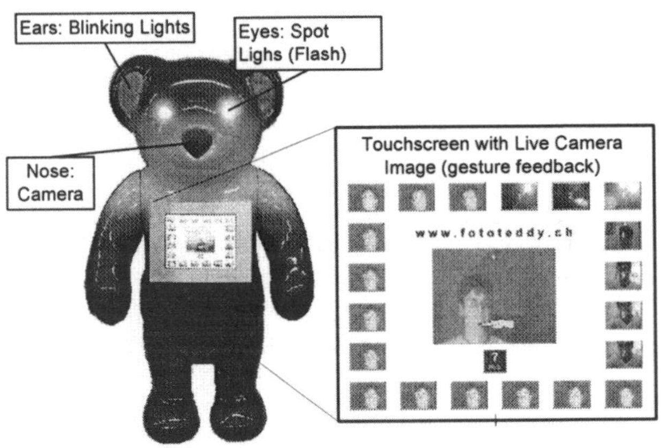

Fig. 3. Fototeddy components and gesture feedback screen

The Fototeddy is controlled by Java programs running on a Shuttle xPC AMD-400 computer, which is mounted in the body of the Teddy.

The Fototeddy software provides the following key functions:

User guidance: graphical user interface with six dialog screens with soft button controls. It instructs the user on how to use the Fototeddy, provides explanatory video sequences and takes the appropriate action when a user successfully carries out the gesture action or uploads a picture.

Gesture control: The main screen shows the live video of the person in front of the Teddy. Gesture control displays a sequence of four green target points and a yellow horizontal hand symbol. The user shall direct this symbol towards the target point by appropriate hand movements (see Fig. 4). The hand movements are detected by the motion detection extracted from the video images and visual gesture feedback is given on the display. The green target points appear at various places of the screen and one has to 'catch' them by moving the yellow hand towards them.

Fig. 4. Sequence of gesture control situations

Local picture gallery: stores all pictures which have not been uploaded to the web server yet. Each stored picture gets a unique picture number as well as a date and time tag. The last 20 pictures taken are displayed on the starting screen and can be browsed locally.

Intelligent picture upload assures that all pictures will be uploaded to the web site and stores the images locally until the connection to the web server is available.

In general, the gesture control involves gesture recognition, i.e. determining the movement of a user's hand, arm, head or body through the use of a camera, or through a device with embedded sensors that may be worn, held or body-mounted. Camera-based gesture recognition, as implemented in the Fototeddy, is still in the research phase. Early commercialization is centred on handheld devices that detect motion, such as Nintendo's Wii 3-D controller or Nokia's 5500 Sport phone. The camera based approach will be interesting when there is a growing need to interact with large-screen environments. In the Gartner Group Hype Cycle 2006 gesture recognition is situated in the "technology trigger phase". Mainstream adoption is not expected before 2011 (Fenn, 2006).

3.3 Web Site Functions and Software

The web site (see Fig.5) offers functions for browsing, searching and mailing pictures:

- The photo gallery page shows the most recent pictures with picture number, date and time tag.
- There is a search function to search pictures by their number.
- There is also a calendar to find and browse pictures by date.
- Once a specific picture is selected, it can be sent to other people by e-mail.
- The navigation bar of the web site leads to detailed information about the technology and construction of the Fototeddy. It also contains a list of project milestones and a link to the web site of the university.

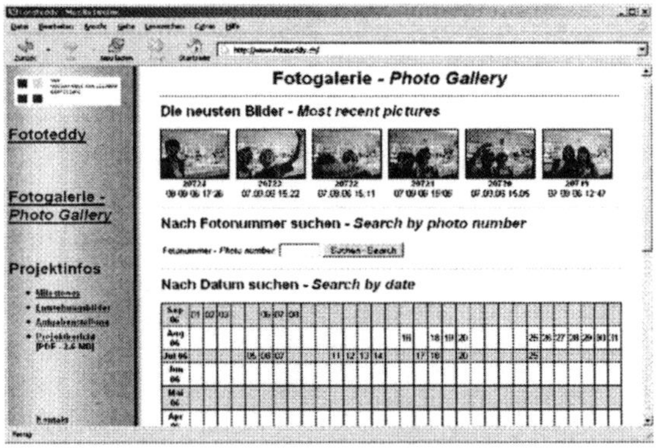

Fig. 5. Web page at www.fototeddy.ch

4 Experience

4.1 Fototeddy in Action

After its first months of life at the "Teddy Summer in Zurich" between May and September 2005 the Fototeddy was used as an attractor at several exhibitions. There were also requests to display it in discos, restaurants, tourist centres or shops.

Especially kids and teens had great fun in taking pictures. They presented themselves in various fun positions, one group even created a sequence of pictures telling a little story. The quality of the pictures depends very much on the illumination around the Teddy. This quality can certainly be improved by using a better camera and more appropriate placement.

Not everybody was immediately able to trigger the photo with the hand movements. Some people had to try several times until they achieved their goal to trigger a photo. Some people gave up and quit. This form of interaction with a physical device has some novelty touch and does create a special user experience, because it is fun to be able to do something which was not possible before or which not everybody can do.

Fortunately, there were little problems with vandals. Every once in a while somebody steeled an eye, i.e. a light bulb, scratched the camera window, or loosened the Teddy's arms.

The Fototeddy got fairly good coverage in the print media and there was even a report on Swiss Television. It was rated as one of the top samples of the Zurich Teddy Summer. The media coverage is also reflected in the number of accesses to the web page during the first weeks of operation (May/June 2006, see Fig. 6).

4.2 Fototeddy (Physical Site) Usage Statistics

The number of pictures taken with the Fototeddy depends on the place where it is installed, on the age of people passing by, on the accessibility, i.e. opening hours of the site and on the time people have to interact with the Fototeddy. At Zurich main station thousands of people passed by the Fototeddy every day. There were up to 293 pictures taken per day with significantly more pictures taken at weekends than on weekdays (see Fig. 6 where the vertical grid lines indicate Sundays). Around the weekend of the 14th of August the Teddy was taken out of service due to the Street Parade Event in Zurich. At smaller exhibitions with hundreds of people passing by there were up to 90 pictures taken per day. Typically, a picture was taken every 5 to 10 minutes.

4.3 Observations at the Physical Site

At a recent exhibition, the GEHLA industrial fair in Chur, Switzerland, the Fototeddy was used as an attractor to promote the Swiss Engineering Association. It was placed near the entrance of the exhibition at a rather noisy place next to a cooling system. Here a human computer interaction (HCI) researcher systematically observed how people interact with the Fototeddy. The observations from Saturday, August 28, 2006 between 14:15 and 16:15 can be summarized as follows:

Not alone: Most people approached the Fototeddy in pairs or in even larger groups. Only 6 people came alone and stayed alone. In 7 other cases first one person came, then friends/family followed. 19 groups of 2 or more people came together from the beginning.

Attractive for children: Mostly children passing by came to the Fototeddy, probably because of its attractive appearance, i.e. the teddy form and the cheerful colours. Children mostly started touching the screen immediately.

Too big for children: However, the Fototeddy was too big for most of the children. They helped themselves by climbing on the foundation, but then they were out of sight of the camera.

Adults read but do not interact: The few adults who came to see the Fototeddy started reading the paper description of the project besides the Fototeddy, and did not immediately start interacting with it. Some only read the description, and did not interact with the Teddy at all.

Too close to the camera: People mostly came too close to the camera. The reason might be that the screen is rather small in order to read/see what is on it.

Touch screen is for touching: Most people, especially children, started the interaction immediately by touching the screen. This is a very natural kind of interaction. It was impressive to see how a one-year-old child in the hand of her mother immediately reached her hand to touch the Teddy. However, this probably underpins the intended interaction which should be touchless, by giving the wrong clues to the kind of interaction (touch instead of hand movement).

Hand movement too fast: Those who understood that they have to move their hand in order to initiate some action moved the hand too fast. Maybe they did not understand that they have to catch the little yellow hand on the screen and 'move it' by the own hand movement.

Posing for a real picture: Once people decided to take a picture, they posed for the picture in a serious manner, like in a normal photo booth. If the picture was not good enough, they did not accept to upload it by touching the appropriate button on the touch screen.

Waiting: Some people were waiting near the Fototeddy, but mostly did not realize what it could be used for.

Frustration: One boy beat the camera, another quit with a dismissive gesture, after not succeeding in making a photo. During the observation time there were rather few manifestations of frustration which could be explained by a relaxed atmosphere and leisure time. Improvements on the success rate of people taking pictures should be possible by better user guidance (e.g. marks on the floor indicating where people should stand for taking the pictures).

4.4 Web (Virtual Site) Usage Statistics

Fig. 6 shows the number of pictures viewed on the web and the number of pictures mailed via web site during the Zurich Teddy Summer Event where the system was installed at Zurich main station. The number of pictures taken at the Fototeddy is given as reference. At the beginning of the period the URL was published in several print media. There is a clear correlation of the number of pictures viewed with the publications of the URL in print media, e.g. Computerworld Schweiz (9'898 print run) published on Saturday 21.05.2005 lead to 513 views the next Monday (23.5.2005).

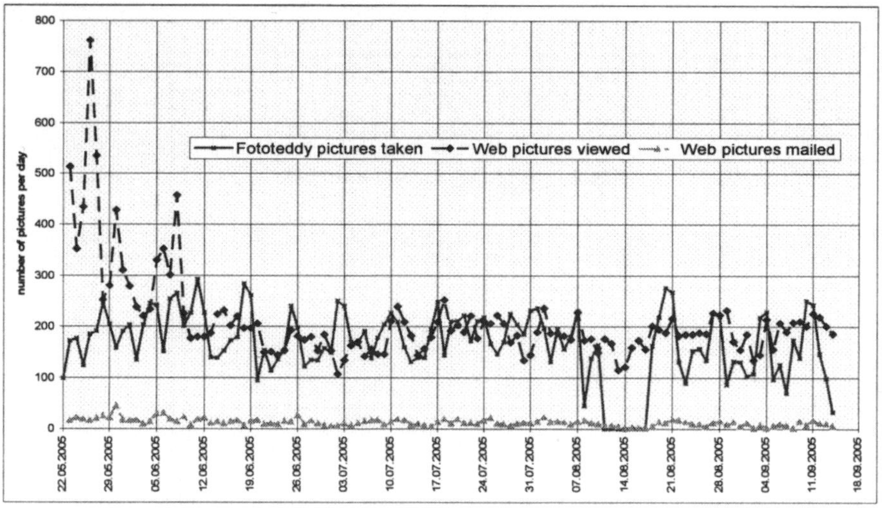

Fig. 6. Number of pictures taken and number of pictures viewed and mailed via Web

There was a clear impact of these publications on the number of web pictures viewed, but the media coverage had no impact on the number of pictures taken. After this starting period with large media coverage and lots of web accesses, the number of accesses remained fairly stable. About 10% of the pictures viewed were also mailed to somebody. The vertical grid lines indicate Sundays. As can be seen, there were significantly more pictures taken on weekends and people tend to visit the web more frequently during weekdays.

The way how people search for pictures on the web site was analyzed. 5% of the picture accesses were done by entering a number which was given at the Fototeddy when the picture was taken. 95% of the people did browse through the gallery using a calendar. 70% of the accesses during the exhibition period did focus on the exhibition period only. 25% of the accesses were on older pictures.

4.5 Physical Site and Web Site Interaction

Due to the anonymous mode of operation it is not possible to exactly track how much an attractive physical site with a high user engagement does lead users to the virtual site. However, comparing the time series of pictures taken per day with the number of pictures viewed per day and e-mailed per day it is estimated that about 10% of the people who take a picture at the Fototeddy do also visit the web site and e-mail a picture. Most pictures were taken on Saturdays and Sundays, which makes sense because people passing at the main station typically have more time for taking pictures on weekends than during working days. This hypothesis is supported by the statistics by day of the week (see Fig. 7). It looks like pictures would be viewed and mailed on the next day after the picture was taken. This is further evidence on the physical site to virtual site coupling.

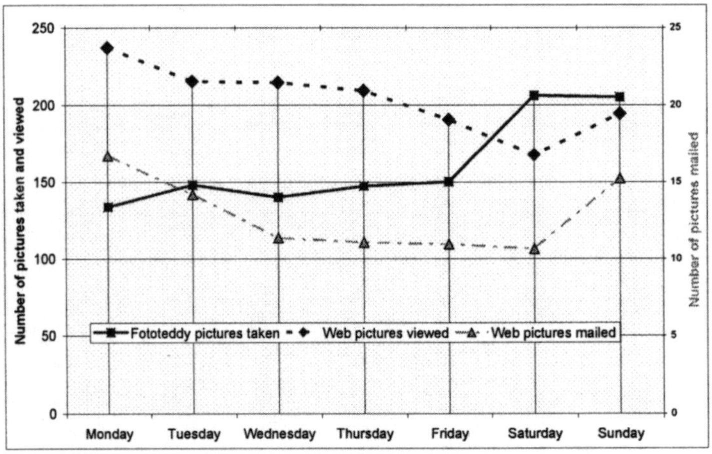

Fig. 7. Average number of pictures taken, viewed and mailed per week day

Fig. 8. shows an overview of the user behaviour concerning visits, picture views and number of other contents viewed during the GEHLA exhibition. The "other contents" denote information on the web site which is not directly connected to their physical visit. In our case this is the description of the Fototeddy project or the list of its milestones. Those pages were not of main interest to the users, and could, in a commercial application, link to other content, e.g. tourist information or advertisements.

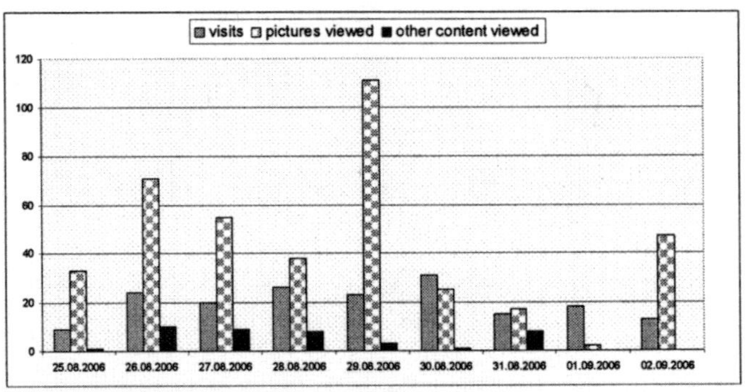

Fig. 8. Number visits and number of views to pictures and other content (during GEHLA 2006)

5 The "Fototeddy Strategy" for Tourism

The following outlines how the "Fototeddy Strategy" could be adapted to other settings. For example in a skiing resort it can be implemented as follows (Berger, 2005):

Attract: The photo booth does not necessarily have to be installed in an attractive housing in form of a Teddy. It could be integrated in a building with a large flat screen. However, selecting an object like a pet – possibly with affinity to the resort – would attract more people, especially children. In a skiing resort people could also be attracted by a photo booth system which shows a spectacular view on the mountains in the background.

Engage: The gesture control is a special experience and exciting for people who use it for the first time. In the skiing environment with low temperatures and people wearing gloves it is more practical than touch screens or buttons.

Lead: Making the pictures only available via the resort's web site, will lead people to visit this site in order to print out the picture or to e-mail the picture to friends. This gives several promotion possibilities for the resort: e.g. the photos may be labelled with resort logos. The guest web site interactions may be used for polls, to make people participate in contests or to ask them to subscribe for newsletters.

Additional functions are possible for the web platform, e.g. setting up an electronic voting to rate the photos and automatically displaying the most recent photos or the photos with the highest ratings at mountain cableway stations. The investments for such a system are estimated to 30kEuro with operational cost in the order of 3kEuro per year.

6 Conclusion

By implementing an attractive photo booth shaped like a Teddy bear, it was possible to let more than 20'000 people take pictures by carrying out a sequence of hand gestures. People got attracted by the colour and shape of the Teddy and many did like to experiment with the novel gesture interface. However, there are also many people who give up when they are not able to control the system properly within about half a minute. About 10% of the people who took a picture at the Fototeddy did also visit the corresponding web site. Thus, it seems to be possible to lead people from the physical into the digital world, e.g. from the Fototeddy object to the web site www.fototeddy.ch. Once on the web site, many people were also willing to explore content not directly related to their previous real-world experience.

This so-called "Fototeddy Strategy" to attract people at a real-world physical object, to get their engagement in interactions with this object, and finally to lead them to a corresponding virtual object is a novel approach to get a high value customer relationship. It was presented how to explore this strategy in tourism by outlining the Fototeddy system application for a skiing resort.

HSR will continue to rent the Fototeddy for events and exhibitions, looking forward to the implementation of the "Fototeddy Strategy" in a tourist resort. All future events shall be accompanied with Human Computer Interaction (HCI) studies based on additional log functions, observations and interviews. This shall give further insight into gesture control user interfaces as well as real-world to virtual-world coupling efficiency.

References

Baumgartner, M. & Höhener, R. (2005). *Fototeddy*. HSR Study Project Report, HSR Hochschule für Technik Rapperswil.

Berger, F. (2005), *Thematisierung der Aussichtsberge in Saas-Fee, Konkrete Massnahmen zur Angebotsinszenierung*. Diploma Thesis, Course TK 0301, International School of Tourism Management, Zurich.

Borchers, J. (2001). *A Pattern Approach to Interaction Design*, Wiley.

Brin S. & Page, L. (1998). The anatomy of a large-scale hypertextual search engine. *Computer Networks and ISDN Systems*, 30, 107-117.

Eran, B. et al (2001), *Urban Simulation and the Luminous Planning Table: Bridging the Gap between the Digital and the Tangible*, Journal of Planning Education and Research, Volume 21 p.195-202.

Fenn, J. et al. (2006). *Hype Cycle for Human-Computer Interaction 2006*. Gartner Group Research Report, G00141150, July 2006

Flickr (2006). *Online photo management and sharing application. Retrieved September 11, 2006 from*, http://flickr.com/

Fraunhofer (2006). *Touch Less Human Computer Interfaces*. Retrieved September 11, 2006 from http://www.imk.fraunhofer.de/en/pointscreen

Hines, B. (2005). *Photo Booth Postcard Book*, Princeton Architectural Press.

Microsoft (2006). *World-Wide Media eXchange (WWMX), Browse photos on a single database indexed by their location*, http://wwmx.org/ (accessed September 11, 2006)

Ratner, B. & Evans, R. (2003). *Hilhaven Lodge: The Photo Booth Pictures*. Powerhouse Books.

Rauterberg, M., Fjeld, M., Krueger, H., Bichsel, M., Leonhardt U., & Meier M.(1998). BUILD-IT: a planning tool for construction and design, CHI '98: CHI 98 conference summary on Human factors in computing systems.

Acknowledgment

The authors wish to thank Marc Baumgartner and Reto Höhener for their tremendous work during their study project.

Integrated Electronic Customer Relationship Management (CRM) for Alpine Tourist Destinations: Drivers and an Adoption Framework

Michael Fux[a]
Daniel S. Mathieu[a]
Frank Go[b]

[a] Institute of Information Systems
University of Berne, Switzerland
{michael.fux, daniel.mathieu}@iwi.unibe.ch
[b] Department of Marketing Management / Centre for Tourism Management
Erasmus University Rotterdam, Netherlands
fgo@fbk.eur.nl

Abstract

Integrated customer relationship management (CRM) processes between service providers and destination management organizations (DMOs) are essential to bring about the cooperation enabling a tourism region to remain competitive. While DMOs face the threat of disintermediation and need to respond with higher level services, service providers, particularly small and medium-sized tourism enterprises (SMTEs) have considerable potential within their CRM processes for efficiency improvement. One possible scenario to solve this dilemma would be a partnership between the service providers and the DMO in the field of CRM processes. In this integrative CRM approach the DMO provides both the required information and communication technologies (ICT) infrastructure and the processing of specific tasks. Currently, the outsourcing of CRM processes is hardly practised in the DMO context. The derived research model explains which factors drive the service providers' intention to increase the outsourcing level, identifies destination management systems (DMS) as enablers of integrated electronic CRM and offers a thorough understanding of the critical factors influencing cooperative CRM between DMOs and SMTEs.

Keywords: Integrated CRM, Destination Management Organization, outsourcing, Small and Medium-Sized Tourism Enterprises

1 Introduction

The success of tourist destinations depends to a large extent on effective relationships between DMOs (Destination Management Organizations) and enterprises, in particular small businesses. In many European regions this relationship and the strategic position of destinations has been altered by two major factors, which are inextricably connected: Internationalization and information and communication technologies (ICT). The emphasis in the 1970s was on Computer Reservation Systems (CRS), in the 1980s it was on Global Distribution Systems (GDS), and in the mid-1990s the centre of gravitation shifted towards the Internet.

The focus of e-tourism has been primarily on marketing and sales and offers vast potential to develop a process of cooperative promotion of a geographic area to lure travellers (Palmer & McCole, 2000). Whilst online booking and reservation services can be said to have been adopted by travellers, the 'e-Business Scoreboard 2005: Tourism' indicates that CRM practices in an electronic environment is not 'widely diffused among the smaller firms' (E-Business Watch, 2005), which 'robs' them of a chance to raise productivity.

CRM is an all-embracing business paradigm, which puts the customer in the centre of all activities and pursues an integration of marketing, sales and service functions facilitated by information and communication technologies (Parvatiyar, 2001; Payne & Frow, 2005; Reinartz, Krafft, & Hoyer, 2004). The customer-centric processes follow the objectives of initiating, developing and maintaining successful long-run relationships with customers (Day, 2000). CRM system assists these strategic goals by providing the enterprise with an integrated view of its customers' socio-demographic profiles, interests and activities, as well as their past and prospective needs (Zikmund, McLeod, & Gilbert, 2003). Electronic CRM (e-CRM) involves mainly the Internet and other interactive technologies to initiate and mediate relationships between the firms and their customers (Feinberg, Kadam, Hokama, & Kim, 2002; Luck & Lancaster, 2003).

So far, smaller tourism firms have been unable to capture the considerable potential that CRM systems offer for efficiency improvement. Due to its complexity, it is unlikely that this situation will change. Therefore, our argument is that the outsourcing of CRM tasks to DMOs enables smaller firms to concentrate on their own core competencies and offers the best chance to improve their efficiency. The purpose of this paper is to help DMOs and small businesses understand the reality of international competition and manage their regional network in the new business context. Subsequently, to demonstrate that an integrated CRM will prove essential to bring about the level of cooperation needed between a destination and enterprises in order to afford a tourism region the opportunity to remain competitive.

The foregoing argument implies an urgent need for a complete redesign of customer-oriented processes that can be seamlessly linked to independent tourism operators in a destination network via intervention and coordination by the DMO. Reengineering is therefore required, in order to redesign inter- and intra-organizational processes taking advantage of newly available technology tools.

The redesign envisioned by the authors is realistic, because the DMS, viewed as the common ICT infrastructure of the DMO, can be leveraged as an enabling mechanism to converge different services and products from a tourist destination (Collins & Buhalis, 2003; Lewis, 2002) and present the destination as a holistic entity (Buhalis & Licata, 2002). Furthermore, the literature describes DMSs as inter-organizational systems (IOS), which allow resource pooling in forms of joint marketing or distribution activities (Hong, 2002). In early stages, DMS consisted mainly of a content management system and a booking engine with a web interface for customers. However, at present, CRM applications are integrated in DMS.

Accordingly, from a technical perspective, the envisioned redesign is quite possible. A successful implementation of a DMS as examined in this paper is primarily dependent on the human factor, i.e. the willingness and ability of stakeholders, especially of accommodation providers and tourist attractions, to participate fully in an integrated CRM initiative. For that reason, the willingness of stakeholders to adopt services hosted in a DMS is crucial for further development and is the focus of the developed adoption model. According to a study in the Canary Islands hotel industry, there is an increasing propensity to outsource services in all departments. Improved quality and services as well as taking advantages of resources and core capabilities are the perceived key advantages and thus correlate with the desire to outsource (Espino-Rodríguez & Robaina, 2005). Research about the acceptance of ASP solutions by small hotels indicates an interest in this model of software delivery, because of expected reductions of labour and ICT costs and improvement of ICT performance. Unease is primary expressed about 'outsourcing' applications that are regarded as business-critical and referring the idea that confidential data is hosted by an external server provider (Paraskevas & Buhalis, 2002).

The driving hypothesis underlying this work is that small and medium-sized tourism enterprises (SMTE), which typically lack specialized resources in the web-based CRM domain, may profit from a DMO's experience by integrating CRM processes by means of inter-organizational systems (IOS) within their own business processes. In a cooperative approach, DMOs are insourcing specific e-CRM activities which are currently handled by service providers. This centralised concept is similar to the segmentation described by Hagel III and Singer (1999), i.e. the unbundling of corporations into three kinds of businesses: customer relationship business, product innovation business and infrastructure business. This model provides a first orientation towards the necessary transformation of business processes in tourist destinations.

Consequently, the objectives of the study are threefold: from a practical perspective, framing the drivers for a cooperative approach in e-CRM and describing an integrated solution with the corresponding potential, and, from a theoretical perspective, identifying antecedents to individual and organizational adoption of innovations such as cooperative e-CRM.

2 Drivers for Collaboration in E-CRM

According to Buhalis, successful realisation of CRM in tourist destinations requires bringing all individual partners together—rather than having them compete against one another—and pooling resources towards developing an integrated marketing mix and delivery system (Buhalis, 2000). Drivers for cooperation in e-CRM in alpine tourist destinations were identified the destination as a whole and from the DMO's and service provider's perspective. The challenges from each perspective are presented in the following sections.

CRM entails building in-depth knowledge of customer needs, motivation and behaviour and applying customer knowledge to improve process performance (Shaw & Reed, 1999). However, the current structure in alpine tourist destinations generates a 'data-ownership dilemma' because CRM applications and adequate processes are established at two levels: the first being between customers and the DMO, and the second between service providers and customers (see Fig. 1). This situation is characterized by a multiplicity of non-integrated customer touch points and makes it impossible to keep track of the information produced through each interaction. The provision of a 'complete tourism experience' through delivery of complementary products is lacking. The required integration of marketing, sales and after-sales activities into a closed loop is difficult to establish (Hirschowitz, 2001). This dilemma and deficient competences in conducting CRM processes at DMOs constitute a barrier to comprehensive CRM initiatives at the level of destination brands.

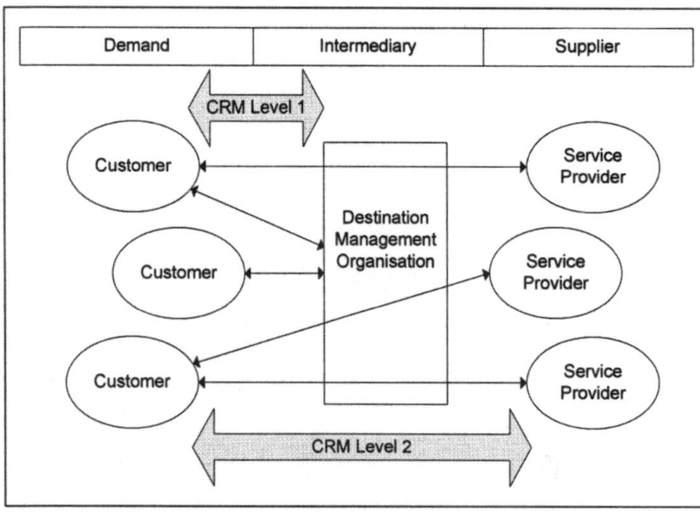

Fig. 1. CRM at different levels in tourist destinations

By failing to cooperate in e-CRM processes, firms could find themselves in a position of "spending more and more resources managing and guarding information silos rather than using them effectively" (Badii & Sharif, 2003: 146). A key to competitive advantage in dynamic destination networks is the inter-organizational coordination of information (Dyer & Singh, 1998). This observation compels the authors to argue, that a DMO should play the coordinator role in e-CRM processes. Our research seeks to provide evidence to underpin our assumption.

Smaller service providers—especially in the accommodation sector—are struggling with customer-oriented processes in an increasingly complex ICT environment. Furthermore, restricted financial resources prevent investments in technology, process design and people. It follows that small tourism operators in the accommodation sector with their need to build up a comprehensive and accurate picture of their clients are not leveraging the potential of CRM applications. Moreover, the websites of small hotels tend to be electronic brochures rather than dynamic and interactive relationship marketing tools (Morrison, Taylor, Morrison, & Morrison, 1999). Beyond having an Internet presence, B2B communication aspects such as interconnectivity and interoperability need to be addressed (Collins & Buhalis, 2003). Various empirical studies reveal the e-mail and e-booking services of SMTEs to be lacking. Besides inadequate online booking facilities (indeed, websites of SMTEs rarely offer this service), problems with answering e-mails or defensive adoption of e-mail marketing are not uncommon (Frey, Schegg, & Murphy, 2003; Murphy, Olaru, Schegg, & Frey, 2003; Schegg, Liebrich, Liu, & Murphy, 2006). As Evans, Bohrer and Richards (2001) have noted, small tourism firms may well remain lost in the electronic marketplace unless they are assisted in the usage of ICT tools and acquire the skills needed to participate in the digital economy. From a global point of view, small and medium-sized accommodation providers lag behind dominant hotel chains, which deploy the technological infrastructure to support CRM processes.

From a DMO perspective, the implementation of a stronger "customer-connected strategy" (Lin & Su, 2003: 718) especially in the field of marketing communications can be seen as an advancement in comparison to the current mass marketing practices (WTO, 2004). Today, DMOs' online marketplaces constitute an important distribution channel for small and medium-sized tourism operators. To keep their standing as preferred distribution partners and to remain competitive among online intermediaries, they need an attractive service bundle for all stakeholders. DMSs have much to offer, i.e., additional applications, beyond online booking engines, to support CRM processes. Experts are postulating a commercialisation of destination management organizations into a leading distribution partner for service providers (Bieger, Laesser, & Weinert, 2006; Pechlaner & Tschurtschenthaler, 2003). The advancement of DMO websites from web portals with limited information to electronic marketplaces with dynamic packaging features indicates a strategic shift towards a more commercial approach. The latter, however, requires accommodation providers to give a DMS an appropriate allocation (Collins & Buhalis, 2003). Where such support is lacking the destination runs the risk of loosing market share (Buhalis, 1996).

3 A Cooperative Approach

The cooperative scenario is based on a CRM infrastructure which is part of a DMS. The CRM system hosted by the DMO consists of three pivotal applications: an online booking engine, an inbound management system and an e-mail marketing system. The booking engine enables customers to check room availability, book accommodation and make arrangements online. Furthermore, the booking engine includes an e-mail workflow: E-mails are generated automatically to thank the guest for his or her reservation just after the booking process, to send the latest information about the destination a few days before arrival, and to request feedback about one week after the stay. The inbound management system sorts incoming e-mails semi- or fully automatically to pre-defined categories and forwards them to relevant team members after analysis for further processing. The application identifies semantic links by analyzing texts and comparing content with data from the internal customer database. These are then used as the basis for intelligent response management and to generate a fully-automatic response for standard customer queries. The e-mail marketing application generates personalised mailings with individual offers and arrangements. The information used to personalise the mailings is stored in a central database. Each of the three applications generates information about the customers to enter in the database. The inbound management system scans e-mails for keywords relating to the customer's interests to include that information, and the booking engine saves all the available information obtained during the booking process. The newsletters generated by the system are interactive: When the customer navigates through the newsletter, the system learns more about her or his interests through click-tracking. The system also maintains the database to avoid duplicate, inaccurate or out-of-date information. Together, the database and the three applications enable integrated e-CRM processes.

On the basis of the characterised CRM system, different cooperative scenarios to conduct e-mail marketing campaigns, manage inquiries and process online bookings are imaginable. In the following three scenarios the DMO takes on specific activities and acts as provider of the application.

(1) E-Mail Marketing: Planning, implementation and analysis are the main process steps during a marketing campaign (MacPherson, 2001; Schumacher & Meyer, 2004). SMTEs and DMOs collaborate to appoint the objectives, the target group, the content and the implementation time of the campaign. During implementation, content is arranged by collaborating partners and customers are selected according to matching profiles from the central database. After transmitting the e-mail on behalf of the service provider or the DMO, customer reactions are stored in the database and the efficiency of the campaigns in terms of opening- and click-rate or bookings is measured. Whereas the first step is not suitable for outsourcing, the subsequent activities have a high potential for standardization and therefore fit better for outsourcing.

(2) Inquiry Management: In a cooperative scenario the DMO acts as the first contact person in handling inbound contacts. In standard cases, such as offer requests, the processing of inbound contact is fully outsourced to the DMO. While processing at the DMO, there is the potential to offer a 'complete tourism experience' by delivering complementary services to a basic product. The DMO is in charge to keep track of the sent offers and arrange follow-up activities for non-booked offers. In non-standard cases the query is forwarded to the service provider in a pre-qualified format and processed by them.

(3) Online Booking: Cooperation in the field of distribution, concerns the participation of service providers on the online marketplace. Derived from the classical room reservation process (Baker et al., 1994), online booking includes the following activities: characterise the product and create offers, maintain room availabilities, conduct online booking with payment, document booking details and confirm booking. The basic offer is created by the service provider and is offered on the electronic marketplace. Predestined for outsourcing to the DMO are booking

transaction and confirmation. Due to comprehensive customer profiles cross- and up-selling possibilities are to realise during the search and booking process.

The following explanation explores if there are any fundamental motives for service providers to consider adopting one of the outsourcing scenarios. Table 1 presents specific potentials for each e-CRM process in the case of cooperation.

Table 1. Potentials of three cooperation scenarios in e-CRM processes

(1) e-mail marketing	- focus on content and strategy - improve quality through state-of-the-art technology - access to marketing expertise of the DMO - increase relevance of campaigns through unified customer profiles - implement advanced segmentation techniques
(2) inquiry management	- reduce destination-specific requests - receive pre-qualified inquiries in a standardised format - obtain more information about customers to create offers - provide access to a multi-channel customer interaction centre
(3) online booking	- profit of an additional distribution channel and market scope - provide complete and up-to-date information about products and availabilities - generate supplier-based packages and more flexible, dynamic packages

In addition to leveraging process-specific potentials, generic advantages of outsourcing like cost reductions, focus on core competences or increase cost transparency may create value for the service providers. In this sense, these co-operation schemes support local enterprises to counteract their lack of economies of scale and strengthen their competitiveness in the international tourism competitive arena (Buhalis, 1996). Outsourcing of CRM applications and processes can lead to the mentioned advantages but it can give rise to significant risks. Commonly quoted disadvantages are the loss of critical capabilities, the risk of sourcing defective capabilities, the loss of cross-functional skills and the loss of control over the supplier (Quinn & Hilmer, 1994).

Although there is obvious potential for service providers, their willingness to cooperate with DMOs is lacking. Reasons therefore are that, SMTE are not intensely engaged in networking and do not consider themselves as part of a destination network. Barriers for entering cooperative initiatives are cultural factors on the one hand and deficient resources as time and staff on the other hand (Evans, 1999). For this purpose, the outlined scenario is used to tackle the factors that influence SMTEs' decision to outsource CRM processes to DMOs and to explore the cooperative CRM adoption research model.

4 Adoption Framework

As CRM outsourcing may be seen as a major organizational innovation, which is hardly practised, it may be more appropriate to explain variations in the SMTEs' attitude towards CRM outsourcing and towards their decision to increase the level of outsourcing rather than variations in the degree of outsourcing. The researchers of this paper have been unable to identify research publications, which report on the adoption of CRM outsourcing in the destination management context. Therefore, the research model that they apply, is based on prior works on similar innovations such as IS outsourcing or the adoption of inter-organizational systems such as EDI.

Besides the technology acceptance model presented by Davis (1989) and Roger's (1995) innovation decision process, the theory of planned behaviour (TPB) (Ajzen, 1985)—as an extended successor of the theory of reasoned action (TRA) (Fishbein & Ajzen, 1975)—has been successful in predicting and explaining behaviour across a wide variety of domains. The objective of the TPB is to predict and understand motivational influences on individual behaviour, where "[...] behaviour involves a choice among two ore more alternatives" (Ajzen & Fishbein, 1980: 79). The TPB postulates that attitude, subjective norm and perceived behavioural control influence the decision to perform a given behaviour.

According to a much-quoted work by Kwon and Zmud (1987), technological, structural, environmental, individual and task-related factors are traditional elements influencing the adoption of innovations. They integrate innovation characteristics from Roger's Innovation Diffusion Theory (Rogers, 1995), task-related factors from Hackman and Oldman (1976), and environmental factors from DiMaggio and Powell (1983). At an aggregate level, technological and task-related factors are considered innovation characteristics, and structural, individual and environmental determinants are regarded as organizational characteristics. These two collections of independent variables are treated as appropriate predictors of both individual and organizational IT adoption (Jeyaraj, Rottman, & Lacity, 2006). By combining Kwon and Zmud's framework and the TPB, the innovation and organizational characteristics form one's attitude towards cooperation in CRM.

To determine innovation characteristics, the concepts of relative advantage and transaction costs are applied. The concept of relative advantage in decision theory compares the expected risks and benefits of a decision. In addition to organizational readiness and competitive pressures, perceived benefits as a characteristic of the innovation are also a major factor explaining the adoption of EDI in SMEs (Iacovou, Benbasat, & Dexter, 1995). Jurison (1995) employed the concept of relative advantage on outsourcing. Applied to the context of collaboration in CRM, this means that a service provider has to evaluate all the potential risks and benefits that may arise as a consequence of a new governance mode and the application of new technologies. To identify the individual risks, the perceived risk concept developed by Cunningham (1967) will be applied to the context of CRM collaboration. He divided perceived risk into six facets, in particular performance risk, financial risk, opportunity/time risk, psychological risk, social risk and safety risk (Gewald, Wüllenweber, & Weitzel, 2006). The major advantages associated with the choice of insourcing versus outsourcing have already been identified. In numerous studies, four motives according to which corporations choose to outsource parts of their business were quoted frequently, in particular cost reduction, gain access to specialised resources, focus on core business and quality improvement (Dibbern, Goles,

Hirschheim, & Jayatilaka, 2004; Lacity & Willcocks, 1998; Matiaske & Mellewigt, 2002).

Transaction-cost analysis supports a general framework for sourcing decisions and is used to examine organizations with regard to their efficient boundary, i.e. which activities should be processed internally and which should be sourced externally (Williamson, 1998). With the transaction-cost approach, an analysis of asset specificity, frequency, and uncertainty of current CRM processes explains the attitude towards collaboration.

Organizational structure is measured by a set of constructs influencing the attitude towards cooperative CRM. These constructs are adopter characteristics, inter-organizational complementarity and environmental influences. "Organization Dispositional Innovativeness", size and structure are used to measure the adopter characteristics (Frambach & Schillewaert, 2002). Inter-organizational complementarity reflects relational perspective among partners in terms of information and control systems, decision-making processes, and organizational culture (Tan & Raman, 2002). Network externalities and competitive pressures are regarded as environmental influences (Frambach & Schillewaert, 2002).

In an organizational context, the subjective norm is determined by the firm's competitive environment. Applied to the context, subjective norm is defined as the degree to which most people who are important to an organization, think that the organization should increase the level of cooperation with the DMO (Dibbern, 2004). Perceived behavioural control reflects the perceived feasibility of performing the behaviour and is thus related to perceptions of situational competence (self-efficacy) (Krueger, Reilly, & Carsrud, 2000). The dependent variable is defined as a person's or organization's intention to use or adopt cooperative CRM processes. This is usually measured using forward-looking statements that capture the intent of the person or organization (Jeyaraj et al., 2006). Hotel size and quality category are used as control variables to establish whether or not these have a systematic influence on intention to cooperate. The theoretical constructs and their relationships are converted and depicted in the following model (Fig. 2).

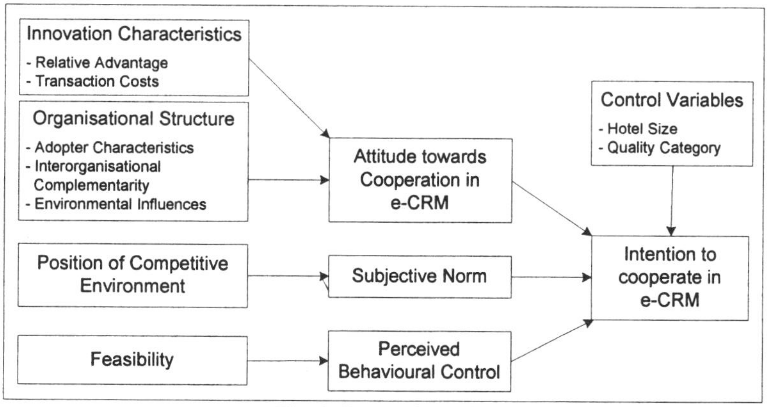

Fig. 2. Research model

5 Further Research and Expected Results

The conceptually derived potentials were validated by focus groups composed of service providers and DMO managers and enabled an evaluation of the chosen determinants influencing the intention to outsource e-CRM processes. Afterwards Structural Equation Modelling (SEM) shall be performed to measure the proposed research model. SEM tests all the hypothesized relationships simultaneously in a multivariate context (Kline, 2005; Schumacker & Lomax, 1996). SEM is used to illustrate, interrelate and explain the relationship between the attitude towards outsourcing, subjective norm, perceived behavioural control and the intention to increase the level of outsourcing. The data collected from hotel managers is analyzed using the Partial Least Squares (PLS) procedure of structural equation modelling. DMSs as enablers of integrated CRM processes are potentially the most important technological instrument for the DMO future, particularly because they enable service providers-destination collaboration ventures; resources pooling, e.g. the sharing of management, marketing and technology expertise. Therefore, identifying the factors influencing adoption of an integrated CRM acceptance by service providers is a crucial issue this research seeks to resolve.

References

Ajzen, I. (1985). From Intentions to Actions: A Theory of Planned Behavior. In J. Kuhl & J. Beckmann (Eds.). *Action-Control: From Cognition to Behavior* (pp. 11-39). Heidelberg: Springer.

Ajzen, I. & Fishbein, M. (1980). *Understanding attitudes and predicting social behavior.* Englewood Cliffs: Prentice-Hall.

Badii, A. & Sharif, A. (2003). Information management and knowledge integration for enterprise innovation. *Logistics Information Management*, 16(2), 145-155.

Baker, S., Bradley, P. & Huyton, J. (1994). *Principles of Hotel Front Office Operations.* London: Cassell.

Bieger, T., Laesser, C. & Weinert, R. (2006). *Wettbewerbsfähige Strukturen und Aufgabenteilung im Bündner Tourismus - Teil 1: Ausgangslage.* St. Gallen: Universität St. Gallen, Institut für Öffentliche Dienstleistungen und Tourismus.

Buhalis, D. (1996). Enhancing the Competitiveness of Small and Medium-Sized Tourism Enterprises. *Electronic Markets*, 6(1), 1-6.

Buhalis, D. (2000). Marketing the competitive destination of the future. *Tourism Management*, 21(1), 97-116.

Buhalis, D. & Licata, M.C. (2002). The future eTourism intermediaries. *Tourism Management*, 23(3), 207-220.

Collins, C. & Buhalis, D. (2003). Destination Management Systems Utilisation in England. In A. J. Frew (Ed.), *Information and Communication Technologies in Tourism 2004* (pp. 202-211). Wien - New York: Springer.

Cunningham, S. M. (1967). The Major Dimensions of Perceived Risk. In D. F. Cox (Ed.). *Risk Taking and Information Handling in Consumer Behaviour* (pp. 82-108). Boston: Harvard University Press.

Davis, F. D. (1989). Perceived Usefulness, Perceived Ease of Use and User Acceptance of Information Technology. *MIS Quarterly*, 13(3), 318-340.

Day, G. S. (2000). Capabilities for Foreign Customer Relationship Managements, Institution.

Dibbern, J. (2004). *The Sourcing of Application Software Services: Empirical Evidence of Cultural, Industry and Functional Differences.* Heidelberg: Physica-Verlag.

Dibbern, J., Goles, T., Hirschheim, R. & Jayatilaka, B. (2004). Information Systems Outsourcing: A Survey and Analysis of the Literature. *The DATA BASE for Advances in Information Systems*, 35(4), 6-102.

DiMaggio, P. & Powell, W. (1983). The Iron Cage Revisited: Industrial isomorphism and collective rationality in organizational fields. *American Sociological Review*, 48(2), 147–160.

Dyer, J. H. & Singh, H. (1998). The relational View: Cooperative Strategy and Sources of interorganizational competitive Advantage. *Academy of Management Review*, 23(4), 660-679.

E-Business Watch (2005). *ICT and Electronic Business in the Tourism Industry, Sector Report No. 09*. Salzburg/Brüssel: ETC - eTourism Center, European Commission, Enterprise & Industry Directorate General.

Espino-Rodríguez, T. F. & Robaina, V. P. (2005). The management perception of the strategic outsourcing of services: An empirical examination in the hotel sector. *Service Industries Journal*, 25(5), 689-708.

Evans, G. (1999). Networking for Growth and Digital Business: Local Urban Tourism SMTEs and ICT. In Buhalis, D. & Schertler, W. (Eds.), *Information and Communications Technologies in Tourism* (pp. 247-258). Wien: Springer.

Feinberg, R. A., Kadam, R., Hokama, L. & Kim, I. (2002). The state of electronic customer relationship management in retailing. *International Journal of Retail & Distribution Management*, 30(10), 470-481.

Fishbein, M. & Ajzen, I. (1975). *Belief, Attitude, Intention, and Behavior: An Introduction to Theory and Research*. Addison-Wesley, Reading.

Frambach, R. T. & Schillewaert, N. (2002). Organizational innovation adoption A multi-level framework of determinants and opportunities for future research. *Journal of Business Research*, 55(2), 163-176.

Frey, S., Schegg, R. & Murphy, J. (2003). E-mail customer service in the Swiss hotel industry. *Tourism & Hospitality Research*, 4(3), 197-212.

Gewald, H., Wüllenweber, K. & Weitzel, T. (2006). The Influence of Perceived Risks on Banking Managers' Intention to Outsource Business Processes - A Study of the German Banking and Finance Industry. *Journal of Electronic Commerce Research*, 7 (2), 78-96.

Hackman, J. R. & Oldman, G. R. (1976). Motivation through Design of Work. *Organizational Behavior and Human Performance*, 16(2), 250–279.

Hagel III, J. & Singer, M. (1999). Unbundling the Corporation. *Harvard Business Review*, 77(2), 133-141.

Hirschowitz, A. (2001). Closing the CRM loop: The 21st century marketer's challenge: Transforming customer insight into customer value. *Journal of Targeting, Measurement & Analysis for Marketing*, 1 (2), 168-178.

Hong, I. B. (2002). A new framework for interorganizational systems based on the linkage of participants' roles. *Information & Management*, 39(4), 261-270.

Iacovou, C. L., Benbasat, I. & Dexter, A. S. (1995). Electronic data interchange and small organizations: Adoption and impact of technology. *MIS Quarterly*, 19(4), 465-.

Jeyaraj, A., Rottman, J. W. & Lacity, M. C. (2006). A review of the predictors, linkages, and biases in IT innovation adoption research. *Journal of Information Technology*, 21(1), 1-23.

Jurison, J. (1995). The role of risk and return in information technology outsourcing decisions. *Journal of Information Technology*, 10(4), 239-247.

Kline, R. B. (2005). *Principles and practice of structural equation modelling*. 2nd ed., New York: The Guilford Press.

Krueger, N. F., Reilly, M. D. & Carsrud, A. L. (2000). Competing models of entrepreneurial intentions. *Journal of Business Venturing*, 15(5-6), 411-432.

Kwon, T. H. & Zmud, R. W. (1987). Unifying the fragmented models of information systems implementation. In R. J. Boland & R. A. Hirschheim (Eds.). *Critical issues in information systems research* (pp. 227-251). New York: John Wiley & Sons.

Lacity, M. C. & Willcocks, L. P. (1998). An empirical investigation of information technology sourcing practices: Lessons from experience. *MIS Quarterly*, 22(3), 308–363.

Lewis, R. D. (2002). Modelling Tourism Impacts Using IT Based Destination Management System. In K. W. Wöber, A. J. Frew, & M. Hitz (Eds.), *Information and Communication Technologies in Tourism* (pp. 97-104). Wien/New York: Springer.

Lin, Y. & Su, H.-Y. (2003). Strategic analysis of customer relationship management—a field study on hotel enterprises. *Total Quality Management and Business Excellence*, 14(6), 715-731.

Luck, D. & Lancaster, G. (2003). E-CRM: customer relationship marketing in the hotel industry. *Managerial Auditing Journal*, 18(3), 213-231.

MacPherson, K. (2001). *Permission Based E-mail Marketing That Works*. Chicago: Dearborn Trade.

Matiaske, W. & Mellewigt, T. (2002). Motive, Erfolge und Risiken des Outsourcings - Befunde und Defizite der empirischen Outsourcing-Forschung. *Zeitschrift für Betriebswirtschaft*, 72(6), 641-659.

Morrison, A. M., Taylor, S., Morrison, A. J. & Morrison, A. D. (1999). Marketing small hotels on the World Wide Web. *Information Technology and Tourism*, 2(2), 97-113.

Murphy, J., Olaru, D., Schegg, R. & Frey, S. (2003). Swiss Hotels' Web-site and E-mail Management: The Bandwagon Effect. *Cornell Hotel and Restaurant Administration Quarterly*, 44(1), 71-87.

Palmer, A. & McCole, P. (2000). The role of electronic commerce in creating virtual tourism destination marketing organisations. *International Journal of Contemporary Hospitality Management*, 12(3), 198-204.

Paraskevas, A. & Buhalis, D. (2002). Outsourcing IT for small hotels: the opportunities and challenges of using application service providers. *The Cornell Hotel and Restaurant Administration Quarterly*, 43(2), 27-39.

Parvatiyar, A., Sheth, J. N. (2001). Conceptual Framework of Customer Relationship Management. In A. Parvatiyar, J. N. Sheth, & G. Shainesh (Eds.), *Customer Relationship Management - Emerging Concepts, Tools and Applications* (pp. 3-25). New Dehli: Tata/McGraw-Hill.

Payne, A. & Frow, P. (2005). A Strategic Framework for Customer Relationship Management. *Journal of Marketing*, 69(4), 167-176.

Pechlaner, H. & Tschurtschenthaler, P. (2003). Tourism Policy, Tourism Organisations and Change Management in Alpine Regions and Destinations: A European Perspective. *Current Issues in Tourism*, 6(6), 508-539.

Quinn, J.B. & Hilmer, F. G. (1994). Strategic Outsourcing. *MIT Sloan Management Review*, 35(4), 43-55.

Reinartz, W., Krafft, M. & Hoyer, W. D. (2004). The Customer Relationship Management Process: Its Measurement and Impact on Performance. *Journal of Marketing Research*, 41(3), 293-305.

Rogers, E. M. (1995). *Diffusion of innovations*. 4, New York: The Free Press.

Schegg, R., Liebrich, A., Liu, F. & Murphy, J. (2006). eService by Swiss and Austrian Hotels: Does Language Matter? M. Hitz, M. Sigala, & J. Murphy (Eds.), *Information and Communication Technologies in Tourism 2006* (pp. 357-368). Wien/New York: Springer.

Schumacher, J. & Meyer, M. (2004). *Customer Relationship Management strukturiert dargestellt*. Berlin/Heidelberg: Springer Verlag.

Schumacker, R.E. & Lomax, R.G. (1996). *A beginner's guide to structural equation modeling*. Mahwah: Lawrence Erlbaum.

Shaw, R. & Reed, D. (1999). *Measuring and Valuing Customer Relationships: How to Develop the Measures That Drive Profitable CRM Strategies*. London: Business Intelligence.

Tan, M. & Raman, K. (2002). Interorganizational Systems and Transformation of Interorganizational Relationships: A Relational Perspective, in: Applegate, L. et al. (Hrsg), International Conference on Information Systems 2002, Barcelona

Williamson, O. E. (1998). *The Economic Institutions of Capitalism: Firms, Markets, Relational Contracting*. New York: Free Press.

WTO (2004). Survey of Destination Management Organisations, 2004.

Zikmund, W. G., McLeod, R. & Gilbert, F. W. (2003). *Customer Relationship Management: Integrating Marketing Strategy and Information Technology*. Hoboken: Wiley, John & Sons, Inc.

Exploring Email Service Quality (EMSQ) Factors

Jamie Murphy[a]
Roland Schegg[b]
Doina Olaru[a]
Charles F. Hofacker[c]

[a] Business School
University of Western Australia, Australia
{jmurphy, dolaru}@biz.uwa.edu.au

[b] Institute Economics & Tourism,
University of Applied Sciences Valais, Switzerland
roland.schegg@hevs.ch

[c]Department of Marketing
The Florida State University, Greece
chofack@garnet.acns.fsu.edu

Abstract

This paper adds to the sparse literature of email service quality. While many studies model website quality or describe the content of email replies, this may be the first study to model dimensions of email service quality (EMSQ). Unlike most website quality studies that ignore email or mix email with self-service technologies, this exploratory study first discusses email's role in service quality. Drawing on data from a study of almost 500 luxury hotels and the SERVQUAL model, a series of structural equations on 25 features of quality email replies suggest four dimensions of service quality – personalisation, responsiveness, reliability and tangibility. These dimensions provide management with insights for improving their EMSQ and provide academics with a theoretical model for further study of EMSQ.

Keywords: Email, Service Quality, e-services, SERVQUAL

1 Introduction

One of the many uses of Google Scholar (scholar.google.com) is its "cited by" feature, which reflects an article's importance (Jacsó, 2006). The results of two September 2006 queries, 1,546 and 1,343 citations respectively, highlight widespread acceptance of Parasuraman, Zeithamal and Berry's (1985; 1988) articles on service quality. While myriad authors have refined and questioned the latter article's 22-item scale and five dimensions of perceived customer service, even its critics acknowledge the SERVQUAL model's impact (Coulthard, 2004; Kettinger & Lee, 2005).

Beginning this century, a burgeoning research stream has applied SERVQUAL to electronic service quality (e.g., Fassnacht & Koese, 2006; Sousa & Voss, 2006). Most studies apply SERVQUAL to websites, but a major limitation is the model's assumption of human interaction (Long & McMellon, 2004). Instruments for measuring perceived offline service quality may be inappropriate for measuring electronic service quality, or eService (Parasuraman, Zeithaml, & Malhotra, 2005). Human interaction such as email communication relates to eService (Yang, Peterson, & Cai, 2003), albeit Fassnacht and Koese (2006, p. 23) define eService as self-service and contend that email applies to service quality only with service recovery.

This narrow perspective, human interaction is relevant only with service recovery, may be a product of the prevailing research. Many studies fail to define eService, or treat it as self-service (Froehle, 2006; Sousa & Voss, 2006). Furthermore, eService studies often focus on the sales aspects of websites and ignore that customers may need service before or after the sale. Consumers may email the company to assist them find information on a website, provide information not on the site or answer routine questions related to their purchase (Bauer, Falk, & Hammerschmidt, 2006; Piccoli, Brohman, Watson, & Parasuraman, 2004; Wolfinbarger & Gilly, 2003).

Email service quality (EMSQ) extends beyond service recovery and merits its own research, rather than appended to website service quality. Email rather than the World Wide Web, remains "the number one activity and time consumer for the vast majority of Internet users (Rainie & Horigan, 2005, p. 63)." In addition, email's human interaction aligns with SERVQUAL's focus on employee-customer interaction.

To the authors' knowledge, the extant eService studies focus on consumer perceptions of website quality. There is little research of email's role in customer service (Froehle, 2006; Hill et al., 2002) and at least one call to investigate the role of response time to customer email queries (Rust & Lemon, 2001, p. 96). A few studies incorporate email into their eService quality models, but often relate email to service recovery rather than to overall eService (J. E. Collier & Bienstock, 2006; Long & McMellon, 2004; Parasuraman et al., 2005; Wolfinbarger & Gilly, 2003; Yang et al., 2003). Studies that include email, however, lead to a conceptual overlap that mixes electronic- and people-based service elements (Fassnacht & Koese, 2006, p. 23).

Rather than consumer perceptions of eService quality, a related research stream examines companies' delivery of EMSQ. The studies provide insights of organisational email use and snapshots of EMSQ in education (Murphy & Gomes, 2003), tourism (Murphy & Tan, 2003) and hospitality (Matzler, Pechlaner, Abfalter, & Wolf, 2005). Yet these articles tend to classify EMSQ on an ad hoc rather than theoretical basis. There is little reliability or validity testing of the ad hoc dimensions, but validity and reliability are important to new measures of technology-mediated customer service (Froehle & Roth, 2004; Kettinger & Lee, 2005).

Thus, the aims of this study are to (a) add to the limited EMSQ research (b) help position email's role in online service quality, (c) explore theoretically-derived dimensions of EMSQ, and (d) test the validity and reliability of these dimensions.

2 Literature Review

Two decades ago, Collier (1983) heralded the industrial revolution's demise, thanks to robotics and computerised manufacturing. While these technologies dealt with the back office, he also predicted wide-ranging outcomes of automated front office services such as pneumatic delivery systems, automated teller machines, phone answering machines and hotel elevators. Unfortunately, or fortunately, his predicted 32 hour work week by the year 2000 (p. 20) failed to eventuate.

Over the next decade, research of automation continued to favour the back office. Noting this limitation, Walley and Amin (1994) developed a conceptual framework suggesting that the more advanced the technology, the lower the customer contact. Vending machines have low technology but high customer contact. A travel agency's IT system has more complicated technology but the customer has no direct contact with that technology. The authors concluded that maximising ease of use was a key to developing these services.

This century, research continues to examine service technologies, shifting from describing technologies to examining their impact on customers (Meuter, Ostrom, Roundtree, & Bitner, 2000). Scholars signalled the new paradigm of eService – providing services over electronic networks (Rust & Kannan, 2003, p. 38) – and its impact on customers (e.g.,.Collier & Bienstock, 2006; Fassnacht & Koese, 2006; Parasuraman et al., 2005). The following sections examine offline service quality, position email's role in eServices and propose four factors of EMSQ.

2.1 SERVQUAL and Offline Factors of Service Quality

Service quality research began in the 1980s, stemming from the product quality and customer satisfaction literature. The research has evolved into competing perspectives of service quality of either categorical or descriptive terms (Brady & Cronin, 2001). The latter, SERVQUAL, describes five service encounter characteristics – tangibility, reliability, responsiveness, assurance and empathy (Parasuraman et al., 1988). The former categorises service quality in either a technical dimension of what the customer receives, or a functional dimension of customer perceptions of interactions during service delivery (Grönroos, 1984).

Brady and Cronin (2001, p. 44) integrate these competing perspectives with "qualitative and empirical evidence that service quality is a multidimensional, hierarchical construct." Their service quality model contains three second-order factors – interaction, environment and outcome quality – based on nine subdimensions. The model uses four of SERVQUAL's five dimensions, albeit not as primary dimensions of service quality. Tangibility is a subdimension, while empathy, reliability and responsiveness serve as descriptors of the nine subdimensions. They dropped assurance from the model as it failed to remain distinct in past studies as well as in their pretest and factor analysis.

Mittal and Lasser (1996) also question assurance, as well as the empathy dimension. They argue that that two of SERVQUAL's assurance items relate to reliability and the other two items relate to a proposed new dimension, personalisation. Furthermore, empathy items overlap with responsiveness and should reflect relating to customers at a personal level. Their literature review highlighted the importance of interpersonal interaction in customer service and proposed that personalisation captures the interaction's social aspect. Personalisation knows the customer as a person engages in friendly conversations and includes aspects such as warmth, politeness and courtesy.

The revised SERVQUAL-P model has four dimensions – tangibles, reliability, responsiveness, and personalisation. In their empirical test of SERVQUAL versus SERVQUAL-P, the latter outperformed the former across five outcomes in a people processing (health care) service and in four of five outcomes in a possession processing (car repair) service. Similarly, a study of information systems services merged empathy and assurance into a rapport dimension that conveys courteous and caring support (Kettinger & Lee, 2005, p. 612).

2.2 Positioning Email Service Quality (EMSQ)

Early conceptualisations of eService tended to focus on the interaction between consumers and the website, with later research going beyond website interactivity and including dimensions such as fulfilment and service recovery (Collier & Bienstock, 2006). Despite many studies, a common definition of eServices has not emerged and the sole similarity seems to be a focus on Internet-based services (Fassnacht & Koese, 2006, p. 23). Yet another eServices definition goes beyond the Internet to include other "electronic environments such as ATMs, smart card networks, kiosks, among others (Rust & Kannan, 2003, p. 38)."

Given the ambiguity of eService, and limited theoretical research of EMSQ, it is important to position email's role in service quality. As noted earlier, a lack of human interaction limits applying traditional service quality models to the online environment. Four other shortcomings of eServices research are the failure to: include outcome quality, recognise multichannel service delivery, operationalise eServices as either services delivered or customer satisfaction with delivered services, and consider that channels can be self-service or have human interaction (Bansal, McDougal, Dikolli, & Sedatole, 2004; Collier & Bienstock, 2006; Froehle, 2006; Froehle & Roth, 2004; Kettinger & Lee, 2005; Sousa & Voss, 2006).

Froehle & Roth's (2004) five archetypes of technology-related customer contact position email as having human interaction. Three of their archetypes involve face-to-face contact, with or without technology. The other two archetypes are face-to-screen and require technology. *Technology-generated* customer contact, self service technology, has no human interaction and could include interactive voice response systems, interactive kiosks, software and the Internet (Meuter et al., 2000). With *technology-mediated* contact – e.g. email, telephone and instant messaging – the customer and service representative rely on technology to communicate.

Similarly, Sousa and Voss (2006) propose two types of service quality, physical and virtual. Physical service has human intervention, either face-to-face or via technology. Virtual service, automated and without human intervention, uses the Web as the main delivery channel. Most eServices research assumes self-service via websites, technology-generated contact or virtual service; there is a dearth of constructs and scales for technology-mediated contact (Froehle & Roth, 2004, p. 3).

Similar to offline research of service quality (Brady & Cronin, 2001), at least two online studies argue that service quality has hierarchical dimensions. Collier and Bienstock (2006) propose nine subdimensions, which form three dimensions – outcome quality, process quality and service recovery – of eService quality. Fassnacht and Koese (2006) propose 11 subdimensions that form three quality dimensions – outcome, environment and delivery.

Common to both models is outcome quality, what the customer has after service delivery (Fassnacht & Koese, 2006) or the outcome of how the service is delivered (Collier & Bienstock, 2006). The latter study, which investigates retail websites, proposes three subdimensions of outcome quality, order timeliness, order accuracy and order condition. The former study of homepage services, sports coverage and retail websites, has three subdimensions of reliability, functional benefits and emotional benefits. Rather than the broad outcome of delivering goods or services, this study focus solely on company emails sent to customers. Furthermore, this study investigates sent emails, not consumer satisfaction with those emails. Given the above discussion, this paper positions email service quality in three ways.

- EMSQ is based on the content of the emails that customers receive.
- EMSQ has human interaction; it is technology-mediated.
- Finally, given the interpersonal nature of email, traditional conceptualisations of service quality such as SERVQUAL should apply (Sousa & Voss, 2006, p. 363).

Thus the following section reviews eServices studies that highlight the importance of email or include email in their SERVQUAL iteration.

2.3 Factors of Email Service Quality (EMSQ)

Few studies highlight an obvious, perhaps understudied area, consumer reactions to email replies. At a basic level, companies should answer emails promptly. Comparing Internet purchasers and non-purchasers, Yang and Sun (2002), found that answering email was significant to buyers, but not significant to non-buyers. A study of over one thousand customer reviews of online retailers showed that consumers want a quick email reply (Yang et al., 2003). With regard to service recovery, answering email complaints – and in a timely manner that addresses the specific problem and includes the employee's name – relates to customer satisfaction and intention to repurchase (Mattila & Mount, 2003; Naylor, 2003; Strauss & Hill, 2001).

Apart from consumer's appreciating a timely reply, the research is sparse and inconclusive on important EMSQ elements. Drawing on media richness, Froehle (2006) investigated six customer service representative characteristics across three media – telephone, email and online chat. Regardless of the medium, thoroughness, knowledgeableness and preparedness by the representatives influenced customer satisfaction, but the other three characteristics – courtesy, professionalism and attentiveness – showed no influence. Two other studies though, suggest that politeness in emails helps build relationships (Bunz & Campbell, 2004) and empathy in online chat helps build trust (Feng, Lazar, & Preece, 2004).

The founders of SERVQUAL used focus groups and survey research to develop and refine scales encompassing all phases of customer-service interaction, E-S-QUAL and E-Recs-Qual, (Parasuraman et al., 2005). Two scales were necessary, with the former encompassing routine encounters and the latter was salient for service recovery. Email responses to customers fell in the latter, E-Recs-Qual. Two other studies include email service recovery in their eService model (Bauer et al., 2006; J. E.

Collier & Bienstock, 2006), and two studies include responses to routine emails in dimensions of responsiveness, empathy (Long & McMellon, 2004) and customer service (Wolfinbarger & Gilly, 2003). A final study includes routine and service recovery emails that could fall in the dimensions of responsiveness, courtesy, personalisation, competence and communication (Yang et al., 2003)

3 Analysis

This paper draws upon data from a study showing how 491 luxury chain hotels in 55 countries responded to a fictitious email requesting information about room availability for a honeymoon weekend, special events and nearby medical facilities (Schegg, Murphy, & Leuenberger, 2003). The study found that North American hotels and hotels affiliated with smaller chains outperformed their South American and larger chain counterparts in some email response features. After eliminating hotels that did not respond or had missing email response features, the data set contained 311 hotels and 25 response features.

The features stem from academic and industry literature suggesting components of proper email responses, such as answering promptly and politely (Murphy, Olaru, Schegg, & Frey, 2003; Zemke & Connellan, 2001). Table 1 lists the 25 response features, along with the percentage of hotels that addressed these criteria in their email reply. For example, 81% of the hotel emails greeted the guest politely, i.e. *Dear*, and 79% addressed the guest by name. With the exception of response time, the features are binary.

Table 1. Proposed dimensions and presence of email features

% of hotel emails with		**% of hotel emails with**	
Personalisation		**Responsiveness**	
polite opening	81 %	answer honeymoon request	35 %
use guest's name	79 %	answer special event request	46 %
say thank-you	67 %	answer hospital request	72 %
sender's position	85 %	response time	
		~~room request~~	~~95 %~~
Reliability		**Tangibility**	
provisional booking	4 %	chain information	6 %
cancellation information	14 %	sender's name	94 %
credit card request	33 %	signature file	43 %
.com domain name	82 %	promotional information	39 %
		~~telephone number~~	~~48 %~~
		~~fax number~~	~~38 %~~
		~~address~~	~~23 %~~
		~~url~~	~~25 %~~
		~~hotel name~~	~~81 %~~
		~~long message~~	~~26 %~~
		~~with attachment~~	~~15 %~~
		~~disclaimer~~	~~12 %~~

Table 1 also shows the provisional and final categorisation of the features into four EMSQ factors. Given email's interpersonal nature, the researchers classified each of the 25 features into SERVQUAL dimensions (Sousa & Voss, 2006), albeit merging empathy and assurance into a personalisation dimension (Kettinger & Lee, 2005; Mittal & Lassar, 1996) in order to highlight the interpersonal nature of email.

After the provisional classifications, the researchers selectively deleted the features, using AMOS6 with tetrachoric, polychoric, and polyserial correlations to assess the measurement models (Hair, Black, Babin, Anderson, & Tatham, 2006; Jöreskog & Sorbom, 1998). For example, the one variable signature file tended to capture other features possible in a signature file – the hotel name, telephone number, fax number, url and address. Similarly, features that failed to add to a factor were dropped from subsequent iterations. These analyses lead to the four unidimensional factors, goodness-of-fit and other measures shown in Table 2.

Table 2. Dimensions of Email Service Quality

Construct (Eigenvalue)	Features	Factor Loading	Composite Reliability	
Personalisation (1.719)	Polite opening	0.759	0.703	$\chi^2 = 1.912$
	Use guest name	0.682		(2 df) p=0.384
	Say thank-you	0.154		CFI=1
	Sender's position	0.342		AGFI=0.983
Responsiveness (1.344)	Answer honeymoon request	0.438	0.522	$\chi^2 = 0.907$
	Answer special event request	0.457		(2 df) p=0.635
	Answer hospital request			CFI=1
	Response time	0.218		AGFI=0.992
		0.279		
Reliability (1.574)	Cancel booking	0.601	0.573	$\chi^2 = 1.553$
	Credit card request	0.631		(2 df) p=0.46
	Provisional booking	0.292		CFI=1
	Global *.com* domain	0.162		AGFI=0.986
Tangibility (1.613)	Sender's name	0.421	0.547	$\chi^2 = 3.135$
	Signature block	0.627		(2 df) p=0.209
	Chain information	0.357		CFI=0.977
	Promotional information	0.352		AGFI=0.972

The latent constructs have reliabilities above 0.5. Discriminant validity was assessed by testing if construct correlations differed significantly from unity, comparing a constrained model (with correlations = 1) and an unconstrained model. The x^2 difference at $p<0.05$ supports the discriminant validity criterion. Correlations between the constructs lower than the reliability coefficients also suggest discriminant validity. As there are no cross-loadings between the indicators of the four constructs, a two-step approach with congeneric models is appropriate (Anderson & Gerbing, 1988). The overall measurement model including the four constructs has a significant χ^2 (p=0.001). Other common indices however – GFI=0.936, CFI=0.833 and RMSEA=0.043 – correspond to a "good" fit model considering the non-normality of binary data and the sample size.

While these results need confirmation by other studies, they do suggest reliable and valid dimensions of EMSQ.

4 Conclusions

Most if not all service quality studies model their dimensions based on consumer perceptions. Furthermore, most if not all eService studies focus on websites. This exploratory study complements previous research by focusing on email and rather than consumer perceptions, investigates email service quality that companies deliver. The four EMSQ dimensions have managerial implications and provide a foundation for future research of email's under-researched role in online service quality.

4.1 Managerial implications

The four dimensions provide a framework for hoteliers to review their own and their competitors' EMSQ. Management should review these dimensions in order to and develop other email features related to EMSQ and improve their EMSQ across at least three categories of email communication: corporate external communication, email marketing and complaint handling. Finally, and as discussed in the academic implications, this exploratory study measured email features that companies deliver, not what consumers expect.

Given the impersonal nature of technology-mediated communication, *personalisation* seems particularly important. Early research suggests that online, politeness and empathy increase trust and build relationships (Bunz & Campbell, 2004; Feng et al., 2004). Finally, the including features comprising personalisation – a polite opening, thanking the customer by name and including the sender's position – should be easy for a business to implement.

Research also supports a *responsiveness* feature, timely email replies can improve customer satisfaction and intention to repurchase (Mattila & Mount, 2003; Naylor, 2003; Strauss & Hill, 2001). The other three features dealt with answering customer's specific questions and underscore the importance of thorough and knowledgeable customer service representatives (Froehle, 2006).

Three *reliability* features related to customers booking a room. The other feature however, related to online branding via the global *.com* domain name. Thus the ABC international hotel in Austria should reflect upon using *abchotel.com* rather than the Austrian *.at* domain as in *abchotel.at*.

Similar to the personalisation features, the *tangibility* features should be easy for hoteliers to implement via signature files. A 2006 study found that almost three out of four organisational emails included these short text blocks at the end of the email (Rains & Young). The study's 193 signature files contained 17 types of information.

4.2 Academic implications and future research

This study adds to the sparse literature of the most popular online application's role in eServices. Although exploratory, the results of this study support applying SERVQUAL to online service with human interaction, such as email and chat

(Froehle & Roth, 2004; Sousa & Voss, 2006). The four EMSQ dimensions align with other studies proposing four service quality dimensions (Kettinger & Lee, 2005; Mittal & Lassar, 1996) and provide a foundation for future EMSQ research.

In addition to replicating this study, future research should examine and develop scaled based on consumer reactions to the proposed four EMSQ factors. Other consumer reactions to investigate include the emotional aspect of EMSQ and EMSQ across the four stages in a transaction, process-based framework (Bauer et al., 2006).

Finally, future research could investigate the relationships between Hofstede's (1980) cultural dimensions and organisations' delivery of the proposed four EMSQ factors.

References

Anderson, J. C., & Gerbing, D. W. (1988). Structural Equation Modeling in Practice: A Review and Recommended Two-Step Approach. *Psychological Bulletin, 103*(3), 411-423.

Bansal, H. S., McDougal, G. H. G., Dikolli, S. S., & Sedatole, K. L. (2004). Relating e-satisfaction to Behavioral Outcomes: An Empirical Study. *Journal of Services Marketing, 18*(4), 290-302.

Bauer, H. H., Falk, T., & Hammerschmidt, M. (2006). eTransQual: A Transaction Process-based Approach for Capturing Service Quality in Online Shopping. *Journal of Business Research, 59*(7), 866-875.

Brady, M. K., & Cronin Jr, J. J. (2001). Some New Thoughts on Conceptualizing Perceived Service Quality: A Hierarchical Approach. *Journal of Marketing, 65*(3), 34-41.

Bunz, U., & Campbell, S. W. (2004). Politeness Accommodation in Electronic Mail. *Communication Research Reports, 21*(1), 11-25.

Collier, D. A. (1983). The Service Sector Revolution: The Automation of Services. *Long Range Planning, 16*(6), 10-20.

Collier, J. E., & Bienstock, C. C. (2006). Measuring Service Quality in E-Retailing. *Journal of Service Research, 8*(3), 260-275.

Coulthard, L. J. M. (2004). A Review and Critique of Research Using SERVQUAL. *International Journal of Market Research, 46*(4), 479-497.

Fassnacht, M., & Koese, I. (2006). Quality of Electronic Services: Conceptualizing and Testing a Hierarchical Model. *Journal of Service Research, 9*(1), 19-37.

Feng, J., Lazar, J., & Preece, J. (2004). Empathy and Online Interpersonal Trust: A Fragile Relationship. *Behaviour and Information Technology, 23*(2), 97-106.

Froehle, C. M. (2006). Service Personnel, Technology and Their Interaction in Influencing Customer Satisfaction. *Decision Sciences, 37*(1), 5-38.

Froehle, C. M., & Roth, A. V. (2004). New Measurement Scales for Evaluating Perceptions of the Technology-mediated Customer Service Experience. *Journal of Operations Management, 22*(1), 1-21.

Grönroos, C. (1984). A Service Quality Model and its Marketing Implications. *European Journal of Marketing, 18*(4), 36-44.

Hair, J. F., Black, W. C., Babin, B. J., Anderson, R. E., & Tatham, R. L. (2006). *Multivariate Data Analysis* (Sixth ed.). Upper Saddle River, NJ: Prentice Hall.

Hill, A. V., Collier, D. A., Froehle, C. M., Goodale, J. C., Metters, R. D., & Verma, R. (2002). Research Opportunities in Service Process Design. *Journal of Operations Management, 20*(2), 189-202.

Hofstede, G. (1980). *Culture's Consequences: International Differences in Work-Related Values*. Beverly Hills, California: Sage.

Jacsó, P. (2006). Google Scholar: The Pros and the Cons. *Online Information Review, 29*(2), 208-214.

Jöreskog, K. G., & Sorbom, D. (1998). *LISREL 8: Structural Equation Modeling with the SIMPLIS Command Language*. Chicago: Scientific Software International.

Kettinger, W. J., & Lee, C. C. (2005). Zones of Tolerance: Alternative Scales for Measuring Information Systems Service Quality. *MIS Quarterly, 29*(4), 607-623.

Long, M., & McMellon, C. (2004). Exploring the Determinants of Retail Service Quality on the Internet. *Journal of Services Marketing, 18*(1), 78-90.

Mattila, A. S., & Mount, D. J. (2003). The Impact of Selected Customer Characteristics and Response Time on E-complaint Satisfaction and Return Intent. *International Journal of Hospitality Management, 22*(2), 135-145.

Matzler, K., Pechlaner, H., Abfalter, D., & Wolf, M. (2005). Determinants of Response to Customer E-mail Enquiries to Hotels: Evidence from Austria. *Tourism Management, 26*(2), 249-259.

Meuter, M., L., Ostrom, A. L., Roundtree, R. I., & Bitner, M. J. (2000). Self Service Technologies: Understanding Customer Satisfaction with Technology-Based Service Encounters. *Journal of Marketing, 64*(3), 50-64.

Mittal, B., & Lassar, W. M. (1996). The Role of Personailzation in Service Encounters. *Journal of Retailing, 72*(1), 95-109.

Murphy, J., & Gomes, L. (2003). E-Mail Customer Service by Australian Educational Institutions. *Australasian Marketing Journal, 11*(2), 56-69.

Murphy, J., Olaru, D., Schegg, R., & Frey, S. (2003). The Bandwagon Effect: Swiss Hotels' Website and E-mail Management. *Cornell Hotel and Restaurant Administration Quarterly, 44*(1), 71-87.

Murphy, J., & Tan, I. (2003). Journey to Nowhere? Electronic Customer Service by Travel Agents in Singapore. *Tourism Management, 24*(5), 543-550.

Naylor, G. (2003). The Complaining Customer: A Service Provider's Best Friend? *Journal of Consumer Satisfaction, Dissatisfaction and Complaining Behavior, 16*, 241-248.

Parasuraman, A., Zeithaml, V. A., & Berry, L. L. (1985). A Conceptual Model of Service Quality and Its Implications for Future Research. *Journal of Marketing, 49*(4), 41-50.

Parasuraman, A., Zeithaml, V. A., & Berry, L. L. (1988). SERVQUAL: A Multiple-Item Scale for Measuring Consumer Perceptions of Service Quality. *Journal of Retailing, 64*(1), 12-40.

Parasuraman, A., Zeithaml, V. A., & Malhotra, A. (2005). E-S-QUAL: A Multiple-Item Scale for Assessing Electronic Service Quality. *Journal of Service Research, 7*(3), 213-233.

Piccoli, G., Brohman, M. K., Watson, R. T., & Parasuraman, A. (2004). Net-Based Customer Service Systems: Evolution and Revolution in Web Site Functionalities. *Decision Sciences, 35*(3), 423-455.

Rainie, L., & Horigan, J. (2005). A Decade of Adoption: How the Internet Has Woven Itself into American Life. In *Internet: The Mainstreaming of Online Life* (pp. 56-69): Pew Internet and American Life Project.

Rains, S. A., & Young, A. M. (2006). A Sign of the Times: An Analysis of Organizational Members' Email Signatures. *Journal of Computer Mediated Communication, 11*(4), http://jcmc.indiana.edu/vol11/issue14/rains.html.

Rust, R. T., & Kannan, P. K. (2003). E-Service: A New Paradigm for Business in the Electronic Environment. *Communications of the ACM, 46*(6), 36-42.

Rust, R. T., & Lemon, K. N. (2001). E-Service and the Consumer. *International Journal of Electronic Commerce, 5*(3), 85-101.

Schegg, R., Murphy, J., & Leuenberger, R. (2003). Five-Star Treatment? E-Mail Customer Service by International Luxury Hotels. *Information Technology and Tourism, 6*(2), 99-112.

Sousa, R., & Voss, C. A. (2006). Service Quality in Mulitchannel Services Employing Virtual Channels. *Journal of Service Research, 8*(4), 356-371.

Strauss, J., & Hill, D. J. (2001). Consumer Complaints by Emails: An Exploratory Investigation of Corporate Responses and Customer Reactions. *Journal of Interactive Marketing, 15*(1), 63-73.

Walley, P., & Amin, V. (1994). Automation in a Customer Contact Environment. *International Journal of Operations & Production Management, 15*(5), 86-100.

Wolfinbarger, M., & Gilly, M. C. (2003). eTailQ: Dimensionalizing, Measuring and Predicting etail Quality. *Journal of Retailing, 79*(3), 183-198.

Yang, Z., & Jun, M. (2002). Consumer Perception of E-Service Quality: From Internet Purchaser and Non-Purchaser Perspectives. *Journal of Business Strategies, 19*(1), 19-41.

Yang, Z., Peterson, R. T., & Cai, S. (2003). Services Quality Dimensions of Internet Retailing: An Exploratory Analysis. *Journal of Services Marketing, 17*(7), 685-700.

Zemke, R., & Connellan, T. (2001). *e-Service*. New York, New York: Amacom.

Take Me Back: Validating the Wayback Machine as a Measure of Website Evolution

Noor Hazarina Hashim[a]
Jamie Murphy[a]
Peter O' Connor[b]

[a] Business SchoolThe University of Western Australia
{hashin01}@student.uwa.edu.au
{jmurphy}@biz.uwa.edu.au

[b] Essec Business School,
Cergy-Pontoise Cedex, France
{oconnor}@essec.fr

Abstract

Drawing on Diffusion of Innovations theory, this study of 175 Malaysian hotel websites validates the Wayback Machine (WM) – a web-based tool that archives websites – as a means to study website evolution. The results support validating the Wayback Machine for studying website evolution, and extend hospitality diffusion research to Malaysia. In line with prior research, there were significant positive relationships between hotel size, category and affiliation with two variables provided by the WM – website age and number of updates. Larger, higher-rated and affiliated hotels launched their websites earlier and updated their sites more often than smaller, lower-rated and independent hotels.

Keywords: websites, Wayback Machine, diffusion of innovations, Internet

1 Introduction

As the Internet grows in importance for tourism and hospitality (O'Connor & Frew, 2002), industry and academics question how to use this medium effectively (Murphy, Olaru, Schegg, & Frey, 2003; Wang & Fesenmaier, 2005). Furthermore, since 1994, academics have investigated evolutionary aspects of business Internet use (Teo & Pian, 2004). For example, tourism websites may evolve from promotional to provisional to processing tasks (Doolin, Burgess, & Cooper, 2002) and hotel websites may incorporate increasingly complex customer relationship management features (Murphy et al., 2003).

Yet the snapshot approach used in most website studies is a major limitation (Morrison, Taylor, & Douglas, 2004). Websites by their very nature evolve. A single evaluation at a single point in time fails to capture such evolution. While longitudinal studies would let researchers track changing website features and functions, performing multiple evaluations is time consuming, some websites may no longer exist and some changes are ephemeral. For instance, in a study of over one thousand websites across six categories, McMillan (2002) found that only about two thirds of the sites still functioned at the same URL five years later.

Domain name age, based on when an organisation originally registered a domain name – such as Hyatt hotels registering Hyatt.com – provides a temporal measure of Internet adoption (Adamic & Huberman, 2000; Gosain & Faraj, 2001). Yet for names registered in the most common domain, .com, changes in registrars can render the age invalid (Murphy, Olaru, & Schegg, 2006). Furthermore, organisations may buy a domain name but wait months or years before hosting a website at that name. Thus, domain name age as a measure of website evolution suffers several limitations.

The Wayback Machine (WM), provided by the Internet Archive (www.archive.org), provides two alternative and complementary measures of website evolution – website age and website updates. Several scholars have used the WM to investigate archived versions of websites (Ryan, Field, & Olfman, 2003; Thelwall, Vaughan, Cothey, Li, & Smith, 2003; Veronin, 2002) and to infer website age (Vaughan & Thelwall, 2003). Yet to the authors' knowledge, no studies have validated the Wayback Machine.

Straub (1989) argues that instrument validation is inadequate in management information system research due to difficulty tracking rapid technological changes. Yet establishing validity is particularly important for new measures (Bagozzi, 1981; Hinkin, 1995). Validation promotes cooperative research by allowing future research to utilise the tested measure in different settings and triangulate results (Straub, 1989). Most importantly, failure to validate an instrument raises trust issues on the research findings (Straub, 1989).

Furthermore, while studies have drawn upon the WM's archived websites and website age, to the authors' knowledge no studies have used the number of website updates provided by the WM. Finally, Internet research in the tourism industry predominately focuses on developed countries (Frew, 2000). This may be in part due to hospitality Internet use being at an infant and formative phase in developing countries, including Malaysia (Thuong & Anthony, 2002). Studies of Malaysia's hospitality industry are limited, particularly on hotel Internet use (Hashim & Murphy, 2005).

Thus, the aims of this study are to:

- Test the website age and website updates provided by the Wayback Machine as a valid tools to measure website evolution,
- Apply Diffusion of Innovations theory (Rogers, 2003) to validate the Wayback Machine and examine evolving hotel industry website use, and
- Add to the paucity of Internet research of Malaysia's hospitality industry.

The following section introduces the Wayback Machine and describes the study population. Next, the paper applies Diffusion of Innovations theory to validate two WM variables – website age and website updates – and investigates evolving website use in Malaysia's hospitality industry. The paper closes with suggestions for industry practitioners and future research directions for academics studying website evolution.

2 Background

The Wayback Machine forms part of the Internet Archive at *www.archive.org*, which amasses websites, moving images, texts, audio and recently, educational resources (FAQs, 2006). Drawing upon the results from the Alexa webcrawler, this US-based non-profit organisation permanently stores publicly accessible websites in an enormous digital archive. By preserving human knowledge and artefacts, and making its collection available to all, the Internet Archive envisions resembling ancient Egypt's legendary library of Alexandria (FAQs, 2006).

The archive contains snapshots of over 55 billion web pages – more information than in any library including the US Library of Congress – even though archiving only began in 1996 (FAQs, 2006). The archive adds about 20 terabytes (10^{12} bytes) of digital content per month (FAQs, 2006), with each sweep of the estimated 16 million archived websites taking over two months (Howell, 2006).

Users can view the original version of each site as well as the dates and content of subsequent updates. To call up the archived websites, users simply type the URL of the desired site into the address box on the WM homepage. The Machine then returns the date of original site creation, of site updates and links to those archived sites. Figure 1 shows the WM homepage and Figure 2 shows the results for a Malaysian hotel, the Timotel in Mersing. The WM also provides information on the number of updates made to a website. The asterisks besides the dates in Figure 2 indicate more than 50% changes to the website since the last visit.

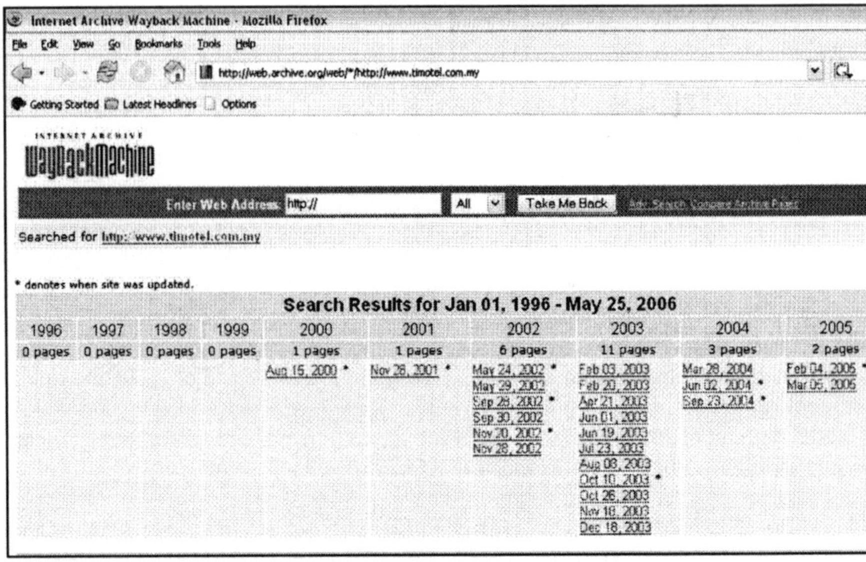

Fig. 1. Homepage of the Internet Archive

Tracking the evolution of a site over time can be useful. For example, a researcher could investigate the evolution of *Hyatt.com*'s online customer relationship programs by examining consecutive archived versions of the company's site. Researchers in the information sciences are increasingly using the WM to help track and measure web content development (Hackett & Parmanto, 2005). The WM is also gaining acceptance in legal cases involving trademark or intellectual property issues (Howell, 2006). In a landmark 2004 US case, the court ruled that pages culled from the WM were admissible as evidence (Anonymous, 2004).

While comprehensive, the WM has limitations. It can archive publicly accessible simple html sites, but has problems archiving password-protected or dynamic sites (Veronin, 2002). Furthermore, sites can decline archiving by either emailing the Internet Archive or using the Standard for Robot Exclusion (see www.robotstxt.org for further information) to specify files or directories not to crawl (FAQs, 2006). Intellectual property owners concerned about infringements on third party sites can also request removal of that content. In each case, such actions will result in both sites not being indexed in the future and removal of past content from the archive (FAQs, 2006).

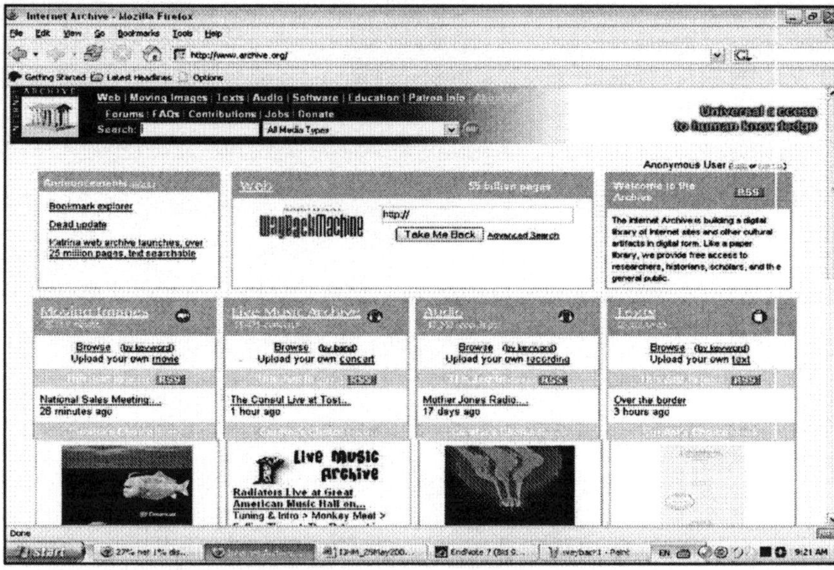

Fig. 2. Wayback Machine results for www.timotel.com.my

Finally, a condition of use of the Alexa webcrawler is that the Internet Archive must wait a minimum of six months after surveying before including site updates in the public archive. Coupled with the requisite time to survey the 55 billion archived pages, this means a time lag of between six to twelve months for an archived snapshot to appear (FAQs, 2006; Howell, 2006).

3 Research Methodology

This study uses Malaysian hotels to validate two variables from the Wayback Machine and to examine evolving Internet use. Given no comprehensive database of Malaysian hotel website addresses, this study began with the 540 hotels registered with Malaysia's Ministry of Tourism and the Malaysian Accommodation Directory (MAD) 2003/2004, which provides about 100 hotel websites addresses. In May 2006, keying the 540 hotels' names into Google and Yahoo! helped find more hotel websites and verify the MAD website addresses, for a total of 310 hotel websites. Of these, the Wayback Machine failed to give results for 19 sites due to trouble locating the site or the site declining to be indexed by the Internet Archive.

Of the remaining 291 websites, some chain hotels shared the same domain name, such as *hyatt.com* or *hilton.com* for all Hyatt or Hilton hotels in Malaysia. To avoid duplication, this study excluded the 116 hotels with the same domain name, for a final sample of 175 hotels. Finally, as explained later, only 79 of these 175 hotels hosted their website in Malaysia's country domain, *.my*.

Table 1 shows the final sample and suggests that the higher rated, chain-affiliated and larger hotels tended to lead in website adoption. The first five-star hotel went online about three years earlier than the first one-star hotel, in early 1997 versus late 2000. The first chain hotel went online just under a year earlier than the first non-affiliated hotel, late 1996 versus mid 1997. Finally, the first online hotel with over 300 rooms was about two years earlier than the first online hotel with less than 200 rooms.

Table 1: Sample Characteristics

	Websites accessible via Wayback	**Sample excluding same domain name**	**Sample with *.my* domain**	**First website**	**Most updates from 1996-2005**
Rating					
1-star	4	4	0	10.11.2000	35
2-star	50	31	12	3.11.1999	35
3-star	95	62	28	27.8.1997	63
4-star	71	48	24	22.12.1996	72
5-star	71	30	15	25.1.1997	60
Affiliation					
Chain	205	89	40	22.12.1996	72
Non-chain	86	86	39	27.8.1997	63
No. of Rooms					
1-99	70	53	16	1.12.1998	63
100-199	84	50	21	25.1.1997	33
200-299	55	35	22	25.1.1998	56
>299	82	37	20	22.12.1996	72
Total	**291**	**175**	**79**		

Similarly, the higher rated, chain-affiliated and larger hotels tended to lead in updating their websites. The five-star hotel with the most website updates from 1996-2006 changed its site 60 times compared to 35 times for the leading one-star hotel. Likewise, the leading chain-affiliated and larger hotel made 72 updates on its website compared to 63 times for the non-affiliated and smaller hotel. The discussion on website age and number of updates in Table 1, however, was just for one hotel in each category. The next section relies upon statistical tests using all hotels to establish the validity of website age and website updates.

4 Validation of Measures

Validation helps determine whether a method or an item is suitable for measuring a construct (Malhotra, Hall, Shaw, & Oppenheim, 2002). The three general approaches to achieve validity range from the weakest – face or content validity – to criterion validity and finally construct validity (Sekaran, 2003; Zikmund, 2000). For new measures, Bagozzi (1981) argues that construct and content validity require substantiation. The following discussion describes the evidence for the Wayback Machine to reflect evolving Internet use according to the three validation criteria.

Face and content validity

As its name demonstrates, face validity relates to face value and relies upon personal evaluations (Zikmund, 2000). Because of vagueness and subjectivity, face validity is the weakest way to demonstrate validity and some researchers question face validity as a validity test (Sekaran, 2003).

Content validity ensures that a measure includes an adequate and representative set of items that cover a concept (Zikmund, 2000). Content validity also relates to sample-population representativeness, that is, the ability of the questionnaire to represent the larger area of the population. When experts agree that a measure provides adequate coverage of a concept, the measure has content validity (Zikmund, 2000).

This study established content and face validity based on literature and experts' agreement. An email invited two Malaysian hoteliers to test their website with the WM; they agreed that the Wayback Machine provided accurate archived versions of their websites. This study further validated the face and content validity of the WM by investigating the four hotel homepages shown in the Murphy, Forrest, Wotring, and Brymer (1996) study. The WM results showed the same homepages as those in the article.

Construct validity

Construct validity is the ability of a measure to provide empirical evidence consistent with relevant theories in a research stream (Malhotra et al., 2002). Convergent and discriminant validity help achieve construct validity. Discriminant validity results when two variables are uncorrelated, indicating that the two variables measure different concepts (Sekaran, 2003).

Convergent validity results when two variables measuring the same construct correlate highly (Sekaran, 2003). A few studies rely upon an organisation's domain name age as for establishing a proxy of Internet adoption (Adamic & Huberman, 2000; Gosain & Faraj, 2001; Murphy et al., 2006; Scaglione, Schegg, & Murphy, 2006). Thus as a test of construct validity, there should be a high correlation between a website's domain name age and that same website's age provided by the WM.

Establishing the age of names in global domains such as *.com* or *.org* is problematic. On 30 November 1999, the Internet Corporation for Assigned Names and Numbers shifted from a sole domain registrar to the Shared Registration System (SRS) and multiple registrars in the *.com*, *.net*, and *.org* global domains (see *www.icann.org* for a history of domain names). SRS makes gathering a valid global domain name age unreliable as companies may change domain registrars, thus 'resetting' the domain name creation date (Murphy et al., 2006).

At the country domain level however, such as *.at* and *.my* for Austria and Malaysia respectively, gathering the age of a domain name can be straightforward. There is usually just one database for a country, such as in Malaysia (www.mynic.net.my).

Thus, due to the inherent difficulty validating ages in the *.com* domain, the study included only the 79 hotels websites with a *.my* domain to test convergent validity. Keying these hotels' domain names into the Mynic whois function (whois.mynic.net.my) yielded the domain name age for these hotels.

Cohen (1988, p. 82) indicates a correlation (*r*) between any two variables above 0.5 as a high correlation. The result of Pearson correlation for the 79 hotels hosted in .my shows that the website age and domain name age are highly correlated, $r = 0.809$, $p<.001$. This significant correlation between website and domain name age supports convergent validity for the website age as provided by the Wayback Machine.

Criterion validity (predictive and concurrent)

Criterion validity measures how well an independent variable or a set of independent variables relate to a criterion (Sekaran, 2003). A criterion could be behaviours, skills or other characteristics of research interest, such as website age and the number of website updates in this study. The two sub-components of criterion validity are predictive and concurrent validity (Sekaran, 2003; Zikmund, 2000).

Predictive validity is the ability of independent variables to predict future criteria. Concurrent validity uses independent variables to predict present criteria. For example, a hotel could evaluate its online reservation system based on the number of website visits and email enquiries. To demonstrate concurrent validity, the hotel would correlate the number of visits and email enquiries with online reservations. A positive and high correlation indicates predictive validity. A positive and high correlation with future online reservation demonstrates predictive validity for the number of web page visits and email enquiries. Depending on the objective of the validity, researchers use correlation or regression analyses to test theory-driven hypothesised relationship (Hinkin, 1995).

Hospitality studies frequently use the diffusion of innovations (Rogers, 2003) to investigate Internet use (Matzler, Pechlaner, Abfalter, & Wolf, 2005; Wang & Fesenmaier, 2005). The theory argues that organisational characteristics – i.e., rating, size and affiliation – relate positively to organisational technology use. US and Swiss studies show that higher rated, larger and affiliated hotels lead in technology adoption (Murphy, Olaru, Schegg, & Frey, 2003; Scaglione, Steiner, Schegg, & Murphy, 2005; Siguaw, Enz, & Navasivayam, 2000). Compared to lower rated, smaller or non-affiliated hotels, these hotels have more resources and expertise to facilitate IT implementation. Similarly, emerging Malaysian research and early global research suggest that larger, higher-rated and chain hotels show more advanced Internet use (Hashim & Murphy, 2005; Wei et al., 2001).

Table 2 shows the results of one-way Pearson correlation tests for the number of rooms, Spearman correlation tests for star rating and independent t-tests for the chain-affiliation category. Because some hotels launched their websites late, the analysis for number of updates uses the average number of annual updates from 2002 to 2005.

Table 2. Correlation and T-test results for website age and number of updates

Correlation coefficient/ t-value, significance level	**Size**	**Rating**	**Affiliation**
Website Age (in days)	0.185, **p = 0.007**	0.236, **p = 0.001**	2.627, **p = 0.004**
Average number of annual updates (2002-2005)	0.129, **p = 0.045**	0.176, **p = 0.01**	1.547, p = 0.06

The results support literature on hotels' Internet use and suggest criterion validity. Website age and website updates help predict hotel size, rating and affiliation. In line with diffusion research, larger, higher-rated and affiliated hotels launched their websites earlier and updated their websites more often than smaller, lower-rated and non-affiliated hotels.

5 Conclusions

5.1 Academic Implications

This study adds to the sparse research on the evolutionary and dynamic nature of Internet use in the hospitality industry. Perhaps most importantly, this study helps address a key limitation of researching the evolution of hospitality Internet use – the prevalent snapshot approach (Morrison et al., 2004) – by introducing and validating the Wayback Machine as a resource for longitudinal studies.

Although the WM has limitations such as not indexing some websites, it serves as a complementary tool to help address limitations of using domain name age. Possibly the first hospitality study to use the Wayback Machine and the first study to validate the WM, the results support it as a simple and valid way to study website evolution via website age, website updates, and the content of archived websites.

MIS researchers frequently adopt previously developed instrument, which can contribute to flawed measures for at least two reasons; the adapted instrument has not been validated or the researcher made major alterations in the validated instrument without re-testing it (Straub, 1989, p.162). This study shows formal validation of the Wayback Machine. The results also help generalise myriad hospitality diffusion studies in developed countries to a developing country, Malaysia. Larger, higher-rated and affiliated Malaysian hotels lead in the adoption and updating of websites.

Managerial implications

Malaysian hoteliers and related authorities such as Tourism Malaysia and Malaysia's Ministry of Tourism can use these results to gauge how Malaysian hotels have progressed in their Internet use. The results show that larger, higher rated and chain hotels lead in Internet usage. As the Internet continues to become an important tourism and hospitality tool, smaller, lower rated and non-chain hotels should reflect upon having a website or updating their website more often to create or maintain their competitive edge. Understanding website evolution allows managers to gauge ideas on previous and present online marketing activities as well as benchmark their website performance based on various metrics such as return of investment and conversion rate.

However, hotels should not adopt Internet simply to follow trends, fashions or imitate their competitors. To leverage their online investment, hotels should have clear aims, objectives and well-planned strategies (Murphy et al., 2003), including updating the website. The dot com crash in 2000 and the saga of failed Internet venture Boo.com exemplify businesses' failures to implement and understand Internet technology (Stockport, Kunnath, & Sedick, 2001).

6 Future Research Directions

Deleting 216 websites limits extending the results to most international chain-affiliated hotels. As this study overlooks hotel websites unlisted with Yahoo! or Google, future research should extend this study to more Malaysian hotels and other Southeast Asian countries such as Singapore, Indonesia and Brunei. Furthermore, the comparative results would illustrate Internet diffusion within the Southeast Asian hospitality industry.

As noted earlier, this study extends diffusion research to Malaysia's hospitality industry, further generalising the relationship of organisational characteristics and having websites. Future studies could replicate this relationship in other countries, but perhaps it is time to move on and examine other aspects. For example, researchers could use the Wayback Machine for longitudinal studies of evolving website features (Morrison et al., 2004; Murphy et al., 2006) or effective website implementation (Murphy et al., 2003; Wang & Fesenmaier, 2005).

Another fruitful research area is aligning technology adoption with business strategy (Rogers, 2003). For example, Miles and Snow's (1978) four business strategies – Prospectors, Analysers, Defenders and Reactors – support a link between technology and strategy. The four strategic types range from Reactor firms with little adaptive capacity to Prospector firms with a high adaptive capacity (Conant, Mokwa, & Varadarajan, 1990). Future research could classify Malaysian hotels into these typologies, and then analyse how they differ in evolving website use.

References

Adamic, L. A., & Huberman, B. A. (2000). Power-Law Distribution of the World Wide Web. *Science, 287*(5461), 2115.

Anonymous. (2004). Internet Archive's Web Page Snapshots Held Admissible as Evidence. *Packets, 2*(3), cyberlaw.stanford.edu/packets/vol_2_no_3/.

Bagozzi, R. P. (1981). An Examination of the Validity of Two Models of Attitude. *Multivariate Behavioral Research, 16*(3), 323-359.

Cohen, J. (1988). *Statistical Power Analysis for the Behavioral Sciences* (2 ed.). Hillsdale, New Jersey: Lawrence Erlbaum Associates Publishers.

Conant, J. S., Mokwa, M. P., & Varadarajan, P. R. (1990). Strategic Types, Distinctive Marketing Competencies and Organisational Performance: A Multiple Measures-Based Study. *Strategic Management Journal, 11*(5), 365-383.

Doolin, B., Burgess, L., & Cooper, J. (2002). Evaluating the Use of the Web for Tourism Marketing: A Case Study from New Zealand. *Tourism Management, 23*(5), 557-561.

FAQs. (2006). *The Wayback Machine: Frequently Asked Questions*. Retrieved 11 August, 2006, from www.archive.org/about/faqs.php

Frew, A. J. (2000). Information Technology and Tourism: A Research Agenda. *Information Technology and Tourism, 3*(2), 99-110.

Gosain, S., & Faraj, S. (2001). *Web Technology Diffusion - Initial Adoption, Assimilation and Network Performance*. Paper presented at the DIGIT, New Orleans, Louisiana.

Hackett, S., & Parmanto, B. (2005). A Longitudinal Evaluation of Accessibility: Higher Education Websites. *Internet Research, 15*(3), 281-294.

Hashim, N. H., & Murphy, J. (2005, 28-29 November). *The Diffusion of Websites and Email among Malaysian Hotels*. Paper presented at the International Conference on Tourism and Hospitality, Penang, Malaysia.

Hinkin, T. R. (1995). A Review of Scale Development Practices in the Study of Organisations. *Journal of Management, 21*(5), 967-988.

Howell, B. (2006). Proving Web History: How to Use the Internet Archive. *Journal of Internet Law, 9*(8), 3-9.

Malhotra, N., Hall, J., Shaw, M., & Oppenheim, P. (2002). *Marketing Research: An Applied Orientation*. New South Wales, Australia: Pearson Education Australia Pty Ltd.

Matzler, K., Pechlaner, H., Abfalter, D., & Wolf, M. (2005). Determinants of Response to Customer E-mail Enquiries to Hotels: Evidence from Austria. *Tourism Management, 26*(2), 249-259.

McMillan, S. J. (2002). Longevity of Websites and Interactive Advertising Communication. *Journal of Interactive Advertising, 2*(2), http://jiad.org/vol2/no2/mcmillan/index.htm.

Miles, R. E., & Snow, C. C. (1978). *Organizational Strategy, Structure and Process*. New York: McGrawHill.

Morrison, A. M., Taylor, J. S., & Douglas, A. (2004). Website Evaluation in Tourism and Hospitality: The Art is Not Yet Stated. *Journal of Travel and Tourism Marketing, 17*(2/3), 233-251.

Murphy, J., Forrest, E. J., Wotring, C. E., & Brymer, R. A. (1996). Hotel Management and Marketing on the Internet : An Analysis of Sites and Features. *The Cornell Hotel and Restaurant Administration Quarterly, 37*(3), 70-82.

Murphy, J., Olaru, D., & Schegg, R. (2006). Investigating the Evolution of Hotel Internet Adoption. *Journal of Information Technology and Tourism., 8*(3/4), forthcoming.

Murphy, J., Olaru, D., Schegg, R., & Frey, S. (2003). The Bandwagon Effect: Swiss Hotels' Web-Site and E-Mail Management. *The Cornell Hotel and Restaurant Administration Quarterly, 44*(1), 71-87.

O'Connor, P., & Frew, A. J. (2002). The Future of Hotel Electronic Distribution: Expert and Industry Perspectives. *Cornell Hotel and Restaurant Administration Quarterly, 43*(3), 33-45.

Rogers, E. M. (2003). *Diffusion of Innovations* (5th ed.). New York: Free Press.

Ryan, T., Field, R. H. G., & Olfman, L. (2003). The Evolution of US State Government Home Pages from 1997 to 2002. *International Journal of Human-Computer Studies, 59*(4), 403–430.

Scaglione, M., Schegg, R., & Murphy, J. (2006). Investigating Website Performance in Valais' Hospitality Industry. In P. Keller & T. Berger (Eds.), *Marketing Efficiency in Tourism - Coping with Volatile Demand* (Vol. 1, pp. 131-142). Berlin: Erich Schmidt Verlag.

Scaglione, M., Steiner, T., Schegg, R., & Murphy, J. (2005, 26-28 January). *Investigating Domain Name Diffusion across Swiss Accommodation Enterprises.* Paper presented at the Information and Communication Technologies in Tourism (ENTER) 2005, Innsbruck, Austria.

Sekaran, U. (2003). *Research Methods For Business: A Skill Building Approach* (4 ed.). New York: John Wiley & Sons Inc.

Siguaw, J. A., Enz, C. A., & Navasivayam, K. (2000). Adoption of Information Technology in U.S. Hotels: Strategically Driven Objectives. *Journal of Travel Research, 39*(2), 192-201.

Stockport, G. J., Kunnath, G., & Sedick, R. (2001). Boo.com - The Path to Failure. *Journal of Interactive Marketing, 15*(4), 56-70.

Straub, D. W. (1989). Validating Instruments in MIS Research. *MIS Quarterly, 13*(2), 147-169.

Teo, T. S. H., & Pian, Y. (2004). A Model for Web Adoption. *Information & Management, 41*(4), 457-468.

Thelwall, M., Vaughan, L., Cothey, V., Li, X., & Smith, A. G. (2003). Which Academic Subjects Have Most Online Impact? A Pilot Study and a New Classification Process. *Online Information Review, 27*(5), 333-343.

Thuong, T. L., & Anthony, C. K. (2002). A Managerial Perspective on Electronic Commerce Development in Malaysia. *Electronic Commerce Research, 2*(1/2), 7-29.

Vaughan, L., & Thelwall, M. (2003). Scholarly Use of the Web: What Are the Key Inducers of Links to Journal Web Sites? *Journal of the American Society for Information Science and Technology, 54*(1), 29-38.

Veronin, M. A. (2002). Where Are They Now? A Case Study of Health-related Web Site Attrition. *Journal of Medical Internet Research, 4*(2), www.jmir.org/2002/2002/e2010/.

Wang, Y., & Fesenmaier, D. R. (2005). Identifying the Success Factors of Web-based Marketing Strategy: An Investigation of Convention and Visitors Bureaus in the United States. *Journal of Travel Research, 43*(3), 1-11.

Zikmund, W. G. (2000). *Business Research Methods* (6 ed.). Chicago: The Dryden Press.

e-Business W@tch in the Tourism Sector

Markus Lassnig
Mark Markus

[a] Salzburg Research Forschungsgesellschaft, Austria
{markus.lassnig, mark.markus}@salzburgresearch.at

Abstract

This paper builds on the findings from e-Business W@tch, a study commissioned on behalf of the European Commission with the main aim of monitoring and analysing the impact of e-business across different sectors of the European economy. One of the sectors surveyed is tourism. Some core results of the study on ICT adoption and e-business activity in tourism in 2006 shall be presented, here. The focus of this paper is on the analysis of selected indicators gathered in a representative survey based on 14,081 interviews with decision-makers in companies from 29 European countries. The main result is that "e-tourism has taken off" in the field of customer-facing activities, while other areas of e-business (like internal business processes or supply-side activities) are still lagging behind. Drivers and barriers for e-business adoption are discussed as well as the effects on competition and business impacts.

Keywords: Market research in e-tourism, e-business survey, e-business maturity indicators.

1 Introduction

The European Commission, Enterprise & Industry Directorate General, launched e-Business W@tch to monitor the growing maturity of electronic business across different sectors of the European economy. Since January 2002, the e-Business W@tch has been analysing e-business developments and impacts in manufacturing, construction, financial and service sectors and has become an essential information source for policy representatives and decision makers in the economy. This article builds mainly on empirical results from a Sector Impact Study on ICT adoption and e-business in tourism conducted in 2006. Salzburg Research authored this study on behalf of e-Business W@tch.

2 Research Issues and Methodology

The objective of the e-Business W@tch's Sector Study on the tourism industry is to describe how and to what extent companies in this sector use ICT for conducting business, to assess the impact of this development for firms and for the industry as a whole, and to indicate possible implications for policy. Analysis is based on literature, interviews, case studies (Several interview-based case studies, including Accor Hotels, Ryanair, CSI-Media, adriatica.net, were conducted on the thematic issues "Dis-intermediation and Re-intermediation", "Dynamic Packaging" and "ICT-related developments in the aviation industry".) and a survey among decision-makers in

European enterprises from the tourism industry about the ICT use of their company. This article focuses on the results from the quantitative survey in 2006.

Methodology of the e-Business Survey 2006

e-Business W@tch collects data on the use of ICT and e-business in European enterprises by means of representative telephone surveys (a comprehensive methodology report, together with the questionnaire is available online at http://www.ebusiness-watch.org/about/methodology.htm). The e-Business Survey 2006 was the fourth of its kind after those of 2002, 2003 and 2005. It had a scope of 14,081 interviews with decision-makers in enterprises from 29 European countries. The survey was carried out as an enterprise survey: data collection and reporting focused on enterprises, defined as a business organisations (legal unit) with one or more establishments. Interviews were carried out in March and April 2006.

To ensure data comparability, most of the tables and diagrams in this article feature a breakdown of the population of enterprises based on the aggregate of 10 EU countries – the "EU-10" (CZ, DE, ES, FR, IT, HU, NL, PL, FI, UK). In these countries the survey covered all 10 sectors of the economy (at least to some extent); therefore comparability of the sample across sectors is ensured. Furthermore, the EU-10 represent more than 80% of the total GDP and inhabitants of the EU-25 and are thus to a large extent representative for the whole EU (Methodology Report, 2006).

Sector definition

For the survey, the tourism sector was defined as specified in table 1.

3 Results of selected indicators in the quantitative survey

e-Procurement

About 39% of all firms active in the tourism industry in the EU-10 countries place orders to suppliers online, compared to a cross-sectoral average of 48%. Frequency of online procurement increases with company size class – from 38% of micro enterprises up to 80% of large companies (see table 2). In terms of employment-weighted data, the results of tourism industry are similar to those of the other sectors (with the companies procuring online representing about 60% of employment in the sector). There are significant differences between tourism sub-sectors: 60% of travel agencies and tour operators, 47% of accommodation companies and 24% of enterprises in gastronomy use e-procurement. However, it is obvious that the industry has started to adopt online sourcing and procurement relatively late.

Table 1. Definition of the tourism sector by e-Business W@tch 2006

NACE Rev. 1.1*		Business activities
Divisions	**Groups**	
H 55		Hotels and restaurants
	55.1	Hotels
	55.2	Camping sites and other provisions of short-stay accommodation
	55.3	Restaurants
	55.4	Bars
I 63		Supporting and auxiliary transport activities; activities of travel agencies
	63.3	Activities of travel agencies and tour operators; tourist assistance activities n.e.c.
O 92		Recreational, cultural and sporting activities
	92.33	Fair and amusement park activities
	92.52	Museums activities and preservation of historical sites and buildings
	92.53	Botanical and zoological gardens and nature reserves activities

* NACE Rev. 1.1 is a 4-digit classification of business activities. It is a revision of the 'General Industrial Classification of Economic Activities within the European Communities', known by the acronym NACE and originally published by Eurostat in 1970.

Table 2. Companies ordering supply goods online

	Place orders online		Place 1-25% of their orders online		Place more than 25% of orders online	
	% of empl	% of firms	% of empl	% of firms	% of empl	% of firms
Tourism (EU-10)	**60**	**39**	**77**	**72**	**23**	**28**
Micro (1-9 empl.)		38		73		27
Small (10-49 empl.)		54		83		17
Medium (50-249 empl.)		61		75		25
Large (250+ empl.) *		80		73		27
Tourism sub-sectors:						
Accommodation sector	68	47	84	79	16	21
Gastronomy	50	24	74	85	26	15
Travel agencies & tour operat.	70	60	60	52	40	48
All 10 sectors (EU-10)	**57**	**48**	**74**	**75**	**26**	**25**
Base (100%)	firms using computers		firms placing orders online		firms placing orders online	
N (for sector, EU-10)	725		418		418	

e-Sales

About 36% of all firms active in the tourism industry in the EU-10 allow customers to order goods or book services online; this figure is significantly higher than the cross-sectoral average of 25% (see table 3).

Table 3. Companies receiving orders and reservations from customers online

	Accept orders from customers online		**Receive 1-25% of orders online**		**Receive more than 25% of orders online**		**Use specific ICT solutions for e-selling**	
	% of empl.	% of firms	% of empl.	% of firms	% of empl.	% of firms	% of empl.	% of firms
Tourism (EU-10)	**49**	**36**	**68**	**72**	**32**	**28**	**28**	**11**
Micro (1-9 empl.)		35		74		26		8
Small (10-49 empl.)		46		69		31		20
Medium (50-249 em)		55		64		36		32
Large (250+ empl.)		61		65		35		50
Tourism sub-sectors:								
Accommodation	73	62	62	66	38	34	41	18
Gastronomy	24	16	72	83	28	17	15	3
Travel ag. & tour op.	53	40	74	78	26	22	26	20
Czech Republic	34	38	68	56	32	44	2	0
Denmark	57	47	77	71	23	29	24	10
Germany	43	19	86	86	14	14	31	15
Estonia	69	68	53	54	47	46	12	7
Greece	35	29	78	60	22	40	14	7
Spain	33	31	65	82	35	18	20	6
France	63	54	53	54	47	46	31	21
Ireland	47	39	56	28	44	72	20	9
Italy	46	41	96	99	4	1	22	1
Cyprus	41	27	78	39	22	61	27	19
Latvia	33	21	71	88	29	12	20	8
Luxembourg	65	56	89	88	11	12	23	15
Hungary	47	25	64	60	36	40	14	6
Malta	61	44	79	88	21	12	24	14
Netherlands	44	18	84	65	16	35	13	0
Austria	65	51	68	63	32	37	28	15
Poland	76	71	65	58	35	42	24	6
Portugal	35	38	94	89	6	11	7	6
Slovenia	52	48	79	75	21	25	16	16
Slovakia	36	37	77	64	23	36	9	4
Finland	68	39	73	65	27	35	35	13
Sweden	44	40	76	76	24	24	19	3
United Kingdom	48	17	74	85	26	15	29	10
Bulgaria	28	14	96	100	4	0	25	7
Romania	53	39	44	74	56	26	30	23
Norway	62	46	70	76	30	24	37	14
All 10 sectors (EU-10)	**35**	**25**	**73**	**75**	**27**	**25**	**18**	**9**
Base (100%)	firms using computers		firms accepting orders online		firms accepting orders online		firms using computers	
N (for sector, EU-10)	725		339		339		725	

However, this average figure conceals some striking results of specific tourism sub-sectors: While online orders and reservations from customers, unsurprisingly, play only a minor role in gastronomy, they are extremely important for travel agencies and tour operators (where 40% of companies accept online orders or reservations), and even more so for the accommodation sector (where a substantial 62% of accommodation providers accept online reservations from customers).

Furthermore, findings have to be put into perspective by the relative share of customer orders received online (as percentage of the total order volume). In tourism, a vast majority of about 72% of those companies that enable customers to order online say that online orders and reservations account for up to 25% of their total orders received. In comparison, about 28% of companies receive more than a quarter of their orders online. These average figures are comparable to results of other sectors. However, there are significant differences with different tourism sub-sectors: Only 17% of companies in gastronomy receive more than a quarter of their orders online, compared to respectable 34% in the accommodation sector. Overall, accommodation providers seem to be the strongest adopters of online bookings. If a company from the accommodation sector accepts orders from customers online, it tends to create considerable volumes of e-transactions. There are only 16% of accommodation providers which generate less than 5% of their reservations online, while 34% generate more than 25% of their bookings online.

e-Business Index and Scoreboard 2006

In a ranking of the 10 sectors studied by *e-Business W@tch* in 2006, the tourism industry scores in the middle field regarding its overall use of ICT and e-business. The tourism sector is clearly lagging behind vanguard industries like the telecommunications sector or ICT manufacturing. Only industries like construction, the food sector or the footwear industry are more hesitant adopters of ICT and e-business than tourism (see figure 1 below).

Similar to findings from previous e-Business Surveys, marketing and sales oriented objectives dominate electronic business in tourism (see figure 2). In three out of four component indicators in the field of e-marketing and sales (i.e. D.1 ‘CRM use’, D.2 ‘Firms accepting orders online’ and D.3 ‘Use of ICT systems for marketing/sales’) tourism results are above the average of all 10 sectors surveyed. The only other component indicator scoring above the cross-sectoral average is an indicator in the field of e-sourcing and procurement (C2 ‘Use of ICT systems for sourcing’). In all other areas, the deployment of ICT and e-business in tourism is below the average of the 10 sectors. In particular, there are shortfalls regarding the infrastructure for ICT networks and regarding the uptake of e-integrated business processes.

Considering the ICT adoption in regard to different size classes of companies, the most striking result is that smaller tourism companies are more active users of e-business compared to their counterparts from other industries. The gap between large and small players in making use of ICT and e-business applications – although it certainly exists in this sector as well – may be relatively smaller than in other sectors.

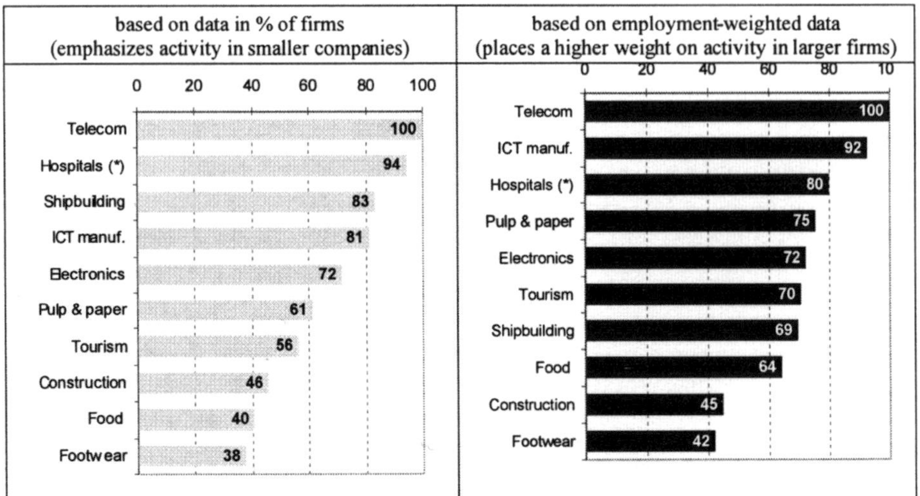

(*) The index for the hospital sector is not fully comparable to the other industries, as there are only few micro and small organisations in this sector. Thus, the apparently more intensive use of ICT is largely an artefact of the specific structure of this sector. When comparing only the large enterprises and organisations, hospitals would not be within the top rank.

Fig. 1. e-Business Index 2006 (based on 16 component indicators of the Scoreboard)

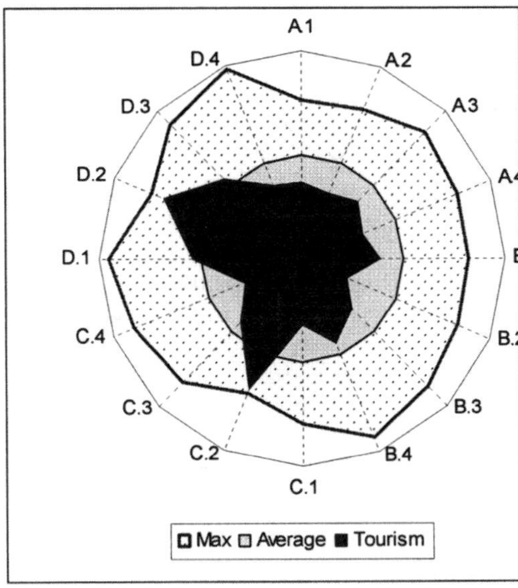

Component indicators
(based on data in % of firms)

A. ICT Networks
A.1 Internet connectivity (index)
A.2 LAN
A.3 W-LAN
A.4 Remote access to company network

B. e-Integrated Business Processes
B.1 Intranet
B.2 ERP systems
B.3 Online tracking of production time
B.4 e-Invoicing

C. e-Sourcing and Procurement
C.1 Firms placing orders online
C.2 Use of ICT systems for sourcing
C.3 ICT system linked with suppliers
C.4 Online inventory management

D. e-Marketing and Sales
D.1 CRM use
D.2 Firms accepting orders online
D.3 Use of ICT systems for marketing/sales
D.4 ICT system linked with customers

Fig. 2. e-Business Scoreboard 2006

Drivers of e-business adoption

Those companies that confirmed that e-business constituted "a significant part" or "some part" of the way they operate were then asked to indicate the rationale for starting their e-business activities. Four main explanations were suggested: a simple imitation of competitors' activities, a reaction to pressure from customers, a reaction to pressure from suppliers, or gaining a competitive advantage. Replies showed that all explanations were perceived as relevant, with customers' expectations and the opportunity to gain a competitive advantage being the most important ones.

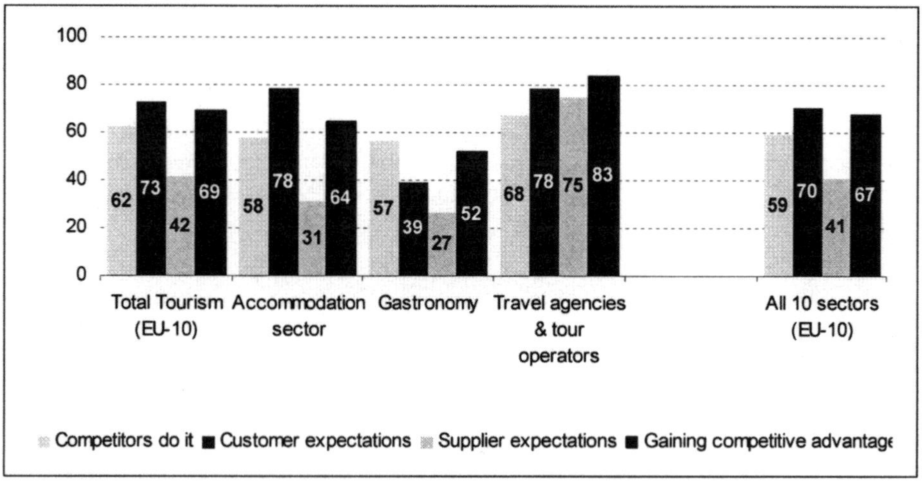

Base (100%): Companies saying that e-business is a part of their operations.
N (for sector, EU-10) = 491. Weighting: Totals (for the sector and for all 10 sectors) are weighted by employment and should be read as "enterprises comprising ...% of employment in the sector(s)".
Figures for tourism sub-sectors are in % of enterprises from the respective sub-sector.

Fig. 3. Companies saying that ... was an important reason for starting e-business.

Thus, the results for the tourism sector are in line with average results for all 10 sectors. Suppliers were not considered as the main driving force, as was the case in other industries (mainly in the manufacturing sectors), which indicates that their influence in this context is limited. Rather, pressure seems to be coming from customers. Imitative behaviour ("... because competitors do it ...") is also an important motive in the tourism industry – 62% of e-business practitioners stated that this was an important reason – but is considered as less relevant than the two main reasons mentioned above (see figure 3).

The situation differs between sub-sectors, in particular concerning supplier expectations: these only play a minor role in the sub-sectors of accommodation and gastronomy, while they are of major importance for travel agencies and tour operators. Customer expectations have exactly the same importance for the accommodation sector as for travel agencies and tour operators, while they are only about half as important for gastronomy. Overall, most drivers are most relevant for the sub-sector of travel agencies and tour operators.

Barriers to e-business adoption

The barriers to e-business adoption in tourism seem to be very similar to the ones of the other economic sectors. The most prominent barrier seems to be that companies consider themselves to be too small to benefit from any e-business activities. Unsurprisingly, especially micro enterprises expressed this argument. This is in line with the findings from other industries – with the important difference that there are many more micro enterprises in tourism than in the other sectors.

The perception that e-business technology is too expensive is stated as the second most important argument (by enterprises constituting about 42% of employment in the sector). About one quarter of companies (weighted by employment) state that e-business technology is too complicated, raises security concerns or major unsolved legal issues. About every fifth company stated that their systems were not compatible with those of suppliers or customers or claimed not to have sufficiently reliable IT suppliers.

Perceived ICT influence on the company's business

ICT influence on tourism companies' business is to a large extent considered positive (see figure 4). As expected, strong ICT influence is perceived particularly in the front-end area, i.e. in the customer service domain, which is probably due – similar to findings from previous e-Business Surveys – to well established online booking and e-marketing activities. Interestingly however, the influence of ICT on the back-end area – internal work organisation, business process efficiency, productivity and revenue growth – has been perceived (almost) equally strong as well. This could be explained by a growing reliance on companies digital business environments (e.g. e-invoicing or e-procurement), and to a smaller extent by the integration of customer-facing operations with back-office systems. Given a fairly low adoption level of software systems for internal process integration (intranet, ERP systems, document management systems, supply chain management and ICT systems linked with customers) and for collaborative B2B processes, there is a large untapped potential. This holds true especially the fact that paper-based processes still dominate financial (and probably other) work flows among companies of the tourism sector.

ICT influence is perceived as fairly low in connection with quality of products or services, which can be ascribed to the nature of tourism services which are not directly associated with ICT, as for instance is the case in the telecommunication industry. On the other hand, the fact that ICT-based search, booking and real-time (dynamic) packaging functionalities have been revolutionising tourism services in recent years is not reflected strongly in the perception of ICT influence on service quality. On the contrary, ICT influence has been perceived most negatively.

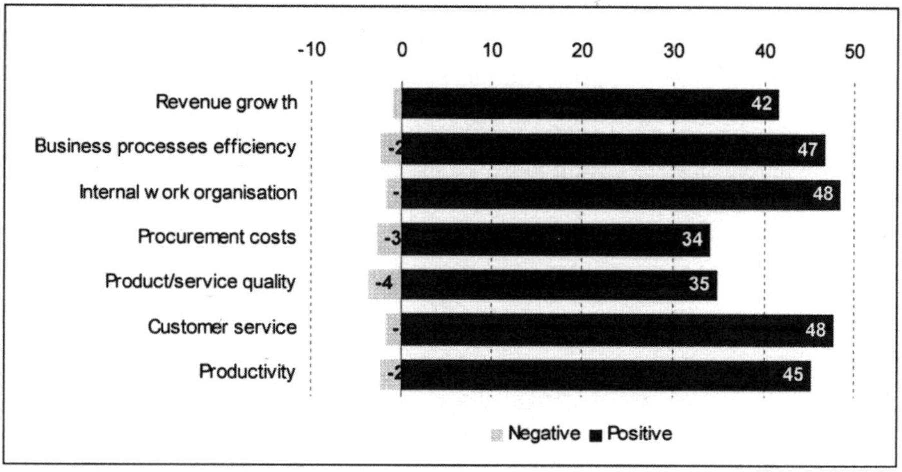

Base (100%): Companies using computers. N (for sector, EU-10) = 725. Weighting: in % of firms.

Fig. 4. Perceived ICT influence on the company's business.

ICT impact on competition

ICT increases competition in the tourism industry slightly stronger than in other sectors. For enterprises comprising 56% of employment in the sector competition has "significantly" or "somewhat" increased due to ICT (see figure 5). Especially affected are small enterprises of which 25% have perceived a significantly increased competition due to ICT. Overall, companies from all size-classes have the impression that the introduction of ICT increases competition.

4 Conclusions

Underpinning the results from previous surveys, tourism is in the vanguard of ICT adoption and e-business in the area of e-marketing and online sales. In the area of customer-facing e-business activities "e-tourism has taken off". Yet, in a ranking of the 10 sectors studied in 2006, the tourism industry scores only in the middle field regarding the overall use of ICT and e-business. Especially regarding the deployment of ICT infrastructure and the adoption of e-integrated business processes, tourism companies are still lagging behind their counterparts in other industries. This finding is supported by several indicators: For example, the overall internet connectivity is still somewhat below the average of the 10 sectors surveyed, also the level of usage of ERP (enterprise resource planning) systems is low, and e-procurement is significantly less developed than in other sectors. Overall, customer expectations and market competition are the main drivers of e-business in the tourism sector, while the small size of most companies and the considerable costs associated with acquiring technologies constitute the main barriers for a stronger uptake of e-business.

Considering the ICT adoption and size of companies, the most outstanding result is that small tourism companies are more active users of e-business compared to their counterparts from other industries. The gap between big and small companies in using ICT and e-business applications is somewhat smaller than in other industries. Furthermore, results broken down by different sub-sectors of tourism show that travel agencies and tour operators seem to be the strongest adopters of ICT and e-business, followed by the accommodation sector and – with much lower adoption rates – by gastronomy.

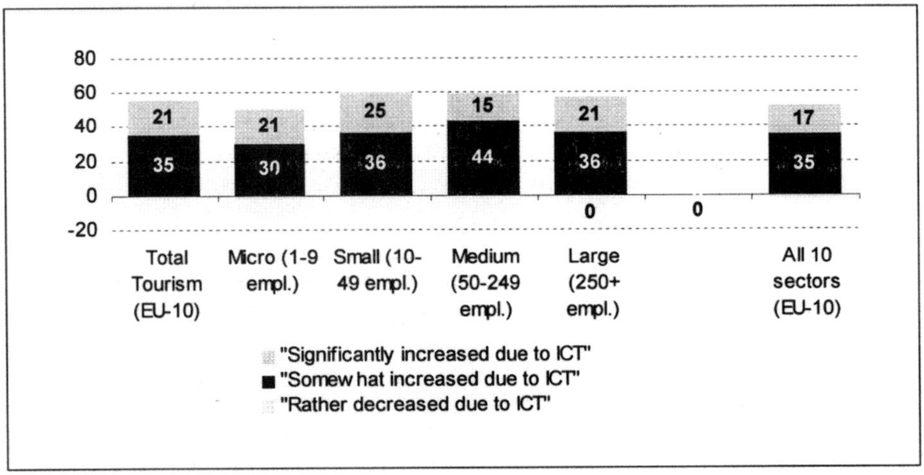

Base (100%): Companies using computers. N (for sector, EU-10) = 725. Weighting: Totals (for the sector and for all 10 sectors) are weighted by employment and should be read as "enterprises comprising ...% of employment in the sector(s)". Figures for size-bands are in % of enterprises from the size-band.

Fig. 5. Perceived impact of ICT on competition in the industry.

References

e-Business W@tch / European Commission (2006). *ICT and e-Business in the Tourism Industry.* Sector Impact Study No. 08, September 2006. Salzburg, Brussels. Retrieved from www.ebusiness-watch.org ('resources')

e-Business W@tch (2006). *e-Business W@tch Survey 2006 – Methodology Report.* Retrieved from www.ebusiness-watch.org/about/methodology.htm.

Acknowledgements

e-Business W@tch is being implemented and operated by empirica Gesellschaft für Kommunikations- und Technologieforschung mbH in co-operation with Berlecon Research, Databank Consulting spa, DIW Berlin – German Institute for Economic Research, IDATE, Lios Geal Consultants, RAMBØLL Management and Salzburg Research.

The Relationship between Business Strategy and Internet Evolution: Investigating the Miles and Snow Typology

Noor Hazarina Hashim[a]
Charles F. Hofacker[b]
Sharon Lu[c]
Sarjit Singh[c]
Shaharudin Md Said[d]

[a] School of Business, University of Western Australia, Australia
{hashin01}@student.uwa.edu.au

[b] College of Business, Florida State University
chofack@cob.fsu.edu

[c]Malaysian Association of Hotels, Kuala Lumpur
sharon, sarjit@hotels.org.my

[d]Malaysian Association of Hotel Owners, Kuala Lumpur
maho@po.jaring.my

Abstract

Based on 13 in-depth interviews, this study explores the relationship between business strategy and hotel Internet use. The findings suggest that depending on their business strategy, hotels take different paths in adopting and using the Internet. Similar to previous Miles and Snow findings, Prospectors lead with advance website features while Reactors are at the other end of the continuum with no adoption. The study adds to the limited studies on the Internet in Malaysia and Miles and Snow in hospitality.

Keywords: Internet evolution, business strategy, hotels, diffusion of innovations. Miles and Snow

1 Introduction

Research in strategic management investigates firm strategic orientations within and across industries. This area of research identified behaviours and common factors in the way firms compete [see for example: Mintzberg (1978); Miles and Snow (1978); Porter (1980)]. Research classifies firms into strategic types based on their environmental adaptation patterns (Moore, 2005) and examines the link between firm strategic types and performance (Croteau & Bergeron, 2001). Nevertheless, research investigating the relationship between strategic types with Internet adoption and usage is limited (Auger, 2003; Teo & Pian, 2004). The sparse research could be attributed to "the existence of, hitherto separate, yet compatible research substream that examines overlapping issues without any attempt to build common ground" (Thomas & Ramaswamy, 1996, p.247). A review of 275 articles on electronic commerce topics indicates that less than 10% of the articles consider business strategy and none address IT alignment (Kearns, 2005, p.1024).

A widely used strategic types classification is the Miles and Snow (1978) typology (Croteau & Bergeron, 2001), yet research on the Miles and Snow (1978) typology in hotel industry (Garrigós-Simón, Marqués, & Narangajavana, 2005) and the Internet (Auger, 2003; Kearns, 2005; Teo & Pian, 2004), and is limited. This study helps address the limited research on business strategy and evolving Internet use. Business Internet use evolves from a simple online presence to the most mature stages when the company website fully integrates with other systems such as enterprise resource planning and customer relationship management (Teo & Pian, 2004).

Similarly, Internet research in the tourism industry predominately focuses on developed countries. Studies on Malaysia's hospitality industry are limited and there is even less on hotel Internet use (Hashim, Olaru, Scaglione, & Murphy, 2006). This study therefore investigates the following questions: (a) Are there distinct strategic types within Malaysian hotels that are consistent with the Miles and Snow theory?, (b) Does each strategic type perceive technology adoption differently?, (c) Does each strategic type differ in their level of Internet usage?

This paper starts with a literature review on Miles and Snow (1978) followed by two propositions. Section four explains the methods applied in this study followed by the findings in section five. The final sections discuss the academic and managerial implications, and future research directions.

2 Literature Review

2.1 The Miles and Snow (1978) business strategy typology

A business strategy describes how a business uses its resources to generate performance (Grover & Saeed, 2004), provides directions for business activities and influences an organisation's technology adoption and use (Osterwalder, Pigneur, & Tucci, 2005). The Miles and Snow (1978) typology, extensively used in various industries, has produced an internally consistent result in describing organisational behaviour (Kearns, 2005). Shortell and Zajac (1990, p.830) concluded that 'a researcher can use this typology with increased confidence in future work on organizations and their strategies'. The Miles and Snow (1978) framework identifies a business strategy through three attributes: product-market domain, technology and administration.

Miles and Snow (1978) view a firm as a complete and integrated system that interacts with its environment. A firm selects the administration and technology that suits its product-market and environment. Product-market refers to goods or services and a target market or market segment (Miles & Snow, 1978). Based on the chosen administration, technology and product-market category, Miles and Snow proposed four types of firms: Prospectors, Defenders, Analysers and Reactors.

Prospectors, the innovators and market leaders, take risks and invest in new technology to explore new market segments (Miles & Snow, 1978). Prospectors constantly monitor the market and respond quickly to changes in market conditions. They take advantage of new opportunities and exploit the benefits of being a pioneer (Slater & Narver, 1993). To maintain the innovator status, Prospectors exhibit a high degree of technological flexibility (Thomas & Ramaswamy, 1996, p.250), a low degree of formalisation, decentralised structure and a low top-down communication (Hambrick, 1983).

Defenders stress cost efficiency and focus on a narrow and stable market through a limited mix of products and customers, and aggressively protect the market from competitors (Miles & Snow, 1978, p.39). Defenders strive for low operating costs and seldom make major changes in their technology, structure or methods of operations. Research and development efforts centre on process improvements rather than product innovation (Slater & Narver, 1993). Defenders adopt a formal hierarchy and high degree of centralisation (Hambrick, 1983).

Analysers pursue a hybrid strategy with Prospector and Defender features. Analysers operate in at least two different product-market areas: one stable and one dynamic (Miles & Snow, 1978). They focus on efficiency and productivity in the stable market, while cautiously moving into a new market when the market is dynamic and turbulent (Slater & Narver, 1993). Analysers adopt technologies that have both stable and flexible components. In a stable market, they operate routinely and efficiently through formalised structures and processes, but are flexible in their turbulent market (Hambrick, 1983).

Reactors follow no conscious strategy and often seem as a dysfunctional organisation type (Miles & Snow, 1978). Reactors fail to develop distinctive competencies and appropriate management structure. They seldom change until forced to do so by environmental pressure (Snow & Hambrick, 1980). Reactors do not attempt to maintain an already acquired market nor do they try to take new opportunities. Their unstable and short-term decisions yield a residual and poorly performing strategy (Slater & Narver, 1993).

Despite the cross industry application, studies on the Miles and Snow (1978) typology in the hotel industry are limited, with one study indicating that Prospector, Analyser and Defender hotels outperformed Reactors in profits, growth and stakeholder satisfaction (Garrigós-Simón et al., 2005). As Zahra and Pearce (1990) suggest, "industry-specific studies should be encouraged to evaluate the relative contribution of strategy and unique environmental forces (p.7634)". Thus, this study uses the Miles and Snow (1978) typology as the theoretical framework to investigate the relationship of business strategy with Internet evolution among Malaysian hotels.

3 Conceptual Development and Propositions

Piccoli et al., (2004) suggest that Internet usage with customers evolves from *experimentation, value creation, focus and differentiation* to *building relationship.* Businesses first use the Internet mainly to publish information (Teo & Pian, 2004). At this stage, businesses are uncertain of their technological goals, value of acquiring the technology, and try to minimise risk by following industry leaders. Later, businesses try to personalise services and raise the barrier to imitation through building relationships with customers and increasing switching costs (Piccoli et al., 2004).

Given the distinct orientations of each strategic type, each business strategy adopts technology for different objectives and purposes. Prospectors tend to place more importance on innovation than the other three strategic types. Prospectors focus on innovation and being first in the market extends to their websites design (Auger, 2003). As such, Prospector hotels should adopt the Internet earlier and incorporate more business activities on their website than Analysers and Defenders. Reactors are less willing to take risks and only respond when forced by environmental pressure (Slater & Narver, 1993). Thus,

Proposition 1: Hotels classified as Prospector will have a higher level of Internet adoption than Analyser and Defender hotels.

Proposition 2: Hotels classified as Reactor will have the lowest level of Internet technology adoption.

4 Methodology

The primary unit of analysis is Malaysian hotels. This exploratory study uses in-depth interviews through snowball sampling to seek information about a hotel's business strategy and Internet use. Snowball sampling suits small and specialised research populations (Malhotra, Hall, Shaw, & Oppenheim, 2002). The interview process began with four experts in Malaysia's hospitality industry. The interviewees later recommended other expert who could provide more information. In total, the researcher conducted 13 interviews with each hotel's CEO or top-level manager, from 4 December 2005 until 4 January 2006.

The face-to-face and tape-recorded interviews relied upon a series of semi-structured questions covering two sections. In the first section, related to the hotel's Internet use, respondents described their hotels' past, present and in the future Internet use. Later, respondents described their hotels' business strategy. The researcher referred to the Conant, Mokwa, and Varadarajan (1990) questionnaire as a guideline to ensure that the interview covered all 11 characteristics of Miles and Snow. Table 1 shows a brief profile of the interviewees. As per the interview protocol, the interviewees' identities are anonymous.

Table 1 Hotel Profiles

Hotel	Profiles			Adopted Internet	Internet Use		
	Star	Affiliation Status	Target market		Email		Web
					Internal	External	
PROSPECTORS							
D	Five	Chain	Business travellers	1998	Extensive	Extensive	A*
E	Five	Chain	Conference, meeting and teambuilding activities	1998	Extensive	Extensive	B
J	Five	Chain	Business travellers	1997	Extensive	Extensive	A
DEFENDERS							
A	Two	Chain	Families and government agencies	1999	Minimal	Minimal	D
B	Three	Chain	Families and government agencies	2000	Moderate	Minimal	C
C	Four	Chain	Top level business travellers	1998	Moderate	Moderate	C
I	Three	Independent	Weekend travellers and privilege card holders	1999	Extensive	Moderate	C
ANALYSERS							
H	Three	Chain	Leisure travellers	1998	Moderate	Moderate	C
K	Four	Chain	Privilege card holders and leisure travellers	1998	Extensive	Moderate	B
M	Five	Chain	Conference and meetings and families	1996	Extensive	Moderate	A
REACTORS							
F	One	Independent	Leisure travellers and travel groups	-	None	None	E
G	Two	Independent	Travel groups	-	Minimal	None	E
L	None	Independent	Students	-	None	None	E

**A: Online reservation, promotion, email marketing and loyalty program*
B: Online reservation, promotion and loyalty program
C: Online reservation, marketing and promotion
D: Brochureware
E: Do not adopt

4.1 Miles and Snow business strategy classification procedure

There are at least five methods to operationalise and classify a Miles and Snow (1978) business strategy: investigator inference, self-typing paragraph, multi-item scale, external assessment and objective indicators. The investigator inference technique allows the researcher to use the available information before suggesting the suitable strategy (Snow & Hambrick, 1980). External assessment relies on expert judgement while objective indicators use published data to help the classification.

The self-typing paragraph, most widely employed, uses a short paragraph describing the four strategic types and then respondents select the description that best characterises their organisation. This method oversimplifies the multi-dimensionality of a business strategy and (Conant et al., 1990; Zahra & Pearce, 1990) managers tend to express strategies into terms of intention or the intended strategy rather than the realised strategy (Snow & Hambrick, 1980). The multi-item scales provide a more comprehensive coverage to the multi-dimensional nature of business strategy construct.

This research employed the multi items scale technique using Conant, Mokwa and Varadarajan (1990) 11 multi-items questionnaire to classify the hotels business strategy. The 11 questions equally cover the three attributes of Miles and Snow (1978). Once completed, the researcher classified the business strategy based on the response option selected most often (Conant et al., 1990). The questionnaire results yielded three Prospectors, four Defenders, three Analysers and three Reactors (see Table 2).

Table 2. Miles and Snow (1978) classification

Hotel	Multi-items Questionnaire	Investigator Inference	Final Classification
Hotel A	Defender	Defender	Defender
Hotel B	Defender	Defender	Defender
Hotel C*	Defender	Analyser	Defender
Hotel D	Prospector	Prospector	Prospector
Hotel E	Prospector	Prospector	Prospector
Hotel F	Reactor	Reactor	Reactor
Hotel G	Reactor	Reactor	Reactor
Hotel H*	Analyser	Defender	Analyser
Hotel I*	Defender	Analyser	Defender
Hotel J	Prospector	Prospector	Prospector
Hotel K	Analyser	Analyser	Analyser
Hotel L	Reactor	Reactor	Reactor

The investigator inference method helps increase the reliability of the coding. The investigator inference resulted in four Prospectors, three Defenders, three Analysers and three Reactors. For the four hotels with conflicting classification, this study assumed the information from the multi items questionnaire was more valid than the investigator inference. Snow and Hambrick (1980) found investigator inference as the weakest and least accurate of the four approaches. Thus, the final classification includes three Prospectors, four Defenders, three Analysers and three Reactors.

5 Results

5.1 Prospectors

The three Prospectors are highly rated international chain hotels. Their main market is business travellers. The Prospector hotels are the trendsetters and already advanced in their Internet use. These hotels were among the earliest in adopting email and websites. For Hotel J, the hotel head office mandated Internet adoption as the general manager recalled: *"I remember during the early days, we were sent to a few Internet courses and learnt how to use and send email"*.

Prospector strengths include the ability to offer new and advanced features on their website. The three hotels agreed that their IT experts and strong financial help support technology changes at their hotel. The three hotels agreed that a good website should be updated regularly and contain only relevant information because consumers scan for information quickly. For Hotels J and D, the headquarters office designs and maintains their websites to ensure consistency and protect the corporate image. In addition, hotel managers frequently contribute new ideas on potential Internet marketing activities and evaluate the website performance.

Hotel E owns and maintains its own Malaysian-based website. In maintaining their website, the hotel management adopted an informal approach, emphasising discussion with the hotel IT expert. The Executive Director in Hotel E commented about their website that, *"We monitor the trends of our website and make sure that latest information is included on the website on a daily basis."* Prospector hotels agreed that the Internet helps them establish closer ties with their customers and makes communication easier. Their websites emphasise building stronger customer relationships through features such as personal login, loyalty point redemptions, newsletters, email marketing, real time information and quick responses to emails.

5.2 Defenders

Defenders include chain and individual hotels ranging from two to four stars. Defenders view the Internet as a cost efficient technology that improves sales and service quality. The four Defenders view their websites as another advertising channel to disseminate information about promotions and discounts. However, the four Defender hotel websites have minimal e-commerce capability. For instance, Hotel A's website is still at a brochureware stage (Hanson, 2000), providing basic information about rooms and facilities. None of the other three hotels goes beyond online reservations. According to the room division manager of hotel B, *"Our online reservation generates less than 5% of our total reservation."*

Their minimum email and website use relates to their main market – government institutions and families that still prefer using letters and fax. When asked about future Internet use, managers of Hotel A and B were unsure as it depends on their customers. If customers are still happy with phone and faxes, there is little benefit for investing much on website and email. The general manager of Hotel A said, "*We have a few loyal customers and we know them very well... whenever they want to stay with us... they just ring and we handle the rest*". However, managers from Hotel I and C agree that industry competition and pressure, and fear of losing their existing customers influenced their decision to go online. As the general manager of Hotel I said, *"We have to follow the trend, otherwise we will lose our existing customers and potential customers as it is easier to find our competitors' hotels on the Net"*

5.3 Analysers

Analysers, from three to five star hotels, operate in two customer markets – one stable and one changing. Analysers assess their competitors closely for new ideas and rapidly adopt those that appear most promising. Commenting about Internet changes, the general manager of Hotel K said, *"We don't just shoot blind bullets, hoping that one will hit. We will do it stage-by-stage. We always look at the successful features adopted by leading hotels and evaluate whether or not it suits us."* The three managers in this category agree that the objective of having a website is to retain existing customers, build loyalty and expand to new potential markets. The hotels however, try to keep their websites as simple as possible to avoid unnecessary design costs. Therefore, at present the Analysers' Internet use is limited to online reservation and promotion.

Analysers, however, feel pressure from changing markets, mainly the younger generation, to provide advanced services online. The general manager of Hotel M commented that, *"Most of our new customers are looking for more features on the web. We need to address this; otherwise we are going to loose"*. Still, Analysers are cautious with their spending for their Internet features. They balance the risk and return by taking and using the leading hotels' most promising ideas.

5.4 Reactors

Reactors comprise the lower rated hotels and do not use the Internet. The three Reactors in the sample are independent hotels, and two of these hotels are family-businesses. Lack of IT expertise and most importantly, customer preferences, are the hotels' reasons to stay offline. The three hotels agree that looking sophisticated and techno-savvy is not an objective. They are happy with their present business. New customers stem from referrals. When asked about potential Internet adoption in the near future, the answer remains negative. The general manager of Hotel F explained: *"I don't think we are going to invest in the Internet within the next couple of years. Business has been very good so why do I have to change?"*

6 Conclusion

The small sample size, however limits generalising Miles and Snow typology for Internet evolution. In addition, the test-retest procedure was not conducted to check the reliability of the multi-items classification. Limitation aside, the results of this study offer important messages for both researchers and managers.

6.1 Academic implications

The results are wholly consistent with the two propositions that Internet adoption and usage differ for each business strategic type. These results support previous findings on the relationship between organisational properties and Internet implementation (Levy & Powell, 2003, p.125), particularly in tourism and hospitality (Garrigós-Simón et al., 2005; Yuan, Gretzel, & Fesenmaier, 2006) and illustrate the evolutionary aspects of Internet adoption. Prospectors lead with advanced website features, while Reactors are at the other end of the continuum with no adoption. Analysers take a safe approach by copying the market leader. As Defenders operate in a stable environment, online changes are slow. Figure 1 illustrates the relationship between hotels' business strategy and their Internet evolution.

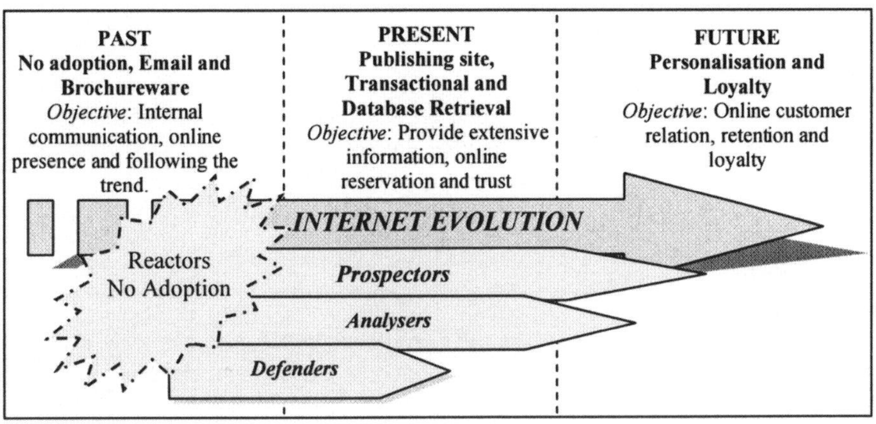

Fig. 1. Hotel business strategy and the Internet evolution timeline

The findings also support Garrigós-Simón et al., (2005) argument that the development of new theories for online studies is not necessary. The apparent link between firms' offline and online characteristics suggest that existing theories to study firms' behaviour offline apply to the online world.

6.2 Managerial implications

Overall, these 13 Malaysian hotels use the Internet in a limited fashion. They focus on exploiting the Internet for disseminating information and taking online reservations. Few hotels use the Internet for advanced activities such as permission email marketing and loyalty programs. The results demonstrate that these hotels have ample room to exploit the Internet further.

As competition intensifies and customers demand more customised and personalised services, hotels should think of enhancing their virtual presence and strategy to provide better services quality and build customer relationship management online. For example, Hyatt has introduced online check-in to make the process easier.

The findings indicate that hotels take different paths in using the Internet. Hotel should take advantage of prior success and must realise that the Internet is not a stand-alone technology to help solve all problems and bring profit. For example, if a hotel aims to increase online visibility and awareness, the hotel should strive for higher ranking on the search results, providing customers with quick access information through sitemaps and anticipating questions via FAQs (Palmer, 2002).

While Prospectors hotels transforms their business activities online, the main challenge is how to benefit from the information obtained. For example, server log files and cookies can provide information about customers' activities on a website (Hofacker & Murphy, 2005). Successful Internet adoption does not replace existing activities but can strengthen organisation present unique activities and develop core competencies. Hotels should avoid making investments simply to follow trends and imitate competitors (Murphy, Olaru, Schegg, & Frey, 2003).

7 Future Research

Future research could investigate factors that encourage advanced Internet use of the Prospectors as compared to Reactors. Research on organisational technology adoption suggests that organisation structural and leader characteristics lead to different technology adoption level (Premkumar, 2003). Investigating the Internet assimilation level (Fichman & Kemerer, 1999) between the four types, business strategy would also be a fruitful research area.

Future research could support these results via quantitative approaches such using questionnaire to identify factors that related to Internet adoption to other Malaysian hotel or other tourism businesses. A content analysis of hotels' website features and email reply quality should provide a more comprehensive view of how each strategic type differs on their Internet use. Future research could also incorporate the domain name age or website age, as a temporal aspect of organisational Internet adoption. Hotels with older domain and website age indicate earlier Internet adoption, a more proactive business strategy than others and thus should reflect more advanced website features and quality email responses.

Another research area is the technical variables of the website such as download time, number of links, the meta tags title and descriptions and via third party tools such Google page rank and Alexa popularity rank (Murphy, Ho, & Chan, 2005) as a measure to the website evolution. Alexa popularity rank shows the popularity of a website, from the first site to millions for rarely visited website while Google rank is a proxy for site visibility, with rankings from a low of zero to a maximum of ten. Hotels at a higher Internet evolution stage should have a better quality on the website's technical aspect.

Lastly, future research could extend the study to more hotels, outside and inside Malaysia to improve generalisability. An extension to hotels in neighbouring countries such as Singapore, Indonesia and Brunei would provide a more comprehensive picture and allow Malaysian hotels to benchmark their Internet diffusion.

References

Auger, P. (2003). An Empirical Investigation of the Miles and Snow Typology for Small Online Businesses. *International Journal of Internet and Enterprise Management, 1*(3), 245-264.

Conant, J. S., Mokwa, M. P., & Varadarajan, P. R. (1990). Strategic Types, Distinctive Marketing Competencies and Organisational Performance: A Multiple Measures-Based Study. *Strategic Management Journal, 11*(5), 365-383.

Croteau, A. M., & Bergeron, F. (2001). An Information Technology Trilogy: Business Strategy, Technological Deployment and Organizational Performance. *Journal of Strategic Information Systems, 10*(2), 77-99.

Fichman, R. G., & Kemerer, C. F. (1999). The Illusory Diffusion of Innovation: An Examination of Assimilation Gaps. *Information Systems Research, 10*(3), 255-275.

Garrigós-Simón, F. J., Marqués, D. P., & Narangajavana, Y. (2005). Competitive Strategies and Performance in Spanish Hospitality Firms. *International Journal of Contemporary Hospitality Management, 17*(1), 22-38.

Grover, V., & Saeed, K. A. (2004). Strategic Orientation and Performance of Internet-Based Businesses. *Information Systems Journal, 14*(1), 23-42.

Hambrick, D. C. (1983). Some Tests on the Effectiveness and Functional Attributes of Miles and Snow's Strategic Types. *Academy of Management Journal, 26*(1), 5-26.

Hanson, W. (2000). *Principles of Internet Marketing*. Cincinnati, Ohio: Southwest College Publishing.

Hashim, N. H., Olaru, D., Scaglione, M., & Murphy, J. (2006). *A Theoretical Framework of Factors Relating to Internet Adoption by Malaysian Hotels*. Paper presented at the ENTER, Lausanne, Switzerland.

Hofacker, C. F., & Murphy, J. (2005). *Contemporary Research in E-Marketing*. Hershey, Pennsylvania: Idea Group.

Kearns, G. S. (2005). An Electronic Commerce Strategic Typology: Insights from Case Studies. *Information & Management, 42*(7), 1023-1036.

Levy, P., & Powell, P. (2003). Exploring SME Adoption: Towards a Contingent Model. *Electronic Markets, 13*(2), 173-181.

Malhotra, N., Hall, J., Shaw, M., & Oppenheim, P. (2002). *Marketing Research: An Applied Orientation*. New South Wales, Australia: Pearson Education Australia Pty Ltd.

Miles, R. E., & Snow, C. C. (1978). *Organizational Strategy, Structure and Process*. New York: McGrawHill.
Mintzberg, H. (1978). Patterns of Strategy Formation. *Management Science, 24*(9), 934-948.
Moore, M. (2005). Towards a Confirmatory Model of Retail Strategy Types: An Empirical Test of Miles and Snow. *Journal of Business Research, 58*(5), 696-704.
Murphy, J., Ho, P., & Chan, C. (2005). Competitive Analyses for Marketing Electronic Wine Tourism. *International Journal of Wine Marketing, 17*(3), 39-54.
Murphy, J., Olaru, D., Schegg, R., & Frey, S. (2003). The Bandwagon Effect: Swiss Hotels' Website and E-mail Management. *Cornell Hotel and Restaurant Administration Quarterly, 44*(1), 71-87.
Osterwalder, A., Pigneur, Y., & Tucci, C., L. (2005). Clarifying Business Model: Origins, Present and Future of the Concept. *Communications of the Association for Information Systems, 15*(May), 1-43.
Palmer, J. W. (2002). Web Site Usability, Design, and Performance Metrics. *Information Systems Research, 13*(2), 151-167.
Porter, M. E. (1980). *Competitive Strategy*. New York: The Free Press.
Premkumar, G. (2003). A Meta Analysis of Research on Information Technology Implementation in Small Business. *Journal of Organizational Computing and Electronic Commerce, 13*(2), 91-121.
Shortell, S. M., & Zajac, E. J. (1990). Perceptual and Archival Measures of Miles and Snow's Strategic Types: A Comprehensive Assessment of Reliability and Validity. *Academy of Management Journal, 33*(4), 817-832.
Slater, S. F., & Narver, J. C. (1993). Product-Market Strategy and Performance: An Analysis of the Miles and Snow Strategy Types. *European Journal of Marketing, 27*(10), 33-51.
Snow, C. C., & Hambrick, D. C. (1980). Measuring Organisational Strategies: Some Theoretical and Methodological Problems. *Academy of Management Review, 5*(4), 527-539.
Teo, T. S. H., & Pian, Y. (2004). A Model for Web Adoption. *Information & Management, 41*(4), 457-468.
Thomas, A. S., & Ramaswamy, K. (1996). Matching Manager to Strategy: Further Tests of the Miles and Snow Typology. *British Journal of Management, 7*(3), 247-261.
Yuan, Y. L., Gretzel, U., & Fesenmaier, D. R. (2006). The Role of Information Technology Use in American Convention and Visitors Bureaus. *Tourism Management, 27*(2), 326-341.
Zahra, S. A., & Pearce, J. A. (1990). Research Evidence on the Miles and Snow Typology. *Journal of Management Information System, 16*(4), 751-768.

Internet Use by Hospitality SMEs in Alpine Destinations

Roland Schegg[a]
Miriam Scaglione[a]
Andreas Liebrich[b]
Jamie Murphy[c]

[a] Institut Economie & Tourisme
University of Applied Sciences Valais, Switzerland
{roland.schegg; miriam.scaglione}@hevs.ch

[b] Institut für Tourismuswirtschaft
Hochschule für Wirtschaft in Luzern, Switzerland
andreas.liebrich@hsw.fhz.ch

[c] School of Business
University of Western Australia, Australia
jmurphy@biz.uwa.edu.au

Abstract

This study examined Internet use by a representative sample of 182 hospitality enterprises from six Alpine destinations – Germany (Allgäu), Austria (Bodensee-Vorarlberg, Kleinwalsertal and Montafon) and Switzerland (Davos and Savognin) – within the framework of the eFitness Benchmarking project. The study adds to the limited research of evolving IT adoption in tourism and shows that the website age reflects the presence of advanced website features and IT usage. Clustering techniques classified the accommodation enterprises into four clusters based on website features. The clusters illustrate how adoption evolves from basic to advanced IT use. In line with prior research, there were significant positive relationships between cluster membership and firm size, category and affiliation.

Keywords: technology adoption, hospitality, website, SME, Switzerland, Austria, Germany

1 Introduction

Research shows that businesses evolve in their use of an innovation, from the initial adoption of a technology to incorporating that technology within their business processes (Rogers, 1995). Similarly, hospitality and tourism websites may start by providing basic information, then in subsequent phases add interactivity and personalisation (Doolin, Burgess, & Cooper, 2002; Hanson, 2000).

Furthermore, early adopters of a technology such as websites may lack a coherent managerial plan (Soutar, Allen, & Long, 2000). Lack of training, traditional ownership and rational management hinder the adoption process by small to medium sized enterprises (SMEs) (Buhalis & Main, 1998). Additionally, rather than a reasoned strategy, fear of being different can pressure organisations to adopt technologies (Abrahamson, 1991; Fichman, 2000), such as website and email in the hospitality industry (Murphy, Olaru, Schegg, & Frey, 2003). Still, emerging research suggests that hotels adopting Internet technologies gain revenue relative to those hotels failing to go online (Scaglione, Schegg, & Murphy, 2006).

Given the range and evolutionary nature of Internet tools, questions remain on what Internet features and functions to adopt (Murphy et al., 2003). Furthermore, the predominant snapshot approach of hospitality website studies fails to consider the dynamics of websites (Morrison, Taylor, & Douglas, 2004). After grouping 182 Alpine SMEs into four clusters based on their usage of Internet tools, the study draws upon a temporal dimension, website age, the Diffusion of Innovations (Rogers, 1995) and organisational strategy (Miles & Snow, 1978) in order to address three research questions.

- What Internet features relate to Internet success?
- What organisational differences relate to the clusters based on Internet tools?
- What temporal differences relate to clusters based on Internet tools?

2 Literature review

A few contributions treat the adoption of information technology (IT) and innovation in hotels. The reasons why small and medium hotels adopt IT to a different stage are manifold and stem from two main factors: economic and managerial. Among the economic factors, lack of financial resources and lack of economies of scale in small hotels are key reasons for not adopting IT. Managerial factors include centralised business structures and lack of professionalism. Although Porter and Millar (1985) claimed over 20 years ago that IT can give companies a competitive advantage, decisions about adopting IT may be irrational (Buhalis & Main, 1998).

With or without facilitation, IT adoption is an evolving process. Murphy, Schegg and Olaru (2006) show that domain name age – when a company first registered a domain name such as *hyatt.com* for Hyatt hotels – correlates positively with the presence of advanced website features. From a simple web-presence to the implementation of e-business processes, company websites go through several development stages (Doolin et al., 2002; Hanson, 2000).

3 Methodology

This paper draws on data from the eFitness® Benchmarking project (www.efitnessbenchmarking.com) of tourism enterprises in six alpine destinations in Germany (Allgäu), Austria (Bodensee-Vorarlberg, Kleinwalsertal and Montafon) and Switzerland (Davos and Savognin). The eFitness objective is to facilitate effective technology adoption by small and mid-sized tourism organisations through online benchmarking and knowledge exchange. A web-based platform facilitates yearly industry comparisons and identifies competitive potentials. The eFitness model (see Tables 1 and 3) links four input factors – eMarketing, IT infrastructure, website quality and email customer service – to Internet success measures.

The study began with a random sample of 182 online accommodation enterprises in the six Alpine destinations, stratified across category (1-5* hotels, non-classified hotel and rental flats). In November 2005, the local tourism organisations administered a written questionnaire for dimensions E1, E2 and E5 of the eFitness model. By February 2005, 110 enterprises had returned the questionnaires, for a 60% response rate.

To investigate the temporal dimension of organisational Internet adoption, the research relied upon data from the *Internet Archive* (www.archive.org), a non-profit organisation that began archiving websites in 1996 (FAQs, 2006). While domain name registration dates suggest when an organisation started to go online (Scaglione, Schegg, Steiner, & Murphy, 2004), ages available through the *Wayback Machine* (WM) in the *Internet Archive* serve as a proxy for the moment when a website first went online. Scholars have used the WM to investigate archived versions of web pages (Ryan, Field, & Olfman, 2003; Thelwall, Vaughan, Cothey, Li, & Smith, 2003; Veronin, 2002) and to infer website age (Vaughan & Thelwall, 2003).

From March-May 2006, two trained researchers content analysed the enterprises' websites for the presence of 92 features (E3) in the eFitness model, either visually and through browser prompts. This study also assessed the same properties' eService (E4), via their responses to a short reservation request for two adults and two children for a pre-Easter weekend in 2006. The dependent eService variables stemmed from past studies (Murphy et al., 2003; Schegg, Liebrich, Liu, & Murphy, 2006), covering responsiveness (e.g. quickly responding, addressing the questions, etc.) and quality (e.g. friendly answers, personal salutations, politely closing with the sender's full name and contact details, etc.).

Table 1. Dimensions of the eFitness® model

	dimension	description	data acquisition	number of criteria
E1	eMarketing	use of eMarketing tools (search engine submission, use of keyword marketing, etc.)	paper questionnaire	9
E2	IT infrastructure and investment	level of IT infrastructure (e.g. software use, Internet access options for guests, etc.); commitment to new media in terms of time and money invested in IT and Internet	paper questionnaire	22
E3	Website quality*	evaluation of the quality, technological standards and strategies of the hotel websites along various dimensions (information provision, transaction/reservation functions, communication and customer service, use of advanced Internet technologies, etc.)	expert check	92
E4	Email service**	eService quality evaluated with a email mystery check	expert check	31
E5	e-Success	outcome in terms of number of online reservation requests, website visitors or search engine ranking	paper questionnaire	10

** evaluation criteria adapted from Schegg et al. (2002), **evaluation criteria adapted from Schegg et al. (2006)*

A disjoint cluster analysis was performed on the Euclidean distances computed from the website feature variables (E3). No other hotel characteristics features were used. Observations close to each other are usually assigned to the same cluster, while observations far apart are in different clusters (SAS, 2004, p. 1380). The cluster centres are estimated using a least-squares method. This clustering method is often called a k-means model, since the cluster centres are the means of the observations assigned to each cluster when the algorithm is run to complete convergence. Every iteration reduces the least-squares criterion until convergence (SAS, 2004).

The "proc fastclust" package in SAS Enterprise Miner© yields this analysis and, after several trials, a decomposition to clusters was chosen.

4 Results

Table 2 shows organisational characteristics of each cluster.

The third cluster, two thirds of all firms, contains mainly rental homes and small, budget hotels (average of 12 rooms). The first cluster, with 28 properties, is mainly large, mid- to up-scale hotels. These properties show the most affiliation and business clients of all clusters. Cluster 2 also has mostly 3-4 star hotels, albeit smaller (32 rooms) than the cluster 1 properties (79 rooms). None of the cluster 2 members is chain-affiliated and their clientele comprises few business guests (9%).

Table 2. Cluster profiles

	cluster 1	**cluster 2**	**cluster 3**	**cluster 4**	**total**
n	28	24	116	14	182
dominant hotel category	4 stars (46%), 3 stars (32%)	3 stars (38%), 4 stars (21%)	rental flats (59%)	rental flats (36%), 4 stars (29%)	
size (room)	**79**	32	*12*	18	25
type of website	own domain	own domain	own website	portal website	
affiliation	**33%**	0%	0%	8%	8%
proportion of business clients	21%	9%	7%	21%	12%
bed occupancy	58%	**66%**	52%	55%	55%
room revenue >1 million Euro	**45%**	15%	*2%*	13%	17%

[numbers in bold (italic) are significantly, $p < 0.05$, higher (lower) than the sample average]

Cluster 4 has a hybrid composition compared to the other groups, mostly rental flat owners and 4 star hotels. Their average property (18 rooms) is much smaller than for clusters 1 and 2. None of these fourth cluster properties has their own website domain, rather they use a portal for website presence. The clusters often differ significantly across results IT usage. Table 3 summarises the clusters performance along the four eFitness dimensions and sub-dimensions.

Table 3. Relative cluster performance along sub-dimensions of the eFitness® model

		cluster 1	cluster 2	cluster 3	cluster 4
eMarketing	e-marketing instruments (10)	80%	40%	10%	40%
	e-mail marketing (3)	100%	100%	0%	33%
IT infrastructure and investment	website maintenance (2)	100%	50%	0%	50%
	Internet access hotel (2)	100%	0%	0%	50%
	Internet guest access (4)	50%	75%	50%	25%
	software (3)	100%	100%	0%	0%
	IT infrastructure (2)	100%	50%	0%	0%
	know-how (3)	100%	67%	0%	33%
	input time & money (6)	100%	50%	0%	17%
website quality	linking strategy (6)	100%	17%	0%	83%
	meta tags (3)	67%	100%	0%	33%
	domain name (2)	100%	100%	50%	50%
	language (4)	100%	100%	0%	25%
	navigation&usability (15)	60%	67%	27%	67%
	design (5)	80%	60%	40%	20%
	hotel information (10)	90%	80%	0%	70%
	image (3)	100%	67%	0%	67%
	visualisation (5)	100%	80%	0%	40%
	service information (4)	100%	75%	0%	100%
	regional information (4)	100%	100%	0%	100%
	accomodation information (4)	75%	100%	0%	75%
	price information (4)	100%	75%	0%	100%
	general sales condition (4)	75%	100%	0%	75%
	booking (5)	100%	20%	0%	100%
	sales motivation (4)	75%	50%	0%	25%
	CRM (8)	88%	100%	13%	25%
	other aspects (2)	100%	100%	0%	50%
email	email responsivness (8)	88%	63%	0%	50%
	email quality (23)	91%	78%	13%	57%
e-success	search engine fitness (3)	100%	0%	0%	0%
	website success & booking request (7)	100%	43%	0%	43%

Legend: Performance levels measure the the number of times a cluster outperforms the sample average on the criteria evaluated in a sub-dimension. Number of criteria given in parentheses. High performance levels indicated by shading of cells.

Miles and Snow's (1978) four strategic business approaches provide a foundation for interpreting technology use (Hashim, Olaru, Scaglione, & Murphy, 2006). Table 4 shows characteristics of each strategy for technological adaptation. *Defenders* constantly try to improve their core product. They are efficient in today's environment, but can have trouble if the environment changes rapidly. *Prospectors*, however, try most everything in order to adapt faster than their competitors do.

Analyzers unify the positive characteristics of the former approaches. *Reactors* have no strategic plan to cope with adaptations.

	Defenders	**Prospectors**	**Analyzers (Mix of defenders and prospectors)**	**Reactors**
Relationship between the environment and the firm	Stable	Highly dynamic	Balanced	Unforeseeable
Technological goals	Efficiency	Pushing the edge	At the edge	Laggard
Business focus	Narrow	Broad	Balanced	Unclear
(Technology) adoption mode	Slow, continous improvement	Fast adoption, sometimes irrational	Imitation of successful innovations	No pattern

Table 4. Adoption strategies according to Miles and Snow (1978)

Cluster 1, Prospectors: Compared to all other clusters, the mid- to up-scale cluster 1 hotels have the most advanced IT use in nearly all aspects. They use eMarketing more than the firms in the other clusters do. Over 90% using CRM and hotel software (PMS) compared to about one third in clusters 3 and 4. That 70% of the cluster members update their website at least monthly suggests professional IT use. Similarly, systematic training of employees in IT and Internet use in every second property reflects the strategic importance of technology for prospector hotels.

Their websites provide detailed information to help build and extend the properties' customer-base, sales and customer relationships via features such as "tell a friend", online help/FAQ and offering subscriptions to electronic newsletter. The booking process on the website is particularly well implemented by prospector hotels. Good practices include well outlined vacancy calendars, and transparent bookings and cancellations conditions on the same page where the online booker is asked to enter a credit card number. Moreover, the user knows at every stage how many steps to finish the process.

The e-services provided by this group exceed the other clusters in most criteria, especially in reply quality. For example, roughly two out of three prospector hotels included a complete signature file with relevant information, compared to one out of four in the third cluster.

Cluster 2, Analyzers: The small 3 and 4 stars second cluster hotels show good performance in website quality and often resemble the performance of hotels in cluster 1. Analyzer hotels, similar to the prospector hotels, provide in-depth hotel and the regional information on the website. They also present the goods and services in visually appealing form through webcams, 360° panoramas and virtual hotel tours. A significant difference however, is booking features. Over nine out of ten analyzer hotels provide simple booking forms whereas the cluster 1 properties have a higher proportion of real-time booking options (29% versus 4% in cluster 2).

Compared to the sample average, the analyzers' eService is good in responsiveness and reply quality. This cluster also lags the first cluster in the IT infrastructure dimension, such as time and money invested, knowledge building and IT process such as website maintenance.

Cluster 3, Reactors: The micro-enterprises in this "rental flat" group show the poorest performance on nearly all dimensions. The websites are generally simple with only basic information and functionalities. Their minimal IT usage and infrastructure may reflect the semi-professional character of numerous properties in this group. A notable exception however, is their free Internet access for guests.

Cluster 4, Defenders: Properties in this group have neither an advanced IT infrastructure nor use the numerous eMarketing possibilities. However, as their website presence is through a travel portal, they show good performance in website aspects related to the portal's booking process – quality of destination information, service and price information, and booking options.

5 Cluster membership and e-success measures

The results show that clusters adopting technology early (i.e. clusters 1 and 2 with the oldest website age) tend to surpass late adopters in all the success measures studied (see Table 5).

Table 5. E-success measures and cluster membership

	cluster 1	cluster 2	cluster 3	cluster 4	total	n	Anova
age of website (days)	1 962	1 901	1 510	1 375	1 637	149	**p<0.001**, F=6.6
Google PageRank	3,00	2,00	1,22	0,71	1,55	182	**p<0.0001**, F=17.08
Unique visitors 2005	72 262	19 264	9 173	3 756	36 841	36	p=0.176, F=1.8
Online booking revenue 2005 (Euro)	268 718	101 941	26 897	13 135	99 585	35	p=0.095, F=2.31
Online booking revenue per room 2005 (Euro)	1 879	1 615	1 368	1 159	1 610	35	p=0,954, F=0.1
Email booking requests 2005	2 996	2 405	685	2 773	1 654	91	**p=0.001**, F=5.7

Search engine popularity, measured via Google PageRank is significantly better in clusters 1 and 2 compared to clusters 3 and 4. Given their lower Google rank, properties in these latter groups have lower chances of discovery by potential clients through search engines. Clusters 1 and 2 also outperform the other groups in unique website visitors and online booking revenues, which suggest that superior eMarketing, quality of eService and websites relate to better online results. The high number of e-mail requests of properties in cluster 4, however, shows that outsourcing the website via a portal may increase market interest.

6 Discussion and conclusions

This study introduces the eFitness® model and investigates IT and Internet use by a representative sample of 182 hospitality enterprises across six Austrian, German and Swiss alpine destinations. Yet as these statistics stem from few observations, particularly the success measures, the results have limited generalisability. The small database, particularly with success indicators, also hinders applying multivariate statistical approaches to identify Internet success factors. Future research should address this point and extend the sample to other locations (e.g. city hotels) in order to improve the generalisability and relevance of the results.

The study adds to the limited research of evolving Internet adoption (Murphy et al., 2006 and references therein). Website age tends to reflect advanced website features and IT usage. Early adopters invest more in these technologies, make better and wider use of them (quality websites, high level of e-service, etc.), and seem to be more successful in website traffic and online bookings. In line with prior research (Murphy et al., 2003; Siguaw, Enz, & Namiasivayam, 2000; Wei, Ruys, van Hoof, & Combrink, 2001), there are significant positive relationships between hotel size, category and affiliation with dimensions of the eFitness performance model. Enterprises of clusters 1 and 2, the top performers, are significantly larger, more frequently affiliated and generally dominated by 3-5 star hotels. These findings align with a Greek study on Internet practices that compares and clusters IT-services of non-chain and chain hotels (Zafirapoulos, Vrana, & Paschaloudis 2006).

Ease of use and information content are important to website success. Huizingh (2000) for example argued that content and design could be determinants of website success. Law & Hsu (2006) support this view with an empirical study indicating that consumers view hotel website dimensions such as "Reservations Information", "Facilities Information", "Contact Information", "Surrounding Area Information", and "Website Management" as important. Prospectors and to a certain extent analyzers, cluster 1 respectively 2, align with these results as enterprises in these groups have an above average performance in nearly all eFitness website dimensions and at the same time show better Internet success results.

Prospectors have been fast and successful in adopting and implementing Internet technologies on a broad scope, from the Internet presence to the eService quality level and IT infrastructure. The analyzers of cluster 2 have good performance in some dimensions, in line with the companies' resources. Reactors of cluster 3 have no clear adoption strategy and use only few opportunities provided by the ICT (e.g. Internet access for customers). Although late in the adoption process, accommodation enterprises of cluster 4, the defenders, seem to focus IT investments on one business processes: online sales. Integrating their website presence into a travel portal allows these enterprises to profit from standardised business procedures, technology and expertise of their business partner.

Tourism enterprises and organizations are more and more challenged by the rapidly evolving technological environment: the skills required for managing electronic business processes – customer services, property and yield management, and booking requests – are increasing and the way of doing business differs from the traditional approach most hotels are used to. Stakeholders and employees must therefore constantly update their knowledge on the use of new media. Tourism enterprises that fail to implement these new media successfully in their work processes face competitive disadvantages.

Management of the cluster 3 reactor hotels must therefore reflect on outsourcing certain IT processes. Their eFitness, and ability to compete, lags compared to the other clusters. One solution, to outsource key functions through an appropriate affiliation or integrated electronic destination management system, gives these properties access to Internet distribution systems as well as a referenced website. Besides enhanced electronic distribution channels, affiliated hotels may often benefit from other advantages such as access to technological knowledge or management systems. Cooperation within local or regional initiatives is another option to overcome this knowledge and technology gap. A website presence using a professional tourism portal provider is another interesting and affordable strategy with low entry barriers. Yet as the results of cluster 4 show, outsourcing fails to solve many IT management issues.

Continuous assessment of email correspondence, website effectiveness, online bookings and guest Internet access (the new media communication portfolio) represents a critical competitive factor. Online benchmarking tools such as the eFitness benchmarking platform allow an objective evaluation and anonymous comparison of ICT use by hotels and destination organisations with other competitors (e.g. hotels of the same category). Such benchmarking tools give enterprises a detailed view of their strengths and weaknesses as well as suggestions for improvements. Online platforms can also share knowledge, networking and co-operation among enterprises.

Another option to improve ICT use among SME hospitality enterprises is to offer seminars/courses, customized consultancy services and contacts to trustworthy specialists. Peters and Mathies (2002) further propose e-learning to spread knowledge among hoteliers. In the case of Kleinwalsertal, the tourist organization has created a free consultancy service (www.kleinwalsertal.com/efitness). The service is run by a full-time employee who is trying to improve the ICT use among all the hotels and guesthouses in the destination.

References

Abrahamson, E. (1991). Managerial Fads and Fashions: The Diffusion and Rejection of Innovations. *Academy of Management Review, 16*(3), 586-612.

Buhalis, D., & Main, H. (1998). Information Technology in Peripheral Small and Medium Hospitality Enterprises: Strategic Analysis and Critical Factors. *International Journal of Contemporary Hospitality Management, 10*(5), 198-202.

Doolin, B., Burgess, L., & Cooper, J. (2002). Evaluating the Use of the Web for Tourism Marketing: A Case Study from New Zealand. *Tourism Management, 23*(5), 557-561.

FAQs. (2006). *The Wayback Machine: Frequently Asked Questions*. Retrieved 11 August, 2006 from www.archive.org/about/faqs.php

Fichman, R. G. (2000). The Diffusion and Assimilation of Information Technology Innovations. Framing the Domains of IT Management. In R. W. Zmud (Ed.), *Projecting the Future through the Past* (pp. 105-128). Cincinnati, Ohio: Pinnaflex Publishing.

Hanson, W. (2000). *Principles of Internet Marketing*. Cincinnati, Ohio: Southwest College Publishing.

Hashim, N.H, Olaru, D., Scaglione, M. & Murphy, J. (2006). A Theoretical Framework of Factors Relating to Internet Adoption by Malaysian Hotels. In M. Hitz, M. Sigala and J. Murphy (Eds.). *Information and Communication Technologies in Tourism 2006, proceedings of ENTER 2006* (pp.196-208), Vienna, Austria: Springer Verlag.

Huizingh, E. K. R. E. (2000). The content and design of web sites: an empirical study. *Information and Management, 37*, 123-134.

Law, R., & Hsu, C. H. C. (2006). Importance of Hotel Website Dimensions and Attributes: Perceptions of Online Browsers and Online Purchasers. *Journal of Hospitality & Tourism Research, 30*(3), 295-312.

Miles, R. E., & Snow, C. C. (1978). *Organizational Strategy, Structure and Process*. New York: McGrawHill.

Morrison, A. M., Taylor, J. S., & Douglas, A. (2004). Website Evaluation in Tourism and Hospitality: The Art Is Not Yet Stated. *Journal of Travel and Tourism Marketing, 17*(2/3), 233-251.

Murphy, J., Olaru, D., & Schegg, R. (2006). Investigating the Evolution of Hotel Internet Adoption. *Information Technology and Tourism, 8*(3/4), Forthcoming.

Murphy, J., Olaru, D., Schegg, R., & Frey, S. (2003). The Bandwagon Effect: Swiss Hotels' Website and E-mail Management. *Cornell Hotel and Restaurant Administration Quarterly, 44*(1), 71-87.

Peters, M. & Mathis, C. (2002). SMART-UP: Zum Nutzen von Informations- und Kommunikationsplattformen für die österreichische Hotellerie. *Wirtschaft im Alpenraum*, August 2002.

Porter, M. E., & Millar, V. E. (1985). How Information Gives You Competitive Advantage. *Harvard Business Review, 63*(4), 149-160.

Rogers, E. M. (1995). *Diffusion of Innovations* (Fourth ed.). New York, New York: The Free Press.

Ryan, T., Field, R. H. G., & Olfman, L. (2003). The Evolution of US State Government Home Pages from 1997 to 2002. *International Journal of Human-Computer Studies, 59*(4), 403–430.

SAS. (2004). *SAS/STAT (r) 9.1 User's Guide*. Cary, NC: SAS Institute Inc.

Scaglione, M., Schegg, R., & Murphy, J. (2006). Investigating Website Performance in Valais' Hospitality Industry. In P. Keller & T. Berger (Eds.), *Marketing Efficiency in Tourism - Coping with Volatile Demand* (Vol. 1, pp. 131-142). Berlin: Erich Schmidt Verlag.

Scaglione, M., Schegg, R., Steiner, T., & Murphy, J. (2004). Internet Adoption by Swiss Hotels: The Dynamics of Domain Name Registration. In A. J. Frew (Ed.), *Information and Communication Technologies in Tourism* (pp. 479-488). Wien-New York: Springer-Verlag.

Schegg, R., Liebrich, A., Liu, F., & Murphy, J. (2006). eService by Swiss and Austrian Hotels: Does Language Matter? In M. Hitz, M. Sigala & J. Murphy (Eds.), *Information and Communication Technologies in Tourism 2006, proceedings of ENTER 2006* (pp. 357-368). Vienna, Austria: Springer-Verlag.

Schegg, R., Steiner, T., Frey, S., & Murphy, J. (2002). Benchmarks of Web Site Design and Marketing by Swiss Hotels. *Information Technology and Tourism, 5*(2), 73-89.

Siguaw, J. A., Enz, C. A., & Namiasivayam, K. (2000). Adoption of Information Technology in U.S. Hotels: Strategically Driven Objectives. *Journal of Travel Research, 39*(November), 192-201.

Soutar, G., Allen, R., & Long, F. (2000). *Does the Pace of E-Commerce Adoption Reflect Considered Strategy or Revolutionary Fervor? Indications from Western Australia and Western Europe.* Paper presented at the The Fifth International Conference on Global Business and Economic Development, Beijing.

Thelwall, M., Vaughan, L., Cothey, V., Li, X., & Smith, A. G. (2003). Which Academic Subjects Have Most Online Impact? A Pilot Study and a New Classification Process. *Online Information Review, 27*(5), 333-343.

Vaughan, L., & Thelwall, M. (2003). Scholarly Use of the Web: What Are the Key Inducers of Links to Journal Web Sites? *Journal of the American Society for Information Science and Technology, 54*(1), 29-38.

Veronin, M. A. (2002). Where Are They Now? A Case Study of Health-related Web Site Attrition. *Journal of Medical Internet Research, 4*(2), www.jmir.org/2002/2002/e2010/.

Wei, S., Ruys, H. F., van Hoof, H. B., & Combrink, T. E. (2001). Uses of the Internet in the Global Hotel Industry. *Journal of Business Research, 54*(3), 235-241.

Zafirapoulos, C., Vrana V., & Paschaloudis, D. (2006). The Internet Practices of Hotel Companies: An Analysis from Greece. *Journal of Contemporary Hospitality Management, 18*(2), 156-163.

The Strategic Impact of the Internet on the Tourism Industry

Dimitrios Buhalis
Marianna Zoge

University of Surrey
d.buhalis@surrey.ac.uk
mariannazoge@yahoo.gr

Abstract

The emergence of the Internet altered the structure of the tourism industry as it changed dramatically best operational and strategic practices. This paper aims at examining these changes by using Porter's model of industry analysis (5 Forces). It identifies how the Internet has changed the five forces and the competitive position of each of the key players and how the tourism industry is shaped. Data were collected by qualitative methods, as the study is exploratory in nature, and were analysed by content analysis. The results depicted the strategic impact of the internet primarily on tourism suppliers such as Hotels, Airlines, whilst intermediaries such as Travel Agencies (TAs) and Tour Operators (TOs) are also examined. The study concludes that rivalry has increased dramatically; bargaining power of both buyers (consumers) and suppliers (principals) has been strengthened due to their ability to communicate directly at the expense of the position of intermediaries.

Keywords: Internet, Strategic analysis, industry structure, five forces, tourism

1 Introduction

Porter's (1979, 1980) model of industry analysis lies upon the existence of Five Forces that collectively determine the profitability and intensity of competition in the industry. The strength and impacts of these forces depend upon many factors. The rivalry among existing competitors and the bargaining power of suppliers and buyers represent the current situation in which an organisation is found, while the threat of new entrants and the threat of substitutes are based on future expectations. The emergence of the Internet affected all Five Forces as it changed the conditions of competition in the marketplace. As far as the threat of new entrants is concerned, the Internet had an effect on entry barriers as it altered economies of scale and the amount of capital required for competing within the industry. Rivalry among existing competitors was also affected as technology and the Internet affected differentiation and cost structures as well as switching costs (Porter, 1985). Changes also appeared to the bargaining power of buyers as the Internet introduced a much higher degree of transparency and lower switching costs. Similarly, a shift in the bargaining power of suppliers has been noticed, as the Internet provided alternatives and reduced the need to buy only from few powerful suppliers. Finally, the emergence of the Internet affected substitution as "it influences both the relative value/price and switching costs of substitutes" (Porter, 1985: 65).

The structure of the tourism industry has been affected dramatically by the Internet (Buhalis, 1998). The Internet changed the sources of competitive advantage, as it increasingly determines firms' cost and ability to differentiate. Tourism businesses may gain competitive advantage by managing information and knowledge through the Internet (Barnes, Mieczkowska, Hinton, 2003) whilst their strategic position has been influenced by the changes of their Five Forces. The Internet altered barriers to entry, minimised switching costs, revolutionised distribution channels, facilitated price transparency and competition, whilst enhancing production efficiency (Kim, Nam, Stimpert, 2004). The bargaining power of suppliers was also enhanced by allowing direct contact with consumers and decreasing distribution costs whilst creating the opportunity for partnerships with countless affiliates and other distributors. Consequently, tourism enterprises for the first time ever did not have to rely exclusively on powerful intermediaries, such as Tour Operators or Global Distribution Systems. As a result, the Internet changed dramatically the strategic position of tourism organisations and forced them to reconsider their strategy. It is only organisations that understand the strategic implications of these changes that will be able to benefit in the future, and hence this research should support decision makers in their strategic decision making.

2 Literature Review

Before the Internet the travel industry was linearly organised with three major components: suppliers, intermediaries and end-consumers. Suppliers (airlines, hotels, rail, ferries and car rental companies) used intermediaries such as Tour Operators (TOs) and Travel Agencies (TAs) for reaching the end-consumer. For leisure tourism TOs were mainly responsible for packaging and administrating services such as transport, accommodation, transfers etc., together for lower prices. TAs were selling those packages or suppliers' products to end-consumers by using GDSs. The distribution of travel was conducted by traditional intermediaries through the use of CRSs, GDSs and Videotext (O'Connor, 2000; Buhalis & Licata, 2002). Therefore suppliers had to pay both fees and commission to both intermediaries and technology companies (Buhalis, 2004). Consumers demand greater value and service from the suppliers of tourism products and the Internet provided the dynamic means of obtaining information and awareness of offerings as well as purchasing products and services instantly, inexpensively and interactively (Garces, Gorgemans, Martinez Sanchez & Perez, 2004).

From the suppliers' perspective, the Internet changed the way that tourism organisations "plan, control, operate and integrate a significant portion of activities" (Garces et al., 2004: 603). It introduced greater flexibility and convenience, global reach, real time representation, the ability to operate at all times whilst it decreased distribution costs, made market targeting easier and allowed the customisation and globalisation of products (Buhalis & Licata, 2002). In addition, the Internet enabled small and independent suppliers to access directly their target markets (O'Connor, 2003) affording them tools and techniques that were until then only available to global players. The Internet increased both transparency in the marketplace and the intensity of competition by enabling suppliers to sell directly to consumers. In some occasions that introduced disintermediation and reduced the number of intermediaries involved per booking, thus saving on transaction fees. The Internet also revolutionised the way that travel industry functioned by rendering the "location" and "distance" factors irrelevant, as distance has no longer effects on costs for the suppliers and location is no longer a barrier for the interaction between suppliers and consumers (Pitt, Berthon & Berthon, 1999). It also enabled marketers to disseminate information between all involved parties cost effectively whilst it enhanced personalisation and value-added services as well as the development of new services (Disney, Naim, Potter, 2004). Despite the predictions for disintermediation, the emergence of the Internet also led to reintermediation through the introduction of new online travel intermediaries such as expedia.com, that provided consumers with the ability to perform online reservations and bookings. "Expedia has been one of the pioneers in changing the business model used to sell travel online, placing emphasis on both the merchant model and dynamic packaging" (O'Connor, 2003: 61). This led to online intermediaries acting as both TAs and TOs (Daniele & Frew, 2005). GDSs also took advantage of the Internet and developed their own booking solutions and either developed or supported Internet portals. For example, SABRE introduced Corporate.Res and developed Travelocity, Amadeus purchased OPODO, Galileo introduced Highware and Worldspan Trip Manager and empowered Expedia (Paraskevas & Baron, 2004, O'Connor, 2000). A number of last minute agencies also occurred aiming at distributing distressed inventories (e.g. lastminute.com and ratestogo.com). Auction websites started selling travel whilst priceline.com reversed pricing by asking consumers what they were willing to pay (Go, Govers, van den Heuvel, 1999). In addition, a number of search and meta-search engines emerged for travel products, such as Yahoo! Travel (http://travel.yahoo.com) which is operated by SABRE and Kelkoo! Shopping and price comparison websites, meta search websites, such as Kayak, Traveljungle as well as online fare predictor Farecast, provided consumers with unprecedented information and travel tools products. All the aforementioned online alternatives resulted in utter transparency and provided consumers with the ability of choosing between travel components dynamically, instantly and interactively. As a result, customers are now able to create a tailored package by selecting among a wide range of alternatives of travel products (O'Connor, 2003). The new online intermediaries naturally pose a threat on traditional intermediaries as well as challenge the profitability of suppliers forcing them to reconsider their competitive positioning and business model (Schertler & Berger-Koch, 1999; O'Connor, 2000).

Porter's Five Forces Model provides a useful framework for analysing the impacts of the Internet on the structure of the tourism industry. Porter (1980:17) states that "*rivalry* occurs because one or more competitors either feels the pressure or sees the opportunity to improve position". The Internet reduced differences among rivals, due to the increased transparency which gave the ability to monitor competitors, imitate innovations and adapt prices. Competition also increased as the Internet speeded up industry growth due to its ability of global representation, of forming partnerships, of direct access to the market and of lowering start-up, distribution, operational and switching costs as well as due to the ability of SMTEs to promote themselves.

The Internet also enhanced the *bargaining power of suppliers* as it enabled them to monitor competitors and offer tailored and differentiated products. As the cost of obtaining and managing information on specific consumer groups was reduced (Kim et al., 2004) and as the option of dynamic packaging was introduced (Go et al., 1999) suppliers are able to meet the changing patterns of demand through mass-customisation, flexible production and personalised offerings at affordable prices. By being able to adjust to changes in demand and by being efficient, suppliers gain important cost savings. Reducing perishable inventory through the increased opportunity of filling up capacity at last minute (Lancioni, Jensen Schau, Smith, 2003) has improved profitability. Some suppliers also managed to reduce costs by reducing their dependence upon intermediaries. Overall, suppliers of travel products enhanced their position within the industry due to the increased possibility of interconnectivity and interactivity with consumers and partners. From a customer perspective, the Internet affected the *bargaining power of buyers*. Buyers gained bargaining power as they now have instant access to information, understand market offers and conditions better and are constantly exposed to special offers. They have more choice and are able to make direct comparisons rising their expectations and demands. As Porter (2001: 70) states "buyers back away from open marketplaces. They may once again focus on building close, proprietary relationships with fewer suppliers, using Internet technologies to gain efficiency improvements in various aspects of those relationships". The increase in buyers' bargaining power is also related to the increased convenience, transparency, flexibility, direct communication with suppliers and depth of the available information. The Internet also enabled them to dynamically package their individualised products by combining different travel products (i.e. accommodation, transportation etc.) (Daniele & Frew, 2005). Access to a greater range of available suppliers also increased their power.

Porter (1985: 65) suggests that "*substitution* is a function of the relative value to price of competing products and the switching costs", and "is the process by which one product or service supplants another in performing a particular function or functions for a buyer" (Porter, 1998: 273). The threat of substitutes depends on factors such as the buyer's willingness to substitute the product, the price and the performance of substitutes, as well as the cost of switching to substitutes. This threat may be lowered by building a strong brand identity or by increasing switching costs. The threat of substitution may be also affected by technological advancements (Porter, 1980). The intensified rivalry led to increased difficulty to create and sustain competitive advantage through differentiation strategies (Go et al., 1999). Tourism organizations compete for time and for money with all other leisure activities. As Schertler & Berger-Koch (1999:23) stated "today's innovation is time-based competition". Time is a driver that is reflected on the operations of both suppliers and intermediaries. Competition on time reflects the ability of offering instant and relevant information to a global marketplace. The Internet enabled tourism suppliers to become flexible, innovative and closer to their market conditions. Constant innovation of both product and process supported by proactive and reactive strategies are some of the few sources of competitive advantage in the Internet era (Buhalis, 2003).

New entrants to an industry bring new capacity, the desire to gain market share, and often substantial resources (Porter, 1979). They are deterred by the existence of barriers to entry, which represent the costs challenges that derive from attempting to join an industry (Porter, 1980). Initially the Internet changed dramatically the barriers to entry and enabled a wide range of players to enter the market. The Internet revolutionised the entire channel of tourism by offering a new direct sales channel to the travel industry and a number of new entries that provided creative distribution opportunities. A fairly simple web page with content and good links was supporting new organisations to gain traffic and revenues in the late 1990s. However the overoptimistic business models combined with a very dynamic global environment meant that many of the new entries were not sustainable and went into bankruptcy in 2000 when the Internet bubble burst. Those new entries with strong brands, appropriate content and business models, such as expedia.com and lastminute.com were able to survive, gain global market share and become global players. Barriers to entry were again raised and it became again difficult to survive unless being innovative. Porter (2001) claimed that building a brand identity and loyalty on the Internet is difficult because online businesses seem intangible to buyers whilst a competitor is only a click away. Although the Internet enabled many travel businesses to "establish good relationships with the customers and strive for enhancing company loyalty through the provision of professional services" (Yu & Law, 2000: 348), it was also evident that consumers will check an average of five web sites before booking. Another barrier to entry is identifying unique product propositions and differentiation. The Internet, supporting utter transparency facilitated competitors to imitate ideas within a short period of time. Hence it enabled established players to cover a wide range of the service spectrum allowing little space for new entry innovation and differentiation (Kim et al., 2004).

Moreover, entrants may be deterred by capital requirements which stem from the heavy investment in technology that is needed in order to compete effectively (Paraskevas & Baron, 2004). A final barrier to entry is government policy, as it has the power to limit the entry in certain industries, e.g. by licensing requirements, limits on access to raw materials or pollution control requirements (Porter 1979; 1980). Government policies are only recently being updated to support the online environment and more importantly in dealing with the global nature of the Internet and eCommerce. Within the context of EU a number of legislations have been created so as to support the online presence of travel businesses. In most European countries SMTEs are offered incentives, such as ICT hardware and implementation subsidies, flexible funding and tax exemptions, initiatives for developing online presence and low start up costs.

Given these changes of the five forces in the external environment, the tourism industry structure has changed dramatically. Several players, such as budget airlines and hotel chains, as well as new entries such as online travel agencies and value added services, have gained in their competitive position. Others, such as traditional suppliers and intermediaries, have lost market share and have had to change their business models dramatically to survive.

3 Methodology

The purpose of this study therefore is to examine how the Internet has affected the structure of travel industry by using Porter's model of industry analysis. Emphasis was given on the strategic position of the supply elements of the travel industry and in particular airlines and hotels. The position of intermediaries (both online and offline TOs and TAs, as well as new intermediaries) was also examined. This research is exploratory and contributes to fundamental knowledge and theory. Data were collected by both primary and secondary resources. A comprehensive secondary research examined journals articles, books and conference papers with special reference to ENTER proceedings as well as data from online travel companies. Qualitative research methods of collecting primary data were used (Patton, 2002). Primary data were collected by conducting interviews using a standardised in-depth semi-structured open-ended interview structure which consisted of 12 questions. This enabled flexibility in the questions asked as interviewees were prompted for further information when they raised interesting issues. To gain the in-depth knowledge required for this research interviewees had to be knowledgeable with several years of experience. Hence non probability, purposeful judgemental sampling was employed and a small number of experts of the travel industry were targeted for in-depth interviews. The sampling criteria were the respondents' experience of online travel, their responsibilities and knowledge with regards to their company's operations on the Internet as well as their overall understanding of the industry. To undertake this research time and cost effectively, interviews took place at the Travel Distribution Conference, held in the Business Design Centre, London, on the 7th & 8th of June, 2005. This conference is a major event for tourism professionals and it gathers some of the top experts on travel and tourism who attend as speakers or delegates. People representing all sectors of tourism including hotels and airlines, online and offline TAs and TOs, GDSs as well as technology providers were targeted. A target sample of 50 senior executives was drawn based on the conference registration and targeted during the conference. Of those 35 agreed to participate in the research and a total of 28 interviews were materialised. The interviews lasted between 15 and 35 minutes and the answers of the respondents were recorded by taking notes and using a tape recorder. Data were analysed using content analysis in order to determine the presence of the most dominant concepts deriving from the interviews. Data were then divided into thematic categories and were summarised in tables by using Porter's framework. Relevant quotations were identified from the transcripts and were also kept within the framework. The main limitation of this research is that many of the executives were unable to operate within the constraints of Porter's framework. They also found it difficult to conceive the notion of 'substitute products' and as a result they may have different interpretations of the term used in the questionnaire. As far as the limitations deriving from Porter's framework are concerned, researchers support the fact that it is adequate for analyzing traditional businesses but there is no unanimous agreement on whether it is adequate for analysing new business models and in particular e-business (Kim et al., 2004). However, Porter's framework has proved to be very helpful in assessing the effects of IT on an industry (Porter, 2001). Hence it allows this paper to offer a comprehensive account of the impacts of the Internet on the tourism industry.

4 Results and Discussion

With regards to the impact of the Internet on the *rivalry among existing competitors*, respondents revealed that rivalry was intensified after the emergence of the Internet due to lowered barriers to entry. That in turn led to an increase in the number of competitors and in supply. New entrants have had the ability to be represented in equal terms with the existing rivals and maximise their market share. Similarly to Porter's (2001) suggestions many new entries in tourism subsided sales for gaining market share endangering the industry's profitability. Interviewees suggested that the emergence of the Internet resulted in major fixed, distribution and organisational cost reductions. Additionally, it offered the ability of real time representation and instant exchange of information thus leading to a higher degree of integration and globalisation, as was mentioned by three respondents. However, established organisations with legacy systems, organisational charts and processes were unable to modernise their operations until they were really threatened by new or innovative rivals. This was evident in the airline business, where flag carriers such as British Airways and Air Lingus had to go through a major business processing reengineering to be able to compete with Easyjet and Ryanair. One of the most frequently mentioned drivers which led to the alterations of the factors affecting rivalry was transparency in terms of offering, availability and prices. The majority commented that the intensity of rivalry leads to price wars, which in turn, increases the bargaining power of buyers, while at the same time, decreases the bargaining power of suppliers. Nevertheless, this statement differs according to the sector that each respondent comes from. The majority of the respondents believed that the Internet resulted in homogenised and undifferentiated products, as rivals compete on price and end up offering similar products. However, several respondents also supported that the Internet led to personalisation and value added offerings, as outsourcing of processes to consumers enabled collection of richer profiles and led to dynamic Customer Relationships Management (CRM) and differentiation.

Respondents' views reflecting the impact of the Internet on the *bargaining power of suppliers* showed that the latter has increased, as it enabled suppliers not only to access more cost effective distribution platforms but also to interact directly with their customers, as transparency, reduced switching costs and price orientation meant that consumers were able to seek alternatives easily. Respondents explained that tourism suppliers were able to address the global market cost effectively through appropriate Internet representations. Their answers are aligned with the literature as they identified distance and location as increasingly less significant competitive factors. As the Internet intensified rivalry, suppliers started to compete on differentiation and personalisation fields. Providing customers with greater value added products enabled many interviewees to offer more expensive, but better value-for-money products. Some of the interviewees suggested that by externalising their yield management, they allowed leisure travellers with flexible travel requirements to purchase cheaper products during quiet periods whilst business travellers with fixed itineraries or late bookings could pay premium prices. Interviewees also emphasised that the wide range of distribution opportunities introduced by the Internet leads to less dependency on intermediaries, cost reductions and increased returns supporting the competitive position of suppliers. The Internet also enhanced the possibility of collaboration between suppliers through co-opetition, collaboration and competition. This was particularly mentioned by hoteliers who claimed that Internet tools should be utilised for clustering similar and complementary products at the destination. This leads to an increase in their bargaining power, as they are able to integrate and form alliances and partnerships that help them maximise efficiency, performance and revenues whilst avoiding competing solely on price. Co-opetition can deter price wars and can encourage suppliers to focus on the collective/destination quality and competitiveness of their product.

As far as the impact of the Internet on *the bargaining power of buyers* is concerned, respondents representing the hotel and airline sectors claimed that the bargaining power of consumers has increased, whereas, intermediaries claimed that it has decreased. The Internet has led to significant savings in terms of money and time for buyers. The increased transparency enhanced the bargaining power of buyers but reduced the bargaining power of suppliers. This is because transparency increased price competition and rivalry, whilst lower barriers to entry enhanced the variety of offerings in the marketplace, decreasing suppliers bargaining power. As a result, buyers are less loyal to specific suppliers as they shift easily to the ones that meet their requirements. Overall, the bargaining power of buyers has therefore increased. Intermediaries are also buyers of tourism, as TAs and TOs have been buying products on behalf of consumers. Interviewees suggested that their position has been changed dramatically as increasingly consumers had access to information, prices and value added products online that often were not even available to traditional travel agencies. Similarly interviewees claimed that consumers dynamically package their holidays reducing the appeal of TOs packages. Hence their bargaining power has been reduced dramatically and as a consequence they lose market share. However, innovative intermediaries such as Thomas Cook and TUI have gradually developed their online presence whilst new intermediaries such as Expedia.com and Lastminute.com have emerged to reintermediate the industry. Therefore interviewees suggested that although the bargaining power of traditional intermediaries that failed to modernise has been reduced significantly, new and innovative intermediaries have gained significant power in the global marketplace.

Respondents had mixed views with regards the *threat of substitution.* Intermediaries felt that the Internet increased the threat of substitution because of the ability to compare non travel offerings and switch to other types of products. However, suppliers (hotels and airlines) claimed that the Internet not only did it not increase the threat of substitution but also that it armours their products against substitutes. One of the respondents claimed that people find it so easy to book a flight and hotel these days that often do that instead of going to their local theatre. CRM and targeted special offers encourage consumers to purchase travel more frequently substituting other products and strengthening the position of tourism suppliers. It was argued that differentiation and decreased threat of substitution enabled suppliers to serve efficiently niches, where buyers are not price conscious.

Interviewees suggested that on the one hand *barriers to entry* have been lowered, as effective distribution platforms mean that tourism suppliers can gain almost instant access to their markets. On the other hand, increased rivalry and lower switching costs rendered retaining customers and remaining profitable more difficult. With the level of consolidation experienced on online travel new entries are often acquired by larger companies. As one interviewee suggested: “If someone has a great idea that brings innovation in the marketplace it is fairly easier now to develop it and try it out fast. If he proves that the concept works, one of the big online travel companies will probably buy them before their second birthday”. Government policy is also a factor that led to lowering barriers to entry as online businesses are often provided with tax exemptions.

5 Impacts of Internet on Tourism Industry Sectors

The impact of the Internet on the key tourism industry sectors, namely hotels, airlines, TAs and TOs is summarised in Table 1.

Table 1. The Impact of the Internet on the tourism industry

<table>
<tr><th>IMPACT ON
FIVE FORCES</th><th colspan="3">HOTELS
(Htl)</th><th colspan="3">AIRLINES
(Air)</th><th colspan="2">Travel
Agencies
(TA)</th><th colspan="2">Tour
Operators
(TO)</th></tr>
<tr><td rowspan="2">RIVALRY AMONG EXISTING COMPETITORS</td><td colspan="3" rowspan="2">↑</td><td colspan="3" rowspan="2">↑</td><td>Off line</td><td>On line</td><td>Off line</td><td>On Line</td></tr>
<tr><td>↓</td><td>↑</td><td>↓</td><td>↑</td></tr>
<tr><td rowspan="2">BARGAINING POWER OF SUPPLIERS</td><td colspan="3" rowspan="2">↑</td><td colspan="3" rowspan="2">↑</td><td>TO</td><td>Htl
Air</td><td colspan="2">Hotel – Air</td></tr>
<tr><td>↑</td><td>↑</td><td colspan="2">↑</td></tr>
<tr><td rowspan="2">BARGAINING POWER OF BUYERS</td><td>TA</td><td>TO</td><td>C</td><td>TA</td><td>TO</td><td>C</td><td colspan="2">C
Consumer</td><td>TA</td><td>C</td></tr>
<tr><td>↓</td><td>↓</td><td>↑</td><td>↓</td><td>↓</td><td>↑</td><td colspan="2">↑</td><td>↓</td><td>↑</td></tr>
<tr><td>THREAT OF SUBSTITUTES</td><td colspan="3">↑</td><td colspan="3">↑</td><td colspan="2">↑</td><td colspan="2">↑</td></tr>
<tr><td rowspan="2">THREAT OF NEW ENTRANTS</td><td colspan="3" rowspan="2">↑</td><td colspan="3" rowspan="2">↑</td><td>Off line</td><td>On line</td><td>Off line</td><td>On Line</td></tr>
<tr><td>↓</td><td>↑</td><td>↓</td><td>↑</td></tr>
</table>

Rivalry in the *hotel sector* has been intensified as transparency reduced switching costs and increased price comparisons. The Internet introduced new ways of competing online through discounts and direct selling. It also lowered the barriers to entry as far as distribution is concerned and encouraged a number of new hotel chains to enter the industry. Also “small and independent hotels have become equal with big ones in exposure” stated a hotel representative. A switch company representative stated that nowadays, “competition is based on quality of information, not quality of product". Competition is further intensified by offering tailored, value added or differentiated products, able to match consumers' needs. One interviewee suggested that "on the one hand hotels reduced their dependence on intermediaries since they have many distribution alternatives and on the other they handed control of their pricing and inventory to online intermediaries through the Merchant Model". Overall, the Internet increased the bargaining power of hotels against their suppliers (procurement) and distributors (TAs and TOs) and reduced it against consumers. Therefore, respondents suggested that innovative and dynamic hotels that take advantage of the emerging technology are in a much stronger competitive position than before the Internet.

The intensity of rivalry in the *airline sector* may be attributed to a number of factors that are interrelated with the Internet. No-frills airlines emerged as the Internet offered them the possibility to communicate directly with consumers. This intensified competition and scheduled airlines had to use technology to add value to their offering by differentiating their product in a number of ways, such as Frequent Flyer Programmes, e–ticketing and in–flight facilities (more space, special catering options, in–flight entertainment). Charter flights owned or operated by TOs also try to attract customers by selling tickets directly on their website. Hence interviewees suggested that the intensification of rivalry led the carriers to follow a cost leadership (e.g. no-frills airlines) or a differentiation strategy (e.g. BA). For airlines, the Internet is a means of reducing costs as they avoid commission fees paid to TAs, reduce the involvement of intermediaries, communicate directly with both their buyers and suppliers and achieve instant distribution of their product through real-time representation. As a result, the Internet has increased the airlines' bargaining power towards their suppliers. At the same time, buyers of airline tickets have also increased their bargaining power as it is much easier for them to switch to another airline. As far as the threat of new entrants is concerned, it is more likely for new no-frills airlines to emerge as they do not have to face the costs of distribution and personnel. The Internet is threatening the existence of traditional *TAs* in the long run as it has facilitated commission capping from airlines, as well as direct access, communication and distribution between suppliers (Hotels and Airlines) and consumers. As a result, TAs have lost their bargaining power and they run the risk of being bypassed unless they reposition themselves as travel advisors and experts that use all available tools online to save time and money for their consumers. The emergence of online TAs both jeopardises the existence of traditional ones as well as demonstrates that there is still space for innovative intermediaries. Consequently, the rivalry has been intensified in the TA sector. As a result, the bargaining power of TAs' suppliers (hotels and airlines) has increased and the threat of entry for the traditional intermediaries has decreased. The emergence of the Internet has also intensified the rivalry on the *TOs* sector. Like TAs, TOs run the risk of disintermediation due to the emergence of new online intermediaries. Tour Operator respondents suggested that traditional TOs increasingly develop their online presence to access their target markets directly, offer tailored and personalised products and reduce distribution and organisational costs. Transparency intensified competition and TOs increased their bargaining power, as they are able to negotiate on lower fares with their suppliers (hotels and airlines) in their effort to maximise revenues and profitability. The bargaining power of their buyers (TAs) has decreased as TOs became less dependent on them in terms of their product distribution. A trend introduced by the emergence of the Internet is dynamic packaging, which enables both TAs and TOs to offer tailored products. At the same time, TOs 'decompose' the original package and are now, selling individual elements separately. Access to more information has increased the bargaining power of end consumers. Hence the competitive position of TOs has been challenged and they need to identify what is the essence of the value they offer.

6 Conclusion

In conclusion, the emergence of the Internet altered the structure of the travel industry. Overall, consumers benefited the most. Their bargaining power increased due to their ability to access accurate and relevant information instantly and to communicate directly with suppliers while benefiting from lower switching costs. The Internet led to the intensification of rivalry among tourism suppliers as it introduced transparency, speed, convenience and a wide range of choice and flexibility in the marketplace. Transparency enabled buyers to increase their bargaining power by facilitating price comparisons and access to instant, inexpensive and accurate information. Respondents demonstrated that the increased transparency introduced by the Internet enhanced the bargaining power of buyers but reduced the bargaining power of suppliers. Rivalry was further intensified because of lowered barriers to entry and because of the possibility of equal representation of SMTEs. However the respondents suggested that innovative suppliers use advanced CRM to gather information on consumers' profile and to offer tailored and value added products whilst expanding their distribution mix widely to harness the marketplace. Suppliers should enhance their direct communications with end consumers and online intermediaries to save on costs, increase profitability and enhance their efficiency. Respondents agreed that the most critical contribution of the Internet is that it enabled suppliers to access their target markets directly thus reducing their dependency on intermediaries for the distribution of their products. Real time representation facilitated instant distribution and led to bypassing the traditional distribution channels. This not only changed the structure of the tourism value system but also raised challenges for traditional intermediaries. The need for traditional intermediaries to shift their role to consumer advisors was further emphasised and interviewees suggested that unless TAs and TOs utilise internet tools for building and delivering personalised tourism products they will be unable to compete in the future. One respondent suggested that "often consumers have more information than travel professionals and this needs to be addressed if traditional intermediaries are here to stay". Although the tourism industry structure has been altered dramatically it is evident that both tourism suppliers and online intermediaries should apply constant innovation, in terms of marketing techniques and technological advancements, in order to be able to offer differentiated, personalised, tailored and value added products. The key point for sustaining their competitive advantage is to focus on their core competencies and to exploit the opportunities that technology offers to improve their strategic position in the tourism value system.

References

Barnes, D., Mieczkowska, S., Hinton, M. (2003). Integrating Operations and Information Strategy in eBusiness, *European Management Journal,* 21(5), 626-634.

Buhalis, D. (1998). Strategic use of information technologies in the tourism industry, *Tourism Management*, 19(5), 409-421.

Buhalis, D. & Licata, M. C. (2002). The Future eTourism Intermediaries, *Tourism Management,* 23, 207-220.

Buhalis, D. (2003), *eTourism: Information Technology for Tourism for Strategic Tourism Management*, Financial Times-Prentice Hall, London.

Buhalis, D. (2004). eAirlines: Strategic and tactical use of ICTs in the airline industry, *Information & Management*, 41, 805-825.

Daniele, R. & Frew, A. (2005). Using Concept Maps to Examine Business Models and Drivers of Competitive Advantage for Travel eMediaries. In A. J. Frew (Ed.), *Information and Communication Technologies in Tourism 2005.* Springer, Vienna, pp.497-507.

Disney, S. M., Naim, M. M., Potter, A. (2004). Assessing the Impact of eBusiness on Supply Chain Dynamics, *International Journal of Production Economics,* 89(2), 109-118.

Garces, S. A., Gorgemans, S., Martinez Sanchez, A., Perez, M. (2004). Implications of the Internet – An analysis of the Aragonese hospitality industry, *Tourism Management,* 25(5), 603-613.

Go, F. M., Govers, P., van den Heuvel, M. (1999). Towards interactive tourism: capitalizing on virtual and physical value chains. In D, Buhalis. & W. Schertler (Eds.), *Information and Communication Technologies in Tourism 1999.* Springer, Vienna, pp.12-24.

Kim, E., Nam, D., Stimpert, J.L. (2004). The Applicability of Porter's Generic Strategies in the Digital Age: Assumptions, Conjectures and Suggestions, *Journal of Management,* 30(5), 569-589.

Lancioni, R., Jensen Schau, H., Smith, M. (2003). Internet Impacts on Supply Chain Management, *Industrial Marketing Management,* 32(3), 173-175.

O'Connor, P. (2000). *Electronic Information Distribution in Tourism and Hospitality,* CABI.

O'Connor, P. (2003) Online Intermediaries – Revolutionising Travel Distribution, *Travel and Tourism Analyst,* February.

Paraskevas, A. & Baron, C. (2004). Online Business Travel Management: Present Practice – Future Promise. In A. J. Frew (Ed.). *Information & Communication Technologies in Tourism* 2004, Springer, Vienna, pp. 283-292.

Patton, M.Q. (2002). *Qualitative Research & Evaluation Methods,* Sage, London.

Pitt, L., Berthon, P., Berthon, J.P. (1999). Changing Channels: The Impact of the Internet on Distribution Strategy, *Business Horizons,* 42(2), 19-28.

Porter, M. (1979). How Competitive Forces Shape Strategy, *Harvard Business Review,* 57(2), March-April, 137-145.

Porter, M. (1980). *Competitive Strategy: Techniques for Analysing Industries and Competitors,* Free Press, New York.

Porter, M. (1985). Technology and Competitive Advantage, *The Journal of Business Strategy,* 5, 60-70.

Porter, M. (1998). *Competitive Advantage: Creating and Sustaining Superior Performance,* 2nd ed, Free Press, New York.

Porter, M. (2001). Strategy and the Internet, *Harvard Business Review,* 103D, March, 63-78.

Schertler, W & Berger-Koch, C. (1999), Tourism as an information business: The strategic Consequences of e-Commerce for Business Travel. In D. Buhalis & W. Schertler (Eds.), *Information & Communication Technologies in Tourism 1999,* Springer, pp.25-35.

Yu, A. K. L. & Law, R. (2000). The Application of E-Commerce to Enhance the Competitive Advantages of Hotels in Hong Kong, *Information & Communication Technologies in Tourism 2000.* In D. Fesenmaier, S. Klein, D. Buhalis (Eds.), Springer, Vienna, pp. 343-35.

Reviewing the Use of Online Services by the Tourism Industry in an Emerging Market: The Case of Thailand

Kenneth Cosh[a]
Ilian Assenov[b]

[a] School of Computing,
Payap University, Thailand
kenneth_c@payap.ac.th
[b] Faculty of Service Industries
Prince of Songkla University, Thailand
ilian@fsi.psu.ac.th

Abstract

This paper investigates the use of online services within the tourism industry in Thailand, by first assessing the adoption of the internet channel by Thai travel-related companies, and secondly evaluating the effectiveness of their Email use. Previous related research has focused on the developed world, where modern information and communication technologies (ICT) are already pervasive; here we focus on an emerging market with relatively lower internet proliferation, IT infrastructure availability and stability. An interesting case study is presented in Thailand, where its well established, mature tourism industry is contrasted by a developing ICT infrastructure still in its infancy. Despite government driven projects to develop Thailand as a regional ICT leader, we find ICT adoption by the tourism sector is low in quantity and poor in quality. As tourism is a key industry for Thailand, we investigate the reasons for our findings and present recommendations for better utilisation of this channel.

Keywords: e-tourism; website evaluation; Email; service quality; Thailand

1 Introduction

Since the advent of the Internet, modern information and communication technologies (ICT) have revolutionised the way business is conducted. As information technology increasingly becomes a cause and driver of corporate strategy, it is used to reengineer the basis for competition throughout all marketplaces (Applegate, Austin, & McFarlan, 2003). Modern information systems change the nature and balance of relationships between buyers and suppliers and are used to create new markets and products while enhancing existing products and services. This trend is pervasive in all industries and marketplaces, with impacts on all business models, and the effects are experienced internationally in developed and developing countries alike. Within the tourism industry, the opportunities afforded by technologies even as well established as the Internet or emails are vast. The tourism industry is an information rich industry; indeed information is the "lifeblood" of the industry, without which hospitality and tourism cannot function. As tourists are unable to pre-test an intangible hospitality or tourism product, they require information before they travel (O'Conner, 1999). Tourism industry operators depend on finding and developing new means to distribute information-based travel products and services, marketing information to customers at their convenience (Zhou, 2004). Clearly the development of internet services by players in the tourism industry assists with this goal as e-tourism offers opportunities for speedy communication and global access with minimal expense (Buhalis, 2001).

As well as providing an opportunity for the tourism industry to market its wares, there is substantial evidence to point to tourists demanding access to travel information through electronic channels (e.g., www.etcnewmedia.com/review/ [Sep 10 2006]). Trends point clearly towards a changing face of the travel industry: for instance the opportunity of disintermediation allows final product or service providers to bypass the services of travel agents to directly target their customers resulting in travel agents being forced to adapt their business model from a intermediary to an infomediary (Nadkarni & Peng, 2001), repositioning themselves as a consultant or trusted, independent advisor (Ching-biu Tse, 2003). The nature of information provision, whether through intermediary or provider, is also changing as new communication tools are developed and offered, with email, live chat rooms or bulletin boards allowing asynchronous or synchronous communication to suit the circumstances (Cox & Koelzer, 2004; Picozzi, 2005).

In this paper we examine the case of Thailand and investigate how effectively Thai tourist businesses have taken advantage of the potential of both the internet channel and electronic communication technology. Thailand is a South East Asian holiday destination popular for its beaches and also its cultural heritage locations. According to the Tourism Authority of Thailand, the number of tourists visiting has been increasing rapidly, with a projected 15 million visitors in 2006 (www2.tat.or.th/stat/web/static_index.php [Sep 9 2006]). Thailand also recently boasted two of the top five voted city destinations in the world, in Bangkok and Chiang Mai (Travel and Leisure, 2006).

Thailand is an emerging market and as such provides a study environment which contrasts most existing case studies. In many, more developed, countries the tourist service providers, such as hotels, airlines and car rental agencies, have aggressively taken advantage of the direct link to customers provided by the internet, forcing intermediaries to reconsider their business model. In Thailand, the use of ICTs is still relatively immature, so there is less incentive for travel agents to modify a currently successful business model. However, recent national developments within the IT sector, as we shall now present, creates an interesting position for the Thai tourist industry, an industry which accounts for 6% of the Thai economy. In 2002 Thailand established the Ministry of Information and Communication Technology, with the mission of developing and supporting comprehensive electronic processes for government, commerce, industry, business and education (Nasingkun, 2003). This ministry is responsible for driving national projects to improve Thailand's ICT infrastructure, for instance through egovernance projects, but also with tourism related projects such as the development of an interactive map of Chiang Mai (http://www.thaitcc.info/ [Sep 9 2006]). Given this scenario, Thailand presents itself as a relevant case study illustrating how the use of ICTs within a developing country's tourism industry could evolve the industry itself.

In this paper we assess the current state of play in Thailand by reviewing many of Thailand's key tourism industry players, analysing the effectiveness of firstly their websites, as the website is the opening to the web channel. We then play the role of prospective customer and having established electronic contact we then present a comprehensive evaluation of the use of email to develop and maintain relationships.

2 Websites in the Thai Travel Industry

We begin our evaluation of Thailand's travel industries use of ICTs by evaluating the websites of travel industry players. Given the incentives for developing a website discussed in the introduction section, in this section we evaluate the current performance of organisations in Thailand. Previous studies have highlighted some criteria for defining a high quality tourism website, derived from investigations into hotel websites (Chung & Law, 2003; Murphy et al., 2003; Kim et al., 2004), travel agents (Nadkarni & Peng, 2001; Limayem et al., 2003) and general tourism agents (Doolin et al., 2002; World Tourism Organisation, 2001). Our criteria were based on those used in the existing investigations surveyed and specialised to the Thai marketplace, resulting in 5 categories.

Category 1: Provision of Information. As the tourism industry is an information rich industry an important element of a web channel is how well information is given. Travel essential information should cover topics like currency, weather, visa and insurance, but should also include information specific to the destination, such as maps, attractions, history or special festivals. Information should also be provided about transportation links.

Category 2: Products and Services Range. The section category of criteria assesses the range of products / services being offered; what package tours or customised tours there are; whether tourists can make a reservation online.

Category 3: Design and Functionality. In this section we evaluate firstly how easy it is to navigate the website, whether navigation tools such as a site map or menu are provided. We assess the layout of content, readability of fonts, placement of graphics, use of colours and contrasts between background and text.

Category 4: Trust and Safety. When marketing a business from Thailand to customers based overseas, the trustworthiness of a site is an important factor. While a potential customer might search for information from a range of sites, persuading them to perform an online transaction often requires more trust. Here we review whether sites have electronic security features such as SSL secure online transactions or privacy protection statements. There are further aspects which can install trust in a site, such as the use of branded emails and URL's (rather than gmail or geocities) and inclusion of a postal address.

Category 5: E-Business Service. The final category investigates the services offered electronically, such as FAQ's, discussion forums, "contact us" forms or whether customers can complete purchases online. Assessment includes whether different contact channels are created by the site, for instance through email, telephone, fax, or physical location. Given these criteria for creating a good quality website, a comprehensive survey of Thailand's online tourism presence was conducted.

3 Methodology

The criteria discussed above were compiled into a website evaluation form which was used to assess 323 websites from organisations offering different business models within the tourism sector. The list includes a stratified random sample of 78 travel agents, 30 online travel agent, and 205 hotels; as well as the entire population of 7 Thai airlines and 3 nationwide car rental companies. Yamane formulae were used to establish the sample size which represents nearly a quarter of the travel businesses with online presence. Currently there are approximately 11,000 travel businesses registered with the Thai tourism authorities, of which just 13% have a web presence. A quantitative assessment was made for each site in the sample based on the criteria discussed previously. For each category, sub criteria were listed and each website was assessed with scores awarded dependent on the features present on their website. For example, a site would score the maximum 3 for the site navigation sub criteria if it had clear navigation tools, a site map and a site search engine. To ensure a fair reflection the sub criteria were then weighted by a focus group of online travel business professionals. To do this the group studied the websites of several globally recognised leaders (such as Travelocity, Expedia, British Airways, Lufthansa, Marriott and Hyatt) and discussed the relative importance of each sub criteria.

4 Findings

The results of the evaluation are summarised in table 1, with the mean results from a Likert scale rating from 1 to 5. Score greater than 4 is considered 'Excellent', while 3-4 is 'Good', 2-3 is 'Average', 1-2 is 'Poor' and below 1 'Needs Significant Improvement'. The mean scores are calculated for each business model. A review of the results indicates that car rental companies have the best web presence, while in general the quality was just average. Unsurprisingly online travel agents have a higher quality website than their traditional 'bricks and clicks' (offering both offline and online services) rivals.

Table 1. Quality of Travel Business Websites

Business Model	Sample Size	Mean Result by Score	Mean Result by Impression
General Travel Agents	78	2.70	2.37
Online Travel Agents	30	3.68	3.37
Hotels	205	2.57	2.65
Airlines	7	3.52	3.57
Car Rental Companies	3	4.42	4.33
Totals	323	2.75	2.68

Looking closer into the weaknesses with the websites, we summarise 6 key areas needing improvement:

- Lack of Essential Travel Information
- Insufficient Transportation Information
- Lack of Navigation Tools
- Lack of Security Features
- Unclear Online Booking Functions
- No Special Features (e.g. FAQ or discussion forums)

This list includes the criteria rated below average across the sample. The lack of security features such as secure transactions remain a weakness for many operators. Surveys in New Zealand (Doolin et al., 2002) and Hong Kong (Limayem et. al., 2003) have also found a lack of general travel information included. These results will be discussed in more detail in section 4. Before that we address email, the second phase of this assessment of online services, which presents a picture of how effectively customers are developed and maintained.

5 Email Customer Service

Having established a web presence and attracted a potential customer to the website, the next step for many organisations is to continue to develop a relationship, providing further information and service to the prospect in order to build a customer base. At the heart of Customer Relationship Management systems is communication, and modern communication technologies offer many innovative means of maintaining contact with customers. Previously limited to face-to-face contact or telephone calls, email or instant messaging has opened up new synchronous and asynchronous communication styles. Email has the unobtrusive properties of traditional snail mail, while allowing much faster answers to questions. Building online relationships is arguably much more difficult than providing offline service (Teal, 2005), as online services tend to be less personalised (Picozzi, 2005), some people are reluctant to communicate through computers (Peacock, 1995), and auxiliary signals such as body language or tone of voice are lost, opening up the possibilities of semantic ambiguity. While email is a valuable tool for building and maintaining customer relationships, it has to be used effectively to be successful. If email is used poorly it can have disastrous effects. Previous studies highlight that poor email response can lead to not only losing guests, but can result in the guest choosing a different destination entirely (Matzler, Pechlaner, Abfalter, & Wolf, 2003). Common problems include late answers, or no answers at all, insufficient information and not following standard email protocol. Providing the wrong or incomplete information can lead to lost customers (Murphy, & Tan, 2003). Minimal efforts to improve email practice can lead to immediate competitive advantages.

In this section we examine how effectively tourism industry players use email. The criteria for effective use are as follows. *(1) Promptness*; 24 hours was our expected reply time. *(2) Politeness*; here we assessed if an appropriate salutation was used and whether the language was polite and appropriate. *(3) Personal Approach*; here we checked if the customer was addressed by name and if the replier identified themselves. *(4) Professionalism*; This crucial area concerned whether the answer had informative content, whether the questions were answered and whether it was presented well, in English with good grammar and spelling. *(5) Promotional*; this criteria assessed whether the travel agent offered extra services, promoted their name and identified their contact address.

6 Method

We contacted travel agents in Thailand using a *mystery guest* approach, by sending emails under alias names, posing as potential customers and inquiring for specific information. We sent two emails, one from a potential Thai customer, and one from a potential foreign customer to allow us to distinguish between service levels. Efforts were made to avoid spam filters by sending to small groups of no more than 10. Of the 5970 travel agencies listed with the Thai tourism authority, 2,258 have listed email addresses. Anticipating a low response rate, we sent emails to every address, rather than just to a sample of the population. Both emails were sent to every address on different days from different pseudo email addresses. Both emails requested specific information regarding flights from Thailand to Switzerland, and regarding a package tour to Disneyland Hong Kong and both emails were written in English. It is common for Thai's to use English when communicating via e-mail, so the Thai customers request was written in broken English to improve authenticity. The results were analysed using several criteria adapted from existing surveys mentioned above and (Lehnert, 2002). Again a focus group of professionals was used to weight the criteria to allow a quantitative assessment, as well as a qualitative assessment.

7 Findings

Comparative surveys in Austria (Matzler et al., 2003) and Singapore (Murphy & Tan, 2003) have found low response rates, speeds and quality, in the case of Thailand the response rate was very poor and the quality of those responses was just average, with no agents performing excellently on our scale. The response rate was extremely low, and only 7% of the emails sent were replied (230 replies to 4516 emails). This suggests that if a potential customer sends e-mails to travel agents randomly, on average about 15 emails need to be sent for just one reply to be received.

A summary of the replies that we received is provided below for each criterion:

Promptness: Half of the replies we received arrived within 24 hours, while on average it was 2.3 days, with one reply arriving 14 days later. *Politeness*: Almost three quarters of responses had appropriate salutations with half of responses thanking the customer for their enquiry. *Personal Approach*: Half of the responses addressed the customer by name, while only a quarter of repliers identified themselves by name. *Professionalism*: Just over half of the responses answered the questions regarding flights, with only a quarter offering more than 2 options. Only 1 in 10 responses included price, schedule and conditions information. The question regarding package tour was answered less frequently (17%), but with more information. Few answers offered further assistance. *Promotional*: 41% of responses identified the travel agents name, with only 17% identifying a physical address.

Table 2 shows a breakdown of the email responses received, with an average quality of 2.82. There were marginal differences between the way Thais and foreigners were dealt with, as more of the foreigners were replied to, while it normally took longer for the replies to arrive. Noticeably those agents using a branded email faired much better than those using a generic email address, perhaps an indication of the priority they pay to their online traffic.

Table 2. Breakdown of Email Responses

Email Breakdown		Response Rate	Speed of Reply (days)	Quality (out of 5)
Nationality Breakdown	Foreigner	7.78	2.52	2.83
	Thai	6.89	1.69	2.80
Location	Bangkok / Central	9.92	2.19	2.80
	South	3.01	2.00	2.79
	North	8.20	1.70	3.00
	Northeast	16.67	2.56	3.00
Reply uses Branded Email Address	Branded	11.11	2.19	2.97
	Unbranded	5.78	2.09	2.72
For All Emails		**7.34**	**2.13**	**2.82**

7 Discussion

Reviewing the results of this survey suggests that there are plenty of ICT opportunities for the Thai travel industry to take advantage of. Before innovative interactive travel technology is implemented, there are clear weaknesses in the basic electronic commerce offerings. With only 13% of travel agents choosing to use the internet channel, here we investigate why more Thai companies don't develop an online presence, and suggest how to develop their ICT practice.

An initial survey of travel agents without web presence suggests several reasons: a lack of knowledge, even fear, of e-commerce, and no web design capabilities; a feeling that the online channel is already overpopulated, while they are already busy satisfying existing physical customers. Our findings suggest that with only 13% of internal industry players offering an online presence and with online service quality rarely above 'average'; there are still opportunities to be gained from developing online presence. Given that there is a market for further online Thai presence, we offer a 5 point good practice guide for companies deciding to use this channel.

Seek External Professional Assistance: While most travel industry players have core competencies within the tourism industry, they are not experts in e-commerce. With government initiatives, ICT expertise is available to ensure that website quality can score higher than the 'average' mark our research awarded. A regular concern when reviewing the websites was the poor design, with poor navigation tools and unnatural mappings between features and their affordances.

Update the Online Channel Regularly: A key finding of our website quality research indicates that websites are out of date, with no current promotions or activities mentioned. Dynamic websites better afford up to date information. Lots of important information was missing from the websites, such as travel information, or information about the services being offered. Timeliness is also important when it comes to answering promptly customers' online enquiries.

Management Driven Online Presence: Corporate culture in Thailand is very hierarchical, with decisions and incentives invariably coming top down. For innovative use of the online channel, activity needs to be encouraged from management.

Training for Employees: There is currently a large skills gap for employees, both in terms of language capabilities and in terms of electronic commerce knowledge. Training in basic information technology is required for organisations to fully take advantage of the online channel. Staff members must appreciate that e-mail is as important as a phone call, fax or letter, and just as easy to use. Better e-mail policies and training should give agents an immediate competitive advantage via improved e-service (Pechlaner et al., 2002).

Security is a Key Issue: Our research found that the majority of websites offered limited if any security for customers. This is a key issue for organisations wishing to encourage remote customers to complete an online transaction, particularly true for those in an emerging market such as Thailand, where remote customers are accustomed to higher levels of security.

Crucially web presence is not just about having a website. Whether it is being used simply as a window to the world, or as a fully functional dynamic e-commerce site, it is only the first step towards generating income; it is the equivalent of the shop window enticing customers to enter. Failing to reply to an email enquiry is akin to ignoring a customer once they've entered the shop; in a physical world it wouldn't be tolerated, and in an electronic world with competition just a click away it is inexcusable. Dissatisfied potential customers will vote with their mice.

Email is a powerful facilitator for building relationships with customers and is available with little investment. As well as enabling potential new customers to easily contact the organisation, email also offers a way of developing existing customers, building future relationships through up selling and cross selling. Using a branded email, along with the security features mentioned above, can increase trust and dependability in the organisation. Our findings indicate that only 20% of registered travel agents have an email address, and our mystery guest experiment highlighted that those who do use email are not taking advantage of its possibilities. With a response rate of just 7% and responses just average, current customer service by email is disappointing.

8 Conclusions

Previous studies into the use of basic e-commerce facilities, such as email and websites, have been conducted into major developed world markets. Thailand differs from these surveys in several ways: firstly, it is an emerging market, and second, it is a predominantly inbound market, with around 15 million foreign tourists expected in 2006. These factors differentiate this case study in important ways. While this research has clearly highlighted weaknesses in Thailand's electronic offerings, further work will be conducted to investigate why this is the case. For now, we can only suggest possible reasons. As most customers for the travel agents are foreign, traditionally their role in servicing their tourism needs has occurred late in the process. Conventionally tourists would seek advice from their local travel agents and would book hotels, car rental etc. through them in the early stages of organising their trips. Travel agents in Thailand traditionally only provide advice and services once the tourists have arrived in the location. Given that most tourists search destination-related information during the planning stage of their vacation, a Thai travel agency with well-developed and presented destination information may be able to develop customers from tourists who had otherwise been just searching for information. While in other markets the disintermediation effect has been noticeable as travel agents change their business model to become infomediaries, in Thailand disintermediation is less pronounced. There is less incentive for a Thai travel agent to change its currently successful business model, when the end service providers still are not directly targeting customers through the web, with the exception of larger hotels and a few companies with nation-wide operations. This research has limitations, which will be developed through future work. Firstly the investigation has only been into Thailand, while a comparative study into further emerging markets would provide interesting data. Our research focussed solely on the online behaviour of travel service providers, it would be interesting to compare their online and offline behaviour, although we assume travel agents respond promptly to offline enquiries. A further investigation into the customer side of the relationship is also necessary, to discover how they select service providers and how they evaluate websites and service quality. Our perspective is based on personal experience and the opinions of a group of researchers, which may create bias in our results. It would also be relevant to distinguish between bigger and smaller market players. Our results suggested that the big car rental companies and airlines tend to have better-quality websites, but we were unable to assess differences between large and small hotels or travel agents. A big advantage of the web is that economies of scale are reduced allowing smaller players access to larger and distant markets, and smaller players can grow through their use of this channel. Ultimately our research has shown that the use of the internet and email by the Thai tourism industry is still immature. Future work is geared towards developing the use of ICT's by the tourism industry in Thailand.

References

Applegate, A., Austin, R., & McFarlan, F. (2003). *Corporate Information Strategy and Management: Text and Cases.* New York: McGraw-Hill.

Buhalis, D. (2001). The future eTourism intermediaries. *Tourism Management,* 23, 207-220.

Ching-biu Tse, A. (2003). Disintermediation of travel agencies in the hotel industry. *Hospitality Management,* 22, 453-460.

Chung, T., & Law, R. (2003). Developing a performance indicator for hotel websites. *Journal of Hospitality Management,* 22, 119-125.

Cox, B., & Koelzer, W. (2004). *Stickiness: Internet marketing in hospitality.* New Jersey: Pearson Education.

Doolin, B., Burgess, L., & Cooper, J. (2002). Evaluating the use of the web for tourism marketing: a case study from New Zealand. *Journal of Tourism Management,* 23, 557-561.

Frey, S., Schegg, R., & Murphy, J. (2002). Email customer service in the Swiss hotel industry. *Tourism and Hospitality Research.* 4(3), 198-212.

Kim, W. G., Ma, X., & Kim, D.J. (2004). Determinants of Chinese hotel customers' e-satisfaction and purchase intentions. *Journal of Tourism Management,* 27(5), 890-900.

Lehnert, G. W. (2002). *Light on the web: essentials to make the network for you.* United States of Americe: Addison Wesley Longman.

Limayem, A., Hiller, M., & Vogel, D. (2003). Sophistication of Online Tourism Websites in Hong Kong: an Exploratory Study. *Americas Conference on Information Systems,* Tampa: USA.

Matzler, K., Pechlaner, H., Abfalter, D. & Wolf, M. (2003). Determinants of response to customer e-mail enquiries to hotels: evidence from Austria. *Tourism Management,* 26, 249-259.

Murphy, J., Olaru, D., Schegg, R. & Frey, S. (2003). The Bandwagon effect: Swiss Hotel's Website and E-mail Management, *Cornell Hotel and Restaurant Administration Quarterly,* 44 (1), 71-87.

Murphy, J., & Tan, I. (2003). Journey to nowhere? E-mail customer service by travel agents in Singapore. *Tourism Management,* 24, 543-550.

Nadkarni, S. & Peng, C. (2001). The relevance of travel agencies in the era of e-commerce and globalization. *http://www.mca.org.mo/*

Nasingkun, K. (2003). How Thailand Should Utilise Information Technology. http://www.cicc.or.jp

O'Connor, P. (1999). *Electronic Information Distribution in Tourism and Hospitality.* Oxford: CABI.

Peacock, M. (1995). Change: Unravelling the process. *Information Technology in the hospitality industry.* England: Redwood Books.

Pechlaner, H., Rienzner, H., Matzler, K., & Osti, L. (2002). Response attitudes and behavior of hotel industry to electronic info requests. In Wober, K. W., Frew, A. J., & Hitz, M. (Eds.), *Proceedings of the ENTER 2002 conference.* Innsbruck: Springer, pp. 177–186.

Picozzi, L. (2005). *Understand Online Customer Service.* http://www.score.org

Rice, S., & Todd, G. (2005). *A guide to becoming a travel professional.* U.S.A.: Delmar Learning.

Teal, K. (2005). *Online worlds and offline worlds – what are some customer service differences.* http://www.netspoke.com

Travel + Leisure, (2006). Florence Named World's Best City. *Travel + Leisure Magazine,* August, 2006.

World Tourism Organization: WTO (2001). *E-Business for Tourism – Practical Guidelines for Tourism Destinations and Businesses.* Madrid, Spain: The World Tourism Organisation.

Zhou, Z. (2004). *E-commerce and information technology in hospitality and tourism.* Canada: Delmar.

Acknowledgements

The authors thank Nutjika Saweksup and Suparat Boonthai for their assistance with data collection.

Developing Web-Based Tourist Information Tools Using Google Map

Bing Pan[a]
John C. Crotts[a]
Brian Muller[b]

[a] Department of Hospitality and Tourism Management
College of Charleston, USA
{panb, crottsj}@cofc.edu
[b] Butterfat LLC
Charleston, USA
muller@musc.edu

Abstract

This paper reports an explanatory study of using Google Map API to develop two destination-specific tourist information tools: a handheld tour guide and an online trip planner for Charleston, South Carolina, USA. The background, development, functionality, and adoption issues were discussed. The handheld tour guide is based on mobile phones with a GPS antenna to communicate with Google Map and deliver real-time and location-sensitive tourist information. Online Charleston trip planner combines destination specific information with Google Map to provide an interactive trip planning tool based on the map metaphor. The handheld tour guide is slow and unstable due to memory limitations and slow Internet connection provided by the mobile phone service. The online trip planner is being adopted by various hotels and conferences. The development effort demonstrated that Google Map API is a flexible tool with reasonable speed for developing destination-specific online services. For mobile tools, the computing power and wireless connections of small devices are the bottlenecks when communicating with online services.

Keywords: GPS, GIS, Google Map, handheld, ubiquitous computing, tourist information.

1 Background

Advancements in technology have changed the way we travel and plan our trips. However, trip planning online has been a frustrating experience (Pan & Fesenmaier, 2006). Information on various aspects of a trip and destination is distributed: travellers may need to book an airline ticket from expedia.com; then he/she goes to Hilton.com to find the hotel room and then switches to a local convention and visitors bureau site to check out destination information. However, travellers need to put together these pieces of tourist information in their trip plans: they need to find out the relevant distance from the airport to the hotel, as well as the distance between different attractions and the accommodations (Duran, Seker, & Shrestha, 2004). Frequently, the travellers will rely on offline tools, such as pencil and paper, to record their locations and then using online mapping tools to piece together the relevant locations (Pan & Fesenmaier, 2006). The current trip planning practices apparently lack the integration of location information of various aspects of the trips.

On the other hand, anecdotal evidence confirmed that with the ubiquitous information access and more hectic life styles, travellers plan less and less ahead of a trip and engage in more on-route and in-destination planning (Fesenmaier & Vogt, 1992; Fesenmaier, Vogt & Stewart, 1993). For example, travellers frequently call hotels to reserve a room while in the car or check out adjacent attractions while touring a city. Ad-hoc decisions on restaurants or attractions are also a part of the fun during a trip which can create pleasant surprises.

However, travellers still could not access all the travel related information as they wish. For example, if a traveller walks around downtown in a destination, and sees a restaurant on the corner of King Street and Calhoun Street, she could not check out the rating and other visitors' comments about the restaurant easily. Similarly, if she sees a beautiful house on Meeting Street, she would like to know when it was built, and its architectural and historical significance. She could not obtain this information without joining a tour group or having a mobile phone with web access. In the latter case, the information access is still awkward since she need to search on the web through her tiny cell phone screen. Thus, providing appropriate destination related tourist information to the right visitors at the right time and the right place is still a challenge and much is needed for next generation of information technologies for tourism industry.

Recent technology developments based on Geographic Information System (GIS) and satellite images have provide a new way of accessing location-based information. Google Map can provide interactive mapping services as well as realistic satellite images. More importantly, the free Google Map Application Programming Interface (API) (Google, 2006) allows thousands of programmers to tap into the powerful Google mapping service by connecting it with various types of data, from sex offenders' addresses to the demographic information of the United States (Darlin, 2005). Combined with destination-specific tourist information, Google Map could provide a new way of trip planning and tourist information accessing. This paper documents the effort in developing two web-based destination information tools for Charleston, South Carolina, USA, based on Google Map API: a handheld Charleston tour guide and an online interactive trip planner to Charleston; it discusses the advantages and limitations of using Google Map API to develop trip planning and tourist information accessing tools.

2 Recent Developments on Ubiquitous Computing and Mapping Services

Recent developments in hardware, software, and openly available geographical data have provided new opportunities for developing location-based tourist information access and trip planning tools. This section briefly reviews the relevant development.

While computing devices are getting smaller, smarter, and more connected, any time and any access to any information during a trip is becoming a reality (Weiser, 1994). Most current models of mobile phones and Personal Digital Assistants (PDA) have the capability to access the Internet through wireless connections. Laptops could also access phone service network for Internet connections while Wi-Fi spots are not available. However, the speed of Internet access on mobile devices vary: the new standard 3G technology could provide download speeds of 150 Kbps to 700 Kbps and a speed of 150 Kbps max for uploading; most current mobile devices can only have a speed of 50Kbps (Null, 2006; Glenn, 2006). None of these standards can rival broadband access through landlines. In addition, the limited screen side of most mobile devices restrict its extensive usage on cognitively intensive tasks.

Geographical Information System (GIS) have been adopted widely in tourism settings, from information kiosks, hiking maps, to web-based maps (Duran, Seker, & Shrestha, 2004). Those online GIS tools combine the power of GIS with the ubiquity of the Internet. Google Map is one web-based tool which can be used to access large amount geographical information as well as routing capability. Google Map Application Program Interface (API) allows a programmer to embed Google Maps in his/her own web pages with JavaScript. A programmer can add overlays to the map, including markers and polylines, and display information windows linked to other data sources. The Maps API is a free service and available for any web site that is free to consumers (Google, 2006).

Recently there have been developments in both integrated and location-based trip planning tools and mobile information access. Duran, Seker, and Shrestha (2004) provided a conceptual model and technical on the uses of integrated web-based GIS system combining geographical data with tourism data for public and management usage. Brisaboa et. al. (2003) developed an interactive map with JavaApplet to access touristic and cultural information of Galicia, Spain. They used GIS technology combined with multimedia databases to present multimedia content. The two interface metaphors they are using are browsing and map metaphor. However, the JavaApplet needs a certain period of downloading time and requires Java Virtual Machine to run on the client side of the computer.

Furthermore, various GPS (Global Positioning System) based technologies are getting more and more affordable. For example, GoCar, A GPS-guided storytelling car, has gained more and more popularity in San Francisco (GoCar, 2005). The small car navigates and shows the driver directions as well as acting as a tour guide for directing the tourists to the best sites and telling the stories that bring San Francisco to life. However, the rental fee of GoCar is relatively expensive and it might not be suitable for use in certain cities which have narrow streets. Using mobile devices to access location-based information might be a good direction for developing tourist information tools. A mobile tour of Cornell campus has been developed in which a mobile phone with location information could guide the visitors of the campus to hidden treasures of Cornell University (HCI Lab, 2005).

3 Theoretical Foundations and Issues

Various theories have pointed to the power of map metaphor and mapping interface. People engage in cognitive mapping as they collect, organize, store, remember and utilize information about their surrounding environment. Travellers build cognitive maps of the destinations through direct experience, roadside signs and tourist maps (Downs & Stea, 1977; Guy, Curtis, & Crotts, 1990). Research has shown that cognitive maps could substantially influence consumer's commerce or interactions with the environment, including exploring, touring, shopping, purchasing, and patronage (Grossbart & Rammohan, 1980; Holahan & Dobrowolyn, 1978; Guy et al., 1990). However, one of the most important tool for building cognitive maps, the physical tourist maps, are usually static, limited in the volume of information, and could be complicated to use for the first-time visitors because the unfamiliarity with the orientation and layout of the city.

We hypothesize that location-based information trip planning and on-route and during-trip information providence could help the visitors to build cognitive maps more quickly and in more details. As a result, those visitors will be more engaged, visit more attractions, spend more on food and entertainments, achieve a higher satisfaction, and become more loyal customers. The goal of the proposed project is to build and test two web-based tools: a GPS-enabled handheld information device for the visitors to tour downtown Charleston, South Carolina, USA; and an online interactive trip planning tool for the same destination. Specifically, Travellers to Charleston complained about the confusing traffic signs, complicated road network, and busy traffic conditions. Pre-trip planning can help to build cognitive maps and reduce stress during the visiting period; these types of information can also be delivered to a traveller in real-time through wireless and location-sensitive information access. The first tool will provide visitors with location-sensitive texts, images, audios, and videos based on their actual physical locations; the second program will help the visitors plan their trips to Charleston using an interactive map prior to their departure or in their hotel rooms. It was expected that these tools could increase the visitors' satisfaction about the destination, promote more visitations to different attractions, increase sales on food, entertainments and attractions, and foster more loyal visitors. Potentially the devices could become a new marketing channel and a new revenue source for the technology services. It should be noted that this study is not a complete research effort on the usefulness of Google Map, but rather an explanatory study on the researchers' and developers' own experience.

4 Developments of Handheld Charleston Tour Guide

4.1 Conceptualization

In the conceptualization stage, the developers are expected to build a piece of software based on a handheld device equipped with GPS. The multimedia content, including text, images, audio and video will be stored on the hard drive of the mobile device. Based on the identification of location through the GPS chip, the mobile device could dynamically update the map location and orientation, and provide multimedia information if requested by the traveller. Furthermore, a website is planned to set up so that various tourism businesses, including hotels, restaurants, and attractions, could update their information on a daily even hourly basis, for example, a special deal for the day if the restaurant is short of customers or a hotel is having a low occupancy rate. It could generate a new type of marketing channel in which the businesses are advertising to the visitors with close spatial proximity and who are likely to be hungry or tired. See Fig. 1 for an initial conceptualization of the device.

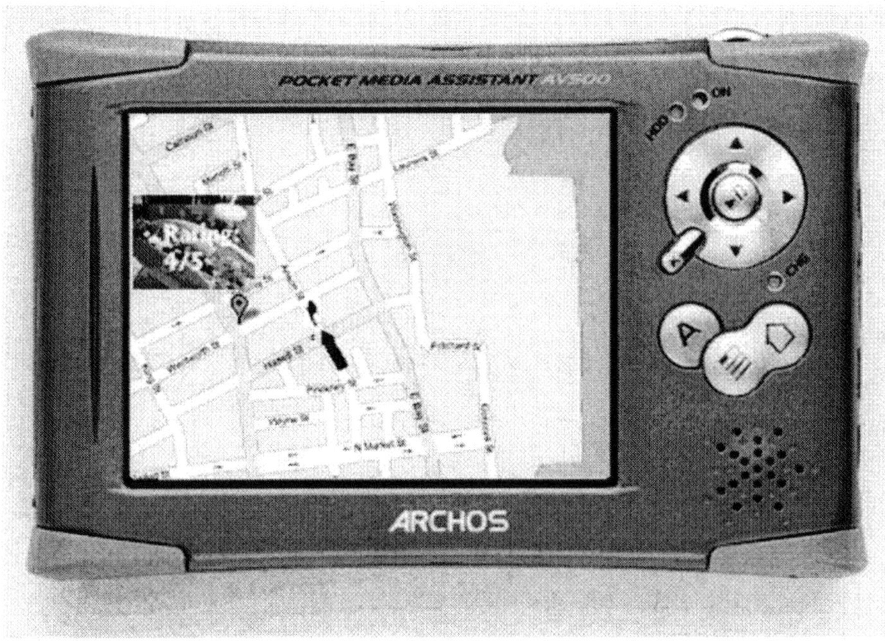

Fig. 1. Conceptualization of Charleston Handheld Tour Guide

4.2 Technical Development

In the actual development stage, the device chose was HP iPAQ hw6500 Pocket PC combined with Cingular network service (HP, 2006). This device runs on Windows Mobile 2003 which ensures maximum development capability; it has a build-in GPS receiver; is uses the integrated GSM/GPRS/EDGE and quad-band GSM phone capabilities which provide reasonable data access through Cingular network. It has 64MB built-in SDRAM and 64M Flash memory. Because of limited financial resources, a stand-alone program is estimated to cost around one year-person programming time and around 70K labour cost since it needs to build a GIS application on this Pocket PC. Thus, a web-based solution is adopted which uses Google Map API.

Technical structure of the device is described in Fig. 2. First, the information about the members of travel council, a destination marketing organization, was collected and a database of attractions, hotels, restaurants, and recreation facilities of Charleston was built with their GPS coordinates. A user interacts with the web browser Minimo on the handheld device. A program on the handheld is developed to retrieve location information from the GPS antenna and then pass the location information to the application web server. The application web server uses the location information to pass it to Google Map server and retrieve map images and routing information. In addition, the application web server retrieves the tourist information database an overlay them with Google Map. It then returns the map images and tourist information to the web browser on the handheld through wireless data transfer. The user of the handheld device could choose to display different types of tourist information at his or her will. The actual user interface is shown in Fig. 3.

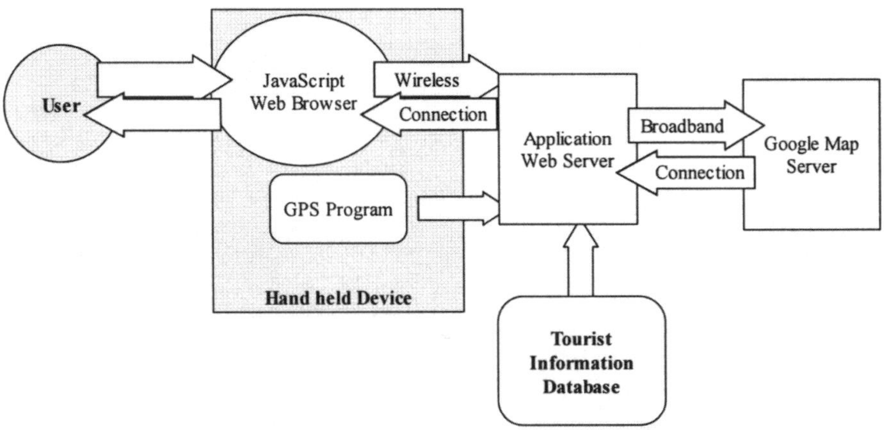

Fig. 2. The Technical Structure of Handheld Charleston Tour Guide

4.3 Problems and Issues in Testing

After the finish of the prototype, a few researchers conducted a few user testing sessions in downtown Charleston. The prototype of the handheld device works with a few limitations. The speed of wireless data connection is low and thus the refreshing of Google Map screen is slow and always lagging behind the walking speed of the testers. In addition, the web browser on the handheld device, Minimo, requires certain amount of memory to run. The existing memory of 128MB is not sufficient and causes frequent crashes. The device needs to restart from time to time. Thus, the speed of wireless connection and the memory of the handheld device are two major bottlenecks of the program. Again, a standalone program without using the web browser and Google Map API may bypass these bottlenecks. However, the cost of developing will rather high and it is not very scalable: for example, a different program will be needed to develop another program for a different destination.

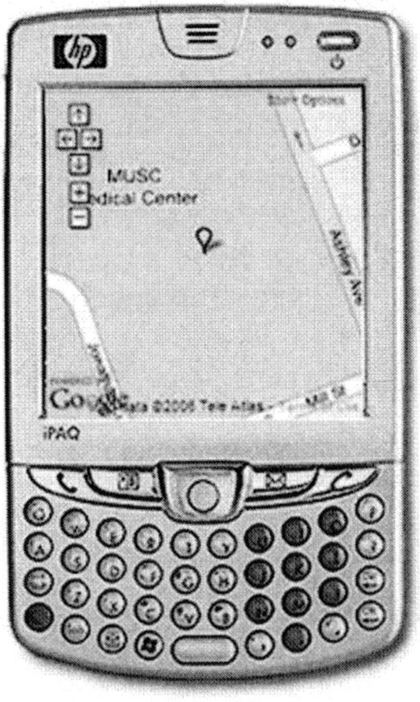

Fig. 3. Handheld Charleston Tour Guide

5 Developments of Interactive Online Charleston Trip Planner

5.1 Conceptualization

As discussed before, online tourist information is distributed in different parts of the web space and an integrated trip planning interface is needed. Also a map metaphor could take advantage of visitors' cognitive mapping capability and increase their satisfaction level, purchase intention, involvement and loyalty in visitation. The online Charleston trip planner is based on the basic structure used in handheld Charleston planner project. Instead of using it during a trip, this tool is intended for the visitors to plan trips before actually leaving their homes or in their hotel rooms. The visitors should be able to plan trips using this interactive interface, save their itinerary, add comments and notes, and print out a paper copy and carry with them to the destination.

5.2 Functionality and Technical Development

Fig. 4 shows a screenshot of the interface. On the left side, various tourist attractions, accommodations, and dining places retrieved from the travel council database, which is built in the first development project for the handheld tour guide. The visitors will be able to add these different properties to their itinerary. When added, the locations of those will show up on the map. When multiple addresses were added, directions between those locations will be automatically displayed at the bottom of the page. The user will also be able to move the locations up and down, rearrange them, and set one of them as default starting point. A user will be able to add another map in which he/she could plan itinerary for another day. When finished, he/she could print the itineraries for multiple days out with each individual itinerary and carry it during the trip.

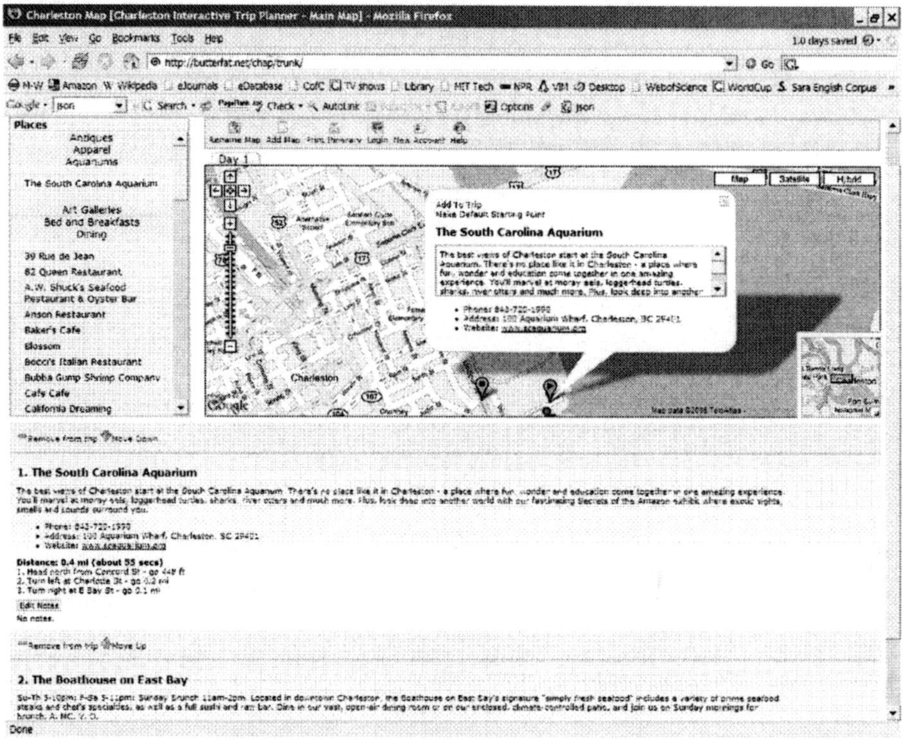

Fig. 4. Online Charleston Trip Planner (http://www.ota.cofc.edu/tripplanner/)

The program uses cookies to track the user session. So a user visits the site for the second time from the same computer will have all the previous selections and routing information retrieved and displayed. In addition, a user will be able to create an account using his/her email address and store all the itinerary information in his/her account. By pressing a button, the itinerary information can be emailed to the user.

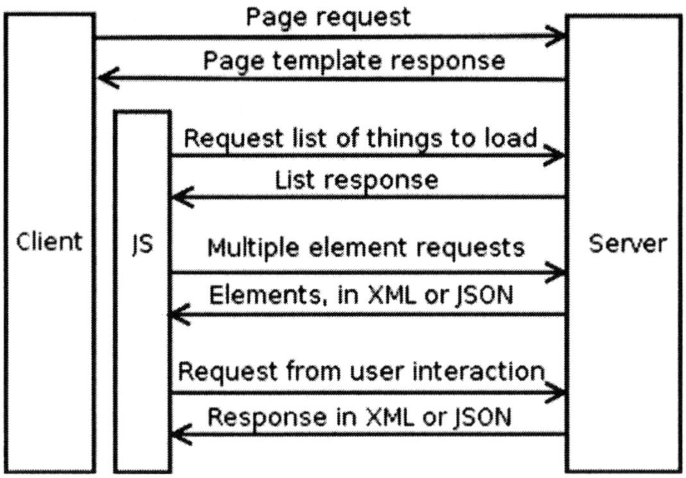

Fig. 5. The Technical Structure of Online Charleston Trip Planner

The software utilizes a Linux/Apache/MySQL/PHP combination on the backend, and asynchronous JavaScript on the front end. The client browser first loads a blank template page that contains layout but no content. The JavaScript then requests different lists of necessary content from the server. Based on these lists, the client can then requests the elements in the list. What is returned in both cases from the server is either in XML or JSON (JavaScript Object Notation) and is dependant upon the existence and content of the client's previous session information. The user interface is then constructed based upon this data. Most interaction between the user and their browser results in communication with the server to maintain a persistent state based upon the client's session. Fig. 5 depicts a diagram of the technical structure.

5.3 Adoption and Promotion

Various conference organizers in Charleston have showed interests to adopt it as a trip planning tool for their participants. A few customized trip planning tools are being developed for a few conferences planned in Charleston area. Initial feedbacks from meeting planners indicate that this is a very useful and intuitive interface for meeting and convention participants.

6 Conclusions and Future Development

This paper documented the effort of developing tourist information tools using Google Map API. This is not a complete research effort on the usefulness of Google Map, but rather an explanatory study on the researchers' and developers' own experience. The program the researchers developed is scalable and can be easily customized to other destinations and areas. For mobile computing devices, the computing power and wireless connections of small devices are the bottlenecks in terms of communicating with online services. More intensive and formal user testing is under the way for the online trip planning tool in order to improve the usability of the interface. Furthermore, with the advancement of hardware, especially faster wireless connections (3G technology) and increased memory of handheld technologies, it is expected that the Charleston handheld tour guide could work more effectively. Combining the tour guide with the trip planning tool could integrate pre-trip plan with during-trip planning and provide more personalized and relevant information during a trip. In addition, post-trip evaluation can be integrated into the system in which the users will be able to rank the different properties they have gone to. Future development can also include an interface for tourism enterprises to update their information daily even hourly (for example, a special deal for the day) to market toward visitors on the road or 100 or 200 yards around them. Location and map-based tourist information tools based on Google Map API opened many opportunities to enhance visitor experience as well as connecting visitors with tourism properties in destinations.

References

Brisaboa, N. R., Farina, A., Luaces, M. R., Parama, J. R., Penabad, M. R., Places, A. S., & Viqueira, J. R. (2003). Using geographical information systems to browse touristic information. *Information Technology and Tourism,* 6, 31-46.

Darlin, D. (2005). A journey to a thousand maps begins with an open code. *New York Times*, October 20, 2005, Technology Column.

Duran, E., Seker, D. Z., & Shrestha, M. (2004). Web based information system for tourism resort: A case study for side/manavgat. In Proceedings for XXth International Society for Photogrammetry and Remote Sensing, Istanbul, Turkey: July 12-23, 2004.

Fesenmaier, D., & Vogt, C. A. (1992). Evaluating the utility of touristic information sources for planning midwest vacation travel. *Journal of Travel & Tourism Marketing*, 1(2), 1-18.

Fesenmaier, D., Vogt, C. A., & Stewart, W. P. (1993). Investigating the influence Of welcome center information on travel behavior. *Journal of Travel Research*, 31(3), 47-53.

GoCar. (2005). GoCar Rentals. Retrieved from http://www.gocarsf.com.

Glenn, F. (2006). Get online from anywhere. *MacWord*, 23(9), 72-73.

Grossbart, S. L., & Rammohan, B. (1980). Cognitive maps and shopping convenience. In K. Moore (Eds). *Advances in Consumer Research*, Association for Consumer Research.

Guy, B. S., Curtis, W. W., & Crotts, J. C. (1990). Environmental learning of first-time travelers. *Annals of Tourism Research*, 17, 419-431.

HCI Lab. (2005). *Hidden treasures.* Available: www.hci.cornell.edu/projects/hidden_treasures.htms.

Holahan, C., & Dobrowolny, M.B. (1978). Cognitive and behavioral correlates of the spatial environment. *Environment and Behavior*, 10(3), 317-333.

HP. (2006). HP iPAQ hw6515a Pocket PC. Retrieved from http://www.shopping.hp.com/webapp/shopping/product_detail.do;jsessionid=FEwhJNXs8NZAedSjCtb9YEJFgaV2uXnAb3wzY1lpsYaPKwkbwDgr!-282458288?storeName=storefronts&landing=storefronts&category=handhelds&orderflow=1&product_code=FA637A%23ABA&catLevel=1

Null, C. (2006). Broadband to go. *PC World*, March, 97-104.

Pan, B., & Fesenmaier, D. R. (2006). Online information search and vacation planning process. *Annals of Tourism Research*, 33(3), 809-832

Weiser, M. (1994). The world is not a desktop. *Interactions*, 1(1), 7-8.

Acknowledgements

Special thanks go to Matthew Gregg (Butterfat, LLC), Christopher Zorn (Butterfat, LLC), Garry Vetter (College of Charleston), Paul Buhler (College of Charleston), and Dr. Frank Starmer (Duke - National University of Singapore Graduate Medical School) for their support and hard work on this project.

Online Pricing Practice of Air Tickets: The Case of Hong Kong

Rob Law[a,]
Mike MS Chang[b]

[a] School of Hotel & Tourism Management,
The Hong Kong Polytechnic University, Hong Kong
hmroblaw@polyu.edu.hk
[b] SPEED, The Hong Kong Polytechnic University, Hong Kong
Mike.Chang@pccw.com

Abstract

This study investigated the online pricing practice, which is defined as the lowest publicly available price, on expedia.com, Zuji.com, and WingOn.com that represent international, regional, and local online travel agencies. Using four most popular outbound travel destinations for Hong Kong travelers including Shanghai, Bangkok, London, and Vancouver, empirical findings indicated that the local online travel agency consistently offered the lowest air fares for all destinations.

Keywords: Air fares, Hong Kong, pricing practice

1 Introduction

Since its commercialization in early 1990s, the Internet has had an unprecedented impact on the world. The technology brings together the geographically isolated computer systems in the world and extends the functions of existing computer systems. With the ongoing use of the Internet, new business models are innovated that revolutionalized people's daily lives. It is well documented that customers can search and purchase their preferred products and services without any geographical and time constraints (Watson, Berthon, Pitt, & Zinkhan, 2000; Wilson & Abel, 2002). In response to the rapid growth of demand from online customers, most businesses in the world have established their online presence for promoting their products and services, and more importantly for facilitating online purchases. Such a behavior of Internet based business directly applies to travel and tourism. In 2002, total online spending on travel comprised 14.7% of the total online spending, which ranked number 3 after books and video, and apparel/clothing (Nielsen/Netratings, 2003). Online spending on travel related products and services, however, ranked number 1 among all product categories in 2005, which was 2.7 times of the second most popular product category (comScore Media Mextrix, 2005). According to Burns (2006) and Cox (2002), reservation of air tickets is the largest business source on travel-related websites.

Taking advantage of the Internet, travellers have been, and will be, searching for their preferred air tickets and with their preferred price on different websites. Price has been demonstrated as one of the most determining factors that could affect customers' online purchase decision (Harris Interactive, 2004; O'Connor, 2002). An intrinsic problem of Internet applications, however, is that the plentiful supply of online sources virtually makes available an unlimited number of ways for travellers to find their favourable websites for the preferred, and often the lowest price, of air tickets. In other words, customers are always overwhelmed by the abundant supply of online information, and are often left helplessly alone without a resolving solution. In spite of the importance of e-business, there has been a limited number of published articles in the tourism literature on online pricing. Although some prior academic studies have investigated online prices for hotel rooms (O'Connor, 2002, 2003; Tso & Law, 2005), these studies did not provide any insight to air travel, the largest business sector in e-tourism. This exploratory study makes an initial attempt to examine the online pricing practice for air tickets on travel agency websites of different scopes in geographical coverage in the context of the outbound industry in Hong Kong, one of the primary travel destinations and outbound travel markets in Asia. In this study, pricing practice refers to the lowest publicly available price that is offered on a travel website at a specific time. This paper would be of interest to the readers who would like to know more about the e-travel business in Hong Kong.

2 Background

The advantages of e-business application are plenty including cost reduction when compared with the traditional offline channels (O'Connor & Frew, 2004; Toms & Taves, 2004). Examples of other advantages include the improvement of reach which enables companies to move into international markets, and the environment to conduct business in an ongoing manner. Using the Internet, consumers can search for information and purchase products or services through direct interactions with online suppliers. However, according to Lohse and Spiller (1998) as well as Kolesar and Galbraith (2000), the experiences of online search and purchase can be largely influenced by the layout of graphical images and textual presentation instead of prior online purchase experience. Somewhat similar to purchase using a printed catalog, online purchase also requires (e-)mail delivery of the purchase. Since both catalog shopping and online shopping do not have any physical contact nor smell of the products and service (Lohse & Spiller, 1998), the success of online shopping basically relies on how satisfied the users' experience in using the website. That is, the outcomes of human computer interaction will be a crucial factor that determines the success of business websites. In their papers, Eggar (2001) and Lee (2002) have stated that the quality of web information and ease of use on an interactive business website are two of the most important factors for trust building. As well, as indicated earlier, price is considered as one of the major determining factors for online purchase. Tourism researchers and practitioners have been, and will be, examining the optimal pricing strategies for e-business in tourism. In a prior study, Quan (2002) showed that pricing strategies in the service industry should provide a form of insurance for price-sensitive customers to have a fixed price for future service. In the context of academic research for hotels, Yelkur and DaCosta (2001) checked the pricing policies for online marketing and found that the existence of differences in segmentation and differential pricing in hotels in the U.S. O'Connor (2002, 2003) examined the prices of hotel brands, and found the majority of hotel brands used multiple online channels and multiple rates on each channel. Likewise, Tso and Law (2005) investigated online prices for different hotel categories on various distribution channels. Empirical findings showed indirect channels offered significantly lower room rates than direct channels. In short, despite the general agreement on the importance of online pricing and the large sales volume of online air tickets, the existing tourism literature has a very limited number of prior research studies, if any, on pricing practice of online air tickets. This study makes an attempt to fill in this void by investigating the issue in the context of Hong Kong which is a key travel destination in Asia – the world's fastest growing region in tourism.

3 Methodology

This study is exploratory in nature, and the data for analysis were collected from different online travel agencies for air tickets to different destinations. Figure 1 shows the flow of the research process.

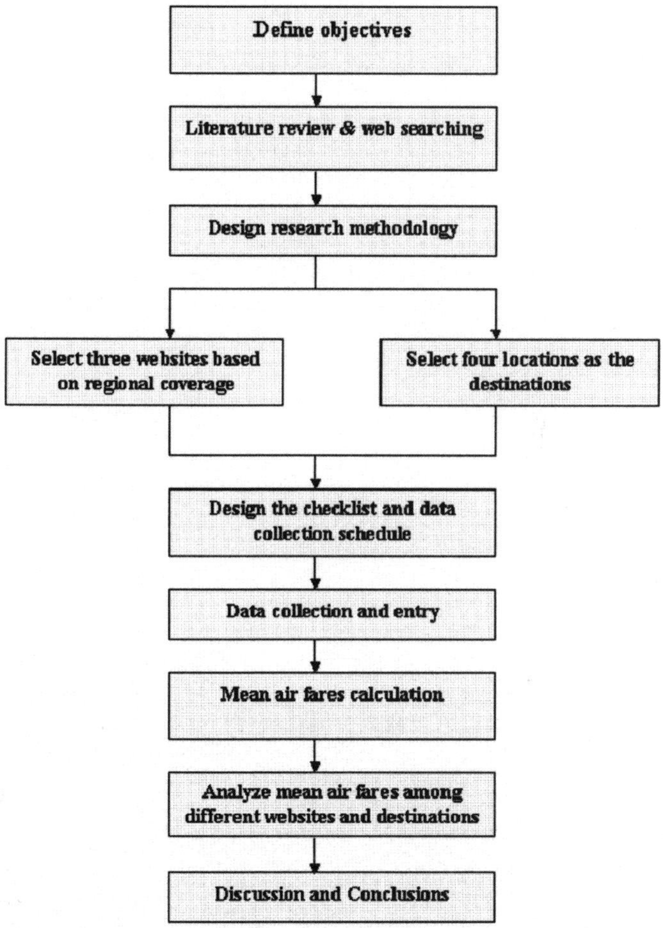

Fig. 1. Research Process flow

3.1 The Channels and Destinations Chosen for Analysis

Data were collected on three travel agency websites, including expedia.com, zuji.com, and wingon.com, representing the key international, regional, and local online travel agencies. Fares of return air tickets from Hong Kong to Shanghai in mainland China, Bangkok in Thailand, London in the United Kingdom, and Vancouver in Canada were checked. These four locations are the most popular outbound short-haul and long-haul destinations for Hong Kong residents to travel within the country (Shanghai), intra-continental (Bangkok), and inter-continental travel destinations in Europe and North America (London and Vancouver).

3.2 Data Collection

Data collection was trial tested in August 2005, and the actual collection was conducted for 90 consecutive days from mid-September to mid-December 2005. There was a computer network problem on one day, leaving 89 days of usable data. Since websites are updated frequently, data were collected within a relatively short period of time to have consistent information, and therefore a fair comparison of results. During the data collection process, the researchers recorded the lowest air fare for a 7-day return air ticket for an adult which was one month after the date for data recording. Additionally, nonstop flights were selected for data collection.

Moreover, in order to reduce the chance of having unnecessary and unexpected variability in air fares, the researchers used the same computer, same Internet Service Provider (ISP), and same Internet browser throughout the entire data collection period. Having collected the necessary data, a comparison was then made among the three websites and for the four destinations.

4 Findings

Flight availability showed all websites had short haul flights at all times but some long haul flights were unavailable on certain days. Although all websites had air tickets that matched the search criteria, there were several days during which air tickets to London were not found on expedia and Zuji. The unavailability of air tickets to Vancouver was also found on all websites. In the case of WingOn, only 71.91% of the 89 days had air tickets available for flights to Vancouver. As a whole, expedia, Zuji, and WingOn had the average availability of 98.03%, 97.47%, and 92.98% respectively. Table 1 shows the availability air tickets on the three websites. It is interesting to note that the days where WingOn could not provide air tickets to Vancouver were all toward the end of the data collection period.

Table 1. Availability of Flights

	Expedia	Availability	Zuji	Availability	Wing On	Availability
Shanghai	89	100%	89	100%	89	100%
Bangkok	89	100%	89	100%	89	100%
London	87	97.75%	83	93.26%	89	100%
Vancouver	84	94.38%	86	96.63%	64	71.91%

Tables 2 to 5 further elaborated the specific airlines that offered the lowest air fares and the conditions imposed by different websites that were related to the lowest air fares.

As indicated in Table 2, when traveling to Shanghai, the dominating airline was the China Eastern Airlines, and both expedia and WingOn had no conditions for purchasing air fares. Zuji, however, had some restricted flights and some flights required the reservations with specific credit cards.

Table 2. Airline summary for flights to Shanghai

Destination	**Agency**	*China Eastern*	*Dragonair*	*Restricted Flight*	*Master Card*	*Visa Card*
Shanghai	Expedia	89	-	-	-	-
	Zuji	39	50	23	7	16
	WingOn	75	14	-	-	-
	Overall	203	64	23	7	16

Table 3 shows that a total of 11 different airlines offered the lowest fare flights from Hong Kong to Bangkok, and the airlines that offered most of these flights were Emirates, Gulf Air, and Orient Thai. Similar to Table 2, expedia and WingOn had no conditions but Zuji had the conditions of e-ticket or paid by Visa card for some flights.

Table 3. Airline summary for flights to Bangkok

Destination	Agency	*Emirates*	*Ethiopian*	*China Airlines*	*Gulf Air*	*Orient Thai*	*Dragonair*	*SriLankan Air*	*Cathay Pacific*	*Thai Air Int'l*	*China Eastern Airlines*	*9I*	*e-ticket*	*Visa Card*
Bangkok	Expedia	72	10	-	2	-	-	3	1	1		-	-	-
	Zuji	11	2	35	31	-	6	-	3	-	1	-	40	5
	WingOn	-	-	-	25	50	-	-	-	-	-	14	-	-
	Overall	83	12	35	58	50	6	3	4	1	1	14	40	5

When flights to London were considered, five airlines had offered flights with the lowest fares (Table 4). While the dominant airlines were British Airways and Cathay Pacific, both Zuji and WingOn had conditions that were associated with their air tickets.

Table 4. Airline summary for flights to London

Destination	Agency	*British Airways*	*Virgin Atlantic*	*Cathay Pacific*	*Qantas Airways*	*Continental*	*e-ticket*	*Master Card*
London	Expedia	40	19	14	14	-	-	-
	Zuji	35	10	18	19	1	55	3
	WingOn	44	1	44	-	-	56	-
	Overall	119	30	76	33	1	111	3

Two airlines offered flights from Hong Kong to Vancouver, and more than 80% of these flights were from Air Canada (Table 5). Like the case of London, expedia was the only website that had no associated conditions.

Table 5. Airline summary for flights to Vancouver

Destination	**Agency**	*Air Canada*	*Cathay Pacific*	*e-ticket*	*Restricted flight*
Vancouver	Expedia	76	8	-	-
	Zuji	49	37	32	6
	WingOn	63	1	-	18
	Overall	188	46	32	24

The collected air fares from the three websites and the four destinations were then compared to evaluate the online pricing practice of these websites. Analysis of Variance (ANOVA) was used to test the existence of significant difference of air fares among different channels. The findings for all channels are presented in Hong Kong currency (HK$7.8 = US$1) in Table 6.

Table 6. Average Air Fares Offered on Different Websites

		Shanghai	*Bangkok*	*London*	*Vancouver*
Expedia	N	89	89	87	84
	mean	3700.81	2171.17	12376.18	13595.12
	s.t.d.	109.96	784.00	3139.76	2982.53
Zuji	N	89	89	83	86
	mean	2240.42	1277.88	7265.88	10221.37
	s.t.d.	242.66	557.10	3778.59	4155.77
WingOn	N	89	89	89	64
	mean	2104.27	1244.38	5444.49	6121.70
	s.t.d.	106.82	255.33	494.03	1739.06
F-value		2538.867	74.512	141.747	97.817
Sig.		0.000*	0.000*	0.000*	0.000*
Post-Hoc		Expedia>Zuji >WingOn	Expedia>Zuji, Expedia>WingOn	Expedia>Zuji >WingOn	Expedia>Zuji >WingOn

* *Significant at 0.05 level*

* *Tukey post hoc comparisons analysis was used*

As revealed in Table 6, WingOn, the local travel agency, consistently offered the lowest air fares for all destinations. Zuji, however, ranked second in terms of the rates of air fares. The Microsoft supported expedia, unfortunately, had the highest air fares for all destinations. Such findings are in accordance with a prior study on online pricing practice for hotels in Hong Kong which stated that expedia had offered unfavorable room rates and local travel agency had offered the lowest room rates (Tso & Law, 2005). Additionally, ANOVA results showed significant differences in air fares among the three websites and for all destinations. Table 6 also showed the significant differences of a post-hoc comparison using a Tukey analysis.

5 Discussion

This study has attempted to provide a clearer picture of online pricing practice of air tickets on travel agency websites with different geographical scope. Findings are expected to provide travelers and practitioners a better understanding of travel agency's online air fares. The price sensitive customers can then choose their preferred websites for making reservations. As well, travel practitioners can establish more appropriate marketing strategies that match these business strategies.

Findings of this study showed the categories of online reservation services provided by any specific website in different destinations were similar. However, the contents of different websites were quite different, ranged from sophisticated (like on expedia) to simple (e.g. on WingOn). Stout (1996) stated that online companies should have the essential components on their websites for promotion of products or services. Apparently, all travel agency websites provided flight schedules and availability (which is equivalent to product information) but not all websites were able to connect to a real time reservation system. Such a difference could be due to the dissimilarity in customers' behavior and technological developments among the three regions of Hong Kong, Asia, and the world. For instance, North America is leading the world in Internet technology, making expedia the most sophisticated website chosen in this study. In contrast, the Hong Kong based WingOn.com is much slower in terms of technological applications.

Information overloading on the Internet becomes an emerging issue in the present era. Findings of this study can, therefore, contribute to provide users a comprehensive view on the selection of websites with the lowest air fares. Drawings on the findings of this study, local intelligence appears outperformed global reach. It is suggested that e-travelers could visit local based websites prior to visiting regional websites in order to search for their air tickets with the lowest fares.

6 Conclusions

With the rapid advancement in computer network technology and the growing popularity of the Internet, Internet shopping is expected to be the next revolution in direct marketing (Jones & Vijayasarathy 1998). This emerging growth is directly applicable to online reservations of air ticket in Asia, the world's fastest growing region in tourism.

There is no doubt that the Internet will be a powerful marketing tool to capture the emerging e-business market in tourism. However, the proficiency of using the Internet needs new skills that are different from traditional skills. This research has tried to analyze the online pricing practice of air tickets on different types of travel agency websites, which serve as a distribution channel for providing online information and reservations of travel-related services and products.

Although empirical findings of this research offer an insight into the issue of online pricing practice of air tickets on selected websites, pricing in other types of services such as hotel room and car rental reservations on these websites remain largely unknown. In other words, the limitations of sample size and investigation scope make the study not possible to generalize the findings in any context. Furthermore, since the content richness and website quality of these travel websites are also important factors that could determine users' purchase inclination, it would be worthwhile to find out the correlation of online price and content as well as design of the websites. Lastly, only the English version of each selected travel agency website was used in this study. A natural extension of this is to examine the pricing practice on other language versions of the websites.

References

Burns, E. (2006). *Online Is Destination For Air Travel Purchase* Retrieved October 18, 2006 from http://www.clickz.com/showPage.html?page=3514481

Cox, B. (2002). *Online Travel – Still an E-commerce Star?* Retrieved June 22, 2005 from http://www.internetnews.com/ec-news/article.php/1437521

Egger, F. N. (2001). Affective Design of E-Commerce User Interfaces: How to Maximise Perceived Trustworthiness. In M. Helander, H. M. Khalid, & Tham (Eds.). *Proceedings of CAHD2001: Conference on Affective Human Factors Design* (pp.317-324). Singapore: ASEAN Press.

Harris Interactive (2004) *One In Four Online Shoppers Have Finished Their Holiday Shopping.* Retrieved June 26, 2006, from http://www.harrisinteractive.com/news/allnewsbydate.asp?NewsID=873.

Jones, J. M., & Vijayasarathy, L. R. (1998). Internet consumer catalog shopping: Findings from an exploratory study and directions for future research. *Internet Research: Electronic Networking Applications and Policy.* 8(4): 322-30.

Kolesar, M. B. & Galbraith, R. W. (2000). A services-marketing perspective on e-retailing: implications for e-retailers and directions for further. *Internet Research: Electronic Networking Applications and Policy,* 10(5): 424-438.

Lee, P. M. (2002). Behavioral model of online purchasers in e-commerce environment. *Electronic Commerce Research.* 2, 75-85.

Lohse, G. L., & Spiller, P. (1998). Electronic shopping: The effect of customer interfaces on traffic and sales. *Communications of the ACM.* 41(7): 81-87.

Nielsen/Netratings (2003). *Books, Music, Video/DVD and Apparel Categories Claim The Bulk of Holiday Consumer spending Online.* Retrieved June 26, 2006, from http://www.nielsen-netratings.com/pr/pr_021220.pdf.

O'Connor, P. (2002). An empirical analysis of hotel chains' online pricing practices. *Information Technology & Tourism* 5, 65-72.

O'Connor, O. (2003). Online pricing: an analysis of hotel-company practices. *Cornell Hotel and Restaurant Administration Quarterly,* February, 88-96.

O'Connor, P., & Frew, A. J. (2004). An evaluation methodology for hotel electronic channels of distribution. *International Journal of Hospitality Management* 23, 179-199.

Quan, D. C. 2002. The price of reservation. *Cornell Hotel and Restaurant Administration Quarterly* June, 77-87.

Stout, R. (1996). *The World Wide Web Complete Reference*. New York: McGraw-Hill.

Tso, A. & Law, R. (2005). An Empirical Study of Online Pricing Practices for Hong Kong Hotels. In A. J. Frew (Ed). *Information and Communication Technologies in Tourism 2005*. ENTER 2005 Proceedings. New York: Springer-Verlag, Wien. pp. 328-337.

Toms, E. G., & Taves, A. R. (2004). Measuring user perceptions of Web site reputation. *Information Processing and Management* 40, 291-317.

Watson, R. T., Berthon, P., Pitt, L. F., & Zinkhan, G. M. (2000) *Electronic Commerce The Strategic Perspective.* Fort Worth, TX: Dryden Press.

Wilson, S. G., & Abel, I. (2002). So you want to get involved in E-commerce. *Industrial Marketing Management* 31, 85-94.

Yelkur, R. & DaCosta, M. M. N. (2001). Differential pricing and segmentation on the Internet: The case of hotels. *Management Decision* 15, 40-50.

eTourism Curriculum Development: A Destination Management Organisation Perspective

Matthias Fuchs[a]
Wolfram Höpken[a]
Peter Mirski[b]
Andreas Lembacher[b]
Bernd Ainedter[c]

[a] eTourism Competence Center Austria (ECCA), Austria
{matthias.fuchs, wolfram.hoepken}@etourism-austria.at
[b] Management and Applied Informatics
Management Center Innsbruck (MCI), Austria
{peter.mirski@mci.edu, a.lembacher@mci4me.at}
[c] International Economics and Business Studies
Leopold Franzens Universität Innsbruck (LFU), Austria
bernd@ainedter.at

Abstract

The paper is presenting results from an information and communication technology (ICT) curriculum development project for the tourism industry, called $_{\text{et}}$Curriculum. After specifying the objectives of the project the various development steps of a curriculum prototype are discussed. Based on Porter and Millar's (1985) *value chain model* the specific (re-)qualification requirements of local tourism organisations in the knowledge field of ICT have been recorded by interviewing a representative number of destination management organisation employees. The curriculum prototype was adapted based on these results.

Keywords: curriculum development; eTourism; further-training; destination management organisation (DMO)

1 Introduction

Mature markets as well as new competitive conditions due to globalization, liberalization and deregulation led to a number of significant changes in the situation of destination management organisations. In particular, information and communication technologies (ICT) have stimulated radical changes in the operation of destination management organisations (DMO). More precise, ICT create new markets, cause new forms of customer relationship (e.g. experiential marketing, eCRM) and support the optimization of (e.g. tourism) business processes (Werthner & Klein 1999). Perhaps the most apparent example is the re-engineering of booking processes, which gradually allowed tourists to experience seamless destination experiences by saving valuable time resources. In the electronic marketplace, however, the visibility for whole destinations becomes a function of ICT and strategically utilized electronic networks (Buhalis 2003). Thus, in order to really achieve competitive advantages from this technological progress, jobholders within destination management organisations should feature adequate ICT knowledge, which, in turn, implies corresponding schooling/training offers and a continuous adjustment, upgrading and even the deletion of existing tourism curricula (Collins & Buhalis 2004).

The paper on hand gives a thorough account on an Austrian tourism curriculum development project, called $_{et}$Curriculum. It intends to develop an eTourism curriculum to prepare and enable both students and employees for their IT-based work (Vogal & Klassen 2001). The paper is structured as follows: After giving a brief overview of curriculum development trends in tourism the need for ICT-related curricula development projects in tourism will be corroborated. Chapter two also highlights the objectives of the project. Chapter three summarizes empirical results of three preparatory studies and is leading to a first version of an eTourism curriculum prototype. Based on the *task-technology fit* approach (Dale, Goodhue, & Thompson, 1995) and on Porter and Millar's (1985) *value chain model* chapter four demonstrates an adaptation procedure to relate the curriculum prototype to the specific (re)qualification requirements of the Tyrolean (Austria) DMO sector. Finally, after having summarized the main findings the conclusion section outlines future research agendas.

2 Curriculum Development Trends in Tourism

Tribe (2001) critically points out that existing curriculum proposals in tourism are predominantly based on the *scientific-positivistic* approach. He concludes that these may have only limited application because of their lack of attention to tourism stakeholders' hidden meaning and values. Thus, he suggests two additional approaches to curriculum design. The *interpretative* approach regards "all relevant participants in the curriculum-event as subjects, not as objects" (Grundy 1987, p. 69) while the *critical* approach supports "emancipation from status-quo and orthodox tourism curriculum" (Tribe 2001, p. 447). The latter approach avoids that individuals behave as "self-forming species by recognising their own capacity of authorship of history" (Young 1989, p. 27). Similarly, Smith and Cooper (2000, p. 92) encourage an evolution of tourism curricular approaches by indicating the growing importance of behavioural autonomy and control for the learning individual. To summarize, only the transmission of a complex of both professional, technical and intellectual skills and concepts through a variety of learning experiences would enable learning individuals to compete successfully in tourism job markets, develop career paths, seek additional education levels, engage in *"life-long learning"* and contribute creatively to a multicultural working society (ibid 2000).

2.1 Curriculum adaptation requirements for DMOs

Tourism services are produced by various subsystems that jointly deliver services along the destination service chain (Bieger 2005). Thus, the primary goal of destination management is to assess the adequacy and effectiveness of tourism products, facilities, programs and destination resources that all together provide memorable experiences for visitors. However, utilization of ICT and growing consideration of tourist destinations as strategically managed territorial systems require more suitable and new ICT-based tasks for DMOs such as:

- Creation & maintenance of an online destination portal
- Electronic sales support for the various destination products
- Web-based promotional campaigns
- Realisation of flexible destination products (e.g. dynamic packaging)
- Promotion of web-based benchmarking projects
- Supply-coordination and international and interregional cooperative initiatives
- Education & training.

For Austria and Italy Pechlaner and Fuchs (2002) have shown empirically that the management of 37 DMOs increasingly perceives the significance of ICTs. From the study also emerged however that the ability to use new ICT-based systems can only be achieved by satisfying the articulated qualification needs in the field of ICT (ibid 2002, p. 52).

From a theoretical perspective adjustment processes regarding a firm's human resource composition can be approached from two vintage points. According to the *market-based* approach (Porter 1991) market forces determine these changes and, thus, explain a firm's behaviour of human resource investments both inside and outside the firm (Becker 1993). In contrast, the *resource-based* approach (Mahoney & Pandian 1992) is based on the notion that demand can only be created by the existence of firm-related resources and their transformation by entrepreneurs in terms of *core-competencies* (Van Krogh & Ross 1996). Thus, innovative schooling and training offers for new vocational fields in tourism (such as ICT) endorse the above described process of *organisational change*.

The aim of the presented $_{et}$Curriculum project is to support the tourism industry with their *"life wide and life long learning"* by working out adequate curriculum adjustments and extensions in the knowledge field of *eTourism* (Buhalis 2003, p. 77). The latter term reflects the "digitalization of all processes and value chains in the tourism industry by bundling together three distinctive disciplines", namely: *Business Management* (e.g. Strategy, Marketing, Finance, Human Resource Management, etc.), *Tourism* (e.g. Transport, Heritage, Hotel, Leisure, Travel, etc.) and *Information Systems and Management* (e.g. Information Systems, Telecommunication, etc.). $_{et}$Curriculum empirically identifies the need for curriculum adjustment from the point of view of the various tourism *stakeholders* (e.g. personnel managers, employees, students, teachers, scientific experts). Doing so, most relevant learning matters and methods for the knowledge-field of eTourism can be deduced from these results (Kyoo 2000). Finally, these new topical areas will be transformed into prototypical teaching materials and put to test in the tourism education system.

3 Preparatory study results

At the very beginning of the $_{et}$Curriculum project an international *"Screening"* of already existing eTourism curricula and the used textbooks at the tertiary level (i.e. 50 universities as well as universities of applied sciences) took place. On the basis of these data, thematically related eTourism topics (e.g. *online marketing, construction &*

evaluation of websites, booking & reservation systems, etc.) were identified and evaluated by 15 internationally well known university lecturers in the field of ICT and tourism (Werthner & Klein 1999; Buhalis 2003). The conducted semi-standardized interviews also allowed to identify additional curriculum topics, such as *content management, recommendation & push technologies, location based services,* as well as to explore an expert-based weighting scheme (i.e. 4 = absolutely important and 1 = absolutely unimportant) for the finally proposed 32 topical areas summarized in Figure 1.

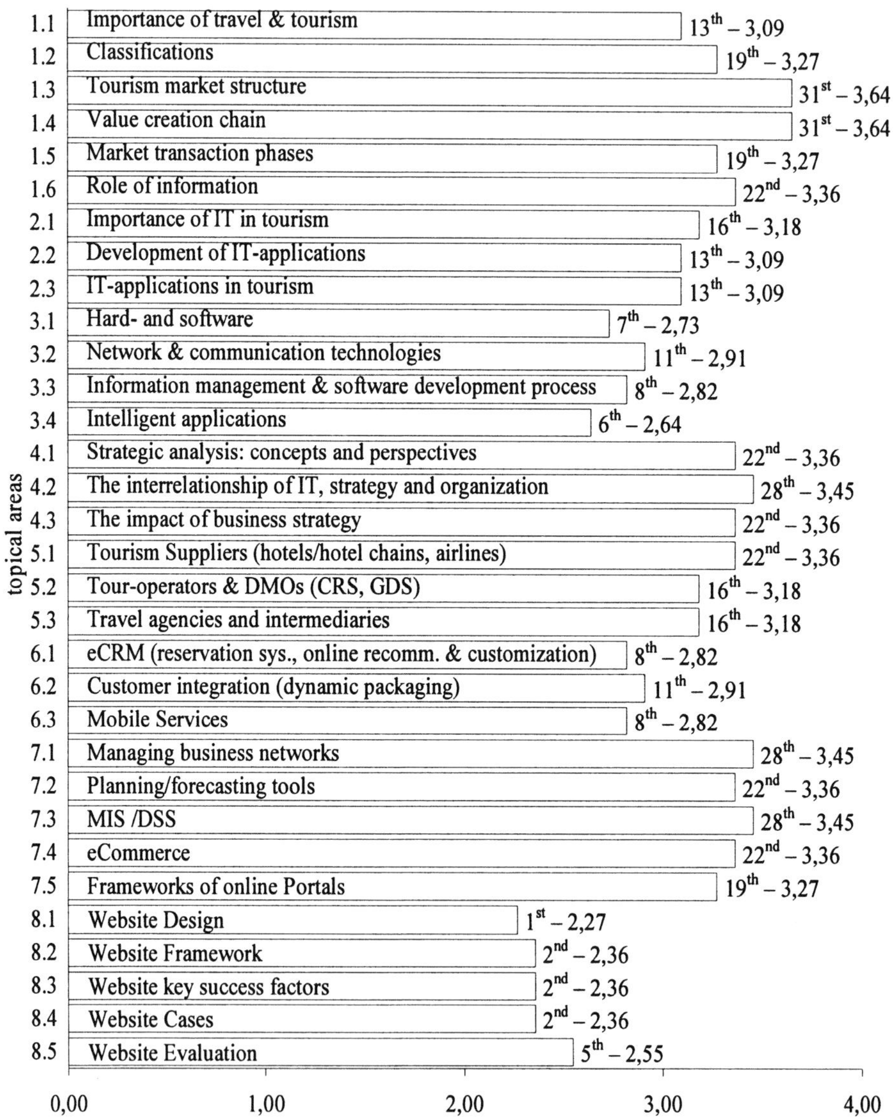

Fig. 1: Expert-based weighting scheme for eTourism curriculum topics

On the base of these initial studies, a first eTourism curriculum prototype version comprising learning objectives, learning levels, assessments (i.e. individual seminar- vs. group-work, etc.) and exam types (e.g. oral/written test, etc.) was generated. The final structure of the prototype, learning matters as well as core target groups, are summarized in Table 1.

Table 1. Structure and learning matters of the $_{et}$Curriculum Prototype

Topic	*Learning Matters (exemplary)*	*Target groups*
1. Introduction	Structure of tourism market and role of information for various market transaction phases; ICT and MIS	A+B, aL
2. ICT & Tourism	Adoption rates & usage trends of ICT applications in tourism; Productivity enhancement through ICT in tourism (Impact Studies), eCommerce/eBusiness in tourism; CRS & GDS	A+B, aL
3. Strategic Tourism Management and ICT	ICT-supported strategy management (segmentation, market share analysis, benchmarking, guest satisfaction); Decision Support Systems concerning controlling, finance and pricing decisions Data Warehousing & Data Mining; Electronic value chains (Smart Business Networks), Strategic ICT applications in tourism (eCRM, recommendation and push, mobile services)	A+B, tL
4. Information Technologie s in Tourism	Network technologies (Inter-/Intranet), data encryption standards (Secure Electronic Transaction) Software architectures for CRS & DMS, data description techniques (XML, UML) & data-base modelling (Entity Relationship Modelling), advanced programming languages (Java, Servlets) & Cocoon frameworks, interoperability & interconnectivity (i.e. harmonisation, Ontologies and Semantic Web technologies)Creation, maintenance and evaluation of websites	B, aL
5. eSolutions	Hotel sector: CRS & GDS, Property Management Systems, Enterprise Resource Planning Systems, eProcurement (Allegro, Fidelio, etc.) Intermediaries: Destination Integrated Computerized Information Reservation Management System (DICIRMS)	A+B, aL
6. Future Trends in eTourism	Ambient intelligence, virtual communities, new market forms (e.g. online auctions, reverse auctions, etc.), hybrid-recommendation, context-sensitive push and pull technologies (e.g. location-based services), re-/disintermediation using agent-technologies	B, aL

Relevant for individuals with tourism (A) and IT (B) background
all educational levels (aL) / tertiary level (tL)

In 2005, the developed curriculum prototype was evaluated by the human resource manager of the largest Tyrolean 5-Star hotel (i.e. 250 employees), by students of the university of applied sciences (i.e. the *Management Centre Innsbruck, Austria*) and by a group of 22 Austrian experts in the field of tourism research, ICT and pedagogy (Brookes 2002). From this evaluation a comprehensive list of *strengths* (e.g. theoretical foundation, practical relevance, problem solving capacity, completeness, etc.) and *chances* (e.g. eLearning support, modularization, opportunity to supply as a further-training offer, etc.) has been deduced. However, also *weaknesses* (e.g. too little time to practice, too large technical focus, etc.) and even *risks* (e.g. barriers of acceptance by educational institutions, students, managers and the requirement for a continuous update, etc.) have been identified in the course of the conducted prototype evaluation.

Following, an empirical procedure to adapt the above elaborated curriculum prototype to the specific needs of (i.e. Tyrolean) destination management organisations (DMOs) for further-training purposes in the knowledge field of *eTourism* is presented.

4 eTourism Curriculum Development for DMOs

The developed eTourism curriculum has yet (only) been evaluated by students, teachers and tourism experts at the post-secondary level (i.e. university of applied sciences). However, in order to minimize observed barriers towards further-training and in conformity with the *interpretative approach* the aim of the following section is to record the specific qualification needs of the DMO-workforce (Grundy 1987; Tribe 2001). Thus, an *online survey* conducted in March 2006 was targeted to both managers as well as employees. According to the *task-technology fit model* (Dale et al. 1995) ICT-applications will be adopted when they effectively support the accomplishment of specific tasks in a pre-specified workplace setting. Therefore, the *task-technology fit model* emphasizes that each organization shows a typical set of workplace-related tasks, which may be supported effectively by the intelligent adoption of new ICT-systems. In order to ensure that data gathering concerning DMOs' further-training requirements within the knowledge-field of ICT would be valid and complete, a systematisation of organisation-specific task-areas was arranged. For this purpose, the illustration of ICT application areas along the various task-areas of a typical DMO was based upon Porter and Millar's (1985) *value chain* model. The latter represents firm-specific activities as interlinked chain of value-adding processes. More precise, *primary activities* comprise "sales activities" (i.e. the intermediation of goods and services to customers), the "production of goods and services" as well as the "delivery of after sales services". In addition, *secondary (i.e. supporting) activities* include intra-destination functions, such as "provision of resource-inputs", "human resource management", "technology management" to support both provision and processing of information and finally "infrastructure management" regarding destination facilities and infrastructures (ibid 1985; Buhalis 2003; Bieger 2005).

Based on required competencies, capabilities and skills to successfully employ ICT within a DMO a total of 26 knowledge areas has been deduced (Werthner & Klein 1999; Buhalis 2003) and arranged below in Figure 2. By anticipating first descriptive findings, figure 2 displays (in parenthesis) both the *priority-ranking* and the corresponding *mean values* quantifying the potential demand for further-training in specific *eTourism* knowledge-areas. Stäudel (1988) defines *competence-levels* as "subjective assessment of own capabilities being at one's command to cope with a specific problem" (ibid 1988, p. 4). According to Aizen and Fishbein's (1980) *theory of reasoned action* a *"self-assessment"*, in turn, results from a subjectively perceived importance level (e.g. attached to a specific knowledge area) and the corresponding *intention* to behave. A survey has been conducted in all the existing 39 Tyrolean Destination Management Organisations including 29 managers and 100 employees. Data gathering took place in March 2006 by means of an *online-survey* (Wilson & Laskey 2003). Based on the above theoretical assumptions the interviewed individuals were asked to quantify their "self-assessment" concerning the above specified (i.e. 26) ICT-knowledge areas using a six-point *Likert scale* (i.e. 1 stands for *highly important* and 6 for *not important at all*). In addition, they were asked to assess their corresponding knowledge-level (i.e. 1 stands for *sufficient knowledge* and 6 indicates *insufficient knowledge levels*).

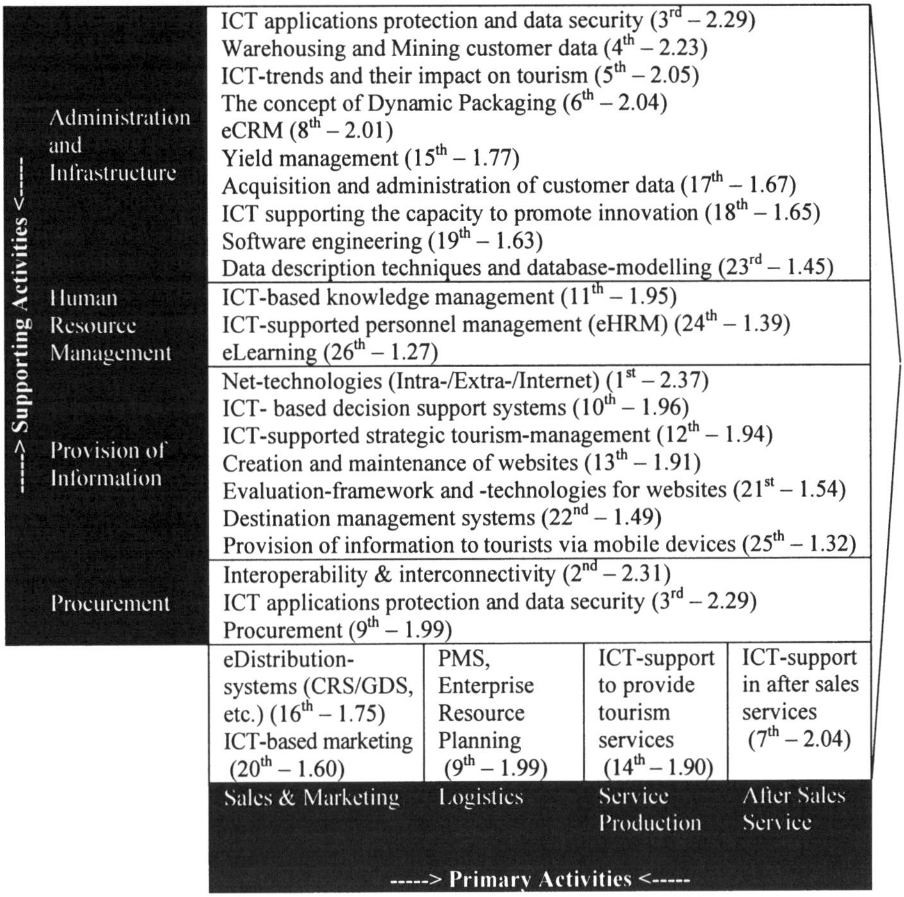

Fig. 2: *Value chain* model & ICT-knowledge areas (adapted from: Porter & Millar 1985)

In order to quantify DMO-specific needs for further-training a *GAP-value* (Parasuraman et al. 1985) was calculated by deducing the "self-assessed importance level" from "self-assessed knowledge". The emerging *GAP-variable* ranges from -5 to +5. More precise, negative values represent a too high knowledge-level compared to the declared importance (i.e. an overinvestment in *human capital*) whereas *zero*-values show a balanced importance/knowledge-level (Becker 1993). The closer the value moves towards +5 the greater the potential demand for further-training (i.e. insufficient knowledge for important task areas). As reported next, an (explorative) *factor analysis* and a *variance analysis* (*ANOVA*) on the base of these *GAP-variables* supported the identification of new training modules in the knowledge-area of *eTourism* (Hair et al. 1995).

5 Empirical Results

The obtained results, first of all, indicate a strong need for further-training with respect to all the proposed 26 ICT knowledge-areas along the DMO-specific *value chain*. More precise, for none of the considered knowledge-areas the average *GAP-value* stood below +1.27. At the aggregate level (e.g. for *all* test persons and *all* ICT-knowledge-areas) the corresponding mean value stood at +1.82. Generally spoken, the need for vocational ICT-training proved to be evenly distributed between both, the *primary* and *supporting activities* of the *value chain* (Porter & Millar 1985, see figure 2). Moreover, based on the obtained GAP values the high-dimensionality of the corresponding 26 DMO-specific ICT knowledge-areas could be reduced to four factors typically by the use of explorative *factor analysis* (Table 2) (Hair et al. 1995).

Table 2. Factor analysis results showing four dimensions of ICT knowledge-areas

	Factor 1	***Factor 2***	***Factor 3***	***Factor 4***
Eigenvalue	14.05	1.52	1.31	1.00
Cronbach Alpha (α)	.92	.91	.86	.85
Destination management systems	.813			
Acquisition and administration of customer data	.745			
Creation and maintenance of websites	.679			
Information provision via mobile devices	.641			
Evaluation-framework for websites	.591			
The concept of Dynamic Packaging	.584			
Warehousing and Mining customer data	.567			
Yield management	.537			
eCRM	.525			
ICT-supported strategic tourism-management	.502			
eLearning		.750		
ICT-support for the provision of tourism services		.732		
ICT-supported personnel management (*eHRM*)		.628		
ICT-based marketing		.613		
ICT-support in after sales services		.612		
Electronic distribution systems (*CRS/GDS*)		.594		
PMS, ERP		.585		
ICT-based knowledge management			.525	
ICT-based business intelligence/decision support			.470	
ICT supporting the capacity to promote innovation			.589	
Interoperability & interconnectivity			.770	
ICT-trends and their impact on tourism			.648	
ICT applications protection and data security				.666
Software engineering				.709
Data description techniques and database-modelling				.596

Extraction Method: *Principal Component Analysis* | Rotation Method: *Varimax*
Total Explained Variance: 69% | Sampling Adequacy: Kaiser-Mayer-Olkin = .922
Bartlett Test of Sphericity = 1679.100 (Sig. = .000)

The four emerging factors presented in table three show a highly satisfactory *construct reliability* as their corresponding *Cronbach Alpha values* stand at 0.92, 0.91, 0.86 and 0.85, respectively. Also the measure for sampling adequacy (i.e. *Kaiser-Mayer-Olkin*) was highly satisfactory, standing at 0.922 (Hair, Anderson, Tatham, & Black, 1995).

- Factor 1 explains 55% of total variance and very consistently integrates „*DMO-to tourist-systems*" (i.e. *destination management systems*) and their various application fields on the customer side, namely: *Acquisition and administration of customer data, provision of information to tourists* (i.e. *websites, mobile devices*), *warehousing and mining customer data,* the use of *methods for electronic customer relationship management* (eCRM) and, finally, the use of specialized tools to approach customers with adequate products and prices, such as *dynamic packaging, yield management* and, consequently, the *ICT-supported strategic tourism management.* In particular, the largest need for further-training can be observed for *warehousing & mining customer data* (GAP Value: 2.23), *dynamic packaging* (GAP Value: 2.04) as well as for *eCRM* (GAP Value: 2.01) (see figure 2).

- Factor 2 was labelled "*Electronic marketing & eHRM*" accounting for 5.9% of total variance. Interestingly enough, the derived training module comprises all those ICT knowledge areas relevant for *primary activities* of the *value chain* (i.e. sales & marketing, logistics, production of the service and after sales service activities). In addition, ICT-based activities necessary to support the important area of human resource management have been attached. Only for *ICT-supported after sales activities* (2.04) and *property management systems* (1.90) large GAP values were identified.

- Factor 3 was labelled „*Learning organisation*" as it interlinks the knowledge creating view of ICT (e.g. *ICT-based knowledge management & decision support systems*, respectively) with the DMO's ability for self-organisation and adaptation (e.g. *innovation, ICT trends* as well as *interoperability & interconnectivity*). Largest further-training needs were registered for the knowledge field of *interoperability & interconnectivity* (GAP value: 2.31) and *ICT trends and their impact on tourism competitiveness* (GAP value: 2.05).

- Factor 4 was labelled „*Technical infrastructure*" and includes all those predominantly technique oriented knowledge fields such as *Inter-, Extra- and Internet-Technologies, ICT application protection and data security* and such knowledge-fields as *software engineering, data description techniques and database-modelling.* Its explanatory power is below 4%. For the curriculum areas of *net-technologies* (GAP Value: 2.37) and *ICT applications protection and data security* (GAP Value: 2.29) the largest further-training need could be identified.

Although with respect to the four ICT qualification-factors no assessment differences between managers and employees could be identified, significant differences exist between various educational groups. More precise, for factor one (i.e. „*DMO-to tourist-*

systems") and two ("*Electronic marketing & eHRM*") the DMO subgroup with a completed tourism education at the secondary level shows the greatest propensity to further education (i.e. sig. = 0.002, and 0.001, respectively). Interestingly enough, for factors three and four no significant differences can be observed among the various educational groups.

In the course of the online survey test-persons were finally asked to evaluate differing training methods (Airey & Frontistis 1997). The option that a "*trainer comes to the organisation*" was considered as most adequate by 86.7% of the interviewed. Similarly, the assessment towards "*training in a training centre*" was judged as rather ideal by 77.5%. In contrast, for "*training on the job*" and "*eLearning*" only low agreement was achieved (i.e. 54.2% and 46.5%, respectively). No differing assessments between managers and employees could again be observed.

6 Conclusions and Outlook

Based on the above results the prejudice that the work-force within the tourism sector would show aversions towards further-training cannot be confirmed for the DMO-sample under study as for none of the 26 ICT knowledge-fields a *GAP value* lower than +1.27 could be realized (see figure 2). As a result from factorial data-reduction, four main subject areas (i.e. "*DMO-to tourist-systems*", "*electronic marketing & eHRM*", "*Learning organisation*" and "*Technical infrastructure*") were identified and thus, as main practical implication, should be "packaged" and delivered in this specific form as new further-training modules to satisfy the ICT-related qualification needs of the (i.e. Tyrolean) DMO sector. Finally, by means of the survey the composition of the elaborated $_{et}$Curriculum *prototype* could be confirmed as being adequate for both, formal education (i.e. schooling) and for vocational further-training. For the latter purpose, due to their corresponding knowledge GAPs perceived by the industry sample, the following curricular sub-topics should be granted highest priority:

Net-technologies (*GAP value* 2.37): The internet combines and integrates equivalently information, collaboration, communication, interaction and transaction. Thus, in contrast to traditional media, the trade-off between the number of attainable persons and information richness (i.e. accuracy, timeliness and customisation) disappeared. Additionally, *intra- and extranet systems* support all the productive areas of a company's *value chain* (Porter & Millar 1985).

Interoperability & interconnectivity (*GAP value* 2.31): The importance of this topic area directly derives from the role of DMOs within the electronic tourism sector (Buhalis 2003). The subtopics are ranging from *standardisation & harmonisation* (e.g. *ontologies*) to the *optimization of data interfaces.*

ICT applications protection and data security (*GAP value* 2.29): The latter knowledge-gap is in line with the final user's few as both the various tourism suppliers as well as tourists within destinations appraise highest priority to this specific topic.

Warehousing and mining customer data (GAP value 2.23): Data mining is defined as the nontrivial extraction previously unknown and potentially useful information from data. It involves the process of analyzing data to show patterns or relationships (e.g. market segments). Application modules can be easily obtained with *Property Management Systems. A data warehouse* can be understood as a copy of enterprise transaction data specifically structured for query, reporting and analysis.

Future research aspects can be sketched as (1) the systematic elaboration and evaluation of "interactive case studies" to foster self-directed e-Learning (Lominé 2002). Thereby, the advantages from *location and time-independency* as well as from the personalisation of learning matters will show the strongest positive impact (Haven & Boterill 2003). Furthermore, (2) the development of approved certification standards in order to boost internationalisation (Black 2004) and individual signalling strategies should be realized (Becker 1993). Finally, (3) the foundation of new business models should be fostered to successfully deliver ICT-related schooling and training measures to future jobholders in the (e.g. Austrian) tourism industry.

References

Airey, D. & Frontistis, A. (1997). Attitudes to Carriers in Tourism: An Anglo-Greek Comparison. *Tourism Management,* 18(3), 149-158.

Aizen, I. & Fishbein, M. (1980). *Understanding Attitudes and predicting Social Behaviour.* Englewood Cliffs: Prentice Hall.

Becker, G. S. (1993). *Human Capital: A Theoretical and Empirical Analysis with Special Reference to Education* (3rd ed.). Chicago: University of Chicago Press.

Bieger, Th. (2005). *Management von Destinationen* (6th ed.). Munich – Vienna: Oldenbourg.

Black, K. (2004). A Review of Factors which Contribute to the Internationalisation of a Programme of Study. *Journal of Hospitality, Leisure, Sport & Tourism Education,* 3(1), 5-18.

Brookes, M. (2002). Evaluating the Student Experience: An Approach to Managing and Enhancing Quality in Higher Education. *Journal of Hospitality, Leisure, Sport & Tourism Education,* 2(1), 17-26.

Buhalis, D. (2003). *eTourism: Information Technology for strategic tourism management.* Essex: Prentice Hall-Pearson.

Collins, C. & Buhalis, D. (2004). Enhancing SMTEs Business Performance through the Internet and Online Learning Platforms. In A. Frew (Ed.). *ENTER Information and Communication Technologies in Tourism,* (pp. 580-591). New York: Springer.

Dale, L., Goodhue, R. & Thompson, L. (1995). Task-Technology Fit and Individual Performance. *MIS Quarterly,* 19(2), 213-236.

Fuchs, M., Höpken, W., Mirski, P., Ainedter, B., Lembacher, A. (2006). eTourism Curricula Development in Tyrol: A Preliminary Report. In proceedings of *3rd China Tourism Forum,* Hong Kong Polytechnic University, Hong Kong, China: December, 15 - 16, 2006 *(in print).*

Grundy, S. (1987). *Curriculum: Product or Praxis.* Sussex, UK: Falmer.

Hair, J.F. Jr., Anderson, R.E., Tatham, R.L. & Black, W.C. (1995). *Multivariate Data Analysis.* New Jersey: Prentice Hall.

Haven, C. & Boterill, D. (2003). Virtual Learning Environments in Hospitality, Leisure and Tourism: A Review. *Journal of Hospitality, Leisure, Sport & Tourism Education,* 2(1), 75-92.

Kyoo, Y.-Ch. (2000). Hotel Management Curriculum Reform based on Required Competencies of Hotel Employees and Career Success in the Hotel Industry. *Tourism Management,* 21, 473-487.

Lominè, L.L. (2002). Online Learning and Teaching in Hospitality and Leisure: Myths, Opportunities and Challenges. *Journal of Hospitality, Leisure, Sport & Tourism Education,* 1(1), 43-49.

Mahoney, J. T, & Pandian, J. R. (1992). The Resource Based View within the Conversation of Strategic Management. *Strategic Management Journal,* 12, 363 – 380.

Parasuraman, V., Zeithaml, A. & Berry, L. L. (1985). A Conceptual Model of Service Quality and its Implications for Future Research. *Journal of Marketing,* 49(4), 41-50.

Pechlaner, H. & Fuchs, M. (2002). Towards new skill rquirements for destination organisations – an exploratory study. *Tourism Analysis,* 7(1): 43-53.

Porter, M. E. (1991). Towards a dynamic theory of strategy. *Strategic Management Journal,* 12, 95 – 117.

Porter, M. E. & Millar, V. (1985). How information gives you Competitive Advantage. *Harvard* Business Review, 63(4), 149-160.

Smith, G. & Cooper, Ch. (2000). Competitive Approaches to Tourism and Hospitality Curriculum Design. *Journal of Travel Research*, 39, 90-95.

Stäudel, T. (1988). Der Kompetenzfragebogen. Ein Verfahren zur Erfassung der Selbsteinschätzung der heuristischen Kompetenz, belastender Emotionen und Verhaltenstendenzen beim Lösen komplexer Probleme. *Diagnostica,* 34(2), 1-12.

Tribe, J. (2001). Research Paradigms and Tourism Curriculum. *Journal of Travel Research,* 39, 442-448.

Von Krogh, G., & Roos, J. (1996). Managing Knowledge – Perspectives on Cooperation and Competition. London: Sage.

Vogal, D. & Klassen, J. (2001). Technology Supported Learning: Status, Issues and Trends. *Journal of Computer Assisted Learning,* 17, 26-35.

Werthner, H. & Klein, S. (1999). *Information Technology and Tourism - A Challenging Relationship*. Wien – New York: Springer.

Wilson, A. & Laskey N. (2003). Internet based Marketing Research. *Marketing Intelligence & Planning,* 21(2), 79-84.

Young, R. (1989). *A Critical Theory of Education.* Hemel Hempstead, UK: Harvester, Wheatsheaf.

E-learning as a Tool for Knowledge Creation in International Hotel Companies

Mohamed F. Hawela
Emily Boyle
Anna Murray

Faculty of Business and Management
University of Ulster
{Hawela-M1, e.boyle and ae.murray}@ulster.ac.uk

Abstract

Knowledge creation (KC) has been identified as a key source of competitive advantage for businesses and e-learning (EL) potentially has a major role to play in this process. In recent years international hotel companies (IHCs) have begun to adopt EL. However, there is little evidence about the extent to which this is being used to support KC. This paper, therefore, focuses on exploring how EL is being utilized by IHCs and suggests ways that further research in this area can help to improve the utilization of EL in the industry. The findings from research that includes a review of literature, internet search, and personal interviews show that EL is seen mainly as a training tool (e-training instead of EL) rather than as a strategic tool to support the creation of new knowledge, innovation, and competitive advantage. There are some limitations of this study; most of the collected data are from the exploratory internet data search. There might be other data related to EL in other IHCs and not included in the internet and therefore, not included in this study.

Key words: e-learning, innovation, international hotel companies, knowledge management, competitive advantage, organisational learning.

1 Introduction

It is increasingly acknowledged that one of the key ways for a firm to sustain and enhance its competitive position is through innovation and KC (Lytras, Naeve, & Pouloudi, 2005; Gupta, Sharma, & Hsu, 2004; Nonaka & Toyama, 2003; Wild, Griggs, & Downing, 2002; Nonaka, Toyama, & Konno, 2000; Teece, 2000; Nonaka & Konno, 1998; Nonaka & Takeuchi, 1995; Nonaka, 1994). Learning is the source of all knowledge and EL refers to the use of digital media to facilitate the learning process. It therefore, follows that EL could have a key role to play in the KC process. To date, however, little research has been carried out to find out the extent to which EL is being used in this way. This paper therefore seeks to clarify the situation in relation to one particular business area, namely, international hotel companies (IHCs). The paper is structured as follows. The next section considers the concept of EL. This is followed by a discussion of the process of KC and the role of knowledge management and the link between EL and the process of KC. The international hotel industry and the factors that favour the use of EL in it come next. There is then a summary of the methodology used, the findings from the research to date and a discussion of their implications in relation to the use of EL as a tool for KC and management among IHCs.

2 The Concept of E-learning (Theory/issues/review of literature)

Writers have suggested that EL can offer firms a number of benefits including reduced costs for staff training and management development, more efficient use of the invested in technology, 'any time, any place learning', flexibility, consistency and customization of materials, improved business agility and opportunities to build communities of practice (Knight, 2005; Rossett, 2002; Rosenberg, 2001; 2006). However, as Alavi & Tiwana (2005) note "despite the growing interest and enthusiasm for the development and application of EL systems, little theoretically grounded and rigorous research guides the development and implementation of these systems in organisation settings". There are a number of reasons for this. Firstly, a wide range of definitions of what is meant by EL exists. Examples of EL definitions can be found in (Kaplan's, 2002; Wild *et al.*, 2002; Collins, Buhalis, & Peters, 2003, Sambrook, 2003; Knight, 2005; McPherson, 2005). All of these definitions are technology focused, neglecting to identify who should be learning and for what purpose. We have therefore developed a more purpose-specific definition of e-learning to support KC. This is *"learning that is facilitated and supported by using internet/intranet as a medium for information and knowledge creation, retention (storage), dissemination, sharing, and support utilization, which provide a base for individual, group and organizational learning. It might be in the form of synchronous or asynchronous communication"*. This definition encompasses multiple perspectives of EL, noting the medium or place for learning (internet/intranet), process outcomes (KC, retention, dissemination, sharing, and supporting application) learner units (individual, group and organizational) and temporal aspects (Synchronous and asynchronous). A second factor hampering EL research is the rapid pace of technological change impacting on it. This has resulted in the advocacy of a variety of approaches to the adoption of electronic media for learning purposes. These include computer based learning, web based learning, blended learning, virtual learning, mobile learning (Tynjala & Haakkinen, 2005; Rosenberg, 2001; 2006). A third obstruction to EL research is that the concept is often interpreted narrowly in terms simply of delivering information through electronic media (Rosenberg, 2006; Tynjala & Haakkinen, 2005; Winch & Ingrm, 2002). Recently, however, Lytras, Naeve, and Pouloudi, (2005) implicitly acknowledged this problem by noting that "the facilitation of learning through technologies requires a multi-fold consideration of issues that fall into cognition, behaviour, beliefs, and attitudes, as well as social constructions such as networks, communities, group formation, recommendations and utilization of human capital". One benefit that a firm can derive from EL that is just beginning to be featured in the literature is the enhancement of its competitive position through the creation of new knowledge (Hawela, 2005; Lytras et al., 2005; Wild et al., 2002).

2.1 The Knowledge Creation (KC) Process

According to (Gupta et al. 2004; Nonaka & Toyama, 2003; and Teece, 2000) a firm's ability to create, capture, share and utilize knowledge at the right time for the right people can be its most important source of sustainable competitive advantage. Despite the importance of KC and management for the firm, (Bouncken, 2002; Yang, 2004; Yang & Wan 2004; and Cooper, 2005) suggest, there is a lack of knowledge management adaptation in tourism and hospitality industry. Therefore, it is vital to develop an understanding of how the process of KC takes place in the firm. Nonaka, 1994; Nonaka and Takeuchi, 1995; Nonaka and Knonno, 1998; Nonaka et al., 2000; Nonaka and Toyama, 2003 have developed the SECI model of KC which argues that new organisational knowledge from which innovations arise occurs when tacit individual knowledge is transformed into explicit organisational knowledge. SECI refers to the Socialization, Externalization, Combination and Internalization processes involved in KC as depicted in Fig. 1. In Fig. 1 the process of KC is manifested as a continuous spiral process where an individual, group and/or organization "transcend the boundary of the old self into a new self by acquiring a new context, a new view of the world, and new knowledge. In short it is a journey from being to becoming" (Nonaka et al., 2000). In this transformation and movement knowledge takes two forms "explicit and tacit knowledge" (Nonaka & Knonno, 1998). Explicit knowledge is codified and is transmittable in formal, systematic language. It can take the form of words, numbers, specifications, manual, electronic databases, articulated online information and courses. Tacit knowledge, on the other hand, is highly personal and not formalized. It is difficult to communicate or share with others. It is deeply rooted in an individual's actions and experience as well as in the ideals, values, or emotions he/she embraces. Subjective insights, intuitions, and hunches fall into this category of knowledge (Deep knowledge, insights, expertise). There are two dimensions of tacit knowledge: the technical dimension, (know how) which encompasses such things as informational personal skills or crafts and the cognitive dimension which consists of beliefs, ideas, values and mental models which are deeply ingrained in us and which we often take for granted. While difficult to articulate, this cognitive dimension of tacit knowledge shapes the way we perceive the world (Nonaka & Takeuchi, 1995; Nonaka & Knonno, 1998; Nonaka & Toyama, 2003). The interaction between tacit and explicit knowledge is referred to as "knowledge conversion" and leads to the creation of new knowledge (Nonaka et al., 2000). The combination of the two categories makes it possible to conceptualize four conversion patterns: *First, Socialisation:* from tacit to tacit knowledge; employees gather information from internal / external sources and direct experience and others acquire it through observation and other non formalised means *Second, Externalisation:* from tacit to explicit knowledge; knowledge can be shared by others and become the basis of new knowledge such as concepts, images, ideas, and written documents. Dialogue is an effective tool to articulate one's tacit knowledge and to share the articulated knowledge with others. To ensure that the knowledge remains explicit it is wise for it to be codified (Gupta, et al., 2004) *Third, Combination:* from explicit to explicit knowledge; the new explicit knowledge is synthesised and disseminated among members of the organization. The creative use of networks and large scale databases can facilitate this mode of conversion. This phase relies on four organisational processes - capturing, and integrating, disseminating and lastly editing. *Fourth,*

Internalisation: from explicit to tacit knowledge; training programs, if properly conducted, help trainees understand the organisation and themselves. Employees can internalise the explicit knowledge gained from the training program and converge it into tacit knowledge with the potential of creating new knowledge.

For a firm to harness individualised tacit knowledge to create new organisational knowledge it needs to manage the process. Knowledge management requires a firm to transform individual tacit knowledge into explicit knowledge through codification, to store it in a repository, to disseminate it throughout the organisation and make it easily retrievable by employees so that it can be exploited and applied (Yang and Wan, 2004).

Of particular importance for creating new organisational knowledge is a shared context. "The knowledge creating process is necessarily context – specific in terms of time, space, and relationship with others. Knowledge cannot be created in a vacuum, and needs a place where information is given meaning through interpretation" (Nonaka & Toyama, 2003). This place can be physical, for example in a meeting room or it can be virtual, for example on the internet with all its communication services. In order to create new knowledge individuals must socialise, interact and create dialogue with each other.

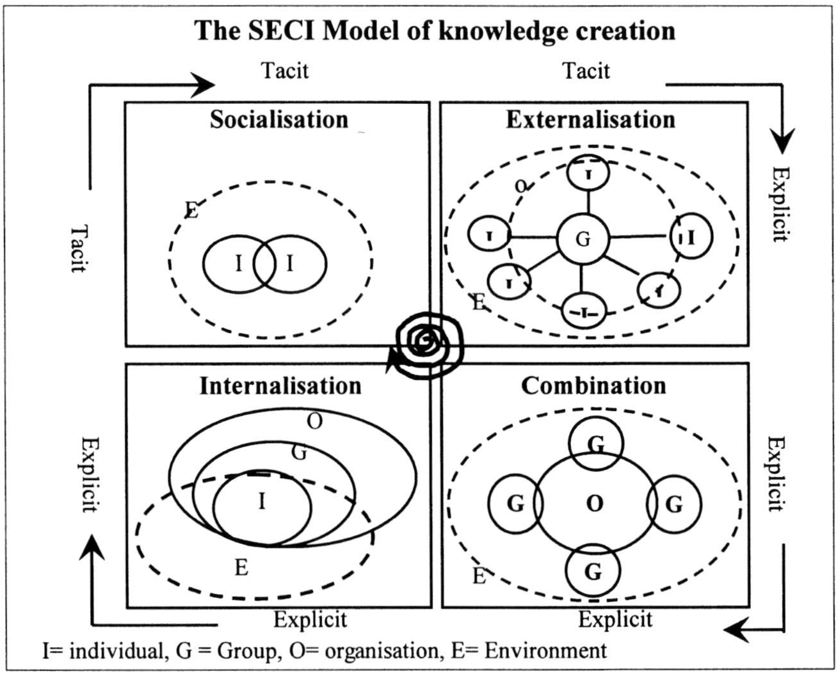

Fig.1. The SECI Model of knowledge creation. Adapted from (Nonaka, 1994; Nonaka & Takeuchi, 1995; Nonaka & Knonno, 1998; Nonaka et al., 2000; and Nonaka & Toyama, 2003)

2.2 The Link between E-learning and Knowledge Creation

EL is recommended as an effective tool for KC and management by Alavi & Leidner, 2001; Marwick, 2001; Alavi & Tiwana, 2005; Lytras et al., 2005; Rosenberg, 2006. By referring to the definition of EL used in this paper and the SECI model for KC, **Fig.** 2 was developed to show the link between EL tools and the SECI model of KC. In this figure EL tools (technologies) are used as mediums for the four processes (internalization, socialisation, externalisation, and combination) of KC. As KC happens within places and it is context-specific (Nonaka & Knonno, 1998), Fig. 2 indicates that the internet/intranet is the place/platform for learning (Lai, 2001). In the internalisation process, where knowledge is transformed from explicit to tacit and from an inter-organisational or intra-organisational level to an individual level online training (library of online courses, simulation, virtual classroom) if properly conducted (Alavi & Leidner, 2001; Marwick, 2001; Alavi .& Tiwana, 2005) could help individuals to reach the needed level of explicit knowledge to reflect upon it, apply it and build their own tacit knowledge.

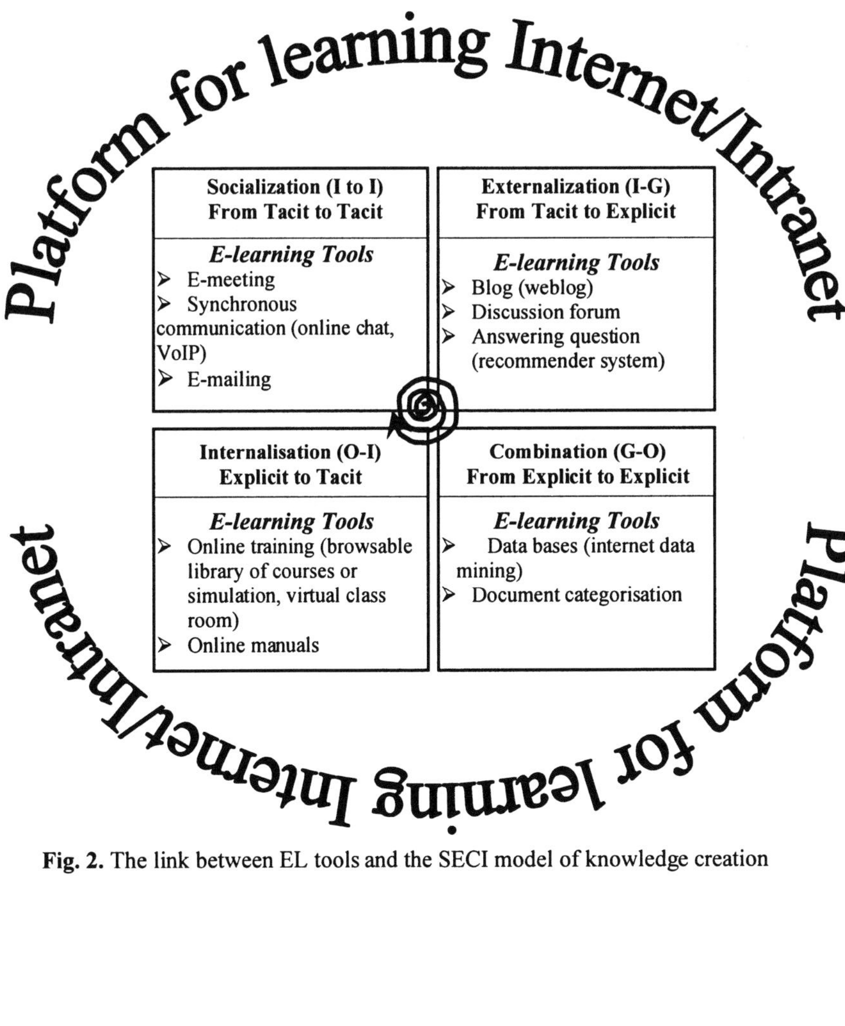

Fig. 2. The link between EL tools and the SECI model of knowledge creation

The socialisation process where knowledge is transformed from tacit to tacit and from individual to individual knowledge can include the usage of electronic meetings and synchronous communication, for example online chat and voice over IP (VoIP) (Varshney, Snow, McGivern, & Howard, 2002) and emailing. "Community of practice or expertise" (Wenger, McDermott, & Snyder, 2002) that use weblogs, online discussion forum and asking and answering questions over an online recommender system (Cayzer, 2004; Farmer, 2004; Herring, Scheidt, Wright, & Bonus, 2005), can play a vital role in the externalization process where tacit knowledge is transformed into explicit knowledge and from individual to group. Data mining tools (Lau, Lee, & Ho, 2005) and updated online data bases help groups in sharing their knowledge in the combination where knowledge is transformed from explicit to explicit and from group knowledge into organizational knowledge (Marwick, 2001). The EL tools can be used for a number of the four KC stages depending on how each tool is perceived.

The International Hospitality Industry Context and E-learning

The international hospitality industry has been in a constant state of flux over the last quarter of a century as a result of continuous consolidation and acquisition. Thus, a small number of firms, approximately a dozen, now dominate the global hotel industry (Zhao & Merna, 1999; Litteljohn, 2000; Dittmer, 2002). According to Strauss & Scoviak (2005) some hotel companies (for example, Intercontinental, Accor, Cendant, Hilton and Marriot) now run hotels in more than 70 countries. For example, the Cendant Hotel Group has nearly 6,500 hotels in over 100 countries on five continents throughout the world (www.ecornell.com/about/news/20060126cendant.jsp [Aug. 3, 2006]) and Starwood Hotels and Resorts has 740 hotels in 80 countries (www.ecornell.com/about/news/starwood-pr.jsp [Aug. 3, 2006]). Furthermore, many IHCs manage multiple brands. For example, Accor has, among others, Sofitel, Novotel, Mercure, Dorint Resorts, Suite hotel, All Seasons and Ibis, whilst Intercontinental has Intercontinental, Crown Plaza, Hotel Indigo, Holiday Inns Hotels, Holiday Inn Express, Staybridge Suites and Candlewood Suites. Previous research by Enz & Siguaw (2003) proposes that high rates of mergers and acquisition among IHC and high staff turnover "make it difficult for the benefits of individual learning to become absorbed into hotel organisational learning systems". In addition, the increasing concentration and intensifying competition in the industry suggests that in order to maintain their competitive positions these IHCs need to be continuously improving quality and reputation, as well as introducing change and innovation (Ottenbacher & Gnoth, 2005; Weinstein, 2005; Tidd, Bessant, & Pavitt, 2003). The use of electronic and digital media could support these efforts. In particular, EL could prove useful for this purpose. However, it is only in recent years that the hospitality industry has begun to adopt EL. This is because, during the1970s and 80s, information technology was complex, expensive, and frustrating. However, as the technology has become increasingly user friendly so the hospitality industry's perception of it has changed (O'Conner and Piccoli, 2003). ICT is now considered to be "the single greatest force affecting change in the hospitality industry" (Connolly & Olsen; 2001). ICT is now one of the most important competitive weapons available to any IHC (Mata, Fuerst, & Barney, 1995; Cho and Olsen, 1998; Connolly & Olsen, 2001; Sigala et al.; 2001; O'Conner & Piccoli, 2003), "if the IHC exploited the ICT networking and information capabilities" (Sigala, 2003). Singh and Kasavana (2005) argue that the increasing ubiquity of the internet and the development of wired or wireless networks is having and will continue to have a major impact on all aspects of the hotel industry. Furthermore, As Cetron (2001) points out the future workforce of the hotel industry will be well able to handle electronic communication. Those currently in their late teens and early twenties, (commonly referred to as Generation Y) have grown up with computer technology, advanced communication and the Internet (McEwen, Fang, Zhang, & Burkholder, 2006).

In summary, globalisation, accelerated number of mergers and acquisition, development in ICT, and changes in workforce's demographics, paved the way for EL to take place. To explain how information relating to the use of EL in IHCs has been collected the next section considers the research methods and procedures used.

3 Methods

There appears to be little published information relating to the use of EL in IHCs. A search in the hospitality index in EBESCO (Business Source Premier) database shows only 10 results for the word elearning. This scarcity of data has resulted in a pragmatism approach being used to collect data to answer the question "Is EL being utilized by IHCs to support KC?" A pragmatic approach is basically concerned with finding out "what works"- and searching for solutions to the problem rather than focusing on the methods being used to answer it. The problem is the most important issue, and researchers use any approach available to try to understand it (Creswell, 2003). When knowledge is relatively undeveloped it is appropriate to use a qualitative research design (Patton, 2002). In this paper a qualitative design was applied. In following the pragmatic philosophy, we followed a mixed methodology (Creswell, 2003); the mix was between three types of data (Patton, 2002), namely, internet exploratory data search, review of literature and semi structured interviews; in an effort to answer the research question. The population of this study is international hotel companies who have representation in more than two continents. A sample of fifteen IHCs has been selected from Strauss & Scovlak (2005) ranking of Top 325 companies. The criteria for selecting the companies were the number of countries they have representation in. Two companies from the sample were contacted for interview and one company accepted. Firstly, a review of literature relating to the adoption of EL in the hospitality industry was conducted. Secondly, because the internet is a rich source of data and information (Best & Krueger, 2004, Marchionini, 2006), an exploratory internet data search for information on EL in IHCs was conducted (Marchionini, 2006). The exploratory internet search *"involves multiple iterations and return of sets of objects that require cognitive processing and interpretation. These objects may be instantiated in various media (graphs, maps, texts, videos) and often require the information seeker to spend time scanning/viewing, comparing and making qualitative judgment*" (Marchionini, 2006). Websites containing relevant information about IHCs adopting EL, as well as two relevant web-based PowerPoint conference presentations were scrutinised. Finally, semi structured interviews were carried out with the director of international learning of one of the IHCs that has adopted EL and with two of its general hotel managers. Each of the general manager's interviews lasted for about an hour. One interview was conducted in November 2005 and the second was conducted in January 2006. The focus of the two interviews was on the history of EL in the company and how it benefits their hotels. In addition they sought to find out if there is any kind of sharing of learnt knowledge between staff in one hotel or between one hotel and others in the IHC. The director of international learning interview was conducted in March 2006 and it lasted for about one hour and forty five minutes. This interview focused on the EL strategy of the company. The interviews were recorded, transcribed and analysed.

4 Results

Evidence suggests that at least eight IHCs have adopted some form of EL so far, from the fifteen internet data searches IHCs. Interest in EL among IHCs can be traced back to the late 1990s when the Marriott hotel group planned and piloted a blended learning programme for fifteen of its junior managers (Ingram, Biermann, Cannon, Neil & Waddle, 2000). The delivery of the programme included use of the internet, e-mail and a virtual library. Much of the learning was done virtually with the support of land based residential face to face sessions. This was followed in 2002 by the launch of the internet-based Hilton University by Hilton International (now merged with Hilton Corporation) (Smethurst, 2006). Hilton chose to launch its virtual university over the internet rather than on its own intranet. This was because some staff were not able to access the intranet at that time. Furthermore initially Hilton International did not adopt a learning management system (LMS). According to Andrea Kluit, the company's Director of International Learning and Development, this was because the company needed time to embed the notion of EL and to make it successful (Kluit, 2004; Smethurst, 2006). However, without an LMS Hilton University was practically unmanageable because the courses it offered came from a range of different providers and therefore had to be accessed through a large number of different web sites (Smethurst, 2006). It was only in 2004 that Hilton University adopted an LMS. Through this the courses provided by Hilton University are now effectively co-ordinated and students learning histories can be easily accessed. Hilton University now operates at three achievement levels: foundation, intermediate and advanced through seven faculties.

The six other IHCs for which there is evidence that some form of EL has been adopted are Four Seasons, the Cendant Group, Shangri-La, Accor, Taj and Intercontinental (www.ecornell.com, [May, 2006]; www.trainingreference.co.uk, [May, 2006]; Dublin, Bellay and Moore, 2005). In all but one of these cases the EL initiative has been introduced at international company wide level. Only in the case of the Taj group was it introduced at individual hotel level. In this case the Pierre Hotel launched the Pierre eKnowledgeSuite in conjunction with eCornell in late 2005 (www.ecornell.com/about/news/20051130pierre.jsp, [Aug. 3, 2006])

Furthermore, in all cases the initiatives are being supported by both external content and LMS providers. Of these the most popular is eCornell, a wholly owned subsidiary of Cornell University. ECornell is acting as content and LMS provider for four of the eight groups identified (www.ecornell.com, May, 2006). Other partners are Sum Total, the LMS provider partnering Accor and Hilton University (www.trainingreference.co.uk/news/lm041008.htm, [June 29, 2006]; Smethurst, 2006). Lance Dublin Consulting is working with Four Seasons Hotels (Dublin, Bellay and Moore, 2005). Kudos is partnering Intercontinental (www.kudos.com/case-Studies/ihg-online-service-info-bulletin.asp, [Sep.17, 2006]) while International Management Centres partnered Marriott (Ingram et al., 2000). The key focus of EL among the IHCs is on staff training and management development (www.ecornell.com, [May, 2006]; Smethurst, 2006; Dublin, Bellay and Moore, 2005; Ingram et al., 2000; www.trainigreference.co.uk, [May 2006]). Evidence from one of the IHCs (Hilton International) indicates that the courses provided through EL are becoming increasingly popular. Between 2002 and 2004 the number of successfully completing EL courses rose from 5,000 to 45,000 (Kluit, 2004).

However the extent to which this learning provides a basis for KC is questionable. The interviews with two general managers from one of the IHCs which has adopted EL indicated that the learning mainly takes the form of reading course content online and then answering questions about it. There were no opportunities for sharing learned knowledge with anyone. Furthermore, they felt that not everything that they had learnt was applicable in reality. The director of international learning of the same IHC noted that sharing knowledge was included on some courses not provided for hotel managers through the use of a discussion forum. However, when she was asked if the shared knowledge was stored by the IHC she explained that the provider kept it for a given period so that the learners could access it but after that it was discarded. She also admitted that from the EL perspective there were no real opportunities for intra-organizational sharing of knowledge in that particular IHC. She commented *"when it comes to creating a learning culture and creating a learning company we are still, we have achieved a lot, but we still have a long way to go to make it perfect and also making it really a learning culture, which is still not".*

5 Discussion

The evidence provided above suggests that no one of the studied eight IHCs by using internet data search; has identified EL as a tool for supporting the knowledge management and creation process. This claim is supported by the interviews conducted in one of those eight IHCs. Firstly, for most of the IHCs the content of the EL experience has been developed by an external provider mainly for training purposes. Thus the knowledge gained is essentially generic, applicable to all IHCs. The IHCs are still in the internalization process of KC and only focus on the individual level of learning, ignoring the group and organisational levels. There are no organised organisational EL tools for the socialisation and externalisation processes. Among IHCs EL is not perceived as a tool for KC and competitive advantage. Rather, it is only perceived as a tool for training large number of employees. Thus, each individual learner's knowledge is likely to remain tacit and in time to be lost to the organisation, especially if the individual leaves.

6 Conclusion

Many IHCs jumped on the bandwagon, and joined other companies in using EL. IHCs do not appear to have appreciated the extent to which EL can be used as a tool for KC. Where it has been used it has been on a very piecemeal basis. What IHCs need to do is to develop a strategy that links KC, knowledge management and EL in a clear and coherent way and which allows for new knowledge and experiences learned by staff through EL to be shared and codified, stored in a repository, where it can be easily accessed so that it can be exploited, applied, and renewed by any other member of the IHC in the world. There is a need for more organised organisational efforts to support socialisation, externalisation, and combination to make EL an effective tool for continuous KC and competitive advantage.

There is very little research to guide and help IHCs to utilize EL as a tool for KC. There is a need for further research in the utilization of EL in hospitality industry. This research should focus on the utilization of EL to facilitate socialisation, externalisation and combination processes of KC. In addition research in the utilisation of EL to support community of practise and/or expertise could help in this process.

References

Alavi, M. & Leidner, D. (2001). Review: Knowledge Management and Knowledge Management Systems: Conceptual Foundation and Research Issues. *MIS Quarterly*, 25 (1), 107-136.

Alavi, M. & Tiwana, A. (2005). Knowledge Management: The Information Technology Dimension. In M, Easterby-Smith and M., Lyles, (eds.), *Handbook of Organizational Learning and Knowledge Management*. (pp. 104 – 120) UK: Blackwell Publishing,

Best, S. & Krueger, B. (2004). *Internet Data Collection*. USA: Sage Publications.

Bouncken, R. (2002). Knowledge Management for Quality Improvements in Hotels. In R. Bounken & S. Pyo (Eds.), *Knowledge Management in Hospitality and Tourism*. (pp. 25 – 59) USA: The Haworth Hospitality press.

Cayzer, S. (2004). Semantic Blogging and Decentralized knowledge Management. *Communications of the ACM*, 47 (12), 47-52.

Cetron, M. (2001) The World of Today and Tomorrow: The Global View. In: A. Lockwood & S. Medik, (Eds.), *Tourism and Hospitality in the 21st Century* (p. 18). UK: Butterworth-Heinemann.

Cho, W. & Olsen M. D. (1998) A Case Study Approach to Understanding the Impact of Information Technology on Competitive Advantage in the Lodging Industry. *Journal of Hospitality & Tourism Research*, 22 (4), 376-94.

Collins, C., Buhalis, D. & Peters, M. (2003). Enhancing SMTEs' Business Performance through the Internet and E-learning Platforms. *Education & Training*, 45 (3), 483-494.

Connolly, D.J. & Olsen, M.D., (2001) An environmental assessment of how technology is reshaping the hospitality industry. *Tourism and Hospitality Research*, 3 (1), 73-93.

Creswell, J. (2003). *Research Design: Qualitative, Quantitative, and Mixed Methods Approaches*. 2nd ed. USA. Sage Publications

Cooper, C. (2005) Knowledge Management and Tourism. *Annals of Tourism Research*, 33(1), 47-64

Dittmer, P.. (2002). *Dimensions of the Hospitality Industry*. 3rd ed. USA: John Wiley & Sons.

Dublin, L, Du Bellay, E. & Moore, C. (2005). A Tale of Two Organizations Getting it right with ASPs. *The LMS/LCMS Implementation and Management Online Symposium*, 27-29 July.

Enz, C. & Siguaw, J. (2003). Revisiting the Best of the Best: Innovations in Hotel Practice. *The Cornell hotel and restaurant administration quarterly*, 44 (5/6), 115-123.

Farmer, J. (2004) Communication dynamics: Discussion boards, weblogs and the development of communities of inquiry in online learning environments. Retrieved October 2, 2006 from https://secure.ascilite. org.au/conferences/perth04/procs/farmer.htm

Gupta, N., Sharma, K. & Hsu, J. (2004). An Overview of Knowledge Management. In Gupta, N., Sharma, K. & Sushi (Eds.) *Creating Knowledge Based Organizations*. (pp. 1-28) USA: Idea Group.

Hawela, M. (2005). Exploring the Usage of E-Learning in the Hospitality Industry in Ireland to Support Organisational Learning and Knowledge Management. Conference on Tourism and Hospitality Research in Ireland: Exploring the Issues, Portrush, June, 2005.

Herring, S., Scheidt, A., Wright, E. & Bonus, S. (2005). Weblogs as a bridging genre *Information Technology & People*, 18(2), 142-171.

Ingram, H., Biermann, K., Cannon, J, Neil, J. & Waddle, C. (2000). Internalizing action learning: a company perspective. Establishing critical success factors for action learning courses. *International Journal of Contemporary Hospitality Management,* 12(2), 107-113.

Kaplan, E. (2002). Glossary [Online] *ASTD Learning Circuits.* Retrieved March 3, 2003 from http://www.learningcircuits.org/glossary

Kluit, A. (2004). Virtual Knowledge Portal For Talent Development. Power Point Presentation in world of learning conference. Nov. 2004. Retrieved August 10, 2005 from http://www.learnevents.com/wol_birm_pres.php

Lai, V. (2001). Intra-organizational Communication with Intranets. *COMMUNICATIONS OF THE ACM,* 44 (7) 95-100.

Lau, K., Lee, K. & Ho, Y. (2005). Text Mining for the Hotel Industry. The *Cornell hotel and restaurant administration quarterly,* 46 (3), 344-362.

Litteljohn, D. (2000). Industry Structures and Competitive Environments. In B. Brotherton, (Eds.), *An Introduction to the UK Hospitality Industry A Comparative Approach (*p. 23) Great Britain: Butterworth Heinemann.

Lytras, M., Naeve, A.,, & Pouloudi, A., (2005) Knowledge Management as a Reference Theory for E-learning: A Conceptual and Technological Perspective. *Journal of Distance Education Technologies*, 3(2), 1-12.

Marchionini, G. (2006). Exploratory Search: from Finding to Understanding. *Communications of the ACM,* 49(4), 41-46

McEwen, W., Fang, X., Zhang, C., & Burkholder, R. (2006) Inside the Mind of the Chinese Consumer. *Harvard Business Review*, 84 (3) 68-67

Mcpherson, M. (2005). E-Learning a Guide to Principles and Practice In: J. Wilson, (eds). *Human Resources Development: Learning & Training for Individual & Organizations.* 2nd ed, (pp. 319-341) London: Kogan Page.

Marwick, D. (2001). Knowledge Management Technology. *IBM Systems Journal,* 40(4), 814-830.

Mata, F., Fuerst, W., & Barney, J. (1995). Information Technology and Sustainable Competitive Advantage: A Resource Based Analysis. *MIS Quarterly*, 19(4), 487-505.

Nonaka, I. (1994). A Dynamic Theory of Organizational Knowledge Creation. Organization Science, 5 (1), 14 – 37.

Nonaka, I. & Takeuchi, H. (1995) *The Knowledge Creating Company*, USA: Oxford University Press.

Nonaka, I. & Konno, N., (1998). The Concept of "Ba" Building a Foundation for Knowledge Creation. *California Management Review,* 40 (3), 40-54.

Nonaka, I., Toyama, R., & Konno, N. (2000). SECI, Ba and Leadership: a Unified Model for Dynamic Knowledge Creation. *Long Range Planning,* 33 (1), 5-34.

Nonaka, I. & Toyama, R. (2003). The Knowledge – Creation Theory revisited: Knowledge Creation as a Synthesizing Process. *Knowledge Management Research & Practice*, 1 (1), 2-10.

O'Connor, P. & Piccoli, G. (2003). The impact of information technology. In B. Brotherton (Eds), *The International Hospitality Industry Structure, Characteristics and Issues.* (p. 110) Great Britain: Butterworth Heinemann.

Ottenbacher, M. & Gnoth, J. (2005) How to Develop Successful Hospitality Innovation. *The Cornell Hotel and Restaurant Administration Quarterly,* 46 (2), 205-222.

Patton, M. Q., (2002) *Qualitative Research & Evaluation Methods* 3rd. edn. USA: Sage Publication.

Rosenberg, M. (2001). *E-learning: Strategies for Delivering Knowledge in the Digital Age.* USA: McGraw-Hill.

Rosenberg, M. (2006) *Beyond E-learning: Approaches and Technologies to Enhance Organizational Knowledge, Learning and Performance.* USA: John Wiley & Sons, Inc.

Rossett, A. (2002). Waking in the night and thinking about E-Learning In: A. Rossett, (eds.) *The ASTD E-learning Handbook.* (pp. 3-18), USA, McGraw-Hill.

Sambrook, S. (2003). E-learning in small organizations. *Education + Training,* 45 (8/9), 506-516.

Sigala, M., Lockwood, A., & Jones, P. (2001). Strategic Implementation and IT: Gaining competitive advantage from the hotel reservation process. *International Journal of Contemporary Hospitality Management* 13(7) 364 -371.

Sigala, M. (2003). The information and communication technologies productivity impact on the UK hotel sector. *International Journal of Operations & Production Management.* 23(10), 1224-1245.

Singh, A. & Kasavana, M. (2005). The impact of information technology on future management of lodging operations: A Delphi study to predict key technological events in 2007 and 2027. *Tourism and Hospitality Research,* 6 (1), 24-37.

Smithurst, S. (2006). Staying Power. *People Management.* Vol. 12 (7), 34-36.

Strauss, K & Scovlak, M. (2005). Giants. *Hotels,* July., 32-50.

Teece, J. D. (2000). Strategies for Managing knowledge Assets: the Role of Firm Structure and Industrial Context. *Long Range Planning,* 33 (1), 35-54.

Tidd, J., Bessant, J. & Pavitt, K. (2003). *Managing Innovation: Integrating Technological, Market and Organizational Change.* GB: 2nd edition, John Wiley.

Tynjala, P. & Haakkinen, P. (2005). E-learning at work: Theoretical Underpinning and Pedagogical challenges. *The Journal of Workplace Learning,* 17(5/6), 318-336.

Varshney, U., Snow A., McGivern, M. & Howard, C. (2002). Voice Over IP. *Communications of the ACM,* 45 (1), 89-69.

Weinstein, J. (2005). What Does Your Brand Stand For? *HOTELS,* July, 7.

Wenger, E, McDermott, R., & Snyder, W. (2002). *A Guide to Managing Knowledge: Cultivating Communities of Practice.* USA: Harvard Business School Press.

Wild, R. H., Griggs, K., & Downing, T. (2002). Framework for e-learning as a tool for knowledge management. *Industrial Management and Data Systems,* 102 (7), 371- 380.

Winch, A. & Ingrma, H. (2002). Re-defining the Focus of Workplace Learning. *International Journal of Contemporary Hospitality Management,* 14(7), 361-367.

Yang, J. (2004) Qualitative knowledge capturing and organizational learning: two case studies in Taiwan hotels. *Tourism Management,* 25(5), 421-428.

Yang, J. & Wan., C., (2004). Advancing organizational effectiveness and knowledge management implementation. *Tourism Management,* 25(5), 593-601.

Zhao, J. & Merna, K. (1999). Impact Analysis and the International Environment. In R. Tear, & M. Olsen (Eds.). *International Hospitality Management* (pp. 3-30) Malaysia: Addison Wesley Longman.

Analyzing Research Collaborations of Information Technology Publications in Leading Hospitality and Tourism Journals: 1986-2005

Rosanna Leung[a]
Rob Law[b]

[a] College of Professional and Continuing Education
The Hong Kong Polytechnic University, Hong Kong
sprosanna@polyu.edu.hk

[b] School of Hotel & Tourism Management,
The Hong Kong Polytechnic University, Hong Kong
hmroblaw@polyu.edu.hk

Abstract

In spite of the existence of many of published Information Technology [IT] related articles in tourism and hospitality research journals, the degree to which the collaboration and social interaction of researchers in IT and tourism remains largely unknown. This paper reports on a study that selected six leading research journals in hospitality and tourism, including *Annals of Tourism Research* [ATR], *Journal of Travel Research* [JTR], *Tourism Management* [TM], *International Journal of Hospitality Management* [IJHM], *Cornell Hotel and Restaurant Administration Quarterly* [CQ], *and Journal of Hospitality & Tourism Research* [JHTR], as the source to analyze research collaboration in the context of IT and tourism research. A total of 4,140 full-length research papers have been published in the period of 1986 to 2005. On the basis of research findings, both national and international research has a significant increase of 154% and 175% between the first and second decades for IT related publications in these six journals. Interestingly, co-authored papers frequently have senior academics' involvement, and that over 90% of the papers had three to four authors have at least one author who is a senior academician.

Keywords: hospitality and tourism research, research collaboration, information technology

1 Introduction

At present, IT has become a major component in tourism business. As such, the tourism industry requires new research efforts on how IT can assist business development. To achieve this, researchers not only conduct research individually but also work with others in order to speed up the research process and to maximize research outcomes. In many cases, academic researchers collaborate within the same institute or different institutes in the same country for the sake of easy communications and resources sharing. With the substantial decrease of communication and travel costs, many research findings from international collaborations are published in the last decade. In addition, publications in academic journals show the collaborative efforts of academics from various backgrounds and positions. Such a phenomenon of single and collaborative efforts also directly applies to IT publications in tourism and hospitality journals. Still, the existing tourism and hospitality literature virtually has no prior studies that made an attempt to examine the issue of collaborations. This study initially analyzes research collaborations on IT related research in the leading tourism and hospitality journals. In addition, this study examines whether there are any relationships of authors' affiliation with North American institutes and the institutes where the chief editors work. This is to investigate the potential linkage with the authors and the world's largest region in research and close proximity with the chief editors. Research findings are expected to shed some insights about the extent to which researchers are working together, and the relationship of these authors' affiliated institutes with the journal and the region.

2 Literature Review

The present tourism industry has been, and will be, enormously affected by advanced technological developments (Bentley, 1996). Technologies have changed the way in which organizations conduct business and compete (Porter, 2001). Although tourism is not an IT oriented industry, Olsen and Connolly (2000) advocated that IT commences and ends with customers in tourism and hospitality, and thus IT use can put knowledge at the core of an organization's competitiveness. Also, as technologies become one of the business components, IT experts cannot purely work on technologies to solve business operations. Instead, they have to integrate IT into their business strategies.

In academia, there are numerous reasons that motivate research collaborations. At first, the establishment of Internet and the substantial fall of travel and communication costs enable researchers communicate and share their expertise easily without any geographic boundaries. (Laudel, 2001; Melin, 2000). Additionally, academic's research performance highly depends on the quality and quantity of their publications. As competitions among universities and researchers become more vigorous, there is an increasing pressure for researchers to publish research outputs in a collaborative way (Wilson, 2001). Lotka (1926) showed that more researchers prefer to collaborate in order to increase their productivity. McKercher (2006) found hat the world's most prolific authors like to co-author. Moreover, Collision and Sheldon (1991) have identified that senior academic have spent more time on research so they have more experience in preparing research publications. Similarly, Håkansson and Snehota (1989) identified that academics and senior personnel of commercial organizations understood the strategic importance of developing collaborations. As an example, commercial organizations can save research and development costs with the assistance of academic research results. Besides, senior academics provide supports to junior scholars by approving their applications for funding and even supervising the junior academics' research (Melin, 2000). Moreover, Kodama (1992) stated that technology research should be in 'fusion' with other fields. As a result, researchers needed to collaborate in order to share knowledge and experience among different areas. A study conducted by Wagner-Döebler (2001) found that at the beginning of the twentieth century, co-authorships accounted for less than 10 percent of publications but at the end of the twentieth century, this percentage had gone up to over 50 percent. In Europe, the growing integration of European Union (EU) encourages researchers in the region to collaborate. (Moed *et al.*, 1991; Marshakova-Shaikevich, 2006).

3 Methodology

On the basis of previous studies on the rating of tourism and hospitality journals (Baloglu & Assante 1999; Bowen & Sparks 1998; Crawford-Welch 1992; Ferreira *et al.* 1994; Jogaratnam *et al.* 2005; Howey *et al.* 1999; O'Connor & Murphy 2004; Pechlaner *et al.* 2004), six leading journals were selected for a content analysis in this study. These journals included ATR, JTR, TM, IJHM, CQ, and JHTR. Only full-length papers were analyzed in this research. Abstracts, book reviews, case studies, conference reports/reviews/proceedings, editors' comments, readers' comments, rejoinders, research notes, and viewpoints were not included.

Specifically, this study analyzed the institutional relationships between authors and editors, identified if the papers had senior researchers, and subsequently to determine if there exists any significant relationship between these factors. More importantly, the study examined the trend of research collaborations on IT-related publications in the selected journals.

In this study, co-authorship was divided into three categories of in-house collaborations, national collaborations, and international collaborations. In-house collaborations refer to the papers in which all authors were from the same university. Publications in single authorship were also grouped in the in-house collaborations. National collaborations refer to the publications in which all authors are from the same country; whereas international collaborations refer to the publications in which the authors were from two or more countries.

When analyzing the relationship between journal editors and authors, all authors' affiliated institutes of each paper were compared with the affiliated institute of the chief editor/s or guest editor/s. Besides, authors were divided into three categories: senior researchers, junior researchers and industrial professionals. In this study, the authors who were full professors, department heads, and associate professors were classified as senior researchers whereas the other academic authors were classified as junior researchers. Authors that were not affiliated with academic institutes were counted as industrial professionals.

4 Findings and Discussions

4.1 Journals Productivity

In total, 4,140 full-length research papers were published in the six research journals, and 195 of them were IT-related publications in the period 1986 to 2005 (Table 1). CQ has contributed the most with 66 IT-related papers (33.85%) whereas ATR had only 5 (2.56%) in the past 20 years.

Table 1. IT Full-length paper ratio in each research journal

Journal	Total Research Paper (a)	Total IT paper (b)	(b) / (a)	(b) / (c)
ATR	841	5	0.59%	2.56%
IJHM	425	32	7.53%	16.41%
CQ	903	66	7.31%	33.85%
JHTR	584	35	5.99%	17.95%
JTR	635	24	3.78%	12.31%
TM	752	33	4.39%	16.92%
Total	4,140	195 (c)	4.71%	100.00%

4.2 Research Collaboration

Leung and Law (2006) identified that the number of co-authorship publications has increased significantly in hospitality and tourism IT research. In other words, more researchers chose to work with others to disseminate their research findings. Figure 1 shows the collaboration of different countries.

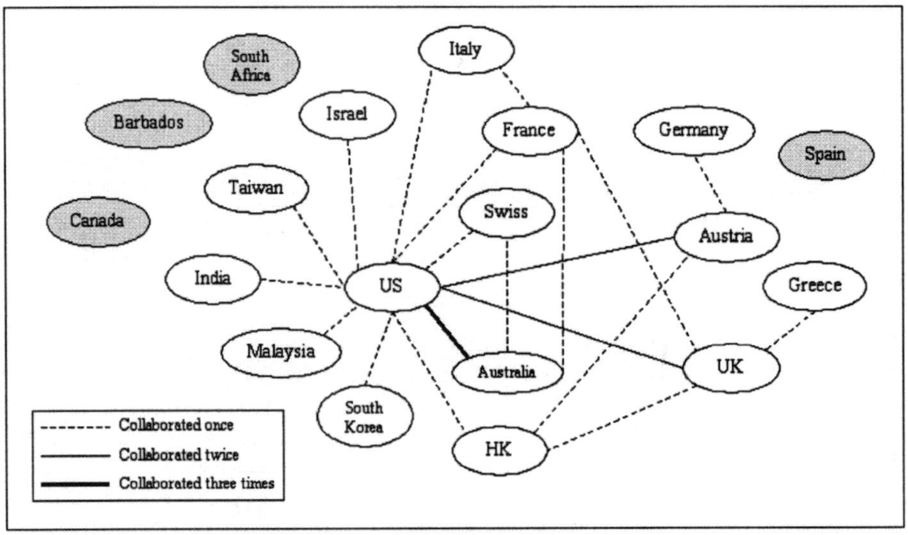

Fig.1. Map of Collaboration

Apparently, the U.S. plays an important role in IT research in hospitality and tourism research as authors from twelve different countries have worked with authors from the U.S. on joint research projects. Within the study period, the U.K. and Austria had two papers that were collaborated with authors from the U.S. Authors from Australia, however, had collaborated with authors from the U.S. for three times. Additionally, there were a large number of collaborations within Europe. Authors from six European countries (Austria and Germany, France and the U.K., France and Italy, and Greece and the U.K.) had co-authored four research papers. Such collaborations are not unexpected as European countries are geographically close to each, which in turn, enable the easily collaborative efforts. Authors from Asian countries, however, were not active in research collaboration. Within the study period, only authors from six Asian countries had published research papers but none of them were collaborated with authors in the same region. Basically, all Asian authors chose to collaborate with authors in the U.S., and authors from Hong Kong had also collaborated with authors in the U.K. and Austria. A reason for Asian authors not collaborating with each other could be due to the immature nature of IT development. Asian researchers would hence prefer to work with authors from the U.S., the most developed country in technology.

As indicated in Figure 1, authors from four countries, including Barbados, Canada, Spain, and South Africa, had published research papers that had no authors from other countries. Among the nine papers in this group, five had single authorship. In Canada, one research paper was the result of an in-house collaboration and another one was the outcome of national collaboration. Among the publications authored by Spanish researchers, two papers were both for publishing findings of in-house collaborations.

Among the 195 papers analyzed in this study, 137 papers (70.26%) had at least one author who was affiliated with North American institutes. Apparently, North American authors had dominated research publications in the samples. Such dominance was particularly true in JHTR and CQ in which only four papers' authors were not affiliated with North American institutes (11.43% and 6.06% respectively). (Table 2) Chi-square test showed the significant relationship between region and authorship.

Table 2. Geographical distribution of authorships

Journals (n=195)	At least one author was affiliated with an institute in North America	None of the authors was North America	d.f.	X^2	Sig.
ATR	2 (40.00%)	3 (60.0%)	5	51.8928	0.0000*
IJHM	13 (40.63%)	19 (59.38%)			
CQ	62 (93.94%)	4 (6.06%)			
JHTR	31 (88.57%)	4 (11.43%)			
JTR	15 (62.50%)	9 (37.50%)			
TM	14 (42.42%)	19 (57.58%)			

* *significant at a 0.05 level*

Since North America plays a leading role in IT and tourism research, many researchers would like to work with researchers in the U.S. because of their richness in resources and advanced technologies. With the popularity of the Internet and the significant decrease in transportation costs, it is common for researchers to form international collaboration networks. Researchers can then easily communicate with each other through email, inexpensive international phone calls, and even low cost air-tickets.

4.3 Authors' Seniority

Among 195 published papers, only 127 had stated the job titles of authors. Within these 127 papers, there were 244 contributing authors and 105 of them were senior researchers whereas the others were junior researchers (43.0% and 57%). Among the six selected journals, four of them showed the majority of publications included at least one senior researcher (ATR, CQ, JTR, and TM) and IJHM and JHTR had published more papers solely by junior researchers. (52.94% and 66.67%). (Table 3)

Table 3. Distribution of Authors' Seniority in six research journals

Journals (n=195)	With at least one author was a senior researcher	No senior researcher on the list of authors	d.f.	X^2	Sig.
Annals	2 (50.00%)	2 (50.00%)	5	8.514	0.130
IJHM	8 (47.06%)	9 (52.94%)			
CQ	46 (69.70%)	20 (30.30%)			
JHTR	2 (33.33%)	4 (66.67%)			
JTR	17 (77.27%)	5 (22.73%)			
TM	6 (50.00%)	6 (50.00%)			

Despite the non-existence of significant relationship between the involvement of senior researchers and publications in Table 3, it was found that there was a higher ratio of having senior researchers in co-authored papers than single-authored papers. Based on the included samples, only 21 papers (41.17%) were written by senior academics whereas 30 papers (58.82%) were authored by junior academics or industrial professional. Among the 25 publications with three authors, all of them had at least one author who was senior academic. In total, 34 authors were senior researchers (45.33%) and 41 of them were junior (54.67%) researchers. Among the 12 publications with four authors, only one paper was authored solely by a junior researcher and the remaining 11 papers (91.67%) had at least one senior researcher. (Table 4) Apparently, senior researchers were experienced in academic publications so their research papers can be prepared in a way that better match journal requirements. Besides, mentorship is also a factor that senior researchers collaborated with junior researchers. As a result, junior researchers would like to collaborate with senior researchers for their experience, mentorship and supervision.

Table 4. Relationship between number of authors and authors' seniority

No. of Authors (n=195)	With at least one author who is a senior researcher	No senior researcher on the list of authors	d.f.	X^2	Sig.	Total
1	21 (41.18%)	30 (58.82%)	3	29.601	0.000*	51 (40.15%)
2	24 (61.54%)	15 (38.46%)				39 (30.71%)
3	25 (100.00%)	0 (0.00%)				25 (19.69%)
4	11 (91.67%)	1 (8.33%)				12 (9.45%

* *significant at a 0.05 level*

In this study, there were 252 authors and 16 of them (6.35%) were industrial professionals. A large portion of these 16 papers were single authored (11 papers,

68.75%) and four of the remaining papers were co-authored with either senior academics (three papers) or another industrial professional (one paper).

4.4 Analysis of Collaboration

As indicated earlier, collaboration was divided into three categories of in-house collaborations, national collaborations, and international collaborations. Based on the findings, there is an increase of national and international collaborations. Figure 2 shows the 5-year moving average patterns of these three categories. Seemingly, there was a large decrease of in-house collaborations but the numbers of national and international collaborations have increased.

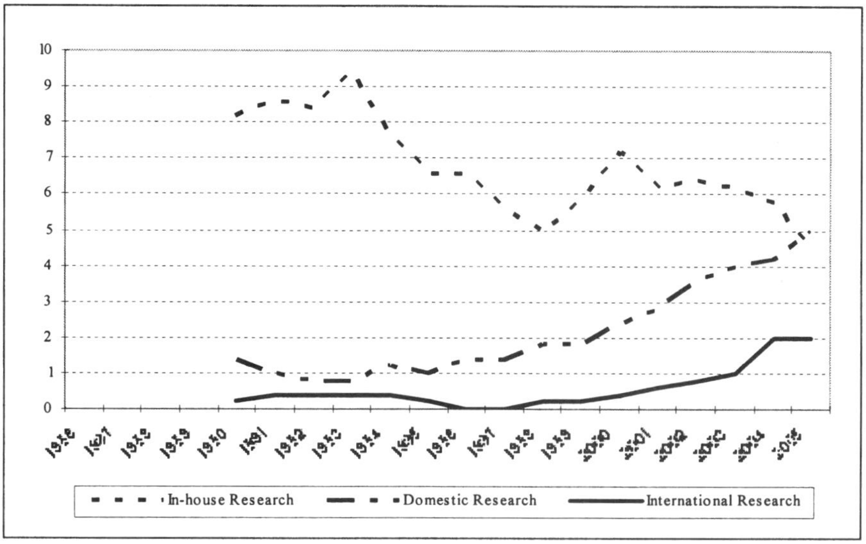

Fig.2. 5-year Moving Average of Three Types of Research

By comparing the research collaboration figures between two study decades, only in-house collaborations had a 22% decrease (from 73 research papers down to 64); whereas national and international collaborations had 2.3-fold and 5-fold increases (from 11 papers to 28, and 4 papers to 15 respectively) (Table 5). Again, the lower costs of telecommunications and traveling had substantially decreased, which helped researchers form national and international research teams. Pooling research funding and maintain networks could encourage researchers to form both domestic and international research teams. As such, the ratio of in-house research had dropped substantially.

Table 5 Distribution of Research Collaboration for past two decade's

		86-95	96-05	% Change
Research Collaborations	In-house	73	64	-12.3
(n=195)	National	11	28	+154.55
	International	4	15	+275.00

4.5 Relationship with Journal Editors

Empirically, the percentage of authors who were affiliated with the institute of journal editors was less than 7% except CQ. ATR and JTR had no publications that the authors' affiliated institutes were the same as journal editors. TM and JHTR had only one publication and IJHM had two publications in this category. However, in CQ 15 papers were authored by researchers from the Cornell University (22.73%). Table 6 shows the significant relationship of the institutes that were affiliated with the authors and editors.

Table 6. Relationship between authors and editors' affiliated institutes

Journals n=195	At least one author's affiliated institute was the same as editor	None of the author's affiliated institute was the same as editor	d.f.	X^2	Sig.
ATR	0 (0.00%)	5 (100.00%)	5	19.8049	0.0014*
IJHM	2 (6.25%)	30 (93.75%)			
CQ	15 (22.73%)	51 (77.27%)			
JHTR	1 (2.86%)	34 (97.14%)			
JTR	0 (0.00%)	24 (100.00%)			
TM	1 (3.03%)	32 (96.97%)			

* *significant at a 0.05 level*

In an attempt to find out whether the authors and editors were from the same country, it was found that more than 50% of the authors for publications in CQ, JHTR and JTR were from the same country as the editors' affiliated institute. In the case of JHTR and CQ, over 85% and 90% of the authors had at least one author who was from the U.S. Again, a significant relationship was found between the countries of authors and editors. (Table 7).

Table 7. Distribution of relationship between authors and editors' affiliated geographic location

Journals (n=195)	At least one author's affiliated institute was from the same country as the editor	None of the author's affiliated institute was from the same country as the editor	d.f.	X^2	Sig.
ATR	2 (40.00%)	3 (60.00%)	5	75.241	0.0000*
IJHM	9 (28.12%)	23 (71.88%)			
CQ	61 (92.42%)	5 (7.58%)			
JHTR	30 (85.71%)	5 (14.29%)			
JTR	13 (54.17%)	11 (45.83%)			
TM	7 (21.21%)	26 (78.79%)			

* *significant at a 0.05 level*

5 Discussion and Conclusions

Based on research findings, more than 70% of research collaborations was associated with authors from the U.S. Consequently, collaboration with authors from North American, especially the U.S., institutes would increase the chance of publication.

The hospitality and tourism industry highly emphasize on industrial applications, so it is necessary for academics to demonstrate their research findings to help industrial practitioners solve managerial or operational problems (Van Scotter & Culligan, 2003; Piccoli & Wagner, 2003). As the requirements of IT research switch from theoretical developments to industrial applications, more researches chose to integrate their work with other areas like Marketing and Revenue Management. In addition, many co-authored papers had the involvement of senior researchers (65.33%), especially for the papers with three or more authors. In some instances, senior researchers authored with their postgraduate students for providing mentorship. As a result, in order to have a higher acceptance rate, junior academics are suggested to collaborate with senior academics because the latter group has the valuable experience in academic publications.

Furthermore, with the rapid development in telecommunication technologies, collaborations at the national and international levels had substantially increased 154% and 275% respectively between the first and second decades during the study period. Finally, although a significant relationship was found between authors and editors within the selected six journals, the ratio of faculty members at Cornell University who published in CQ was much higher that other journals.

Findings of this research, albeit limited in scope of journal coverage and time frame, do provide some useful findings for researchers in general, and academics in particular, to set their strategies for publications of IT-related papers in first-tier journals in tourism and hospitality. Specifically, the factors that authors need to consider relate to the level of collaborations and their geographical proximity with the journal and the journal editor. To provide a broader view, future researches are recommended to include journals such as IT&T or ENTER proceedings and content analysis on research topics.

References

Baloglu, S., & Assante, L. M. (1999). A content analysis of subject areas and research methods used in five hospitality management journals. *Journal of Hospitality & Tourism Research*, 23(1), 53-70.

Bentley, R. B. (1996). Information technology and tourism: An update. *Tourism Management*, 17(2), 141-144.

Bowen, J. T., & Sparks, B. A. (1998). Hospitality marketing research: A content analysis and implications for future research. *International Journal of Hospitality Management*, 17(2), 125-144.

Collision, F. M. and Sheldon, P. J. (1991). An Empirical Study of Employment Conditions for Tourism and Hospitality Faculty. *Journal of Travel Research.* 29(4), 40-46.

Crawford-Welch, S. (1992). An identification of the subject areas and research techniques used in five hospitality journals. *International Journal of Hospitality Management*, 11(2), 155-167.

Ferreira, R. R., DeFranco, A. L., & Rappole, C. L. (1994). Rating the hospitality journals. *International Journal of Hospitality Management*, 13(3), 209-218.

Håkansson, H. & Snehota, I. (1989). No business is an island: The network concept of business strategy. *Scandinavian Journal of Management, 5* (3), 187-200.

Howey, R. M., Savage, K. S., Verbeeten, M. J. and Van Hoff, H. B. (1999). Tourism and hospitality research journals: cross-citations among research communities. *Tourism Management, 20* (1), 133-139.

Kodama, F. (1992). Technology fusion and the new R&D, *Harvard Business Review, 70*(4), 70-78.

Laudel, G. (2001). Collaboration, creativity and rewards: why and how scientist collaborate. *International Journal of Technology Management, 22(8)*, 762-781.

Leung, R. & Law, R. (2006). Analyzing the Authorship of Information Technology Publications in Leading Hospitality and Tourism Journals. pp. 13-25. In M. Hitz, , M. Sigala, & J. Murphy (Eds). *Information and Communication Technologies in Tourism 2006*. ENTER 2006 Proceedings. New York: Springer-Verlag, Wien.

Lotka, A. J. (1926). The frequency distribution of scientific productivity, *Journal of the Washington Academy of Science, (16)*12, 317-323.

Melin, G. (2000). Pragmatism and self-organization Research Collaboration on the individual level. *Research Policy, 29*(1), 31-40.

Jogaratnam, G., Chon, K. & McCleary, K., Mena, M., Yoo, J. (2005). An analysis of institutional contributors to three major academic tourism journals: 1992-2001. *Tourism Management, 26* (5), 641-648.

Marshakova-Shaikevich, I. (2006). Scientific collaboration of new 10 EU countries in the field of social sciences. *Information Processing & Management, 42*(6), 1592-1598.

McKercher, B. (2006). A study of prolific authors in 25 tourism and hospitality journals. *Proceedings of CATHE2006,* Melbourne, pp. 166-178.

Moed, H. F., de Bruin, R. E., Nederhof, A. J., and Tijssen, R. J. W. (1991). International scientific cooperation and awareness within the European Community: Problems and perspectives. *Scientometrics, 21* (3), 291-311.

O'Connor, P., & Murphy, J. (2004). Research on information technology in the hospitality industry, *International Journal of Hospitality Management*, 23(5), 473-484.

Olsen, M. D., & Connolly, D. J. (2000). Experience-based travel: how technology is changing the hospitality industry. *Cornell Hotel and Restaurant Administration Quarterly*, *40* (1), 30-40.

Pechlaner, H., Zehrer, A., Matzler, K, & Abfalter, D. (2004). A ranking of international tourism and hospitality journals. *Journal of Travel Research*, 42 (4), 328-332.

Piccolo, G. & Wagner, E.L. (2003). The Value of Academic Research. *Cornell Hotel and* Restaurant Administration Quarterly. April, 29-38.

Porter, M. (2001). Strategy and the Internet. *Harvard Business Review*, 79(3), 63-78.

Scotter, J. R. & Culligan, P. E . (2003). The Value of Theoretical Research and Applied Research for the Hospitality Industry. *Cornell Hotel and Restaurant Administration Quarterly*. April, 14-27.

Wilson, R. (2001). A higher bar for earning tenure. *Chronicle of Higher education, 47* (17), 12-14.

Wagner-Döebler, R. (2001). Continuity and discontinuity of collaboration behaviour since 1800-from a bibliometric point of view. *Scientometrics, 52* (3), 503-517.

Alfred Taudes (ed.)

Adaptive Information Systems and Modelling in Economics and Management Science

2005. XIV, 276 pages. 68 figures.
Hardcover **EUR 65,–**
(Recommended retail price)
Net-price subject to local VAT.
ISBN-10 3-211-20684-1
ISBN-13 978-3-211-20684-3
Interdisciplinary Studies in Economics and Management, Volume 5

Learning and adaption are key features of "real economies". Studying interesting real phenomena like innovation, industry evolution or the role of expectation formulation in financial markets thus necessitates novel methods of data analysis and modelling. This title covers statistical models of heterogeneity, artificial consumer markets, models of adaptive expectation formulation in financial markets and agent-based models of industry evolution, product diversification and energy markets. The joint findings are presented in a manner that is interesting both for readers with a background in economics/management and mathematics and statistics and also for non-expert readers because it allows them to grasp the ideas of modern management science. This book thus provides a unique integrated toolbox for building realistic agent-based models of learning and adaption in a variety of settings based on sound data analysis.

Springer and the Environment

WE AT SPRINGER FIRMLY BELIEVE THAT AN INTERnational science publisher has a special obligation to the environment, and our corporate policies consistently reflect this conviction.

WE ALSO EXPECT OUR BUSINESS PARTNERS – PRINTERS, paper mills, packaging manufacturers, etc. – to commit themselves to using environmentally friendly materials and production processes.

THE PAPER IN THIS BOOK IS MADE FROM NO-CHLORINE pulp and is acid free, in conformance with international standards for paper permanency.